D1595233

Studies in Targum Jonathan
to the Prophets
and
Targum Jonathan to the Prophets

THE LIBRARY

OF

BIBLICAL STUDIES

Edited by

Harry M. Orlinsky

Studies in Targum Jonathan
to the Prophets

by Leivy Smolar and Moses Aberbach

and

Targum Jonathan to the Prophets

by Pinkhos Churgin

KTAV Publishing House, Inc.
and The Baltimore Hebrew College
New York and Baltimore 1983

NEW MATTER
COPYRIGHT © 1983
BALTIMORE HEBREW COLLEGE

Library of Congress Cataloging in Publication Data

Smolar, Leivy.
  Studies in Targum Jonathan to the Prophets.

  (The Library of Biblical studies)
  "Pinkhos Churgin's Targum Jonathan to the Prophets,
originally published in 1927 by Yale University
Press"—Pref.
  Includes bibliographical references and indexes.
  1. Bible. O.T. Prophets (Nevi'im). Aramaic. Targum
Jonathan—Criticism, interpretation, etc. 2. Rabbinical
literature—History and criticism. I. Aberbach, Moses.
II. Churgin, Pinkhos, 1894– . Targum Jonathan to the
Prophets. 1983. III. Title. IV. Series.
BS1286.A4A7 1983   224'.042   83–15759
ISBN 0–87068–109–5

MANUFACTURED IN THE UNITED STATES OF AMERICA

*This volume is
dedicated
to the Memory of
Maurice A. Stiller,
devoted and faithful
husband and father,
warm and loving Jew.*

Table of Contents

Preface

The authors wish to pay tribute to Professor Harry M. Orlinsky, editor of the Library of Biblical Studies published by KTAV, and to Mrs. Orlinsky. This volume will appear during the year of Dr. Orlinsky's seventy-fifth birthday. Dr. Orlinsky is one of the world's most distinguished scholars and the recognition of his mastery as researcher and teacher increases from year to year. Less known, perhaps, is the unique and deeply admired Mrs. Donya Orlinsky. While it is doubtful that she has directly contributed to Dr. Orlinsky's intricate Septuagint, Masoretic and other studies, those who know the Orlinskys recognize the luminous affection that dominates their life and the support that he always receives from her. The scholarly efforts of the authors in this volume are in the form of a birthday tribute to the Orlinskys.

This study, which was begun at the invitation of Dr. Orlinsky, is part of the Library of Biblical Studies and was to include only a prolegomenon to and reprinting of Pinkhos Churgin's *Targum Jonathan to the Prophets,* originally published in 1927 by Yale University Press. It soon became apparent that a fuller, independent study was required. Dr. Orlinsky and Bernard Scharfstein of KTAV, publisher of the Library of Biblical Studies, agreed that the new study and the Churgin volume would be printed in a single volume. Mr. Shale Stiller, who established the Maurice A. Stiller Fund of Baltimore Hebrew College in honor of his father, graciously agreed that the Fund would assist in the publication of the volume. The Fund supports the well-known Maurice A. Stiller Prize which has been awarded to Meyer Levin, Karl Shapiro, Aharon Appelfeld, and John Hersey by the College.

The authors wish to record their deepest appreciation to the editor and publisher of the Library of Biblical Studies and to Mr. Stiller.

The research for this work was done in Baltimore and Jerusalem. We would like to thank the staff of the Joseph Meyerhoff Library of the Baltimore Hebrew College and its director, Dr. Jesse Mashbaum; of the Schocken Library of the Jewish Theological Seminary of America in Jerusalem and its director, Dr. H. Jacob Katzenstein; of the Yeshurun Synagogue Library on King George Street and its director, Rabbi S. Staw; of the Olin-Sang

Library of the Jerusalem School of Hebrew Union College—Jewish Institute of Religion and its director, Curt Arnson.

Special gratitude is also due to Mrs. Lily Resneck, whose patience in preparing a successions of revisions of the typescripts was almost endless.

All of the indexes were prepared by the authors' student, Rabbi Jan Caryl Kaufman, who has been associated with this project since her undergraduate years. Rabbi Kaufman's work is particularly appreciated. Thanks are also due to Robin Smolar and Arlene Cohen for their typing and proofreading of the indexes.

Finally, we are grateful to our dear colleague, the Dean of the Baltimore Hebrew College, Professor Samuel Iwry, who generously shared his expert knowledge of the field of Biblical and post-Biblical Aramaic with the authors.

Sivan 5743
Baltimore

Introduction

In recent years, Targum Jonathan to the Prophets (TJ) has emerged as one of the most important sources for early Rabbinic Judaism and nascent Christianity in the first centuries of the common era. This volume includes two studies of TJ: a detailed analysis of halacha, theology, and historical and geographical allusions of TJ, and a reprint of the 1927 edition of Targum Jonathan to the Prophets by Pinkhos Churgin.[1]

The overall characteristics of Targum Onkelos (TO) and TJ, the very similar, almost twin-like,[2] official Targumim recited in the Synagogue, have briefly been noted by H. M. Orlinsky: "To prevent misconceptions, they [the authors of the Targumim] expanded and explained what was obscure, adjusted the incidents of the past to the ideas of later times, emphasized the moral lessons to be learned from the national history and, finally, adapted the rules and regulations of the Holy Scriptures to the conditions and requirements of their own age ..." In TJ, Orlinsky continued, "anthropomorphisms, as a rule, are avoided ...; expressions derogatory to the dignity of God, or of the heirs of the nation are softened down ... There is, further, a tendency to interpret the prophetic utterances so as to make them applicable to the immediate enemies of the Jewish people."[3] While there is no

1. Leivy Smolar and Moses Aberbach, *Studies* in *Targum Jonathan* (pp. 1–227) followed by Pinkhos Churgin, *Targum Jonathan to the Prophets* (Yale University Press: New Haven, Conn., 1927) [= Yale Oriental Series, 14], hereafter cited as Churgin.

2. Y. Komlosh, *The Bible in the Light of the Aramaic Translations* (Tel Aviv, 1973), pp. 19,57 (Hebrew); see M. McNamara, *Targum and Testament: Aramaic Paraphrases of the Hebrew Bible. A Light on the New Testament* (Irish University Pess, 1972) pp. 14, 15: "No two texts of the Palestinian Targum (Targums?) are verbally identical over very many verses ... But it is equally clear that, despite their differences, all the texts in questions represent the same tradition of translation. There is a certain family unity among them." See also Churgin, p. 35: "There was a common source for the official Targumim. They were originated in one and the same time; in one and the same way, under one and the same circumstances and share a common history."

3. "Targum," *EB* (1961; 1973), Vol. 21, 697a–698a. Cf. R. Le Déaut, "Les études targumiques — Etat de la récherches et perspectives pour l'exégèse de l'Ancien Testament," *ETL* 44 (1968), pp. 30–31.

disagreement on the general pattern of exegesis found in TO or TJ,[4] controversy has existed with regard to such matters as TJ's use of anti-anthropo-
morphisms, the dating of TJ, the authority of TJ in the Synagogue,
divergences of TJ from the so-called Masoretic text, and the authorship of
TJ.

Orlinsky has also convincingly argued that the proposal that the Targumim in general exhibit a consistent anti-anthropomorphism "is little
more than a gratuitous assumption."[5] Orlinsky's student, Leo R. Wolkow,
demonstrated that while TJ to Is. 1–39 "scrupulously avoided the repetition
of anthropomorphisms . . . he reproduces literally almost all anthropopathic
references to God." Wolkow rejects both B. J. Roberts' claim that anthropomorphisms and anthropopathisms are "usually paraphrased"[6] and Louis
Ginzberg's argument that TJ avoids anthropomorphisms and anthropopathisms "whenever the Biblical expressions seem such."[7] Similarly, another
of Orlinsky's students, Robert D. Schreibman, concluded: "The evidence . . .
makes it impossible to accept the generally held theory that the Targumim
avoided all anthropomorphisms and anthropopathisms."[8] In Schreibman's
view, TJ's renderings were largely based on "stylistic considerations."

It is indeed quite evident in the Targum of the Latter Prophets, that
colorful, poetic, and metaphorical language was flattened by TJ into a prose

---

4. M. McNamara, *Targum and Testament*, pp. 69–78. The major stylistic attributes of
TJ were recognized by W. Bacher, "Targum," *JE XII*, 612, cols. 61 a–b; idem, "Kritische
Untersuchungen zum Prophetentargum," *ZDMG* 28 (1874), pp. 1–58. An excellent and
comprehensive listing of examples which characterize various aspects of style, grammar and
approaches of TJ is found in E. Z. Melamed, *Bible Commentators*[2] (Jerusalem, 1978) I, pp.
281–341 (Hebrew).

5. "Introductory Essay: On Anthropomorphisms and Anthropopathisms in the Septuagint and Targum," in Bernard M. Zlotowitz, *The Septuagint Translation of the Hebrew
Terms in Relation to God in the Book of Jeremiah* (New York, 1981), p. xxiii.

6. B. J. Roberts, *The Old Testament Text and Versions* (1951), p. 198.

7. Cf. art. "Anthropomorphisms and Anthropopathisms," *JE* I, 623a; Leo R. Wolkow,
Anthropomorphisms and Anthropopathisms in the Targum of Isaiah 1–39 (Hebrew Union
College — Jewish Institute of Religion, 1962; unpublished master's thesis).

8. *The Treatment of Anthromorphisms and Anthropopathisms in the Targum of Jeremiah*
(Hebrew Union College — Jewish Institute of Religion, 1962; unpublished master's thesis),
p. 48; see also Michael L. Klein, "the Preposition קדם ('Before'): A pseudo anti-
anthropomorphism in the Targum," *JThS* (1979), pp. 502–507 idem, "The Translation of
Anthropomorphisms in the Targumim," in *Congress Volume* (Vienna, 1980) [= *SVT* 32], pp.
162–177; Harry Fox, "'As if with a Finger'—the Text History of an Expression Avoiding
Anthropomorphisms," *Tarbiz* 49 (1980), pp. 278–291 (Hebrew).

style that would be understood by worshippers in the Synagogue. The earlier historical books largely contain narrative verse and required comparatively less recasting, although the Biblical descriptions and stories of leading characters in the Former Prophets were more than occasionally in need of editing to achieve the hagiographical status with which TJ attempted to adorn them.

Until ten years ago, the prevailing opinion regarding the dating — and usefulness — of the official Targumim was voiced by Paul Kahle: "Das TO ist dann in den nächsten Jahrhunderten weiter in Babylonien auf Grund von Mischna und Talmud ausgebildet worden."[9] To Kahle, the name Jonathan in TJ was a Hebraized form of Theodotion that was used to identify the Babylonian *Verfasser* with Jonathan b. Uzziel. In his Schweich lectures on the Cairo Genizah, Kahle had maintained that TO, and for that matter TJ, "cannot have been introduced into Palestine" and that Gustav Dalman had committed a "fatal mistake to take the language of the TO as characteristic of Aramaic as spoken in Palestine at the time of our Lord."[10]

By 1967, following the death of Kahle, Matthew Black, who considers himself one of the main proponents of the "Kahle school of Targumic and Aramaic studies," had moved away from full support of Kahle's position. "We need not . . . be so sceptical," he wrote, "about the value of Dalman's 'Aramaic Grammar' as Kahle was. . . ." Particularly with respect to the Qumran Targum to Job, Black maintained that "it is abundantly clear that linguistically, these newly discovered Aramaic scrolls belong to the period of the Daniel-type or Reichsaramäisch (or classical Aramaic)." Black continued to reject E. Y. Kutscher's arguments against Kahle's view, preferring the work of G. J. Kuiper, written under Black's supervision, which regarded TO as "an authoritative redaction of the same kind of Palestinian Targum tradition which is preserved" in the Genizah fragments and Targum Neofiti I.[11]

The evidence for an early dating and Palestinian provenance for TO and TJ had been building up especially since the Pesher Habbakuk had come to light among the Qumran Scrolls. For example, the clear relationships between Pesher Habakkuk and TJ have been noted by W. H. Brownlee and

---

9. Paul Kahle, "Das palästinishcen Pentateuchtargum u. das zur Zeit Jesu gesprochene Aramäisch," *ZNW* 49 (1958), pp. 103–104, 126–127, 130; Cf. Kutscher's reply to Kahle, E. Y. Kutscher, "Das zur Zeit Jesu gesprochene Aramäisch," *ZNW* 51 (1960), pp. 46–54.

10. Paul Kahle, *The Cairo Genizah*[2] (Oxford, 1959), p. 130.

11. M. Black, "Aramaic Studies and the Language of Jesus," in M. Black and G. Fohrer, eds. *In Memoriam Paul Kahle* (Berlin, 1968) [= *BZAW* 103], pp. 17, 19–21, 26.

N. Wieder.[12] There is further evidence in his *Antiquities* that Josephus followed the interpretation of TJ in various places.[13]

The early existence of TJ is strongly supported by the researches of Etan Levine and Abraham Tal who have concluded that the language of TJ belongs to the later strata of Old Aramaic and is akin to Nabatean, Palmyrene, and the Aramaic of Qumran. E. Y. Kutscher earlier demonstrated that the close relationship between TJ and the language of the Genesis Apocryphon unambiguously points to TJ as a product of the land of Israel at the end of the Second Commonwealth.[14] Levine's study of TJ to Jonah underscores TJ's use of Middle Aramaic pronouns as evidence that "its thrust is Western, not Eastern."[15] Komlosh affirms M. H. Segal's view that TJ, which includes "the ancient Palestinian tradition," dating from the days of the Second Temple into the Tannaitic period, should be considered as a legitimate aspect of the Oral Law.[16]

There has been serious dispute over whether the Palestinian Targum (PT) is earlier than TJ. McNamara has argued that "in the Palestinian Targum, we have a very ancient and possibly, if not probably, pre-Christian work,"[17] that has proven to be extremely useful in attempting to reconstruct

---

12. W. H. Brownlee, "The Habakkuk Midrash and the Targum of Jonathan," *JJS* 4(1953), pp. 14–18; Roberts, *The Old Testament Text and Versions*, p. 197; Kahle, *The Cairo Genizah*, p. 196.

13. S. Rappaport, *Aggada und Exegese bei Flavius Josephus* (Vienna, 1930), p. xxi f.

14. E. Y. Kutscher, "The Language of the Genesis Apocryphon: a Preliminary Study," *Scripta Hierosolymitana* 4 (1965), pp. 10, 44; see also A. Tal, "Inquiries into the Aramaic of the Land of Israel," *Lèshonénu* 44 (1979), pp. 43–65 (Hebrew). G. J. Kuiper, "A Study of the Relationship between *A Genesis Apocryphon* and the Pentateuchal Targumim in Genesis 14, 1–12," in Black and Fohrer, *In Memoriam Paul Kahle*, p. 161, maintains, however, that the Genesis Apocryphon "lies behind the authoritative translation of [Onkelos]." See also M. R. Lehman, "IQ Genesis Apocryphon in the Light of the Targumim and Midrashim," *RevQ* 1 (1958), pp. 249–263. J. A. Fitzmeyer, *The Genesis Apocryphon of Qumran Cave I* (Rome 1966) [= *Biblica et Orientalia*, 18], p. 13, has indicated that the palaeographical date of his copy of the Apocryphon is to be set at the end of the first century B.C.E. or the first half of the first century C.E. Fitzmeyer agrees with Kutscher against Kahle: "the glaring non-sequitur of many of Kahle's arguments were easily disposed of by Kutscher," p. 15. As for the Targum to Job, see Michael Sokoloff, *The Targum to Job from Qumran Cave XI* (Bar Ilan University: Ramat Gan, Israel, 1974), p. 25: "if a date may be hazarded — probably sometime in the late second century B.C.E."

15. Etan Levine, *The Aramaic Version of Jonah* (Jerusalem, 1975), pp. 21–22.

16. Komlosh, pp. 21, 61–63.

17. McNamara, *Targum and Testament*, p. 16.

the Aramaic *Vorlage* of the Gospels and other parts of the New Testament.[18]

In Tal's view, however, the official Targumim are equally of Palestinian origin and are to be dated earlier than PT, while the close relationship between the language of the Palestinian Targumim and that of the Jerusalem Talmud and similar sources, and their distance from earlier Aramaic sources, indicate a dating of the third century onward for PT.[19] Moreover, Kutscher's analysis has undermined the Geiger-Kahle thesis of the Babylonian compilation of TO and TJ, although Kahle's view that the Palestinian Targumim were older than the official Targumim, indeed, pre-Christian in origin, and hence valuable for an understanding of early Christianity, received new life with the publication by A. Díez Macho of the Neofiti Targum.[20] Tal, however, is not convinced of the antiquity claimed for Neofiti. He believes that Matthew Black's argument for an early dating of PT is forced, since even Black admits that the Aramaic portions of the Jerusalem Talmud and the Palestinian Midrash, with which Black feels Neofiti has the most affinity, are themselves products of the fourth to the sixth centuries.[21]

Roger Le Déaut[22] is convinced that an Aramaic version of the Bible was in circulation before the first century. W. H. Brownlee has raised the possibility that the Pesher Habakkuk presupposes an extant Targum, that TJ, or a part of it, was pre-Christian, and that TJ may rest upon a "very early Targum (or possibly, upon a prototargum in writing)."[23] Le Déaut also argues that the dominance of Aramaic in Christian Palestine as well as the NT evidence (Luke 4:16 f.) that the reading of the Prophets in the Synagogue was already established during the period of the NT,[24] are sufficient evi-

18. McNamara, p. 57; cf. R. Le Déaut, "Les études targumiques," *ETL* (1968), p.7 n.10.

19. A. Tal, *The Language of the Targum of the Former Prophets and its Position within the Aramaic Dialects* (Tel Aviv, 1975), p. 216 (Hebrew).

20. Alejandro Díez Macho, "Magister-Minister, P. E. Kahle through Twelve Years of Correspondence," in *Recent Progress in Biblical Scholarship* (Oxford, 1965), pp. 13–67. Cf. A. Díez Macho, "The Recently discovered Palestinian Targum: Its Antiquity and Relationship with the Other Targums," in *Congress Volume: Oxford, 1959* [= *SVT* 7] (Leiden, 1960), p. 245, that TO is later than PT. Fitzmeyer argues, however, that "Díez Macho's date for Codex Neofiti I Targum (2nd century A. D. or even earlier) is almost certainly too early," *Genesis Apocryphon,* p. 27.

21. Tal, pp. כו־כה.

22. Ed., *Targum de Pentateuque,* Vol. I: *Génèse* (Les Editions du Cerf: (Paris, 1978) [= Sources Chrétiennes, no. 245], p. 17.

23. Brownlee, "The Habakkuk Midrash," pp. 169–186; Wieder, "The Habakkuk Scroll," pp. 14–18.

24. Le Déaut, *Targum du Pentateuque,* pp. 16, 43.

dence to assume that the Targum to the Prophets was recited at the time, probably from memory.[25]

S. A. Kaufman's argument that TO and TJ are early Palestinian Targumim is most telling. Based on the work of Kutscher, which for Kaufman provides "the strongest evidence" for dating the Genesis Apocryphon in the first century C. E., Kaufman places the Targum to Job in the first century B.C.E. In addition, Kaufman refers to Kutscher's identification of the connections among TO, TJ and the Genesis Apocryphon, and to his own discovery of clear lexical connections between the Targum to Job and TO and TJ. As a consequence, Kaufman concludes that "the final Palestinian form of Targums Onkelos and Jonathan must, therefore, date between 70 C.E. and the fall of Bar Kochba [135 C.E.]."[26]

Although TJ may very well be dated as early as the first century of the common era, the final redaction of a fixed text of the Targum took place centuries later in Babylonia not earlier than the fifty century C.E.[27] TJ continued to be read in the Babylonian synagogues during worship as late as the eleventh century, but the use of the Targum declined in the Land of Israel during the end of the ninth and early tenth centuries. H. Z. Hirschberg[28] argues that with the Arab conquest and the further dispersion of the Jews in Arab lands, the use of Arabic as the vernacular among Jews rendered the Targum unnecessary. The study of the Targumim and the use of Aramaic were further reduced as a result of the renewed interest in the Hebrew lan-

25. Le Déaut, *Introduction à la Littérature Targumique* I (Rome, 1966), pp. 38–51; whether written Targumim existed in the Tannaitic period is discussed by Anthony D. York, "The Targum in the Synagogue and in the School," *JSJ* 10(1979), pp. 77, notes 8, 9.

26. "The Job Targum from Qumran," *JAOS* 93(1973) pp. 326–327. The literal character of the translation of the Qumran Targum to Job has completely negated Kahle's premise that the freer translations were the earlier ones (Kahle, *Cairo Geniza*, pp. 197–198). Black remained of two opinions: that "it must be admitted with Kahle that the more idiomatic and freer Aramaic of the pre-Onkelos Palestinian Targum tradition . . . is a much better source of knowledge for the Aramaic of the New Testament period" ("Aramaic Studies," pp. 19–20; cf. also M. Black, "The Recovery of the Language of Jesus," *NTS* 3[1957], p. 306), while at the same time maintaining that "the new Qumran Aramaic texts . . . [serve] as a much closer prototype of the Aramaic portions and especially the original Aramaic poetry of the Gospels" ("Aramaic Studies," p. 21).

27. Bernard Grossfeld, "The Targum to the Prophets," *EJ* 4, cols. 846–848, 851.

28. "On the Place of the Aramaic Targumim in the Life of our People," *Annual of Bar-Ilan University: Studies in Judaica and the Humanities* I [= Pinkhos Churgin Memorial Volume] (Jerusalem, 1963), pp. 16–23 (Hebrew); cf. M. Martin, "The Babylonian Tradition and Targum," in R. de Langhe, ed. *Le Psautier* (Louvain, 1962), pp. 435–438.

guage, grammatical research, and the develoment of new commentaries on the Bible.[29] Churgin[30] was of the opinion that the *terminus ad quem* preceded the Arab invasions. S. H. Levey,[31] citing TJ at Is. 11:46, dates TJ's redaction to the era of Saadia Gaon, while Bacher[32] was convinced that "certainly by the middle of the eleventh century, the reading of the Targumim was fairly well abandoned."

The question of the authority of TO and TJ has produced much discussion, particularly on the importance of the divergences of the Targum from the Halacha, i.e., Rabbinic Law. H. Albeck[33] strongly maintained that the Targum represents the personal opinion of the Targumist, while J. Faur,[34] reflecting JT Megilla, IV, 1, has argued that the Targum had to conform closely to the accepted Halachic norm; even "subtle nuances" in deviation were "censured." Le Déaut maintains that Targumic adaptation "consiste aussi à conformer les textes aux usages contemporains, spécialement en matière de halakha ... Dans la transmission du NT on trouverait peut-être de pareils 'aggiornamenti' halakhiques."[35] But J. Heinemann[36] argued quite firmly that the Targum would not idiosyncratically contradict the Halacha "since the Aramaic Targum had a permanent and definite function in the prescribed liturgy of the Synagogue, and its task was to render faithfully into the vernacular the written text read in public." This view gained support from P. S. Alexander[37] who considers the Targum to have been "reasonably stable by the late Tannaitic period," and that "in the lists of forbidden Targumim, we have solid evidence that already in the early Tannaitic period a movement had gone out from the religious authorities to control the Targum." On the other hand, despite the prohibitions and circumstances relating to the reading and use of TO, H. Z. Hirschberg[38] placed TJ in the category of Palestinian Agada, the development of which was different from

29. Hirschberg, p. 23 n. 17.

30. Churgin, pp. 28–30.

31. "The Date of the Targum Jonathan to the Prophets," *VT* 21(1971), 193–194.

32. Bacher, "Targum" *JE*, p. 58b.

33. "Apocryphal Halacha in the Palestinian Targums and the Haggada," in J. L. Fishman, ed. *B. M. Lewin Jubilee Volume* (Jerusalem, 1940), pp. 93–104 (Hebrew).

34. "The Targumim and the Halacha," *JQR* 66 (1974/76), pp. 19–26.

35. Le Déaut, "Un phénomène spontané de l'herméneutique juive ancienne: le targumisme," *Biblica* 52 (1971), p. 520 n. 2.

36. "Early Halakhah in the Palestinian Targum," *JJS* 25(1974), pp. 117–118.

37. "The Rabbinic Lists of Forbidden Targumim," *JJS* 27(1976), p. 182 n. 8.

38. See above, n. 28, "On the Place of the Aramaic Targumim," pp. 20–21.

that of TO and "was not subject to the limitations that bound TO." Moreover, in the opinion of Michael L. Klein,[39] "no single standard of translation prevailed" and "even individual Targumim are rarely consistent in their translational methods."

The recitation of the Targum to the Prophets was in fact carefully regulated by Halacha so that it would not compete with the primary authority of the Biblical text in the minds of worshippers. Only three verses were permitted to be read at a time before being translated, so that even unsophisticated Synagogue audiences might recognize a deviation of TJ from the Biblical text (M. Meg. 4,4). In addition, care was taken not to lower the morale of the worshippers by dwelling on the more embarrassing chapters in Biblical history.

Hence, the story of Reuben (Gen. 35:22), the second part of the narration of the Golden Calf episode (Exod. 32:21–25), and the story of David and Bathsheba (2 Sam. 11:2–17) were read but not translated. The story of Amnon and Tamar was neither read nor translated (2 Sam. 11:2–17), nor was the three-fold benediction (Num. 6:24–27) read or translated for the masses (M. Meg. 4,10; Meg. 25 a–b).

The dangers of promoting misunderstanding were also present as, for example, in translating the Book of Isaiah, especially the so-called Messianic passages, where TJ is paraphrastic and contains no small amount of deviations from the Masoretic text.[40] Thus, R. P. Gordon[41] has called attention to the "certainty of non-masoretic variants of pre-Christian origin" in TJ and to the existence of such variants in the *Vorlage* of the Targum to Isaiah

39. "Converse Translation: a Targumic Technique," *Biblica* 57(1976), p. 515.

40. J. F. Stenning, *The Targum of Isaiah* (Oxford, 1949), pp. xvii–xix; cf. Y. Komlosh, "The Aramaic Translation of the Book of Isaiah as a Commentary," in *Papers of the Fourth World Congress of Jewish Studies* I (Jerusalem, 1967), Hebrew Section, p. 75; J. Shunary, "Insertions of MSYH in Targum Jonathan to the Prophets," *Tarbiz* 42 (1973), pp. 259–265 (Hebrew); D. Dimant, "Targum Jonathan to Isaiah XVI 6 and Jeremiah XLVIII 29f," *JSS* 18(1973), pp. 55–56; E. R. Rowlands "The Targum and the Peshitta Version of the Book of Isaiah," *VT*9(1959), pp. 178–191. E. Levine, *The Aramaic Version of Ruth* (Rome, 1973) [= *Analecta Biblica,* 58], p. III, has neatly described the problem: "Unlike midrash texts, the targum incorporated its material directly into the Biblical translation; thus, the listener (and the casual reader) was unable to discern the distinction between translation of, and commentary upon the scriptural reading."

41. R. P. Gordon, "The Citation of the Targums in Recent English Bible Translations (RSV, JB, NEB)," *JJS* 26 (1975), pp. 50–60. The authors did not have the benefit of Gordon's unpublished thesis, *A Study of Targum Jonathan to the Minor Prophets, from Nahum to Malachi* (Cambridge, 1973).

which has been borne out by the Isaiah Scroll (IQIsa). Additionally, Talmon points out how IQIsa "reflects in some cases examples of Jewish exegesis different from the Masoretic tradition but in accord with similar traditions in LXX and Targum, e.g., Is. XIX 10."[42]

Despite the precautions that were taken to assure that the authority of the Targum would not be equated with that of the Biblical text itself,[43] TJ was accorded an historical importance as the work of the greatest pupil of Hillel the Elder, Jonathan ben Uzziel, who had received the Targumic tradition "from the mouths of Haggai, Zechariah, and Malachi" (Meg. 3a; Sukk. 28a). In the Talmudic account, Jonathan ben Uzziel's audacity in translating the Biblical text is defended against the protestations of a divine voice that cries out: "Who has revealed My secrets to mortal man? Jonathan ben Uzziel arose and said, '. . . I am the one who revealed Your secrets to mortal man . . . but for Your glory, so that dissension in Israel might not increase'" (Meg. 3a). While scholars have not accepted Jonathan ben Uzziel as the compiler of TJ,[44] the tradition expressed in the Talmud was designed — by attributing authorship to Jonathan ben Uzziel in defiance of the divine voice — to provide TJ with credence and authority. However, it is generally agreed that the author of TJ is unknown. Neither Jonathan ben Uzziel nor the fourth century Babylonian Amora, R. Joseph b. Hiyya, is acknowledged (Sanh. 94b);[45] nor, incidentally, is Jonathan to be identified with Theodotion.[46]

In light of our survey of recent discussions and conclusions regarding Targum Jonathan to the Prophets, the work of Pinkhos Churgin, published in 1927, takes on a remarkable significance. Churgin was a creative and independent scholar. Among Churgin's predecessors in the study of Targum Jonathan were the pioneers in Jüdische Wissenschaft — such men as Isaac Hirsch Weiss, Zechariah Frankel, Abraham Berliner, and, above all, Abraham Geiger. Churgin also wrote at a time when Christian New Testament scholars such as Dalman, Nöldecke, and Schürer were beginning to explore

---

42. S. Talmon, "DSI as a Witness to Ancient Exegesis of the Book of Isaiah," *ASTI* I (1962), p. 66.

43. Levine, *The Aramaic Version of Jonah*, p. 11.

44. Komlosh, p. 39.

45. M. McNamara, *Targum and Testament*, p. 206; Stenning, *The Targum of Isaiah*, pp. vii — xviii; McNamara, *The New Testament and the Palestinian Targum*, pp. 230—233; Churgin, pp. 9—14.

46. D. Barthelemy. *Les dévanciers d'Aquila* (Leiden, 1963), pp. 148—156; Churgin, p. 15, considers this identification to be a "fanciful hypothesis."

the possible Aramaic background of the Gospels in search of the language that Jesus spoke.[47]

Many of Churgin's conclusions ran counter to the prevailing opinion of the time. Churgin argued that the official Targumim were not suppressed in Palestine (Churgin p. 10), and that the "theory of Palestinian disregard for the Targum" was "erroneous" (p. 16). He rejected the traditional dating for the Targum in the days of Ezra and Nehemiah and argued that TJ did not originate before the Maccabean period (p. 37). He maintained that the Palestinian Targum to the Pentatecuh was not older than TJ on the grounds that the generation of the Return to Zion still used Hebrew as the vernacular and would have had no use for an Aramaic version of the Pentateuch (pp. 37–38). Churgin rejected the idea that the freer midrashic style of the Palestinian Targum necessarily made it earlier than the more literal official Targumim (p. 36), and proposed that TO and TJ were "in definite shape in the time of R. Akiba" (p. 42).

In all, Churgin's study of TJ was a singular contribution to scholarship in calling attention to a major Rabbinic source. For TJ represents a significant dimension of Rabbinic opinion which emerged during the same five hundred years that witnessed the development of Tannaitic and Amoraic literature. Churgin based his study on a careful analyis of the Targum and its Rabbinic parallels. He was at home in manuscript criticism and was careful and adept at separating various strata of Rabbinic opinion. His dissection and dating of passages in the Targum is most impressive.

Pinkhos Churgin came to his study of the Targum with two very powerful resources: a considerable knowledge of Rabbinic texts that was not untypical of the carefully schooled students of the Yeshivot (rabbinical academics) of Eastern Europe, and the methodology which Churgin learned from his American professor, one of the most unorthodox Biblical critics of twentieth century American scholarship, Charles Cutler Torrey.

These two unlike mentors, the Rabbis of the Yeshivot and Torrey of Yale, influenced Churgin's work. A brief examination of Churgin's background and his reaction to Torrey may help illustrate the scholarly controls that were operative in Churgin's works, especially in his studies of the Second Temple period in Jewish history and, less obviously, in his work on TJ, which he intially wrote as a doctoral dissertation under Torrey's supervision.[48]

47. M. McNamara, "Targumic Studies," *CBQ* 28 (1966), pp. 9–13.

48. The choice of TJ as the topic for Churgin's dissertation was made with Torrey's approval and the work done under Torrey's supervision, see H. L. Hirschberg, "On the Place of the Aramaic Targumim in the Life of our People," p. 161.

Pinkhos Churgin was brought up in the unique atmosphere of modern traditional Judaism which combines religious orthodoxy with a belief in the return to a Jewish polity in Israel, and not in "the end of days" but in the near future. In fact, Churgin's entire life was dedicated to modern Zionism as well as to the revival in a free, independent Israel of a Jewish religious community.

The influences that moved Churgin to a lifetime devoted to religious Zionism are clear. Churgin was born in Pohost, Russia in 1894.[49] As a child of nine, he was taken by his parents to Jerusalem. Churgin's parents were religious Zionists who belonged to the Mizrachi movement that had been founded by Rabbi Isaac Jacob Reines in 1902.[50] The Mizrachi movement maintained that while political Zionism *per se* could be left in the hands of secular Jews, the cultural rebuilding of the land of Israel could not. Although the World Zionist Congress and the modern Zionist movement were already under way under the leadership of Theodor Herzl, the leaders of the Mizrachi believed that an accompanying and cooperating but parallel and autonomous movement of religious Zionism was required. It was in this atmosphere that Churgin was reared.

Churgin was sent back to Russia by his parents to study Talmud and other Rabbinic codes and commentaries in the famed Yeshiva of Volozhin in Lithuania.[51] Volozhin was an unusual place of study whose renowned academic head at the end of the nineteenth century, Rabbi Naftali Zevi Berlin, had been an early advocate of religious Zionism. At Volozhin, Churgin became interested in modern Hebrew literature and religious Zionist thought. Churgin returned to Jerusalem at the end of 1912 and might have remained in Jerusalem. But in 1914, with the advent of World War I, the Turkish Government decreed that all former inhabitants of enemy countries, among them Czarist Russia, had to leave the country or become subjects of

49. Cf. the biographical note by Sidney B. Hoenig, "Pinkhos Churgin (1894–1957)," *Jewish Book Annual* 16 (1958/1959), pp. 105–108.

50. Samuel Rosenblatt, *The History of the Mizrahi Movement* (New York, 1951); Pinkhos Churgin and Leon Gellman, eds. *Mizrahi Jubilee Publication* (New York, 1936).

51. Cf. Samuel K. Mirsky, "The Yeshiva of Volozhin," in S. K. Mirsky, ed. *Personalities and Recollections in Jewish Scholarship in Eastern Europe Before Its Decline* (Jerusalem: 1959), pp. 1–86 (Hebrew); Churgin was a student during the tenure of Rabbi Raphael Shapiro as head of the Yeshiva; Meir Berlin, *From Volozhin to Jerusalem* (Tel Aviv, 1939), Vol. 2, pp. 307–320 (Hebrew). For a view of the philosophy of the Yeshiva of Volozhin, see Walter S. Wurzburger, "Rabbi Hayyim of Volozhin," in Leo Jung, ed. *Guardians of Our Heritage, 1924–1953* (New York, 1958), pp. 189–206; Joseph Litvin, "Rabbi Naphtali Tzevi Berlin," in Leo Jung, ed. *Men of the Spirit* (New York, 1964), pp. 287–299.

the Ottoman Empire.[52] Churgin stayed in Alexandria, Egypt, for a short time and then sailed to the United States.

Churgin received his undergraduate education at Clark College in Worcester, Massachusetts, and pursued his graduate studies at Yale.[53] Churgin earned his doctorate in 1922; his thesis on the Targum to the Prophets was published by Yale in 1927.

In 1920, Churgin was appointed to the faculty of the Teachers Institute in New York City. The Teachers Institute and the Rabbi Isaac Elhanan Theological Seminary became the nuclei of the institute of higher learning now known as Yeshiva University.[54] Churgin became Dean of the Teachers Institute in 1924 and quickly emerged as one of American Jewry's leading educators and proponents of religious Zionism.

Churgin's entire scholarly career was connected with Yeshiva University. He was appointed Assistant Professor of History and Literature in 1924, Associate Professor in 1930, and full Professor in 1933. As a young man, he published frequently in the Hebrew language journals *Haivri* and *Hatoren,* edited by Meir Berlin. In 1934, Churgin established *Horeb* magazine as a forum for the study of Biblical and rabbinic texts within the framework of Orthodox Judaism. Most of Churgin's scholarly articles first appeared in *Horeb.* Churgin published studies of the Targum on the Hagiographa (1935), the Syriac version of the Five Scrolls (1936), a history of the Hasmonean dynasty (1938), and a collection of his essays on the period of the Second Commonwealth (1949). He frequently used the results of his research to illustrate and support his popular essays and as a conceptual framework for his communal efforts on behalf of the State of Israel and a rejuvenated modern Orthodox community in the new State.

In 1949, he was elected President of the Mizrachi movement in North America. Within a year, following a visit to Israel, Churgin began to press

52. Samuel K. Mirsky, "A Friend Who Died," *Hadoar* (January, 1958), pp. 174–175 (Hebrew).

53. Z. Ravid, "A Note Illustrating the Character of Pinkhos Churgin," *Hadoar* (December, 1977), p. 141 (Hebrew).

54. For a description of the precursors of Yeshiva University in the 1920's, particularly the Rabbi Isaac Elhanan Rabbinical Seminary, and the struggle of formulate an educational philosophy which would include secular as well as religious studies, see Aaron Rothkoff, *Bernard Revel: Builder of American Jewish Orthodoxy* (Philadelphia, 1972), pp. 79ff. In 1928, Torrey was a member of the Yeshiva College Advisory Council on the Liberal Arts, Rothkoff, p. 83. On the early history of Teachers Institute, see Samuel Rosenblatt, *History of the Mizrahi* p. 31; Isidor Margolis, *Jewish Teacher Training Schools in the United States* (New York, 1974), pp. 149, 158–159.

for the establishment of a university in Israel which would be under Orthodox Jewish auspices. Churgin was the person most singly responsible for the
founding of Bar-Ilan University, named after Meir Berlin. In 1955, Churgin
became its first chancellor. He died in 1957.[55]

Churgin's approach to the post-exilic period is particularly evident when
contrasted with Torrey's. Torrey took the most radical position in Biblical
scholarship in repudiating the historicity of the Babylonian exile and the
return to Zion. In Torrey's reconstruction, "there was no return of exiles, no
scribe-potentate Ezra, no law brought from Babylonia, no wholesale expulsion of Gentile wives and children"[56] and the Babylonian exile "was in
reality a small and relatively insignificant affair."[57] Torrey's argument
regarding the unhistorical descriptions of the Chronicler rested on his conviction that the Chronicler had rewritten history in order to undermine the
legitimacy of the Samaritans by creating a history of a continuous Jewish
existence in Babylonia.[58] On the contrary, as Torrey put it, "The 'priestly
law' was neither edited in Babylonia nor brought to Jerusalem from that
country. Hebrew literature contains no 'exilic' elements. Every part of our
Old Testament was written in Palestine; if Jews of the dispersion influenced
its growth at any point, we have at least no evidence of the fact."[59]

Torrey argued that after the destruction of the Temple, Judaism continued to develop in the land of Israel. Foreign elements played a "relatively
small part." The outlook of the people was "becoming broader all the time.
The religion of Israel — meaning that of the whole people — was more
liberal and more spiritual in the fourth century than it had been in the fifth
... the ceremonial law played no such part in thought and activities of the

---

55. Hayim Leaf, "Dr. Pinkhos Churgin — The Man and His Vision," *Hadoar* (December
1977), p. 135 (Hebrew); A. Pattashnik, "A Man of Secure Belief," *Hadoar* (January, 1958), p.
175 (Hebrew).

56. Charles C. Torrey, *Ezra Studies* (1910; reissued by Ktav Publishing House, New
York, 1970, with a Prolegomenon by William F. Stinespring. [= Library of Biblical Studies,
ed. Harry M. Orlinsky], Stinespring, p. XXXI. Cf. also C. C. Torrey, *Pseudo-Ezekiel and the
Original Prophecy* (1930; reissued by Ktav, 1970 [Library of Biblical Studies]), pp. 104–108,
112–113 for a concise summary of his views. For the refutation of Torrey's thesis that there
was no widespread destruction in 586 B.C.E., no exile, and no restoration, see Harry M.
Orlinsky, "The Destruction of the First Temple and the Babylonian Exile in the Light of
Archaeology," in *Essays in Biblical Culture and Bible Translation* (New York, 1974), pp.
144–161.

57. Torrey, *Ezra Studies*, p. 285.

58. Torrey, p. 287.

59. Torrey, p. 288 n. 8.

people in general as the modern theory has assumed. The catastrophe which included the destruction of the Temple and the extinction of the monarchy was indeed a crushing blow, which left its deep and permanent imprint on the religious literature of the Jews. But the dispersion was a calamity which was far more significant and whose mark on the heart of Israel was much deeper."[60]

And Torrey made it a point that the diaspora had become far more important in Jewish life than Zion and that the Jews themselves realized that living in the cities of the diaspora was preferable to living in Zion.[61] Moreover, Torrey stressed, "no Jew in Babylonia, for instance, could ever have thought of advising the colonists there to return; nor would any member of the presumably still larger *gola* in Egypt have counseled his countrymen to make their way back to Palestine, though they might perhaps have found it possible to do so."[62]

Torrey was also convinced that Israelite nationalism began to fade after the destruction of the First Temple, resulting in the abandonment of nationalist elements in Israelite prophecy, the end of the nation as a political entity, and the assumption of a universal role for Israel. Torrey argues that the standard for the religion of Israel was the universalism of the prophets exemplified by Second Isaiah, "the teachers of the restoration period, and those who wrote the best part of the Psalter." Indeed, Torrey saw the religion of Israel growing and evolving along an inclined plane as it rose to its level of highest achievement, the birth of Christianity. Thus Torrey wrote, "Jesus of Nazareth was the true child of his people, the best fruit of its sublime religious growth which in modern times has been seriously misunderstood."[63]

Although Churgin accepted a number of Torrey's assumptions, e.g., that the Restoration was not commemorated as a time of great rejoicing or celebration, he never doubted the historicity of the entire era and its leading characters as depicted in the genuine accounts of the Books of Ezra, Nehemiah, and Chronicles.

So far as Churgin was concerned, the destruction of the First Temple and the Babylonian exile constituted a massive catastrophe in the history of ancient Israel that even the return to Zion could not overshadow. The

---

60. Torrey, p. 289.
61. Torrey, p. 294.
62. Torrey, p. 310.
63. Torrey, p. XXXII.

destruction of the First Temple was an enormous blow to the people of
Judah who had not recovered their political independence as a result of the
return, and consequently never considered the return worth celebrating. As a
result, there is no mention in the Bible of a festival which would mark the
official end of exile. The exiles did not regard the permission to rebuild their
land and Temple as the fulfillment of the prophetic promise of ultimate liber-
ation and restoration. Nor did the remnant which remained in the land of
Israel consider the return of the exiles to Zion as heralding the end of exile
itself, which they interpreted as the return to a state of political freedom.
The new Temple did not heal the sorrow over the destruction of the first
sanctuary and the Second Temple was not regarded as the First being
rebuilt; hence, there was no consecration of the new Temple.

Churgin repeatedly argued that the centuries following the destruction of
the First Temple and the expulsion to Babylonia represented a single un-
broken exile which would only end with the restoration of an independent
monarchy. He agreed with Torrey that the dispersion of the Jews was an
even greater disaster than the destruction of the Temple and the end of the
monarchy. In fact, Churgin maintained that the dispersion was the essence
of the exile and that so long as a diaspora existed involving one member of
the Jewish people, even the existence of a Second Temple and a rebuilt Jerusalem would not satisfy their hope for a total redemption and a return of all
the exiles.[64]

Churgin never insisted that the evidence from the Bible was clear and
fully evident in its support of his position. In his comment on the Book of
Judith, Churgin wrote, "The entire essence of the story is wrapped in fog."[65]
Nevertheless, he argued strongly that the Books of Judith, and Tobit, and
the Epistle of Jeremiah stemmed from the Jewish community of Babylonia,
demonstrating that the period was not altogether bereft of historical
evidence.[66]

Churgin opposed the view that the Samaritans were remnants of the
Northern Tribes or that the Samaritans already had their own cultic practice
on Mount Gerizim when the exiles returned from Babylonia. He repudiated
the argument that the cause for the opposition of the returned exiles to the

64. Churgin, "The Period of the Second Temple — An Era of Exile," *Horeb* 8 (1944), pp.
1–16. Unless otherwise indicated, Churgin's articles are in Hebrew.
65. Churgin, "The Book of Judith," *Horeb* 1 (1934), pp. 48–76.
66. Churgin, "The Great Phenomenon of the Exile of the Children of Israel to Babylonia," *Horeb* 2 (1938), pp. 37–55, especially p. 53; Churgin, "Judith," pp. 48–71.

Samaritans was the ancient hatred between North and South, particularly the animosity of the South — for which Churgin finds no basis whatever.[67] There was no threat to the historic legitimacy of the returnees from exile and certainly no need for the Chronicler to have fabricated a history, as Torrey had claimed.

Churgin's religious traditionalism does not seem to have played an inhibiting role in his treatment of Targum Jonathan. Churgin rightly called TJ "a mine of Aggadic exegesis" and therefore an essential part of Aggadic literature. As we have noted, Churgin repeatedly stressed that TJ is an early Palestinian Targum, (Churgin, pp. 10, 14, 16, 19) which reached a definitive stage of development at the time of R. Akiba and its final shape in the period before the Arab invasion — although there are a few references (TJ to Is. 49:24, 25 and 66:5) that, in his view, reflect the Arab Period (pp. 30, 42, 152). Quite definitely, Churgin argued that the official Targumim were not suppressed in Palestine and the Talmud's ascription of the authorship of TJ to R. Joseph is insufficient evidence that TJ was of Babylonian origin (pp. 10, 14, 16).

In dealing with textual deviations in TJ from MT, Churgin set up three categories: A) different reading and pointings from those in MT which cannot be explained away; B) rather "arbitrary and haphazard" attempts to eliminate grammatical discrepancies, e.g., in number and gender, in a Biblical verse; C) attempts by TJ to smooth out or do away with differences between two versions of the same event in the Biblical text (pp. 53—54). Churgin focused on the development of the text of the Targum, arguing that later Midrashim were superimposed on the "original, simple exegesis." He admitted that in most of these cases it was impossible to "release the original from the new forms. Few additions can be safely pointed out" (p. 126).

On the basis of an examination of variant manuscript readings, Churgin separated one layer of exegesis from another. Here, one sees Churgin at his best, moving securely through ancient and medieval exegetical and liturgical sources and their versions and identifying the sources for variations within the text of TJ and divergences from MT. Churgin provided lists of terms which he identified as interpolations in the form of duplications (pp. 139—141) and insertions (pp. 142—145); variant readings of TJ found in the Talmud; and quotations from TJ found in the medieval Rabbinic commentaries of Rashi, David Kimchi, and others, which differ from the text of TJ. He argued that the antiquity of TJ, which Rabbinic tradition dated back to

---

67. Churgin, "The Separation of the Samaritans," *Horeb* 1 (1934), pp. 127—150.

the era of the Restoration, was enough to render the Targum immune from questioning and certainly from emendation even when the deviations from MT were particularly striking (pp. 17–20, 78). Nonetheless, despite all the internal variations in TJ and TJ's deviations from the Biblical text, Churgin asserted that all the Targumic texts "may have a common source" (p. 151).

Churgin's chapter dealing with the approach of TJ is useful. Churgin provided illustrations of how TJ converts the poetry of the Prophets into literal, detailed, pedestrian prose (p. 79); explains allegories, describes metaphors in their plain sense, and makes explicit what appears implicit in prophetic language. He regarded all of TJ's interpretations as falling within the broad category of the early Palestinian exegesis largely found in the Agada (p. 93). Churgin did not find any strong attempt to conform to the existing Halacha, except in several cases in Ezekiel (p. 123). He also considered TJ's view of messianic expectations as part and parcel of Rabbinic hopes for divine deliverance and as highly expressive of the hope for national redemption which characterized the Roman era in Jewish history (pp. 123–125).

Churgin's work is helpful in depicting various aspects of TJ's treatment of the Biblical text. Thus, Churgin pointed out how TJ used different terminology to distinguish between the sacred and the profane within Israelite religion and to differentiate between the religion of Israel and those of other nations (pp. 111–119). He pointed out how TJ offers renderings which blunt the force of prophetic condemnations of Israel while sharpening the attacks of the Prophets against Israel's enemies (pp. 119–122). The veneration of the Torah is also given primacy in TJ as it is throughout Rabbinic literature (ppp. 122–23).

Much attention was also devoted by Churgin to the question of whether TJ was supposed to be recited orally or could it also be committed to writing. His conclusion that the prohibition against the written Targum was confined to the public reading in the service and was designed to avoid attributing to the Targum the same sanctity as the original Hebrew Bible seems reasonable. To the extent that the Targum was used in teaching, it could be written down.

Churgin's assignment of various historical allusions in TJ to the Hasmonean Period is unconvincing. So is Churgin's identification of Bavel/ Babylon in TJ on Isaiah 21:9 with Persia. It is well known that Bavel in Rabbinic literature stands for Rome, and Churgin's heroic attempt to introduce references to Sassanid Persian persecutions into the text of TJ reflects more ingenuity than substance.

An important observation noted by Churgin is that, originally, any portion from the Prophets could be recited at the end of the Torah reading, and "hence the rise of a Targum to all the prophetical works." Later, when the official Targum assumed a fixed form, different translations of the same words in different contexts reflected, in Churgin's opinion, different Targumim (pp. 39—41). However, whether any Targum was so rigidly fixed that it could not choose synonyms whenever appropriate, seems rather doubtful. Churgin does provide an impressive array of examples to illustrate his view.

Nonetheless, Churgin's pioneering work, however questionable in detail, remains a major reference work containing many illustrations of exegetical methods, textual variations and comparisons with other ancient translations of the Bible and various types of textual deviations and interpolations.

Whether one begins with Churgin's work or with the research of the past decade or so, the conclusions are broadly similar. TJ is a late first century-early second century work which originated and was first developed in the land of Israel before being brought to Babylonia where it was redacted prior to the Arab invasion. As such, it is a prime resource for the study of early Rabbinic Judaism and early Christianity.

It was, therefore, the intention of the editor of the Library of Biblical Studies, Dr. Harry M. Orlinsky, to include a new study of TJ in the series which would provide a detailed, systematic synthesis of major concepts of TJ that would complement the growing spate of textual studies. The authors — L. Smolar and M. Aberbach — consequently set forth to examine TJ as a whole, as a compendium of Rabbinic Judaism. The authors agreed that Sperber's edition would be used, although it has been subjected to much criticism.[68] M. Martin pointed out that in the edition of the *Targum to the Former Prophets* (1959), Sperber described his ms. as "belonging to the Babyonian trend," while actually using Yemenite Targum texts of "an impure strain."[69] R. P. Gordon[70] supports Martin's view that Sperber

---

68. Among Sperber's early critics, see W. E. Barnes, "The Targum on the Later Prophets," *JThS* 28 (1927), pp. 283—285; idem, "The Targum on the Later Prophets," *JThS* 29 (1928), pp. 331—333. The latter is a rebuttal to Sperber's "Zur Sprache des Prophetentargums," *ZAW* 45 (1927), pp. 268—287; cf. A. Sperber, "Zur Textgestalt des Prophetentargums," *ZAW* 44 (1926), pp. 175—176. See also J. van Zijl, "Errata in Sperber's Edition of Targum Isaiah," *ASTI* 4 (1965), pp. 189—191; idem, "A Second List of Errata in Sperber's Edition of Targum Isaiah," *ASTI* 7 (1968/69), pp. 132—134.

69. "The Babylonian Traditin and Targum," *Le Psautier*, pp. 425—451.

70. "Sperber's Edition of the Targum to the Prophets: a Critique," *JQR* 64 (1973—74), p. 315.

assumed that the Babylonian supralinear vowel-signs in the Yemenite text were actual representations of "the authentic Babylonian text-tradition." Gordon and Martin also argue, independently of each other, that Sperber's mss. are too young and far removed in time from the most productive era of the Babylonian academies to be of use in reflecting the Babylonian system of vocalization or text-tradition. Nevertheless, Gordon concludes that Sperber's reproduction of the consonantal text of ms. Or. 2210 of the British Museum, dating from the middle of the fifteenth century — which Sperber used for his edition of TJ — may "be regarded as sufficient for most purposes."[71]

Studies in Targum Jonathan includes sections on the Halacha in TJ (pp. 1–61), historical and geographical allusions (pp. 62–128), and such theological concepts found in TJ as the concept of God, God and man, idolatry, fear of God and sin, Torah and good deeds, prayer, reward and punishment, divine justice relating to individuals, to nations in general and Israel in particular, and mysticism and eschatology (pp. 129–227).

The Halacha in Targum Jonathan is that of Judaism as defined by R. Akiba and his school. Since Biblical practices often differed from those considered proper in Rabbinic times, the Targumists deliberately changed the text whenever necessary to bring it into conformity with Rabbinic Halacha. Historical accuracy was often sacrificed for the sake of Halachic expediencey and need.

This is particularly evident in the case of cultic Halacha, i.e., laws and practices relating to sanctuaries, sacrifices, priesthood, etc. It is also followed consistently in describing the practices of outstanding Biblical personalities such as Samuel, Saul, David, and many others, who are made to conform to Halachic rules which did not exist in their time. From the Rabbinic point of view, it was essential that Biblical heroes, who served as role models for future generations, should behave, as far as possible, in accordance with what was believed to be a virtually unchanging Halacha. Of course, the sinful practices of some of these Biblical personalities could not be entirely ignored, especially in a translation of the text. But, wherever possible, such wrongdoing was toned down, particularly in Midrashic and Aggadic texts where apologetic tendencies could be given free rein.

Rabbinic Halacha regarding the position of women — including marriage, divorce, and sexual morality — is also reflected in numerous TJ renderings of suitable Biblical passages. Here, too, the guiding principle is the

---

71. Martin, p. 448; Gordon, pp. 315–320.

assumption that the unchanging Halacha must have prevailed in Biblical times. Therefore, Rabbinic rules gverning the status of women were assumed to have been equally applicable in Biblical times.

Other Halachic problems alluded to in TJ include proselytization, circumcision, sickness, death, and mourning customs. Since the Halacha was concerned with every aspect of life from the cradle to the grave, TJ naturally reflects the contemporary state of Jewish law in its numerous deviations from, and homiletic additions to, the plain meaning of the Biblical text.

Targum Jonathan on the Prophets is a rich fund of allusions to historical events and geographical sites of the Hellenistic Roman period. The recitation of Prophetic passages in the Synagogue service was, together with the reading of the Torah, the most important educational tool of the Jewish community. The translators interpreted the Biblical text with contemporary events in mind. As a result, deviations from the literal meaning of the Biblical text are often pregnant with significant allusions to contemporary history.

The events "covered" by TJ range from the time of the persecution of the Jews under Antiochus IV (168—165 B.C.E.) and the Hasmonean Age, including in particular, the reign of Alexander Jannaeus (103—76 B.C.E.), down to the middle of the second century C.E. when the Jewish community of the land of Israel was beginning to recover from the disaster of the Bar Kochba war.

TJ interprets historical events and social customs recorded in the Bible either homiletically or in terms of contemporary conditions and norms. TJ likewise clarifies obscure verses which are often unintelligible without Targumic explanation. Indeed, a large number of Targumic expressions used in a variety of passages reflect the Roman period. This tendency to contemporize the Biblical material is particularly evident in the translation of place names which are usually identified with "modern" (i.e., Talmudic) localities and translated accordingly.

Among the events on which light is shed in TJ are the foundations of the city of Tiberias; the Roman-Jewish war, especially the civil war in Jerusalem and the siege of the city by the Roman legions under Titus (66—70 C.E.); Trajan's Parthian campaign; the Bar Kochba revolt; the Hadrianic persecution and its aftermath; and the Patriarchate of R. Judah ha-Nasi. There are also allusions to Agrippa II, the High Priests in the Temple, corrupt leaders, judges, and informers — as well as to the Samaritan dove cult.

There is an abundance of material shedding light on the theology of TJ in all its aspects. The theology of TJ is in agreement with Rabbinic Judaism as represented by R. Akiba and his school. The Hebrew Bible, reflecting as it does the religious ideas and culture of an earlier age, contains an extensive number of expressions and concepts which were later refined by Rabbinic exegesis. The numerous deviations of TJ from the literal meaning of the Biblical text were designed with a view to elevating the religious understanding of the Jewish people. Biblical concepts of God are considerably refashioned to leave no doubt about the unity, incorporeality, eternity, omniscience, and unlimited power of the Almighty. In the relations between God and man, TJ is anxious to avoid or circumvent the easy familiarity so often displayed in the Bible. In TJ, God and and are kept strictly apart, even while divine Providence permeates human affairs. God cares for every individual and supervises his every activity; but there can be no relationship between a humanly inconceivable spiritual force encompassing the universe and a weak, mortal earth-bound creature like man.

God's perfection and justice cannot be contested in TJ. Prophetic complaints against divine injustice and indeed any criticism voiced of the divine will are suppressed in TJ's rendering of the Prophets. Divine justice in the form of appropriate reward and punishment for each individual — as well as for nations in general — is a basic doctrine enunciated in the Bible and Talmud, and fully accepted by TJ. Hence, it is impossible for the wicked to prosper or the innocent to suffer — all evidence to the contrary notwithstanding.

The uniqueness of God requires, in TJ's theology, the elimination of all expressions which may even remotely suggest the reality of any other God. Poetical devices and rhetorical questions in the original Hebrew must yield to prosaic interpretations which even the most simple-minded could not possibly misunderstand. Idolatry in any manner or form is wholly rejected in TJ, sometimes to the point of being unmentionable.

Among features often emphasized in TJ are the fear of God and the fear of sin; the study of Torah and the performance of good deeds; and the value of prayer, including intercessory prayer by worthy men, in helping man to escape his troubles.

As already mentioned, the concepts of reward and punishment are basic to Rabbinic theology, and are given due emphasis in TJ. In line with Rabbinic concepts, TJ recognizes that divine reward and punishment are not necessarily confined to this world. There is another world where the wrongs of this world will be rectified. The righteous are to be rewarded in paradise, and the wicked will be duly consigned to Gehenna where they will be punished for the evils wrought by them in this world. Ritual and moral offenses alike are liable to cause the punishment of their perpetrators. Like ordinary individuals, Israel and the nations of the world are subject to reward and punishment, including exile, a topic on which TJ dwells at great length.

The antidote to sin and punishment is repentance; and in keeping with both Biblical and Rabbinic theology, repentant sinners are generally welcomed back to the fold and their sins are forgiven. Israel, too, will be forgiven.[72]

In the vast majority of instances, therefore, we have concluded that the theology of TJ is "identical with orthodox Judaism as developed by the Pharisees and rabbis. . . . It was precisely because the Bible frequently expresses concepts and views which were later rejected by the rabbis that TJ, which was designed for the religious edification of the masses, significantly changes the translation, with a view to eliminating all traces of unorthodox theology."[73]

72. Cf. R. P. Gordon, "The Targumists as Eschatologists," in *Congress Volume,* 1977 (Leiden, 1978) [= *SVT* 29], p. 130: "The Targumists were not content with the mere repetition of eschatological credenda and they set themselves the more rewarding task of encouraging the faithful, and of rallying the wavering to orthodoxy of belief and to rectitude of conduct."

73. See below, *Studies in Targum Jonathan,* pp. 129–130. A seperate study on messianic concepts in TJ is in progress.

The following abbreviations are used above:

ASTI	*Annual of the Swedish Theological Institute*
Bib	*Biblica*
BZAW	*Beiheft das Zeitschrift das Altestamentliche Wissenschaft*
CBQ	*Catholic Biblical Quarterly*
EB	*Encyclopedia Britannica*
EJ	*Encyclopedia Judaica*
ETL	*Ephemerides Theological Lovanienses*
JAOS	*Journal of the American Oriental Society*
JE	*Jewish Encyclopedia*
JBL	*Journal of Biblical Literature*
JJS	*Journal of Jewish Studies*
JSS	*Journal of Semitic Studies*
JQR	*Jewish Quarterly Review*
JSJ	*Journal for the Study of Judaism in the Persian, Hellenistic and Roman Period*
JThS	*Journal of Theological Studies*
NTS	*New Testament Studies*
Rev Q	*Revue de Qumran*
VT	*Vetus Testamentum*
SVT	*Supplements to Vetus Testamentum*
ZDMG	*Zeitschrift der Deutschen Morgenlandischen Gesellschaft*
ZNW	*Zeitschrift das Neutestamentliche Wissenschaft*

Studies in
Targum Jonathan
to the Prophets

by
Leivy Smolar and Moses Aberbach

The Halacha in Targum Jonathan

Targum Jonathan on the Prophets was recognized as the official Aramaic translation authorized for use in the synagogue. Since it was designed to educate and enlighten the masses of synagogue worshippers, the Halacha reflected in this translation had to be, as it were, above board. It had to reflect not the laws or customs prevailing in biblical times, but rather the rabbinic interpretation of the Scriptures. Not only was it essential to reinterpret passages which plainly contradicted rabbinic Halacha, but it was sometimes considered necessary to depart from the literal text even when there was no direct contradiction of later Halacha involved. If, for example, rabbinic Midrash had utilized the passage in question for a halachic conclusion, the Targum might well reflect the Midrash, even though there was no inherent need to depart from the literal meaning of the Hebrew text.

The Halacha represented in the Targum Jonathan on the Prophets is undoubtedly that of the school of R. Akiba—the same halachic school which set its stamp on the Mishnah and which also exercised a decisive influence on the Targum Onkelos.[1] The evidence for this assertion is quite conclusive. Thus, for example, TJ interprets I Samuel 21:6b—". . . how much more today will their vessels become holy"—as follows: ". . . on this day it (viz., the shewbread) is eaten and it is not rendered unfit through a vessel."

To understand this enigmatic interpretation, we have to refer to the explanation of this verse given in T.B. Menahot 95b:

"R. Judah maintains that he (viz., David) found them (i.e., the priests of Nob) baking it (viz., the shewbread) on a weekday.[2] So he said to them, 'You are baking it on a weekday?!' But since it has been sanctified this day in the

---

1. Cf., e.g., Y. Komlosh, המקרא באור התרגום (Tel Aviv 1973), pp. 159 f., where, however, a number of exceptions are pointed out as far as Targum Onkelos is concerned.

2. Cf. Rashi *ad loc.*: "David found the priests baking it (viz., the shewbread) on the eve of the Sabbath."

I

vessel (i.e., in the baking-oven) it will become unfit by being kept over-night![3] R. Simeon maintains that he found them baking it on the Sabbath and said to them, 'Should you not have baked it on a weekday?[4] After all it is not the oven that hallows the bread but the table!'"[5]

Both R. Judah and R. Simeon were disciples of R. Akiba,[6] but it was R. Simeon who (along with R. Meir) was R. Akiba's disciple *par excellence,* following him even to prison to study Torah under his guidance.[7] TJ agrees with R. Simeon's opinion that the oven (= "a vessel") does *not* cause the shewbread to be hallowed and, hence, to become ritually unfit through over-night stay outside the inner sanctuary.

It is noteworthy that earlier in the same verse (1 Sam. 21:6), MT ["the vessels of the young men were holy,] though it was but a common journey," is rendered in some TJ manuscripts: ". . . and he (viz., David) was *not* going on a profane journey." The purpose of this manifestly deliberate change was no doubt to account for the consumption of the sacred shewbread by per-sons who were not priests. Only a sacred purpose might justify this breach of the law in an emergency. It was with this problem in mind that the tal-mudic aggadah relates that David was in danger of his life because he had been seized by a ravenous hunger which had to be satisfied—if no other food was available—even with sacred or ritually unfit food in order to save his life.[8]

This aggadah as well as the above-cited targumic variants are all the more significant in view of the use made of this passage (1 Samuel 21:4 ff.) in the Synoptic Gospels. There the plucking of grain on the Sabbath by Jesus' hungry disciples is defended by Jesus on the ground that David, too, and his men were permitted to trespass the law when they were hungry.[9] The rabbinic response to this argument was that David's act was halachic-

---

3. It follows that it is wrong to bake the shewbread on a weekday, since it is not placed on the table in the sanctuary before the Sabbath (cf. Lev. 24:8).

4. I.e., on the eve of the Sabbath.

5. It should therefore have been baked before the Sabbath and kept for the Sabbath; for it is not hallowed until it is set on the table.

6. Cf. T.B. Yev. 62b; Sanh. 86a; Gen. R. LXI, 3; Eccl. R. XI, 10.

7. Cf. T.B. Pes. 112a; Git. 67a; Nid. 52b; T.Y. Sanh. 1, 2, 19a; Lev. R. XXI, 8: Pesik. R.K. 27, edit. Buber 176b.

8. Cf. T.B. Men. 95b-96a; M. Yoma VIII, 6.

9. Cf. Matt. 12:1-4; Mark 2:23-26; Luke 6:1-4.

ally above board—which was presumably not the case with Jesus' disciples who were not in danger of their lives.

The influence of R. Akiba's school is even more evident in TJ's astonishing version of Malachi 2:16a— "For he hates (or: I hate) divorce"—which turns out to be the very opposite of the plain meaning of the verse: "For if you hate her, divorce her." The passage is discussed in T.B. Git. 90b, where R. Judah (who was, as has already been pointed out,[10] one of R. Akiba's disciples) interprets it: "If you hate her, divorce her."[11] This agrees with R. Akiba's ultra-liberal view on divorce, permitting it "even if he found another woman more beautiful than she is (i.e., than his wife)."[12]

Although the view of the school of Hillel permitting divorce "even if she spoiled his (cooked) food" [13] may seem equally liberal, allowing a mere pretext to serve as a cause of divorce, R. Akiba's attitude is in fact considerably more liberal, since he does not require any fault on the part of the wife or even a pretext. A man may divorce his wife because he dislikes her—and he need not justify his feelings. This is also the import of R. Judah's interpretation: "If you hate her, divorce her"; no grounds are needed.

The purpose of this tendencious explanation of a biblical verse (which manifestly fails to take into account the context and meaning of the passage) was apparently to counter sectarian—Christian opposition to divorce,[14] which was contrary to the law of the Torah[15] and to the accepted norm in Jewish society.[16] Since Malachi 2:16 provided at least moral support to the contention that divorce was an odious practice and contrary to morality even if legally permissible, R. Akiba and his school may have deliberately rendered divorce easy in order to counteract "heretical" concepts.[17]

The stamp of R. Akiba's school can also be seen in TJ's rendering of Ezekiel 34:31, where MT "... you are men" is translated: "... you are the

---

10. See above, n. 6.

11. This interpretation was opposed by the third century Amora R. Johanan who explained Mal. 2:16 as meaning: "Hateful is he that divorces (viz., his wife)"; cf. T.B. Git. 90b.

12. M. Git. IX, 10.

13. *Ibid.*

14. Cf. Matt. 5:31 f.; 19:3-9; Mark 10:2-12; Luke 16:18; Romans 7:2 f.; I Cor. 7:10 f.

15. Cf. Deut. 24:1 ff.; cf. Matt. 5:31; 19:7; Mark 10:4.

16. Cf., e.g., Is. 50:1; Jer. 3:1; Ecclesiasticus 25:26.

17. For similar demonstrative reactions to heretical views, cf. M. Ber. IX, 5; Parah III, 7; Tos. Parah III, 8: T.B. Yoma 2a; 53a; Hag. 23a; Zev. 21a; Men. 65a.

house of Israel."[18] This agrees with R. Simeon's exegesis of the same verse: "You are called men, but the nations of the world are not called men, but beasts."[19] R. Akiba's attitude toward Gentiles, including pagan women, was not much different.[20]

In general, TJ tends to introduce a proper legal order ensuring that whatever transpired in these areas during biblical times conformed to the legal requirements of the Halacha.

David's general, Joab, was thus assumed by the rabbis to have conducted military affairs—as well as his personal vendettas—in accordance with the Halacha.[21] In regard to Isaiah 3:9a, where MT reads, "Their partiality testifies (or : witnesses) against them", TJ adds the significant word בדינא ("in judgment"). It is therefore not partiality in general that is denounced by the prophet, but, more specifically, partiality in court procedure—which is the only kind of favoritism prohibited by law.[22]

Legal order is also introduced in TJ's rendering of Jeremiah 6:19a, where God is threatening to bring evil upon Israel—the disaster being "the outcome of their devices (or: schemes)". The Hebrew פרי מחשבותם means literally, "the fruit of their thoughts", thus implying divine punishment for mere intention to commit a wrong. This, however, is contrary to rabbinic doctrine that only evil intention which "bears fruit"—i.e., which is followed by action—is punishable, while "intention which does not bear fruit the Holy One, Blessed be He, does not combine with deed." In other words, God does not punish evil schemes which are not carried into effect.[23]

Jeremiah 6:19a is indeed cited as proof-text for this doctrine,[24] which although of primarily theological import, undoubtedly has its legal ramifica-

---

18. Similarly, Ezek. 36:38, where MT "flocks of men" = TJ "Men of the house of Israel."

19. T.B. B.M. 114b; cf. also Yev. 60b—61a, where the words "but beasts" are omitted. Although the statement is designed for halachic purposes, namely to exclude Gentiles from the rules of levitical impurity, its spirit reflects R. Simeon's bitterness against the pagan persecutors of the Jews. For other dicta by R. Simeon expressing similar sentiments, cf. Mekhilta on Exod. 14:7 (edit. Lauterbach I, 201); T.Y. Kid. IV, 11 66c; Soferim XV, 9: Lev. R. XIII, 2; Esther R. Proem 3.

20. Cf. Aboth-de-R. Nathan, ch. 16, edit. Schechter, Version I, p.63.

21. Cf. T.B. Sanh. 49a; B.B. 21a-b; cf. M. Aberbach היחסים בין עירא היארי ודוד לפי האגדה התלמודית, in *Tarbiz* XXXIII, No. 4 (Tammuz 5724 [1964]), p. 358 f., especially, n. 3.

22. Cf. Exod. 23:3; Lev. 19:15; and especially Deut. 1:17 and 16:19. Cf. also Sifra on Lev. 19:15; T.B. Ket. 105b; 106a; Sanh. 7b.

23. Cf. T.B. Kid. 39b; 40a; Hul. 142a.

24. Cf. T.B. Kid. 40a.

tions. For in Jewish law, no penalties can be imposed even for the openly expressed intention to commit an unlawful act, unless there are witnesses who are able to pass a rigorous cross-examination. In fact, where capital offenses are concerned, the would be criminal must be warned about the nature and consequences of the act he is about to carry into effect prior to its commission.[25] TJ, therefore, renders פרי מחשבותם as the recompense for their *"deeds"*. The emphasis is on deeds which alone can make one liable to either divine or human "recompense."

Halachic order is also applied by TJ to the story about the destruction of the altar of Baal and the Asherah by Gideon.[26] Joash, Gideon's father, determined to defend his son, ridiculed Baal, saying, "Will you contend for Baal or will you save him? Whoever will contend for him shall be put to death by morning."[27] However, according to the Mishnah,[28] capital punishment required a trial that would last at least two days. Since the targumist could not imagine Joash's suggesting a course of action contrary to the Halacha, TJ renders: "Whoever will take vengeance for him (viz., Baal), shall be put to death; but an extension shall be (lit., is) given to him until morning." In other words, his case shall not be disposed of immediately, but must be continued during the following day.[29]

Strict regard for the precise language required for legal order is also observed in TJ's translation of several passages in Ezekiel[30] which have the words "blood" or "bloodshed" in common. In all these cases "bloodshed" or "the bloody city" are denounced. The targumist, concerned as he is with the legal aspect of the matter, cannot leave it at that, especially since the blood of Jerusalem (i.e., shed in Jerusalem) is depicted as an unforgivable

---

25. Cf. Deut. 17:6; 19:15; M. Sanh. III, 6; IV, 1.5; V, 1-4; VII, 10-11; M. Mak. I, 8 f.; Tos. Sanh. VI, 3; VIII, 3; IX, 1; XI, 1 ff.; T.Y. Sanh. V, 1, 22c-d; T.B. Sanh. 29a-b; 37b; 40b; 41a; 61a; Cf. also Sifre Num. 15:33, par. 133. Cf. also Maimonides, *Mishneh Torah, Hil. Sanhedrin XII*, 1-3; XVI, 4; Encyclopedia Talmudit (Jerusalem 1965), Vol. XI, p. 291 ff.

26. Cf. Jud. 6:25 ff.

27. *Ibid.* 6:31.

28. Cf. M. Sanh. IV, 1 (end) and V, 5 (beg.).

29. The entire account of Gideon's sacrifice following the destruction of the Baal altar and the Asherah teems with halachic irregularities—no less than eight according to the Talmud (cf. T.B. Tem. 28b-29a), which were, however, permitted on that special occasion (cf. *ibid.*). It is presumably in accordance with this view that through most of the passage TJ does not attempt to change the literal meaning of the text.

30. Cf. Ezek. 22:6. 9.12; 23:27.45; 24:6-9; 36:18.

sin, for which severe punishment would be exacted.[31] Yet, halachically, while the shedding of blood is usually repugnant, it is not always a crime.[32] Hence, where it is denounced as a major transgression in the biblical text, TJ usually adds "innocent" (זכי or זכאי), i.e., the blood of innocent people was shed. Dire predictions of punishment of the perpetrators of innocent bloodshed are to be expected and would be legally and morally unimpeachable.

Similarly, in historical situations, any criminal accusation which could not be substantiated would be reinterpreted by TJ to conform to proper legal procedure. Thus, for example, Shimei the son of Gera was cursing David, calling him, "you man of blood,[33] implying—and indeed stating almost explicitly in the following verse[34]—that David had slain (or at least caused the violent deaths of) Saul and his family. The targumist, aware that the historical record knows of no such crime on the part of David, deliberately softens Shimei's accusations. David is described by TJ not as a "man of blood," but as a man who deserves to be put to death." Likewise, in II Samuel 16:8, it is not "the blood of the house of Saul" that God has avenged upon David, but rather, in TJ's formulation, "the sins of the house of Saul." TJ thus implies, admittedly with scant regard to the logic of the situation, that David was now being saddled with the sins of Saul's family whom he had displaced.[35]

A concern for proper legality in capital cases is also shown by TJ in connection with the strange prediction in Zechariah 13:3, where we are told that "if anyone again appears as a prophet, his father and mother who bore him will say to him, 'You shall not live, for you speak lies in the name of the

31. *Ibid.* 24:7-14.
32. Cf., e.g., I Chron. 22:8; 28:3, where David is told that he would not be permitted to build the Temple because he had shed much blood in the course of his wars. Significantly, the Targum Rab Joseph, *ad. loc.,* renders literally, it being assumed that, while a warrior king like David might not be suitable for building the Temple of peace, he had not shed "innocent" blood, which would have required a far more serious penalty.
33. II Sam. 16:7.
34. *Ibid.* v.8.
35. This curious interpretation may have been influenced by the description, in II Sam. 21:1, of Saul's dynasty as his "bloody house"—rendered by TJ, "the house that deserves to be put to death." Since Saul's bloodguilt in slaying the Gibeonites is clearly stressed in the same verse, it was natural for TJ to apply the same interpretation to the somewhat different situation described in II Sam. 16:7.

Lord'; and his father and mother who bore him shall pierce him through when he prophesies." The idea that anyone could be killed—and, of all people, by his own parents—without due process or even a semblance of a trial, was an anathema to the targumist who first of all softens the words, "You shall not live" to "You shall not be preserved"—or, possibly, "It (viz., your prophecy) shall not be fulfilled." The last clause of the verse is rendered in such a way as to agree with the Deuteronomic prescription for "the stubborn and rebellious son"—where his parents are instructed to "*take hold of him* and bring him to the elders of his town."[36] TJ, accordingly, reads: ". . . and his father and mother who bore him shall *seize* (or: *take hold of*) *him* when he prophesies."

A halachic nuance is also introduced by the targumist in his interpretation of another passage dealing with capital punishment, namely II Samuel 14:11, where MT reads as follows:

"Pray, let the king invoke the Lord your God, that the avenger of blood slay no more, and my son be not destroyed." TJ, alluding to Deuteronomy 19:6a,[37] where provision is made for setting up cities of refuge for people involved in unintentional homicide, renders: "May the king now remember that which is written in the book of the Law of the Lord your God that the way should be made long before (i.e., for) the avenger of the blood (who is out) to destroy."[38] The wise woman of Tekoa is reminding David that the Law provides for the protection of the manslayer against the private vengeance of the blood-avenger.

Yet another example of careful regard for legal order in cases where a public execution of a malefactor has occurred is to be found in TJ's rendering of Joshua 7:25. According to MT, "all Israel stoned him (viz., Achan who had unlawfully taken some of the spoils of Jericho) with stones, and they burned them with fire, and stoned them with stones." The severe punishment of Achan—and apparently also of his family—is discussed at length in the Talmud,[39] and an attempt is made to soften the harsh impact of the nar-

36. Deut. 21:19.

37. ". . . Otherwise the avenger of blood may pursue the manslayer in hot anger and overtake him, because the distance is great (or: because the way is long) and kill him."

38. Since Deut. 19:6a does not speak about making the way long for the blood avenger, but, on the contrary, to make it short (by providing a near-by city of refuge) for the inadvertent manslayer, some TJ versions read: ". . . that the way should *not* be made long (viz., for the manslayer) before the avenger of the blood . . ." Cf. Komlosh, *op. cit.*, p. 318.

39. Cf. T.B. Sanh. 44a.

rative. According to one opinion, Achan had been guilty of cohabitation with a betrothed maiden—a sin equivalent to adultery for which the penalty of stoning was provided by both Biblical and Talmudic law.[40] Achan was, therefore, stoned instead of burned for misappropriating the spoils of Jericho which were under the ban.[41] The question was also raised why Achan's sons and daughters should have suffered the death penalty for their father's sin.[42] Since, however, "all Israel" is also mentioned in the same passage,[43] the retort was made that Achan's family, like the rest of the people, were only brought along to witness the execution so as to be warned against a repetition of such an offense.[44]

There was also the problem of what at first glance looks like a threefold execution, namely stoning, burning, and—once again—stoning.[45] The solution offered in the Talmud is that "those suitable for burning[46] were burned, and those suitable for stoning[47] were stoned.[48]

The targumist was concerned not so much with the moral problems posed by the narrative as with the logical and legal impossibility of a threefold execution. TJ's solution is original, though it may be based indirectly on the Deuteronomic legislation providing for temporary impaling on a stake of a person put to death for a capital crime.[49] A second "execution" may thus serve the purpose of degradation and warning "to all Israel." Similarly, TJ renders in our case: "And all Israel stoned him with stones; and they burned them with fire *after* they had stoned them with stones."[50] Thus, according to TJ, the burning was to serve as an additional punishment and a most impressive warning to the survivors.

In Biblical times, cremation was, it seems, a humiliation inflicted on

40. Cf. Deut. 22:23 ff.; M. Sanh. VII, 4.

41. Cf. Jos. 7:15 and 7:25.

42. Cf. T.B. Sanh. 44a.

43. Cf. Jos. 7:24.

44. Cf. T.B. Sanh. 44a.

45. Cf. Jos. 7:25.

46. According to Rashi on T.B. Sanh. 44a, this refers to Achan's inanimate property, e.g., silver, gold and garments.

47. A reference to Achan, his oxen, and cattle in general.

48. T.B. Sanh. 44a.

49. Cf. Deut. 21:22 f. According to the Mishnah, only those sentenced to be stoned—and not necessarily all of them— were to be impaled after the execution.

50. Cf. Komlosh, *op. cit.,* p. 274.

criminals and enemies of Israel.[51] Normally, however, cremation, though not explicitly prohibited by law, was contrary to Jewish custom. The Halacha provides only for the interment of the body, and burial was sometimes regarded as a positive commandment of the Torah.[52]

It is in accordance with the customary disapproval of cremation that the otherwise praiseworthy act of the men of Jabesh-gilead in rescuing the bodies of Saul and his sons from the wall of Beth-shan and ultimately providing honorable burial for them[53] was marred from the halachic point of view by their burning of the bodies prior to the interment of the bones.[54] TJ, alluding perhaps to the ancient and well-established practice of burning the royal accoutrements in honor of a deceased king,[55] translates MT ". . . and they burned them there"[56] by ". . . and they made a fire for them there as one makes a fire for kings." Thus, a halachically dubious act became one which was definitely permitted and, indeed, considered the proper thing to do.

TJ carefully adhered to a basic halachic attitude regarding vows, which were generally considered to be ill-advised. A halachic and moral problem was posed by Jephthah's foolish vow to sacrifice as a burnt offering "Whoever comes forth from the door of my house to meet me when I return victorious from the Amnonites"[57]—which resulted in the sacrificial death of his own daughter.[58] The rabbinic view of this terrible episode was that, according to the Halacha, Jephthah could easily have been absolved from his vow—even assuming that it was formally valid—, if he had consulted the high priest Phineas (who is assumed to have survived up to Jephthah's time). His failure to do so—and the equally unforgivable refusal of Phineas

51. Cf. *Enc. Jud.* V, 1072 ff.

52. Cf. T.B. Sanh. 46b (with reference to Deut. 21:23). Tacitus, Hist. V, 5, attributes the Jewish custom of burying rather than cremating the dead to Egyptian influence. Cf. especially M. Higger, הלכות ואגדות (New York 1933), pp. 161-183, where the literature on the subject is fully surveyed and analyzed.

53. Cf. I Sam. 31:11 ff.

54. Cf. *ibid.*, vv. 12 f. Significantly, the Chronicler (I Chron. 10:12) omits the cremation episode in his account of the death of Saul and his sons and the ultimate disposal of their bodies by the men of Jabesh-gilead.

55. Cf. Jer. 34:5; II Chron. 16:14; 21:19; Tos. Shab. VII (VIII), 18; Sanh. II, 4; T.Y. Sanh. II, 8, 20c; T.B. Sanh. 52b; A.Z. 11a.

56. I Sam. 31:12.

57. Jud. 11:30 f.

58. Cf. *ibid.* 11:34 ff.

to intervene of his own accord—were due to the intolerable arrogance of the two leaders, each of whom considered it beneath his dignity to take the first step and thus symbolically submit to the jurisdiction of the other. According to the Midrash, Phineas was punished by the loss of divine inspiration which he had previously enjoyed, while Jephthah was smitten by a loathsome disease which caused his body to disintegrate limb by limb, so that the organs of his body were interred in different places.[59]

One TJ version on Jud. 12:7 (where MT, translated literally, reads: "... and he (viz., Jephthah) was buried in the *cities* of Gilead")[60] adds the same homiletical interpretation:

"... and Jephthah the Gileadite died of bad afflictions because he had not taken compassion on his daughter and had not gone to urge Phineas the priest to annul his vow. Therefore, his limbs fell off from him, and they (literally: and his limbs) were buried in the cities of Gilead.[61]

A similar homiletical interpretation is to be found in Judges 11:39b, where MT "... and it became a custom in Israel" is rendered by TJ: "... and it became a decree[62] in Israel, so that no man should offer up his son or his daughter as a burnt offering, as was done by Jephthah the Gileadite without consulting Phineas the priest; for if he had consulted Phineas the priest, he would have redeemed her for money."[63]

The negative halachic attitude to vows is also indicated in TJ's rendering of Malachi 1:14, where MT reads: "Cursed be the cheat who has a male in his flock, and vows it, and yet sacrifices to the Lord what is blemished ..." TJ renders the last clause: "... and he is obligated to make a vow, and yet sacrifices before the Lord that which is blemished..." Since, according

---

59. Cf. Gen. R. LX, 3; Lev. R. XXXVII, 4; Eccl. R. X, 15; Midr.Tanh. בחקותי 5, edit. Buber, p. 112. f.

60. Heb. בערי גלעד —usually rendered, "in *one of* the cities of Gilead" or emended to בעירו גלעד —"in his city of Gilead."

61. Cf. Churgin, p. 129, who rightly points out that this Aggadah as well as the one cited in the next paragraph imply agreement with the view that a vow like Jephthah's was legally valid and had to be redeemed with money (or nullified by a priest or a sage). There was also another view, namely that a vow which involved the commission of an act prohibited by the Torah—in Jephthah's case, the killing of his daughter—was null and void *ab initio* and did not require any formal annulment; cf. Gen. R. LX, 3; Lev. R. XXXVII, 4; Tanh. בחקותי 5, edit. Buber, p.113. See also Komlosh, *op cit.*, p. 293.

62. Aram. גזירא—a literal translation of Heb. חק (statute, custom).

63. Cf. Churgin, p. 129; Komlosh, *op cit.*, p. 292.

to Deuteronomy 23:23, it is by no means sinful if one does not make any vows (a view which is to some extent confirmed in Ecclesiastes 5:4), TJ has to emphasize the obligatory character of the vow in question, thereby stressing the seriousness of the offense in offering blemished animals.

While vows of thanksgiving and similar offerings were acceptable,[64] there was a tendency, by no means universally shared, to regard a Nazirite, whose vow prevented him from drinking wine or eating grapes,[65] as requiring atonement for his self-imposed abstention.[66] It is this view which is reflected in TJ's translation of the word נזרים in Amos 2:11 and 12. MT—"I raised up some of your sons for prophets, and some of your young men for Nazirites... But you made the Nazirites drink wine"—clearly implies that the Nazirites, like the prophets, were a highly regarded element and given to Israel as a mark of divine favor. To circumvent this unpalatable description, TJ renders: "I raised... some of your young men to be teachers... But you led your teachers astray with wine..." This novel interpretation manages to ignore the Nazirites altogether, while placing teachers virtually on a level with the prophets. It is a view which agrees with the rabbinic opinion that "since the day when the Temple was destroyed, prophecy has been taken from the prophets and given to the wise.... A wise man is superior to a prophet."[67]

The rabbinic tendency to frown on vows applied equally to oaths. There was a strong aversion even against true oaths because of the possibility, however remote, that they might involve unintentional falsehoods.[68] Because of this attitude, there was a natural reluctance to accept the literal meaning of a verse implying that (true) oaths uttered in the name of the Lord were unobjectionable. Thus, Isaiah 48:1b—where those who "swear by the name of the Lord" are implicitly praised, though they are reprimanded at the end of the verse because of lack of truth and sincerity—is changed by TJ into "those with whom a covenant was made in the name of

---

64. Even so, there were many rabbinic warnings against habitually making vows which one might not be able or willing to fulfill; cf. M. Dem. II, 3; T.B. Ned. 20a; Derech Eretz R. 1, 13; Midr. Tanh. ויקרא 7, edit. Buber, Lev., p. 10; מטות I, edit. Buber, Num. p. 157.

65. Cf. Num. 6:1 ff.

66. Cf. Sifre to Num. 6:11; T.B. Nazir 19a. For a contrary view, cf. T.B. Ber. 63a; Sot. 2a; Naz. 2a.

67. T.B. B.B. 12a

68. Cf. T.B. Git. 35a. Cf. also Num. R. XXII, 1; Midr. Tanh. ויקרא, edit. Buber, Lev., p. 10.

the Lord." In this amended version there is no trace of any oath, let alone express or implied approval.

Of course, not all passages which mention oaths will necessarily bear out our contention that the targumists objected even to true oaths.[69] Thus, it is arguable that Hosea 4:15b—". . . and swear not, 'As the Lord lives'"—ought to have been translated literally in view of this seemingly clear rejection of any oath whatsoever. Yet, in point of fact, TJ renders: ". . . and swear not *falsely,* 'The Lord lives'." Hence it would follow that a true oath in the name of God was quite in order. However, this passage has to be seen in its proper context. It is preceded by the words, "Enter not into Gilgal, nor go up to Beth-aven." These were centers of what the prophet regarded as idolatrous cults. To have this followed by a prohibition of swearing in the name of the Lord would sound paradoxical and absurd, since it would seem to put true oaths on a par with idolatry. The unsophisticated synagogue audiences, for whom TJ was originally designed, could not be expected to understand that Hosea was objecting not to true oaths as such, but to the hypocrisy of invoking the name of Yahweh, while at the same time making pilgrimages to idolatrous cult centers. It was, therefore, necessary to make a clear distinction between the former (i.e., true oaths) and the latter, and that could be done only by depicting the prophetic denunciation as being directed against *false* oaths in the name of God—which were indeed just as repugnant as the preceding pilgrimages to Gilgal and Beth-aven.

One of the main problems facing the targumists was to reconcile the Biblical Temple practices and, especially, the sacrificial cult, with the occasionally rather different rabbinic rules governing this area of Jewish religious law. As a matter of fact, even the later books of the Bible, written under the influence of the Priestly Code and the Deuteronomic school, sometimes found it difficult to reconcile earlier practices with the strict centralization of the sacrificial cult required by Deuteronomic legislation.

Thus, II Samuel 8:18b—". . . and David's sons were priests", which was unacceptable from the point of view of the Priestly Code which had decreed that "the stranger (i.e., non-priest) who comes near (viz., to sacrifice on the

---

69. It must be conceded that Targum Onkelos, which generally shares the halachic concepts of TJ, renders literally both Deut. 6:13b and Deut. 10:20b—". . . by His (viz., God's) name you shall swear" (implying unqualified approval of true oaths uttered in the name of God). However, it must be borne in mind that Targum Onkelos is far more literal than TJ, deviating from MT only when the need for reinterpretation is very cogent indeed.

altar) shall be put to death"[70], was changed in the parallel passage in I Chronicles 18:17b to "... and David's sons were the chief officials next to (i.e., in the service of) the king".[71] The same interpretation is implied in the Mekhilta on Exodus 18:1, where R. Eleazar of Modi'im, citing II Samuel 8:18 as his proof-text, explains that Jethro "the priest of Midian" was in reality no priest but a ruler. As one might expect, TJ on II Samuel 8:18b follows the same ideological trend: "... and David's sons were officers (or: great men)."

The exclusive privilege of Aaronide priests to have access to the inner sanctuary and to minister in it is repeatedly indicated in TJ's rendering of ambiguous verses where a wrong impression might be conveyed by a literal translation. For example, when David was fleeing from Absalom, he urged Zadok the priest to carry the ark of God back to Jerusalem rather than take it with him to exile; for, as he put it, "If I find favor in the eyes of the Lord, He will bring me back and let me see both it (Heb. אתו) and His habitation.[72] The Hebrew אתו could refer either to the ark or to God. The latter was inconceivable in view of the unequivocal statement that "man may not see me and live."[73] But even the ark, which was in the Holy of Holies,[74] was supposed to be inaccessible to laymen; in fact only the high priest was permitted to approach it and then only on the Day of Atonement.[75] If David adhered to the Halacha—and it was taken for granted that he did[76]—he could not possibly have expressed the hope that God would let him see the ark. TJ therefore renders: "If I find mercy before the Lord, He will bring me back and let me be seen before him, and I will worship before Him in His sanctuary." David will be seen—and he will worship—in the sanctuary; but he can never see the ark which remains hidden in the Holy of Holies.

TJ is also concerned with the halachically unauthorized wearing of the

---

70. Num. 1:51; 3:10,38; 18:7. The Talmud (T. B. Shab. 31a) goes out of its way to emphasize that this severe rule applied even to David king of Israel who was not of priestly descent.

71. It is noteworthy that AV, too, renders II Sam. 8:18b; "... and David's sons were chief rulers"— evidently to harmonize it with I Chron. 18:17b.

72. II Sam. 15:25.

73. Exod. 33:20.

74. *Ibid.* 26:33 f.; Lev. 16:2.

75. Cf. Lev. 16:2 ff.; M. Yoma V,1.

76. Cf., e.g., T.B. Ber. 3b-4a; Shab. 56a.

linen ephod by David[77] and by Samuel[78], who was only a Levite,[79] not a priest. In both cases TJ renders: כרדוט דבוץ, i.e., a tunic with sleeves made of fine linen.[80]

The sensitivity of TJ where priestly privileges are concerned is also indicated in TJ's rendering of a seemingly inoffensive clause in Malachi 2:12, where the prophet denounces him who marries a foreign wife, cursing him, among other things, to have none (presumably, no offspring) "to bring (ומגיש) an offering to the Lord of hosts." If the Hebrew for "bring" had been מבי[א], there would have been no objection; anyone may bring an offering. The Hebrew מגיש, on the other hand, has the connotation of "presenting," i.e., offering it on the altar.[81] In that case there would be no point in the exclusion from the privilege of offering a sacrifice on the altar, unless the offender happened to be a priest. Hence both the Talmud[82] and TJ agree that this clause deals with a priest who has married a foreign wife: ". . . and if he is a priest, he shall have none (i.e., no son) to offer a sacrifice in the Temple of the Lord of Hosts." Where Halacha and history do not agree, rabbinic exegesis invariably sacrificed authentic history on the altar of undeviating Halacha. True to this principle, TJ insists on keeping a clear distinction between priests and Levites, a distinction which hardly existed in the earlier biblical period. For instance, Joshua 18:7a—"For the Levites have no portion among you, for the priesthood of the Lord is their inheritance"—could, if translated literally, imply that the Levites were entitled to the privileges of the priesthood. Such aspirations undoubtedly existed. Thus, the story of Korah and his fellow rebels[83] who asserted that "all the congregation are holy, every one of them"[84] was designed as an object lesson of what may

---

77. Cf. II Sam. 6:14; cf. also I Chron. 15:27, where the ephod is replaced by "a robe of fine linen."

78. Cf. I Sam. 2:18.

79. Cf. I Chron. 6:7-13. 18-23.

80. Churgin, p. 116, notes that TJ differentiates in rendering אפוד in a holy sense and in a profane sense; but he fails to point out that this distinction does not necessarily correspond to the original meaning of MT, but reflects later halachic propriety.

81. Cf., e.g., Mal. 1:7 f.; Exod. 32:6; Lev. 8:15.

82. Cf. T.B. Shab. 55b; Sanh. 82a: "If he is a priest, he shall have no son to offer an offering [to the Lord of hosts]." Churgin, p. 110, lists this passage as an example of parallel exegesis in TJ and Talmud or Midrash. He does not, however, subject the exegesis as such to a historical analysis.

83. Cf. Num. 16:1-35.

84. *Ibid.* 16:3.

85. Cf. also II Chron. 26:16-21, where it is related how King Uzziah of Judah was punished with leprosy for venturing to enter the temple and burn incense on the altar.

happen to Levites or any other non-Aaronides who attempt to perform sacerdotal functions.[85] So also Josephus, who prided himself of his priestly descent[86] sharply criticized the Levites who in his own time successfully usurped the right to wear linen robes, a privilege hitherto reserved exclusively for the priests.[87]

TJ, determined to keep the Scriptures in line with the Halacha, interprets Joshua 18:7a: "The gifts which the Lord gave them they are their inheritance."[88] Here there is no longer any reference to priesthood. The Levites have to content themselves with the "gifts" (i.e., the tithes) which God allocated to them.

A similar problem arose with the Biblical description of Samuel "lying down within the Temple of the Lord, where the ark of God was."[89] Since Samuel was a Levite,[90] he had no business lying down—and, presumably, sleeping—in the sanctuary, least of all in the Holy of Holies where the ark was placed.[91] In a somewhat different form this question was raised in the Talmud:

"Surely sitting (and, by analogy, lying down and sleeping) was permitted in the Temple only to the kings of the Davidic dynasty?!"[92]

The answer given was that the reading of the text should be changed to: "Now the lamp of the Lord had not yet gone out in the Temple of the Lord, and Samuel was lying in his place."[93] In a similar but more explicit vein TJ renders:

"Now Samuel was lying in the court of the Levites, and a voice was heard from the Temple of the Lord where the ark of the Lord was."

This version keeps Samuel out of the inner sanctuary and confines him to the court of the Levites, where he belongs. As for the ark in the Holy of Holies, it is the source of the divine voice heard by Samuel[94] which happens to agree with the description in Numbers 7:89:

"When Moses went into the tent of meeting to speak with Him (viz.,

86. Cf. *Vita* I, 1, beginning.

87. Cf. *Ant.* XX, 9, 6, pars. 216-218.

88. Churgin, p. 70, rightly points to the semantic influence of Jos. 13:33 (and, he could have added, of Deut. 18:2) on TJ's wording. Yet, he fails to explain the basic reason for the deviation from the original.

89. I Sam. 3:3.

90. See above, n. 30.

91. See above, notes 25 and 26.

92. T.B. Kid. 78b.

93. *Ibid.*

94. Cf. Komlosh, *op. cit.*, p. 329, where this problem is briefly discussed. See especially the literature cited there.

God), he heard the voice addressing him from above the cover that was upon the ark of the testimony. . . ".

The unhalachic behavior of Samuel and his disciples, especially his habit of offering sacrifices on *bamoth* ("high places"),[95] was disturbing from a halachic point of view. TJ is not very consistent in the translation of *bamah*, (or *bamoth*) which is normally rendered במתא, not only when semi-idolatrous "high places" are referred to,[96] but also when Solomon is recorded as having offered hecatombs of sacrifices on the Great *bamah* of Gibeon.[97] Yet, where Samuel is concerned, TJ goes out of its way to clear the prophet of any deviation from later Halacha by rendering Heb. במה by בית— אסחרותא a place of feasting.[98]

To be sure, after the destruction of the central sanctuary at Shiloh by the Philistines, the "high places" were supposed to have become halachically acceptable[99] which may account for the lack of consistency in TJ's rendering of במה. Still, there were other "deviations" from the orthodox practice of Talmudic Halacha during the age of Samuel which could not be glossed over so easily.

Thus, the offering of cows as burnt offerings when in fact only bulls were supposed to be offered[100] was explained away as a special ruling for that occasion.[101] Similarly, Samuel's sacrifice of a suckling lamb, which, according to one opinion, was a female animal, was eventually considered permissible on a private "high place".[102] But none of this really solved the problem as to how Samuel as a non-Aaronide was qualified to offer any sacrifices at all.

A certain sensitivity about Samuel's sacrificial activities can also be detected in the addition of the Aramaic *Sheru* ("meal" or "banquet") before the literal rendering of *Zevah* (sacrifice) in I Samuel 20:6,29—as if to emphasize that this was really an ordinary banquet rather than a formal

95. Cf. I Sam 9:12-14, 19,25; 10:5,13. Cf. also Komlosh, *op. cit.,* p. 306.

96. Cf., e.g., I Kings 3:2; 13:32-33; 15:14; 22:44 *et passim*

97. Cf. *ibid.* 3:4.

98. See above, note 95; cf. also Churgin, p. 116.

99. Cf., e.g., Tos. Men. XIII, 4-5; M. Meg. I, 10; T.B. Meg. 10a; Zev. 112 b; Bekhor. 4b.

100. Cf. Lev. 1:3; I Sam. 6:14.

101. Cf. T.B. A.Z. 24b.

102. *Ibid.*

sacrifice. However, unaware of the ancient custom of annual family sacrifices,[103] and sensing perhaps a parallel to I Samuel 16:2-5, where Samuel is engaged in offering a sacrifice (though not necessarily carrying out the entire cultic ritual), TJ depicts the sacrifice as "holy", even though this is not stated in the text. This addition may have been designed to counter any idea that the "sacrifices" were of less than sacred character.

In one passage, though, TJ attempts to circumvent the concept that Samuel may have offered sacrifices. In I Samuel 9:13, we are informed that Samuel was "to bless the sacrifice." Since there is no evidence in halachic literature that a prophet—or, for that matter, a scholar—was to make a formal blessing over the sacrifices, TJ changes the clause to the point where it assumes an entirely new meaning:

"He breaks the food" (i.e., the bread)—which presumably means that the prophet had the privilege of reciting grace before the meal.[104]

As already indicated, it was sometimes difficult to reconcile later biblical and rabbinic Halacha relating to the sacrificial cult with the actual practices depicted by some of the biblical writers. Thus, Isaiah's prediction that there would be "an altar to the Lord in the midst of the land of Egypt, and a pillar to the Lord at its border"[105] flatly contradicted Deuteronomy 12:5-14, which prohibited sacrifices outside "the place which the Lord your God will choose.[106] It also contradicted Deuteronomy 16:22, where it is expressly stated that "you shall not set up a pillar, which the Lord your God hates." Both Josephus[107] and the Talmud[108] recognize in Isaiah 19:19 an allusion to the Temple of Onias in Leontopolis, Egypt, though they also criticize its existence. The Mishnah,[109] however, records different views regarding the legitimacy of certain vows, the fulfillment of which required sacrificial acts in the Temple of Onias. Significantly, R. Simeon—whom we have already

---

103. Cf. I Sam. 1:3 ff.; 20:6.

104. It is noteworthy, that, according to the Talmud (T.B. Ber. 48 b), the obligation to recite a blessing before the meal is derived from this verse.

105. Is. 19:19.

106. See, especially, Deut. 12:13: "Take heed that you do *not* offer your burnt offerings at every place that you like." Cf. also M. Zev. XIV, 10; Tos. Zev. XIII, 8.

107. *Ant.* XIII, 3,1-3, pars. 62-73; *Bell.* VII, 10, 2-3, pars. 423-432.

108. T.B. Men. 109b.

109. M. Men. XIII,10.

identified as an outstanding representative of the school of R. Akiba—states that vows relating to the Temple of Onias had no validity whatsoever.[110] It is in line with this view that TJ renders:

"... there shall be an altar *prepared before* the Lord within the land of Egypt, and a pillar by its border *before* the Lord." Although the Aramaic קדם (before) is frequently used in the sense of "to", the combination of מתקן (prepared) with קדם amounts to a deliberate circumlocution, which also applies to the last clause of the verse. The implication seems to be that neither the Temple nor the pillar were recognized as being dedicated *to* the Lord. They were merely there *before* the Lord, but did not enjoy any legitimacy.

A similar difficulty seems to have arisen with the tacit permission evidently granted by the prophet Elisha to the Aramean general Naaman to use earth from the Land of Israel to build an altar in Syria for the purpose of offering sacrifices to God.[111] Accordingly, a marginal note (Targum Yerushalmi) adds the following to II Kings 5:20 (5:19 in Sperber's edition of TJ):

"[And he said to him, 'go in peace]; for an altar before the Lord is not proper in a foreign country, only in the Land of Israel. If, however, it is your wish to send burnt offerings and holy sacrifices to offer up before the Lord year by year in the place where it is his wish to cause His divine presence to rest, we shall accept them from you.'"

This marginal note neatly disposes of all the objections that could be raised against the Hebrew text.

Not only animal sacrifices, but also drink offerings, including even water libations, were prohibited outside of the central sanctuary or during times not set aside for this purpose. When, for example, the Israelites "gathered at Mizpah, and drew water and poured it out before the Lord and fasted on that day,"[112] they were obviously not observing the joyful water libation rites customary in the Temple on the seven days of the festival of Succot.[113] TJ therefore turns the verse into a suitable homily so as to remove any suggestion of a formal, religiously valid ceremony:

110. *Ibid.*
111. II Kings 5:17-19.
112. I. Sam. 7:6.
113. Cf. M. Suk. IV, 1. 9. 10; Tos. Suk. III, 3.14-16.

"... and they poured out their hearts in repentance like water before the Lord."

The same problem arose in connection with David's pouring of the water from the well of Bethlehem "to the Lord."[114] Since David was at the time at the cave of Adullam,[115] he was not even at a recognized sanctuary where libations might be in order. TJ, accordingly, renders:

"... and he *said that he would* [or: he *promised to*] pour them out before the Lord." In other words, David was going to offer this libation only in the central sanctuary and, presumably, in accordance with halachic requirements.

There is evidence that, according to TJ, not only Jews but even Gentiles were not supposed to offer sacrifices to God outside the Temple of Jerusalem. Thus, in Jonah 1:16, we are told that the foreign sailors on Jonah's ship "offered a sacrifice to the Lord." As in the previous example, TJ subtly changes this to "... and they said that they would [or: They promised to] offer a sacrifice to the Lord." Mere intention to make a sacrificial offering—presumably later in Jerusalem—was of course in no way reprehensible. Thus, in TJ, even non-Jews are made to adhere to the Halacha.

Perhaps the most difficult halachic problem faced by the targumist was to be found in that enigmatic verse in Malachi (1:11), where we are informed that "... in every place incense is offered to my name, and a pure offering...." If this is a reference to non-Jews, it implies that their idolatrous cults are ultimately directed towards the God of heaven and earth. Athough this is contrary to the entire trend of Biblical theology which absolutely negates idolatry in all its form, denounces its obscenities and barbarities, and ridicules its absurdity,[116] nevertheless, one Talmudic and one medieval interpretation do indeed run along these lines:

"From Tyre to Carthage they (viz., the nations) know Israel and their Father who is in heaven... ... They call him the God of Gods."[117]

A similar interpretation, though couched in poetical style, is to be found in Solomon Ibn Gabirol's *Keter Malchuth:*

---

114. II Sam. 23:16.
115. Cf. *ibid.* v. 13.
116. Cf., e.g., Lev. 18:3. 24-30; 20:2-6. 22-27; Deut. 7:1-5,25 f.; 12:1-3, 30 f.; 13:2-8; 17:2-7; 18:9-14; 20:16-18; 29:15-27; 32:15 ff.; Jud. 2:2-14; 3:5-8; I Sam 12:21; I Kings 18:27; II Kings 17:7-18; 21:1-15; Is. 40:18-20; 44:9-20; 45:20; 66:1 f., 5-7; 65:3-7; 66:3 f. 17; Jer. 2:10-13.20-28; 3:1-13; Ezek. 16:16-25; Hos. 4:12 f.; 8:4-6.
117. T.B. Men. 110a.

"Thou art God—and all beings are Thy servants and Thy worshipers. Yet Thy glory is not diminished in the assembly of[118] those that serve others besides Thee; for the intention of them all is to come to Thee."[119]

If, on the other hand, Malachi 1:11 refers to Jews, it would mean that incense and "a pure offering" were acceptable all over the world and did not necessarily have to be brought to the Temple of Jerusalem.

To obviate both these explanations with their theological and halachic problems, R. Jonathan (not to be confused with Targum Jonathan) homiletically interpreted Malachi 1:11 as follows:

"This refers to scholars who engage in the study of the Torah in whatever place they are. [God says,] I account it unto them as though they burned incense and offered it unto my name. '... and a pure offering'—this refers to one who studies the Torah in purity, that is, one who takes a wife and afterwards studies the Torah."[120]

TJ adopts a similar homiletical interpretation, except that here the emphasis is on prayer rather than on study, possibly because for unsophisticated synagogue audiences prayer was indeed of overriding importance:

"... and whenever you perform (lit., do) my will, I shall accept your prayer, and my great name shall be sanctified through you, and your prayer is like a pure offering before me...."[121]

---

118. Heb. בקהל. According to Israel Davidson's edition (in collaboration with Israel Zangwill, *Selected Religious Poems of Solomon Ibn Gabirol, Philadelphia 1944, p. 86),* בגלל ("on account of").

119. Cf. Hayyim Schirmann, השירה העברית בספרד ובפרובאנס (Jerusalem-Tel Aviv, 1961), Vol. I, p. 261. It is highly probable that this represents Ibn Gabirol's interpretation of Malachi 1:11.

120. T.B. Men. 110a.

121. Although TJ on this verse is quoted three times by Churgin (pp. 28, 91, 110), it is not explained in terms of its halachic significance, but as an indication of post-Second Commonwealth prevenance (p. 28). Yet, this is by no means certain, since in Temple times the importance of sacrificing only in the Temple of Jerusalem—and not, for example, in the Temple of Onias in Egypt—would tend to be emphasized even more than later when sacrifice had ceased in any case.

Churgin (p. 110) also cites Num. R. XIII, 4 (not 2 as printed erroneously) where, in reference to Mal. 1:11, the question is asked: "... But are incense and oblations offered in every place to the name of the Holy One Blessed be He? But (the meaning is:) wherever Israelites stand and recite the afternoon prayer (Minhah)—the term Minhah (offering, oblation) in its literal sense is applied to it ... 'is offered'—this refers to the morning service ... 'incense'—this refers to the evening service ..."

It should be noted, however, that the Midrash on Numbers is of very late provenance (cf.

A major problem for the targumists was the negative prophetic attitude to the sacrificial cult, thereby contradicting the Priestly and Deuteronomic Codes of the Pentateuch which not only favor sacrifices, but prescribe them for a large variety of occasions. TJ could not, of course, entirely ignore the Prophetic texts, and a consistent re-writing in the Aramaic translation of anti-sacrificial passages was not to be expected. There are, nevertheless, a few significant deviations from the original Hebrew indicating that the halachic problems of prophetic denunciations of the prevailing cult were not being ignored.

Thus, Isaiah 1:13—"Bring no more vain offerings"—implies that bringing oblations is futile.[122] Since this could not possibly be reconciled with the minute commandments in the Torah to offer sacrifices on every conceivable occasion, TJ renders: "Bring no more oblations of oppression (i.e., of ill-gotten wealth)"—which is, of course, halachically unimpeachable. The same verse continues: "Incense is an abomination to me." Taken literally this contradicts Exodus 30:7 f., 31:8,11; 35:8,15 as well as other passages showing that incense-burning was an integral part of the sacrificial cult required by the Law. TJ therefore avoids this difficulty by rendering: "It is an abominable sacrifice[123] before me," thus referring it to be the previous clause which had been translated, "Bring no more oblations of oppression." Such an offering would indeed be "an abominable sacrifice."

Similarly, Hosea 6:6—"For I desire steadfast love and not sacrifice"—is rendered theologically acceptable by TJ's translation: "I desire those that do acts of kindness *more than* him that sacrifices." With this slight change, outright rejection of sacrifices has been replaced by a fully justified value judgment.

Another example of a seemingly disdainful prophetic stance regarding the Temple cult is to be found in Malachi 1:10, where the prophet, disgusted with the blemished sacrifices accepted by the priests for the altar, calls upon them that they should "not kindle fire upon my altar in vain." In terms of Halacha, the kindling of the fire was independent of the sacrifices

---

H.L. Strack, *Introduction to the Talmud and Midrash,* Eng. transl., Philadelphia 1945, pp. 214 f.), and it was undoubtedly influenced by TJ, not vice versa.

122. This is indeed the exact wording of the new JPS translation, which may not be a precise rendering of the Hebrew, but it correctly expresses the spirit of the original.

123. The usual Aramaic translation of the Hebrew קטורת is קטורת בוסמין or קטורת בוסמיא ; cf., e.g., I Sam. 2:28 *et passim.*

that might or might not be offered on the altar: "The fire on the altar shall be kept burning on it, it shall not go out.[124] It follows that the altar-fire does not actually need to be lit at all; it need only be maintained by adding firewood. Hence TJ's evasive rendering: "... and you shall not offer an abominable sacrifice upon my altar."

A different halachic problem connected with the altar was posed by Ezekiel 43:17b (end), where we are told that "... its (viz., the altar's) steps shall face east." Since the altar was not supposed to have steps leading up to it,[125] TJ simply eliminates the steps by translating:

"... and from the place where one goes up to it one turns to the east".

Sometimes, TJ is influenced not so much by halachic contradictions as by certain unrelated halachic practices which for some reason are connected in the mind of the targumist with the verse in question. For example, in I Samuel 25:18 we are told that Abigail brought David, among other things, "five sheep ready dressed" (עשׂויות), which means that the culinary preparations had been made and that they were ready to be eaten. TJ, associating the Hebrew עשׂויות (root עשׂה) with the identical verb used frequently in connection with the Paschal lamb,[126] which was roasted with its legs and entrails partly stuffed in and partly hanging out,[127] renders: "... and five stuffed (תכברא) sheep.[128]

It may seem strange that a specific mode of preparing the Paschal lamb should be associated with a secular act in the story of David and Abigail. Any imitation of the Paschal lamb outside Jerusalem was considered reprehensible even deserving excommunication. The difficulty is, however, more

---

124. Lev. 6:5; cf. *ibid.* vv. 1 and 6.

125. Cf. Exod. 20:26: "You shall not ascend my altar by steps..." This difficulty was noted by Rashi and Kimchi in their commentaries on Ezek. 43:17b, and they both suggest— Rashi by implication, Kimchi explicitly—that the "steps" may actually have been made in the form of a slanting ascent. This conforms to the traditional rabbinic view; cf., e.g., M. Yoma II, 1-2; Suk. IV, 9; Zev. III, 6; V, 3; VI, 5; Tam. I, 4; III, 1; IV, 3 (end); V, 2; VII, 3; Mid. V, 2). Kimchi also quotes a different version of TJ, where the "steps" of the Hebrew text are retained in the translation. Accordingly, Kimchi offers an alternative interpretation, namely that the steps in question led to the Temple court, *not* to the altar.

126. Cf. Exod. 12:48; Num. 9:2,4,5,6.10.14; Deut. 16:1; Jos. 5:10 f.; II Kings 23:21,23; Ezra 6:19; II Chron. 30:1,2,5; 35:1,16,17 ff.

127. Cf. M. Pes. VII, 1.

128. Cf. Rashi on T.B. Pes. 74a, where he cites—and connects with I Sam. 25:18— a similar reading (תכבר) in the talmudic text (which differs from ours) in R. Ishmael's description of the Paschal lamb.

apparent than real. For such imitation was forbidden only on the first night of Passover, while it was definitely permitted on the last night of Passover.[129] By implication, it was permitted during the rest of the year when there could be no conceivable appearance of eating the Paschal lamb outside Jerusalem. TJ's translation therefore remains strictly within the bound of halachic propriety.

This characteristic feature of targumic Halacha is also true in the case of TJ's rendering of Ezekiel 44:18, where the priests are commanded not to "gird themselves with anything that causes sweat". Although the priestly girdles were made of linen,[130] and not of heat-inducing wool, there is no specific commandment in the Torah prohibiting a woolen girdle for priestly use. Possibly for this reason, the Talmud interprets this verse rather differently:

"They shall not gird themselves in the place where they sweat.[131] As it was taught (in a Baraitha): When they gird themselves, they must not do so either below their loins or above their elbows, but (in the place) corresponding to their elbows."[132] TJ, while not exactly following this interpretation, comes reasonably close to it:

"... and they shall not gird themselves on their loins, but on their hearts", meaning, one may reasonably assume, the entire area of the chest, which is close to the area above the loins.[133]

Another example of adherence to halachic propriety in regard to sacerdotal vestments can be found in TJ's rendering of I Samuel 22:18b, where MT "... on that day he put to death eighty-five men who wore the linen ephod" becomes in TJ: "... and he slew on that day eighty-five men *who were fit to wear* the linen ephod". Since, according to Exodus 28:6 ff., the ephod was worn only by Aaron (i.e., the high priest),[134] while "Aaron's sons" (i.e., ordinary priests) wore only four garments which did not include the ephod,[135] eighty-five ephod wearers could not have been put to death;

---

129. Cf. Tos. Yom Tov II, 15; T.Y. Pes. VII, 1, 34a; T.B. Pes. 53a.

130. Cf. Exod. 39:26; Lev. 16:4.

131. Rashi: "... where flesh folds over flesh, so that one gets heated up and perspires."

132. T.B. Zev. 18b–19a.

133. Churgin (p. 124) assumes too readily total agreement between TJ and the talmudic Baraitha.

134. Cf. also M. Yoma VII, 5.

135. *Ibid.*; cf. also Exod. 28:40 ff.

for obviously there could be only one high priest at any given time. By adding one word, דכשרין *who were fit,* TJ—ignoring, as usual, the possibility of deviant Halacha during the early history of Israel—, makes it clear that the murdered priests were not actually wearing the ephod, but that they were great men worthy of the high priestly honor.[136]

It is noteworthy that even seemingly innocuous statements which would hardly appear to qualify for halachic interpretations are sometimes considered by TJ unacceptable in their literal form. Thus, in I Samuel 21:10, we are informed that Goliath's sword was kept in the sanctuary of Nob "behind the ephod". This would imply that the ephod was not constantly worn by the high priest as he was supposed to do,[137] but was kept somewhere in the sanctuary, except, presumably, on special occasions when the ephod, to which the breastplate with the Urim and Thummim oracle stones was attached,[138] was required for predicting the future.[139] It might even be inferred, as has been done by some modern commentators, that the ephod was not necessarily set on a garment at all, but that it was a metal object, possibly an image made of gold, which served as an oracle.[140]

To counter such halachically unacceptable conclusions, TJ changes MT "behind the ephod" to "after he had inquired for him by the ephod". This was in accordance with the Talmudic concept that nothing of importance may be undertaken by a king or a leader of the people without consulting the Urim and Thummim.[141]

Another example of this type is to be found in Hosea 4:8, where we are told that "they (viz., the priests) feed on the sin of my people; they are greedy for their iniquity". This may superficially be acceptable as a denunciation of priestly corruption. But considered from a halachic point of view, it is difficult to see how the priests can be condemned for eating the sin-offerings brought to the sanctuary, seeing that both the written and oral law

136. The same interpretation is also given in T.Y. Sanh. X, 2, 29a, where the question is posed, "Did not R. Hiyya teach, One many not appoint two high priests at the same time? (How, then, could there be eighty-five priests who wore the ephod?) But this is to teach that they were all worthy of being high priests."

137. Cf. Exod. 28:29 f.; I Sam. 2:28.

138. Cf. Exod. 28:6-30.

139. Cf., e.g., I Sam. 23:9 f.; 30:7 f.; see also Num. 27:21; I Sam. 14:41; 28:6.

140. Cf. אנציקלופדיה מקראית (Jerusalem 1965), Vol. I, col. 496.

141. Cf. M. Yoma VII, 5; T.B. Ber. 3b.

require male priests to eat the flesh of the sin offerings.[142] TJ, therefore, changes the translation to: "The priests have committed desecration by eating the sin-offerings of my people in order to add sins to the guilt of their souls". True, TJ still leaves us in blissful ignorance as to *how* the priests desecrated the sacrifices, and *what* sins precisely they added to *what existing guilt*. Nevertheless, between the lines one can read the suggestion that the priests were guilty of sins analogous to those committed by Hophni and Phineas, the sons of Eli.[143] In TJ's *Weltanschauung* the priests could be accounted guilty only if they ate of the sin-offering beyond what they were permitted and commanded, thereby desecrating the holy sacrifices.

Another aspect of alleged priestly wrongdoing is homiletically clarified in TJ's interpretation of Zechariah 3:3, which reads in the original: "Now Joshua was clothed in filthy garments." This would hardly seem to be a promising area for halachic implications, except for the fact that the entire statement would seem to be pointless. One could also question why a high priest should wear such garments in the first place, even in a vision. TJ, in full agreement with the Talmud,[144] renders: "Now Joshua had sons who had taken themselves wives that were unfit for the priesthood". What may appear to be a homily against priests marrying unsuitable wives which, standing by itself, is quite feasible, may well have been meant as a warning against contracting marriages which could not be recognized according to the Halacha.

Naturally, the following two verses had to be adapted to fit in with this interpretation. hence MT—"Remove the filthy garments from him" (*ibid.* 3:4)—becomes in TJ: "Tell him that he should remove the women who were unfit for the priesthood out of his house". Finally, in v.5, MT "and they clothed him with garments" is turned by TJ into "and they gave him a wife to marry who was fit for the priesthood".

Halachic considerations sometimes intrude in passages where one would least expect them. For example, David's poetical outburst against the mountains of Gilboa where Saul and Jonathan had been slain comprises an execration against the mountains that had witnessed and, as it were, permitted the outrage against the Lord's annointed: "Let there be no dew or rain upon

142. Cf. Lev. 6:19.22; M. Zev. V, 3.
143. Cf. I Sam. 2:12-17.
144. Cf. T.B. Sanh. 93a: "... His (viz. Joshua's) sons married wives unfit for the priesthood, and he did not protest...."

you, nor fields of offering" (שדי תרומות). The latter phrase is rendered by TJ:

"Let there be no harvest on you (even) sufficient for making *Hallah* from it". Since *Hallah* was a small dough cake[145] of minimal quantity—one twenty-fourth part of the dough for the ordinary householder[146]—given to a priest, the curse that the mountains of Gilboa should not yield grain enough for a single Hallah offering, became a striking and familiar illustration of the Biblical malediction.[147]

An even more glaring example of halachic intrusion in unexpected places is a midrashic addition to TJ (on II Kings 4:7) quoted by Kimchi:

"And when that miracle (viz., the oil bounty) happened to her (i.e., the unnamed prophet's widow), she said to the prophet of the Lord (=Elisha): 'Is it incumbent upon me to offer a tithe from this oil or not?' He said to her, 'your husband (identified with Obadiah, Ahab's steward[148]) fed the prophets with food (lit., a thing) for which tithing was not obligatory.[149] You, too, are not obligated to give a tithe, for it (viz., the oil) was produced through a miracle' ".

The halachic problem introduced here is whether food which did not originate naturally needs to be tithed. The answer given is really twofold. First there is a kind of aggadic analogy between the widow and her late husband, on the principle of measue for measure. She did not have to render any tithes just as her husband had fed the prophets with food that did not require tithing, presumably because it was regarded as equivalent to the poor tithe which replaced the so-called second tithe every third and sixth year of the Sabbatical cycle.[150] Alternatively, it was tacitly assumed that the "bread" provided by Obadiah to the prophets hiding in the two caves was really grain taken directly from the field to the caves. This meant that there was no tithing liability, since the grain had to be stacked smoothly in the threshing floor and even, according to one opinion, brought into the house of the owner before being liable to tithing.[151]

The second answer is more prosaic and less complicated. Miraculous

---

145. Cf. Num. 15:17-21.
146. Cf. M. Hal. II, 7.
147. Cf. also Komlosh, *op. cit.*, p. 235.
148. Cf. I Kings 18:3 ff.
149. *Ibid.* 18:13.
150. Cf. Deut. 14:28 f; 26:12 f.; T.B. R. Ha. 12b.
151. Cf. M. Peah I, 6; Ma'as. I, 6; T.B. Ber. 35b; Git. 81a; B.M. 87b-88a.

food is not subject to the laws of tithing, possibly because the tithes are a tax on the fruit of the land. Miraculous food, on the other hand, is not derived from the soil.

In TJ, all arrangements for the sacrificial cult of the Temple had to conform to the Halacha as established towards the end of the Second Commonwealth. Thus, Ezekiel 40:41b—". . . eight tables, *on* which the sacrifices were to be slaughtered"—is slightly but significantly changed in TJ to: ". . . eight tables, *between* which the sacrifices were to be slaughtered". The reason for this change is that the tables in the slaughtering-place were used for rinsing the entrails of the sacrificial animals,[152] not for slaughtering, which was done on the north side of the altar[153] on metal rings to which the animals were attached[154] or, in the case of sacrifices of a minor degree of holiness, anywhere in the Temple court.[155]

A similar adaptation of the description of the future Temple in Ezekiel to the rules and conditions prevailing during the final phase of the Second Temple can be seen in TJ's rendering of Ezekiel 40:43a. MT "And hooks, a handbreadth long, were fastened round about within" becomes in TJ, "And hooks protruding one handbreadth were fastened to the pillars of the slaughter house within the halls round about". This description agrees exactly with that given in several passages of the Mishnah.[156]

The widespread custom of praying in the direction of Jerusalem and the Temple,[157] which was codified into law[158], is clearly reflected in TJ's rendering of II Kings 20:2 (= Isaiah 38:2), where MT reads: "Then Hezekiah turned his face to the wall, and prayed. . ." TJ significantly adds: "Then Hezekiah turned his face to the wall *of the Temple* and prayed. . ." The reasoning behind this addition is that there was no special virtue in turning one's face to the wall of one's house during prayer and there was certainly no need to inform us concerning such a trivial matter. If, on the other hand, the wall was that of the Temple, it follows that Hezekiah was obeying an impor-

---

152. Cf. M. Shek. VI, 4.
153. Cf. Lev. 1:11; 6:18; 7:2; M. Zev. V, 1-5.
154. Cf. M. Mid. III, 5.
155. Cf. Lev. 3:8; M. Zev. V, 6-8.
156. Cf. M. Pes. V, 9; Tam. III, 5; Mid. III, 5.
157. Cf. I Kings 8:35; II Chron. 6:26; Dan. 6:11.
158. Cf. M. Ber. IV, 5-6; Tos. Ber. III, 16; T.B. Ber. 30a; and especially T.Y. Ber. IV, 5, 8c.

tant halachic rule, thus setting an example to others to do likewise.

In addition to TJ's concern with the reconciliation of the Biblical text with rabbinic Halacha as it pertained to various aspects of the Temple cult, TJ also attempted to correct the Biblical descriptions of personal customary practices so that they, too, conformed to Halacha.

The custom of tying a girdle or putting on a special garment for prayer, which was based on Amos 4:12—"Prepare to meet your God, O Israel"— had also become a halachic ruling in Talmudic times[159] and was, accordingly, reflected in TJ's rendering of that same verse in Amos: "Adorn yourself to receive the teaching of the Law of your God, O Israel.[160] The act of "adorning" is not just a form of preparing "to meet God", a manifest anthropomorphism to be carefully avoided. It is at the very least a halachic custom, usually associated with prayer, but in this case attributed to study. Such a custom was as good as a valid ruling for future generations.

Among the major precepts to which considerable importance was attached by the rabbis was the wearing of phylacteries,[161] which was naturally attributed to the ancient heroes of Israel. Most of them were imagined to have been strict observers of the Halacha. Thus, in connection with the account of the Amalekite reporting to David that he had taken from Saul's body "the crown which was on his head and the bracelet (or: armlet) which was on his arm,"[162] the targumist was evidently unable to comprehend how a king of Israel could possibly wear an ornament more fit for a woman[163]— thereby, moreover, transgressing the Biblical commandment, "A woman shall not wear a man's apparel, nor shall a man put on a woman's garment."[164] But since II Samuel 1:10 mentions the crown on Saul's *head* and an ornament on his *arm*, the connection with phylacteries which are worn on the head and on the (left) arm easily suggested itself. TJ, imagining Saul to have worn phylacteries even while fighting his battles, renders accordingly: ". . . and I took the crown[165] which was on his head and the frontlet[166] which was on his arm."

159. Cf. T.B. Shab. 10a.
160. This is cited by Churgin (p. 108) without comment.
161. Cf. Exod. 13:9,16; Deut. 6:8; 11:18.
162. II Sam. 1:10.
163. Cf. Is. 3:20.
164. Deut. 22:5.
165. Here translated literally, but probably taken as an allusion to the phylactery of the head, as indicated by the sequel.
166. Aram. טוטפתא ; cf. טוטפת [ל] in Exod. 13:16; Deut. 6:8; 11:18.

The Halacha exempts mourners from wearing phylacteries[167]—in fact it prohibits it[168]—on the ground that they constitute an ornament which mourners are not supposed to wear. The Biblical proof-text provided is Ezekiel 24:17a[169], where the prophet is commanded not to mourn the loss of his wife. Among other mourning customs that he is to disregard is the removal of his turban. On the contrary, he was told by God, "Bind on your turban."[170] This was to serve as a symbol of the approaching catastrophe which would be so overwhelming that the people would be unable to observe the normal mourning customs.[171] TJ translates Ezekiel 24:17a—as well as 24:23a—in accordance with the Talmudic Halacha: MT "Bind on your turban" becomes in TJ: "Your phylacteries shall be upon you."[172] Likewise, in 24:23a, MT "... and your turbans shall be on your heads" becomes in TJ, "... and your phylacteries shall be on your heads."

Another important halachic field was the regulation of the calendar, and especially the intercalation of years and months, which was necessary to keep the Hebrew lunar calendar in line with the solar year. TJ interpolates this halachic practice in the translation of I Samuel 20:27a, where MT "Now it came to pass on the second day, the morrow after the new moon" is rendered by TJ: "Now it came to pass on the following day which was the intercalated second (new moon) day of the month." The targumist assumes that the previous day, which is indeed described as the New Moon,[173] was the thirtieth day of the previous month, but was celebrated as New Moon just in case witnesses arrived to testify before the high court that they had seen the "new" moon on the previous evening.[174] If the "new" moon was not seen or if witnesses did not arrive in time, the following day would be the first of the next month and observed as the second day of the New Moon celebration. TJ implicitly assumes that this is what happened in the story of David and Jonathan.

167. Cf. T.B. Ber. 11a; 16b; Suk. 25b; Ket. 6b; cf. also T. Y. M.K. III, 5, 82b.
168. Cf. T.B. M.K. 15a.
169. Cf. Churgin, p. 123 f.
170. Ezek. 24:17a.
171. *Ibid.* 24:22 ff.
172. Other TJ versions: "upon your head;" but since the plural form יהון ("they shall be") is used in all versions, the literal translation would obviously be unsuitable. By way of contrast, in 24:23a, where the people are addressed, all TJ versions have, "... and your phylacteries shall be on your heads."
173. Cf. I Sam. 20:24.
174. Cf. M. R. H. I, 4 ff.; II, 1.5 ff.

Consistent with this view, TJ also changes I Samuel 20:34b—MT
". . . and he (viz., Jonathan) ate no food on the second day of the month"—
to: ". . . and he ate no food on the day which was the intercalated second
(new moon) day of the month."

As befits a Targum emanating from the school of R. Akiba, TJ displays a
keen interest in educational matters, even where the plain meaning of the
text would hardly suggest such an interpretation. Thus, in II Kings 22:14,
we are informed that the prophetess Huldah dwelt in Jerusalem "in the
second quarter" (Heb. במשנה). Since משנה in the talmudic age meant teaching by repeated recitation—and hence traditional oral law—, TJ renders:
בבית אולפנא ("in the house of instruction").[175] The implication that a woman,
albeit a prophetess, could study in an institution of higher learning is somewhat startling and clearly betrays the influence of R. Akiba's school. For in
opposition to R. Eliezer's view that "whoever teaches his daughter Torah is
as though he had taught her lechery (or: obscenity)",[176] Ben Azzai, R.
Akiba's disciple and junior colleague[177] as well as his prospective son-in-
law,[178] was of the opinion that "it is a man's duty to teach his daughter
Torah. . ."[179]

The "House of Instruction" also appears in TJ in connection with the
account of David's stay with Samuel at Naioth,[180] which is rendered by TJ
not as a place name, but as בית אולפנא. The assumption was that Samuel was

---

175. It is noteworthy, though, that in Zephaniah 1:10, where the prediction is made that
wailing would be heard "from the second quarter" (מן המשנה), TJ translates: "from Ophla
(other versions: Opha), evidently a gate (Rashi: "second gate)" of Jerusalem. The inconsistency in TJ's interpretation is almost certainly due to the understandable desire not to
associate wailing with an institution devoted to the study of Torah. On the precise meaning
of בית אולפנא , cf. M. Aberbach, "Educational Institutions and Problems during the Talmudic
Age," in *HUCA* Vol. XXXVII (1966), pp. 107-111.

176. M. Sot. III, 4.

177. Cf. Sifra on Lev. 1:1, edit. Weiss, p. 4a; T. Y. Shek. III, 1, 47b; B.B. IX, 9, 17b; T.B.
Sot. 4b; B.B. 158b. See also W. Bacher, *Die Agada der Tannaiten* (Strassburg 1903), second
edit., I, pp. 415-419. There are some indications, however, that Ben Azzai was R. Akiba's
junior colleague rather than his disciple; cf. T.B. Ned. 74b; Bekhor. 58a. See also M.S.
Zuckermandel, *Monatsschrift,* 1873, p. 374.

178. Cf. Ket. 63a and Tosafot *ad loc.* (s.v. ברתיה). Ben Azzai seems, however, to have
remained a bachelor; cf. T. Yev. VIII, 4 (end); T.B. Yev. 63b.

179. M. Sot. III, 4.

180. Cf. I Sam. 19:18f., 23; 20:1.

the head of a college, and that David was studying Torah under Samuel's guidance.[181]

During the Talmudic age, attendance upon a teacher (שימוש תלמידי חכמים or שימוש חכמים) was a *sine qua non* of higher education. R. Simeon ben Yohai who, as we have seen, was a disciple of R. Akiba, went so far as to state that attendance upon scholars was more important than study itself.[182] As already pointed out, David's relationship to his contemporaries was viewed by the rabbis not in historical perspective, but primarily in halachic terms. It was, therefore, natural to regard David's service at Saul's court as one of personal attendance upon a master. Hence I Samuel 16:21, MT "... and he (i.e., David) entered his (viz., Saul's) service" (lit., "and he stood before him") becomes in TJ: "... and he ministered before him." Likewise, I Samuel 16:22b—"Let David be (or: remain) in my service" is transformed in TJ to "Let David now minister (ישמיש) before me."

The counterpart to the disciples' attendance upon their teacher was selfless, unrequited teaching on the part of the master. Ideally, the Torah was to be imparted free of charge, and while this was an impractical ideal where younger pupils were concerned, older and more mature students were in fact taught without any financial obligations on their part.[183] So far from having to pay fees, in many cases, especially if they attended one of the major colleges, they were given what would today be described as scholarships or fellowships; or else they were maintained directly by their teachers.[184] The

---

181. Cf. T.B. Zev. 54b. Cf. also Yev. 77a on Samuel's *Beth Din*—an institution which in talmudic times usually served also as a college. According to Maimonides, who evidently reflects a Talmudic tradition, David received the tradition of the Law from Samuel; cf. Introduction to *Mishneh Torah*.

182. T.B. Ber. 7b. For a detailed discussion of the theory and practice of שימוש חכמים (or: שימוש תלמידי חכמים), cf. M. Aberbach, "The Relations between Master and Disciple in the Talmudic Age" in *Essays presented to Chief Rabbi Israel Brodie on the Occasion of His Seventieth Birthday*, edit. H. J. Zimmels, J. Rabbinowitz and I. Finestein (London 1967), pp. 2-6; and, at greater length, in Hebrew, היחסים בין הרב והתלמיד בתקופת התלמוד , *in Sheviley Hahinuch*, Vol. XXXII, No. I, pp. 9-12; Vol. XXXII, No. 2, pp. 77-81; Vol. XXXIV, No. 1, pp. 5-10. See also Churgin p. 94.

183. Cf. T.B. Ned. 37a; Bekhor. 29a; T.Y. Ned. IV, 3, 38c; Sifre Deut. 48, edit. Friedmann, p. 84a; Der. ER. Z., ch. 4; cf. also M. Avoth IV, 5.

184. Cf. M. Aberbach, "The Relations Between Master and Disciple in the Talmudic Age," *op. cit.*, p. 4, especially notes 28-31. Cf. also M. Aberbach היחסים בין הרב והתלמיד בתקופת התלמוד , *Sheviley Hahinuch*, Vol. XXXIII, No. 2, pp. 77f.

rabbis would have liked to extend this system to all levels of education and
were rather unhappy that it was unworkable at the elementary level and was
not followed even at the secondary Mishnah schools.[185]

This attitude is reflected in TJ's translation of Micah 3:11a, where MT
"... and her (Jerusalem's) prophets divine for money" is rendered,"... and
her prophets *teach* for money". Since they are not depicted as false prophets,
and since, moreover, divination is expressly prohibited in Deuteronomy
18:10, and frequently criticized elsewhere,[186] the prophetic strictures against
divination for money—implying as it does that unpaid divination was acceptable—was logically untenable and contrary to the Halacha. By changing
"divine" to "teach", these difficulties are avoided, while at the same time the
halachic principle of the desirability of unpaid teaching is given Scriptural
support. In line with this reasoning, "divination" and "diviners", mentioned
respectively in Micah 3:6 and 3:7, become in TJ "teaching" and "teachers".

The free instruction given by the teacher to his students and the devotion shown by the master to them necessitated a reciprocal attitude on their
part. Discipline and obedience to the command of the teacher were in-
grained habits among students of the Torah in the Talmudic age, and those
few who failed in their duties were severely taken to task. It was, for example, strictly forbidden to oppose one's master: "Whosoever contends
against (the ruling of) his teacher is as though he contended against the
divine presence".[187] To transgress the halachic pronouncements of scholars
in general (not to mention one's own master) was considered a heinous offense virtually deserving the supreme penalty: "Whosoever transgresses the
words of the sages deserves to die".[188]

It was this ideology that influenced some versions of TJ on II Kings
4:31, where Gehazi's fruitless attempt to revive the son of the Shunammite
woman is described. Since he had apparently acted in accordance with
Elisha's instructions,[189] Gehazi's failure would inevitably reflect on his master. The homiletical versions of TJ accordingly explain that "Gehazi went on
ahead and found a dead lion in the field. He thereupon placed the staff (viz.,

185. Cf. T.Y. Pe'ah VIII, 7, 21a; Hag. I, 7, 76c; Ned. IV, 3, 38c; T.B. Ned. 37a; M. Ned.
IV, 2-3; T.B. Bekhor. 29a; Lev. R. XXX,1.
186. Cf., e.g., I Sam. 15:23; Jer. 14:14; Ezek. 12:24; 13:6f., 23; cf. also Num. 23:23.
187. T.B. Sanh. 110a.
188. T.B. Ber. 4b; Eruv. 21b.
189. Cf. II Kings 4:29.

of Elisha) upon it so as to try it out, and he revived it (viz., the lion). But because he had transgressed the words of his master and had not done as he had commanded him, he went etc., (i.e., he failed in his mission). . . "[190]

The concept of strict obedience to the precepts of one's teacher was thus applied to the prophets who were regarded as masters of their disciples. Moreover, the Deuteronomic law prescribing that nothing was to be added to or taken away from the divine commandments given in the Torah,[191] was extended to include the prophets who were to be obeyed and whose precepts were to be carried out in their entirety without any change whatsoever. Thus, I Samuel 15:23a, where MT reads: "For rebellion is as the sin of divination, and stubbornness is as iniquity and idolatry," is homiletically reinterpreted in TJ: "For like the sin of men who make inquiry through divination, so is the son of every man who is unwilling to obey the words of the Torah; and like the sins of people that go astray after idols, so is the son of every man who takes away from, or adds to, the words of the prophet".[192]

Discipline and obedience were required not only from students, but even from the highest office holders, including the king himself who in both biblical and rabbinic political theory was not free to do as he pleased, but was bound by the Law.[193] It seemed, therefore, that Samuel's suggestion to Saul, whom he had just anointed king, that he should "do whatever your hand finds to do"—implying whatever he liked and was able to do—was inconsistent with the strict rules by which the king was supposed to abide. TJ, accordingly, renders in a novel manner: "Prepare yourself royal garments". This interpretation served a double purpose. It eliminated any suggestion that the king could do as he pleased. At the same time, it introduced the

---

190. It is noteworthy that in rabbinic literature Gehazi is the prototype of the unworthy disciple; cf. T.Y. Yev. II, 4, 3d; Sanh. X, 2, 29b; T.B. Ber. 10b; Sot. 47a; Sanh. 100a; 107b; Lev. R. XXIV, 6.

191. Cf. Deut. 4:2; 13:1.

192. Cf. Komlosh, *op. cit.,* p. 305, where there is, however, no reference to the halachic import of TJ's interpretation.

193. Cf. Deut. 17:16 ff.; I Sam. 10:25, 12:25, 13:13 f., 15:22-29, 28:16 ff.; II Sam. 12:7 ff.; I Kings 11:9 ff., 31 ff., 14:6 ff., 16:1-4, 21:19 ff.; II Kings 1:3-16, 9:6 ff.; Jer. 22:2-5,13-19; 27:12 ff., 36:30 ff., 38:17 ff.; Ezek. 17:11 ff.; M. Sanh. 11, 2-5; Tos Sanh. IV, 2-8; T.Y. Sanh. II, 3-8, 20a-d; T.B. Sanh. 18b-22b; Maimonides, *Mishneh Torah, Hilchot Melachim*, chs. I-IV on the general question of royal privileges, restrictions and obligations in ancient Israel. Cf. L. Smolar and M. Aberbach, הגות עברית באמריקה in המלוכה בהשקפת עולמו של אברבנאל (Jerusalem-Tel Aviv, 1978), pp. 134 ff.

principle, repeatedly enunciated in the Talmud, that the king had to maintain an appearance consonant with his high station in life;[194] for "your eyes shall behold the king in his beauty".[195]

One restriction, which equally applied to a king, general or anyone engaged in warfare on behalf of the state, was that of refraining from attacking an enemy stronghold without offering peace terms first:

"When you approach a town and fight against it, offer terms of peace to it".[196] This halachic principle is introduced by the targumist in the story of Sheba the son of Bichri who rebelled against David and fled to the northern town of Abel of Beth-maacah. Joab pursued him, and on arrival at Abel instantly commenced the siege of the city.[197] At this point a "wise woman" addressed Joab from the wall, saying, "They were wont to say formerly, 'Let them but ask counsel at Abel'; and so they settled the matter. . ."[198] This enigmatic verse is followed by a protestation of loyalty to David and a plea to spare "a city which is a mother in Israel."[199] TJ reads into the wise woman's opening remarks a subtle reminder that Joab had omitted to follow the Deuteronomic precept of offering peace terms before laying siege to the town.[200] TJ's interpretation of II Samuel 20:18 is thus as follows: "Remember now that which is written in the book of the Law, (namely) to offer first peace, that is to say, you surely should have inquired like this in Abel whether they are offering peace."

During the Biblical period, idolatry was considered the epitome of evil, the source and origin of all wickedness. Yet, at least in an earlier age, idolatry was to some extent recognized and tolerated outside the Land of Israel.[201] The emigrant was more or less expected to "do in Rome as the Romans do," and pay his respects to the local deities. This is clearly implied in I Samuel 26:19, where David is reported to have cursed those who had incited King Saul against him; "for they have driven me out this day that I should have no share in the heritage of the Lord, saying, 'Go, serve other

194. Cf. T.Y. Yoma VIII, 1, 44b; T.Y. Sanh. II, 8, 20c; T.B. Yoma 78b; Sanh. 22b; Taan. 17a.

195. Is. 33:17a.

196. Deut. 20:10.

197. Cf. II Sam. 20:1-15.

198. *Ibid.* 20:18.

199. *Ibid.* v. 19.

200. Cf. Komlosh, *op. cit.*, pp. 328 ff.

201. Cf., e.g., Jud. 11:24. See also Deut. 4:19.

gods' ". In other words, David was being forced to emigrate and thus, as a matter of course, to "serve other gods."

In the Talmudic age, such an interpretation was unthinkable: "Is it conceivable that David would be an idolator? But David expounded, saying, Whosoever leaves the Land (viz., of Israel) in time of peace and goes abroad, it is as though he worshipped idols".[202] In full agreement with this Midrash, which was undoubtedly designed to discourage emigration for economic reasons, TJ renders I Samuel 26:19b: "... 'Go dwell among nations that worship idols' ".

Idolatry itself was a subject occupying considerable halachic attention. Although even the making of idols was prohibited by the Torah,[203] it required an overt act of worship to be liable to capital punishment.[204] Yet, in Ezekiel 22:3-4 ("A city that sheds blood in the midst of her... and that makes idols to defile herself. You have become guilty by the blood you have shed and defiled by the idols you have made"), the juxtaposition of bloodshed and the production of idols would seem to be singularly ill-matched. For murder, capital punishment could be exacted,[205] while the making of idols merely constituted transgression of a negative commandment punishable by 39 stripes.[206] To make this distinction clear, TJ changes the *making* of idols into the *worship* of idols,[207] which constituted a capital

---

202. Tos. A.Z. IV (V), 5. Cf. Avoth-de-R. Nathan, edit. Schechter, Vers. I, ch. 26, p. 82, where "in time of peace" is omitted, implying that even in wartime it was forbidden to escape abroad. Cf. also T.B. Ket. 110b: "Who told David, 'Go serve other gods'? But this is to tell you that whoever lives outside the Land (viz., of Israel) it is as though he worshipped idols." It is noteworthy that in this Babylonian Talmud version, which was primarily designed for Babylonian Jews, the emphasis is shifted from discouragement of emigration from the Land of Israel—a major problem at the time—to mere residence in the Diaspora by those already born there.

203. Cf., e.g., Exod. 20:4. 23; Deut. 4:16.25; 5:8 *et passim*. Cf. also Mekhilta on Exod. 20:3, according to which even keeping in one's possession idols made by others was prohibited.

204. Cf. Tos. Sanh. X, 3; T.B. Sanh. 63a, 65a.

205. Cf. Gen. 9:6; Exod. 21:12 ff.; Lev. 24:17 ff.; Num. 35:16 ff.; Deut. 19:11 ff.; M. Sanh. IX, 1; Tos. Sanh. XI, 4.

206. Cf. Tos. Sanh. X, 3; Tos. Mak. V (IV), 7,10; T.B. Mak. 13b; T.B. Shevuot 21a; T.B. Tem. 3a; Cf. M. Mak. III, 10.

207. Cf. TJ on Ezekiel 22:3: "... and they that *worship* idols within it (viz., the city) in order to defile it." Cf. *ibid.* v. 4: "... and by the *worship* of your idols whom you served , you have become defiled."

crime for which one was liable to incur the penalty of stoning.[208]

The Targum Jonathan draws a clear distinction between a proper priest descended from Aaron and suitable for his sacred office and an idolatrous or otherwise unfit priest who had no right to the title.[209] While a legitimate Aaronide priest (Heb. כהן) is always rendered כהין or כהנא (plural כהניא), the idolatrous priest, even though accorded the title כהן in MT, often becomes a despised כומרא (plural כומרין or כומריא) in the Aramaic translation.

Thus, in the charming story of Micah's image[210], Micah's son, promoted to the priesthood by his father's fiat,[211] as well as the more eligible Levite from Bethlehem,[212] are at least in some versions of TJ referred to as כומרא instead of כהין[213], while in the case of the sacerdotal dynasty of Dan, which was associated with the calf-cult established there by Jeroboam[214], all TJ versions render MT כהנים by כומרין.[215] Needless to say, in TJ the priests of Baal and other foreign cults—as well as the priests of the calf-cult—are never elevated to the position of כהנין or כהניא,[216] even if MT does not distinguish them from the legitimate priests of Yahweh by depicting them as כמרים.[217]

There is less consistency where the priests of the "high places" (other than those involved in the calf-cult) are concerned. It was often difficult to

208. Cf. M. Sanh. VII, 4-7; Tos. Sanh. X, 2 ff.

209. Cf. Churgin, p. 115 f. As the following pages will show, the entire subject, which involves halachic considerations, is far more complex than Churgin's relatively brief treatment would indicate.

210. Cf. Jud. chs. 17-18.

211. Cf. *ibid.* 17:5.

212. Cf. *ibid.* 17:6ff.

213. Cf. *ibid.* 17:5,10,12 f.; 18:4,6,17-20,24.

214. Cf. *ibid.* 18:30; I Kings 12:29 f.

215. Cf. Jud. 18:30. J. Levy, *Chaldäisches Wörterbuch über die Targumim* (Leipzig 1881), I, 369, s.v. כומרא, ingeniously suggests that where the idolatrous character of the priest is less obvious, כהין is used instead of כומרא. Although this view is not without merit, it is based on inadequate use of available MSS which have כהין as well as כומרא readings in all the passages in question. Only where the idolatrous character of the priest (or priesthood) is unmistakable, do all TJ versions agree in rendering כומרא or כומרין. Micah's sanctuary, though illegitimate according to the Deuteronomic centralization of the cult legislation (cf. Deut. 12:5-18), was not in itself an idolatrous cult center, the graven image used in it notwithstanding; otherwise the author of the story or at least the editor would not have failed to denounce it. Only the calf-cult introduced there by Jeroboam amounted to genuine idolatry in the eyes of the Deuteronomic authors of the book of Kings. The same, of course, also applies to the Baal cult.

216. Cf., e.g., I Sam. 5:5; I Kings 12:31 f.; 13:2,33; II Kings 10:19; 11:18; 23:20.

217. Cf. II Kings 23:5; Hos. 10:5.

decide whether they were really idolators pure and simple or perhaps merely misguided priests of Yahweh who ignored or were ignorant of Deuteronomic legislation relating to the centralization of the cult. Thus, in II Kings 23:8, we are told that King Josiah "brought all the priests out of the cities of Judah and defiled the high places where the priests had burned incense." Since the impression is conveyed that these "high places" were indeed centers of idolatry—otherwise why did Josiah "defile" them?—the כהנים are depicted as כומריא by TJ. But in the following verse (v. 9), we are given the supplementary information that "the priests of the high places did not come up to the altar of the Lord in Jerusalem, but they ate unleavened bread among their brethren." Although they are manifestly identical with the priests mentioned in the previous verse, they are not altogether rejected as idolators. Instead, they are permitted to share "unleavened bread" and, according to the Mishnah,[218] all sacred food, as if they were blemished priests who could not perform the sacrificial service, but were allowed to "eat of the food of his God".[219] The dichotomy of the situation, which is also evident in the Talmud where the acceptability of a sacrificial animal slaughtered by a repentant idolatrous priest is disputed,[220] is reflected in the TJ rendering of the כוהני הבמות. Some TJ versions continue to refer to them as כומרי במתא, while others, inconsistently but following the inherent logic of the verse, depict them as כהניא.

A similar problem faced the targumist in II Kings 17:32, where we learn that the converted foreign settlers in Samaria "feared the Lord, and appointed from among themselves all sorts of people[221] as priests of the high places. . . ." Since the entire passage (vv. 28-41) is designed to portray the Samaritans as playing a double game—"these nations feared the Lord, and also served their graven images"[222], their "priests of the high places" must have been a thoroughly unsatisfactory lot, most probably outright idolators. Accordingly, most TJ versions, reflecting this mode of thinking, render: כומרי במתא. In one TJ MS, however, they are depicted as presumably God-fearing, though misguided, כהני במתא.

Occasionally, the targumist could not resolve the problem how to render

218. M. Men. XIII, 10.
219. Lev. 21:17-23.
220. Cf. T.B. Men. 109a.
221. Heb. מקצותם. Meaning doubtful.
222. II Kings 17:41.

the Hebrew כהן or כהנים, so that the only recourse left was to deviate altogether from the Hebrew original. Thus, Amaziah, the priest of Bethel, who
tried to stop Amos from prophesying at the royal sanctuary,[223] was undoubtedly an unpleasant establishment figure and presumably a priest of the
idolatrous (or quasi-idolatrous) calf-cult at Bethel. On the other hand, even
Amos did not accuse him of idolatry, and the targumists could not, therefore, portray him as a כומרא on the basis of unsubstantiated circumstantial
evidence. Neither could they see their way to granting him the honorable
title of כהין or כהנא. Taking perhaps their cue from II Samuel 8:18 (where, as
we have seen, the halachically inconceivable priesthood of David's sons was
changed, both in the parallel passage in I Chronicles 18:17 and in TJ to "chief
officials and great men [or: leaders], respectively), the targumists transformed
Amaziah into a רבא-"a great man (or: a leader) of Bethel."[224] This semantic
unfrocking of Amaziah neatly disposed of the problem of defining the character of his priestly status.

An even more complicated problem for the targumist was posed by
Zephaniah 1:4, where we are told that God would cut off, along with "the
remnant of Baal," את שם הכמרים עם הכהנים (lit., "the name of the idolatrous
priests with the priests"). Since the *Cohanim* are distinguished from the
K'marim, the former must be presumed to be non-idolatrous priests. But if
so, why are they to be destroyed? TJ's bold solution is to render *Ha-
K'marim* by פלחיהון ("their worshippers", viz., of the Baalim), and *Ha-
Cohanim* by כומריהון ("their idolatrous priests").[225]

The same distinction that was observed by TJ as between legitimate and
idolatrous priests was also followed in regard to the altars. A legitimate altar
of Yahweh is rendered מדבחא, while idolatrous altars, including those devoted
to the calf-cult, are contemptuously referred to as אגורא or איגורא (plural
אגורין or א[י]גוריא)—lit., a pile of stones. This designation may have been
inspired by Hosea 12:12b: ... "their altars also shall be like stone heaps."[226]

223. Cf. Amos 7:10 ff.

224. Cf. *ibid.* v. 10.

225. A similar association—though a contrasting one—between the idolatrous *K'marim*
and the ordinary worshippers of idols is to be found in T.B. A.Z. 51a: "The term 'advantage'
(used in M. A.Z. IV, 3) means that payment is made to the כומרין, and 'Not to its
advantage' (*ibid.*) means that no payment is made to the כומרין. This excludes the case where
payment is made to *idol-worshippers,* which is permitted."

226. It is significant that, according to the Tosefta (A.Z. VI [VII],4), "all places named in
honor of idols should be given derogatory names instead." The Targumic denigration of idolatrous altars is thus in line with rabbinic Halacha.

In addition to the examples cited by Churgin (p. 113), the following are noteworthy: Jud. 2:2, 6:25,28 (where the altar of Baal=איגורא, while Gideon's altar of Yahweh=מדבחא), 31f.; I Kings 12:32f.; 13:1f.4; II Kings 11:18; 21:4f.; 23:12,15-17,20; Ezekiel 16:24; Hos. 4:19; 10:1f.8; Amos 3:14.

All these מזבחות (altars) are unmistakably idolatrous in character, so that the distinction between them and legitimate altars presents no problem. The only passage where there appears to be some confusion is I Kings 13:1-5. There we are told how an anonymous prophet from Judah appeared in Bethel just as Jeroboam was about to offer incense on the altar he had built, and that the prophet predicted the defilement and destruction of the altar. As long as the story is told in the third person, TJ renders MT המזבח by איגורא.[227] But when reporting the actual words of the prophet, TJ changes the translation to מדבחא.[228] In I Kings 13:4, which is entirely in the third person, Jeroboam's altar is depicted alternately as both איגורא and מדבחא; while in the following verse (which is also in the third person) the same altar is twice rendered מדבחא.

J. Levy[229] has attempted to explain the מדבחא rendering in relation to an idolatrous altar as an indication of Jeroboam's point of view or, where the prophet is addressing Jeroboam, as an expression of the prophet's respect towards the king. However, the first explanation is both inconsistent (in view of the change from איגורא to מדבחא, and vice versa) and logically untenable; for there is no reason why the prophet or the narrator should tell the story from Jeroboam's point of view. On the contrary, virtually the entire account of Jeroboam's career after he came to power is told from an antagonistic viewpoint, and chapter 13 is no exception. As for the second explanation, it could apply only to verses 2-3, not to verses 4-5, quite apart from the fact that a prophecy concerning the defilement and destruction of the royal altar is not—and cannot be—respectful towards the builder of the altar.

A careful analysis of the passage, including I Kings 12:32-33 which immediately precedes it, may yield a clue to the solution of the problem. As long as the story is told in the third person, Jeroboam's altar, devoted as it was to the calf-cult, is quite naturally described as איגורא. But in verse 2, the prophet is addressing the altar, and in the following verse he is evidently addressing the king and the assembled congregation. In both these verses

---

227. One TJ version, though, renders MT המזבח in I Kings 13:1 by מדבחא.
228. Cf. I Kings 13:2 f.
229. *Op. cit.* i, 9, s. v. אגורא.

the prophet is speaking "by the word of the Lord (בדבר ה׳). . . thus says the
Lord." The emphasis on "the word of the Lord" is significant. The prophet
is not merely inspired to speak on behalf of Yahweh. Far more than divine
inspiration, his is his Master's voice, the authentic voice of the Lord. The
targumist was, therefore, faced with the problem of translating the very
words of God recorded out of the mouth of the prophet. Here accuracy was
indispensable. Using contemptuous terms in the translation might be pass-
able in Biblical passages inspired by God, but not where God Himself was,
as it were, the speaker. If God employed the word מזבח in relation to an idolatrous altar, the Aramaic equivalent (מדבחא) had to be used to render God's
word accurately.

Once מדבחא had become, so to say, respectable, the targumist continued
to use it in verses 4 and 5, since it was the same altar that God had spoken
about in the previous two verses. The only exception is the reference to "the
altar in Bethel" in verse 4. Since Bethel and the sinful calf-cult were almost
synonymous in First Commonwealth literature,[230] it was virtually impossible to mention Bethel and its idolatrous altar, in the same breath, as it
were, without denigrating the latter. Hence על איגורא בבית אל in TJ on verse 4.

The Targum Jonathan also makes a clear distinction between statutes
(חקים) and ordinances (משפטים) emanating from God for the benefit of His
people and those issued by idolators—or even by God but designed for the
punishment of Israel for rebelling against the divine law. The חקים and
משפטים of the Almighty are usually rendered קימיא and דינין, i.e., binding
covenants and detailed laws to be observed in daily life.[231] By way of contrast, חקים and משפטים emanating from pagans or associated with idolatry or
other sinful behavior, or else imposed by God as a punishment for Israel's
misdeeds, are translated גזירת and נימוסין, lit., decrees and foreign laws and
usages.[232] In other words, they do not really have the force of law in the
sense of prescribing a righteous, law-abiding life. They are external decrees
imposed by idolators or evil men, unless, of course, they happen to be a
divine visitation for the sins and transgressions perpetrated by the people.

---

230. Cf. Hos. 10:5,15; Amos 3:14; 4:4; 5:5.
231. Cf., e.g., II Kings 17:37; Ezek. 20:19. 21.24.
232. Cf. II Kings 17:33f., 40; Ezek. 20:18, 25. See also I Sam. 2:13, where MT משפט
הכהנים (TJ= נמוסא דכהניא) introduces the evil habits of the wicked priests Hophni and Phineas,
sons of Eli. Similarly, I Samuel 8:9, where MT משפט המלך (= TJ נמוסא דמלכא) adumbrates the
royal tyranny described in the rest of the chapter.

Of special interest in this connection is Ezekiel 23:24b, where MT ". . . and they (viz., the Babylonians, Assyrians and others) shall judge you according to their judgment" is rendered by TJ: ". . . and they shall *punish* you according to their laws (בנימוסיהון)." The implication is that judgment in accordance with pagan laws constitutes punishment rather than fair and impartial justice. It is possible that this interpretation was designed to discourage resort by Jews to non-Jewish courts; a course of action strongly frowned upon by the rabbis, even if non-Jewish law happened to be identical in certain respects with Jewish law.[233]

Just as TJ distinguishes between legitimate and idolatrous priests, altars and laws, so, in translating אלהים, TJ (like Targum Onkelos) insists on rendering foreign gods by טעון (lit., errors), thus depriving them of the dignity of divine designations. The subject is adequately discussed by Churgin (pp. 111 ff.), and all that remains to be added is to point to Exodus 23:13—"Make no mention of the names of other gods; they shall not be heard out of your mouth (or: on your lips)"—as the probable source for the targumists' reluctance to mention the names of idols[234] or accord them the respect implied by the word אלהים.[235] Finally, Hosea 2:19: "For I will remove the names of the Baals from her mouth, and they shall be mentioned by name no more", though only a prediction rather than a precept, may have influenced TJ's practice to substitute derogatory terms for the names and designations of idols.

In addition to what one may term cultic Halacha dealing with laws relating to the sanctuaries, altars and priests, TJ also includes a good many Halachot concerning women: marriage, divorce, sexual morality and so on. An interesting link between these two principal topics of Halacha is provided by Ezekiel 44:22, where we are told that the priests "shall not marry a widow or a divorced woman, but only a virgin of the stock of the house of Israel, or a widow who is the widow of a priest (Heb. אלמנה מכהן) they may take".

---

233. Cf. T.B. Git. 88b; Midr. Tanh. משפטים, 3.

234. It is noteworthy that even in the Bible we meet with this phenomenon, e.g., the substitution of בשת (shame) for Baal; cf. Jer. 3:24; 11:13; Hos. 9:10. Even names such as Eshbaal (I Chron. 8:33; 9:39) and Meribbaal (*ibid.* 8:34; 9:40) are, in II Samuel, regularly referred to as Ish-bosheth and Mephibosheth, respectively. On one occasion, even Gideon-Jerubbaal is renamed Jerubbesheth (II Sam. 11:21).

235. Cf. Tos. A.Z. VI (VII), 11; T.B. Sanh. 63b: "A man must not say to his neighbor, 'Wait for me at the side of this idol, and I will wait for you at the side of that idol, for it is written, 'Make no mention of the names of other gods' (Exod. 23:13)."

This does not harmonize with Leviticus 21:7, which does not include widows among prohibited marriages for ordinary priests. Only the high priest was forbidden to marry a widow[236], and nowhere in the Priestly Code is a distinction made between the widow of a priest and the widow of a Levite or Israelite.

The contradiction is noted in the Talmud,[237] where the problem is "solved" by restricting Ezekiel 44:22a—i.e., the prohibition of marriage to a widow—to high priests only; while the second half of the verse is assumed to refer to priests in general. Since there is no room in Halacha for the widow of a priest to be treated differently from other widows, the Talmud reinterprets v.22b to read: ". . . or a widow—those of the other priests (who are not High Priests) may take". The letter מ of Hebrew מכהן is taken as a partitive preposition, and the word מכהן is understood in the plural sense: משאר כהנים ("those of the other priests"). TJ's solution of the problem is identical with that of the Talmud: ". . . a widow the other priests (שאר כהניא) may take".[238]

Intermarriage with unconverted non-Jews was, at least since the time of Ezra and Nehemiah, strictly prohibited. Rare, occasional affairs between Jewish men and pagan women, or vice versa, did occur, but were sharply condemned.[239] According to the Mishnah,[240] Zealot lynch law was applied against anyone caught in the act of cohabitation with a non-Jewish woman. While such summary justice was subsequently discouraged,[241] there were repeated warnings against liaisons with pagan women, including female slaves.[242] Some Bible interpreters, who translated the weekly portions of the Law for the benefit of Aramaic-speaking synagogue audiences, went so far as to provide a homiletical rendering of Leviticus 18:21a—"You shall not give any of your offspring to be offered up to Molech." Since the Molech cult had long ago become extinct, some translators tried to "modernize" the Biblical injunction by rendering: "You shall not give any of your offspring to a heathen woman causing her to become pregnant." Such a "translation" was,

---

236. Cf. Lev. 21:14.

237. Cf. T.B. Kid. 78b.

238. Some TJ versions include the partitive prepositional מ (משאר), just as in T.B. Kid. 78b.

239. Cf., e.g., T.B. Sanh. 82a.

240. M. Sanh. IX, 6.

241. Cf. T.B. Sanh. 82a.

242. *Ibid.* Cf. Lev. R. IX, 5; XXV, 8.

to be sure, condemned, and anyone offering this rendering in the synagogue was supposed to be silenced with a sharp rebuke.[243] Unofficial targumists nevertheless continued to use this midrashic interpretation, and it is still to be found with minor variations in the Targum Pseudo-Jonathan on Leviticus 18:21.

It is against this background that TJ's rendering of Hosea 5:7a—"They have dealth faithlessly with the Lord; for they have borne alien children" —is to be evaluated. While the plain meaning of the text is that the children of the people of Israel have become idolators, TJ significantly renders: "children of the daughters of the Gentiles they have kept (or: raised) unto themselves". Thus, the historical reality of the eighth century B.C.E. was ignored—idolatry after all was no longer the major problem facing the Jews, and there was no tendency to become addicted to it[244]—and the more topical reality of extra-marital relations with non-Jews was substituted. The purpose was of course to discourage such affairs, which were regarded as far more sinful than the seduction of unmarried Jewish girls.[245]

Elsewhere, too, TJ tends to stress the seriousness of immoral conduct, even where the Hebrew text uses more restrained language. Thus, Hosea 2:15—"... and she went after her lovers"—is given a more serious dimension in TJ's rendering: "... and she went *astray* (וטעת) after her lovers". Clearly the targumist was not satisfied with a simple matter-of-fact statement that Israel followed alien cults. The verb indicating the act had to express a value judgment.

Far more problematic to the rabbinic moralists was the divine command to the prophet Hosea to marry "a wife of harlotry" and beget "children of harlotry";[246] and then, again, to "love a woman who is beloved of a paramour and is an adulteress".[247]

According to the Halacha, a woman who commits adultery is forbidden to her husband as well as to her paramour,[248] in other words, her marriage is dissolved and she cannot marry or re-marry either of them. Patriotic aggadists, who were primarily concerned with maintaining the morale of the

243. Cf. M. Meg. IV, 9.
244. Cf. T.B. Yoma 69b; Sanh. 64a; A.Z. 17a-b.
245. Cf. Exod. 22:15 f.; M. Ket. III, 4; T.B. Sanh. 82a.
246. Hosea 1:2.
247. *Ibid.* 3:1.
248. Cf. M. Sot. V, I.

people by emphasizing God's unfailing love for Israel, were prepared to ignore the halachic problems involved. They regarded the entire episode as a salutary lesson to Hosea who, instead of praying for Israel that their sins might be forgiven, suggested to God that He should "exchange them for a different nation". Thereupon, God ordered him to marry a harlot and beget "children of harlotry". After the harlot had borne him three children, God told Hosea to part from his wife. The prophet demurred: "Master of the Universe! I have children by her. I cannot expel her or divorce her!" This, of course, exposed Hosea to a well-deserved rebuke for having proposed that God should choose a different people, thereby ignoring the divine love for Israel and, especially, for the meritorious Patriarchs, whose descendants the Israelites were.[249]

A long midrashic version of TJ on Hosea 1:2 repeats, with slight variations, the talmudic Aggadah, and it is evident that they are both derived from the same source. The main TJ text, however, is clearly concerned with the halachic-theological aspects of the case, namely the manifest impossibility of God commanding anyone, least of all a prophet, to marry a harlot, an adulteress, and beget "children of harlotry."[250] TJ gets round the problem by providing a relatively brief allegorical interpretation of the text.[251]

A halachic principle, and perhaps also a degree of moral sensitivity, may be involved in TJ's rendering of II Samuel 1:26b, "Your love to me was wonderful, passing the love of women." In TJ's translation, MT מאהבת נשים becomes מרחמת תרתין נשין ("than the love of *two* women"). The Talmudic principle invoked here would seem to be that the minimum of any plural form (in the Bible) implies two;[252] that is to say, when a plural form is used and no specific number is given, we may assume that the reference is to two.

Since David was the author of the above-quoted elegy, TJ's rendering

---

249. Cf. T.B. Pes. 87a-b.

250. Concern about the halachic irregularity of God's commandment to Hosea is also expressed by the medieval commentators Ibn Ezra and Kimchi (on Hosea 1:2). They both assume that the entire episode was a dream vision, which never happened in real life.

251. For the translation, see Churgin, p. 82. The translation, unfortunately, leaves much to be desired. Thus, the inhabitants of the city did not "increase" in sin, but "continued" (מוסיפן) to sin. Similarly also in verse 3, "They increased and committed evil deeds," should read: "and they continued (ואוסיפו) to commit evil deeds." In verse 8a, TJ הדריהון דאיתגליאו לביני עממיא—"and their scattered ones that were exiled among the nations"—is erroneously translated by Churgin: "and their *generation* exiled among the peoples."

252. Cf., e.g., T.Y. Sanh. III, 10, 21c; T.Y. Shev. IV, I, 35b; T.B. Kerit. 6b; Nid. 38b.

may also have been influenced by the repeated references to his "two wives", Abigail and Ahinoam of Jezreel.[253] Actually, David had previously been married to Michal, Saul's daughter, and since he never divorced her, and was soon to take her back,[254] David was legally married to three wives at the time. In view of the fact that Saul had given Michal to Palti(el) son of Laish, clearly without obtaining a bill of divorce from the fugitive David, Michal's relationship with her second husband was adulterous, and her subsequent return to David—illegal.[255] The rabbis, therefore, used all their ingenuity to absolve everyone concerned of any wrongdoing. One imginative explanation was that Palti(el), aware that Michal was still David's wife, refused to consummate his "marriage" to her.[256] Undefiled, she could therefore be taken back by David without transgressing any law.

Another explanation, which ties in with TJ's rendering of II Samuel 1:26b, is apparently based on the rabbinic interpretation of II Samuel 12:8a—"and I gave you your master's wives into your bosom." According to R. Judah, this means that David married Saul's widows, though ordinary men were not permitted to marry a king's widow. Most rabbis, however, considered that even a king must not marry a king's widow,[257] and that David married "women of the house of the king (viz., Saul) who were permissible to him," namely Merab and Michal.[258]

This raises the problem of the prohibition of marrying two sisters.[259] One answer was that he married Michal after Merab's death; the other, that his marriage to Merab was not valid in the first place.[260] This still left Saul's

253. Cf. I Sam. 25:43 f.; 27:3; 30:5.18; II Sam. 2:2. The latter reference follows almost immediately after David's lamentation, and is only three verses after II Sam. 1:26, where David speaks about Jonathan's love having been "wonderful, passing the love of women."

254. Cf. II Sam. 3:14-16. This however, raises a hornet's nest of moral-halachic problems, which may not have unduly bothered either Saul or David or any of their contemporaries, but immensely disturbed the rabbis who could not imagine Saul or David acting contrary to the Halacha and moral propriety.

255. Cf. I Sam. 25:44; II Sam. 3:15 f.; M. Sot. V, I. Even if Michal had been divorced by David, she could not have legally remarried him after being married to another man; cf. Deut. 24:1-4.

256. Cf. T.B. Sanh. 19b.

257. Cf. M. Sanh. II, 2.

258. Cf. T.B. Sanh. 19b. It is noteworthy that here, again, *two* wives of David are inferred from the plural form in II Sam. 12:8.

259. Cf. Lev. 18:18.

260. Cf. Tos. Sot. XI, 16: T.B. Sanh. 19b.

high handed act in marrying off Michal to another man while she was still married to David, halachically unacceptable. It was, therefore, explained that Saul may have had halachic reasons to consider David's betrothal to Michal to be invalid.[261] She could, therefore, marry Palti(el), and, by the same token, David could eventually marry Michal (presumably after Palti[el] had divorced her), since he had never been legally married to her before. TJ on II Samuel 1:26b, which ignores David's original marriage to Michal, may have been based on the same assumption.

In addition to these purely legal considerations, there may have been a vague feeling that "the love of women" might suggest a somewhat loose moral code on the part of David, which was rather unseemly for the ideal king of Israel and reputed author of the book of Psalms.[262] By limiting the number of women to two, by implication the two wives he actually had at the time, the sting of moral laxity was effectively removed.

We have already seen that on the question of divorce, TJ adheres to the lenient views of the school of R. Akiba. In this connection, a midrashic version of TJ (known as Yerushalmi) on I Samuel 17:18b (MT . . ."and bring some token from them [or:". . . and take their pledge"] is of some interest. MT is rendered by TJ Yerushalmi: ". . . and take the bills of divorcement of their wives and bring them." This agrees with the Talmudic statement that the soldiers of David, and hence, by presumption, his contemporaries in Saul's army, would give conditional divorces to their wives whenever the men went off to war.[263] In case they failed to return without clear evidence that they had been killed, their wives would thereby not be "tied" and thus prevented from remarrying. While this was, of course, a purely imaginary retrojection of rabbinic law to Biblical times, it testifies to the importance attached by the rabbis to the humanitarian problems of society as well as to the preservation of the highest moral standards in Jewish family life.

The strictness of the moral code of the rabbis is not infrequently reflected in TJ. For example, dancing women and girls, though mentioned a few

261. Cf. T.B. Sanh. 19b. In spite of the apologetic tendencies in all these forced and manifestly unhistorical interpretations, we also find a more candid appraisal by R. Jose— incidentally, a historian and reputed author of the historical work *Seder Olam*—who bluntly states that the marriages of Michal to Palti and of Merab to Adriel (cf. I Sam. 18:19) were both unlawful; cf. Tos. Sot. XI, 15; T.B. Sanh. 19b.

262. Cf. T.B. Shab. 56a: "Whoever says that David sinned (in the Bathsheba affair) is utterly mistaken."

263. Cf. T.B. Shab. 56a; Ket. 9b. See also Churgin's pertinent observation, p. 152.

times in the Bible,[264] and once even in the Mishnah (but only as a custom of the past prior to the destruction of the Temple)[265], were not the kind of spectacle relished by the rabbis. Jeremiah's prediction that "the virgin Israel ... shall go forth in the dance of merrymakers"[266] could therefore not be left to stand literally in the Aramaic translation. TJ, accordingly, renders: "... O congregation of Israel, you shall yet ... go forth in the company of those that praise (viz., the Lord)". The secular "dance of merrymakers" thus became a religious group of hymn-singers—a remarkable transformation.

Similarly, Jeremiah 31:12a—"Then shall the maiden rejoice in the dance" becomes in TJ: "Then shall the congregation of Israel rejoice as in dances." Although the dancing does not altogether disappear, it is used only as a simile. The "congregation of Israel" rejoices without actually indulging in dancing.

If female dancing was considered incompatible with modesty, singing in the presence of men was frowned upon even more as coming close to indecency: "A woman's voice constitutes sexual incitement."[267] The refusal of the eighty year old Barzilai to accept David's invitation to his court because he was too old (and presumably too hard of hearing) to enjoy, among other things, "the voice of singing men and singing women",[268] implied that, if he had been younger, he would have enjoyed listening to female singers. Worse still, it clearly indicated that "singing women" were employed at David's court. Since the rabbis could not imagine David or indeed any Biblical hero failing in the strict observance of Halacha, TJ changes the "singing men and singing women" to "harps and praises" (viz., of God).

The rabbis generally preferred women to stay indoors and not to be gadabouts. Respectable women would, in fact, stay at home, and the Halacha was often adapted to this end to avoid situations where women might have to leave the protective shelter of the home.[269] Outside the home, moral perils were lurking everywhere, and the only thing for a decent woman to do was to stay at home and never go out unchaperoned. This concept is clearly re-

264. Cf., e.g., Exod. 15:20; Jud. 11:34; 21:21ff.; I Sam. 18:6f.
265. Cf. M. Taan. IV, 8.
266. Jer. 31:3 [4].
267. T.B. Ber. 24a.
268. II Sam. 19:36.
269. Cf. M. Ket. XIII, 3; B.B. IX, 1; T.B. Yev. 77a; Git. 41a; Shev. 30a; Gen R. VIII, 12; XVIII, 2; LXX, 2-5; Ruth R. IV, 6; Eccl. R. X, 8; Midr. Tanh. וישלח 6-7, edit. Buber, Vol. I, pp. 170 f.; Tanh. במדבר 3.

flected in TJ on Isaiah 44:13b, where MT "... according to the beauty of a man (אדם) to dwell in the house"—is rendered, "according to the praise (כתשבחת) of a *woman* who dwells in the house". This interpretation, which may have been prompted by the fact that "man" (איש) is already mentioned in the previous clause,[270] agrees with a midrashic statement to the same effect:

"R. Huna said, Where do we find that Eve was called man (אדם)? '... according to the beauty of a man, to dwell in a house.'"[271]

Since women were supposed to stay at home for their own moral welfare, it was out of question for them to bear arms like men or go out to fight the enemy.[272] As a matter of fact, Zealot women fought the Romans side by side with men, defending the besieged city of Jerusalem in 70 C.E.[273] But since the rabbis for the most part disapproved of the war, which they regarded as suicidal,[274] it goes without saying that they frowned upon the participation of women in any warlike activities.

It was in line with this firmly held rabbinic attitude that several TJ versions contain a homiletical translation of Judges 5:24 and 26a. The Hebrew text praises Jael's martial qualities:

"Most blessed of women be Jael, the wife of Heber the Kenite, of tent-dwelling women most blessed ... She put her hand to the tent-peg, and her right hand to the workmen's mallet ..."

On the face of it this looks suspiciously like a violation of the prohibition of female participation in fighting. It is probably for this reason that TJ transforms Jael into a pious woman serving scholars (presumably with food and drink) in the houses of study, while a number of TJ versions interpret verses 24 and 26 as follows:

"Blessed be Jael, the wife of Heber the Shalmaite,[275] who fulfilled what

270. Cf. Komlosh, *op. cit.*, p. 396.

271. Gen. R. XXI, 2.

272. Cf. T.B. Naz. 59a. Cf. also Targum Onkelos on Deut. 22:5a, where MT "A woman must not wear man's apparel" = Targum Onkelos "The equipment of a man's weapons shall not be worn by a woman."

273. Cf. Tacitus, Hist. V, 13.

274. Cf. T.B. Git. 56a; Avoth de-R. Nathan, edit. Schechter, Vers. I, ch. 4, p. 22 f.; Vers. II, ch. 6, p. 19; Lam. R. I, 5, par. 31.

275. TJ's identification of the Kenites with the Arab tribe of the Shalmaites (cf. also TJ on I Sam. 15:6 and Targum Onkelos on Gen. 15:19 and Num. 24:21) is in line with that given in the Talmud and Midrash; cf. T.Y. Sheviith VI, I, 36b; Kid. I, 9, 61d; T.B. B.B. 56a; Gen. R. XLIV, 23.

is written in the book of the Law of Moses, 'The equipment of a man's weapons must not be worn by a woman ... '[276]; but she put her hand to the tent-peg ... " Thus, by shunning the usual weapons employed by men, Jael was in fact fulfilling the Law in accordance with its rabbinic interpretation.

While strict puritanism was the hallmark of rabbinic thinking, marriage and procreation were considered to be not only permissible, but meritorious and, indeed, mandatory. Procreation was after all enjoined by the very first commandment of the Torah,[277] and it was accordingly regulated by the rabbis.[278] It is in line with this principle that TJ renders Isaiah 45:18: ". . . he formed it (viz., the earth) to be inhabited" by ". . . he established it to multiply people on it." Significantly, this interpretation agrees with one of the early halachot formulated by the School of Shammai, with the ultimate agreement of the opposing School of Hillel. Accordingly, a slave belonging to two masters, who had been manumitted by one, must also be freed by the other, the reason being that otherwise the slave would be unable to marry either a free woman or a bondwoman. As for the possibility that he might remain single, it was dismissed on the grounds that "surely the world was created only for the purpose of procreation, as it is stated, 'He (i.e., God) did not create it (viz., the earth) to be void, he formed it to be inhabited.'"[279] TJ's identical interpretation of this verse is obviously not accidental, but stems from the same rabbinic ideology.

Although the Talmud and Midrash are often very explicit in referring to bodily functions and sexual activities,[280] the targumists, who had to translate and expound the Scriptures for the masses, felt that what might be suitable for lecture halls and houses of study could not be applied in synagogues while rendering Holy Writ into the vernacular. The relatively unrestrained language of the prophets, and the rough language to be found occasionally in various parts of the Bible could not be conveyed literally to the ordinary people who might all too easily mistake linguistic frankness and sexual imagery for license. At the very least such language might arouse the prurient interests of the licentious. It, therefore, became necessary to censor the

276. Cf. Deut. 22:5a and Targum Onkelos *ad loc.* See above, n. 272.
277. Cf. Gen. 1:28.
278. Cf. M. Yev. VI, 6.
279. M. Git. IV, 5; M. Eduy. I, 13.
280. Cf. S. Glasner, "Judaism and Sex" in *The Encyclopedia of Sexual Behavior,* edit. Albert Ellis and Albert Abarbanel, pp. 575 ff.

Biblical text and alter it in such a way that rough expressions and sexual imagery were eliminated in favor of various euphemisms and circumlocutions characterized by clear, unimpeachable language.

As a matter of fact, the rabbis no less than the targumists were profoundly committed to clean language and to the avoidance of gross expressions, even when discussing potentially titillating themes. Refined terminology and generally decent language were to be used at all times,[281] even when referring to topics where such primness was not altogether suited for the employment of honest, explicit language.

In line with this puritan, moral thinking, TJ carefully avoids any suggestion of improper expressions, no matter what the circumstances. For example, in Joshua 7:15b, where MT reads: ". . . he (viz., Achan) has done a shameful thing (נבלה) in Israel, TJ renders נבלה by "that which is not proper", evidently because נבלה has sometimes a sexual connotation.[282]

Another example of extreme care to avoid using rough language is TJ's rendering of Isaiah 6:5a:

"I am a man of unclean lips and I dwell in the midst of a people of unclean lips."

Isaiah's language in this context was criticized both in the Talmud and in the Midrash.[283] TJ, accordingly, renders: "I am a man in duty bound to rebuke, and I dwell amidst a people that is polluted by its sins." Thus, Isaiah is not only represented as having confined himself to clean language, but the prophetic castigator is clearly separated from the sinful masses.

More serious than these cases was that recorded in Judges 5:30, where Sisera's mother and her "wise ladies" are trying to explain the delay in Sisera's return by the need to divide the spoil of the (presumably) defeated Israelites, including female captives: "a maiden or two (רחם רחמתים) for every man." The Hebrew could more accurately be translated, "a wench or two for every man", a most objectionable terminology and indeed an insult to Israelite womanhood. The targumist, therefore, had to soften the harshness of the original,[284] rendering it: "They give a man and his house to

---

281. Cf. T.B. Pes. 3a.

282. Cf., e.g., Deut. 22:21, where MT נבלה (= TO קלנא) depicts the disgrace of adultery. It is significant that, based on the coincidence of the same word—נבלה—being used both in Deut. 22:21 and in Jos. 7:15b, one talmudic opinion attributes adultery with a betrothed (i.e., legally married) girl to Achan; cf. T.B. Sanh. 44a.

283. Cf. T.B. Yev. 49b; Cant. R. I, 6, 1,; Midr. Tanh. וישלח ,2.

284. Cf. Komlosh, *op. cit.,* p. 291.

everyone." There is no philological basis for this translation.[285]

A similar softening of a harsh expression is to be found in TJ's rendering of I Kings 22:38,[286] where we read that harlots washed themselves in the blood of King Ahab. Since in Talmudic times the rabbis displayed considerable respect even for non-Jewish kings and rulers,[287] such degradation of a deceased king of Israel was more than the rabbis and targumists could allow. One view expressed in the Talmud was that Jezebel had painted pictures of two harlots on Ahab's chariot in order to arouse his desire, and that it was these pictures, and not real live harlots which were "washed" (i.e., smeared) with Ahab's blood.[288] On the other hand, connecting זנות (harlots) with זינא (arms, weapons) TJ renders: ". . . and they washed the weapons (viz., in the blood)." The embarrassment and disgrace of harlots washing themselves in the blood of a king of Israel was thus avoided.

No less embarrassing was the advice given by his courtiers to the aged and cold king David to let a young maiden "lie in your bosom, that my lord the king may be warm."[289] The Talmud discusses the reason for David's failure to marry the "young maiden", Abishag, who had been chosen to lie in his bosom. It was not old age or impotence that prevented him from marrying Abishag; on the contrary, his virility was as strong as ever. But since he already had eighteen wives, he was not permitted, according to the rabbinic interpretation of the Deuteronomic law of kingship, to exceed this number.[290] TJ, however, softens the language of the original by omitting the royal "bosom": ". . . and let her lie *with* you".[291]

It goes without saying that a vulgar expression like משתין בקיר (lit., "one that pisses against the wall")[292] could not be translated literally into Aramaic.[293] Not only was it liable to scandalize synagogue audiences, but its

285. *Ibid.*

286. Cf. Komlosh, *op. cit.*, p. 337.

287. Cf. Mekhilta on Exod. 12:31; T.Y. Ber. III, 1, 6a; T.B. Ber. 9b, 19b, 58a; Zev. 102a; Men. 98a; Exod. R. XVIII, 1.

288. Cf. T.B. Sanh. 39b.

289. I Kings 1:2.

290. Cf. Deut. 17:17; T.B. Sanh. 21a, 22a.

291. Cf. Komlosh, *op. cit.*, p. 337. Cf. also Targum Onkelos's rendering of Gen. 16:5, where MT בחיקך ("in your bosom") is altogether omitted in Targum Onkelos's translation.

292. I Sam. 25:22,34; I Kings 14:10, 16:11, 21:21; II Kings 9:8.

293. Cf. Komlosh, *op. cit.*, p. 325, where, however, no attempt is made to explain TJ's rendering other than as a softening of a harsh expression.

exact meaning was obscure.[294] TJ renders it ידע מדע (lit., "one who has knowledge"), a euphemism for a male adult capable of "knowing" a woman sexually.[295] TJ may have been influenced by Num. 31:17 f. and Jud. 21:11f., where a distinction is made between virgins "who had not known man by lying with him" and were, therefore, spared, and non-virgins who were slain, as well as by Deuteronomy 24:16 and Ezekiel 18:20[296] which prohibit the punishment of fathers for the sins of their children and vice versa. It was thus inconceivable that David should threaten, and that prophets like Abijah, Elijah and Elisha's disciple should predict in the name of God, that entire families, including infant children, would be wiped out because of the wrongdoing of the head of the clan or dynasty. Hence the distinction in TJ between infants (concerning whom nothing is said) and adults who have had carnal knowledge of women and are presumed to be sinners and therefore deserving of total annihilation.

The vivid sexual metaphors employed in the sixteenth and twenty-third chapters of Ezekiel were utterly unsuitable for puritan synagogue audiences, quite apart from the fact that biblical poetical metaphors are invariably translated by TJ in terms understandable by the simple masses. In the case of Ezekiel chapter 16, there was the additional factor in that it constituted a ruthless denunciaton of Jerusalem and the people of Judah, which R. Eliezer, for example, felt was sufficient reason for omitting the entire chapter from synagogue readings.[297] While this view was not universally accepted, it obliged the targumists to take special precautions in their translations, if they were to avoid undermining the morale of the people as well as titillating their audiences with explicit sexual imagery. Examples of such verses abound, and naturally TJ's renderings are almost invariably homiletical. Only a small selection can be cited here:

Ezekiel 16:7b: MT". . . your breasts were formed, and your hair had grown; yet you were naked and bare." TJ: ". . . and through the good deeds

---

294. Significantly, medieval commentators could not agree on the precise meaning of this expression, which some took to mean a person endowed with reason or, alternatively, a dog (Rashi, Kimchi) or else a male person (Gersonides).

295. Cf. J. Levy, *op. cit.*, I, 327, s.v. ידע. For the verb ידע in the sense of carnal knowledge, cf. Gen. 4:1.17.25; 19:5.8; 24:16; 38:26; Num. 31:17 f., 35; Jud. 11:39; 19:22.25; 21:11 f., I Sam. 1:19; I Kings 1:4.

296. Cf. also II Kings 14:5 f. = II Chron. 25:3 f.

297. Cf. M. Meg. IV, 9; Tos. Meg. IV (III), 34; T.Y. Meg. IV, 12, 75c; T.B. Meg. 25b.

of your forefathers the time of your congregation's redemption has come; for you are enslaved and afflicted."[298]

Ibid. 16:8: MT "...you were at the age for love; and I spread my skirt over you, and covered your nakedness." TJ: "... The time for your redemption had come; so I protected you with my *Memra*,[299] and I removed your sins".

Ibid. 16:22b: MT "... when you were naked and bare." TJ: "... when you were exiled and forsaken."

Ibid. 16:25a: MT "... and you have opened your feet to everyone that passed by." TJ "... and you joined yourself with everyone that passed by to worship idols".

Ibid. 23:3b: MT"... there their breasts were pressed, and there their virgin bosoms were handled." TJ: ".... there she worshipped idols, and there her deeds became corrupt."

Ibid. 23:8: MT "She did not abandon her harlotry (which she had practiced) since (her days in) Egypt; for in her youth men had lain with her, and they handled her virgin bosom and they poured our their lust upon her." TJ: "She did not abandon the worship of idols, which she had practiced (literally, that was with her) since (her days) in Egypt; for they made her worship idols, and they taught her evil deeds, and they poured their idols upon her."

Ibid. 23:17a: MT "And the Babylonians came to her into the bed of love, and they defiled her with their lust." TJ: "... and the Babylonians came to her to make love, and they defiled her with their idols."

Ibid. 23:18a: MT "... and she uncovered her nakedness." TJ: "... and her disgrace was seen."

Ibid. 23:21b: MT "... when the Egyptians handled your bosom, to squeeze[300] your young breasts." TJ: "... when you made love ever since (your days in) Egypt on account of the sins of your youth."

Ibid. 23:34a: "... and you shall tear your breasts." TJ: "... and you shall tear your flesh."

It is noteworthy that in all these cases TJ displays an aversion to any

---

298. This is, incidentally, also a good example of patriotic sentiments—the anticipation of redemption at an early date—and of the theological emphasis on זכות אבות ("the merit of the fathers"), which plays an important role in rabbinic thinking.

299. The Targumim use God's *Memra* (lit., "the word," Greek *logos*) in the sense of the creative or directive power of God's speech, as a substitute for anthropomorphic expressions. Cf. *Jewish Encyclopedia* (New York and London 1905-1912), Vol. VIII, p. 464 f.

300. Reading למען instead of למען ("for the sake of") which is unsuitable in this context.

sort of sexual imagery. Sexual acts as well as female breasts and nakedness are unmentionable.[301] Even a "bed of love" was not included in TJ's restricted vocabulary.

In addition to the Halacha relating to legal procedure, the Temple cult, marriage laws and sexual purity, the Targum Jonathan contains allusions to various aspects of the course of the life of the individuals.

Thus, circumcision of a male child on the eighth day after his birth is a basic law of Judaism, the sign of the covenant between God and the seed of Abraham.[302] How this law was to be carried out is not specified in the Bible, though Moses' wife, Zipporah, is depicted as having used a flint (MT צר = Targum Onkelos טנרא) to circumcise her son.[303] In Talmudic times, however, it would appear that it was customary to use a surgeon's knife or a scalpel (איזמל),[304] and this is reflected in TJ's rendering of Jos. 5:2 f. where MT חרבות צרים ("flint knives") is translated אזמילון חריפין ("sharp scalpels").

Throughout the Talmudic period, the problem of converting non-Jews to Judaism, usually through immersion and circumcision[305] occupied the attention of the rabbis. It was a period of major crisis in the religious world of the Roman empire. Oriental mystery cults—as well as Judaism and Christianity—were popular and, indeed, fashionable among all classes of society, especially in urban communities. Yet, many of the numerous converts to Judaism were somewhat less than sincere, and most of them were not really prepared to accept the full burden of the Law in all its ramifications. Inevitably, some rabbis questioned the sincerity of would-be converts; tried to discourage them;[306] and were suspicious even of those who had already converted.[307]

301. In this connection, TJ's translation of Is. 3:17b—"and the Lord will lay bare their (viz., the daughters' of Zion) secret parts"—is noteworthy. Here, in addition to the unmentionable female genitals, there is the additional difficulty that it is none other than the Almighty Himself who is uncovering the nakedness of the daughters of Zion. This is hardly a suitable occupation for a God who was imagined by the rabbis as a great scholar regularly engaged in the study of the Torah and in teaching it to children or attempting to resolve (not always successfully) disputed issues of Halacha (cf., e.g., T.B. A.Z. 3b; Eruv. 13b; B.M. 59b). TJ, accordingly, renders: ". . . and the Lord will remove their honor (or: glory)." This is so innocuous that even the Almighty has nothing to be embarrassed about.

302. Cf. Gen. 17:9 ff.

303. Cf. Exod. 4:25.

304. Cf. T.Y. Shab. XIX, I, 16d; T.B. Shab. 130a-b.

305. Cf. T.B. Yev. 46a.

306. Cf. T.B. Yev. 24b; 47a; A.Z. 3b; Eccl. R. I, 8, 4.

307. Cf. T.Y. Pes. VIII, 7, 36a; T.B. Yev. 47b; 48b; 109b; Kid. 70b; B.M. 59b; B.B. 109b; Sanh. 94a; Nid. 13b; Gen. R. LXX, 5; Pesik. R. 22, edit. Friedmann 111b.

These doubts and hesitations—as well as the more positive attitude of the majority—are reflected in some TJ renderings of the Hebrew גר—lit., resident alien, but almost invariably rendered גִּיוֹר or גִּיוֹרָא ("proselyte") by the major Targumim, especially Targum Onkelos on the Pentateuch and Targum Jonathan on the Prophets. The positive aspect is accentuated in Isaiah 14:1b, where MT ". . . and strangers shall join them" is translated by TJ: ". . . and proselytes shall be added to them" (viz., to Israel).

Similarly, in Isaiah 19:21, MT "And the Lord will make Himself known to the Egyptians, and the Egyptians will know (or: acknowledge) the Lord,"—becomes in TJ a welcome and promise to the Egyptians, who do not merely "acknowledge" the Lord, but "fear" him—a technical term for the numerous Judaizers and semi-proselytes known as "God-fearers".[308] TJ accordingly renders: "And the might of the Lord shall be revealed to do good to the Egyptians, and the Egyptians will know to fear (from before) the Lord."

Various stages in the conversion of proselytes are reflected in TJ's translation of Isaiah 44:5:

"One (or: This one) shall say, 'I am the Lord's,' another shall call himself by the name of Jacob; and another shall write on his hand, 'of the Lord', and surname himself by the name of Israel". TJ renders as follows: "This one shall say, 'I am of those that fear the Lord,'[309] and another shall pray in the name of Jacob; and another shall offer his sacrifice before the Lord,[310] and in the name of Israel he shall draw nigh".[311]

A positive attitude to the proselyte is also indicated in TJ's rendering of Ezek. 22:29b where MT ". . . and they shall oppress the stranger (or: extort from the sojourner—Heb. גר) unlawfully (Heb. בלא משפט)"—is translated:

308. Cf. Josephus, *Ant.* XX, 9, 11, par. 195; *Bell.* II, 18, 1, par. 463; 20, 2 par. 560; VII, 3,3, par. 45; II *Apion* 39, par. 282. Cf. also G.F. Moore, *Judaism* (Cambridge, Mass. 1927), Vol. I, pp. 325 ff.; S.W. Baron, *A Social and Religious History of the Jews,* second edit. (Philadelphia 1952), Vol. II, p. 283 f.; L.H. Feldman, "Jewish 'Sympathizers' in Classical Literature and Inscriptions," *Transactions of the American Philological Association* LXXXI, 1950, pp. 200-208.

309. As above, "those that fear the Lord" is a technical term for semi-proselytes.

310. Sacrifices offered by non-Jews were accepted in the Temple of Jerusalem; cf. Is. 56:7; Josephus, *Bell.* II, 17, 2-3, pars. 409-414; Sifra on Lev. 22:18; Tos. Men. IX, 1; T.B. Men. 73b. Komlosh (*op. cit.,* p. 372) plausibly suggests that the targumist may not have understood the meaning of MT "shall write on his hand," and possibly considered it in its literal sense a violation of the prohibition of tattooing (cf. Lev. 19:28).

311. A similar interpretation of Is. 44:5 is to be found in the Mekhilta on Exod. 22:20 and in Avoth-de-R. Nathan, edit. Schechter, Vers. I, ch. 36, p. 107. Cf. also Churgin, p. 103.

". . . and they shall oppress the proselyte improperly". Normally, the Hebrew בלא משפט should have been rendered בלא דינא. The intentional avoidance of דינא may plausibly be connected with the halachic rules relating to the robbery of proselytes who subsequently die without Jewish heirs. While the repentant robber is expected to make restitution to the priests and offer a sacrifice at the sanctuary,[312] no legal proceedings are initiated against him in view of the absence of any legal claimants to the proselytes' estates, which can be acquired by anyone without requiring special authority.[313]

Thus, while there was moral opprobrium in robbing proselytes, the legal protection accorded to them did not extend beyond their death, unless they left Jewish heirs. TJ's rendering may therefore be regarded as a deliberate widening of the scope of the prophetic strictures to include the free-for-all which was, indeed, permitted after the proselyte's death, but is likely enough to have started while he was still alive but stricken with terminal illness. From the targumist's point of view, any improper act against the proselyte was reprehensible and illegal.

A less favorable attitude towards certain proselytes is implied in a midrashic version of TJ (known as Yerushalmi) on I Sam. 11:2, where we are told that the Ammonite ruler Nahash was willing to accept the surrender of Jabesh-Gilead only on condition that all the right eyes of the city's inhabitants be gouged out. The homiletical version reads as follows:

"(On this condition I will make a covenant with you) if you will erase from your Torah the commandment wherein it is written that the Ammonites and Moabites shall not be cleansed to enter the assembly of the Lord".[314]

This enigmatic midrash can perhaps best be understood in the light of the incident that occurred around 100 C.E. when an Ammonite proselyte asked whether he would be permitted to enter the assembly of the Lord, i.e., marry into a native Jewish family. After a long debate, the lenient view of R. Joshua b. Hananiah was accepted, namely that the inquirer was indeed permitted to intermarry with Jews—the reason being that Sennacherib had transplanted the nations and confused their boundaries, so that the people

312. For details and source references, cf. *Encyclopedia Talmudit,* edit. S. Zevin (Jerusalem 1953), Vol. V, pp. 495 ff.

313. Cf. M. B.B. III, 3; T.B. Git. 39a, For further details, cf. *Encyclopedia Talmudit,* Vol. VI, 279 ff.

314. Cf. Deut. 23:4; M. Yev. VIII, 3.

living in the territories of Ammon and Moab were not necessarily descended from the ancient Ammonites and Moabites.[315]

It must, however, be borne in mind that the inhabitants of Ammon and Moab during the Talmudic period were predominantly Nabatean Arabs,[316] whose hostility to the Jews was notorious, surpassing as it did that of any other ethnic group, with the possible exception of the Syrians.[317] While it was impossible to stop any individual Nabateans from converting to Judaism, there was an understandable reluctance to permit them to intermarry with native-born Jews. By translating the planned atrocity of the Ammonite ruler—reminiscent, incidentally, of Arab atrocities during the siege of Jerusalem—as an attempt to remove a divine precept from the Torah, thus enabling Nabatean "Ammonites" to become full-fledged Jews with the privilege of intermarrying with Jews, the homiletical targumist is in effect voicing a protest against the halachic leniency of the Sanhedrin, which had in effect agreed to do precisely that which Nahash the Ammonite had vainly sought to force upon his Israelite contemporaries.

Popular dislike of hostile foreigners was, if anything, surpassed by the animosity towards evil individuals, irrespective of their religious status. They were morally so repulsive that one was not even supposed to look into their wicked faces: "The Holy One, Blessed be He, said, I cannot look at the wicked".[318] R. Joshua ben Korha attributed his longevity to the fact that he would never gaze at the countenance of a wicked man.[319] R. Johanan, citing Elisha's outburst against the wicked king Jehoram of Israel—". . . I would

---

315. Cf. M. Yad. IV, 4.

316. There were of course Hellenistic cities, especially the Decapolis in Northern Transjordan. The Greek-speaking elements, however, constituted only a small minority of the population.

317. Arab auxiliaries, especially archers, played a prominent role in the Roman-Jewish war of 66-70 C.E. They (as well as the Syrians) committed some horrible atrocities against the Jews (cf. *Bell.* III, 7, 9, par. 168; 7, 18, par. 211; 7,26, par. 262; V, 6, 5, par. 290; and especially 13, 4-5, pars. 551-561. Cf. also Midr. Tanh. יתרו 5; Gen. R. LIII, 14; and Lam. R. II, 2, 4, for an example of Arab cruelty toward Jewish captives, supposedly in 587 B.C.E., but probably reflecting an incident around 70 C.E.

As early as the time of Herod, the Nabateans had massacred Jewish envoys (cf. *Ant.* XV, 5, 2, par. 124; 5, 5, 156; *Bell* I, 19, 3, par. 371). The Jewish attitude to the Nabatean Arabs is well illustrated in the anti-Arab speech put by Josephus into Herod's mouth; cf. *Ant.* XV, 5, 3, 127-146; *Bell* I, 19, 4, pars. 373-379.

318. T.B. Shab. 104a.

319. Cf. T.B. Meg. 28a.

neither look at you nor see you"[320]—stated that it was forbidden to gaze at the countenance of a wicked person.[321] R. Eleazar went so far as to claim that one who failed to heed this injunction would lose his sight, as had in fact happened to Isaac "because he used to gaze at the wicked Esau".[322]

The idea behind this seemingly childish prohibition was, of course, not so much avoiding an accidental look at the face of a morally depraved individual but rather shunning his company and his potentially contagious influence for evil. In line with this concept (as well as in accordance with TJ's preference for concrete facts as against abstract ideas), MT Isaiah 33:15b—". . . and he shuts his eyes against looking at evil"—is translated by TJ: ". . . and he restrains his eyes against looking at evil-doers".

The Halacha was concerned not only with ritual and religious laws and customs. It embraced every aspect of life, including major crises in human experience such as sickness and death. This brings us to the concluding examples of targumic halacha. Visiting the sick was always considered an act of kindness enjoined by Jewish ethics,[323] even toward Gentiles[324] and even on the Sabbath[325], one that was also of considerable therapeutic value,[326] and hence rewarded both in this world and in the world-to-come.[327] It was in fact of such outstanding importance that God Himself had set the example when he visited Abraham on the third day after the Patriarch had had himself circumcised;[328] and the Divine Presence was still continuing to sustain the sick.[329]

Particularly significant is a story about a disciple of R. Akiba's who fell sick and was not visited by his fellow scholars. R. Akiba personally visited him and, evidently finding the room in a state of neglect, gave orders to have it swept and cleaned—whereupon the patient recovered.[330]

It is perhaps with this story in mind that TJ's translation of II Kings

320. II Kings 3:14.
321. Cf. T.B. Meg. 28a.
322. *Ibid.*
323. T.B. Ned. 39b-40a; Sot. 14a; B.K. 100a; B.M. 30b.
324. Cf. T.B. Git. 61a.
325. Cf. T.B. Shab. 12b.
326. Cf. T.B. Ned. 39b-40a; B.M. 30b.
327. Cf. T.B. Shab. 127a; Ned. 39b-40a.
328. Cf. T.B. B.M. 86b; Gen. R. VIII, 13; Midr. Tanh. וירא 2 (end).
329. Cf. T.B. Ned. 40a; Gen. R. VIII, 13.
330. Cf. T.B. Ned. 40a.

8:29 and 9:16—in both passages we are informed that Ahaziah King of Judah went to visit his wounded uncle, Joram, King of Israel—is to be seen. Where MT merely speaks about Ahaziah going to "see" (לראות) Joram, TJ renders: למסעד ("to support" or "to help").[331] In other words, visiting the sick is not meant to be confined to inactively seeing the patient or chatting with him, but includes aiding and nursing him to speed his recovery.

If the patient did not recover from his illness and died, it was considered essential—if he was a righteous man—not to bury him together with a wicked person or, for that matter, with anybody unworthy of being buried in his immediate vicinity: "A wicked man may not be buried beside a righteous one."[332] Both the Talmud[333] and the Midrash[334] explain the resurrection miracle of the man whose body had been thrown into Elisha's grave[335] as a purely temporary phenomenon designed to keep his body apart from that of the great prophet.

A midrashic version of TJ has preserved a similar legend, though there are some differences: "Now it happened that, while they were burying a man, lo, they saw troops. So they threw the man into Elisha's grave. But in order that Elisha's bones should not be defiled by a dead person, a miracle happened to him, so that when the man touched the bones of Elisha, he revived and stood on his feet. He then went out from the grave, yet he did not go to his home; but he went down to his burial place which he chanced to find and fell down and died there."

It should be noted that this version does not denigrate the dead man, even by implication, and nowhere is there any hint that he was a wicked

331. Similarly, II Kings 10:13b, where "to see" or "to visit" is implied in MT, while TJ renders: למסעד ("to support" or "to aid").
332. T.B. Sanh. 47a.
333. *Ibid.*
334. Eccl. R. VII, 10; Midrash Shoher Tov, ch. 26, edit. Buber, p. 220.
335. Cf. II Kings 13:21. According to Midrash Shoher Tov, *ad loc.*, the man in question was the son of the Shunammite woman who had been revived by Elisha (cf. II Kings 4:8-37). His death after his second resurrection was due to his wickedness. A different tradition is mentioned by Rashi on T.B. Sanh. 47a, according to which the man was identical with the old—and false—prophet of Bethel (cf. I Kings 13:11 ff.) who, it should be noted, had requested to be buried in the grave of the anonymous prophet from Judah (*ibid.* v. 31) whom he had brought back to Bethel under false pretenses. This request may have originated the tradition reported by Rashi.

person. His temporary revival was due solely to the need to keep Elisha's bones free from contact with the dead—presumably, *any* dead, including righteous ones. This, of course, implies that Elisha's own bones were ritually pure[336]—a unique halachic stance for which there is no parallel[337]—and had therefore to be kept apart from unclean bodies.

Death was usually followed by a period of mourning, during which certain customs would be observed, including "sackcloth and ashes." These were also followed on other sad occasions and were symbolical of mourning for a variety of reasons not necessarily connected with bereavement. In Biblical times, the usual custom was to spread ashes on the ground and sit or lie on them[338] and/or cast dust on the head.[339] This is in fact expressly stated in Ezek. 27:30: "They cast dust on their heads and wallow in ashes."[340]

In the Talmudic age, it was customary to cast wood ashes—not dust—on the heads of the congregation on a public fast when prayers for rain would be offered.[341] It may be assumed that this was also the custom on other mournful occasions—and even on some joyful ones. Thus, wood ashes were strewn on the head of the bridegroom on his wedding day—a poignant reminder (like the breaking of the glass which is still the norm at Jewish weddings) of the unabated national mourning for the Temple that was burnt down by the Romans.[342]

Is is this custom which is reflected in TJ's translation of Jeremiah 6:26a, where MT reads: "... gird on sackcloth and wallow in ashes." TJ renders: "... Tie on sackcloth and *cover your heads* with ashes." The change from "wallowing," i.e., rolling on ashes spread on the ground, to covering the head

---

336. Conceivably, this idea is based on the talmudic statement that "the righteous are called living (even) in their death" (T.B. Ber. 18a).

337. Normative Judaism does not distinguish between the dead bodies of righteous and wicked people—they are all impure and convey levitical impurity through touch as well as through being under the same roof or cover; cf. Num. 19:11-14; M. Ohol. I, 4; II, 1 *et passim*.

338. Cf. Is. 58:5; Jer. 6:26; Ezek. 27:30; Jon. 3:6; Job 2:8; Esther 4:3.

339. Cf. Jos. 7:6; Ezek. 27:30; Job 2:12; Lam. 2:10. Cf. also Amos 2:7.

340. Only in II Sam. 13:19 do we find that Tamar, having been raped and humiliated by her half-brother Amnon, casts ashes rather than dust on her head. However, because of the euphonic similarity between עפר (dust) and אפר (wood ashes), one must allow for occasional confusion between the two; cf. T.B. Sot. 16a; Hul. 88b.

341. Cf. M. Ta'an. II, 1.

342. Cf. T.B. B.B. 60b.

with ashes is not accidental. Once the Biblical custom of sitting or lying on ashes and covering the head with dust had been superseded by the simpler and less excitable Halacha of sprinkling wood ashes on the head, TJ had to adapt the Biblical meaning to the new legal order.

Summing up, it may be confidently stated that the evidence leaves no doubt that the laws and customs depicted in TJ are not necessarily what they were in biblical times, but a retrojection of halachic practice in the Talmudic age. It cannot be sufficiently emphasized that the central purpose of the Aramaic translation of Biblical texts was not to provide an accurate rendering for the benefit of scholars, but to instruct the masses with an up-to-date version of the Scriptures, one which perforce had to agree with current laws and customs. Inevitably, accuracy and historical truth had to be sacrificed on the altar of halachic orthodoxy.

Historical and Geographical Allusions in Targum Jonathan

There are numerous allusions to historical events in TJ as well as retrojections to Biblical times of political, social and economic conditons which prevailed in the Talmudic age. The problem is to identify correctly the event or situation hinted at in TJ or in the midrashic additions to TJ, whose provenance and genuineness are often obscure. Inevitably, identifications are sometimes tenuous and, to the extent that they have not been established already, they may well be little more than intelligent speculation. In some cases, indeed, alternative possibilities must be taken into account, and dogmatic conclusions should be carefully avoided.

There are, nevertheless, certain basic rules which ought to be applied. Where, for example, probability and some (albeit inconclusive) evidence point in a certain direction, the fact that absolute certainty is unattainable should not prevent us from drawing at least tentative conclusions. Secondly, where the alternatives to be weighed are far apart in time, and there are no cogent reasons to pick the earlier date, the later date is generally to be preferred. Just as Mishnaic references to the Temple, the Temple cult, Jerusalem and its Sanhedrin undoubtedly reflect the last decades of the existence of the Second Temple,[1] so, with rare exceptions, TJ reflects the events and conditions of the centuries coinciding with, and following, the destruction of the Second Commonwealth.

Hence, where we have descriptions of religious persecution, with the clear choice between the proscription of Judaism by Antiochus IV (168–165 B.C.E.) and the equally vicious Hadrianic persecution following the Bar Kochba War (135–8 C.E.), the inherent probability is that the reference in TJ is to the latter. As the Talmud eloquently puts it, "Israel's later troubles

---

1. Cf., e.g., A. Büchler, *Die Priester und der Cultus im letzten Jahrzehnt des Jerusalemischen Tempels* (Vienna, 1895), p. 10; A. Büchler, *Das Synedrion in Jerusalem* (Vienna, 1902), pp. 96ff.; 228-240.

make them forget the earlier ones".[2] Thus, even existing Targumic material relating to earlier persecutions is likely to have been reworked and revised in the light of later events.

Where the Targumic Midrash also mentions the interruption of the study and teaching of Torah during the persecution, probability becomes almost certainty; for although such statements are not entirely inapplicable to the Maccabean age, the emphasis on the dissemination of learning is far more characteristic of the age of R. Akiba and his disciples (who, as already pointed out, decisively shaped the entire ideology of TJ) than of any earlier period. During Antiochus's persecution, men and women were tortured and killed because they refused to transgress the Law; because they circumcised their children; and because they would not desecrate the Sabbath and the festivals or eat the meat—usually swine's flesh—of pagan sacrifices or participate in any heathen cult.[3] Although Torah scrolls were torn up and burnt,[4] there is no record of any martyrs who died because they studied or taught the Law. We do *not* hear of Maccabean scholars who, like R. Akiba and R. Hanina ben Teradyon during the Hadrianic persecution, were put to death because they openly defied the edict prohibiting the teaching and dissemination of Judaism.[5]

Here and there one, nevertheless, meets with allusions to earlier times, including the Hasmonean epoch. Thus, we read about those that "act truthfully" and "observe faithfulness" hiding themselves and being unable "to show themselves."[6] Granted that this description equally fits the persecutions of 168-5 B.C.E. and 135-8 C.E., the emphasis on truth and faithfulness and the absence of any reference to the study and teaching of Torah[7] points to the earlier persecution when mass education had not yet been developed.

There are strong indications of allusions to the Hasmonean age in TJ's rendering of Isaiah 22:22 f. While the prophet predicts that his con-

---

2. T. B. Ber. 13a.
3. Cf. I Macc. 1:6ff.; 2:29-38; II Macc. 6:10-7:42.
4. Cf. I Macc. 1:56.
5. Cf. T. B. Ber. 61b; A. Z. 18a.
6. Cf. Is. 59:14b (MT "... for truth has fallen (or: stumbled) in the public square, and uprightness cannot enter" = "... for those that act truthfully have stumbled in the street, and they that observe faithfulness were not able to show themselves"); *ibid.* 59:15a (MT "Truth was missing" = "Those that act truthfully were hiding themselves").

7. For example, "they that observe faithfulness" could easily have been modified to "they that study (or: teach) the Torah faithfully."

temporary, Eliakim the son of Hilkiah, would inherit the position of steward of the royal household and be given charge of "the key of the house of David," TJ speaks of giving Eliakim the key of the Temple as well as the dominion of the house of David.[8] In addition, he is to be appointed as "a faithful trustee" (אמרכל)[9]—a position which is known to have been held by members of the high priestly families during the last decades of the Second Commonwealth.[10] TJ's description fits no one but the Hasmonean rulers, who combined the high priesthood with temporal power, having assumed the authority which traditionally belonged to members of the Davidic dynasty.[11] TJ, however, adds a postscript to Is. 22:25. Accordingly, the "faithful trustee who ministers in the permanent place" would be removed, "and the burden of prophecy concerning him will be annulled."[12] This can

8. Cf. Is. 22:22a (MT "And I will place on his shoulder the key of the house of David" = "And I will give the key of the Temple and the dominion (or: rule) of the house of David in his hand").

9. Cf. *ibid.* 22:23a (MT "And I will fasten him [viz., Eliakim] like a peg in a sure place" = TJ "And I will appoint him a faithful trustee, ministering in the permanent place" [i.e., the Temple]).

10. Cf. T. B. Pes. 57a; Hor. 13a. Cf. also M. Shek. V, 2; Tos. Shek. II, 15 and Num. 3:32a, where Eleazar son of Aaron, who subsequently became his father's successor as high priest, is depicted in Targum Onkelos as "the trustee (אמרכלא) who is appointed over the chiefs of the Levites."

11. Cf. I Macc. 14:25-47; Josephus, Ant. XIII, 11, 1, par. 301; Strabo, Geog., XVI, 2, 40, par. 762. On general Aggadic material relating to the Hasmoneans, cf. J. Heinemann, האגדה אגדות חשמונאיות ואנטי־חשמונאיות?, in מולד IV (5731-1971), No. 19-20, pp. 150-160. See also V. Aptowitzer, *Parteipolitik der Hasmonäerzeit im rabbinischen und pseudoepigraphischen Schrifttum* (Vienna, 1927), and A. Marmorstein's criticism in *MGWJ*, 73 (1929), pp. 244ff.

12. Cf. Is. 22:25 (MT "In that day ... the peg that was fastened in a sure place will be removed [or: will give way]; and it will be cut down and fall, and the burden that was upon it will be cut off ..." = TJ "At that time ... the faithful trustee who ministers in the permanent place will be removed, and he will be plucked off and fall, and the burden of prophecy concerning him will be annulled").

On the entire passage, see also Lev. R. V, 5, and Churgin, p. 100, who points out that Shebna's position, which was supposed to be transferred to Eliakim (cf. vv. 20-1) was that of high priest (cf. v. 18a, where MT "He will whirl you round and round" (צנוף יצנפך צנפה) is rendered by TJ, "He will remove the mitre from you"); while Eliakim himself is granted no more than the position of trustee. It is likely that this seeming contradiction partly explains the different views of R. Eleazar (according to whom Shebna was high priest) and R. Judah (who maintains that Shebna was only a trustee) in Lev. R. V, 5. However, the contradiction is more apparent than real. TJ's "mitre" (מצנפתא) was undoubtedly influenced by the homophony

only refer to the post-Hasmonean period after Herod had defeated the last Hasmonean ruler, Antigonus, and had caused him to be executed,[13] following this up by arranging the murder of his brother-in-law, Aristobulus, whom he had been forced to appoint high priest.[14]

The ease with which this TJ postscript makes null and void the earlier prophecies regarding the "faithful trustee," i.e., the Hasmonean priest-rulers adumbrated by Eliakim is understandable in the light of the moral deterioration of the later Hasmoneans, notably Judah Aristobulus I and Alexander Jannaeus, who became typical Hellenistic tyrants who mercilessly oppressed the people. This is admirably reflected in TJ's rendering of Zech. 11:4b and especially 11:7, where the "leaders," whom God had appointed over the people are denounced for having ruled over them as over "the flock doomed to slaughter;" exiled them;[15] and "rejected the kingdom of the house of David concerning whom it is my wish that they should be leaders over my people."[16] Although ostensibly directed against those who "divided the house of Israel against the house of Judah,"[17] this Targum passage, which

---

with MT צנפה יצנפך צנוף, without necessarily implying that Shebna was high priest. As we have seen (supra, n. 10) Eleazar son of Aaron who was heir to the high priesthood is also depicted in Targum Onkelos as אמרכלא.

13. Cf. Ant. XIV, 16, 2-4, pars. 468-490; XV, 1, 2, pars. 8-10; Bell. I, 18, 1-3, pars. 347-357.

14. Cf. Ant. XV, 2,5-3,3, pars. 23-55; Bell. I, 22, 2, par. 437.

15. Cf. Ant. XIII, 13, 5-14, 2, pars. 376-383 and Bell. I, 4, 4-6, pars. 91-98, where we are informed that Alexander Jannaeus, fighting for six years a ferocious civil war against his own people, slew 50,000 Jews, and, on attaining victory, had 800 of his opponents—evidently the leaders of the Pharisees—crucified, slaughtering their wives and children before their eyes. Thereupon, we are told, some of his remaining opponents fled and remained in exile as long as the king lived. Among those hiding or in exile were the spiritual leaders of the Pharisees, Simeon ben Shatach and Judah ben Tabbai; cf. T. Y. Ber. VII, 2, 11b; T. Y. Hag. II, 2, 77d; T. B. Ber. 48a; Sot. 47a; Sanh. 107b; Gen. R. XCI, 3.

16. Cf. Zech. 11:4b (MT "Feed the flock doomed to slaughter" = TJ "Prophesy concerning the leaders who were appointed to provide for the people, but they rule over them as over sheep [destined] for slaughter"). Cf. especially *ibid.* 11:7 (MT "So I became the shepherd of the flock doomed to slaughter, even you, O poor of the flock. And I took unto me two staffs; one I named Grace [or: Pleasantness], and the other I named Bands [or: Binders], and I tended the flock" = TJ "And I appointed leaders over the people, but they ruled over them as over the poor sheep [destined] for slaughter, and they carried away [or: exiled] my people; they were divided before me into two parts. The house of Israel was divided from the house of Judah; they rejected the kingdom of the house of David concerning whom it is my wish that they should be leaders over my people").

17. There is a strong possibility that this clause alludes to the Samaritan schism, with the

has only the vaguest connection with the Hebrew original, clearly refers to contemporary issues. Now, it is well known that the assumption of royal power by the later Hasmoneans provoked profound hostility, the reason being that this was considered to be the exclusive privilege of the Davidic dynasty.[18] There is thus every reason to assume that the entire passage—or most of it—represents a Targumic denunciation of Alexander Jannaeus.

In 6 C.E., a little over four decades after the extinction of the Hasmonean dynasty, Judaea became a Roman procuratorial province. A census for taxation purposes was carried out against violent opposition, which was ruthlessly suppressed.[19] According to Churgin,[20] it is this event which gave rise to TJ's interpretation of Hab. 3:17b, namely, that the Romans would be destroyed and would no longer collect the tribute from Jerusalem.[21] It is a plausible suggestion, but not absolutely convincing. After all, the Romans continued to collect taxes right down to 66 C.E., when the initially successful Jewish rising temporarily put an end to the Roman occupation. It is quite possible that it was at that time or soon thereafter that this "prediction" about the "destruction" of the Romans was made as a *vaticinium post eventum*.

About half a century earlier, one of Herod's sons, Herod Antipas,

---

Samaritans cast in the role of "splitters" who "divided the house of Israel against the house of Judah."

18. Cf. II Sam. 7:13ff.; Jer. 33:17, 20-26; Ezek. 37:24; Pss. 89:21-38; I Chron. 17:12ff.; Psalms of Solomon 17:4-6. See especially Soferim XIII, 13: "Gladden us . . . with the kingdom of the house of David thine annointed . . . Suffer not a stranger to sit upon his throne . . ." Cf. also S. Zeitlin, *The Rise and Fall of the Judaean State* I (Philadelphia, 1962), p. 318; S. Zeitlin and S. Tedesche, *The First Book of the Maccabees* (New York, 1950), Introduction, p. 31.

19. Cf. Ant. XVII, 13, 5, par. 355; XVIII, 1, 1, pars. 1ff.; Bell. II, 8, 1, pars. 117-118; Acts 5:37.

20. Cf. Churgin, pp. 22f. See especially p. 23, n. 34. Cf. also Komlosh, *op. cit.*, p. 60.

21. Cf. Hab. 3:17b (MT ". . . the flock shall be cut off from the fold, and there shall be no herd in the stalls" = TJ ". . . the Romans shall be destroyed, and they shall not collect the tribute [Aramaic קיסומא = rakings] from Jerusalem"). Cf. also Is. 3:6b where MT והמכשלה הזאת (and this ruin) = TJ ומגביתא הדא (and this collection [*viz.*, of the tribute]). The collection of tribute, which was often carried out with extraordinary cruelty, was rightly regarded as a "ruin." (For a different interpretation of this verse, cf. T. B. Shab. 119b-120a; Hag. 14a; Git. 43a). By way of contrast, the future age of Israel's glory would be characterized by the payment of tribute to Israel by foreign nations; cf. Is. 55:5a (MT ". . . nations that knew you not shall run to you" = TJ ". . . a people that did not know you shall run to bring [up to] you taxes").

tetrarch of Galilee and Peraea, founded the city of Tiberias which was to be the spiritual capital of Palestinian Jewry for some eight centuries. Yet, both Josephus[22] and the Talmud[23] inform us that priests and other observant Jews originally refused to settle in Tiberias because it was supposed to have been built over graves, thus polluting everyone stepping over them. It was only about the middle of the second century c.e. that R. Simeon bar Yohai, who had been cured of a skin disease by bathing in the hot springs of Tiberias, found a way to declare Tiberias to be levitically clean.[24]

The unfavorable orthodox attitude towards Tiberias at the time of its foundation and probably for some considerable time thereafter appears to be reflected in TJ's rendering of Is. 65:4a, where the prophetic censure of the superstitious and idolatrous practices in MT is transformed in TJ into a denunciation of people "staying in houses built of the dust of graves, and . . . dwelling with the corpses of the sons of men."[25]

About 52 c.e., a trial took place in Rome of Jews, Samaritans and Romans involved in a series of bloody encounters between the Jews and the Samaritans. Among the sentences passed by the emperor Claudius was one that a tribune by the name of Celer, who had evidently been guilty of some grave offenses against the Jews, should be brought to Jerusalem and there dragged through the city and slain.[26] It is quite possible that this extremely rare incident of a Roman tribune being given such exemplary punishment in Jerusalem for offending the Jews—which undoubtedly made a deep impression upon the people,—is reflected in TJ's rendering of II Sam. 12:31a, where MT " . . . he (viz., David) made them (i.e., the Ammonites) pass

---

22. Cf. Ant. XVIII, 2, 3, pars. 36-38.

23. Cf. T. B. Shab. 33b-34a.

24. *Ibid.*

25. Cf. Is. 65:4a, where MT reads: "Who dwell in tombs, and spend the night (or: lodge) in secret places (or: monuments)". Churgin, p. 25, rightly regards TJ's interpretation as "a valuable historical statement on the erection of Tiberias." He is, however, on very uncertain ground when he assigns this Targumic passage to 28 c.e. Tiberias was founded about a decade earlier, and the Targumic comment could have arisen then or soon after. As far as we know, 28 c.e. has no particular significance in the history of Tiberias.

26. Cf. Ant. XX, 6, 3, par. 136; Bell. II, 12, 7, par. 246. Cf. also M. Aberbach, "The Conflicting Accounts of Josephus and Tacitus concerning Cumanus' and Felix' Terms of Office," *JQR* XL, 1949, 1-14. For a Talmudic Agadah relating a similar punishment, cf. Sanh. 26b, where we are told that the Assyrians "bored holes through his (Shebna's) heels, tied him to the tails of their horses, and dragged him over thorns and thistles." This form of punishment was undoubtedly derived from contemporary experience.

through (or: toil at) the brick-kilns" is rendered by TJ, " . . . he dragged them through the streets."

A few years after this event, apparently shortly before the outbreak of the Roman-Jewish war in 66 C.E., King Agrippa II, following, it seems, the wishes of Cestius Gallus, the Roman governor of Syria, ordered the priests to take a census of the Passover pilgrims by retaining a kidney from each Paschal lamb brought to the Temple.[27] This event is almost certainly reflected in TJ's interpretation of I Sam. 15:4a, where we are told that Saul numbered his army "in Telaim," a place which is probably identical with Telem mentioned in Joshua 15:24.[28] Since Telaim can also mean lambs, TJ renders, " . . . he counted them by the Passover lambs."[29]

It is probably King Agrippa II who is again alluded to in TJ on Is. 28:1a, where MT reads: "Woe to the proud crown of the drunkards of Ephraim, and to the fading flower of its glorious beauty." This is homiletically expanded in TJ to "Woe to him that gives the crown to the arrogant, the big fool of Israel, and (that) gives the mitre[30] to the wicked of the Temple." Churgin (p. 23), who is followed by Komlosh,[31] identifies this reference to a priest-king with Alexander Jannaeus who—judging by the description given of him in Josephus—was indeed both arrogant and wicked. However, this explanation, plausible though it may seem, is untenable for three reasons:

1. Nowhere in our sources is Alexander Jannaeus depicted as a fool. On the contrary, both Josephus and the Talmudic sources agree that, with all his ferocity, he was a highly intelligent ruler as well as a successful conqueror.

2. Most MSS have the plural form of "to the wicked" (לרשׁיעיא), not the

---

27. Cf. Bell. VI, 9, 3, pars. 420-7; Tos. Pes. IV, 3; T. B. Pes. 64b; Lam. R. I 1 (2). A similar interpretation is also given in T. B. Yoma 22b.

28. Cf. H. W. Hertzberg, *I and II Samuel*, Eng. Transl. (London, 1964), p. 125. Among medieval commentators, Kimchi considers Telaim to be the name of a place.

29. Cf. Komlosh, *op. cit.*, p. 321. Churgin, p. 27, discusses this interpretation as a possibility, but adds: "I would not, however, stress this evidence. A later Targumist might as well have used for exegetical purpose a current Agada." Churgin's caution is perhaps overdrawn. It is more probable that an earlier Targumist, who witnessed or remembered Agrippa's census, would utilize it for exegetical purposes rather than a later one.

30. Aramaic מצנפתא; cf. מצנפת in Exod. 28:4.39, where it describes the headgear of the high priest. The connecting link with our word is the Hebrew word ציץ, which in this context means "flower" or "blossom," but happens to be also the word used for the "forehead plate" worn by the high priest (*ibid.* 28:36ff.).

31. *Op. cit.*, p. 60.

singular לרשיעא. If לרשיעיא is correct, the reference cannot be to Alexander Jannaeus.

3. Alexander Jannaeus was never "given" the crown by anybody. He inherited it from his brother Judah Aristobulus who, according to Josephus,[32] was the first to assume the royal title in addition to his high-priestly functions.

It is more probable that the king in question is Agrippa II, who was appointed king of northeastern Galilee and other neighboring territories by the Romans.[33] He was also granted the right to supervise the Temple and to appoint high priests, and most of the high priests he appointed in rapid succession were Boethusian Sadducees[34]—described as "wicked" in the Talmud,[35]—among them Anan son of Anan whose high-handed methods, culminating in the judicial murder of the saintly James, aroused the law-abiding citizens of Jerusalem against him and led to his deposition.[36]

Although Agrippa was a man of weak character, a number of incidents in his career would justify depicting him as arrogant and foolish. Thus, he was suspected of indulging in an incestuous relationship with his sister Berenice.[37] He aroused unnecessarily the opposition of the priests of Jerusalem by attempting to watch the proceedings of the Temple from an adjacent tower and trying—unsuccessfully as it turned out—to stop the priests from building a high wall to protect the privacy of the Temple service.[38] Even more seriously, he offended the priests by permitting the Levites to wear the linen garments which only priests were supposed to wear. According to Josephus, this was such a serious religious transgression that the disastrous war which followed soon after was a well-deserved punishment.[39] Agrippa's role when the question of providing employment for 18,000 workmen was being considered by the Temple authorities was hardly helpful.[40]

Finally, his ineffectiveness in persuading the zealot rebels to lay down

32. Cf. Ant. XIII, 11, 1, p. 301; Bell. I, 3, 1, par. 70.

33. Cf. Ant. XX, 7, 1, par. 138; *ibid.* 8, 4, par. 159; Bell. II, 12, 8, pars. 247f.; *ibid.* 13, 2, par. 252.

34. Cf. Ant. XX, 5, 2, par. 103-4; *ibid.* 8, 8, par. 179; Bell. II, 12, 1, par. 223.

35. Cf. Tos. Yoma I, 8; T. B. Yoma, 9a; 18a; 19b; Pes. 57a; T. Y. Yoma I, 5, 39a. Cf. also Ant. XX, 8, 8, par. 180; *ibid.* 9, 2, pars. 206-7.

36. Cf. Ant. XX, 9, 1, pars. 200ff.

37. Cf. *ibid.* XX, 7, 3, par. 145; Juvenal, *Satires*, VI, 156-160.

38. Cf. Ant. XX, 8, 11, pars. 189ff.

39. Cf. *ibid.* XX, 9, 6, pars. 216ff.

40. Cf. *ibid.* XX, 9, 7, pars. 219-222.

their arms in 66 C.E.—the speech delivered by him on that occasion, though freely invented by Josephus, undoubtedly represents Agrippa's true sentiments[41]—stamps him as a foolish as well as arrogant ruler who completely failed to recognize that the revolutionaries had valid grievances which ought to be redressed. His attempt to force the people to submit not only to Rome but also to Florus, the most rapacious and most hated of all the procurators,[42] was certainly the height of folly. Add to this the fact that he and his entourage engaged in acts of violence and oppression,[43] while displaying excessive munificence to foreign cities which, we are told, "made him more than ordinarily hated by his subjects,"[44] and the description of Agrippa in TJ is more than justified, since it fits him better than any other Jewish king during the Second Commonwealth.

The TJ version of Is. 28:1 may, therefore, be interpreted as follows: "Woe to him (viz., the Roman emperor) who gives the crown to the arrogant, the big fool of Israel (i.e., to Agrippa II), (and woe to him [viz., Agrippa II]) who gives the mitre (i.e., the high-priesthood) to the wicked ones of the Temple."

In the speech attributed by Josephus to Agrippa II on the occasion of the outbreak of the Roman-Jewish War in 66 C.E., there is a reference to Jewish complaints that "Servitude is hard"[45]—or, in other words, it is intolerable to be subjected to arbitrary Roman rule. This situation, which became considerably aggravated during the procuratorship of Gessius Florus,[46] seems to be reflected in TJ's rendering of Is. 28:20:[47] "For their strength shall be

---

41. Cf. Bell. II, 16, 4, pars. 345-401. Cf. also M. Aberbach, *The Roman-Jewish War* (London, 1966), p. 51, n. 196.

42. Cf. Bell. II, 17, 1, par. 406.

43. Cf. Ant. XX, 9, 4, par. 214.

44. *Ibid.* XX, 9, 4, pars. 211-212.

45. Bell. II, 16, 4, par. 365.

46. Cf. Ant. XX, 11, 1, pars. 252-257; Bell. II, 14, 2ff., pars. 277ff.; Tacitus, Hist. V, 10.

47. MT: "For the bed is too short to stretch oneself on it, and the covering too narrow to wrap oneself in it." Komlosh (*op. cit.*, p. 60), following Churgin, p. 29, regards this verse as a reflection of the oppression suffered by the Babylonian Jews at the hands of the Sassanid dynasty in the third century C.E. (cf., e.g., T. B. Yeb. 63b; Git. 17a; Kid. 72a; B. K. 117a). This view is based on the reading, ושלטון בבלאי מעיק—"and the oppressive rule of the Babylonians"—which is not to be found in Sperber's edition of TJ. However, even if the addition בבלאי is correct, it could not be attributed to the Persians who in the Talmud are described as פרסאי or חברי (Guebers), never as בבלאי. It is, furthermore, well known that in rabbinic literature "Babylonia" and "Babylonians" often stand for Rome and Romans, respectively. (For a detailed discussion, cf. *Encyclopedia Judaica* [Jerusalem 1971], vol. 16, s. v. Mesopotamia

reduced because of hard servitude, and an oppressive ruler shall increase his
tyranny." Although, theoretically, several possibilities are conceivable, none
fits the occasion so precisely as the governorship of Florus who was an "oppressive ruler" *par excellence* and who most certainly did "increase his
tyranny" and imposed "hard servitude" on the people.

To the same period of conflict between the Jews and the Romans belongs a midrashic addition to the Targum on I Sam. 17:43 ff. David and
Goliath are cast in the roles of Jews and Romans, and their Targumic propaganda war prior to the duel fought between them is reminiscent of the arguments used by the protagonists of peace and war during the Roman-Jewish
war of 66-70 C.E.[48] Surprisingly, Goliath plays a rather sympathetic role in
this midrash. First, he warns David about the inevitable consequences of his
rashness in opposing the Philistine champion, and he exhorts him over and
over again to pity his youth:[49] "Woe unto you, O lamb," exclaims Goliath,
"that you are attacking (or: provoking a fight with) a bear, and there is no
lamb that can stand up against a bear."[50] David fearlessly answers: "The

[subsection, In the Aggadah], cols. 1512-14). The attribution of TJ on Is. 28:20 to Persian
oppression is also inherently unlikely; for under the Sassanids the Jews endured religious
persecutions, not social-economic oppression. The expression "hard servitude" (שעבוד תקיף) is
manifestly unsuitable and in fact never used for deprivation of religious rights.

48. Cf., e.g., Bell. II, 16, 4, pars. 345-404; *ibid.* V, 9, 3, pars. 361-419; *ibid.* VI, 2, 1, pars.
93-110.

49. Significantly, it was the youthful elements who were always in the forefront of the
anti-Roman agitation; cf. Bell. II, 7, 2, par. 409; *ibid.* 13, 7, par. 267; *ibid.* 14, 5, 8, pars. 290
and 303; *ibid.* 16, 4, par. 346; *ibid.* IV, 3, 2, par. 128. Cf. also M. Aberbach, *The Roman-
Jewish War*, pp. 30-31. In a Midrashic version of the story of Hannah and her seven mar-
tyred children (Lam. R.I, 16, par. 50) we read that the "emperor" told the youngest son,
"Your brothers were full of days and years, and enjoyed a good life; but you are young, and
you are not full of days and years, and you did not enjoy a good life . . ." Although, ostensibly,
the story is identical with that told in II Macc., ch. 7, there are subtle differences (including
the change of Hannah's name to Miriam and the absence of any reference by Antiochus to the
youthfulness of the youngest son in II Macc. as well as the transformation in the Midrash of
Antiochus into a Roman emperor), which clearly stamp it, in its final form, as a late rework-
ing of the earlier material in the light of conditions under the Romans.

50. The lamb-bear metaphor was evidently influenced by I Sam. 17:34-37, where David
relates his exploits in saving lambs from a bear and a lion (or: bears and lions). The reason
why Goliath is represented as a bear and not as a lion is probably that the lion, the king of the
animal world, is the symbol of the tribe of Judah (cf. Gen. 49:9) as well as of Israel as a whole
(Num. 24:9) and therefore unsuitable as a metaphor for Goliath. The frequently cited homiletical metaphor of Israel being "a lamb enduring among seventy wolves" (i.e., powerful

Memra of my God who is coming with me—it shall save the lamb from the mouth of the bear."

Goliath alternates his threats with expressions of concern for David and his family: "Your father is crying and your mother is wailing, 'Woe, woe' ... Your heart that has been exalted, the Lord shall humble it." This sounds suspiciously like the exhortations of men like Agrippa II and Josephus who warned the Zealots against bringing calamity upon themselves and their country by their heedless rush into war with Rome.[51]

Among Goliath's threats is a fanciful warning that he might spit at David, thereby causing him to drown in spittle—an unmistakable allusion to the legend that Daniel's three companions, Hananiah, Mishael, and Azariah, were drowned in spittle—a metaphorical expression for contempt—after being rescued from the fiery furnace.[52] The implication of this threat is therefore that the Zealots, by their foolhardy venture in challenging the might of Rome, would bring upon themselves the contempt and derision of the world.

David's five smooth stones with which he armed himself before the duel with Goliath[53] provide additional grist to the homiletical mills of the Targumist. Accordingly, the names of Abraham, Isaac, Jacob, Moses and Aaron were inscribed, respectively, on these five stones, which vied with one another for the privilege of being the first to be cast upon Goliath:

"There was a great commotion (or: excitement) among the five stones; for one said to the other, 'I will go up first.'"[54]

Abraham's stone demanded to be the first to be slung at Goliath, "so that I may destroy this uncircumcised one together with his foreskin and remove disgrace from the house of Israel"[55]—possibly an oblique allusion to the prohibition of circumcision during the Hadrianic persecution. Even-

---

nations; cf. Esth. R., ch. 10 on Esth. 9:2) would have made a wolf-lamb metaphor eminently suitable, but for the reason given at the beginning of this note.

51. Cf. *supra*, n. 48.

52. Cf. T. B. Sanh. 93a.

53. Cf. I Sam. 17:40a.

54. This is clearly reminiscent of the well-known Aggadah that when Jacob came to Bethel on his way to Haran and "took of the stones of the place" to lay his head on (cf. Gen. 28:11), the stones quarreled with one another, each one saying, "Upon me shall this righteous man rest his head" (cf. T. B. Ḥul. 91b).

55. Cf. Jos. 5:9, where, following the circumcision of the Israelites, God tells Joshua, "This day I have rolled away the reproach (or: disgrace) of Egypt from off you."

tually, in accordance with the will of God, it was Aaron's stone which killed Goliath, "because he used to pursue peace."[56] This revealing paradox abundantly clarifies the political stance of the Targumic author of this midrash. Peaceful methods and reliance on divine intervention against the enemies of Israel will ultimately be more effective than the armed struggle advocated by the Zealots. This also explains, at least in part, why Goliath is given such a remarkably friendly treatment by the Targumist who evidently agreed with some of the anti-war arguments put into Goliath's mouth, which actually represented the views of the peace party.

The midrash concludes with the equally revealing sentence: "And what happened to that generation (viz., of David), shall happen to us—forever." In other words, as in David's time, Israel's freedom shall be regained—no doubt, by divine aid—from the hands of Israel's enemies.

An allusion to Vespasian's conquest of Galilee and other parts of Palestine between 67 and 69 C.E. may be contained in TJ on Amos 8:8b[57] and 9:5b:[58] "And a king shall come up against it (viz., the land of Israel) with his army which is great like the waters of the river, and he shall cover it all and drive out the inhabitants . . ."

It is noteworthy that the only ruler who personally conducted a major campaign against the Jews in the land of Israel was Vespasian.[59] Admittedly, he was only a general, not an emperor, during his entire campaign. But, just as R. Johanan ben Zakkai hailed him as emperor even though he had not yet been officially proclaimed as such,[60] so the Targumist, with the

56. Cf. M. Avot I, 12: "Hillel used to say, Be of the disciples of Aaron, loving peace and pursuing peace . . ."

57. MI: "And all of it (viz., the land) shall rise like the river (i.e., the Nile), and it shall be tossed about and sink again, like the river of Egypt."

58. MT: "And all of it shall rise like the river (viz., the Nile), and it shall sink again, like the river of Egypt."

59. During the other anti-Roman rebellions in Palestine, it was invariably one of the imperial governors or generals who were sent to put down the risings. It is true that King Antiochus IV invaded Palestine "with a great army" (I Macc. 1:20ff.) and carried out a massacre in Jerusalem during a second campaign in 168 B.C.E. when he also came "with a great host" (I Macc. 1:29ff.; II Macc. 5:12ff.); but on those occasions there was no general expulsion or deportation of the inhabitants. It is, nevertheless, possible, that an earlier version of TJ did indeed refer to Antiochus, but did not mention anything about the explusion or deportation of the inhabitants; while a later version applied the verse to Vespasian, adding the deportation statement at the end.

60. Cf. T. B. Git. 56a-b; Avot-de-R. Nathan, ed. Schechter, Vers. I, ch. 4, p. 23; Vers. II, ch. 6, p. 19; Lam. R. I, 5, par. 31.

added advantage of hindsight, would regard Vespasian, retrospectively, as emperor (= king). Vespasian and his son Titus did indeed bring large armies with them,[61] and they deported into slavery many tens of thousands of people.[62] Moreover, since Amos's prophecy refers to the northern kingdom, Vespasian's campaigns in Galilee and central Palestine would have been regarded as especially appropriate fulfillment of the prediction by the prophet of Tekoah who had repeatedly pronounced the doom of the northern kingdom of Israel.[63]

Allusions to various incidents during the great Roman-Jewish war can be found in TJ on Is. 22:5 and 29:1 ff. Josephus tells us that the hill fortress of Jotapata, which was situated on a precipitous cliff and which he defended for 47 days during the spring and summer of 67 C.E., was provided with strong defense towers.[64] Josephus also informs us that, following the capture of Jerusalem, the Roman soldiers searched the houses for loot,[65] and it is well known that plundering a captured city was the normal practice after every successful siege.[66] Thus, TJ on Is. 22:5b,[67] "searching the houses (and) besieging (or: surrounding) the towers on top of the mountains" has the authentic ring of contemporary events.

Prior and during the siege of Jerusalem in 70 C.E., a terrible civil war raged in the city. Following the proscription of the peace party, the Zealots fought bloody battles among themselves, uniting only when Titus arrived before the walls of Jerusalem. We are told that the captured war engines were used by one of the Zealot leaders, John of Gischala, to hurl missiles at the Temple area held by another faction. Many pilgrims and other worshippers were killed and, in Josephus's words, "they fell before (offering) their sacrifices and sprinkled with libations of their own blood that altar universally venerated by Greeks and barbarians. The dead bodies of natives and

---

61. Cf. Bell. III, 1, 3, pars. 6ff.; *ibid.* II, 4, pars. 29f.; *ibid.* 4, 1-2, pars. 59-69; *ibid.* IV, 11, 5, pars. 658f.; *ibid.* V, 1, 6, pars. 40 ff.; *ibid.* 2, 1, pars. 47ff.; *ibid.* 2, 3, par. 67.

62. Cf. Bell. III, 10, 10, par. 540; *ibid.* VI, 9, 2, par. 418.

63. Cf., e.g., Amos 2:6a; 3:14f.; 5:2.27; 7:8f.; 8:2b; 9:1ff. 8ff.

64. Cf. Bell. III, 7, 7, par. 158; *ibid.* 7, 10, par. 174.

65. Cf. *ibid.* V, 1, par. 271; *ibid.* 6, 3, pars. 354f.; *ibid.* VI, 8, 5, par. 405.

66. Cf., e.g., Ant. XIV, 16, 3, pars. 484f.; Bell, I, 18, 3, pars. 355f. (Roman looting in Jerusalem after capturing the city in 37 B.C.E.) and especially Tacitus, Hist. II, 100; III, 15-33, where the sack of Cremona in Italy by Vespasian's troops in 70 C.E.—the same year in which Jerusalem was destroyed—is graphically described.

67. MT: ". . . a battering down of walls and a shouting to the mountains . . ."

aliens, of priests and laity, were mingled in a mass, and the blood of all manner of corpses formed pools in the courts of God."[68]

It is this situation and the siege of Jerusalem and the destruction of the Temple which followed soon after which are clearly reflected in the Targumic version of Is. 29:1-3:[69] "Woe, O altar, altar which was (lit., they) built in the city in which David dwelt. Because of a gathering of armies that are assembling against it, within a year the festive offerings will cease upon you.[70] (v. 2): And I will distress the city in which there is the altar, and it shall be desolate and empty,[71] and it shall be surrounded before me with the blood of the slain as the altar is surrounded with the blood of the holy sacrifices slaughtered all around on the day of the festival. (v. 3) And I will cause armies to encamp against you, and I will build siege works against you, and heap up a mound ... "

Here we have a precise description of events in Jerusalem, virtually in their chronological order. After the slaughter in the Temple area and elsewhere caused by the civil war, the Roman legions under Titus arrived in the spring of 70 C.E.[72] and immediately began the siege of the city. There are some transparent allusions to Titus's march upon Jerusalem in another

68. Bell. V, 1, 3, pars. 16-18.

69. MT: "Ho Ariel, Ariel, the city where David encamped! Add year to year; let the feasts run their round. (v. 2) Yet I will distress Ariel, and there shall be moaning and lamentation, and she shall be to me like an Ariel. (v. 3) And I will encamp against you round about, and besiege you with towers; and I will raise siege works against you." Significantly, in Avot-de-R. Nathan, ed. Schechter, version 1, ch. 1, p. 4, Titus is represented as denouncing the Temple altar, while citing Isaiah 29:1. In Lam. R., Proem 26, Is. 29:2 is connected with the destruction of both the first and second Temples.

70. The reference appears to be to 69 C.E.—one year before the sacrifices in the Temple were suspended—,though it was probably committed to writing only after the destruction of the Temple. It is actually not even necessary to assume a *vaticinium post eventum*. The approaching doom was clearly visible in 69 C.E., and the prediction of the end of the sacrificial service hardly required prophetic insight. According to the Talmud and Midrash (T. B. Yoma 39b; Git. 56b; Avot-de-R. Nathan, ed. Schechter, I, ch. 4, p. 23; II, ch. 6, p. 19; Lam. R. I, 5, par. 31) R. Johanan ben Zakkai predicted the fall of Jerusalem and the destruction of the Temple long before the event, and R. Zadok was said to have fasted for forty years to prevent this calamity. Josephus (Bell. VI, 5, 3-4, pars. 288-315) as well as Tacitus (Hist. V, 13) relate accounts of prophecies, signs, and omens that preceded the destruction of the Temple.

71. The order of the description, which is generally chronological, deviates here from the norm, the final result of the war being predicted first, while some of the details are filled in afterwards.

72. Cf. Bell. V, 2, 1ff., pars. 47ff.

midrashic addition to TJ—namely, on Is. 10:32a.[73] The Biblical Sennacherib is transformed in the Targumic midrash (which has been transmitted in two similar versions) into a Roman general who looks suspiciously like Titus.[74] Having prepared three lodging-places[75] for his forces, he led with him an assorted army consisting of 4000 (another version has 40,000) crowned princes, many thousands of swordsmen, archers and spearsmen as well as 100,000 warriors "as swift as an eagle." At this point the figures tend to assume fantastic proportions, running into millions, while the length of the army is said to have extended over 400 Persian miles, and the horses standing neck to neck formed a line forty Persian miles long.[76] More accurately, we are then told that the entire host was divided into four armies—which agrees with Josephus's account,[77] according to which Titus "had three legions which under his father's command had previously ravaged Judaea, and the twelfth . . . ," and that it was these four legions that converged upon Jerusalem.

Reverting to fantasy, the Targumic midrash informs us that when the

73. MT: "This very day he shall halt at Nob." As pointed out by Churgin, pp. 132f., this Midrash is based on a modified version in T. B. Sanh. 95b, where Sennacherib's march on Jerusalem is depicted in vivid details, including a reference to female camp followers and harlots. It is noteworthy that Titus, too, is said to have brought a harlot—according to another version, two harlots—to the Holy of Holies, desecrating it by fornication with the harlot(s) on a Torah scroll or, according to the other version, on the altar; cf. T. B. Git. 56b; Gen. R. X, 7.

74. Cf. Avot-de-R. Nathan, ed. Schechter, Vers. II, ch. 7, p. 20, where Titus is depicted as blaspheming God whose alleged destruction of Sisera and Sennacherib he ridicules. Here a direct Midrashic link between Titus and Sennacherib has been preserved.

75. On the surface, the three lodging places would seem to be those listed in Is. 10:29 (Geba, Ramah and Gibeah of Saul, though only Geba is mentioned as having been used by the enemy as "their lodging"). Josephus (Bell. V, 2, 1, pars. 50-51) lists two stops—Gophna and the "Valley of Thorns" near Gibeath-Shaul—during Titus's march on Jerusalem; but he subsequently reports that one day later Titus moved his camp from the "Valley of Thorns" to Mt. Scopus (*ibid.* 2, 3, par. 67)—which thus constituted the third "lodging place" of the Romans.

76. The graphic (though greatly exaggerated) description of Sennacherib's host is in some ways similar to the vivid eyewitness account given by Josephus of Titus's army marching into Judaea; cf. Bell. V, 2, 1, pars. 47-49. Josephus also relates the tremendous impression made upon the people of Jerusalem by a full-dress parade of the Roman army organized by Titus during the siege of the city (cf. Bell. V, 9, 1, pars. 348ff.). The Talmudic and Midrashic accounts of Sennacherib's army may well reflect the impact made by the Romans on these and other occasions on the popular imagination.

77. Cf. Bell. V, 1, 6, pars. 41,2,3, 67ff.

first army crossed the Jordan, the men (or: their horses) drank all the water of the Jordan. The second army had to raise the hooves of the horses before being able to draw water—apparently by making the horses dig with their hooves. The third army found no more water and had to dig wells before they were able to find water.[78] The fourth army included Sennacherib and Nebuchadnezzar "his son-in-law"[79] as well as Adrammelech and Sharezer[80] and Esar-Haddon[81] his sons.

Allowing for the inevitable exaggerations to which Aggadah is prone, the basic fact remains that this remarkable Targumic midrash depicts in graphic language Titus's march on Jerusalem in 70 C.E. The description does not of course agree in every detail with the known facts of history; but the similarity is close enough to warrant the positive conclusion that the midrash reflects faithfully the impression made upon contemporaries of the advance upon the Holy City of the Roman legions under Titus.

Another possible allusion to Titus's preparations for the siege of Jerusalem may be found in TJ's rendering of Is. 10:28b:[82] ". . . at Michmash he appoints the leaders of his army." We have already seen that three verses later (v. 32) Sennacherib is depicted in terms which strongly suggest that the Targumist had Titus in mind. It is therefore highly probable that here, too, the Assyrian ruler is but a thin disguise for the Roman general—all the more so in view of the fact that in verse 29 Gibeah of Saul (the same place where Titus encamped on his way to Jerusalem)[83] is expressly mentioned as having been in Sennacherib's line of advance, so that the inhabitants fled in terror. Whether Titus appointed any generals at Michmash, about nine Roman miles north of Jerusalem[84] and thus in Titus's line of advance, cannot be

78. Although Josephus does not mention any shortage of water among the Romans prior to or during the siege of Jerusalem, he does give a similar description of the increasing shortage of timber for the battering rams, which eventually had to be brought from a distance of ninety or even 100 furlongs; cf. *Bell.* V, 12, 1, pars. 494f.; *ibid.* 12:3, pars. 523f.; *ibid.* VI, 1, 1, pars. 5f.; *ibid.* 2, 7, par. 151; *ibid.* 8, 1, par. 375.

79. Although the parallel is not precise, the close relationship between Vespasian and Titus is evidently indicated by the Sennacherib-Nebuchadnezzar legend. Nebuchadnezzar, as the destroyer of the first Temple, is frequently a transparent disguise for Titus; cf. *Encyclopedia Judaica* (Jerusalem, 1971), vol. 16, cols. 1512-13.

80. Cf. II Kings 19:37; Is. 37:38.

81. Cf. II Kings, *ibid.;* Is. *ibid.*

82. MT : ". . . at Michmash he (viz., Sennacherib) stores his baggage."

83. Cf. *Bell.* V, 2, 1, par. 51.

84. Cf. Eusebius, *The Onomastikon* (Heb. Trans. by E. Z. Melamed, Jerusalem 1950), p. 64, No. 695. Cf. also I Sam. 13:2ff.

ascertained from the sources;[85] but since our information is rather limited, the possibility that TJ has preserved a significant item in the history of the Roman-Jewish war is not to be discounted.

Among the horrors of the siege of Jerusalem in 70 C.E., Josephus mentions how the Arab and Syrian auxiliaries, expecting to find swallowed gold coins in the intestines of Jewish fugitives from the besieged city, ripped up in one night no less than two thousand of these unfortunates.[86] "It seems to me," Josephus adds, "that no more cruel calamity befell the Jews than this."[87]

Another horror story which deeply impressed itself upon the minds of contemporaries as well as later generations was an act of cannibalism by a woman named Mary daughter of Eleazar, who, crazed by the pangs of prolonged famine, slew her infant son and devoured his flesh.[88]

It is evidently these incidents that the Targumist of Is. 51:20a had in mind when he rendered MT "Your sons have fainted" by "Your children shall be torn to pieces."

More doubtful is another possible allusion to the siege of Jerusalem in TJ on Is. 22:6b,[89] where TJ translates, ". . . and upon the wall they affixed (their) shields." According to Josephus, the Romans planted their standards on Jerusalem's towers after capturing the walls of the city.[90] On the other hand, there is no doubt that the Targumist who rendered Is. 51:19a[91] by "Two afflictions (or: troubles) have come upon you, O Jerusalem," was thinking of the destruction of Jerusalem in 587/6 B.C.E and 70 C.E.

Similarly, the devastation of the country all around Jerusalem during the

---

85. Conceivably, TJ connects MT יִפְקֹד (Hiphil) with יְפַקֵּד (Pi'el), thus changing the meaning to "appoint."

86. Cf. Bell. V, 13, 4, pars. 551f.

87. *Ibid.*, par. 552.

88. *Ibid.* VI, 3, 4, 201-213; T. B. Yoma 38b; Lam. R. I, 16, par. 51. Although in the latter source the reference is ostensibly to the siege of Jerusalem by Nebuchadnezzar in 587 B.C.E., the context leaves no doubt that it was the Roman siege in 70 C.E. that the Midrashist had in mind.

89. MT: ". . . and Kir uncovered the shield."

90. Bell. VI, 8, 5, par. 403. The differences between Josephus and TJ may be due to exegetical reasons, TJ being unable to ignore MT קִיר (which can be rendered "wall," but not "tower") and מָגֵן (shield) which cannot be translated as "standards."

91. MT: "These two things have befallen you." Similarly also Ezek. 24:6f, where MT "Take out of it (viz., Jerusalem) piece after piece " is renderd by TJ "Exile upon exile (i.e., 587/6 B.C.E. and 70 C.E.) was endured (*lit.*, taken out) by its people." The partial exile of 597 B.C.E. is unlikely to have been recalled by TJ as a major disaster.

siege of the city and after it had been taken[92]—as well as the destruction of
many other Jewish towns prior to the siege of Jerusalem—may well be
alluded to in TJ on Jer. 4:26:[93] "And, behold, the land of Israel, which had
been cultivated like Carmel (or: fruitful land), turned back to be like a wilderness, and all its cities are desolate . . ." On the other hand, it must be
conceded that the even greater devastation of much of the country during
the Bar Kochba war (132-135 C.E.) could be equally alluded to by the Targumist.

Somewhat doubtful, too, is the allusion in TJ on Jer. 9:18b,[94] which is
rendered: "For our land is destroyed, for our (other version: its) castles are
desolate." These "castles" (בירניתנא or ברניתהא) could be fortresses such as
Jotapata in Galilee, Herodium in Judaea, and Machaerus and Masada, east
and west, respectively, of the Dead Sea. On the other hand, they could
equally allude to the numerous fortresses conquered by Julius Severus during the Bar Kochba war.[95] Indeed, as already mentioned, the devastation of
the country as a result of the Bar Kochba war was, if anything, even worse
than during the Roman-Jewish war of 66-70 C.E. The mountainous areas of
Judaea, especially, were, with few exceptions, virtually denuded of their
Jewish inhabitants.[96]

A major event in the history of the Middle East was Trajan's Mesopotamian campaign during the years 114-117 C.E. For a time he succeeded in
extending the Roman empire to its utmost limits, incorporating most of
Mesopotamia, which had been a Parthian province for centuries, within the
Roman empire, and he succeeded even in capturing Ctesiphon, the capital
of the Parthian empire. At this point, however, the Babylonian Jews, along
with the non-Jewish population of Mesopotamia, rebelled against the
Romans. This threat to his rear, coupled with Jewish risings in Egypt,
Cyrene and Cyprus, forced Trajan to withdraw, though the Jewish rebels in

---

92. Cf. Bell. V, 6, 2, par. 264; VI, 1, 1, pars. 5-8; VII, 1, 1, pars. 1-4.

93. MT: "I beheld, and, lo, the fruitful land was a desert, and all its cities were laid in
ruins . . ."

94. MT: ". . . for we have left the land, because they have cast down our dwellings."

95. Cf. Dio Cassius LXIX, 13; Eusebius, Hist. Eccl. IV, 6; Lam. R. II, 1-2, pars. 71-2;
T. B. Git. 57a; T. Y. Taan. IV, 8, 68d-69a. Cf. also E. Schürer, *Geschichte des Jüdischen
Volkes im Zeitalter Jesu Christi*, 5th ed. (Leipzig 1901), Vol. 1, pp. 690f., n. 122; Graetz,
Geschichte der Juden (Leipzig 1908), Vol. IV, Note 16, pp. 424ff.

96. Cf. M. Avi-Yonah, בימי רומא וביזאנטיון, 4th ed. (Jerusalem, 1970), pp. 21f.

Mesopotamia were ruthlessly destroyed by Trajan's general, Lucius Quietus.[97]

The profound impression made by Trajan's Parthian campaign seems to be reflected in TJ's rendering of II Sam. 8:3b:[98] ". . . as he (viz., Hadadezer) went to change his border (or: territory) at the river Euphrates."[99] The Targumist naturally assumes that a ruler marching from Syria to the Euphrates must have territorial conquest in mind.

Several TJ passages probably contain allusions to the Bar Kochba war or its aftermath. Thus, II Sam. 1:19a and 25b[100] are, respectively, rendered by TJ, ". . . upon your stronghold ye have been cast down slain" and ". . . upon your stronghold you were slain." The Targumic transformation of the Biblical high places into what appear to be fortified strongholds where Israel's warriors were slain—though not inapplicable to the earlier stages of the Roman-Jewish war of 66-70 C.E., especially Vespasian's Galilean campaign in 67 C.E.—fits best the Bar Kochba war when the Jewish defenders of the Judaean hill fortress of Bether were slain almost to a man.[101]

The mass slaughter that characterized the Bar Kochba war is apparently also alluded to in TJ's translation of Is. 22:3b, where MT ". . . all that are found within you were bound (or: imprisoned) together" is significantly changed in TJ to ". . . all that were found within you were slain." Although the passage ostensibly refers (according to the traditional interpretation) to Jerusalem, it fits the period of the Bar Kochba war far better than that of the fall of Jerusalem in 70 C.E. For then vast numbers were also taken prisoner—no less than 97,000, according to Josephus,—[102] so that there would have been no reason for TJ to change the straightforward meaning of the text from "imprisoned" (אסרו) to "slain."

---

97. Cf. Eusebius, Hist. Eccl. IV, 2; Orosius VII, 12; Dio Cassius LXVIII, 32.

98. MT: ". . . as he (viz., Hadadezer) went to restore his power at the river Euphrates."

99. Although a number of Parthian (and subsequently Persian) wars were conducted by Roman generals during the first century B.C.E. and the first three centuries C.E., none left such a deep mark on the Jews as Trajan's. Hence, while other possibilities cannot be entirely discounted, they are not very probable.

100. MT: ". . . slain upon your high places."

101. See *supra,* n. 95. It is noteworthy that the singular form in TJ (בית תקפכון and בית תקפך, respectively) indicates a major battle for one fortress, not, as in 67 C.E., a considerable number. The Bar Kochba war, moreover, impressed itself far more deeply in the minds of the Rabbis than Vespasian's relatively remote Galilean campaign of 67 C.E.

102. Cf. Bell. VI, 9, 3, par. 420.

Of considerable interest in this connection is TJ's homiletical rendering of Jud. 5:11a:[103] "For the place where they would rob them (i.e., the Israelites) and take what was in their hands, the seat of publicans (or: tax-collectors) and the dwelling-place of highwaymen, at the pits (or: cisterns) of the watering troughs; the place where miracles were wrought for them, and mighty acts for the house of Israel in olden times; the place where the daughters of Israel would go out to fill (viz., their pitchers) with water, where they were unable (other version: afraid) to let the sound of the tread (lit., rapping) of the soles of their feet be heard because of the ambush of the enemy and the oppressor . . ."

The targumist provides several clues in his midrashic expansion of MT. 1. It was a period of unrest and insecurity, with highwaymen and tax-collectors robbing the people. 2. Women and girls were afraid of being ambushed by the enemy and attacked whenever they ventured out from their homes to get water from the wells.

While it is difficult to date the historical allusions in this passage with any degree of precision—the "publicans" (or: tax-collectors) are depicted as sinners and robbers both in the New Testament[104] and in the Talmud[105]— it is a fact that Mishnaic and Talmudic legislation, most of which was later than the Bar Kochba war, specifically deals with the מוכסין (tax-collectors), and that R. Jose, who flourished in the middle of the second century C.E., reports a case of a girl who went to get water from a well and was raped.[106] Furthermore, most of the midrashic Targum on Judges 5, refers to the period of persecution which followed the Bar Kochba war. It is therefore

103. MT: "Louder than the noise of archers, by the watering-troughs . . ." The exact meaning of the Hebrew is uncertain, and many different renderings have been offered.

104. Cf. Matt. 9:10-11; Mark 2:15-16; Luke 5:30; 15:1; 19:1-8.

105. Cf. M. B. K. X, 1-2; Tos. B. K. X, 22; T. B. B. K. 113a, Sanh. 25b. Churgin, pp. 26-7, identifying the מוכסין with the Sicarii who, according to Josephus (Ant. XX, 8, 5, par. 163ff.; *ibid.* 9, 10, pars. 186ff.; *ibid.* 9, 2, par. 204; *ibid.* 9, 3, pars. 208ff.; Bell. II, 13, 3, pars. 254ff.), afflicted Judaea during the procuratorships of Felix and Festus, regards TJ as reflecting the vehement reaction of the targumist's generation. However, the Talmud clearly distinguishes between the מוכסין and the Sicarii who are called סיקרין or סיקריקין or סיקריקון in the Mishnah (cf. M. Bik. I, 2; II, 3; Git. V, 6; Makhshirin I, 6). Cf. also Komlosh, *op. cit.,* p. 288. The respective roles played by the מוכסין and the Sicarii were totally different, since the former served the interests of the Roman occupation regime, while the latter attempted to overthrow it by force and violence, though concentrating their revolutionary activities against Jewish collaborators with the Romans. There is thus no room for any confusion between the two mutually antagonistic groups.

106. Cf. M. Ket. I, 10.

reasonable, though by no means certain, to regard this passage as reflecting the conditions of that time.

Inadequate enthusiasm for the war which Bar Kochba castigated in his letters discovered in the Nahal Hever area south of En-Gedi in 1960/1[107] may be alluded to in TJ's homiletical rendering of Jud. 5:15b-16:[108] "In the family of Reuben there were many plots of the heart. (v. 16) Why did you return[109] from the battle camps (or: armies) to dwell between the borders, so as to hear tidings (and) to know which army is victorious (and then) to join (lit., be with) it?[110] Is it right for you to do such a thing? O house of Reuben, do you not know that before Him (viz. God) the thoughts of the heart are revealed?!"

Although the general context would seem to point to the Bar Kochba rising—to which must be added the significant fact that the people of En-Gedi who were the principal objects of Bar Kochba's wrath lived in an area which was quite close to the ancient territory of the tribe of Reuben,[111]— the possibility remains that the targumist, alluding to events in 67 C.E., is directing his denunciation at Galilean cities such as Sepphoris or Tiberias. Sepphoris, which had supported the anti-Roman elements way back in 4

---

107. Cf. Bar-Kochba's complaint that the people of En-Gedi had failed to carry out their duties and supply food for the army: "You are living well, eating and drinking off the property of the house of Israel, and care nothing about your brethren" (cf. S. Abramsky, בר כוכבא - נשיא ישראל [Tel Aviv, 1961], p. 200).

108. MT (v. 15b): "Among the clans of Reuben there were great searchings of heart. (v. 16) Why did you tarry among the sheepfolds, to hear the piping for the flocks? Among the clans of Reuben there were great searchings of heart."

109. TJ may have read שַׁבְתְּ (you returned) instead of MT יָשַׁבְתְּ (you dwelt, tarried).

110. Some versions add here: "To Barak you are saying, We are yours; and to Sisera you are saying, We are yours."

111. It should be noted that the Reubenite clans of Hezron and Carmi (cf. Gen. 46:9; Exod. 6:14; Num. 26:6; I Chron. 5:3) were eventually absorbed by Judah (cf. I Chron. 4:1; cf. also *ibid.* 2:5.9.18.21ff.). This was presumably due to their westward migration across the Jordan and the Dead Sea as a result of the encroachments on their territory by neighboring peoples (cf. Deut. 33:6; II Kings 10:33). It is noteworthy that the Reubenites are conspicuous by their absence in the Moabite Stone inscription, while the Gadites who were further north are prominently mentioned. What is more, Mesha king of Moab boasts that he occupied a number of Israelite cities which, according to the territorial division described in Joshua (13:15ff.), belonged to Reuben. Evidently those Reubenites who were still in Transjordan had been absorbed by the Gadites before their conquest by the Moabites and subsequently by the Arameans (cf. II Kings, *ibid.*). If the people of En-Gedi were indeed of Reubenite stock, TJ's interpretation of Deborah's criticism of the Reubenites would be particularly apt.

B.C.E.,[112] and had suffered as a result destruction and enslavement at the hands of the Romans,[113] appears to have sided with the Romans during the great Roman-Jewish war.[114] Yet, in one seemingly contradictory passage, Josephus states that "the inhabitants of Sepphoris . . . even without orders (viz., from Josephus who had been appointed governor of Galilee by the Sanhedrin), were eager for hostilities with the Romans."[115]

This could be a tendencious falsification perpetrated once by Josephus in the *Bellum* because of a personal vendetta against Sepphoris, but—with characteristic inconsistency—not continued thereafter. If, on the other hand, there was an anti-Roman party in Sepphoris which was indeed "eager for hostilities with the Romans," but failed to act in the face of Roman superiority, the targumist's complaint about fence-sitting and waiting to see who would win would ideally fit the people of Sepphoris.

Another contemporary candidate for targumic castigation would be the city of Tiberias, where mutually antagonistic factions were pulling in different directions.[116] On two occasions Tiberias rebelled against Josephus— at that time the revolutionary governor of Galilee—either because the party which opposed the war against Rome had gained the upper hand or because Josephus's loyalty to the revolutionary government was doubted.[117] The erratic behavior of the leaders and people of Tiberias; their shifting loyalties; their numerous plots and counterplots;[118] and their constant changes of mood and allegiance would provide adequate grounds for targumic criticism.

If TJ on Jud. 15b-16 is open to different interpretations, there is little doubt that the targumist's homiletical rendering of Jud. 5:9[119] alludes to the Hadrianic persecution which followed the disastrous Bar Kochba war:

112. Cf. Bell. II, 4, 1, par. 56.

113. Cf. *ibid.* II, 5, 1, par. 68.

114. Cf. Bell. II, 11, 10, pars. 645f., *ibid.* 18, 11, par. 511; *ibid.* III, 2, 4, pars. 30-34; *ibid.* 4, 1, pars. 59-61; Vita 8, par. 30; 9, pars. 38f.; 22, pars. 104f.; 45, par. 232; 65, pars. 346ff.; 67, pars. 373ff.; 71, pars. 394ff.; 74, par. 411.

115. Cf. Bell. II, 20, 6, par. 574.

116. Cf. Josephus, Vita 9, pars. 32ff.

117. Cf. *ibid.* 32, pars. 155ff.; 63, pars. 326ff.; 65, pars. 340ff.; *ibid.* pars. 349ff.; 68, pars. 381ff.; 70, pars. 391ff.; Bell. II, 21, 8, pars. 362f.; 21, 10, pars. 645f.; III, 9:7-8, pars. 445-461.

118. Note TJ's charge (on Jud. 5:15b) about "many plots of the heart," i.e., secret conspiracies.

119. MT: "My heart goes out to the commanders of Israel who offered themselves willingly among the people."

"Deborah said through prophecy: I am sent to praise the scribes (or: teachers) of Israel. For when that trouble happened, they did not cease from expounding the Torah. But now it is fitting (or: good) for them that they are sitting openly in the synagogues and teaching the people the words of the Torah; and they are blessing and giving thanks before God."

The revealing expression, "that trouble" (עקתא ההיא), indicates a familiar calamity of relatively recent vintage and still well-remembered by contemporaries. According to the targumist, "they did not cease (viz., during that troubled period) from expounding the Torah"—which is precisely what happened during the Hadrianic persecution when martyr-rabbis such as R. Akiba and R. Hanina ben Teradyon openly defied the Roman authorities by continuing their public teaching of Judaism.[120] After the death of Hadrian, the persecution ceased and the surviving rabbis assembled at Usha in Galilee where they resumed their public teaching of the Torah.[121]

As already pointed out in the beginning of this chapter, the only alternative conceivable—the proscription of Judaism by Antiochus IV in 168-165 B.C.E.—is unlikely to be alluded to in this context where the emphasis is on the public dissemination of the Torah, which is characteristic of the Talmudic period but hardly of the early Hasmonean age.

The Hadrianic persecution is apparently also indicated in TJ's homiletical interpretation of Is. 32:2:[122] "And the righteous who are hiding from the wicked shall be as though they were hiding from a tempest; they shall return and they shall be made great (or: they shall multiply), and their teaching shall be accepted (or: received) quickly like streams of water that flow in a thirsty land."

But for the emphasis on the "teaching," which is characteristic of a later age, TJ might just as well be referring to Antiochus' persecution of the Jews in 168-165 B.C.E.[123] Indeed, there is a distinct possibility that the original version did allude to the earlier persecution;[124] but after the Hadrianic

120. Cf. T. B. Ber. 61b; A. Z. 18a.

121. Cf. Cant. R. II, 5, 3.

122. MT: "Each will be like a hiding place from the wind, a covert from the tempest, like streams of water in a dry place . . ."

123. The Hellenizers are consistently referred to as "sinful," "wicked" or "lawless" in the first book of the Maccabees (cf., e.g., I Macc. 1:11.34; 2:44; 6:21; 7:5; 9:25.58.69.73; 10:61; 11:25. We are also told that the Jews were hiding from their enemies; cf. *ibid.* 1:53; 2:31; II Macc. 14:30.

124. It should be noted, though, that the context indicates a post-Second Common-

persecution this was brought up-to-date by the addition of the "teaching" which had become a *sine qua non* in rabbinic ideology.

The conditions of secrecy which characterized the study and teaching of the Torah during the Hadrianic persecution[125] are reflected in TJ's version of Is. 26:16b:[126] ". . . in their trouble[127] they used to teach the instruction of your Torah[128] in secret." Here, too, the persecution under Antiochus, though not inconceivable, is less likely to be alluded to.

The restoration of Torah instruction after the Hadrianic persecution seems to be hinted at in TJ on Joel 2:23a[129]—"He has given you back your teachers . . ."[130]—as well as in TJ's homiletical version of Jud. 5:2a,[131] which must be regarded as the key to the understanding of TJ's interpretation of the entire chapter:

"When the house of Israel rebelled against the Torah, the nations came upon them and drove them out from their cities; but when they returned to fulfill (lit., do) the Torah, they prevailed against their enemies, and drove them out from the territory of the land of Israel.[132] Therefore, for the visitation of misfortune upon Sisera and his army and for the miracle and re-

---

wealth date; for a few verses later (32:14a), MT "For the palace will be (or: is) forsaken" is rendered by TJ, "For the Temple is destroyed."

125. Cf. T. Y. Yev. XII, 6, 12d; T. B. Pes. 112a; Yev. 108b. The deliberate martyrdom of R. Akiba and R. Hanina ben Teradyon must be regarded as exceptional. The majority, no doubt, continued to disseminate the study of Judaism in secret, and even R. Akiba was anxious to avoid anything which might jeopardize the lives of his students; cf. T. B. Pes. *ibid;* T. Y. Yev. *ibid.*

126. MT: '. . . they poured out a prayer when your chastening was upon them."

127. Cf. Komlosh, *op. cit.,* p. 360, who points out that TJ connects MT צקון, which is a *hapax legomenon,* with מצוקה (trouble). So also LXX and Peshitta.

128. TJ takes MT מוסרך (your chastening) in the sense of "instruction" which usually went hand in hand with "chastisement." Similarly also LXX. Cf. Komlosh, *ibid.*

129. MT: ". . . he has given you the early rain."

130. TJ takes MT המורה (the early rain) in the sense of "teacher."

131. MT: "When men grow their hair long (or: That the leaders took the lead) in Israel, when (or: that) the people offered themselves willingly . . ."

132. The views offered so far, though substantially in accord with the theology of the Prophetic books in general (cf. Komlosh, *op. cit.,* p. 284) and of the book of Judges in particular, nevertheless appear to allude to a historic event. It could be either the Hasmonean victories against the Syrians and the Jewish Hellenizers (though there was hardly anything resembling a general explusion of the Jews from the cities of the Land of Israel) or Bar Kochba's initial victories, while the explusions would be those that occurred during the Roman-Jewish war of 66-70 C.E. The verse may also have been used for both events in succession. Similar interpretations are also offered by TJ on verses 4 and 8.

demption that were wrought for Israel, (namely) that the sages have come back to sit in the synagogues openly and to teach the people the words of the Torah . . ."

The last clause, which could have been added after the termination of the Hadrianic persecution, almost certainly refers to the resumption of public teaching by the rabbis following the death of Hadrian and the reconstitution of the Sanhedrin in Usha. We may, therefore, conclude that the targumic midrash on the Song of Deborah, while in all probability retaining allusions to earlier events, notably the persecution under Antiochus IV and the Hasmonean victories, represents in its final form a characteristic rabbinic reaction to the aftermath of Hadrian's persecution. Notwithstanding the disastrous loss of life sustained during and after the Bar Kochba war, and in spite of the utter devastation of the country, the targumists and rabbis, who ordained a special blessing of thanks for the permission that was eventually granted after a long delay to bury the Jews who had been slain at Bether,[133] were equally grateful that at least the proscription of Judaism had been discontinued, so that the teaching of the Torah could be resumed and the Jewish faith could survive within "the four cubits of the Law."

Together with the restoration of religious freedom after the Hadrianic persecution, there was a resumption of the activity of the rabbinical courts which had been unable to function for some years. The various *Takkanot* (ordinances) of Usha[134] bear witness to the legislative and judicial vitality of the Sanhedrin, which was probably reflected in the lower courts wherever they were able to exercise their judicial activities. With few well-defined exceptions, the judges were unpaid,[135] and often had to neglect their own work in order to maintain Jewish judicial autonomy, which was one of the few—and highly prized—privileges left to the Jews after the destruction of the Second Commonwealth.

It is highly probable that the resumption of judicial activity after 138 C.E. is alluded to in TJ's midrashic version of Jud. 5:10:[136] "They who neglected their (private) business (or: occupations) . . . and were going through all the territory of the Land of Israel, and would join themselves to sit for

---

133. Cf. T. B. Ber. 48b; Taan. 31a; B. B. 121b.

134. Cf. Cant. R. II, 5, 3; Tos. Shev. IV, 21; T. B. Ket. 49b-50a; Shab. 15b; R. H. 15a.

135. Cf. M. Bekhor. IV, 6; T. B. Ket. 105a; T. Y. Sanh. I, 1, 18b.

136. MT: "You who ride on tawny asses, you who sit on rich carpets, and you who walk by the way . . ."

judgment . . ."[137] Since we have already seen that the context of this TJ passage generally alludes to the Hadrianic and immediate post-Hadrianic
period, it is reasonable to assume that here, too, the age of the synod of Usha
is reflected in TJ's homiletical expansion.

Not all judges were as selfless and devoted to the cause of justice as those
alluded to in TJ's interpretation of Jud. 5:10. In the third century especially,
we hear about unworthy and corrupt judges being appointed by the finan-
cially hard-pressed Patriarch in return for monetary contributions. The
rabbis denounced this practice and strongly criticized and ridiculed the
ignorant judges who were making a mockery of the administration of
justice.[138]

It is this state of affairs which is reflected in TJ's rendering of several
verses. Thus, TJ on Is. 1:23a[139] reads: "They all love to receive a bribe,
saying to one another, 'Do something for me in my court case, so that I may
recompense you in your court case.'" In other words, a judge who happened
to be involved in litigation would approach the colleague who was assigned
to deal with the case with an offer to exchange corrupt favors.

Similarly, on Hos. 5:11b,[140] TJ refers to judges who "turn to go astray
after the money of falsehood."[141] Likewise, on II Sam. 14:14b,[142] TJ adds a
moralistic homily, ". . . like water that is poured to the ground so that it
cannot be gathered (again), so it is impossible for a true judge[143] to accept
money of falsehood." It is clear that corrupt judges who accepted bribes
were a source of anxiety and irritation to the people—and hence to the targumists,—and, not surprisingly, TJ also manages to provide divine punish-

---

137. TJ takes MT מדין ("rich carpets") in the sense of "judgment" (דין). TJ's interpretation
is similar to that given in T. B. Eruv. 54b: "'You who ride on tawny asses'—this refers to the
learned men who travel from town to town and from province to province to study (or: to
teach) the Torah . . .'who sit on rich carpets'—(this means) that they give true judgment for
the sake of the truth (or: a perfectly true judgment)."

138. Cf. T. Y. Bik. III, 3, 65d; T. B. Shab. 139a; Sanh. 7a-b; Lev. R. III, 2. Cf. Avi-
Yonah, *op. cit.,* pp. 101f.

139. MT: "Every one loves a bribe and runs after gifts."

140. MT: ". . . because he willingly walked after vanity (or: filth [reading צואה instead of צו,
lit., commandment])."

141. The connection with the judicial administration is established by the first half of the
verse, "Ephraim is oppressed, crushed in judgment."

142. MT: ". . . like water spilt to the ground, which cannot be gathered again; but God
will not take away the life . . ."

143. TJ takes MT אלהים (God) in the sense of "judge"; cf. Ex. 22:8.

ment for such evil judges. Thus, on Zephaniah 3:15a,[144] TJ renders, "The Lord has exiled false judges from your midst."

It was because of the corruptibility of certain judges that the exceedingly strange statement was made that only wealthy men, people of means, should be appointed judges[145]—no doubt because such men would be unlikely to be tempted by bribes. In line with this idea, TJ on Jud. 4:5a adds a remarkable midrashic exposition that Deborah, who, we are told in the same verse, functioned as a judge, "made her living from her own means. She had palm trees in Jericho, fruit orchards in Ramah, oil-producing olive trees in the valley, a well-watered field in Bethel, light-colored land (lit., earth) on the Mountain of the King . . ." This enumeration of Deborah's wealth was presumably designed to emphasize that her judicial career was blameless, since with her enormous wealth she had no need to accept bribes.

A favorable allusion to the Houses of the Patriarch as well as the Babylonian Exilarch is to be found in TJ's rendering of II Sam. 7:29b:[146] ". . . and with your blessing shall the Houses of your righteous servants be blessed forever." The change from the singular of the Hebrew—בֵית עַבְדְּךָ—to the plural form, with the significant addition of צַדִּיקַיָּא (righteous), is obviously deliberate. It is in all probability a midrashic attempt to counteract the opposition which occasionally manifested itself against the autocratic behavior of the Patriarch and Exilarch, who headed semi-royal dynasties enjoying the support of the Roman and Parthian (later, Persian) governments, respectively. This opposition came out in the open when Judah and Hezekiah, the sons of R. Hiyya,[147] stated during a banquet hosted by R. Judah the Patriarch that "the son of David (i.e., the Messiah) cannot appear before the two ruling Houses in Israel shall have come to an end, namely, the Exilarch in Babylonia and the Patriarch in the Land of Israel.[148] R. Judah the Patriarch, surnamed "our holy master,"[149] was visibly upset by this expression of antagonism among his close disciples, and he told them, "My

---

144. MT: "The Lord has taken away the judgments against you."

145. Cf. Mekilta on Exod. 18:21.

146. MT: ". . . and with your blessing shall the house of your servant be blessed forever."

147. R. Hiyya was a close friend and confidant of R. Judah the Patriarch; cf. T. Y. Kil. IX, 4, 32b; T. Y. Ket. XII, 1, 35a; T. B. Hag. 5b; Ned. 41a; Ket. 103b; B. M. 85b; Gen. R. XXXIII, 3; XCVI, 5.

148. T. B. Sanh. 38a.

149. Cf. T. B. Shab. 156a; Pes. 37b; cf. also Shab. 118b; T. Y. Meg. III, 2, 74a; T. Y. Sanh. X, 6, 29c; T. Y. A. Z. III, 1, 42c.

children, you are casting thorns in my eyes!"[150] It was evidently to counteract such subversive sentiments that the Targumist altered the plain sense
of II Sam. 7:29b to stress the permanence of God's blessing upon the two
"righteous" dynasties of Israel—the epithet "righteous" being of course
particularly apt in the case of "our holy master."

It was during the early years of the life of R. Judah the Patriarch that an
incident occurred which caused the Samaritans, who had previously been
recognized as Jewish in some respects,[151] to be proscribed as if they were
gentiles. We are told that the Samaritans worshipped the figure of a dove on
Mt. Gerizim—whereupon R. Meir excluded them from all religious fellow-
ship with the Jews.[152] The question was, however, not finally resolved before the third century,[153] and R. Simeon ben Gamaliel, the father of R.
Judah the Patriarch, actually declared the Samaritans to be "like Israelites in
every respect."[154]

It is apparently the above-mentioned dove cult incident that is alluded to
in a midrashic version of TJ on II Kings 17:30a;[155] "And the men of Babylon made the dove and its young[156] (i.e., for cultic purposes); and the men of
Cuth made the foot of Jacob[157] and the foot of Joseph,[158] and they set up
over them the image of a cock."[159] Bearing in mind that the passage in

150. T. B. Sanh. 38a.

151. Cf., e.g., M. Ber. VII, 1; VIII, 8; M. Dem. III, 4; T. Y. Shek. I, 5, 46a; T. B. Ber.
47b; Nazir 62a; Git. 10a; Kid. 75b-76a; Sanh. 85b; Hul. 3a-b; 4a; Nid. 56b.

152. Cf. T. B. Hul. 6a.

153. Cf., e.g., *ibid.* 5b.

154. T. Y. Shek. I, 5, 46a.

155. MT: "The men of Babylon made Succoth-benoth, and the men of Cuth made Nergal" (i.e., idols of these Mesopotamian deities).

156. Heb. בנות (lit., daughters) is connected with the chicks of doves.

157. TJ: ריגלוייהי דיעקב, derived from MT נרגל, but etymologically connected with Gen.
30:30a, where Jacob tells Laban, "God blessed you on account of me" (לרגלי). According to
this Midrash, the men of Cuth worshipped an image shaped like a foot (or leg)—presumably
as a form of sympathetic magic to obtain divine blessings. Cf. on this T. Y. A. Z. III, 2,
42b-c, and P'nei Moshe, *ad loc.*

158. According to P'nei Moshe, *op. cit.,* this is connected with Gen. 39:5a, where we are
told that "the Lord blessed the house of the Egyptian because of Joseph (MT בגלל יוסף)—
which, on the analogy of Jacob in Gen. 30:27b (ויברכני ה' בגללך) is also connected with the
image of a foot used as a cult object.

159. Here MT נרגל is connected with Heb. תרנגול (cock). On the homiletical interpretation
of the entire passage, cf. T. Y. A. Z. III, 2, 42b-c; T. B. Sanh. 63b, where a Midrash is presented which is remarkably similar to that offered in TJ—both in this verse and in v. 31,
though the latter does not concern us here.

question is supposed to refer to the reputed Babylonian ancestors of the Samaritans (=Cuthians), it is fairly evident that the targumist had the dove cult incident in mind.

Throughout the Roman period, the people suffered from the depredations of violent men and oppressors who robbed the weak, seized land illegally, and generally deprived the masses of the fruits of their labor. Sometimes these powerful "robber barons" and men of violence (אונסין or אונסין) were gentiles,[160] but quite frequently they were Jews.[161] Side by side with the fight for independence there was also a never-ending struggle against individual men of violence who, protected as they often were by the authorities, were able to lord it over the Jewish people. This constant fight against both Jewish and non-Jewish oppressors is reflected in TJ's rendering of Jud. 5:26a, where MT "the workmen's mallet" is rendered, "the hammer (some versions add: of the smiths) to break the wicked and the men of violence." Thus, Jael was imagined not only as a liberator of the nation from the yoke of Sisera, but also as one whose hammer would smash other "men of violence" as well. Similarly, too, Is. 29:20, MT "the scoffer is destroyed and all who watch to do evil shall be cut off" undergoes a remarkable change in TJ, which translates, "the plunderer is destroyed and all those that seek to do violence have perished." Clearly, if the heretical scoffers, normally a popular target of rabbinic denunciation, are replaced by "the plunderers" and the indeterminate שקדי און are defined as the familiar plague of violent men, the problem must have assumed very serious proportions.

The depredations of these elements, which were not only tolerated but also supported and encouraged by corrupt leaders,[162] evoked some protests,[163] which seem to be reflected in TJ's rendering of Ezek. 34:16 ff. Although TJ is actually conveying the general sense of Ezekiel's metaphorical description of the shepherd and the flocks (i.e., the leaders and the people), the fat sheep and the lean sheep (i.e., the wealthy and the poor), there are a

160. Cf., e.g., T. B. Hul. 94b and, especially, B. B. 45a, where gentiles are generally depicted as violent men who are liable to seize Jewish property at will.

161. Cf., e.g., TJ on Is. 5:7b; Jer. 6:6b; Hos. 6:8a. Cf. in particular, Tos. Ter. I, 6, where we are told that the tithes given by a thief, a man of violence (אנס—here one who is in possession of forcibly seized land) or a robber were valid tithes, even though they might have been stolen from their rightful owners. Similarly also T. Y. Kid. I, 4, 60c.

162. Cf., e.g., the excesses and forcible tithe confiscations perpetrated by the High Priestly families shortly before the destruction of Jerusalem; cf. T. B. Pes. 57a; Jos., Ant. XX, 8:8, par. 181; *ibid.* 9, 2, pars. 206f.

163. Cf. e.g., T. B. Pes. *ibid.*

couple of instances where TJ goes beyond the requirements of the text.
Thus, on Ezek. 34:18-22,[164] TJ renders, "Is it a little thing that you are sustained in good prosperity, and the rest of your sustenance is eaten by your
servants?[165] And you drink proper drink, and the rest is drunk by your servants? (v. 19) And my people eat the rest of the food of your servants, and
they drink the rest of the drink of your servants. (v. 20)... I will judge
between a rich man and a poor man. (v. 21) Because you push with wickedness and (your strong) arm; and by your power you break all the sick ones
until you scatter them among the (different) countries. (v. 22) Therefore I
will deliver my people ... and I will judge between man and man." Although
this may best fit the late Second Commonwealth, there is a timelessness in
the sharp social protest, which could be appropriate for the entire Hellenistic-Roman period.

One of the perennial problems which plagued the Jewish community was
that of informers (*delatores* — hence דלטורין, also מוסרים) who collaborated
with the Romans and brought great misery upon their fellow Jews by their
tale-bearing and slander. The numerous denunciations of the *delatores* in
the Talmud and Midrash[166] testify to the seriousness with which this problem was viewed by the rabbis. TJ, too, reflects profound indignation in its
rendering of Mic. 7:2b:[167] "They lie in wait to shed innocent blood; they
deliver (מסרין) one another (lit., each man his brother) for destruction."

Occasionally, TJ attempts to clarify obscure or logically incoherent verses
by identifying historical situations or individuals allegedly alluded to or by
altering the wording sufficiently to make the Biblical personality in question
behave in accordance with the logic of the situation. Taking the examples

---

164. MT: (v. 18) "Is it not enough for you to feed on the good pasture, that you must
tread down with your feet the rest of your pasture; and to drink of clear water, that you must
foul the rest with your feet? (v. 19) And must my sheep eat what you have trodden with your
feet, and drink what you have fouled with your feet? (v. 20)... I will judge between the fat
sheep and the lean sheep. (v. 21) Because you push with side and shoulder, and thrust at all
the weak with your horns, till you have scattered them abroad, (v. 22) I will save my flock
... and I will judge between sheep and sheep."

165. Cf. Jos., Ant. 9, 2, pars. 206f., where we are told that the slaves of the High Priest
Ananias would take the tithes by force and beat up those who refused to give them. Cf. T. B.
Pes. 57a: "...their (viz., the High Priests') servants beat the people with staves."

166. Cf. T. B. Sanh. 11a; 43b; T. Y. Peah I, 1, 16a; Lev. R. XXVI, 2; Deut. R. V, 10;
Esther R., Introd. 8; Tanh. שמות, 10.

167. M "They lie in wait for blood, and each hunts his brother with a net."

we have in chronological order, we find that TJ on Jud. 5:14a[168] provides, in homiletical form, a coherent rendering which makes good sense within a midrashic frame of reference: "From the house of Ephraim there arose Joshua the son of Nun, (and) he was the first to wage war (or: engage in battle) against the house of Amalek. After him arose King Saul from the house of Benjamin. He slew those of the house of Amalek and waged war (or: engaged in battle) against other peoples."[169]

Another attempt to relate a somewhat obscure reference to a Biblical personality to a known historic event is to be found in TJ's interpretation of Jer. 41:17a, where MT "Geruth Chimham" is explained, ". . . in Geruth (or: the dwelling-place) which David gave to Chimham son of Barzilai the Gileadite." The reference is to the account of David's special favor to Chimham son of Barzilai,[170] though there is nothing mentioned there about an estate being granted by David to this loyal favorite. It is, nevertheless, a legitimate and indeed highly probable inference.

TJ is generally distinguished by scrupulous adherence to the logic of the context. A good example of this characteristic is provided by I Kings 2:30a, where Joab, responding to Benaiah son of Jehoiada's summons to leave the sanctuary to be executed, says defiantly, "No, I will die here." But since Joab did not die a normal death, but was slain by Benaiah,[171] TJ renders, "No, but here I will be put to death."

Another characteristic feature of TJ is clarification of obscure or partly obscure passages. Thus, we learn in Jer. 41:9a about a cistern that had been made by Asa king of Judah "because of (מפני) Baasha king of Israel." To us who are familiar with the story of the wars between Asa and Baasha,[172] it is fairly obvious that Asa had prepared the cistern to collect rainwater, thereby enabling the Judahite defenders to withstand a prolonged siege. In the Talmudic age, when books were rare and expensive, the reader of one Biblical

---

168. MT: "From Ephraim their root in Amalek, following (or: after) you Benjamin, with your kinsmen."

169. Cf. Komlosh, *op. cit.*, p. 289, who points out that the Targumist prefers to identify general names with individuals. Accordingly, Ephraim alludes to Joshua (who was an Ephraimite, cf. Num. 13:8.16; I Chron. 7:20-27), while Benjamin alludes to the Benjamite king Saul (cf. I Sam. 9:1f. 21; I Chron. 8:1-33).

170. Cf. II Sam. 19:38-39; cf. also I Kings 2:7.

171. Cf. I Kings 2:34.

172. Cf. *ibid.* 15:16ff.

book was not necessarily familiar with other books of the Bible. To clarify matters, TJ translates the above-mentioned clause, "...the cistern (or: pit)...was the one that had been made by king Asa when Baasha king of Israel besieged him."

Occasionally, TJ provides a midrashic rendering for additional names (or titles) of Biblical personalities. For example, in Jer. 46:30a, "Pharaoh Hophra" is translated by TJ, "Pharaoh the Lame" (תבירא)—possibly because of the legends told about another Pharaoh of a generation earlier, Necho (Heb. נכה) who was said to have become lame (Heb. נכה) as a result of his attempt to ascend Solomon's throne.[173] Another possible reason for TJ's rendering is that, according to Herodotus II, 169, Pharaoh Hophra was strangled.[174]

Highly instructive is TJ's expanded translation of Zech. 12:11,[175] where we have a rather obscure allusion to an event unknown to us:[176] "In that time there shall be great mourning (or: lamentation) in Jerusalem like the mourning (or: lamentation) over Ahab son of Omri whom Hadadrimmon son of Tabrimmon had slain in Ramoth Gilead,[177] and like the mourning (or: lamentation) over Josiah son of Amon whom Pharaoh the Lame (חגירא)[178] had slain in the plain of Megiddo."[179]

The events of the last days of the First Commonwealth are, according to TJ on Ezek. 21:31-32,[180] alluded to in these somewhat obscure verses: "Re-

173. Cf. Pesik. de-R. Kahana XXVII, p. 168a; Lev. R. XX, 1; Tanhuma Deut., edit. Buber, p. 7, Koheleth R. IX, 2.

174. Aramaic תבירא usually means "broken," which comes close to strangulation.

175. MT: "On that day the mourning in Jerusalem whill be as great as the mourning for Hadadrimmon in the plain of Megiddo(n)."

176. So according to Kimchi and Ibn Ezra, who dismisses the Targumic interpretation as pure midrash. Cf. also T. B. Meg. 3a; M. K. 28b, where the Babylonian Targum expert, Rab Joseph, states, "Were it not for the Targum of this verse, I would not know what it means."

177. Cf. I Kings 22:34ff.; and II Chron. 18:33f., where the unknown archer who mortally wounded Ahab is not named. According to Targum Rab Joseph on II Chron. 18:33, it was the Aramean general Naaman (cf. II Kings 5:1ff.) who killed Ahab. So also Josephus, Ant. VIII, 15, 5, par. 414 and Midrash Pss. ch. 78, edit. Buber, p. 350.

178. Pharaoh Necho (נכה), homiletically expounded as גבה (lame).

179. Cf. II Kings 23:29; II Chron. 35:20ff.

180. MT: "...Remove the turban, and take off the crown; things (lit., this) shall not remain as it is; exalt that which is low, and abase that which is high. (v. 32) A ruin, ruin, ruin, I will make it; there shall not even be a trace of it (lit., not be even this) until he comes whose right it is; and to him I will give it."

move the turban from Seraiah the High Priest,[181] and put an end to the crown of King Zedekiah; neither the one nor the other shall endure in his place, (but) they shall surely be exiled. Gedaliah son of Ahikam to whom it (viz., royal authority) did not belong shall take it.[182] Zedekiah to whom it belonged—from him it shall be taken. (v. 32) Their sins which they committed—it is according to their sins that I shall punish them; but also for this one (viz., Gedaliah) it shall not endure, until I bring upon him the calamity of Ishmael son of Nethaniah[183] and deliver him (viz., Gedaliah) into his hand."

Very frequently TJ retrojects the conditions existing in the Talmudic period way back to the Biblical age. As throughout rabbinic literature, so also in TJ, ideas, practices, customs, and even the linguistic characteristics of a later age are attributed to Biblical times. Thus, TJ on II Kings 12:5a, identifying the money brought to the Temple with the half-shekels rendered annually by every adult male,[184] renders MT עובר כסף (lit., "money that passess") by "the money of the Shekalim." Although the half-shekel tribute is traditionally a commandment enjoined by the Torah, the primitive economic conditions of a Biblical peasant society leave a good deal of doubt whether this precept, even if known among the masses, was strictly observed.[185] In the Second Commonwealth, on the other hand, the half-shekel was rendered not only in Judaea, but by Jewish communities throughout the world. TJ, however, assumes—in line with rabbinic thinking on the subject—that the money referred to must have been the shekel tax.[186]

181. Cf. II Kings 25:18ff.; Jer. 52:24ff. On the turban (מצנפת(א as the headgear of the High Priest, cf. Exod. 28:4; 39:28.

182. Cf. II Kings 25:22; Jer. 40:5ff.

183. Cf. II Kings 25:25; Jer. 41:1ff.

184. Cf. Exod. 30:11ff. Actually, this passage does not speak of an annual tax but of a onetime measure for the purpose of a popular census. It was, however, from here that the Rabbis derived the Scriptural basis for the annual half-shekel tax; cf., e.g., T. Y. Shek. I, 1, 45d-46a; *ibid.* II, 4, 46d; T. B. Meg. 29b.

185. The passages cited in this connection (II Kings 12:5-17; 22:3-7; II Chron. 24:5-14; 34:8-18; Nehem. 10:33f. [where a third part of a shekel is mentioned]) do not prove that the money in question was the helf-shekel annual tax. The fact that Nehemiah (*op. cit.*) had to introduce a tax of a third of a shekel would rather indicate the contrary. Cf. Schürer, *Geschichte des Jüdischen Volkes*⁴, II, 314, n. 49.

186. Cf. Matt. 17:24; Ant. XVIII, 9, 1, par. 312; Bell. VII, 6, 6, par. 218; Cf. also Cicero, Pro Flacco 28; Dio Cassius, 66, 7.

TJ also sometimes translates Biblical coins and weights in terms of those familiar in Talmudic times. Thus, in Ezek. 45:12,[187] shekel is rendered "sela," while gerah becomes "me'ah." On the other hand, in Ezek. 4:10a,[188] where shekel denotes a weight, not a monetary unit, TJ translates פילס—a corruption of the Greek *phollis* ($\phi\acute{o}\lambda\lambda\iota s$). The same is also true of measures. For example, in Ezek. 45:10-14, the Biblical ephah and homer become "a measure" (מכילתא)[189] and a "kor," respectively, and TJ even renders MT "one tenth of a homer" (v.11) by a much more familiar expression—"an amount of three se'ahs."[190]

The ubiquitous Roman army—admired and imitated by Josephus even when he was fighting it[191]—inevitably left its mark on TJ, just as it did on one of the major Dead Sea Scrolls, "The War of the Sons of Light against the Sons of Darkness," which is replete with Roman military terms. Such expressions are to be found particularly in TJ's interpretation of a number of metaphorical passages in Ezekiel, but also elsewhere in the Prophets. Thus, we find TJ translating MT בצים ("in ships")[192]—בלגיונין ("in [or: with] legions").

Even more visible than the Roman legions were the local and imported auxiliaries and mercenaries,[193] especially the ruthless Syrian and Arab auxiliary forces employed by the Romans both before and during the Roman-Jewish War of 66-70 C.E.[194] The Aramaic equivalents of auxiliaries, סומכיון or סומכותא (with appropriate suffixes) are introduced by TJ in a number of passages,[195] in most cases without any exegetical justification. The promi-

---

187. MT: "The shekel shall be twenty gerahs; twenty shekels, twenty-five shekels, fifteen shekels shall be your mina." For the rabbinic interpretation of this rather difficult verse, cf. T.B. B.B. 90a b.

188. MT: "And the food which you shall eat shall be by weight, twenty shekels a day."

189. Either a familiar, defined measure, or an indeterminate one, due to the absence of any corresponding measure in the Talmudic age.

190. On the correlation of Biblical and Talmudic measures, cf. M. Men. VII, 1 and especially T. B. Men. 77a, where Ezek. 45:11 is discussed in detail.

191. Cf. Bell. II, 20, 7, pars. 577ff.

192. Ezek. 30:9a.

193. Cf., e.g., Ant. XVII, 10, 3, par. 266; 10, 9, pars. 286f.; XVIII, 8, 2, par. 262; XIX, 9, 1-2, pars. 357ff.; 365f.; XX, 8, 7, par. 177; Bell. II, 5, 2, par. 74; 12, 5, par. 236; III, 6, 2, pars. 116 and 126; V, 2, 1, par. 47ff.

194. Cf., e.g., Ant. XVII, 10, 9, par. 287; Bell. II, 3, 4, par. 52; 4, 2-3, pars. 58, 63; 5, 1, pars. 67ff.; 5, 3, par. 76; 10, 1, par. 186; 13, 7, par. 268; 18, 9, pars. 500ff., 506; III, 7, 9, par. 168; 7, 26, par. 262; V, 13, 4-5, pars. 551,556.

195. Cf. Ezek. 24:5a; 31:4a.5b.7a.8a.12b; 32:2b.

nent role played by Arab auxiliaries in the Roman-Jewish wars[196] is reflected in TJ's translation of I Kings 10:15b, where MT "all the kings of Arabia" becomes "all the auxiliary kings" in TJ. Likewise, too, the recurrent expression, "all the mingled (or: foreign) people" (כל הערב)[197] is consistently rendered סמכותא by TJ.

With remarkable disregard of logic and theology, TJ translates Jer. 24:10a,[198] "And I (viz., God) will hire against them those that kill with the sword." Mercenaries were such a common feature of the Roman (as well as Hellenistic) armies that even the Almighty was imagined as a supreme military commander who has to strengthen his army by hiring mercenaries.

Military runners who would carry despatches announcing victory were common characteristics of ancient armies. Hence TJ on Jud. 5:28b[199] renders, "Why are the runners delayed who would bring me a letter (or: despatch) of victory?"

In a land occupied by Roman soldiers, the equipment of the Roman army would naturally be familiar. Sometimes this knowledge would be applied to Biblical exegesis—it being assumed that ancient armies must have been similarly equipped and would be so in the future. Thus, TJ on Ezek. 38:4b[200] renders, ". . . armed with round shields and (rectangular) shields." Likewise, in the following verse,[201] TJ translates, ". . . all of them armed with round shields and helmets." Round shields were typical of the equipment used by the Roman army. Similarly also Roman camp chairs (or footstools), which one version of TJ introduces in the translation of Jer. 43:10b:[202] ". . . and he will tie his camp chair"—presumably with ropes required for such a portable piece of army furniture..[203]

---

196. See *supra,* n. 194.

197. Jer. 25:20a; 50:37a; Ezek. 30:5a. Note that Hebrew ערב (ignoring the vocalization) can also mean "Arabia."

198. MT: "And I will send the sword upon them . . ."

199. MT: "Why tarry the hoofbeats of his chariots?" This question repeats, in different words, the previous clause, "Why is his chariot so long in coming?" Unnecessary repetition, even for the sake of poetical parallelism, is not accepted as valid in rabbinic exegesis, which therefore tends to look for additional meanings in the "extra" clause. Cf. also Komlosh, *op. cit.,* p. 291.

200. MT: ". . . with buckler and shield."

201. Cf. Ezek. 38:5b: ". . . all of them with shield and helmet." On the various types of shields used in Palestine during the Roman period, cf. M. Kel. XXIV, 1.

202. MT: ". . . and he (viz., Nebuchadrezzar) will spread his canopy (or: royal pavilion) over them."

203. On this type of foot-stool or camp chair, cf. also Tos. Kel. B. M. VIII, 6.

The Roman practice of crucifixion was also assumed to have been used in Biblical times. Thus, the עצים (wooden stakes) on which Joshua hanged (or impaled) several Canaanite kings[204] are rendered in TJ צליבא or צליבין— almost certainly T-shaped crosses to which slaves and rebels were nailed.[205]

As part of the retrojection of later conditions to Biblical times, TJ very often applies the linguistic usages of Mishnaic Hebrew to Biblical exegesis. For example, MT צדקה means "justice" or "righteousness" and is frequently indistinguishable from משפט (law, judgment, justice), and the two expressions are usually closely associated.[206] But in post-Biblical Hebrew, צדקה assumes different meanings—"merit," "virtue" and, especially "charity." Yet, it is in this sense that TJ renders צדקה by Aramaic זכו instead of the more accurate דינא.[207]

A similar change of meaning happens to the word גר—"stranger" or "resident alien" in Biblical Hebrew, but always, "proselyte" in Mishnaic Hebrew. TJ, like other Targumim as well as the Talmud,[208] almost invariably renders גר by גיור or גיורא (proselyte).[209] Strangers that sojourn (or: reside) among the Israelites become, in TJ's version, "proselytes who are converted."[210]

Out-of-date Biblical expressions are sometimes given contemporary meanings in TJ. Thus, the Biblical "Hebrews" (עברים) is rendered "Jews" (יהודאי) by TJ.[211] The Northern Kingdom of Israel and its people—often

---

204. Cf. Jos. 8:29a; 10:26f.

205. For references to crucifixion in the Talmud and Midrash, cf., e.g., M. Shab. VI, 10; M. Yev. XVI, 10; M. Ohol. III, 5; Tos. Ohol. IV, 11; Tos. Git. VII (V), 1; T. Y. Git. VII, 1, 48c; Gen. R. LVI, 3. Cf. also Targ. Onkelos on Deut. 21:22b.

206. Cf., e.g., Gen. 18:19a; Is. 1:27, 33.5; Jer. 22:15b; 23:5b.

207. Cf. Is. *ibid.; ibid.;* Jer. 23:5b. By way of contrast, cf. Targ. Onkelos on Gen. 18:19a, where MT צדקה is rendered accurately צדקתא.

208. Cf., e.g., M. B. M. IV, 10; T. B. Pes. 21b; Meg. 17b; Yev. 47b; 48b; Kid. 20a; 70b; B. K. 113b; B. M. 59b; 71a; 111b; Sanh. 56a; Mak. 9a.

209. Cf. TJ on Jos. 8:33a.35b;20:9a; II Sam. 1:13b; Is. 14:1b; Jer. 7:6a; 22:3b; Ezek. 14:7a; 22:7a.29b; 47:22a.23a; Zech. 7:10a; Mal. 3:5b. A significant exception is Jer. 14:8b, where the prophet addresses God, "Why should you be like a stranger in the land . . .?" Since this simile is somewhat anthropomorphic, TJ transfers the "strangeness" to Israel, rendering it, however, כתותבין ("like sojourners").

210. Cf. TJ on Jos. 20:9a; Ezek. 14:7a; 47:22a.23a.

211. Cf., e.g., I Sam. 4:9a; 13:3b,7a,19b; 14:11b,21a; 29:3; Jon. 1:9a. A notable exception is TJ's translation of העברי והעבריה in Jer. 34:9a and העברי in v. 14a *ibid.* Since the release of Jewish slaves after six years' service applied only to slaves of Jewish birth and not to "Canaanite" slaves converted to Judaism by their masters (cf. Lev. 25:44-46), TJ renders,

poetically referred to as Ephraim in the Bible—are frequently, though not always, given their proper name, Israel, in TJ.[212]

Within a midrashic context, we find that on one occasion the anachronistic Biblical system of describing the months of the year according to number is abandoned in TJ in favor of the Babylonian name of the month adopted by the Jews during the Babylonian captivity. Thus, in Ezek. 1:1a, the "fourth month" of MT becomes Tammuz in TJ.

Throughout the late Second Commonwealth and the Talmudic period, Greek cultural influences were all-pervasive in Eretz Israel,[213] and the large number of Greek words in the Talmud and Midrash represents adequate testimony to the direct linguistic influence of Hellenism on both Halachic and Aggadic literature. The Targumim, on the other hand, tend to ignore such Greek influences, possibly because they are after all *Aramaic* translations designed for the unsophisticated masses among whom Greek was less common than among the upper and middle classes. Only one Greek word, *strategos* (general, military governor), became popular in TJ and is found several times as the rendering for the Hebrew (ים) נציב.[214]

One of the major developments of the Hellenistic-Roman age was the foundation or re-establishment of cities, coupled with a general tendency at urbanization. Anachronistic Biblical references to "tents"—a linguistic heritage of the nomadic period of Israel's early history, which had been out of date even during the First Commonwealth—, became too glaring to be retained in TJ. Hence, in numerous passages, the "tent" (אהל) of the Hebrew text became a "city" in TJ.[215] "Modern" urban influence can also be detected

---

"the son of an Israelite and the daughter of an Israelite" (בר ישראל ובת ישראל). So also Targ. Onkelos on Exod. 21:2a and Deut. 15:12a.

212. Cf., e.g., Is. 7:2a,8b,17a; 28:1a.3b; Jer. 7:15b; 31:5(6)a,17(18)a,19(20)a; Hos. 4:17a; 7:8a,11a; 8:9b; 9:8a,11a,13a,16a; 10:11; 11:3a,9a; 12:2a; 14:9a; Zech. 9:13a. The rendering is not always consistent, and there are many exceptions, though in most cases there are reasons why the literal translation is retained. Noteworthy is TJ on Is. 17:3a, where MT "The fortress will disappear from Ephraim" is rendered in TJ, "Rulership (or: power) will cease from Ephraim." Since there were many fortresses in Samaria, the former territory of Ephraim, "fortresses" is taken in a metaphorical sense. Ephraim, on the other hand, is retained, perhaps because of the anti-Samaritan tendency of the Targumist.

213. Cf. S. Lieberman, *Greek in Jewish Palestine* (N. Y. 1942); *Hellenism in Jewish Palestine* (N. Y. 1950).

214. Cf. II Sam. 8:6a,14a; 23:14b (Heb. ומצב = ונציב; cf. the parallel passage in I Chron. 11:16b); I Kings 4:7a,19b; 5:7a,30a; 9:23a; 22:48b.

215. Cf. Jos. 22:4b,6b,7b,8a; Jud. 7:8a; 19:9b; I Sam. 4:10a; 13:2b; IISam. 20:1b; I

in TJ's translation of Is. 32:18b, where MT ". . . and in quiet resting places" is rendered ". . . and in their cities at ease."

There are some allusions in TJ to characteristic features of the Roman administration of Judaea. Thus, TJ on I Sam. 10:27a[216] refers directly to the Roman custom of *salutatio*, i.e., the habit of "clientes"—proteges and dependents of the emperor or of some other wealthy and powerful patron—to pay their daily respects by offering their "greetings" to their protector.[217] TJ accordingly renders, ". . . and they did not come to inquire concerning his welfare." Moreover, the "present" which was supposed to be brought to Saul in MT was too reminiscent of the corruption typical of Roman administrators. It was therefore inconceivable that an Israelite king of unblemished character as Saul was supposed to have been[218] should have had to be placated with gifts and bribes. TJ's rendering implies that the "worthless fellows" did not come to pay their respects, i.e., to follow the custom of *salutatio*.

The Roman tax system seems to have influenced TJ's translation of the recurrent phrase על המס ("in charge of forced labor").[219] Although in Roman times the pernicious *angaria* (corvée) system was still widespread, it was not nearly as important or pervasive as the numerous monetary impositions and taxes which burdened the provinces of the Roman empire, all too often beyond their capacity. We have already seen that the tax collectors were regarded as sinners and reprobates,[220] and it is not surprising, therefore, that TJ invariably renders על המס by על מסקי מסין ("in charge of the tax-collectors").

Another administrative feature of imperial Rome was the burgeoning bureaucracy, both in Rome and in the various provincial centers. The emperor had a considerable number of recorders, secretaries, and other public

---

Kings 12:16. In Jos. 3:14a, MT "from their tents" is rendered by TJ in two versions—the literal (ממשכניהון) and the one considered more suitable for a settled, urbanized people (מקרויהון = from their cities). Similarly, also, TJ on Ob. 19a translates MT "land" (lit., field) of Ephraim and the "land" of Samaria as "the cities of Ephraim and the cities of Samaria;" while in the last clause of the verse ("and Benjamin shall possess Gilead"), TJ adds, "the cities of the inhabitants of the land of Gilead."

216. MT: ". . . and they brought him (i.e., the "worthless fellows" to Saul) no present."

217. That this was customary in Jewish Palestine, too, is indicated by the phrase משכים לפתחו (lit., "rising early to [go] to someone's door"); cf. T. B. Ber. 14a; 28a; Sanh. 70b.

218. Cf. T. B. Yoma 22b.

219. Cf. II Sam. 20:24a; I Kings 4:6b; 12:18a.

220. See *supra*,p.

servants at his disposal.[221] It was therefore inconceivable for TJ to imagine that David king of all Israel had only one "recorder"[222] or, for that matter, that Hezekiah king of Judah, who was also distinguished for his piety and statesmanship,[223] should likewise have been limited to one "recorder."[224] TJ, accordingly, renders in each case that the recorder in question "was appointed over the recorders." In other words, only the chief recorder is mentioned, but, of course, there must have been a bureaucracy of subordinates.

In the Roman period, scribes were equipped with a folded writing tablet, the so-called *pinax,* which is frequently referred to in Talmudic and Midrashic literature.[225] Inkwells or inkhorns were indeed used,[226] but they were not normally carried on one's "loins," i.e., on the side. It was the *pinax* which was carried in this manner. TJ therefore renders Ezek. 9:2a.3b.11a, where the prophet describes a man "with a writer's inkhorn by his side": ". . . and the *pinax* (פנקס) of the scribe was on his side (lit., loins)".

The scribe, who also functioned as teacher,[227] played such a vital role in post-biblical times that—in line with the Talmudic principle that "a sage is superior to a prophet"[228]—the teacher would sometimes displace the prophet of the original text.[229] Similarly, the "vision" (חזון) of the prophet occasionally becomes "instruction" (אלפן) in TJ,[230] while those who "see" visions in MT are sometimes transformed in TJ into those who "teach"—either the truth or lies.[231] The "priest," too, was on at least one occasion seen as a teacher in TJ[232]—a role which was indeed played by the priests of the Biblical age.[233] Even false divination was regarded as false teaching by TJ, while

221. Cf. Tacitus, Ann. XII, 60; XIV, 39; Hist. II, 57, 95.

222. Cf. II Sam. 8:16b; 20:24b.

223. Cf. II Kings 18:1-8; 20:20; II Chron., chs. 29-32.

224. Cf. II Kings 18:18.

225. Cf. B. Kossowsky, אוצר לשון התלמוד, Vol. 31 (Jerusalem 1973), p. 305, s.v. פנקס; M. Jastrow, *op. cit.,* s.v. פנקס; S. Krauss, *Talmudische Archäologie* III, 144f., 160.

226. Cf. Krauss, *ibid.* p. 156.

227. Note that in the Talmudic age, סופר (Aram. ספרא) means both "scribe" and "Bible teacher."

228. T. B.B. B. 12a. Cf. *ibid.*: "Since the day when the Temple was destroyed, prophecy has been taken from the prophets and given to the sages."

229. Cf. Is. 3:2b; Jer. 8:10b; 26:7a,8b,11a,16a; Ezek. 7:26b. In all these cases MT נביא and נביאים are rendered in TJ ספר and ספריא, respectively.

230. Cf. Ezek. 7:26b; 12:27a.

231. Cf. *ibid.* 12:27a; 13:8a.

232. Cf. Hos. 4:4b.

233. On the priest as teacher, cf. Deut. 17:8ff.; 24:8b; 33:10a; II Kings 17:27f.; Ezek. 7:26b; Mic. 3:11a; Mal. 2:7a; II Chron. 15:3b.

diviners or sorcerers were simply false teachers[234]—a remarkable testimony
to the overwhelming influence of education and teaching during the Talmudic age.

Finally, even Amos's "prudent one" (משכיל)[235] becomes, after being
turned into the plural form, "teachers" who are advised to keep silence "because of the wicked ones." Whether this alludes to the religious persecution
by Antiochus IV[236] or Hadrian or to ill-treatment by the patriarchal authorities—and there were such notorious cases in the third century during the
patriarchate of Judah II,[237]—cannot be established with any certainty. The
context of the passage in Amos—social injustice by the Israelite upper
classes—would seem to favor the latter alternative.[238]

The overwhelming importance of Torah study and schools in the lives of
the Rabbis is reflected in TJ's interpretations of a number of passages. Thus,
Ezek. 14:4b[239] is rendered by TJ, ". . . who comes *to ask for instruction* from
me, although he is very much involved in the worship of his idols." According to TJ, therefore, the repentant sinner who comes to return to God is in
reality coming to study under his Creator's guidance.

The familiar practice of disciples to welcome their master on his arrival
in town or visit him at his home[240] is indicated in TJ's interpretation of
Ezek. 33:31a:[241] "And they shall come to you as men (who are) disciples
come."

Teachers and students alike would of course spend most of their time in
the Beth Hamidrash or Yeshivah, sometimes also called בית אולפנא.[242] Hence

---

234. Cf. Ezek. 13:6a,7a,8a,9a,23a; Mic. 3:6a,7a,11a.

235. Cf. Amos 5:13a.

236. It is perhaps noteworthy that the six chapters of the Hebrew part of the book of
Daniel, which was written or at least assumed its final form during Antiochus's persecution,
contains no less than ten forms of both nouns and verbs derived from the root שכל (cf. Dan.
1:4.17; 8:25; 9:13.22.25; 11:33.35; 12:3.10). Particularly important in this connection is Dan.
12:10, where the contrast between the משכילים and רשעים is vividly drawn.

237. Cf., e.g., T. Y. Sanh. II, 1, 19d-20a; *ibid.* 8, 20d; Gen. R. LXXVIII, 12; LXXX, 1.
Cf. Avi-Yonah, *op. cit.*, pp. 101ff.

238. It should be remembered that TJ was designed above all for the masses, and the Targumists may well have shared the anti-Patriarchal tendency of certain popular preachers; see
previous note for references.

239. MT: ". . . that comes with the multitude of his idols."

240. Cf., e.g., Tos. Negaim VIII, 2; T. Y. Eruv. V, 1; T. B. Pes. 108a; Yoma 77b; Suc.
27b; R. H. 16b; Tem. 16a.

241. MT: "And they come to you as people come . . ."

242. Cf., e.g., Targum Onkelos on Gen. 25:27b, where MT "dwelling in tents" is rendered

we find in one expanded TJ version on I Sam. 10:22b,[243] "Behold he (viz., Saul) is in the house of instruction (בבית אולפנא), hiding and praying, and reading the Torah (clad) in precious garments." Even the prophetess Huldah was, according to TJ on II Kings 22:14a,[244] "dwelling in Jerusalem in the house of instruction (בבית אולפנא)[245]—another example of TJ's practice to attribute to Biblical times not only the actual customs current in the Talmudic age, but even, by implication, those considered proper or desirable in the future. Needless to say, women did not attend schools in Talmudic times; but if Huldah was assumed to have done so hundreds of years earlier, the implicit idea was no doubt that at least some women of exceptional intellectual capacity—e.g., Beruriah, the scholarly wife of R. Meir[246]—might indeed be admitted to the houses of study to listen to the teachings and discussions of scholars.

One of the basic equipment items of the school in the Talmudic age, namely the writing tablet (לוח) is presumed by TJ to have existed in Biblical times. Hence TJ's translation of עץ ("stick") in Ezek. 37:16 f. and v. 20a is consistently לוחא ("writing tablet"), though this rendering is hardly suitable in this context.[247]

Finally, the all-embracing importance of the Torah is indirectly emphasized in TJ's addition to the translation of Hos. 10:2a.[248] The "divided heart" of the Israelites is interpreted in TJ as "Their heart is separated from (or, according to another version, against) the Torah."

The Temple hierarchy of the late Second Commonwealth was assumed to have been in existence during the First Commonwealth as well as in the early days of the Second Temple. Accordingly, TJ introduces the Captain of the Temple (סגן) as well as the Temple trustees (אמרכלין) in a number of Bib-

---

משמש בית אולפנא = "(who) ministered at the house of instruction." On the precise meaning of בית אולפנא, cf. *Hebrew Union College Annual* 36 (1966), pp. 107-111.

243. MT: "Behold, he has hidden himself among the baggage."

244. MT: "...now she dwelt in Jerusalem in the Second Quarter."

245. So also Targ. Rab Joseph on II Chron. 34:22a, where MT is the same as in II Kings 22:14a. Cf. also Komlosh, *op. cit.*, p. 337, who explains that TJ's interpretation is based on the later meaning of the verb שנה (to study, teach). He considers that TJ's explanation is due to the Aggadic tendency to attribute some sort of holiness to the daily activities of Biblical heroes.

246. Cf. *Jewish Encyclopedia* Vol. III, pp. 109f., s.v. Beruriah.

247. It is true that Ezekiel is told to write on the עץ (v. 16). But the context indicates that this was no writing tablet, but a wooden stick.

248. MT: "Their heart is divided (i.e., false)".

lical passages, in some of which such interpretations are entirely unwarranted. Thus, TJ on II Kings 23:4a[249] renders, "the captain (or: deputy) of the priests and the trustees." Likewise, TJ on II Kings 25:18 and Jer. 52:24[250] translates, "the captain (or: deputy) of the priests and the three trustees."[251] That mere guards of the threshold should be promoted to the high position of Temple trustees[252] may seem surprising. The key to the riddle is to be found in Tosefta Shek. II, 15, where we are informed that the trustees were in charge of the keys of the Temple court.[253]

With some plausibility, Jeremiah's contemporary, Pashhur the son of Immer, a priest who is described as "chief officer" (פקיד נגיד) in the Temple,[254] becomes in TJ a "captain of the priests." Similarly, another of Jeremiah's contemporaries, Zephaniah the son of Maaseiah, who is vaguely depicted in Jeremiah 29:25-26 as "having charge" (להיות פקדים) in the Temple, is defined more precisely in TJ's rendering as having been "appointed captain of the priests of the Temple of the Lord."[255]

Where there are descriptions of the Temple in the Bible, TJ pictures them in terms appropriate to the topography of Herod's Temple which is described in Josephus and the Mishnah.[256] Accordingly, TJ on Ezek. 40:15a, renders "the gate of (or: at) the entrance" as "the middle gate,"[257]—

---

249. MT: ". . . the priests of the second order and the keepers of the threshold."

250. MT: ". . . the second priest and the three keepers of the threshold."

251. Cf. also II Kings 12:10b, where MT "the priests who guarded (or: who were keepers of) the threshold" = TJ "priestly trustees." According to other TJ versions, they were "Temple guards" (נטרי היכלא). So also Jer. 35:4b (MT: "the keeper of the threshold" = TJ "the trustee"). A remarkable instance of the term אמרכל where we would not expect it is TJ on Zech. 11:13, where MT "into the treasury" (אל היוצר = אל האוצר) is rendered by TJ, "under the authority of the (chief) trustee." Here the trustee acts also as Temple treasurer.

252. Cf. T. B. Hor. 13a: "The trustee . . . commands all . . . The trustee takes precedence over the Temple treasurer." Cf. also M. Shek. V, 2. According to T. B. Pes. 57a, where we are told that the sons of the high priests were Temple treasurers, and their sons-in-law trustees, the order of precedence would seem to have been reversed.

253. Cf. A. Büchler, *Priester und Cultus*, p. 96, who cites Josephus, C. Ap. II, 8, par. 108: ". . . other priests assemble together at midday and receive the keys of the Temple and the vessles." It is likely that even the Biblical threshold keepers were not mere guards but high Temple officials.

254. Cf. Jer. 20:1a.

255. II Kings 25:18a and Jer. 52:24a.

256. Cf. Bell. V, 5, 1ff., pars. 184ff.; M. Midoth I, 3ff.

257. Cf. T. Y. Eruv. V, 1, 22c, where the eastern gate of the Temple is said to have had seven names, including "the gate of the entrance," "the middle gate," "the upper gate" (cf., e.g., M. Suc. V, 4) and "the new gate" (cf. Jer. 26:10b). See also n. 259.

evidently because the Targumist identifies it with the famous Nicanor gate, called by Josephus, "the Corinthian gate" because it was made of Corinthian bronze which glittered like gold and was indeed more beautiful and more valuable than gold.[258] It could be described as "the middle gate," either because it was the main gate in the east at which ceremonial processions would take place[259] or because it was flanked by two large chambers[260] or else because it was situated between two gates.[261] Conceivably, it may also have been identified with the "middle gate" mentioned in Jer. 39:3a[262]—rendered by TJ תרעא מציעאה(ב), exactly the same as in Ezek. 40:15a.

The "New Gate" of the First Temple mentioned in Jer. 26:10b is translated "the Eastern Gate" by TJ—which also agrees with the identification given in the Jerusalem Talmud.[263] This would of course make it identical with "the gate of (or:at) the entrance" in Ezek. 40:15a. Thus, TJ, in line with rabbinic thinking on the subject, identifies the Eastern, middle gate of the First Temple with the entrance gate of Ezekiel's vision, and this in turn is seen as the same as the Nicanor gate of the Herodian Temple.

While, topographically, these assumptions may have some validity, TJ's rendering of Ezek. 42:12b[264]—"... before the platform of the Levites"[265]—seems implausible.[266] TJ's identification is probably due to the reference to "chambers" in the same verse (as well as the preceding verses)—which the targumist may have identified with the "chambers under the Court of the Israelites" where "the Levites played upon harps

258. Cf. Bell. V, 5, 3, par. 201; M. Shek. VI, 3; M. Mid. I, 4; II, 3; Tos. Yom ha-Kip. II, 4; Tos. Shek. VI, 3; Tos. Sot. I, 5; Tos. Neg. XIV, 8; T. Y. Yoma III, 8, 41a; T. B. Yoma 38b.

259. Cf. M. Suk. V, 4; M. Sot. I, 5. On the Nicanor Gate, cf. Maimonides, *Yad*, Hilchot Beth Ha-Behirah V, 5; VII, 5; Tosafot Yom Tov on M. Suc. V, 5; *Encyclopaedia Judaica* (Jerusalem 1971) XII, 1133f.; H. Graetz in *MGWJ*, Vol. 25 (1876), pp. 434f.; and, especially, A. Büchler in *JQR*, Vol. 11 (1898/99), pp. 46-62. See also A. Schalit, הורדוס המלך (Jerusalem 1964), pp. 204, 464, n. 792.

260. Cf. M. Mid. I, 4.

261. So according to T. Y. Eruv. *op. cit.* The two gates were, according to קרבן העדה *ad loc.*, the gate of the sanctuary and the gate leading to the women's court. This seems to agree with the description in Josephus, Bell. V, 5, 3, par. 204.

262. Cf. קרבן העדה on T. Y. Eruv. *op. cit.*

263. See *supra*, n. 257.

264. MT: "... before the dividing wall."

265. Cf. M. Mid. II, 6. Cf. also M. Kid. IV, 5; M. Arak. II, 6; T. B. Meg. 3a; Arak. 4a.

266. Cf. Kimchi *ad loc.*, where the problem is discussed in great detail.

and lyres and the cymbals and all instruments of music."[267]

The institution of the synagogue was generally assumed to go back to the earliest period of the history of Israel.[268] Hence TJ on Am. 5:12b[269] renders, "... they pervert the cause of the needy in their synagogues." Likewise, TJ on Am. 5:15a[270] translates, "... establish justice in your synagogues." By way of contrast, though, a few verses earlier, TJ on Am. 5:10a[271] renders, "They hate him who admonishes them in court with words of the Torah."[272] In the following chapter, however, TJ on Am. 6:3b[273] reverts to the synagogue as the center of injustice by translating, "... and you bring near robbery in your synagogue." In this connection it must be borne in mind that in the Talmudic age synagogues, academies and houses of study served, among other things, as venues for courts of justice.[274]

Hellenistic-Roman architecture is sometimes reflected in TJ's renderings of words which did not originally have the connotation attributed to them by the targumist. Thus, Solomon's בית יער הלבנון[275] becomes "the summer house (lit., cooling place) of the kings" in TJ. Although royal summer and

---

267. M. Mid. II, 6; cf. also M. Arak. II, 3 ff. and M. Tam. VII, 3.

268. Cf. T. Y. Meg. IV, 1, 75a; T. B. Sanh. 94b; Gen. R. XLII, 2; LXIII, 6 (where, however, the existence of the synagogue in Patriarchal times is questioned); Targ. Ps.-Jon. on Exod. 18:20; Pesik. R. XXVI, 129b; Philo, De Vita Mosis III, 27; Jos., C. Ap. II, 17, par. 175; Acts 15:21.

269. MT: "... they turn aside the needy in the gate" (viz., from their right—in other words, the courts pervert justice).

270. MT: "... establish justice in the gate."

271. MT: "They hate him who reproves in the gate."

272. While TJ is in this case keeping close to the plain meaning of the text, this is not the case in vss. 12 and 15. Possibly the Targumist felt that, unlike Amos 5:12.15 and 6:3, where the absence of justice is deplored by the prophet—which could be imagined to apply to synagogues where courts of justice would meet (see *infra*, n. 273),—v. 10 was in a different category. For in the Talmudic age synagogue audiences are not known to have entertained hatred toward rabbis or preachers who admonished or reproved worshippers at the synagogue. Hence a more literal translation was in this case preferable.

273. MT: "... and you bring near the seat of violence."

274. Cf., e.g., Jos., Vita 54, pars. 277-279 (boulè [=council which also served as a court] meeting at the synagogue of Tiberias); T. Y. Taan. I, 2, 64a ("the synagogue of the Boulè"); T. B. Sanh. 32b. Houses of Study also served as prayer centers, in effect as synagogues; cf. T. Y. Ber. V, 1, 9a; T. B. Ber. 8a; 30b. In most communities, the synagogue was the only public building available for a court of law.

275. I Kings 7:2a; 10:17b.21a.

winter palaces existed as early as the time of Amos,[276] they were far more frequent in the Hellenistic-Roman age when not only kings but also wealthy and aristocratic families would, as a matter of course, acquire villas in the mountains or near the sea, in addition to their town houses, where they would live most of the year.[277]

Particularly anachronistic is TJ's identification of the Biblical Temple "pillars"[278] with the Hellenistic stoa (portico, colonnade) which was indeed a prominent feature of Herod's Temple.[279] Likewise, the capitals on the Corinthian columns built in the Hellenistic-Roman period were attributed by TJ to Ezekiel's future temple vision.[280]

The changing social conditions of women are occasionally reflected in TJ's renderings of verses where women are represented in a manner which differed from that customary in the Talmudic age. Thus, TJ on I Sam. 8:13, where Samuel warns the Israelites that the king they want to saddle themselves with would take their daughters "to be perfumers and cooks and bakers," changes the "perfumers" to "attendants" (or: servants—Aram. שמשין). The reason for this change is that in Talmudic times the trade of perfume-making was a highly respected occupation for males,[281] and in the Temple the priestly family of Abtinas was renowned for its unmatched expertise in preparing the incense used in connection with the sacrificial cult.[282] It would thus have been absurd for Samuel to threaten that the king would employ the daughters of the Israelites as "perfumers." If, on the other

276. Cf. Am. 3:15a. Apparently, King Ahab already built himself a winter palace in Jezreel and a summer palace in Samaria; cf. I Kings 21:1; II Kings 10:1ff.

277. Cf. T. Mommsen, *Das Weltreich de Caesaren* (Vienna 1933), p. 50; Tenney Frank, *An Economic Survey of Ancient Rome*, Vol. I (New York 1933, reprinted 1975), p. 295; M. Rostovtzeff, *The Social and Economic History of the Roman Empire*, second edition (Oxford 1957), Vol. I, p. 263; Vol. II, p. 660f., n. 21.

278. Cf. II Kings 11:14a; 23:3a.

279. Cf. Ant. XV, 11, 5, par. 411; XX, 9, 7, par. 220f. (where, significantly, the portico is assumed by Josephus to have been built by King Solomon); Bell. V, 5, 2, par. 190ff.; VI, 4, 2, pars. 232ff.

280. Cf. Ezek. 40:16b,22a,6b,31a,34a,37a; 41:18a,19a,20a,25a,26a.

281. Cf. T. B. Kid. 82b: "Happy is he whose craft is that of a perfume-maker."

282. Cf. M. Shek. V,1; M. Yoma III,11; Tos. Yom Ha-Kippurim II,6; T. B. Yoma 38a. It is highly improbable that any women were employed in preparing the incense, which required absolute levitical purity at all times. If, moreover, the incense was prepared within the inner area of the Temple, women would not even have been allowed access beyond the women's court; cf. Jos., Bell. V,5,2, par. 199; M. Mid. II, 5.

hand, the free daughters of Israel were going to be reduced to the status of attendants or servants, it was indeed a matter of concern and, Samuel may have thought, might cause the Israelites to have second thoughts about the monarchy.

It is well known that in Biblical times women would use timbrels on joyful occasions, for example, to welcome conquering heroes with song and dance.[283] In the more puritan Talmudic age, on the other hand, no such custom is recorded; and if it existed at all, it must have been discouraged, since it was considered safest from the point of view of morality for women to stay at home—a concept well rooted in Talmudic legislation.[284]

Hence Jeremiah's prediction about Israel that "Again you shall adorn yourself with timbrels, and shall go forth in the dance of the merrimakers,"[285] was not quite to the taste of the targumist who takes the entire verse to be a metaphor and allegorizes accordingly: "Again I will establish you, and you shall be established, O congregation of Israel. Again you will adorn yourself with ornaments and go forth in the company of those that give praise."

Puritan rabbinic morality is also reflected in TJ's rendering of Jud. 14:10a.[286] Samson's father Manoah, who is considered an ignorant עם הארץ in the Talmud for doing nothing worse than going "after (i.e., behind) his wife,"[287] could not have flouted traditional propriety by going to a strange woman—and a Philistine at that,—even though his purpose was to arrange his son's marriage. In normal circumstances, the father of the groom would never go to his prospective daughter-in-law, but to her parents, so as to negotiate the bride-price and make the necessary arrangements for the wedding. TJ therefore changes the translation to read, "And his father went down on account (or: with regard to the business) of the woman." Manoah, then, did not improperly go to see his future daughter-in-law, but, presumably, her parents, with a view to arranging the marriage.

Occasionally, TJ allows Biblical women to engage in public service or to minister to teachers and students in the houses of study. Thus, TJ on II

---

283. Cf., e.g., Exod. 15:20; Jud. 11:34a; I Sam. 18:6.

284. Cf., M. Ket. XIII, 3; M. B. B. IX, 1; T. Y. Sanh. II, 8, 20d; T. B. Yev. 77a; Git. 12a; Shevuoth 30a; Gen. R. VIII, 12; Num. R. I, 3; Ruth R. IV, 6; Eccl. R. X, 8; Tanh. וישלח 5-6; ed. Buber, I,17of.; *ibid.* במדבר IV, 5a.

285. Jer. 31:3 (v. 4 in AV, RSV and TJ).

286. MT: "And his father went down to the woman."

287. Jud. 13:11a; cf. T. B. Ber. 61a; Eruv. 18b.

Kings 4:13b[288] renders, "I am bearing the burden in the affairs of my people"[289]—presumably, charitable activities among neighbors and friends who were in need of assistance. This was more or less the limit of female public service tolerated by rabbinic morality. In addition, women also served teachers and students, apparently by providing them with food and drink. This is reflected in TJ's rendering of Jud. 5:24b:[290] "... like one of the women who minister in the houses of study she shall be blessed."[291]

According to the Talmud and Midrash, there was a great increase in sexual immorality especially in Jerusalem, during the years preceding the destruction of the Temple.[292] Later, we also hear about men exchanging their wives.[293] It is this degeneration of morality which is reflected in TJ's expanded interpretation of Hos. 4:2, where MT "committing adultery, they break all bounds" is rendered by TJ, "committing adultery, they beget children by the wives of their fellows."

The distinction between cult prostitutes (קדשות) and common whores (זונה) in the Bible was no longer familiar in Talmudic times. They were all tarred with the same brush. Also, men who patronized prostitutes did not offer sacrifices as part of the liaison. Hence TJ translates Hos. 4:14b,[294] "... and with whores they eat and drink." Thus, the prophetic denunciation of cult prostitution and participation in idolatrous sacrifices is brought up-

288. MT: "I dwell among my own people."

289. Cf. Komlosh, *op. cit.,* p. 346, who considers TJ's translation to be a fair rendering of the primary meaning of this clause. This is, however, unlikely. Heb. עמי ("my people") really means here, "My kinsfolk"; and what the Shunammite woman meant to say was that she needed no special assistance or recommendation to the authorities, since she was fully protected by her family.

290. MT: "... of tent-dwelling women most blessed."

291. Komlosh, *op.cit.,* p. 290, citing T. B. Nazir 23b and Rashi *ad loc.* as well as Gen. R. XLVIII, 16 (cf. Ginzberg, *Legends* VI, p. 198), believes that TJ alludes to the Hebrew matriarchs—Sarah, Rebekah, Rachel and Leah—whose "tents" (cf. Gen. 18:9b; 24:67a; 31:33) are identified with the Beit Ha-Midrash, a characteristic feature of the Aggadah (cf. Ginzberg, *op. cit.,* V, p. 274). It seems, however, more likely that TJ is alluding to contemporary women, especially since כחדא מנשיא ("like one of the women") clearly refers to a type rather than to the matriarchs as such.

292. Cf. M. Sot. IX, 9; T. B. Shab. 62b-63a; Tanh.עירית, 11.

293. Cf. T. B. Shab. 62b. R. Abbahu, who reports this in expounding Am. 6:4a, lived in Caesarea towards the end of the third century C.E. He probably had members of his assimilated community in mind. Cf. T. Y. Sot. VII, 1, 2, 21b; cf. also S. Lieberman, יוונים ויוונות בארץ ישראל (Jerusalem, 1962), p. 23.

294. MT: "... and with cult prostitutes they sacrifice."

to-date, as it were, by the omission of what was no longer topical. Instead, the targumist concentrates on the real moral problem of the time— associating and feasting with whores.

According to the Mishnah,[295] certain criminals were imprisoned in a narrow vaulted chamber (כפה), where there was no room to move[296] and where they were given a barley and bread-and-water diet.[297] It is this black-hole type of prison which is retrojected to Jeremiah's time in TJ's translation of Jer. 29:26b:[298] "... and you should put him into the vaulted prison chamber" (לכיפתא).

A more pleasant habit of the Hellenistic-Roman age was to recline during meals—a well-known custom still preserved to some extent during the Passover seder meal.[299] TJ repeatedly assumes that people who sat down to dine in Biblical times must also have done so in reclining fashion, and translates accordingly.[300] The dining furniture of the Roman *triclinium* is similarly retrojected by TJ to the early 6th century B.C.E.[301] Likewise, too, the siesta custom, which in Roman times appears to have been confined to the aristocracy and other wealthy elements, is assumed in TJ to have been the more or less exclusive privilege of royalty during the age of the early Israelite monarchy.[302]

Occasionally, economic developments in the Talmudic age are faithfully reflected in TJ. We have already seen that the targumic midrash on Debo-

295. Cf. M. Sanh. IX, 3.5.

296. Cf. T. B. Sanh. 81b.

297. Cf. *ibid.*

298. MT: "... that you should put him in the stocks."

299. Cf., e.g., M. Pes. X, 1 and Passover Haggadah - מה נשתנה.

300. Cf. Jud. 19:6a: MT "They sat down to eat [lit., They ate]" = TJ "They reclined and ate." Cf. I Kings 10:5a: MT "And the food of his table and the seating of his officials [lit., servants]" = TJ "And the food of his table and the reclining of his servants." Cf. *ibid.* 13:20a: MT "As they sat at the table" = TJ "While they were reclining round the table." Cf. also Targ. Onkelos on Gen. 27:19 and 37:25. Even where altogether inappropriate, as in II Sam. 18:30a, MT "Turn aside (סב) and stand here" is rendered, "Recline and stand in readiness" in TJ. This absurd translation is due no doubt to the linguistic similarity of סב and מסב ("recline"), which have the same root סבב.

301. Cf. Ezek. 23:41a (MT "You sat upon a stately couch with a table spread before it" = TJ "You raised up upholstered couches with expensive cushions filled with all good things you have set before them"). The last clause reflects luxurious Roman dining.

302. Cf. II Sam. 4:5b, where MT "as he was taking his noonday rest" = TJ "as he was sleeping the sleep of kings."

rah's wealth, in TJ on Jud. 4:5,[303] is an accurate, though obviously incomplete, map of the economic geography of the Land of Israel in Talmudic times. Other anachronistic examples are the fine wool of Miletus,[304] which was highly prized throughout the Roman empire,[305] and sleeved tunics (כרדוטין), which, in TJ, replace the cakes offered to the Queen of Heaven[306] as well as the linen ephod (TJ: כרדוט דבוץ) worn by Samuel and David.[307]

Of considerable interest is TJ's identification of ancient tribes and place names with contemporary peoples or places. Most of these identifications ard correct or at least feasible. Others are unlikely or even definitely incorrect.

Starting with Jerusalem, we find that the ancient locations were by and large well remembered. Thus, "the Potsherd Gate" in Jer. 19:2a is rendered "the Dung Gate" in TJ, in accordance with the name given to one of the southern gates of Jerusalem since the time of Nehemiah.[308] Similarly, the Tower of Hananel[309] is in TJ plausibly identified, in terms of its location, with the Tower of "Picus" (=Hippicus) built by Herod.[310] Likewise, too, the commerical suburb of Jerusalem known as "the Mortar" (המכתש)[311] is correctly identified by TJ with the Kidron Valley. Undoubtedly accurate is

---

303. Cf. Komlosh, *op. cit.*, p. 293, who considers it likely that this Targum version is the original source of the legend of Deborah's wealth. Noteworthy, too, in this connection is TJ's rendering of Amos 7:14b, where MT "a dresser of sycamore trees" is rendered by TJ, "I have sycamore trees in the Shephelah"—an assumption unwarranted in the case of the prophet from Tekoa, but reflecting the economic geography of the Talmudic age; cf. T. B. Ned. 38a and Churgin, p. 148.

304. Cf., e.g., Ezek. 27:18b (MT ". . . and white wool" = TJ ". . . and fine wool [ועמר מילח] = lit., "and wool of Miletus"] wrapped up [or: covered]); Hos. 2:7b (MT: ". . . who give me . . . my wool" = TJ ". . . who provide me with fine [=Miletus] wool); *ibid.* 2:11b (MT ". . . and I will take away my wool = TJ ". . . and I will take away my fine (=Miletus) wool"). Cf. T. B. Shab. 10b; 30b; Ket. 111b; Nid. 17a; Ruth R. III, 7 on Ruth 1:19. On the high value set on wool from Miletus or fine wool produced by covering the sheep from birth so that they should develop wool of a fine, silky texture, cf. T. B. Shab. 54a.

305. *Cambridge Ancient History* III (Cambridge 1925), p. 510; *ibid.* IV (Cambridge 1926), p. 89; S. Krauss, *Talmudische Archäologie*, Vol. I, pp. 531f., n. 92.

306. Cf. TJ on Jer. 7:18b; 44:19b. Cf. also Krauss, *Lehnwörter*, p. 295; Komlosh, *op. cit.*, p. 409.

307. Cf. I Sam. 2:18; II Sam. 6:14b.

308. Cf. Neh. 2:13a; 3:13b.14a; 12:31b; cf. also M. Ed. I, 3.

309. Cf. Jer. 31:37b; Zech. 14:10b.

310. Cf. Josephus, Bell. V, 4, 3, par. 161.

311. Cf. Zeph. 1:11.

TJ's rendering of "the mountain which is on the east side of the city"[312] as "the mount of olives which is east of the city."

The spring of Gihon—where Solomon was crowned[313] and which was diverted by Hezekiah king of Judah to provide water for Jerusalem during the anticipated siege of the city by the Assyrians, while denying it to the enemy[314]—becomes the Shiloah in TJ.[315] Although actually not identical, the fact that the Gihon waters flow into the pool of Shiloah (= Siloam) evidently influenced TJ's translation.[316]

More doubtful is TJ's identification of the "Second Quarter" of Jerusalem mentioned in Zeph. 1:10a with the Ophel or "hill"[317] referred to repeatedly in Nehemiah[318] and Chronicles.[319] Doubtful, too, is TJ's updating of "the Serpent's Stone which is beside En-Rogel"[320]—which is rendered, "the stone of the watchpost (סכותא - lit., outlook) which is on the side of En-Katzra (עין קצרא)." Since there is no linguistic connection between MT הזחלת and TJ סכותא,[321] one must assume that a topographical identification is attempted by TJ. It would seem that there was in fact a stone in the area used as a watchpost in the Talmudic age. As for En-Katzra, it could be a slight variation on En-Castra ("fountain of the [Roman] camp")[322]—possibly, the one used by the tenth legion left by the Roman authorities to garrison Jerusalem in 70 C.E.[323] But, more probably, עין קצרא should be translated, "the

312. Ezek. 11:23b.

313. Cf. I Kings 1:33b,38b,45a.

314. Cf. II Chron. 32:30; cf. M. Pes. IV, 9; Ab. R. N., edit. Schechter, vers. I, ch. 2, p. 12.

315. Cf. Is. 8:5a; cf. also T. Y. Taan. II, 1, 65a.

316. So according to Z. Vilnay, אריאל: אנציקלופדיה לידיעת ארץ ישראל ג־ו, II (Tel Aviv 1976), col. 1319.

317. The text of TJ is not altogether certain. The MS readings vary between עולפא and עופא; but it seems highly probable that these are Aramaic versions of Heb. עפל. The difference between TJ's rendering of MT משנה in this case and that in II Kings 22:14a (where, as we have seen above, TJ translates בית אולפנא) is due to the context in our verse—"a wail from the Second Quarter,"—which precludes a repetition of the בית אולפנא rendering. The Targumist could not let the prophet predict wailing in the House of Study. See *supra*, n. 242.

318. Cf. Neh. 3:26a.27b; 11:21a.

319. Cf. II Chron. 27:3b; 33:14a.

320. I Kings 1:9a. En-rogel is also mentioned in Jos. 15:7b; 18:16b; and II Sam. 17:17a.

321. Cf. אנציקלופדיה מקראית, Vol. I, col. 47, where it is conceded that the basis for TJ's interpretation is not clear, and that the exact meaning of the word סכותא is also unknown.

322. For examples for קצרא in the sense of "camp" or "fort," cf. Jastrow, *op. cit.*, pp. 1408f., s.v. קצרא III.

323. Cf. Bell. VII, 1, 2, par. 5.

fountain of the fuller (or: washer)," which has been plausibly identified with Bir Ayub, at the junction of the Valley of Hinnom with the Kidron Valley, used by Arab women for washing of clothes even in modern times.[324] It is impossible to establish with any degree of certainty whether TJ's identification in this case is accurate.

Doubtful, too, is TJ's identification of Beth-car, where the Israelites under Samuel's leadership pursued the Philistines,[325] with Beth Sharon—or, more probably Beth-horon[326]—which fits the strategic situation, though it is difficult to accept this emendation from a paleographic point of view.[327]

Even more doubtful—indeed, almost certainly wrong—is TJ's identification of Baal-shalishah[328] with "the land of the south." According to Eusebius,[329] Baal-shalishah is in the area of Lydda (Diospolis), which is usually identified with the "South" (דרום) in rabbinic literature. It would seem that Eusebius followed rabbinic ideas on the identification of Baal-shalishah. The rabbis, who generally considered איש (plural אנשים) to designate righteous and important men,[330] could not imagine that the man (איש) from Baal-shalishah who had brought food supplies to Elisha would reside anywhere but at a place distinguished by Torah learning. Since Baal-shalishah was clearly not in Galilee, the only suitable place left was the area of Lod (Lydda) which was the center of the so-called "Elders (or: Rabbis) of the South."[331] This entire theory is, however, midrashic in character, and, according to other sources, it would appear that Baal-shalishah was in the Jordan Valley, probably in the area of Jericho.[332] It has so far not been possible to pinpoint the location of Baa-shalishah.

In the extreme south, the area of Shur near the Egyptian border[333] is plausibly rendered Hagra by TJ,[334] though the precise identification and location of Hagra is a matter of scholarly dispute.[335]

---

324. Cf. S. Klein, ארץ יהודה (Tel Aviv 1939), p. 116.

325. Cf. I Sam. 7:11b.

326. Cf. F. M. Abel, *Géographie de la Palestine,* II (Paris 1938), p. 269.

327. Cf. אנציקלופדיה מקראית, II, col. 84.

328. Cf. II Kings 4:42a; cf. I Sam. 9:4a, where MT בארץ שלשה = TJ בארע דרומא.

329. Onomasticon, 21-23.

330. Cf. Tanhuma שלח 3; cf. also Num. 13:3 and Rashi *ad loc.*

331. Cf. T. B. Yev. 45a; Zev. 22b; 23a; Hul. 132b; T. Y. Pes. V, 3, 32d; T. Y. M. K. III, 2, 82d; Lev. R. XX, 4; cf. also T. B. B. B. 25b; 96a; Lam. R. III, 17; Pesik. R., ch. 29, 138b.

332. Cf. Tos. Sanh. II, 9; T. B. Sanh. 12a; S. Klein, *op. cit.,* pp. 146 and 189. See, especially, אנציקלופדיה מקראית, II, col. 292, where the problem is discussed in detail.

333. Cf. I Sam. 15:7b; 27:8b.

334. So also Targ. Onkelos on Gen. 16:7b; 25:18a; and Exod. 15:22a.

335. Hagra is probably identical with חגר listed in M. Git. I, 1 (and also in Sifre, Deut. עקב

Turning to central and northern Palestine, we find that "the palm of Deborah," which was situated "between Ramah and Bethel in the hill country of Ephraim,"[336] ceases altogether to be a palm tree in TJ. Instead, Deborah is depicted as dwelling "in the city in Ataroth." For an Israelite judge, even if she was a mere woman, to dispense justice while sitting under a palm tree was inconceivable in the urbanized Talmudic age. Since, according to Jos. 16:2, the border of the territory of Ephraim, "going down from Bethel to Luz, it passes along to Ataroth," TJ plausibly identifies the location of Deborah's judicial activity with Ataroth, which, in line with the later practice of setting up courts in towns but not in villages, is duly elevated into a city.

In the same verse, TJ transforms "the hill country of Ephraim" to "the mountain of the king" (טור מלכא)—which was the name given to the central mountain range of Eretz Israel during the Talmudic period.[337]

Further north, in Galilee, TJ identifies Chinneroth[338] with Ginnosar, a fruitful valley along the shores of the lake of Tiberias or Kinneret.[339]

51, where it is misspelt (החגרא) as a Palestinian border area. It is identified by Hildesheimer, *Beiträge zur Geographie Palästinas,* pp. 53 and 68 with the wilderness of Shur. According to S. Klein, ספר הישוב (Jerusalem 1939), I, 43, (א) חגת was in Transjordan, south of Damascus. C. Albeck, in his edition of J. Theodor's בראשית רבא II, p. 949 (on LXXIX, 7), points out that— as suggested by Tosafot on T. B. Git. 2a (ד"ה ואשקלון)—there were two localities by the name of חגרא, one in Transjordan called חגרא דערבא (Hagra of Arabia), the inhabitants of which were Nabateans; while the other Hagra was presumably identical with the Biblical Shur, on the south-western border of Palestine. A different possibility is proposed by Skinner, ICC, *Genesis,* p. 287. Accordingly, חגרא may be a translation of שור in the sense of "wall." (This may explain the definite article החגר in M. Git. I, 1). The problem is discussed in great detail by B. Maisler (Mazar), הרקם וההגרא *Tarbiz* XX (1949), pp. 316-319, where the relevant litera- ture is cited. According to Maisler, החגר (=חגרא) is to be identified with the Roman *limes* in the Negev, which was built to protect the area against the bedouin. Hence also the definite article החגר (Aram. חגרא).

336. Jud. 4:5a.

337. Cf. T. B. Git. 55b; 57a; cf. also M. Shev. IX, 2, where the Hebrew name of "the mountain of the king" (הר המלך) is given. On the geographical identity of "the mountain of the king," cf. A. Büchler, "Die Schauplätze des Bar-Kochba krieges," *JQR,* XVI, pp. 180ff.

338. Cf. Jos. 11:2a; 12:3a; I Kings 15:20b. Cf. also Jos. 13:27b, where the vocalization is slightly different to read Chinnereth. Cf. also Targum Onkelos on Deut. 3:17a, where MT "Chinnereth" is likewise rendered Ginnosar.

339. So also T.Y. Meg. I, 1, 70a; T.B. Meg. 6a. On the fertility of the Valley of Ginnosar, cf. Sifre ברכה, par. 355; T.B. Pes. 8b; Meg. 6a; Gen. R. XCVIII, 22; XCIX, 12; Tanh. ויחי 13; Midr. Hag. Gen. ויחי, par. 21, edit. M. Margulies (Jerusalem 1947), p. 853. On the history of the valley of Ginnosar, cf. Z. Vilnay, אריאל: אנציקלופדיה לידיעת ארץ ישראל, Vol. II (ג-ד) (Tel-Aviv, 1974), cols. 1323–1327, s.v. גינוסר.

As far as Transjordan is concerned, TJ regularly renders the northern province of Bashan — "Mathnan" (מתנן)[340]—evidently because this was the common Aramaic designation of the area during the Talmudic age. It was probably another form of Batanaea, which is mentioned in different transliterations in the Jerusalem Talmud and the Targumim.[341] Reasonably accurate is also TJ's rendering of MT "the region of Argob"[342] as "the district of Trachonitis."

Further south, in the Land of Moab, "the road to Horonaim"[343] is transformed by TJ into "the declivity (or: descent) of Horonaim," no doubt because the parallel passage in Jer. 48:5b reads במורד חרונים. It has been identified with the village of Al-Iraq in southern Moab,[344] though Z. Vilnay[345] considers that its exact location is unknown.

Another Moabite town, Kerioth,[346] is rendered כרכא ("the city") in TJ, which evidently connects קריות with קריה ("city"). The major Moabite city of Ar[347] is transformed by TJ into a "fort" or "fortress" (לחית),[348] possibly through confusion with nearby Aroer, translated לחית by Ps.-Jon. and Targ. Yer. on Num. 32:34b, and by the latter also on Deut. 4:48a. As we shall presently see, Aroer itself is erroneously introduced by TJ into its rendering of Jer. 48:6b.[349]

Foreign cities and countries are also depicted in terms more suitable for the Talmudic age than for the Biblical period. In the case of Egypt, for example (Is. 19:13b),[350] the Biblical "tribes," which no longer existed in Egypt, are turned into "provinces," and the metaphorical "cornerstones" become "governors." Since Egypt was a Roman province, administered by Roman governors, TJ's rendering—"the governors of her provinces"—is eminently up-to-date.[351] The ancient Egyptian cities of Zoan and Noph are often

---

340. Cf., e.g., TJ on Jos. 9:10b; 12:4a.5a; 13:11b.12a.30a; *et passim*.

341. Cf. Jastrow, *op. cit.*, I, 151, s.v. בותניי

342. I Kings 4:13b; cf. also Targ. Onkelos on Deut. 3:4b.13b.14a.

343. Is. 15:5b.

344. Cf. Press, *op. cit.*, Vol. II, p. 365.

345. *Op. cit.*, Vol. III (ח-ך), col. 2263.

346. Cf. Jer. 48:24a.41a; Am. 2:2a.

347. Cf. Is. 15:1a.

348. So also Targ. Onkelos, Targ. Ps.-Jon. and Targ. Yer. on Num. 21:15a.28b; Deut. 2:9b.18b.

349. See *infra*, p.

350. MT: "...those who are the cornerstones of her tribes."

351. Cf. Komlosh, *op. cit.*, p. 297.

given in TJ their contemporary Hellensitic names, Tanis and Memphis, respectively.[352] Is. 19:18b, where there is an unmistakable allusion to Heliopolis,[353] is homiletically rendered in TJ, "the city of Beth-shemesh (=Helio-polis) which will in future be destroyed."[354]

The targumists were apparently familiar with the Arab tribes of the North Arabian and Syrian desert. For example, "the kings of the mixed tribes (הָעֶרֶב) that dwell in the desert"[355] become in TJ "the kings of the Arabs who dwell in tents in the desert."[356] While TJ ערבאי ("the Arabs") is no doubt a result of the linguistic similarity with MT הערב, the addition of the word בשכונין ("in tents") must be regarded as a logical explanation, since there was no point in mentioning the obvious and universally known fact that the Arabs dwell in the desert. But while everybody knew that the Arabs were "children of the desert," not all Arabs lived in tents—the settled Nabatean Arabs being the obvious exception. Hence the addition of the "tents" to depict the nomadic tent-dwelling Arabs.

Logical consistency as well as familiarity with contemporary geographical conditions are also evident in TJ's rendering of Jud. 8:24b[357]— "... because they were Arabs."[358] Since, according to Gen. 25:1-2, Midian was Abraham's son by Keturah, the Midianites could not be accurately described as Ishmaelites.[359]

TJ also provides us with the contemporary name of an otherwise unknown geographical area in North Arabia. The Biblical Ephah,[360] which was undoubtedly in or near the ancient territory occupied by the nomadic or

352. Cf. Is. 19:11a,13a; 30:4a; Jer. 2:16a; 44:1b; 46:14a,19b; Ezek. 30:13a,14a,16b.

353. MT: עיר ההרס (= "the city of destruction")—probably a deliberate change from עיר החרס (= "the city of the sun") = Heliopolis.

354. Cf. Rashi's perceptive commentary, *ad loc.* Connecting TJ's interpretation with Jer. 43:13a ("He shall break the obelisks of Beth-shemesh [=Heliopolis]), and citing Job 9:7a ("who commands the sun [לחרס], and it does not rise"), Rashi points out that TJ provides a twofold explanation based on two readings, ההרס ("the destruction") and החרס ("the sun"). Cf. also T.B. Men. 110a, where the Job passage is cited in the exegesis of our verse.

355. Jer. 25:24b.

356. Similarly, too, TJ on Jud. 8:11a, where MT "... by the way of them that dwelt in tents" = TJ "... by the way of the camp of the Arabs who dwell in tents in the desert."

357. MT: "... because they (*viz.*, the Midianites) were Ishmaelites."

358. According to another version, "... because they had slain Arabs."

359. It is noteworthy, though, that Targ. Onk. on Gen. 37:25ff. consistently translates MT "Ishmaelites" as "Arabs."

360. Cf. Is. 60:6a.

semi-nomadic Midianite tribes,[361] is translated Hawalad in TJ, presumably as a result of identification of a familiar contemporary Arab tribe (or its territory) with ancient Ephah. Another tribe related to the Midianites, that of the Kenites,[362] is identified in TJ with the Arab tribe of the Shalmaites[363]— which is in line with the views expressed in the Talmud and Midrash.[364] The bedouin tribe of Kedar is usually rendered "Arabs" by TJ,[365] though in Jer. 49:28, "Kedar" is twice left unchanged from the original; while in Ezek. 27:21a, where "Arabia" (ערב) is mentioned in the beginning of the verse, Kedar is translated נבט, i.e., the Nabateans, who were also Arab tribes but of a more settled character.

The commercial activities of the Sabeans, a well-known Arab trading people, are reflected in TJ's rendering of Is. 45:14a,[366] according to which the Sabeans were not "men of stature," but "men of business." As pointed out by Komlosh,[367] the word וסחר ("and the merchandise of") at the beginning of the verse, which refers to כוש, is taken by TJ as applying also to "the Sabeans." Moreover, Heb. מדה ("stature") may also have been connected by TJ with the root מדד ("to measure")—an activity characteristic of "men of business."

Northwest of ancient Eretz Israel, the city of Tyre, "that was mighty on the sea"[368] becomes in TJ "a city . . . that was dwelling in the fortress of the sea." Tyre was situated on an island, but from the time of Alexander the Great, the city was linked to the mainland by a dyke, which over the centuries became ever wider through alluvial deposits, so that it eventually became part of a peninsula.[369] TJ, evidently unaware that Tyre was once an island, changes the translation to adapt it to a fortress situated on the seashore. Similarly also in Ezek. 27:32b, where MT "Who was ever destroyed

361. Cf. Gen. 25:4a; I Chron. 1:33a.

362. Cf. Jud. 1:16a; 4:11a.

363. *Ibid.; ibid.;* 4:17; 5:24a; I Sam. 15:6; 27:10b; 30:29b. Cf. also Targ. Onk. on Gen. 15:19a; Num. 24:21a.22a.

364. Cf. T.Y. Shev. VI, 1, 36b; T.Y. Kid. I, 9, 61d; T.B.B.B. 56a. Komlosh, *op. cit.,* p. 219, cites an opinion connecting the Shalmaites with "the sons of Salma" mentioned in I Chron. 2:54a (cf. v. 51a).

365. Cf. Is. 21:16b.17a; 42:11a; 60:7a; Jer. 2:10a.

366. MT: ". . . the merchandise of Ethiopia (Heb. כוש —possibly an Arab tribe by that name), and the Sabeans, men of stature."

367. *Op. cit.,* p. 632. Cf. also אנציקלופדיה מקראית, Vol. V, col. 993, s.v. סבא.

368. Ezek. 26:17b.

369. Cf. H. Jacob Katzenstein, *The History of Tyre* (Jerusalem, 1973), p. 9.

like Tyre in the midst of the sea?" = TJ "Who is like Tyre? There is none like it[370] in the midst of the sea." Thus, it is not Tyre that is in the midst of the sea, but other places, presumably islands to which Tyre is compared.

Turning to the ideal northeastern border of ancient Palestine, "the river" is nearly always correctly identified in TJ as the Euphrates,[371] though occasionally the identification hinges on somewhat doubtful midrashic exegesis.[372] Even more doubtful is TJ's identification of Canneh (כנה) in Ezek. 27:23a with Nisibis in northern Mesopotamia. Since Canneh is probably a spelling error for Calneh (כלנה)—the precise location of which has never been ascertained,[373]—we find that the ancient Targumim apparently contradict one another in identifying this ancient Mesopotamian city with places familiar in the Talmudic period. Thus, both Targ. Ps.-Jon. and Targ. Yer. on Gen. 10:10a, render "Calneh" by "Ktesiphon," a city on the left bank of the Tigris in central Mesopotamia, which sometimes served as the capital of the Parthian Empire; while in the same clause Accad is translated "Nisibis." It is clear that all the Targumists were able to do was to offer conjectures based on contemporary conditions. They evidently had no reliable traditions to fall back upon.

Very doubtful, too, is TJ's identification of Ararat[374] with Kardu, the district of Cordyene, which was situated east of the Tigris in northern Mesopotamia, roughly corresponding to modern Kurdistan. If the area of Mt. Ararat in north-eastern Turkey corresponds more or less to the Biblical Ararat, then the Targumic identification with Cordyene is clearly erroneous; but since the exact location of Biblical Ararat cannot be ascertained, Cordyene is not altogether inconceivable, though in fact highly improbable.

Several places in Asia Minor are identified by TJ more or less plausibly, though by no means reliably, such as Togarmah (or: Beth-togarmah) in Ezek. 27:14a and 38:6a, which is rendered, "the province of Germamia;"[375]

370. TJ takes MT כִּדְמָה (*lit.*, "like one that is destroyed") in the sense of כִּדְמֵה (*lit.*, "like similar").

371. Cf. Jos. 24:2a.3a.14b.15a; II Sam. 10:16a; I Kings 5:1a.4a; 14:15a; Is. 11:15a; 27:12a; Jer. 2:18b; Mic. 7:12b; Zech. 9:10 b.

372. Cf. Is. 48:18b; 59:19b; 66:12a.

373. Cf. אנצוקלופדיה מקראית, Vol. IV, col. 186, s.v. כלנה.

374. Cf. II Kings 19:37a; Is. 37:38a; Jer. 51:27a; cf. also Targ. Onk. on Gen. 8:4b.

375. Cf. Gen. R. XXXVII, 1, where Togarmah in Gen. 10:3b is identified with "Germania" (not to be confused with European Germania), though, according to one opinion, Togarmah was in fact in Germanicia (so also T.Y. Meg. I, 10, 71b), a town and district in

and "the men of Gamad," in Ezek. 27:11a, who are identified with the Cappadocians. Both the reading and the meaning of Gamad are highly doubtful.[376] In north-eastern Asia Minor, TJ identifies Minni[377] with Armenia, a plausible conjecture which is likely to be correct. On the other hand, TJ's rendering of "Harmon"[378] as Armenia is highly improbable, even if the reading is correct—itself a rather doubtful proposition.

A considerable number of geographical identifications in TJ are demonstrably wrong. Thus, "the Horse Gate" northeast of the Temple area mentioned in Jer. 31:39a, 40a[379] was obviously not, as maintained by TJ, "the race-course of the king," i.e., the hippodrome built in all probability by Herod,[380] and situated south of the Temple area.[381] The association with horses in both cases undoubtedly caused this erroneous identification.

Almost certainly mistaken is TJ's identification of "Hazerhatticon which is on the border of Hauran"[382] with "the pool (or: pond) of the Agebeans (or: Agbeans)." Despite various attempts, neither this tribe (or: its territory) nor Hazerhatticon nor the nearby Hazar-enon have been satisfactorily identified.[383]

Another characteristic misidentification is TJ's rendering of the southern border town of Tamar (תמר), in Ezek. 47:19a as Jericho, presumably because

---

Commagene; cf. Levy, NHW, p. 155, s.v. גרממיא. Jastrow, *op. cit.*, p. 270, s.v. גרממיא, identifies Germamia with the land of the Cimmerii (on whose history and migrations in Asia Minor, cf. Pauly-Wissowa-Kroll, *Real-Encyclopädie der Classischen Altertumswissenschaft*, Vol. I, cols. 397ff., s.v. Kimmerier). On the other hand both Talmudim identify Gomer, not Togarmah, with Germamia; cf. T.Y. Meg. *ibid.;* T.B. Yoma 10a.

376. Cf. אנציקלופדיה מקראית מקראית, Vol. II, cols. 518—519, s.v. גמדים. If, as some think, the correct reading is גמרים (from גמר, cf. Gen. 10:2—3), TJ's rendering would hardly be tenable. In any case it is probably little more than guesswork.

377. Cf. Jer. 51:27b. TJ also assumes that מצור (= מצרים = Egypt) in Mic. 7:12b, refers to Armenia Major—a manifest impossibility.

378. Cf. Am. 4:3b.

379. On the probable location of the Horse Gate, cf. also Neh. 3:26—29.

380. Cf. Josephus, Ant. XV, 8, 1, par. 268 (Loeb Classical Library edition, pp. 128f., n. b); XVII, 10, 2, par. 255; Bell. II, 3, 1, par. 44. Cf. also Gen. 14:17b, where MT "the King's Valley" = Targ. Onk. "the place of the race-course of the king."

381. Cf. Bell. *ad loc.*

382. Ezek. 47:16b.

383. Cf. *ibid.* 14:17a; Num. 34:9a. Cf. אנציקלופדיה מקראית, Vol. III, cols. 275—6, s.v. חצר עינון and חצר התיכון; cf. Press, *op. cit.*, vol. I, Introd., p. 37. Quite improbable are the identifications mentioned by H. Bar-Daroma in his work, זה גבול הארץ (Jerusalem 1958), p. 262, n. 268.

Jericho is described as עיר התמרים ("the city of palm trees") in Deut. 34:3 and II Chron. 28:15a.[384] It is also possible that, since MT speaks of the area as "... southward from Tamar," the Targumist had in mind Hazazon-Tamar,[385] i.e., En-gedi,[386] which is indeed south of Jericho.

Equally mistaken is TJ's identification of Baal-tamar, near Gibeah in Benjamin[387] with "the plain of Jericho."[388] The same holds true for TJ's rendering of Ezek. 39:11a[389]—"the valley of the ford (or: pass) east of the sea of Ginnosar." Since MT undoubtedly refers to the area east of the Dead Sea, TJ's translation is likely to have originated at a time when the Palestinian Jewish community was concentrated mainly in Galilee (i.e., after the Bar-Kochba war of 132-135 C.E.) so that "east of the sea" would immediately bring to mind the sea of Galilee rather than the remote Dead Sea much further south.

In the extreme south, too, TJ regularly misidentifies Kadesh, which is situated in the Negev wilderness,[390] with Rekem,[391] a place in Transjordan, identified with Petra by Josephus,[392] and regarded as part of the eastern boundary of Eretz Israel.[393]

As one would expect, errors of identification in TJ are even more frequent where foreign countries are concerned. For example, the Egyptian city of No-amon,[394] which is undoubtedly the ancient city of Thebes in Upper Egypt, becomes in TJ Alexandria, a great port founded by Alexander the

384. Jericho was internationally famous for its palm trees in the Roman period; cf. Pliny, Hist. Nat. V, 14; Tacitus, Hist. V, 6. Cf. also Jud. 1:16a, where MT "from the city of palm trees" = TJ "from the city of Jericho." This identification is, however, rather doubtful; cf. D. W. Nowack, *Handkommentar zum Alten Testament, Richter-Ruth* (Göttingen 1900), p. 7; אוציקלופדיה מקראית, Vol. VI, col. 218, s.v. עיר התמרים. On the actual location of Tamar, cf. *ibid.* and Press, *op. cit.*, vol. IV, p. 975, s.v. תמר.

385. Cf. Gen. 14:7b.

386. Cf. II Chron. 20:2b.

387. Cf. Jud. 20:29—33.

388. Cf. אנציקלופדיה מקראית, Vol. II, cols. 292—3.

389. MT: "the Valley of the Travellers (or: of Abarim) east of the sea" viz., the Dead Sea.

390. Cf. Press, *op. cit.*, IV, pp. 816f. and bibliography cited there.

391. Cf. Jud. 11:16b.17b; Ezek. 47:19a; 48:28b. So also Targ. Onk. on Gen. 14:7a; 16:14b; 20:1a; Num. 13:26a; 20:1a.14a.16b.22a; 33:36b.37a; Deut. 1:46a.

392. Cf. Ant. IV, 7, 1, par. 161.

393. Cf. M. Git. I, 1—2. For a full discussion of the problem, cf. B. Maisler (Mazar), in *Tarbiz* XX (1949), p. 316.

394. Cf. Nah. 3:8a. Elsewhere it is referred to briefly as No; cf. Jer. 46:25a; Ezek. 30:14b,15b,16a.

Great and situated on the Mediterranean near the Nile delta, hundreds of miles north of Thebes. The district of Pathros in Upper Eyypt, though usually rendered literally, is transformed in a marginal note of TJ[395] on Is. 11:11b to נסיוטאי (correct reading: גסיוטאי), i.e., the inhabitants of Casiotis, a district surrounding Mt. Casius, east of Pelusium in northeastern Egypt.[396]

Even more erroneous is TJ's occasional identification of Cush (usually rendered Ethiopia, i.e., Nubia, though occasionally identical with Arabian tribes[397]) with India.[398] The reason for this extraordinary confusion may be twofold. On the one hand, no Jews were known to be living in Ethiopia during the Talmudic age, while some Jews did get as far as India; on the other, there was an opinion expressed in the Talmud[399] that India and Ethiopia mentioned in Esther 1:1b were actually close to one another. Even so, it is a rather strange identification, all the more surprising since it is not followed consistently.

Turning north to Syria, we find that in Isaiah 11:11b, a TJ marginal note misidentifies Hamath in central Syria, with Antioch, the Seleucid capital in extreme northwestern Syria. Rather improbable, too is TJ's identification of the territory of the Maacathites in Jos. 12:5a—which was situated in the extreme northern Golan—with the Hellenistic city of Epicoerus (or: Epikairos), which was apparently further south, east of the Jordan.[400]

Some very bad misidentifications were also made by TJ in Mesopotamia. Thus, the area of Kir, which was probably in Assyria, and from where the Arameans were said to have originated,[401] is rendered Cyrene (pronounced Kyrene)[402]—a north African town west of Egypt—probably because of homophony. The north Syrian district of Eden, on the banks of the Euphrates, known in antiquity as Bit Adini and mentioned in Ezek. 27:23a, is identified by TJ with Adiabene, which was situated on the left bank of the upper Tigris. Inconsistently, Ashkenaz, in Jer. 51:27a, is also translated Adiabene in

---

395. Cf. Sperber's edition of נביאים אחרונים, p. 28.

396. So according to Jastrow, p. 261, s.v. גסיוטא. Cf. also Gen. 10:14a, where MT פתרסים = Targ. Ps.-Jon. נסיוטאי (i.e., גסיוטא).

397. Cf. אנציקלופדיה מקראית, Vol. IV, cols. 65–69, s.v. כוש.

398. Cf. Is. 11:11b; 18:1b; Zeph. 3:10a.

399. Cf. T.B. Meg. 11a.

400. So according to Ptolemy V, 16, 9. Cf. also Targ. Onk. on Deut. 3:14a and S. Klein, עבר הירדן היהודי (Vienna 1925), p. 79.

401. Cf. Am. 9:7b.

402. Cf. II Kings 16:9a; Am. 1:5b; 9:7b.

TJ,[403] although the proximity of Ashkenaz to the territory of various peoples in Anatolia and Armenia[404] renders this identification very doubtful if not altogether untenable.

Further west, Sepharad in Ob. 20a—which is probably identical with Sardis, the capital of Lydia in Asia Minor[405]—is rendered "Ispamia" (= Spain) by TJ—an error which has stuck to Sepharad to the present day. Turning towards Europe, we find that TJ identifies the island of Caphtor (= Crete) with Cappadocia in Asia Minor,[406] the error being due no doubt to homophony. Similarly, TJ misidentifies "the isles (or: coasts) of Chittim"—either Cyprus[407] or the Aegean islands—with Apulia in Italy.[408] Similarly, TJ wrongly identifies the "coastlands" (or: islands) of Elishah, in Ezek. 27:7b, with Italy.

Finally, Tarshish, in I Kings 10:22; 22:49a; and Jer. 10:9a—the identity of which has never been satisfactorily determined[409]—is arbitrarily rendered "Africa" in TJ; while elsewhere[410] it is translated ימא ("sea").[411]

Very rarely, we come across a TJ rendering, which changes a generic term into a place name. Thus, in Jer. 48:6, where the Moabites are urged to flee in order to save themselves, they are told that they would be "like a tamarisk (כערוער; LXX and Aquila: "like a wild ass"—reading כערוד instead of כערוער) in the wilderness." Since Aroer was also a border town on the river Arnon which frequently changed hands between the Israelites and the Moabites,[412] there may indeed be a word play intended. At any rate, TJ renders, "like the tower of Aroer that is situated (lit., rests) alone in the wilderness."

---

403. Cf. also Gen. R. XXXVII, 1 (on Gen. 10:3), where Ashkenaz = Asia, and Riphath = Adiabene.

404. Cf. Gen. 10:3.

405. Cf. אנציקלופדיה מקראית, Vol. V, col. 1100.

406. Cf. Jer. 47:4b and Am. 9:7b. So also LXX as well as Targ. Onk. on Deut. 2:23b.

407. So already Josephus, Ant. I, 6, 1, par. 128. On the problem of the identity of כתים, cf. אנציקלופדיה מקראית, IV, cols. 394–398, and the bibliography cited there.

408. Cf. Num. 24:24a, where כתים is identified with the Romans by Targ. Onk. and Targ. Yer., and with Italy by Targ. Ps.-Jon.

409. Cf. *Encyclopaedia Judaica*, Vol. 15, col. 825, s.v. Tarshish. It is likely that the meaning varies in different contexts.

410. Cf. Is. 2:16a; 23:1a,14a; 66:19a; Ezek. 27:12a,25a; 38:13a; Jonah 1:3b; 4:2a.

411. Cf. Churgin, p. 44. See also Pss. 72:10a, where MT Tarshish is rendered טרסיס.

412. Cf. Press, *op. cit.*, IV, p. 755, s.v. ערער-ג; cf. אנציקלופדיה מקראית, VI, cols. 397–399, s.v. 2-ערער.

Another example of such an unusual rendering is Is. 10:29a, where MT עברו מעברה ("they are gone over the pass," i.e., a mountain pass) is translated by TJ, "they pass the Jordan." TJ's rendering, which does not fit the context at all, was evidently influenced by the expression מעברות הירדן ("fords of the Jordan") in Jud. 3:28b.[413]

Finally in Jon. 2:6b, MT "Reeds (סוף) were wrapped about my head" becomes in TJ "the Red Sea (ימא דסוף) is suspended above my head." Here we have in effect a homiletical interpretation of סוף, which is due exclusively to the partial homophony of סוף and ים סוף. TJ's interpretation is probably the basis of a Midrash preserved in Pirkei de-R. Eliezer, ch. 10, according to which God showed Jonah the Red Sea through which the Israelites had passed.

In most cases, however, the process is reversed and geographical names are translated into generic terms, which often border on Midrash. For example, in Jerusalem a locality by the name of Goah (געה), mentioned in Jer. 31:38(39), which was evidently no longer known by that name in the Talmudic age,[414] is transformed in TJ to "the calf's (or: heifer's) pool." TJ connects געה with the verb געה ("to low"), usually associated with the sound produced by young cattle. It has been surmised that the place may have been near a slaughter-house.[415]

Another, more homiletical interpretation is provided by TJ on Joel 4:2a.12a, where MT "the valley of Jehoshaphat" is rendered, "the valley where judgment is given." Although this rendering may not be as far-fetched as it sounds, since the context refers to God judging the nations in the valley of Jehoshaphat,[416] — it is on the whole more likely that the valley in question was meant to be the valley of Hinnom (or: Ben-hinnom) south of Jerusalem.[417] Similarly, too, "the valley of decision" (עמק החרוץ) in Joel 4:14b, is rendered by TJ "the valley where judgment is given." Here again, although TJ's translation may be reasonably accurate, it is noteworthy that Eusebius[418] identifies the valley with that dividing Jerusalem from the

413. Cf. also T.B. Ber. 28a: הרואה . . . מעברות הירדן ("He who sees . . . the fords of the Jordan").

414. Goah has not been satisfactorily identified; cf. אנציקלופדיה מקראית, Vol. II, cols. 539–40, s.v. געה.

415. *Ibid.*

416. Jehoshaphat means literally, "The Lord judges."

417. Cf. Eusebius, Onomasticon 170, 1.10; cf. also אנציקלופדיה מקראית, Vol. VI, s.v. עמק יהושפט, cols. 297–298.

418. *Op. cit.*, 118, 1.18; cf. אנציקלופדיה מקראית, *ibid.*

Mount of Olives, i.e., the Kidron Valley. Although couched in homiletic terms, the prophet probably had a real locality in mind when he thought of a place where God would judge the nations. Since the valley of Hinnom was notor-ious for the human sacrifices offered there,[419] while the valley of Kidron served as a burial place for the dead since time immemorial, these valleys must have seemed eminently suitable as the venue for the Last Judgment.

East and southeast of Jerusalem, the geographic depression known as the Aravah is almost invariably rendered as "the plain" not only by TJ,[420] but by all the Targumim.[421] The real meaning of Aravah is in all probability "a dry, desolate region,"[422] which is also indicated by the fact that it is frequently mentioned in apposition or parallel to "desert."[423] Possibly, the definite article usually attached to Aravah (הערבה) may have induced the targumists to render a geographic term as if it were a generic one.

Due east of the southern Aravah, the part of Edom known as Teman is invariably rendered "south" (דרומא) in TJ.[424] The same applies to the Negev, which is always translated "south," even where the geographical area of the Negev is undoubtedly indicated.[425]

In southern Judah, Kiriath Sepher, the erstwhile name of Debir,[426] is rendered "the city of the court" (קרית ארכי) in TJ, presumably because the targumist could not imagine Sepher in a Canaanite city to have any other meaning. Sepher in the sense of "book" was confined to sacred literature in the Talmudic age. The only alternative, however, would be secular court records.

Further north, the locality known as "the cistern of Sirah"[427] is rendered

---

419. Cf. Jer. 7:31f.; 19:6; 32:35a.

420. Cf., e.g., Jos. 3:16a; 8:14a; 11:16a; 12:1b; 12:3a; 18:18a; *et passim.* The only exceptions, due no doubt to the context, are Jer. 50:12b and 51:43a, where MT "Aravah" = TJ "destroyed."

421. Cf., e.g., Targ. Onk., Targ. Ps.-Jon. and Targ. Yer. on Deut. 1:1b.7a; 2:8a; 3:17; 4:49a; 11:30a; *et passim.*

422. Cf. אנציקלופדיה מקראית, VI, col. 364, s.v. ערבה.

423. Cf., e.g., Is. 35:6b; 40:3; 41:19; 51:3a; Jer. 2:6b; 17:6; 50:12b; 51:43a.

424. Cf. Jos. 12:3b; Jer. 49:7a,20a, Ezek. 25:13a; Am. 1:12a; Ob.9a; Hab. 3:3a.

425. Cf. Jos. 10:40a; 12:8a; 15:19a; Jud. 1:9b,15a; I Sam. 30:1b; Is. 21:1b; 30:6a; Jer. 13:19a; 17:26a; 32:44a; 33:13a; Zech. 7:7b.

426. Cf. Jos. 15:15b; Jud. 1:11b.

427. II Sam. 3:26a. On the exact location of the cistern of Sirah—approximately 3700 meters north of Hebron—, cf. Josephus, Ant. VII, 1, 5, par. 34; Press, *op. cit.,* I, p. 64, s.v. בור הסרה; cf. אנציקלופדיה מקראית, Vol. II, col. 43, s.v. בור הסירה.

by TJ "the cistern of the thorn." TJ's translation is undoubtedly due to one of the meanings of the word סיר (plur. סירים).[428] The valley of Repahim near Jerusalem is turned by TJ into "the valley of the warriors,"[429] evidently because "the Rephaim" mentioned in Gen. 14:5a and Deut. 2:11a (rendered גברין or גבריא by Targ. Onk. and Targ. Ps.-Jon.) were believed to have been mighty giants.

North of Judah, in the territory of Benjamin, the town of Bahurim[430] is rendered "young men" in TJ—just as if it were a generic term. Not far from there, Shebarim, a locality between ancient Ai and Jericho[431] is derived by TJ from the root שבר ("to break") and rendered "they broke (or: "destroyed") them."

Purely midrashic designations are given in TJ to the two rocky crags Bozez and Seneh[432] near Michmash and Geba in the land of Benjamin.[433] According to TJ, Bozez was "slippery" (or: "a smooth slope"), while Seneh was "a well trodden place." It has been suggested[434] that Seneh (סנה) is associated by the Targumist with מסנאי ("shoes" in Aramaic)—hence "a well trodden place."

A homiletical interpretation is also offered by TJ on the locality—or, more probably, two localities—known as Ebenezer.[435] TJ's rendering, "Stone of Help," while in agreement with that given in I Sam. 7:12, is nevertheless midrashic in character, since the places in question were of course described by their Hebrew names, not by any Aramaic equivalents.

Typically midrashic is TJ's rendering of "the land of Zuph"[436] as "the

428. Cf. Is. 34:13a; Hos. 2:8a; Nah. 1:10a; Eccl. 7:6a.

429. Cf. Jos. 2:16a; II Sam. 5:18b.22b; 23:13b; Is. 17:5b. On the location of the Valley of Refaim, cf. אנציקלופדיה מקראית, VI, cols. 299–300.

430. Cf. II Sam. 3:16b; 16:5a; 17:18b; I Kings 2:8a.

431. Cf. Jos. 7:5a.

432. Cf. I Sam. 14:4b.

433. *Ibid.*, v. 5.

434. Cf. אנציקלופדיה מקראית, V, col. 1061, s.v. סנה.

435. Cf. I Sam. 4:1b; 5:1b; 7:12a. Cf. Y. Elitzur, אבן העזר, in ספר זיידל (Jerusalem 1962), pp. 111–118. According to Elitzur, there were two places by that name, neither of which was inhabited. They were named after (altar?) stones called symbolically אבן העזר ("stone of help," cf. I Sam. 7:12). The one mentioned in connection with the battle of Aphek was situated near Tel Rosh Ha-ayin, in south-western Ephraim, while Samuel's victory against the Philistines was gained in the area of another Mizpah, in the mountains of Benjamin.

436. I Sam. 9:5a. Zuph was near modern Ramallah, due north of Jerusalem; cf. Press, *op. cit.*, pp. 51–2.

land in which there is a prophet." As pointed out by Rashi, TJ connects Zuph (צוּף) with צוּפה (lit., "watchman") used in connection with the prophet Ezekiel.[437] Similarly, "of Ramathaim-zophim," in I Sam. 1:1a, is homiletically interpreted to read in TJ: ". . . from Ramah, of the disciples of the prophets." In this way Elkanah is transformed into a prophetic figure.[438]

A rather difficult problem is posed by TJ's interpretation of "the land of Shaalim," in I Sam. 9:4b—an area believed to have been in the southeastern section of the territory of Ephraim.[439] TJ renders, ארע מתברא (lit., "broken land"), which is hard to explain either topographically or etymologically. There is no possible connection between שעלים and תבר (Heb. שבר). On the other hand, an alternative reading of TJ, ארע מדברא - "land of the wilderness"—would make good sense, since the area in question is on the edge of the wilderness.

Some identify "the land of Shaalim" with "the land of Shual" mentioned in I Sam. 13:17b.[440] TJ, however, translates the latter, "the land of the south." One must assume that TJ misplaced the land of Shual into the area of Lod (Lydda), which, as we have seen, was known as הדרום (Aram. דרומא)—"the South."

Religious reasons rather than topographical or homiletical ones seem to have determined TJ's rendering of Baal-hazor, north of Bethel, in or near the territory of Ephraim,[441] as "the plain of Hazor." Since Baal-hazor was actually situated on a high mountain according to most scholars,[442] the motivation for the change must have been a disinclination to use Baal in a name—just as in the book of Samuel names like Esh-baal and Merib-baal[443] are changed to Ish-bosheth and Mephibosheth, respectively.

Further north, Harosheth-ha-goiim[444] is transformed in TJ into "the might of the cities of the nations"—a midrashic explanation only partly

437. Cf. Ezek. 3:17a; 33:7a.
438. Cf. also T.B. Meg. 14a, where Elkanah is depicted as "one of two hundred prophets who prophesied for Israel . . ."
439. Cf. Press, *op. cit.*, Vol. I, p. 52; Z. Vilnay, *op. cit.*, Vol. I (א-ה), col. 333.
440. Cf. *ibid.*
441. Cf. II Sam. 13:23a.
442. Cf. אנציקלופדיה מקראית, II, col. 288, s.v. בעל חצור; Press, *op. cit.*, I, p. 113, s.v. בעל חצור.
443. Cf. I Chron. 8:33–34.
444. Cf. Jud. 4:13b. Its exact location has been disputed, though it is likely to have been south-east of Haifa; cf. Press, *op. cit.*, p. 366, s.v. חרשת הגוים; Vilnay, *op. cit.*, col. 2512, s.v. חרושת הגוים.

based on etymological grounds. Almost equally difficult to explain is TJ's rendering of MT "the hill of Moreh (גבעת המורה) in the valley,"[445] which turns out to be "the hill that overlooks the valley." Possibly, TJ connects "Moreh" in the sense of "indicating," "showing," with "overlooking."

TJ provides a rather complicated as well as inconsistent rendering of "the oak in Zaananim"—a locality in Galilee near Kedesh on the southern border of Naphtali[446]—mentioned in Jos. 19:33a (where TJ translates literally) and Jud. 4:11b. In the latter verse, TJ renders, "the plain of marshes," which happens to agree more or less with the interpretation given in the Jerusalem Talmud[447]—"the marshes (אגניא) of Kedesh." S. Klein[448] has plausibly suggested that אגניא was the Aramaic equivalent of Heb. בקעה, which could be either a plain or a marsh. In any case, both the Targumist and the Rabbis evidently connected בצעננים with בצעי המים (watery swamps) mentioned in the Babylonian Talmud.[449]

Some place names are provided with literal (though not necessarily accurate) translations in TJ, and, conversely, unnamed geographical areas are given names which seem suitable to the Targumist in the light of the description and context of the verse. Thus, "the stronghold of Zion"[450] becomes the "fortress (חקרא) of Zion" in TJ, possibly because of the phonetic coincidence with the Greek *achra,* the notorious Hellenistic fortress in Jerusalem during the Maccabean age. David's desert "stronghold"[451] is also rendered חקרא in TJ. Similarly, Geba, where the Israelite and Philistine armies faced each other[452] becomes "the hill" in TJ. The valley of Elah where David slew Goliath[453] is translated "the plain of the terebinth" in TJ. Likewise, too, Jeremiah's "salt land"[454] is turned in TJ into "the land of Sodom"—no doubt because the salty soil near the Dead Sea happens to be in the general area where ancient Sodom used to be situated.

Another attempt at a literal rendering of a topographical designation is

---

445. Jud. 7:1b. The hill of Moreh faces Mt. Gilboa, north of the Valley of Jezreel.
446. Cf. אנציקלופדיה מקראית, I, cols. 327–8; Press, *op. cit.,* I, p. 19.
447. Cf. T.Y. Meg. I, 1, 70a.
448. ארץ הגליל (Jerusalem, 1946), p. 133.
449. Cf. T.B. Sanh.96a; cf. also T.B. Shav. 16a: ביצעין.
450. II Sam. 5:7a; cf. also v. 9a.
451. Cf. I Sam. 22:4b.5a; II Sam. 5:17b.
452. Cf. I Sam. 14:5b.
453. Cf. *ibid.* 17:2a.19a; 21:10a.
454. Jer. 17:6b.

made by TJ in its interpretation of "the stone Ezel" (האבן האזל) in I Sam. 20:19b,[455] which is rendered, "the stone of coming," taking אזל as a verbal noun from the Aramaic root אזל ("to go").

Finally, TJ identifies "the graves of the common people," where Josiah king of Judah cast the ground dust of the Asherah,[456] with the graves of an idolatrous shrine (לקברי גליא), possibly at Beit Jalla near Jerusalem.[457]

455. According to LXX, apparently based on a *Vorlage* אבן הגל, the meaning is "the stone heap."

456. Cf. II Kings 23:6b.

457. Cf. T.B. Meg. 6a; A.Z. 46a; cf. also S. Horowitz, Palestine, p. 129.

The authors would like to express their gratitude to Prof. Yehudah Elitzur and Dr. Zev Vilnay who have kindly provided us with up-to-date information on the precise locations of a number of biblical places mentioned in Targum Jonathan under different names.

Theological Concepts in Targum Jonathan

INTRODUCTION

There is no theme in TJ which can compare in sheer abundance of material with the subject of theology. There is hardly a chapter in the Prophets where TJ does not deviate from the literal meaning of the text in order to bring home a theological concept. Indeed, there are numerous chapters where almost every verse is utilized to emphasize certain theological views which are not implicit in MT, which may indeed contradict it. It would be virtually impossible even to enumerate, still less scrutinize and analyze, all the anthropomorphisms and anthropopathisms in TJ. Only a relatively small selection of the more significant material will be made in this chapter. Neither will it be possible to provide the direct textual evidence in each statement on the theological concepts of TJ. For the most part, all that can be done is to provide the Biblical references which can then be checked whenever desired.

The theology of TJ, is, with rare exceptions, identical with orthodox Judaism as developed by the Pharisees and rabbis. As in other areas, it is the religious ideology of the school of Rabbi Akiba which prevails throughout.[1] It was precisely because the Bible frequently expresses concepts and views which were later rejected by the rabbis that TJ, which was designed

---

1. Cf., for example, I Kings 12:15, where the Hebrew text explicitly states that Rehoboam's refusal to accede to the request of the people was "brought about by the Lord." Since this would imply predestination and thus contradict Rabbi Akiba's doctrine of free will (cf. M. Aboth III, 15), TJ renders, "For there was a division before the Lord." In other words, the division of the kingdom took place with God's knowledge and concurrence, but was not predetermined by him. Similarly, in I Kings 12:24, where God is represented as saying, "For this king (viz., the division of the kingdom) is from me," TJ weakens the theological impact by rendering, "For this thing is from before my *Memra*" (i.e., the divine logos). The unorthodox concept of divine predestination is thus circumvented.

for the religious edification of the masses, significantly changes the translation, with a view to eliminating all traces of unorthodox theology.

1. THE CONCEPT OF GOD

In accordance with basic Jewish religious thinking, TJ stresses the exclusive existence of one God, appropriately changing passages where ambiguity or imprecise language might lead to doubt.[2] Thus, the frequent oath introduced with the words, "as the Lord lives"—implying a comparative or possibly conditional statement—is invariably rendered by a declarative asertion of faith in a living God: "The Lord exists."[3]

Similarly, Jeremiah's prediction (16:14–15) that ". . . it shall no longer be said, 'As the Lord lives . . .'"—which could initially mislead the reader to imagine that the existence of a living God would no longer be averred—is judiciously changed by TJ to ". . . They shall no longer speak of the might of thp Lord . . ."

Where God's exclusive existence and power are implied in the form of a question, TJ takes care to change the question into a positive statement asserting these basic theological principles and flatly denying the existence of any other divinity or power.[4] Even when we are explicitly informed that the Israelites "did not believe in the Lord their God,"[5] TJ, horrified no doubt at such impiety, weakens the devastating effect of the biblical denunciation by introducing the *Memra* (word, logos) of God as the object of their disbelief. In other words, while one might disbelieve the word of God, which was presumably transmitted by a prophet, it was inconceivable to deny belief in God Himself.

Even a negatively phrased question such as Rabshakeh's statement—"Is it without the Lord that I have come up against this place (or: land) to destroy it?"[6]—was considered unacceptable despite Rabshakeh's unam-

---

2. Cf., e.g., Is. 44:8b, where MT ואין צור בל ידעתי could be misunderstood to imply divine *ignorance* of other gods, but not an unqualified denial of their existence. TJ accordingly renders: ". . . and there is none that is strong, unless strength is given to him from before Me."

3. Cf., e.g., I Sam. 25:26; II Sam. 12:5; 14:11; 15:21; I Kings 1:29; 17:12; 18:10,15; 22:14; II Kings 2:4,6; 3:14; 4:30; 5:16,19; Jer. 12:16; 38:16.

4. Cf. II Sam. 22:32.

5. II Kings 17:14.

6. II Kings 18:25 = Is. 36:10.

biguous clarification that "God said to me, 'Go up against this land and destroy it.'"[7] TJ, sensing in Rabshakeh's rhetorical qustion a possible denial of the divine role in history,[8] counters by substituting the *Memra* for God: "Is it without the *Memra* of the Lord that I have come up ...?"

Just as it is inconceivable to deny God, it is impossible to speak falsely,[9] loathe,[10] act with effrontry,[11] reject,[12] devise evil,[13] deal treacherously[14] or rebel[15] against the Almighty. Where such expressions do occur, TJ substitutes the divine *Memra* for God. The *Memra*, like the *Shechinah* (Divine Presence) often acts as a sort of lightning conductor drawing away unseemly expressions from God.

Even less offensive acts against God—such as forsaking,[16] ignoring[17] or

---

7. *Ibid.* = *ibid.*

8. TJ generally emphasizes God's active role in history. Cf., e.g., Is. 48:21a, where MT "They thirsted not" is changed by TJ to "He (viz., God) did not suffer them to thirst." Similarly, Is. 49:25a—"Even the captives of the mighty shall be taken, and the prey of the tyrant shall be rescued—is transformed by TJ from the passive to the active state, with God as the active subject force: "Even that which the mighty have taken captive I will restore, and the prey which the powerful have taken I will deliver." Likewise, Hos. 10:10b, MT "... nations shall be gathered against them," becomes in TJ (where the tense is understood to be the perfect rather than the imperfect), "I gathered nations against them." See also *infra*, n. 29.

9. Cf. Jer. 5:12a (MT "They have spoken falsely of the Lord" = TJ "They have spoken falsely of the *Memra* of the Lord").

10. Cf. Zech. 11:8b, where MT "I became impatient with them and they also loathed Me" is doubly unacceptable, since it attributed impatience—a human failing—to God, and an attitude amounting to blasphemy to Israel. These objections are eliminated in TJ: "My *Memra* detested them because their soul abhors My worship."

11. Cf. II Kings 19:22 = Is. 37:23. MT "Against whom have you raised your voice and (haughtily) lifted your eyes? Against the Holy One of Israel," is significantly altered in TJ: "Before whom have you raised your voice and lifted your eyes, and said words that are not proper? Before the Holy One of Israel." Cf. also I Kings 14:9b and Ezek. 23:35a, where MT "... you have cast Me (viz., God) behind your back" is softened by TJ to "... you have removed My worship (Ezek. 23:35a: "the fear of Me") from before your eyes."

12. Cf. I Sam. 8:7b: (MT "... they have rejected Me [viz., God] = TJ "... they have detested the worship of me").

13. Cf. Hos. 7:15b (MT "... they devise evil against me = "... they continue to devise [or: they are devising to add] evil things before Me").

14. Cf. TJ on Jer. 3:20; 5:11; Ezek. 20:27; Hos. 5:7; 6:7.

15. Cf. TJ on Jer. 3:13; 33:8; Ezek. 20:25; Hos. 10:9; 14:1; Zeph. 3:11.

16. Cf. TJ on Jud. 10:3,6,10; I Sam. 8:8; I Kings 9:9; II Kings 22:17; Is. 1:28; Jer. 1:16; 2:13,17,19; 5:19; 15:6; 16:11; 19:4; Hos. 4:10. A notable exception to the rule is TJ on Is. 17:10a, where MT "... you have forgotten the God of your salvation" is rendered by TJ, "... you have *forsaken* the God of your salvation."

17. Cf. TJ on Is. 57:11; 65:12; 66:4.

forgetting[18] Him—are inadmissible in the theological system of TJ, which substitutes the worship or fear of God—or else the divine law—for the Almighty Himself. TJ indeed frowns on any act or saying involving disrespect towards God, either directly or indirectly. The detailed treatment of this complicated topic will be reserved for the next section entitled "God and Man."

TJ also maintains firmly the eternity of God and of the kingdom of God. Hence the divine declaration, "I am the first and I am the last,"[19] which implies a beginning and an end—an impossible theological proposition,—is subtly altered by TJ into, "I am from of old, yea, the everlasting ages are mine." Similarly, a prediction such as Micah 4:7b ('. . . and the Lord will reign over them"), connoting a *future* reign of God and its absence in the past and present, was unacceptable in TJ's orthodox theology. TJ, therefore, renders: ". . . and the kingdom of the Lord shall be revealed unto them."[20] It follows that God *always* reigns, but His kingdom will be revealed to those who through ignorance are unaware of it.

For exactly the same reason, Obadiah 1:21b—"And the kingdom *shall be* the Lord's"—which could be misintrepreted to mean that only in the future would the kingdom be the Lord's, but not in the past or the present—is homiletically expanded by TJ: "And the kingdom of the Lord shall be revealed to all the inhabitants of the earth" (Some versions add: "And the kingdom of the Lord shall endure forever and unto all eternity").

The incomparability of God is another basic doctrine strictly adhered to by TJ.[21] It is likewise impossible to compare anything to the divine

---

18. Cf. TJ on Jud. 3:7; 8:34; 12:9; I Sam. 12:9; Is. 17:10; 51:13; 57:11; Jer. 2:11; 13:25; 18:15; 23:27; Ezek. 22:12; 23:35; Hos. 2:15; 8:14; 13:6. Even an expression like "remembering" God (cf. Jon. 2:8; Zech. 10:9)—implying as it does previous oblivion—is unacceptable to TJ, which therefore replaces "God" by the "worship" and "fear" of God, respectively. So also Targum Onkelos on Deut. 32:18.

19. Is. 44:6; 48:12.

20. Cf. also Exod.15:18, where MT, "The Lord shall reign forever and ever" is translated by Targum Onkelos: "The Lord—His kingdom endures forever and unto all eternity."

21. Cf., e.g., Hos. 14:9b, where MT compares God to an "evergreen cypress." TJ changes this to "I, by my *Memra*, will make him (viz., Ephraim = Israel) like a beautiful cypress." Even the familiar metaphor of God as Father or (in one case) Master, and Israel as his children is often interpreted by TJ in a homiletical fashion or else changed into a theologically acceptable simile. Cf. Is. 1:2b (MT "Sons have I raised and brought up" = TJ 'My people the house of Israel—I have called them children; I have loved them"); *ibid.* 63:16; 64:7a (MT ". . . You are our Father" = TJ ". . . You are the One whose mercies upon us are greater than

attributes.[22] Even a seemingly innocuous statement—such as "There is none like you"[23]—could leave open the possibility of the existence of inferior gods who are indeed not to be put on the same level as the God of Israel, but might yet exercise certain divine functions. However remote such a meaning might seem to a sophisticated theologian, the targumist, who served the unsophisticated synagogue audiences, could not afford to take any risk. Hence the rendering, "There is no one apart from you." Thus, the very existence of other divinities is catagorically denied.

It was for the same reason that Elijah's appeal to the Israelites to make up their minds whether to follow the Lord or Baal[24] was unacceptable in terms of orthodox theology. Clearly, the Israelites could not be left to their own devices to determine whether to worship God or an idol. The very wording of Elijah's call—"If the Lord is God, follow him; but if Baal, then follow him"—was an unheard-of effrontery and came close to blasphemy. There could obviously be no ifs and buts about who was the true God. TJ accordingly renders: "Surely the Lord is God, worship before him alone. Why, then, do you go astray after Baal who is useless?"

Targum Jonathan puts special emphasis on God being the wise and thoughtful Creator of the universe,[25] which he would form anew, i.e., reshape and renew, for the benefit of the righteous.[26] God is the ultimate cause of all "natural" phenomena,[27] and everything in the world belongs to Him.[28] God controls, owns and indeed originates everything that happens in

---

those of a father upon his children"); Jer. 3:4 (MT "...you called to Me, 'My father, you are the friend of my youth'" = TJ "...you prayed before Me, 'My master, you are my redeemer from of old'"); Mal. 1:6b (MT "If I am a father ... and if I am a master" = TJ "If I am *like* a father ... and if I am *like* a master").

22. Cf. Ezek. 10:5, where "the sound of the wings of the cherubim" is compared in MT to "the voice of God Almighty." In TJ, this theologically inadmissible comparison is changed to "like a voice from before the Almighty."

23. I Kings 8:23a.

24. Cf. I Kings 18:21.

25. Cf. Is. 28:29; Jer. 23:23.

26. Cf. Jer. *ibid.*

27. Cf. Ezek. 30:18a, where MT "At Tehaphnehes the day shall be dark = TJ "On Tehaphnehes I will bring darkness by day." In other words, darkness will not come by itself, but will be brought about by God. Similarly, on Jer. 14:22a ("Can the skies give showers?"), TJ adds significantly, "Except by your *Memra.*"

28. Cf., e.g., Is. 14:25a, where TJ changes MT "my mountains" (suggesting the existence of other mountains not belonging to God) to "the mountains of my people." Cf. also *infra*, n. 42.

the world.[29] There is much stress on God's power,[30] which is sometimes exercised through the agency of men;[31] and it follows hence that with divine aid the weak can overcome the strong.[32] God's omnipotence is indeed boundless and unquestionable.[33] Whenever God "speaks"—and He does not directly speak to man,[34]—His words are unalterable decrees.[35] He faithfully fulfills his promises,[36] and He does not "repent" or change His mind.[37] God's ways—which are invariably explained by TJ as "the ways that are

29. Cf. Hos. 8:4a (MT "They made kings, but not through me" = TJ "They made kings, but not through my *Memra*"). Cf. *ibid.* 10:10b, where MT "and nations shall be gathered against them" is changed by TJ from the imperfect passive to the perfect active form: "and I gathered nations against them." The change in tense may have been designed to avoid a prediction of a future calamity. In any case, it is God who determines history — things do not just "happen." For a similar deliberate change from the impersonal to a form indicating divine control of historic events, cf. TJ on Amos 5:9b. See also Jer. 5:10b, where MT "they (viz., the Israelites) are not the Lord's" could create the erroneous impression that Israel was not under the authority of the almighty. Hence TJ's "correction:" "there is no desire in them before the Lord." See also *supra*, n. 8.

30. Cf., e.g., TJ on Nah. 1:2.

31. Cf., I Sam. 12:6a, where MT "It is the Lord who made Moses and Aaron"—an obvious statement of fact which hardly needs reiterating in view of the commonly known concept of God as the universal "Creator"—is remarkably changed by TJ to "It is the Lord who wrought mighty deeds through Moses and Aaron."

32. Cf., e.g., Amos 5:9a: MT "Who makes destruction (Heb. שׁד) flash forth against the strong" = TJ "He makes the weak (apparently reading שׁדוד instead of שׁד) prevail against the mighty."

33. Cf. Is. 14:27b: "His hand is stretched out, and who can turn it back?" The "hand" is symbolic of God's power, and the question in MT is turned by TJ into a categorical negative: ". . . and there is none who can turn it back." Cf. also Jos. 7:9b, where the rhetorical question, ". . . what will You do for Your great name?"—implying the possibility (or at least the appearance) of divine impotence—is changed by one version of TJ into a positive statement, leaving no room for doubt: ". . . You *are* doing for Your great name."

34. Cf., e.g., Hab. 2:16, where MT quotes "what He (viz., God) will speak to me" is changed in TJ to "what will be spoken to me."

35. Cf., e.g., TJ on I Kings 14:11; Ezek. 5:13,15,17; 6:10; 7:8; 21:22,37; 22:14; 23:34; 24:14; 26:5,14; 28:10; 30:12; 34:24; 36:5,6,36; 37:14.

36. Cf. TJ on Zeph. 3:7a and Ezek. 5:13b.

37. Although this is an explicit biblical doctrine (cf. Num. 23:19 and I Sam. 15:29), there are numerous passages which appear to contradict it. Both Targum Onkelos (cf., e.g., Gen. 6:6-7) and TJ invariably reinterpret such passages, so as to avoid anything that might suggest divine changeability or "repentence;" cf., e.g., TJ on Jud. 2:18; I Sam. 15:11,35; Is. 57:6; Jer. 4:28; 15:6; 18:8,10; 20:16; 26:3,13,19; 31:18; 42:10; Hos. 13:14; Joel 2:13-14; Amos 7:3,6; Jon. 1:6; 3:9-10; 4:2; Mal. 3:6.

right before me"[38]—are perfect, and the right way for man is, therefore, to follow the way that is approved by God.[39]

Other basic attributes of God are His omnipresence[40]—implied, though not expressly stated, in a number of passages in which TJ carefully avoids literal renderings indicating that God was "near" or "far" or that He could be "sought" or "found"[41] or that he was a territorially limited deity;[42]—His omniscience at all times of the thoughts and deeds of men[43]—a concept pre-

38. Cf., e.g., Jos. 22:5; Jud. 2:22; Zech. 3:7. Similarly, also Targum Onkelos on Gen. 18:19 *et passim*.

39. Cf., e.g., TJ on Jos. 22:5; Jud. 2:22.

40. Although God's "place" in Hos. 5:15a ("I will return again to my place") is defined in TJ, *ad loc.*, as being in heaven, it is really the *Shechinah* (mentioned by TJ in the beginning of the verse) that is, as it were, allocated heavenly headquarters. This can be clearly seen in TJ on I Kings 8:23a, where "God in heaven" is replaced by the *Shechinah* in TJ. Cf. also Targum on Ps. 115:3.16. God himself is assumed to be everywhere, not only in heaven. Elsewhere, God's "place" is defined by TJ as being in the Sanctuary; cf. Jer. 7:12a, where MT ". . . to My place that was in Shiloh" is rendered in TJ, ". . . to the place of My sanctuary that was in Shiloh." The unorthodox doctrine of pantheism, which could, theoretically, be derived from Jer. 23:24b ("Do I not fill heaven and earth? says the Lord"), is rejected in TJ, where the "glory" of God—not God Himself—fills the heaven and the earth. Because of the concept of God's omnipresence, various divine activities depicted in the Bible which happen to involve movement or confinement to a given place are usually circumvented in the Aramaic Targumim so as to avoid creating the impression that there is any place without the Divine Presence.

41. Cf. TJ on II Kings 2:14; Is. 30:27; 45:19; 55:6; 65:10; Jer. 2:6,8; 10:21; 12:2; 21:2; 23:23; 29:13,14; 37:7; 50:4; Ezek. 20:1,3,31; Hos. 3:5; 5:6,15; 10:12; Amos 5:4,6.

42. Cf. Jos. 22:31a (MT ". . . the Lord is in the midst of us" = TJ ". . . among us dwells the *Shechinah* of the Lord"); I Sam. 26:19b (MT "the inheritance of the Lord" = TJ "the inheritance of the *people* of the Lord"); Is. 66:1 (MT "The heaven is My throne, and the earth is My footstool; . . . and what is the place of My rest?" = TJ "The heaven is the throne of My *glory*, and the earth is a footstool before Me; . . . and where is the dwelling-place of My *Shechinah?*"); Jer. 3:17a (MT "Jerusalem shall be called the throne of the Lord" = TJ "Jerusalem shall be called the place of the house of the Lord's *Shechinah*"); Ezek. 43:7a (MT "This is the place of My throne and the place of the soles of My feet where I dwell" = TJ "This is the house of the throne of My *glory*, and this is the dwelling-place of My *Shechinah* where I will cause My *Shechinah* to dwell"); Hos. 9:3a (MT ". . . the land of the Lord" = TJ ". . . the land of the *Shechinah* of the Lord"); cf. also Jer. 2:7; 7:2,12; 8:19; 16:18; Ezek. 7:22; 36:5,20; 38:16.

43. Cf. TJ on I Sam. 2:8b, where MT ". . . the pillars of the earth are the Lord's "becomes in TJ: ". . . before the Lord are revealed the deeds of the sons of man." Cf. also Jer. 23:24, where MT unequivocally expresses, in words only slightly different from those used by TJ, God's capacity to see even the most "hidden" things. Similarly, TJ on I Sam. 16:7; 24:16; II

cluding the idea of God "forgetting" or "remembering;"[44] His invisibility[45]—occasional statements to the contrary notwithstanding;[46] His
providence, which excludes any possibility that man should ever be, as it
were, out of the Almighty's sight;[47] and His inaudibility,[48] at any rate by
anyone not endowed with the gift of prophecy.[49]

Kings 9:26; Is. 40:10; 62:11; 65:7; Jer. 11:20; 12:3; 18:19; Ezek. 20:32; 35:10; Zech.
4:10.
    Any statement even remotely implying a limitation of God's knowledge or perception is
studiously avoided; cf. Amos 3:2a (MT "You only have I known . . ." = TJ "You only have I
desired"); Hab. 1:2b (MT ". . . You will not hear" = TJ ". . . surely, it is revealed before
You"). Similarly, Hos. 8:4a (MT ". . . they set up princes, but without My knowledge" = TJ
". . . they set up princes [or: they raised to power], but not according to My will"); *ibid.*,
13:5a (MT "I knew you in the wilderness" [leaving open the possibility that God did not know
Israel elsewhere] = TJ "I supplied your needs in the wilderness"); Jer. 20:12b (MT ". . . to
You I have revealed my cause" [implying that God would not otherwise have been aware of
Jeremiah's plea] = TJ ". . . before You I have stated [i.e., complained about] my humiliation"). See also Jer. 23:11b, where MT ". . . I have *found* their wickedness" (implying that
God needs to "find" or discover) is changed in TJ to ". . . their wicked deeds are revealed
before Me." Cf. also Jer. 32:17b,27b, where God's omnipotence is stressed in MT, while TJ's
translation emphasizes God's omniscience. Similarly, also, Targum Onkelos on Gen. 18:14.
    44. Cf. Isaiah 49:14b, where MT ". . . my Lord has forgotten me"—becomes in TJ,
". . . the Lord has rejected me." Similarly, Is. 49:15b. (MT "I will not forget you" = TJ
"My *Memra* will not reject you"); Hos. 4:6b (MT "I will forget your children" = TJ "I will
reject your children"); Amos 8:7b (MT "Surely I will never forget any of their deeds" = TJ
"Surely none of their deeds will ever be forgotten"). How careful the targumists were in their
treatment of such anthropomorphic expressions can be seen in TJ on Jer. 23:39a, where MT
ונשיתי—here used in the sense of "remove" or "tear out," but theoretically capable of bearing
the meaning, "I (i.e., God) will forget"—is homiletically interpreted in TJ, "I will send My
wrath." Noteworthy, too, is Is. 63:11a, where MT "He remembered the days of old" is
convoluted by TJ into "He had pity for the glory of His name because of the remembrance of
His goodness." Finally, Samson's prayer, "O Lord God, remember me" (Jud. 16:28b) is similarly convoluted in TJ: ". . . may the rememberance of me come up before You."
    45. Cf., e.g., Is. 64:3b, where MT ". . . no eye has seen a god besides You" (which could
be interpreted to mean that God can be seen) is given a homiletical twist by TJ: ". . . no eye
has seen what Your people saw—the *Shechinah* of Your glory, O Lord." The concept of
God's invisibility is based on Exod. 33:20b: "Man can not see Me and live."
    46. Cf. Jud. 13:22b (MT "We have seen God" = TJ "We have seen an angel of the Lord");
I Kings 22:19b and Is. 6:1a (MT "I saw the Lord" = TJ "I saw the glory of the Lord");
Ezek. 1:1b and 8:3b (MT "visions of God" = TJ "a vision of prophecy that rested upon me
from before the Lord"). Cf. also Is. 64:3; Zech. 9:14; Mal. 3:2; and Targum Onkelos on
Exod. 24:10a.
    47. Cf. Jon. 2:5a (MT "I am cast out from before your eyes" = TJ "I am cast out from
before your *Memra*"). To say, as the Israelites did, that "the Lord does not see" (Ezek. 9:9b)

As is done by all the Targumim, TJ consistently emphasizes God's incorporeality, and there is hardly a chapter where one or several instances of anthropomorphic expressions suitably changed by TJ cannot be found.

In line with TJ's exalted conception of God, it is impossible to "know" Him,[50] except through His miraculous intervention in history[51] or His more prosaic instruction as revealed in the Torah.[52] One can also approach a degree of the knowledge of God through the fear of God.[53] A special section will be devoted to this topic later in this chapter.

2. GOD AND MAN

By virtue of man's creation by God, there is, in TJ as in the Hebrew Bible, a more or less direct relationship between man and God. However, unlike the Bible, TJ takes immense care to keep this relationship, as it were, at a safe distance.[54] God does *not* do things that man in his simplicity may

---

is blasphemous and hence unrepeatable. Therefore, TJ weakens it to ". . . this is not revealed before the Lord." Similarly, Ezek. 8:12b, MT "The Lord does not see us" = TJ "Our deeds are not revealed before the Lord."

48. Cf. TJ on Is. 64:3a (MT "From of old no one has heard or perceived by the ear" = TJ "From of old no ear has heard the voice of Might [i.e., of the Divine Power]"). Cf. also Ezek. 43:2b, where MT ". . . His voice (or: sound) was like the sound of many waters" is radically transformed by TJ to ". . . the voice (or: sound) of those that bless(ed) His name was like the sound of many waters." Cf. also TJ on I Sam. 12:14-15; Jer. 1:4,11,13; 2:1; 3:13,25; 11:2,6,7; 38:20; Zech. 1:4. See also Targum Onkelos on Gen. 3:8 and Exod. 20:16.

49. The *Bath-Kol* (echo of a heavenly voice) of the post-prophetic talmudic period (cf., e.g., M. Aboth VI, 2; T. B. Ber. 17b; Eruv. 13b; Yoma 9b; Git. 56b; Sanh. 11a; T. Y. Taan. IV, 8, 68d) was a non-prophetic substitute for a divine communication, since no one was qualified to hear or otherwise receive a direct message from God.

50. Cf. Hab. 2:14a, where MT ". . . the earth shall be filled to know the glory of the Lord" = TJ ". . . the earth shall be filled to know the fear of the Lord." TJ also emphasizes that it is impossible to know the "thoughts" or "designs" of the Almighty which are always secrets hidden from man; cf. Mic. 4:12a, where MT "the thoughts of the Lord" = TJ "the secrets of the Lord."

51. Cf. TJ on I Kings 18:37 and Ezek. 20:9.

52. Cf. TJ on Hos. 5:4.

53. Cf. TJ on I Sam. 2:12; Is. 11:9; 45:19; 65:10; Jer. 22:16; 29:13; Hos. 2:22; 4:1; 6:3; 8:2. See also *supra*, n. 50.

54. See *infra*, notes 71-80.

imagine Him to do, neither can man establish any kind of close and intimate relationship with God.

God cannot be identified, even indirectly, with any object, not even with a sacred object like an altar devoted to God.[55] No human activities can be attributed to Him. For example, God does not borrow[56] or stand security for anybody.[57] He does not "shine"[58]—a concept associated primarily with the sun—and He certainly needs no light Himself.[59] God requires no watchman to guard His holy city of Jerusalem,[60] and, generally, He needs no intermediary or assistant to effect his purpose in the world.[61]

God does not, in TJ, communicate directly with man, not even with a prophet, and it is therefore inappropriate to say that He "hides" anything

---

55. Cf. Jud. 6:24a, where Gideon names the altar he had built in honor of God "The Lord is peace." To obviate the impression that the altar may somehow be identified with God, TJ renders: ". . . he worshipped on it before the Lord who had made (or: wrought) peace for him."

56. Cf. I Sam. 1:28 (MT "I have lent him to the Lord; . . . he is lent to the Lord" = TJ "I have handed him over that he should serve before the Lord; . . . he is serving before the Lord").

57. Cf. Is. 38:14b (MT ". . . You be my security" = TJ ". . . answer (lit., do) my prayer" [or: "carry out my request"]).

58. Cf. *ibid.* 60:2b (MT ". . . upon you [viz., Israel] the Lord will shine" = TJ ". . . in you shall dwell the *Shechinah* of the Lord").

59. Cf. I Kings 6:4, where MT "He made for the house (viz., the Temple) windows with recessed frames (lit., translucent [and] closed)" is homiletically expanded by TJ to "He made for the house windows (that were) open on the inside and closed on the outside, and the poles covered the tops of the cedar beams." TJ's explanation agrees with that offered in the Talmud (T. B. Men. 86b), where God is depicted as saying, "I do not need light." See also Rashi, *ad loc.*, who explains that the windows were narrow within because God needs no light, and wide on the outside "to bring light out into the world." The talmudic text is not quite clear—there are in fact two contradictory versions,—but the general import that the windows of the sanctuary were not designed to provide illumination is clear.

60. Cf. Is. 62:6a (MT "Upon your walls, O Jerusalem, I have set watchmen" — TJ "Behold, the righteous works of your fathers, O Jerusalem, are set in order and preserved before Me").

61. Cf. Hos. 12:14a (MT "By a prophet the Lord brought Israel up from Egypt" = TJ "Yea, when your forefathers went down to Egypt, the Lord sent a prophet and brought Israel up from Egypt"). Note that in TJ the role of the prophet (viz., Moses) is left ambiguous, and it is actually God, not the prophet, who brought Israel out of Egypt. Cf. Passover Haggadah: "I, and not a messenger (brought Israel out of Egypt)." Cf. Is. 63:5a (MT "I looked, but there was no one to help; I was appalled, but there was no one to uphold" = TJ "It was revealed before Me that there was no man who had good deeds (to his credit), and it was known before Me that there was no man who would arise and pray for them").

from man.[62] It is also inconceivable for God to hide His face, and TJ invariably explains this gross anthropomorphism as an act of removing the *Shechinah*—usually from Israel.[63]

In His omnipotence it is also impossible to say that God "hearkens" to the voice of a man (in effect, obeys the command of man), not even if that man happens to be Joshua.[64] Being omniscient, God does not have to "look" at men,[65] still less to search for them.[66] When man cries out for help, it is clearly inappropriate to say that God does or does not "hear" or, for that matter, that He does or does not "answer." With rare exceptions, God's "hearing" or "answering" becomes an "acceptance" of prayer in TJ.[67]

Nothing is too "marvelous" or difficult for God;[68] and it is therefore self-evident that He does not have to toil and that He cannot ever be faint or weary—even when bearing the burden of hypocritical religiosity or lack of faith offered by an ungrateful nation.[69] Since God needs no rest, it is obviously quite improper to say that He should be given no rest.[70] In short, God does not behave the way humans do.

Conversely, the distance between God and man in TJ also finds expression in man's incapacity to engage in any act which may appear to bring him physically closer to God. It is impossible for man to literally wait for God;[71]

---

62. Cf. II Kings 4:27b (MT '. . . the Lord has hidden it from me and has not told me" = TJ ". . . from before the Lord it has been hidden from me and it was not told me").

63. Cf. TJ on Is. 8:17; 54:8; 57:17; 59:2; Jer. 33:5; Ezek. 39:23,24,29; Mic. 3:4. Cf. also Targum Onkelos and Targum Pseudo-Jonathan on Deut. 31:17,18; 32:20.

64. Cf. Jos. 10:14a (MT ". . . the Lord hearkened to the voice of a man" = TJ ". . . the prayer of man was accepted before the Lord"). Cf. also TJ on Jud. 13:9; I Kings 17:22.

65. Cf. Hos. 14:9b (MT "I look at him" = TJ "I shall have mercy on them (viz., Israel)".

66. Cf. Amos 9:3a (MT ". . . I will search out" = TJ ". . . I will appoint searchers").

67. Cf. TJ on Jud. 9:7; 11:10; I Sam. 7:9; 8:18; 14:37; 23:4; 28:6,15; II Sam. 22:7.42; I Kings 8:29,30,32,34,35,36,39,43,45,49,52; 18:24,37; II Kings 13:4; Is. 1:15; 41:17; 46:7; 49:8; 58:9; 65:24; Jer. 11:11; 33:3; Ezek. 8:18; Hos. 2:23; 14:9; Amos 5:23; Jon. 2:3; Mic. 3:4; 7:7; Hab. 1:2; Zech. 7:13; 10:6; 13:9; Mal. 3:16. Where there is no prayer for God to "answer," TJ renders either literally (cf., e.g., Jer. 23:35.37; 42:4; Joel 2:19; Zech. 1:13; 3:4; 4:6) or in a convoluted form such as "from before the Lord" (cf., e.g., I Sam. 9:17; Hab. 2:2).

68. Cf. Zech. 8:6b, where MT גם בעיני יפלא, though meant as a question, is grammatically ambiguous, since it is not introduced with the interrogative Hé. TJ therefore renders, "Shall they also be precious before Me?" Cf. also Gen. 18:14.

69. Cf. TJ on Is. 1:14; 40:28; Jer. 15:6; Mal. 2:17.

70. Cf. Is. 62:7a (MT ". . . give Him no rest" = TJ ". . . let not their memorial cease from before Him").

71. Cf. Zeph. 3:8a (MT ". . . wait for Me" = TJ ". . . hope for My *Memra*").

turn to Him;[72] follow Him;[73] draw near;[74] come or stand before Him;[75] walk or generally be with God;[76] remove or draw away from Him;[77] wander or stray or be far from Him;[78] hide from Him[79] or, for that matter, return to

72. Cf. Is. 45:22a (MT "Turn to Me" = TJ "Turn to My *Memra*").

73. Cf. Jer. 3:19b (MT ". . . and you would not turn from following Me" = TJ "and you would not turn from (following) after My worship"); cf. II Kings 23:3a (MT "to walk after the Lord" = TJ "to walk after the worship of the Lord").

74. Cf. Jer. 30:21 (MT ". . . he shall approach Me, for who would dare of himself to approach Me?" = TJ ". . . they shall follow My worship eagerly, for who is it whose heart would desire to draw near to My worship?"); Ezek. 46:9a (MT "When the people of the land come before the Lord" = TJ "When the people of the land come to worship before the Lord"). TJ does not permit even the priests to approach God; they have to be satisfied with "drawing near to the worship of God"; cf. Ezek. 42:13; 43:19; 44:13,15.

75. Cf. Mic. 6:6 (MT "With what shall I come before the Lord? . . . Shall I come before Him . . . ?" = TJ "With what shall I worship before the Lord? . . . Shall I worship before Him . . . ?"); Zeph. 3:2b (MT "She does not draw near to her God" = TJ "She does not draw near to the worship of her God"). Cf. I Sam. 16:6b, where MT "Surely, the Lord's annointed is before Him" is changed in TJ to "Surely His annointed one is established before the Lord." Cf. also Is. 45:24b (MT "To Him shall come . . ." = TJ "By His *Memra* shall come" [other versions: "shall confess"]).

76. Cf. Jud. 6:12b (MT "the Lord is with you" = TJ "the *Memra* of the Lord is in support of you"); *ibid.*, 6:13a (MT ". . . if the Lord is with us . . ." = TJ ". . . the *Shechinah* of the Lord is in support of us"); *ibid.* 6:16a (MT "I will be with you" = TJ "My *Memra* will be in support of you") *et passim*.

God does not "dwell" among men, but causes His *Shechinah* to dwell among them; cf. TJ on I Kings 6:13; 8:12; Ezek. 43:9; Zech. 2:14,15; 8:3. See also Targum Onkelos and Targum Psuedo-Jonathan on Exod. 25:8; 29:45,46; Num. 5:3; 35:34; Deut. 12:5.

77. Cf. Ezek. 43:9a (MT "Now let them remove . . . the dead bodies of their kings far away from Me" = TJ "Now let them remove . . . the dead bodies of their kings, so that they should not sin before Me").

78. Cf. Jer. 2:5a (MT ". . . they went far from Me" = TJ ". . . they went far from the fear of Me" Ez.44:10a (MT ". . . the levites who went far from Me" = TJ ". . . the Levites who went astray from My worship"); *ibid.* 44:15a (MT ". . . when the people of Israel went astray from Me" = TJ ". . . the Levites who went astray from My worship"); *ibid.* 44:15a (MT ". . . when the people of Israel went astray from Me" = TJ ". . . when the people of Israel went astray from My worship").

79. Cf. Jer. 23:24a, where the very question posed by MT—"Can a man hide himself in secret places so that I cannot see him?"—is regarded as somewhat derogatory towards God. TJ accordingly renders, "If a man *imagines* to hide himself *as though* in secret, is it not revealed before Me?" Similarly, Amos 9:3 (MT "Though they hide themselves on the top of Carmel . . . and though they hide from My sight at the bottom of the sea . . ." = TJ "If they imagine to hide on the tops of the city towers . . . and if they hide from before My *Memra* on the islands of the sea . . .") It is characteristic of TJ's prosaic understanding of the Bible that the top of Mount Carmel and the bottom of the sea are considered unsuitable hiding places— hence their transformation into city towers and islands, respectively.

God.[80] It goes without saying that man cannot "encompass" God, least of all, with lies.[81] Most of these acts may be explained in a spiritual sense; but the unsophisticated masses might take them literally and thus obtain a totally wrong impression of the deity. TJ therefore systematically provides alternative—usually homiletical—explanations more attuned to the refined concept of God held by the rabbis in the talmudic age.

TJ frequently emphasizes the immense, unbridgeable difference between man and God by refusing even to mention the two together. Since man is like clay in the hands of the potter,[82] man cannot be put on a par with God or referred to in identical terms.[83] Any human boasts, whether real or imagined, are quickly put down by TJ, whose homiletical comments stress the physical as well as spiritual limitations of man.[84] Even the wisest of

---

80. Cf., e.g., TJ on Jer. 3:7; Ezek. 14:6; Hos. 2:9; 5:4,15; 6:1; 11:7; 14:2; Amos 4:6,8,9,10,11; Zech. 1:3; Mal. 3:7. In all these cases, TJ changes the return to God to a return to the worship of God. Conversely, God does not "return" to man; instead it is through His *Memra* that man's return to the worship of God is rewarded; cf., e.g., Mic. 7:19; Zech. 1:3; Mal. 3:7.

81. Cf. Hos. 12:1 (MT "Ephraim has encompassed Me with falsehood" = TJ "The house of Ephraim has multiplied lies before Me").

82. Cf. Is. 29:16a (MT "Shall the potter be regarded as clay?" = TJ "Behold, like the clay in the potter's hand, so are you considered before Me"). TJ's interpretation, which is virtually a quotation from Jer. 18:6, implies that a question relating to human equality with God, even though phrased in such a way that the answer is clearly negative, is inadmissible.

83. Cf. Jud. 7:18b,20b. (MT '... For the Lord and for Gideon" = TJ "... a sword [v. 18: that slays] from before the Lord and victory through Gideon"). The implication of TJ's rendering is that Gideon is an instrument of God's will, since it is God who, as it were, supplies Gideon's "sword." Cf. Jud. 9:9a (MT "... fatness (from the olive) by which God and men are honored" = TJ "... from which honor is paid before the Lord, and in it men [other versions, great men] indulge themselves"). Similarly, *ibid.* 9:13a (MT '... wine which cheers God and men" = TJ "... wine from which libations are offered before the Lord and by it rejoice great men"). Cf. I Sam. 2:26, where MT "... Samuel continued to grow in stature and favor both with the Lord and with men" is expanded in TJ to "Samuel continued to grow, and his name was good, and his ways were right before the Lord, and his deeds were upright among men." Even an oath in the name of God must not be coupled with a human being; cf. *ibid.* 25:26a (MT "... as the Lord lives, and as your soul lives" = TJ "... the Lord exists, and as your soul lives"). Significantly, TJ makes appropriate changes in the translation even where the Hebrew text as such is unimpeachable; cf. *ibid.* 3:1a (MT "Samuel was ministering to the Lord before Eli" = TJ "Samuel was ministering *before* the Lord during Eli's lifetime"). Since direct service *to* God had to be avoided as anthropomorphic, TJ's "before" the Lord would have been identical in wording to the immediately following "before Eli." Hence TJ's "during Eli's lifetime."

84. Cf. TJ's homiletical rendering of Ezek. 28:13b, where MT reads: "... and your engravings; on the day that you were created they were prepared" = TJ "... your (viz., the prince of

men cannot make a judgement by his own intelligence. He must be aided by the echo of a divine voice; for God alone is in possession of the truth, while no earthly judge, however wise, can issue, by his own unaided efforts, a perfect verdict.[85]

Likewise, any act of disrespect to or blasphemy of God can never be mentioned in the same breath with the act of cursing a human being, even if he happens to be a king.[86] Indeed, TJ is reluctant even to use the expression of blasphemy, and where Israel is concerned, the terminology employed is softened both out of reverence for God and respect for Israel.[87]

It goes almost without saying that, as far as TJ was concerned, Jere-

---

Tyre's) heart was lifted up; yet you did not look at your body, seeing that you are made of channels and orifices of which you are in need and without which it would be impossible for you to exist. Ever since the day you were created they were prepared"). See also the vastly expanded marginal note in TJ Codex Reuchlianus on Ezek. 28:13, where man's physical limitations in contrast to God's unlimited power are particularly emphasized. How sensitive TJ is about human boastfulness can be seen in the expanded translation of II Sam. 3:12a, where MT reads: "To whom does the land belong?" Although the text is probably corrupt, as it stands Abner appears to be bragging that he controls the land. Historically, this was true enough; but it ill-behooved a hero of ancient Israel to use such boastful language. TJ therefore renders; "I swear in the name of Him who made the earth." A pious oath is made to replace human arrogance.

85. Cf. I Kings 3:27b, where Solomon gives his celebrated verdict in the case of the two women, each of whom claimed she was the mother of a newly-born child. While MT simply concludes, "She is its mother," some versions of TJ, unwilling to permit even King Solomon to make a categorical statement like this without legal proof, render homiletically: ". . . and the echo a heavenly voice came down from heaven and said, 'She is its mother.'" This agrees with Midr. Eccl. R. X, 16: "The Holy Spirit was crying, saying, 'She is its mother.'" In the same Midrash Solomon is severely criticized for his unconventional and potentially dangerous method of solving the case: "R. Judah said in the name of R. Elai, 'If I had been there, I would have tied a woolen rope round his (viz., Solomon's) neck. When he said, 'Bring me a sword' (I Kings 3:24a), if the mother had not been filled with compassion for him (i.e., the child), he would have been slain.'"

86. Cf. I Kings 21:10 and 13, where we are told that Naboth was falsely charged with having "cursed God and the king." This juxtaposition is unacceptable to TJ, which separates God and king by explaining that (according to this false accusation) Naboth had "blasphemed before God and cursed the king." It is noteworthy that TJ avoids mentioning direct blasphemy—an unimaginable crime—by charging Naboth with blasphemy *before* (not against or towards) God.

87. Cf., e.g., Ezek. 20:27b (MT ". . . your fathers blasphemed Me" = TJ '. . . your fathers have aroused anger before Me"). Similarly, I Kings 21:10.13, where Naboth's alleged blasphemy of God is softened in TJ to blasphemy *before* God.

miah's bitter complaint that God had become to him "like a deceitful brook, like waters that fail"[88] came close to blasphemy, especially when uttered by a prophet. TJ accordingly changes the entire sense of the verse by rendering, "Your *Memra* shall *not* be false unto me, like a spring of water whose water ceases." Even a false prophet cannot "pervert" the words of the living God."[89] It is likewise inconceivable for Israel to "lift up her voice" against God[90] or to "abandon" Him.[91] No criticism of God is tolerated in TJ. To say, as the Jews said to Ezekiel, that "The way of the Lord is not just (or: right),"[92] was quite inadmissible. TJ changes this to "The ways of the Lord's goodness are not expressed clearly"—a harmless request for clarification of the Almighty's good attributes. TJ will not permit even a prophet to express implied criticism of God by his anguished cry, "O Lord, how long shall I cry for help, and you will not hear? Or cry to you 'Violence!' and you will not save?"[94] In TJ this is completely reversed to ". . . how long shall I˙pray? Surely before you my complaint is revealed concerning matters of violence. Surely there is ability before you to deliver!"

Divine justice is generally unquestionable. Habakkuk's outburst that "justice never goes forth"[95] is regarded as theologically unacceptable and hence changed by TJ to "justice does not come forth clearly." As in Ezekiel 18:25,29, TJ's version no longer questions God's justice. In effect, it reduces the prophetic outcry against God's apparent indifference to the reign of injustice and violence to a minor grievance concerning lack of clarity in the divinely ordered system of justice. Actually, there is perfect justice, ines-

88. Jer. 15:18b.

89. *Ibid.* 23:36b. TJ renders: ". . . you (viz., the false prophets) imagine that you can bring to naught the words of the enduring God."

90. *Ibid.* 12:8b (MT ". . . She has lifted up her voice against Me" = TJ ". . . She has raised a commotion before Me").

91. Cf. *ibid.* 15:6a (MT "You have abandoned Me" = TJ "You have abandoned [or: forsaken] My worship").

92. Ezek. 18:25a,29a.

93. TJ's alteration of the meaning of the clause is all the more noticeable when one compares the rendering used (מפרשן) with that employed in the next clause where the prophet retorts that it is Israel's ways that "are not right" (*ibid.* v. 25b; 29b). There, the same Hebrew expression used in the plural form (יתכנו) is accurately translated תקנן.

94. Hab. 1:2.

95. *Ibid.* 1:4a.

capable,[96] never delayed,[97] but we are unable to perceive it clearly until God reveals Himself to judge the world.[98] Unlike human judges, God is a true judge;[99] and—where Israel is concerned—the only one, any others being merely instruments of divine displeasure.[100] The question posed by the people in Malachi 2:17b—"Where is the God of Justice?"—is considered unsuitable for literal translation, not only because it seems to contradict the concept of God's omnipresence, but also because it implicitly casts doubt on divine justice. TJ therefore renders, "How (or: Where) is it that God does justice?" The popular discontent with a less than perfectly managed judicial system, for which God is ultimately responsible, is reduced to a reasonable request for information on the workings of divine justice.

In view of God's perfect justice, it is impertinent for man, even if he happens to be a prophet, to "contend" with God or even to explain why he cannot do so.[101] Conversely, it is inconceivable for God to "contend" or "plead" with man.[102] It goes without saying that God cannot be "judged,"[103] even if

---

96. Cf. Hos. 6:4a, where MT "What shall I do with you, O Judah?" is rendered by TJ, "In the face of (lit., From before) true judgement, what shall I do for you, of the house of Judah?" In other words, the prophet is powerless to intercede against the divine verdict.

97. Cf. TJ on Zeph. 3:5b.

98. Cf. TJ on Zeph. 3:8.

99. Cf. TJ on Hos. 6:4a and Hab. 1:12a.

100. Cf. Ezek. 24:14b, where TJ substitutes God for the Babylonians in MT as the source of punishment for Jerusalem. On the concept of Israel's or Judah's enemies (in this case, Assyria) being the rod of divine anger, cf. Is. 10:5.

101. Cf. Jer. 12:1a (MT "Righteous are you, O Lord, when I contend with you" = TJ "Righteous are you, O Lord, so that one cannot contend against your word").

102. Cf. *ibid.* 2:9 (MT '. . . I will contend with you, says the Lord, and with your children's children I will contend" = TJ ". . . I will punish you, says the Lord, your children's children . . . I will punish"); *ibid.* 25:31a (MT '. . . the Lord has a contention against the nations" = TJ ". . . there is a judgement before the Lord against the nations"); cf. *ibid.* 50:34a (MT "He will surely plead their cause" = TJ "He will surely avenge their insults"); cf. *ibid.* 51:36a (MT "Behold, I will plead your cause" = TJ "Behold, I will judge your case"); cf. Is. 49:25b (MT "I will contend with those who contend against you" = TJ "Your calamity I will avenge"); cf. Hos. 4:1b (MT ". . . the Lord has a contention against [or: controversy with] the inhabitants of the land" = TJ ". . . there is a judgement before the Lord with the inhabitants of the land"); cf. *ibid.* 12:3a (MT "The Lord has a 'contention' against Judah" = TJ "There is a contention before the Lord with those of the house of Judah"); cf. Mic. 6:2b (MT "Hear, you mountains the contention of the Lord" = TJ "Hear, you mountains the judgements of the Lord"); cf. *ibid.* 7:9b (MT ". . . until he pleads my cause" = TJ ". . . until he judges my case"). See also TJ on I Sam. 25:39a.

103. Cf. Is. 66:16a (MT ". . . by fire will the Lord enter into judgement" = TJ ". . . by fire

He Himself is represented as calling upon people to "judge" between Him and Israel.[104]

Just as God cannot be imagined as engaging in litigation, "pleading" or "contending" against man, so it is impossible for man to provoke God to anger[105]—numerous biblical statements to the contrary notwithstanding.[106] TJ gets round this difficulty by making the offenders "provoke anger *before*" God, i.e., engage in sinful activities calculated in human terms to provoke divine wrath.

No evil courses of any kind may be attributed to God.[107] In TJ's renderings of biblical texts, which would appear to contradict this assumption, God usually emerges unstained by any improper course of action. Thus, in TJ God does not give "statutes that are not good and ordinances by which they cannot have life,"[108] neither does he "make sport"[109] of anybody or

---

will the Lord judge in future"). The Hebrew for "enter into judgment," נשפט, is in the passive form, so that its literal meaning could be taken as: "is judged." Cf. also Jer. 25:31a (MT "He is entering into judgement (Heb. נשפט) with all flesh" = TJ "He is executing punishment upon all flesh").

104. Cf. Is. 5:3b (MT "...judge, I pray you, between me and my vineyard [i.e., Israel]" = TJ "... pronounce judgement now before me upon my people").

105. Cf. Jer. 7:19a (MT "Is it I whom they provoke to anger?" = TJ "Do they imagine that it is before Me that they are provoking anger?").

106. Cf. TJ on Jud. 2:12; I Kings 14:9,15; 15:30; 16:2,7,13,26.33; 21:22; II Kings 17:11,17; 21:6,15; 22:17,54; 23:19,26; Is. 65:3; Jer. 7:18; 8:19; 11:17; 25:6,7; 32:30,32; 44:3,8; Ezek. 8:17; 16:26.

107. Cf., e.g., Amos 3:6b, where MT "Can evil be in a city, unless the Lord has done it?" is somewhat softened by TJ: "Can evil be in a city, unless it was done from before the Lord?" The passive form as well as the words: "from before" remove God from direct responsibility for the evil that befalls the city. (It is, however, noteworthy that Is. 45:7, where the doctrine of God as the author of everything, including evil, is enunciated, is translated literally by TJ—no doubt because in this context it is implicit in the concept of the unity of God). Cf. also Jer. 2:5a, where the prophet daringly asks in the name of God, "What iniquity have your fathers found in Me?" Although the question clearly presumes a negative answer, it is nevertheless inappropriate to link God with iniquity. TJ accordingly substitutes the *Memra* for God; "What falsehood have your fathers found in My *Memra?*" See also Hab. 1:3a, where MT "Why do You make me see iniquity?" is substantially changed in TJ to "Why do I see violent men?" In this version, God is not directly involved.

108. Ezek. 20:25. TJ explains this theolgoically unacceptable statement as follows: "... since they rebelled against My *Memra* and did not want to accept My prophets, I have rejected them and delivered them into the hands of their foolish impulse, so they went and made decrees that were not right, and laws by which they cannot live."

109. Cf. I Sam. 6:6b (MT "...He made sport of them" = TJ "...He punished [or:

"incite" men to do what they are not supposed to do.[110] He certainly does not instruct a prophet to tell the poeple to "hear indeed, but do not understand; see indeed, but do not perceive;"[111] for this would deprive them of their moral choice, which would be contrary to R. Akiba's authoritative dictum that "Everything is forseen, yet freedom of choice is given."[112] TJ therefore renders: ". . . who hear indeed, but do not reflect; and see indeed, but do not know." Thus, free will is preserved, and it is the people, not God, who must bear the blame for their moral shortcomings.

The Almighty cannot be depicted as "alluring" Israel to return to his fold, especially as the Hebrew expression used (מפתיה) often signifies "seduction,"[113] a most inappropriate term in this context. Indeed, according to a homiletical version of TJ on I Kings 22:21-22, the spirit that offered to "entice" (אפתנו) Ahab by becoming "a lying spirit in the mouth of all his prophets," so far from being encouraged in this design by the Almighty, as the text clearly states, was in fact sharply rebuked and expelled from the heavenly yeshivah; "for the Holy One, Blessed be He, does not desire those who make that which is true false, and He takes no delight in them."[114]

---

wrought vengeance upon] them"). Similarly, Is. 66:4a (MT "I also will choose to make sport of them" = TJ "I also will take pleasure in their destruction"). Although divine *Schadenfredue* may hardly seem an improvement upon the original, it represents sound biblical doctrine that "When the wicked perish, there are shouts of gladness" (Prov. 11:10). In this connection, Ps. 2:3a, where God is represented as laughing and deriding the kings and rulers plotting against him and his annointed king. Cf. also Targum Onkelos on Exod. 10:2a.

110. Cf. I Kings 18:37b, where MT: ". . . You have turned their hearts back" is transformed and expanded by TJ: ". . . You in Your mercy let Yourself be entreated by them through Your *Memra* to bring them back to the fear of You, but they let their hearts remain divided." TJ's explanation agrees with one opinion in the Talmud (T.B. Ber. 31b), according to which Elijah had indeed been guilty of reproaching the Almighty. According to another view, however, God Himself admitted that Elijah had been right (*ibid.*).

111. Is. 6:9.

112. M. Aboth III, 15.

113. Cf. Ex. 22:15; Job 31:9. TJ renders MT "alluring" by "subject to the Torah"—a far more appropriate divine act. There are two other examples of the verb פתה being used in connection with God. In Jer. 20:7a, the prophet complains of having been "deceived" by God. This harsh accusation is radically transformed in TJ to "persuaded." On the other hand, in Ezek. 14:9, where God is depicted as saying that he had "deceived" the false prophet, TJ only softens the somewhat ungodly act by substituting "caused him to err." Presumably, false prophets deserve to be misled.

114. It should, however, be noted, that the main versions of TJ render almost literally, "causing to err." The only exception to this tendency of raising the moral standards of bibli-

Although in biblical theology God is the ultimate cause of both good and evil,[115] in TJ's system God does not personally and directly bring evil upon people.[116] Even where God seems to admit that He did cause affliction upon individuals, TJ manages to absolve Him from unjust behavior by adding, "because of the sins of my people."[117] In a subsequent section, we shall see that reasonable and well-deserved punishment, without any arbitrary infliction upon the innocent is a basic doctrine of TJ.

Divine "jealousy" is inconceivable to TJ—and that in spite of the fact that God Himself claims to be "a jealous God."[118] Instead, TJ transforms verses depicting God's jealousy into descriptions of punishment for those who deserve it.[119] Alternatively, the Almighty's jealousy signifies in TJ divine anger[120] or God's judicial function.[121] Ignoring several biblical statements to the contrary, TJ does not allow God to bear a grudge[122] or pursue vengeance. All He does is to inflict legal punishment[123] upon the wicked.[124]

---

cal history is to be found in TJ on II Kings 10:19b, where Jehu is depicted as employing "cunning in order to destroy the worshippers of Baal." TJ, evidently approving of Jehu's draconian measures, renders "cunning" (Heb. עקבה) by "wisdom." Cf. also Targum Onkelos on Gen. 27:35; 34:13.

115. Cf. Is. 45:7.

116. Cf. Is. 66:4a ("... their fears I will bring upon them" = TJ "... from that which they dreaded they shall not be delivered"); cf. I Sam. 1:5b and 6b (MT '... the Lord had closed her womb" = TJ "... from before the Lord a child was witheld from her"). In addition to God not being represented as the direct author of Hannah's childlessness, there is the fact that metaphors are generally avoided in TJ. Moreover, from a puritanical point of view, there is some indelicacy in depicting the Almighty as closing a womb.

117. Cf. Mic. 4:6b. Note the Hebrew הרעתי—lit., "I have done (or: caused) evil."

118. Exod. 20:5; Deut. 5:9. Significantly, Targum Onkelos *ad loc.* leaves the Hebrew אל קנא untranslated, possibly because "a jealous God" was too embarrassing and no longer corresponded to the elevated concepts of the divine prevailing in the talmudic age.

119. Cf. TJ on Is. 63:15; Ezek. 23:25; 36:5; Zeph. 1:18; Zech. 1:14.

120. Cf. TJ on Ezek. 36:6.

121. Cf. Nah. 1:2a (MT "A jealous God" = TJ "God is judge").

122. Cf. Jer. 3:5a (MT "Will He bear a grudge forever?" = TJ "Is it possible that your sins will be kept against you for ever?"); *ibid.*, 3:12b (MT "I will not bear a grudge for ever" = TJ "Your sins will not be kept against you for ever"). In both passages, the passive form removes the connection with God.

123. Cf. especially TJ on Jer. 20:12b, where MT "Let me see Your vengeance upon them" is channeled by TJ into proper legal form, "Let me see the punishment of Your Law upon them." See also TJ on Is. 1:24b.

124. Cf. TJ on Jud. 11:36; I Sam. 24:13; II Sam. 4:8; 22:48; II Kings 9:7; Is. 34:8; 35:4;

The primitive concept of God's "fighting" His "enemies" or "adversaries"[125] is carefully avoided in TJ, where God's opponents usually become enemies or adversaries of Israel, and "the Lord's battles"—"the battles of the people of the Lord.[126] Occasionally, the divine *Memra* is substituted for God when He is dealing with His enemies.[127] Where the anthropomorphic context does not permit such a solution, TJ resorts to homiletical expansion, with a view to mitigating the prophetic attribution to God of acts suitable only for a human warrior.[128]

Although there are many passages where we read that God "drives out" the enemies of Israel, there is at least one instance where TJ replaces God by the *Memra*—the reason apparently being that God is Himself the speaker instead of being referred to in the third person.[129] It goes without saying that God does not "throw stones" or require arrows in order to defeat the enemies of Israel,[130] neither can he be imagined as being cruel.[131] On the

---

47:3; 59:17; 61:2; 63:4; Jer. 5:9,29; 9:8; 11:20; 15:15; 20:12; 46:10; 50:15,28; 51,6,11,36; Ezek. 25:14,17; Mic. 5:14; Nah. 1:2.

125. Cf., e.g., Exod. 14:14; 15:3; Num. 21:14; Deut. 32:41 and Targum Onkelos *ad loc.*, where the literal meaning is virtually preserved. This is one of the few instances where TJ's theology, which is generally identical with that of Targum Onkelos, shows remarkable differences. Only on Exod. 17:16, where MT reads, "The Lord will have war with Amalek from generation to generation," does Targum Onkelos provide a convoluted rendering designed to lessen the impression that God has to wage war against the Amalekites generation after generation, without, presumably, being able to finish them off in one blow. Targum Onkelos therefore translates: ". . . a battle will be waged before the Lord against the house of Amalek to destroy them from the inhabitants of the world."

126. Cf. TJ on Jos. 10:14; Jud. 5:13.31; I Sam. 18:17; 25:28; 30:26; II Sam. 14:12; Is. 1:24; 59:18; 64:1; Nah 1:2.

127. Cf. TJ on Jos. 10:42; Is. 63:10; 66:6.

128. Cf., e.g., Is. 42:13 (MT "The Lord goes forth like a mighty man, like a man of war He stirs up His fury; He cries out, He shouts aloud, He prevails against His enemies" = TJ "The Lord has revealed Himself to do mighty acts; to do mighty acts He reveals Himself in anger, in speech, and agitation, too, against His enemies He reveals Himself in His might").

129. Cf. Jos. 13:6a (MT "I will Myself drive them out from before the children of Israel" = TJ "By My *Memra* I will drive them out from before the children of Israel"). The emphasis in MT on God personally (אנכי) driving out the people of Canaan renders it too anthropomorphic for TJ's taste—hence the introduction of the *Memra*.

130. Cf. Jos. 10:11a (MT ". . . the Lord threw down great stones from heaven upon them" = TJ ". . . from before the Lord great stones from heaven were thrown down upon them"); cf. II Kings 13:17b (MT "The Lord's arrow of victory" = TJ "This arrow shall be made a redemption for us from before the Lord").

131. Cf. Jer. 6:11a (MT "I am full of the wrath of the Lord; I am weary of holding it in.

contrary, God is always good, bountiful and compassionate towards man,[132] and He is bound to save him in time of trouble.[133] He is truthful at all times;[134] hence absolutely trustworthy;[135] and His promises of benefactions are invariably fulfilled.[136] It is therefore inconceivable that man should abandon hope in God's salvation.[137] The Almighty is the source of whatever success man may be able to attain.[138] Thus, victory in war cannot be achieved without divine aid, and the people of Israel certainly cannot defeat their enemies by their own unaided efforts.[139]

'Pour it out upon infants in the street . . . . = TJ "I am full of the prophecy of the Lord with power from before the Lord; I am weary of holding it in, and I *cannot* pour it out upon infants in the street"). TJ's complete reversal of the original text is remarkable, since it indicates that the harsh sentiments expressed by the prophet in the name of God were totally irreconcilable with TJ's refined concepts of divine justice.

132. Cf., e.g., TJ on Is. 1:9; 55:8-11; 63:16; 64:7; Jer. 3:12; Hos. 14:9.

133. Cf. II Kings 6:27a (MT "If the Lord will not save you . . ." = TJ "Surely, the Lord will save you . . ."). The Hebrew text is not quite certain. As it stands, it could even be rendered "Let not the Lord save you"—a logical absurdity, though linguistically accurate. TJ rejects any possibility of God's *not* helping one who calls upon Him with all his heart, which is good biblical doctrine; cf., e.g., Ps. 37:2 ff.; 145:18. Cf. also Hab. 1:2b, where MT ". . . You will not save"—an unacceptable complaint from TJ's point of view—becomes in TJ, ". . . surely there is ability before You to save."

134. Cf. II Sam. 7:28a, where MT ". . . Your words *shall be* true" (implying the future, not necessarily the past and present) is rendered by TJ, ". . . Your words *are* ture," i.e., at all times.

135. Cf. Zeph. 3:2b where MT "She (viz., Jerusalem) does not trust in the Lord" is considered inadmissible by TJ, which softens it to "She did not trust in the *Memra* of the Lord."

136. Cf. Is. 55:11a (MT ". . . My word that goes forth from My mouth, it shall not return to Me empty" = TJ ". . . it is impossible that the word of My goodness that goes forth from before Me should return before Me empty"). TJ's "impossible" rather than the plain imperfect tense of MT is designed to avoid the impression that the divine promise will only in future be fulfilled, not necessarily in the present or in the past.

137. Cf. II Kings 6:33b (MT "Why should I hope for the Lord any longer?" = TJ "What else can I pray before the Lord?"). TJ's version obviously sounds much better and is theologically unobjectionable.

138. Cf. TJ on II Sam. 22:28.

139. Cf. Jud. 5:13 (MT "Then down marched the remnant of the mighty ones; the people of the Lord marched down for Him against the warriors" = TJ "Then down came one of the armies of Israel and broke the power of the mighty ones of the nations. Behold, not because of (their) strength was this, but the Lord broke before His people the power of the mighty ones of their enemies"). Cf. also TJ on Jud. 5:3-4. On the concept of God's alone being the author of Israel's victories, see especially Deut. 18:17-18.

God is not only man's benefactor; He is also his teacher,[140] and it is therefore man's duty to reciprocate by his love and reverence for his Creator, expressed by his devotion to the service of God.[141]

3. IDOLATRY

Although, ideally, man should devote himself entirely to the service of God, in practice, as the targumists were well aware, the world was filled with idolatry and idolatrous superstitions with all their hideous features. True, during the talmudic age, idolatry had long ceased to represent a serious threat to the survival of Judaism; but in times of persecution it could undermine the resolve of weaker characters who might also be attracted by the outward glitter and unrestricted hedonism of the pagan world.

The targumists, therefore, waged an unrelenting battle against any interpretation of the Scriptures which might mislead simple people who attended synagogue services and Bible readings to imagine that there might be something in idolatry after all; that the whole pagan world could not be altogether wrong; that perhaps the idols were not so dead as they were made out to be; that some mystic powers might indeed reside in them; and that the cult of the heathen gods might be profitable to its followers. Was it not a fact that it was precisely the idolators who were going from strength to strength, while the Jewish people, burdened though they were with innumerable precepts and restrictions imposed by their one and only God, had been forsaken and humiliated by the very God whom they had faithfully worshipped for centuries?

Arguments along these lines were not lacking in the polemics directed by educated pagans against Judaism,[142], and there was certainly a potential danger that circumstances might arise when a demoralized Jewry—or a sub-

---

140. Cf. TJ on Is. 28:26 (MT "For he instructs [lit., chastises] him aright, his God teaches him" = TJ "Behold, all these are meant for them instruction in judgement, so that they may know that God chose them the way that is right that they should walk therein"). Note how in TJ God does not "chastise," but teaches and judges. On God's being the source of instruction, cf., TJ on I Sam. 9:9; II Kings 22:18; Is. 9:12; 31:1; Jer. 10:21; 37:7; Ezek. 20:1. Cf. also Targum Onkelos and Targ. Pseudo-Jonathan on Gen. 25:22 and Ex. 18:15.

141. Cf., e.g., I Kings 3:3a (MT "Solomon loved the Lord" = TJ "Solomon loved the worship of the Lord").

142. Cf., e.g., Cant. R. VII, 1.

stantial proportion of the Jewish people—might yield to the pressures and attractions of paganism.

The targumists—and TJ in particular—therefore took great care to leave no shadow of doubt that idolatry was utterly useless and sinful, and would carry severe punishment in its wake. Of course, the Hebrew Bible is replete with denunciations of idolatry. Nevertheless, here and there the text of the Bible, representing an earlier period when the prevailing concepts of monotheism were as yet unrefined and certainly less than perfect, could give rise to misconceptions. TJ was therefore anxious to avoid any renderings which, because they are accurate and literal, could foster ideas that might turn out to be perilous from the point of view of pure monotheism.

Thus, as already pointed out, there could be no possibility of offering a choice between God and Baal, as Elijah seems to do at the great convocation on Mt. Carmel.[143] It was likewise inconceivable for a prophet to suggest that the exiled Jews would "serve other gods day and night" once they were exiled from their land. TJ changes this unfulfilled prediction to ". . . you shall serve there nations that worship idols."[144]

In TJ's theological thinking there could be no toleration of idolatry, even for non-Jews. Micah's seemingly tolerant statement—". . . all the peoples walk each in the name of its god"[145]—was unacceptable to TJ, which renders, ". . . all peoples shall be guilty because they worshipped idols." Another version of TJ is even harsher: ". . . all peoples shall go to perdition because they worshipped idols." The prophet may not have been as tolerant of idolatry as he seemed to be; but he certainly had not intended such a sharp denunciation of the pagan nations.

TJ carefully eliminates all biblical expressions which may convey the impression that idols are real or have any form of life in them. Even though the idols are in fact invariably ridiculed and denounced in the Scriptures, some verses could still be misleading and therefore had to be duly altered to

143. Cf. TJ on I Kings 8:23. See *supra*, p. 6.

144. Cf. Jer. 16:13. Cf. also Deut. 28:44b, where MT ". . . you shall serve there other gods" is transformed by Targum Onkelos to ". . . you shall serve there nations that worship idols." Except for the singular form of the verb required by the text, Targum Onkelos' rendering is identical with that of TJ on Jer. 16:13b.

145. Micah 4:5. Heb. ילכו could also be rendered, "shall walk," i.e., "let them walk" or, in other words, they are free to follow their pagan cults, while we "walk in the name of the Lord our God" (*ibid.*). Although this interpretation is almost certainly wrong, it is linguistically sound and therefore dangerously misleading.

leave no room for misunderstanding. Thus, TJ could not accept, even in a purely poetical sense, that "the Seraphim utter nonsense"[146] or that "Bel is put to shame, Merodach is dismayed."[147] Still less could TJ render literally, "... my graven image and my molten image commanded them"[148]—even though the prophet, speaking in the name of God, is in fact expressing objections to such hypothetical assertions.

Ambiguous prophetic statements, which, rightly or wrongly, could lend themselves to theologically absurd conclusions are reinterpreted in TJ so as to make sure that they confirm to a pure monotheistic theology. Thus, on Hosea 8:5a—"He has spurned (or: forsaken) your calf, O Samaria,"—TJ was evidently well aware that an alternative translation was possible and had in fact equal merit; "Your calf has forsaken (viz., you), O Samaria." This would imply that the calf was real and could engage in rational acts such as forsaking its followers in Samaria. TJ therefore renders, "They went astray after the calf of Samaria."

Similarly, TJ does not allow questions relating to idols to be put where the answer must be obvious. For example, Jeremiah's rhetorical question, "Are there any among the false gods of the nations that can bring rain?"[149]—though clearly anticipating a negative answer—is nevertheless objectionable; for a question like this would never have been asked by Jews living in the talmudic age, not only because the answer was self-evident, but also because the very question was an insult to an absolute, uncompromising monotheistic fatih. TJ's improved version eliminates such objections: "Behold, the idols of the nations are of no use to bring down rain."

A similar transformation had to be performed with Elijah's suggestion to the prophets of Baal—"You call on the name of your god, and I will call on the name of the Lord; and the god who answers by fire, he is God."[150] Such an either/or solution was inappropriate from TJ's point of view. Clearly, there could be only one God who would anser by fire, and it hardly required a divine miracle to prove that Baal was a fraud. TJ therefore renders: "You

---

146. Zech. 10:2a. TJ renders: "... those that worship images utter violence."

147. Jer. 50:2b. TJ's translation avoids attributing human feelings to Babylonian gods: "Those that worship Bel are put to shame, those that worship Merodach are broken."

148. Is. 48:5b. TJ eliminates the images' "command" by rendering, "... my graven image and my molten image have molten them."

149. Jer. 14:22a.

150. I Kings 18:24.

call on the name of your idol and you will not be answered since there is no profit in it. I, however, will pray in the name of the Lord, so that He may send his *Memra* and bring down fire; for the Lord He is God."

TJ is also unwilling to tolerate sarcastic statements against idolatry, not because such irony was not appreciated, but because it might be lost on simple souls who might all too easily take them at face value. Thus, Elijah's mocking reaction to the failure of the prophets of Baal to be answered by their god[151] happens to be linguistically ambiguous and hence liable to be misunderstood: MT "Cry aloud, for he is a god" could perhaps be mistaken for a statement of fact. In any case, whatever the intention, it is out of the question to say about Baal, even in just, that "he is a god." TJ therefore adds, ". . . for you say that he is a god."

Even the Almighty Himself has to be censored, as it were, when he says to the errant Israelites who had been worshipping idols "Go and cry to the gods whom you have chosen; let them deliver you in the time of your distress."[152] The second half of the verse is clearly not to be taken literally, and to make quite sure no one does, TJ renders, "Can they (viz., the idols) deliver you in the time of your distress?"

For TJ, the idols are so detestable that they cannot be depicted, even ironically, as "delectable,"[153] neither can the offerings brought to them be described as having "a pleasing odor."[154] No less loathsome are the worshippers of idols who are violent men,[155] disgraced by their folly,[156] which is so enormous that they in effect bear witness against themselves.[157]

---

151. *Ibid.* 18:27.

152. Jud. 10:14.

153. Cf. Is. 44:9a (MT ". . . the things they delight in [i.e., the idols] do not profit" = TJ ". . . they that worship them [will find that] they do not profit them").

154. Cf. Ezek. 16:19a, where MT ". . . you set before them (viz., the idols) for a pleasing odor" is put into more prosaic language by TJ: ". . . you set before them offerings for worship."

155. Cf. Zech. 10:2a (MT "For the teraphim utter nonsense" = TJ "For the worshippers of images speak violence").

156. Cf. TJ on Jer. 50:2b.

157. Cf. Is. 44:9b (MT ". . . they [viz., the idols] are their witnesses" = TJ "they (viz., the idolators) are witnesses against themselves"). The radical transformation made in the translation—the subject changes from the idols to their worshippers—is partly due to the fact that, in TJ's view, idols could not act as "witnesses." Metaphors are generally replaced by concrete statements in TJ.

Those that carry idols, so far from being helped by the objects of their worship, are in effect wearied by them. Deutero-Isaiah's vivid description of the Babylonian idols being borne into captivity on beasts of burden exhausted by their load,[158] which must have seemed immaterial to the prosaic targumist, is given a novel interpretation in TJ's version: "Their images were in the likeness of beasts and cattle; the burdens of their idols are heavy on those that bear them, and they are weary."

Idolatrous priests are almost everywhere distinguished from priests of God by being described as כומרין instead of כהנין or כהניא.[159] Likewise, idolatrous altars are, as a rule, אגורין (lit., heaps, viz., of stones) rather than מזבחות.[160] As for the idols themselves, they are invariably טעוון or טעוותא— lit., errors or goings astray,—never אלהין or אלהיא. Even in Jeremiah 10:11, the only Aramaic verse in the Prophets, the original אלהיא is transformed in TJ's homiletical interpretation into טעון.

Idolatry, in TJ, is the sin *par excellence,* equivalent to all other sins.[161] Inexorable punishment is exacted upon Israel for this unforgivable crime— such as loss of freedom and property to the enemies of Israel[162] as well as

---

158. Cf. Is. 46:1f.

159. Cf., e.g., TJ on Jud. 18:30b; II Kings 11:18a. It is worth noting that Jonathan, the idolatrous priest of the Danites, is earlier accorded the title of כהין (Jud. 17:10,13), perhaps because his service in Micah's private sanctuary was not yet held to constitute idolatry in the full sense of the word. Only the sanctuary at Dan, where the calf-cult was subsequently introduced (cf. I Kings 12:28-30), was regarded as an idolatrous center *par excellence.*

160. Cf. especially TJ on Jud. 6:24-25, where the contrast between the altar of the Lord (מדבחא) and the altar of Baal (אגורא) is clearly stressed. Cf. also TJ on I Kings 12:32f.; 13:1ff,32; 16:32; 18:26; II Kings 11:18; 21:3; 23:12,15 ff.; Is. 17:8; Amos 2:8; 3:14. The only notable exception is to be found in TJ on II Kings 16:10 ff., where the altar of Damascus and its imitation in Jerusalem are rendered מדבחא, not, as we would expect, אגורא. This probably due to the fact that the biblical author describes the entire event *sine ira et studio* and fails to make clear that the altars in question were devoted to idolatrous cults. While the Damascus altar cannot have been anything but idolatrous, its Jerusalem counterpart was undoubtably devoted to the service of Yahweh and hence unobjectionable, except from a narrow legalistic point of view, which was opposed to any imitation of foreign cults.

161. Cf. Jer. 15:13b (MT "... for all your sins ..." = TJ "... for the sins that you [committed by] worshipping idols"); *ibid.,* 17:3b (MT "... for the sin" = TJ "... for the sins that you were worshipping idols").

162. Cf. *ibid.* 15:13a-b: (MT "Your wealth and your treasures I will give as spoil ... for all your sins") (see previous note); *ibid.* 17:3 (MT "... On the mountains in the open country; your wealth and all your treasures I will give for spoil; your high places for the sin ..." = TJ "Because you worshipped on the mountains, in the field, your possessions and all your trea-

exile from their land.[163] According to TJ's interpretation of a passage in Hosea, it was the calf-cult in Bethel that was the cause of Israel's exile.[164]

In line with Exod. 12:12, where God promises that he will "execute judgments" on all the gods of Egypt, TJ also puts into the mouth of the prophet Habakkuk a prediction that all the idols would be destroyed.[165] Indeed, in accordance with the commandment in Exod. 23:13b—"make no mention of the names of other gods, nor let such be heard from your mouth,"[166] the very names of foreign deities were to be consigned to oblivion. Just as the author (or redactor) of the book of Samuel changed the names of Esh-baal[167] and Merib-baal[168] to Ishbaal[169] and Mephibosheth,[170] respectively, so TJ sometimes changes place names associated with idolatrous cults.[171] So hateful were the pagan cults to the targumists that, when-

---

sure houses I will deliver, for the sins that you were worshipping idols . . ."); Mic. 1:14b (MT "The houses of Achzib shall be a deceitful thing to the kings of Israel" = TJ "The houses of Achzib shall be delivered to the nations because of the sins that the kings of Israel worshipped idols in them"); Hab. 3:7a (MT "I saw the tents of Cushan in affliction" = TJ "When the house of Israel worshipped idols, I delivered them into the hands of Cushan the sinner").

163. Cf. Zech. 11:10 (MT ". . . I took my staff Grace, and I broke it, annulling the covenant with all the peoples" = TJ ". . . I brought Sennacherib king of Assyria upon the king of Israel, and I exiled him because they changed the covenant which I had made with them not to worship idols; therefore they went into exile among the nations").

164. Cf. Hos. 10:5a, where MT "The inhabitants of Samaria tremble for the calves of Beth aven" is homiletically expanded in TJ: "Because they worshipped the calves in Bethel, a king will come up against them with his army and will exile them. They will take the calf of Samaria from them." Significantly, even non-Jews, who are not bound by the covenant such as that between God and Israel, are liable to be punished for idolatry as well as for their arrogance; cf., Hab. 1:11 (MT "Then they [viz., the Chaldees] sweep by like the wind and go on, guilty men [lit., and they are guilty], whose own might is their god" = TJ "Then, because their spirit was lifted up upon them, they passed away [i.e., were removed] from their kingdom, and they were guilty because they gave much honor to their idol.").

165. Cf. Hab. 2:20b (MT "Let all the earth keep silence before him" = TJ "All the [idolatrous] deities shall perish from before Him").

166. Cf. also Jos. 23:7b: ". . . you shall not make mention of the names of their gods."

167. Cf. I Chron. 9:39.

168. Cf. *ibid.* 9:40.

169. Cf. II Sam. 2:8 ff.; 4:5 ff.

170. Cf. *ibid.* 4:4; 9:5 ff.; 16:1 ff.; 19:25 ff.

171. Cf. Jos. 11:17a; 12:7a (MT "Baal-gad" = TJ "the plain of Gad"); II Sam. 5:20b (MT "Baal-perazim" = TJ "the plain of Perazim"); Is. 65:11b (MT ". . . who set a table for Gad and fill cups of mixed wine for Meni" = TJ ". . . who set tables for idols and mix wine in basins for their deities"). Meni was the god of destiny, while Gad was the god of fortune; cf.

ever possible, they were not even to be mentioned. Along with the destruction of idolatry, its memory, too, would pass from history.

4. FEAR OF GOD AND SIN

The best antidote to idolatry was the fear of, and reverence for, the one
and true God. As already emphasized in biblical Wisdom Literature, the fear
of God is the beginning of wisdom and knowledge,[172] and TJ adds that lack
of wisdom and rejection of knowledge really mean absence or ignorance of
the fear of God.[173] Reverence for God is more precious than gold,[174] and it
makes the remnant of Israel more precious in the sight of the Almighty.[175] It
is a divine gift expressed in the prophetic prediction of a new heart and a
new spirit to be given to Israel.[176] Fear of God is the best method to come
spiritually close to Him.[177] Conversely, lack of reverence for God leads one

---

Gen. 30:11 (though Targum Onkelos *ad loc.*—*like* TJ on Jos. 11:17 and 12:7, see *supra*—
seems to be unaware of this meaning of Gad); T. B. Shab. 67b; Sanh. 63b. Cf. also Jud.
3:19a.26b, where MT הפסילים ("the sculptured stones" or: "the carved images") is rendered "quarries" by TJ, no doubt because TJ was reluctant to associate Ehud, a presumably
pious judge of Israel, with idolatrous images. Otherwise the innocent reader or listener
might ask what Ehud was doing at what seems to have been an idolatrous cult center. On the
question of the permissibility of mentioning idols by their names, see especially T.B. Sanh.
63b.

172. Cf. Ps. 111:10; Prov. 1:7.

173. Cf. Hos. 13:13b (MT "... he is an unwise son" = TJ "... he is a son who was raised
but has not learned to know the fear of me"); *ibid.* 4:6b (MT "because you have rejected
knowledge" = TJ "because you have rejected the knowledge of the fear of me").

174. Cf. Is. 13:12a (MT "I will make men more rare than fine gold" = TJ "I will love
those that fear me more than gold with which people adorn themselves").

175. Cf. Zech. 8:6 (MT "If it is marvelous in the sight of the remnant of this people in
these days, should it also be marvelous in My sight?" = TJ "When the fear of Me will become
precious in the sight of the remnant of this people in these days, they will also be precious
before Me").

176. Cf. Ezek. 36:26 (MT "I will give you a new heart, and a new spirit I will put within
you; ... and I will give you a heart of flesh" = TJ "I will give you a reverential heart, and a
reverential spirit I will put within you; ... and I will give you a spirit fearful before me to do
my will"); *ibid.* 11:19 (MT "I will give them one [another reading: a new] heart, and put a
new spirit within them; ... and I will give them a heart of flesh" = TJ "I will give them a
reverential heart, and a reverential spirit I will put within them; ... and I will give them a
spirit fearful before Me to do My will").

177. Cf. Jos. 22:5a (MT "... to cleave to Him" = TJ "... to draw near to the fear of

away from Him.[178] It is the highest expression of both human perfection[179] and humility.[180] Attainable through observing nature and reflecting on the creation of the hosts of heaven,[181] the fear of God must always be before one's eyes,[182] especially since it also adds a greater spiritual dimension to God's power and glory.[183]

Failure to show adequate reverence for the Creator forms, in TJ's interpretation, part of the prophetic denunciation of Israel in general[184] and of the priests in particular.[185] Jerusalem was punished because of lack of fear of God,[186] and even when the righteous perish, TJ makes the prophet lament that nobody takes the fear of God to his heart.[187]

Closely associated with the fear of God is the fear of sin. In TJ the two are sometimes interchangeable,[188] no doubt because the effectiveness of one

Him"). So also Targum Onkelos and Targum Pseudo-Jonathan on Deut. 11:22; 30:20.

178. Cf. Jer. 2:5a (MT "... they went far from Me" = TJ "... they removed themselves from the fear of Me").

179. Cf. II Sam. 22:24a (MT "I was blameless [lit., perfect] before Him" = TJ "I was perfect in the fear of Him").

180. Cf. Mic. 6:8b (MT "... to walk humbly with your God" = TJ "... be humble to walk in the fear of your God").

181. Cf. Is. 40:26a (MT "... see who created these" = TJ "see to fear before him who created these").

182. Cf. Jer. 2:19b (MT "the fear of God is not within you" = TJ "you did not put the fear of me before your eyes").

183. Cf. Is. 12:2b (MT "... the Lord God is my strength and song" = TJ '... the fear of the Lord is my strength and my praise"). Cf. also Exod. 15:2a, where Targum Onekos' rendering is identical with that of TJ here.

184. Cf. Jer. 2:6a (MT "They did not say, 'Where is the Lord ...?" = TJ "They did not say, 'Let us fear from before the Lord'"); *ibid.* 12:11b (MT "The whole land is made desolate, but no man lays it to heart" = TJ "The whole land is made desolate; for there is no man who puts the fear of Me on his heart").

185. Cf. *ibid.* 2:8a (MT "The priests did not say, 'Where is the Lord?'" = TJ "The priests did not say, 'Let us fear from before the Lord'").

186. Cf. *ibid.* 2:19 (MT "...it is evil and bitter for you to forsake the Lord your God; the fear of Me is not in you ..." = TJ "... evil and bitterness I will bring upon you, O Jerusalem, because you forsook the worship of the Lord your God, and you did not put the fear of Me before your eyes").

187. Cf. Is. 57:1a (MT "The righteous man perishes, and no one lays it to heart" = TJ "The righteous ones are dying, and there is no man who puts the fear of Me in his heart").

188. Cf., e.g., I Kings 18:3b (MT "Now Obadiah revered [or: feared] the Lord greatly" = TJ "Now Obadiah was exceedingly fearful from before the Lord"). It is noteworthy that Obadiah, Ahab's steward, is identified with the prophet Obadiah in the Talmud (T. B. Sanh. 39b).

depends on the other. The quality of sin-fearing is so highly valued in TJ that the Shunammite woman, who had gained special merit through her hospitality for the prophet Elisha,[189] is considered by TJ not simply as "a wealthy woman,"[190] but as a "sin-fearing woman."[191]

The only fear that is of any consequence is the fear of sin. Accordingly, the prophetic prediction that Israel's "heart shall thrill and rejoice" (lit., "fear and be enlarged") is given a novel interpretation in TJ: ". . . and you (viz., Israel) shall fear, and your heart shall be enlarged for fear of sins."[192]

Fear of sin is sometimes equated in TJ to power—spiritual, to be sure—but power nonetheless. Thus, the "mighty man of valor," who appears so frequently in the Hebrew Bible, is occasionally depicted in TJ as a sin-fearing man. For instance, Benaiah son of Jehoiada is described in MT as "the son of a valiant man."[193] TJ, however, influenced perhaps by the extraordinary praise bestowed on Benaiah by the rabbis,[194] renders: ". . . the son of a sin-fearing man." Similarly, Joab's welcoming address to Jonathan son of Abiathar, "Come in, for you are a valiant man and bring good tidings,"[195] is changed by TJ to "Come in, for you are a sin-fearing man and bring good tidings."[196] Likewise, when Solomon promises that no harm

189. Cf. II Kings 4:8 ff.

190. *Ibid.*

191. Cf. *ibid.* TJ's rendering of אשה גדולה (lit., "a great woman"). Where a biblical personality was worthy, "greatness" in TJ means moral superiority. Where no such praise is indicated, TJ renders MT "great" literally; cf. e.g., I Sam. 25:2, where Nabal is described as "very wealthy" (גדול, lit., great). But since Nabal is depicted as a most unattractive type, TJ renders literally (רב). Similarly, II Sam. 19:33, where Barzilai is described as "a very wealthy (גדול) man." However, since Barzilai is criticised in the Talmud as a liar and morally dissolute man (cf. T.B. Shab. 152a), TJ keeps to the literal meaning (רב).

192. Cf. Is. 60:5a. Cf. also M. Sot. VIII, 5, where the "fearful and fainthearted" man who is to be exempted from the army (cf. Deut. 20:8) is identified with "one who is afraid because of the sins he has committed."

193. So according to the most likely reading of II Sam. 23:20a. Another reading is "the son of Ish-hai." Possibly, the description of "valiant man" (or: "man of valor") refers to Benaiah himself, not to his father.

194. Cf. T.B. Ber. 18a-b.

195. I Kings 1:42b.

196. There is a *non sequitur* in the literal meaning of Joab's words. Being an איש חיל (a "valiant man") is no guarantee of being the bearer of good news. If, on the other hand, he is a sin-fearing man, he stands a better chance of becoming a divine instrument of good tidings. TJ may also have been influenced by the similarity of חיל, which can also mean "trembling" and דחיל (fearing).

would befall Adonijah "if he will be 'a valiant man'" (lit., "a son of valor"),[197] TJ once again makes this promise conditional on Adonijah being "a sin-fearing man."[198]

Finally, David's testament to Solomon urging him, among other things, to "be a man,"[199] while comprehensible in a general way as a metaphor for wielding the power of a man, nevertheless makes little sense if taken literally. TJ, as usual, provides a spiritual interpretation—"be a sin-fearing man." The fear of sin is thus elevated to be the most important injunction left to his son and successor by Israel's greatest king.

5. TORAH AND GOOD DEEDS

According to the rabbis, the best method of preventing sin is to engage in the study of the Torah.[200] "If that ugly one (viz., the tempter working through the evil impulse) meets you, drag him to the house of study."[201] Thus, the Torah is the best antidote to sin, and TJ fully concurs with this verdict. The importance of studying and teaching Torah is repeatedly emphasized.[202] According to a homiletical addition in one manuscript of TJ on Judges 5:4, God had offered the Torah to other nations, but they contemptuously rejected it, and only Israel accepted the Torah without reservations.[203] God Himself instructed Israel in the Torah,[204] and hence Israel

197. *Ibid.* 1:52a.

198. Here, again, the logical sequence of MT seems to be deficient. There is no obvious connection between being "valiant" and maintaining loyalty to the king. A sin-fearing man, on the other hand, may be presumed to be loyal and trustworthy.

199. *Ibid.* 2:2b.

200. Cf., e.g., T.B. Ber. 5a.

201. T.B. Kid. 30b.

202. Cf., e.g., Is. 55:1 (MT "Ho, every one who thirsts, come to the waters; and he who has no money, come, buy and eat! Come, buy wine and milk without money and without price" = TJ "Ho, whoever desires to learn, let him come and learn; and he who has no money—come ye and learn without price and without money—instruction that is better than wine and milk"); *ibid.* 57:14a (MT "And it shall be said, 'Build up, build up'" = TJ "And it shall be said, 'Teach ye and exhort'").

203. This aggadic midrash which was designed to provide a rational explanation for Israel's election, occurs in numerous other sources, too; cf., e.g., T. B. A. Z. 2b; Mekhilta on Exod. 19:2 and 20:1; Sifre, par. 311, on Deut. 32:8; Lev. R. XIII, 2; Midr. Tanh. edit. Buber, Lev. p. 28; Deut. pp. 54-55; Midr. Tanh. יתרו 14; שמיני 6; ברכה 4.

204. Cf. Hos. 5:9b (MT "Among the tribes of Israel I declare (or: I have made known)

must be subject to the Torah; and God in turn would reward Israel by performing miraculous acts for His people.[205]

The reward of Torah study for the righteous who long for it will be great. They will constantly acquire new teachings,[206] wisdom and riches,[207] and God will accept their prayers.[208] Not only that, but even their children and children's children will be endowed by the Almighty with knowledge and understanding of Torah.[209] For Israel's leaders, the study of the Torah is its own beautiful reward.[210]

By way of contrast, refusal to study and obey the Torah constitutes an act of rebellion —Jerusalem, for example, was guilty of this sin[211]—for which punishment will be exacted.[212] While ignorance of the Torah is for-

---

what is sure" = TJ "Among the tribes of Israel I have made known the Torah").

205. Cf. Hos. 2:16a (MT ". . . behold, I will allure her, and bring her into the wilderness" = TJ ". . . I will subject her to the Torah and perform miracles and mighty acts for her, as I did for her in the wilderness").

206. Cf. Is. 12:3 (MT ". . . you will draw water with joy from the wells of salvation" = TJ ". . . you will receive a new teaching from the most chosen righteous men" [presumably, the greatest scholars]).

207. Cf. *ibid.* 40:29 (MT 'He gives power to the faint, and to him who has no might he increases strength' = TJ "He gives wisdom to the righteous who faint [i.e., yearn] for the words of the Torah, and to those who have no might He increases riches").

208. Cf. *ibid.* 41:17 (MT 'The poor and needy seek water, and there is none, and their tongue is parched with thirst; I, the Lord, will answer them . . ." = TJ "The humble and poor who desire instruction as one who is thirsty for water, but they do not find it, [while] their spirit faints with affliction—I, the Lord, will accept their prayer . . .").

209. Cf., *ibid.* 40:14 (MT "Whom did He consult that He might make Him understand . . . and who taught Him knowledge, and showed Him the way of understanding?" = TJ "Those who asked of Him—[to them] he explained wisdom . . . and He gave Torah to their children, and the way of understanding He made known to their children's children"). TJ's rendering is obviously influenced by Is. 59:21.

210. Cf. Zech. 9:17a (MT ". . . how great is His goodness, and how great is His beauty!" = TJ ". . . how good and how beautiful is Torah instruction for the leaders"). The "leaders" (נגודיא), who are nowhere alluded to in the text, may have suggested themselves to the targumist because of the first word in the second half of the verse—דגן (grain)—which by metathesis approximates Aramaic נגוד (leader).

211. Cf. Jer. 8:5 (MT "Why has this people turned away, Jerusalem in perpetual backsliding? They hold fast to deceit, they refuse to return" = TJ "Why is this people hardening itself so as not to return to My worship? [Why] have the inhabitants of Jerusalem turn back to rebel against the Torah, and [why] do they not desire to return?").

212. Cf. Hos. 4:14b (MT ". . . a people that does not understand shall come to ruin" = TJ ". . . a generation that does not reflect upon the Torah—shall it not be abandoned?").

givable, refusal to ask for instruction and accept it when given is not, and therefore deserves harsh prophetic censure.[213]

For TJ, the Torah is *the* book, par excellence, and no other book of any value is conceivable.[214] It is the authentic word of God;[215] the revelation of his work[216] and of His commandments, which are to be found only in the Torah.[217]

Because the Torah is perfect, TJ adopts a fundamentalist view that the entire Torah, including the last verses, were written by Moses, while Joshua, who, according to some rabbis, added the last eight verses referring to Moses' death,[218] merely laid aside whatever he had written along with the scroll of the Torah, which Moses had already completed.[219]

---

213. Cf. *ibid.* 5:4b (MT "... they do not know the Lord" = TJ "... they did not ask for instruction from before the Lord"); cf. Jer. 13:17a (MT "But if you will not hear it [or: listen]..." = TJ "But if you will not accept instruction ...").

214. Cf. Jos. 10:13a and II Sam. 1:18b, where MT "Book of Jashar" is rendered "Book of the Law" by TJ. In the Talmud and Midrash (T.B.A.Z. 25a; T.Y. Sot. I, 10, 17c; Gen. R. VI, 9) different views on the identity of the "Book of Jashar" are put forward. They amount to little more than guesswork.

215. Cf. II Sam. 22:31b (MT "the word of the Lord" = TJ "the Torah of the Lord").

216. Cf. Is. 5:12b (MT "... they do not regard the work of the Lord" = TJ "... they do not reflect upon the Torah of the Lord"). It is interesting to compare this somewhat narrow interpretation with that propounded in the Talmud (T.B. Shab. 75a), where this verse is used to stress the importance of studying astronomy—"the work of the Lord" being equated to the science of the "calculation of (astronomical) cycles and planetary courses." Cf. also Is. 5:13a, where MT "Therefore My people are gone into exile for want of knowledge" is rendered in some manuscripts of TJ, "Therefore My people are gone into exile because they did not know the Torah."

217. Cf. Jer. 7:31b (MT "... which I did not command" = "... which I did not command in My Torah"); *ibid.* 32:35a (MT "... which I did not command them" = TJ "... which I did not command in My Torah"). Conceivably, this emphasis on divine commandments being found only in the Torah was directed against sectarian, and especially Christian, antinomian tendencies. In effect, TJ preaches that only in the Torah is God's will revealed, and His precepts cannot be found anywhere else. Cf. T.B. B.M. 59b, where we are told that R. Joshua denied the validity of the mystical *Bath Kol* (the echo of an heavenly voice) if it happened to contradict the Torah. The rabbis considered that even God was subject to the Torah and had to submit to its rules, as He Himself admitted when He responded to R. Joshua's challenge by saying, "My children have prevailed against Me" (*ibid.*).

218. Cf. T.B. B.B. 15a; Mak. 11a. On the perfection of "the Law of the Lord," cf. Ps. 19:8.

219. Cf. Jos. 24:26a (MT "Joshua wrote these words in the Book of the Law of the God" = TJ "Joshua wrote these words and laid them aside with [or: hid them in] the Book of the Law of the Lord").

In line with rabbinic thinking on the subject, TJ envisages a Messianic future in which people will long, hunger and thirst for Torah instruction.[220] Indeed, Israel as a whole will yearn for and follow eagerly the Torah.[221] Israel's repentance will find a fitting expression by a return to the Torah.[222] In that blessed messianic age, Torah learning will spring forth like a fountain of water,[223] and the expansion of learning will be such that all the children will be engaged in the study of Torah.[224] The dream of universal religious education—which in those days constituted virtually all available knowledge that might be useful for the application of law and ethics in Judaism—was perhaps the greatest rabbinic concept, for which both rabbis and targumists labored unceasingly.

Important as the study of the Torah was in the eyes of the Targumists and Rabbis, it was not enough. The Torah also had to be practiced. In line with the rabbinic dictum that "not expounding the Torah is the main thing, but practicing it,[225] TJ interprets II Sam. 22:23a—MT "For all his

220. Cf. Amos 8:11-12. The prophetic prediction of hunger and thirst for the word of the Lord, so that people will wander everywhere and run to and fro "to seek the word of the Lord," is explained by TJ (in v. 12b) in the sense of "to ask for instruction from before the Lord." This passage is interpreted along similar lines in the Tosefta (Eduy. I, 1) and Talmud (T.B. Shab. 138b-139a). Cf. also Is. 32:6b (MT '...to make empty the soul of the hungry, and to deprive the thirsty of drink" = TJ "...to weary the souls of the righteous who crave for instruction as one that hungers for bread, and for words of the Torah which they desire [lit., which are] as one that thirsts for water—they plan to render void").

221. Cf. Jer. 31:21b (MT "a woman shall compass a man" = TJ "the people of the house of Israel will long for [or: follow eagerly] the Torah").

222. Cf. Is. 31:6 (MT "Return ... O children of Israel" = TJ "Return to the Torah ... O children of Israel").

223. Cf. Zech. 13:1a (MT "On that day there shall be a fountain opened for the house of David and the inhabitants of Jerusalem" = TJ "At that time the instruction of the Law shall be revealed like a fountain of water").

224. Cf. Is. 54:13a (MT "All your sons shall be taught by the Lord" = TJ "All your sons shall be learning the Torah of the Lord"). On the rabbinic concept of universal education, cf. T.B. Sanh. 94b, where Hezekiah king of Judah is depicted as having "planted a sword by the door of the house of study and proclaimed, 'Whosoever will not study the Torah shall be pierced with this sword. Thereupon search was made from Dan to Beer sheba, and no ignorant person was found; from Gabbath to Antipatris, and no boy or girl, man or woman was found who was not thoroughly versed in the laws of ritual impurity and purity ...'" The attribution to the biblical past of a state of affairs which was not achieved even in the talmudic age clearly demonstrates the educational ideal of the rabbis which they sought to realize, as, supposedly, it had been in the distant past.

225. M. Aboth I, 17.

ordinances were before me"—in the sense of "For all His judgments are revealed before me *to carry them out.*" To do right is to observe, not merely study the Torah, and those who "store up violence and robbery in their palaces"[226] because "they do not know how to do right"[227] are, in TJ's interpretation, those who "do not know to carry out (the precepts of) the Torah."

A God-fearing man is expected to observe the Torah even when subjected to intense suffering.[228] Israel, when exiled among the nations, will be put under pressure to abandon the practice of the commandments of the Torah; but they must respond with unconditional obedience to the Torah.[229] When Israel was afflicted in Egypt and subjected to slavery, it was due to the observance of circumcision and of the sacrifice of the Paschal lamb that the Almighty redeemed Israel from bondage.[230] Conversely, it was the refusal to observe the commandment of tithing which was the cause of the failure of the grape harvest.[231] Generally, good deeds are the surest protec-

---

226. Amos 3:10b.

227. *Ibid.* v. 10a.

228. Cf. Is. 50:10 (MT "Who among you fears the Lord ... who walks in darkness ...?" = TJ "Who among you of those that fear the Lord ... who has practiced [the commandments of] the Torah [while] in affliction like a man who walks in darkness?"). Cf. Aboth VI, 4: "Such is the way of (studying) Torah: a morsel of bread with salt you shall eat, and water by measure you shall drink, and on the ground you shall sleep, and a life of affliction you shall live—while in the study of Torah you toil ..."

229. Cf. Is. 8:20 (MT "To the teaching and to the testimony! Surely for this word which they speak there is no dawn" = TJ "Thus you shall say to them, 'We obey the Law that was given to us as a testimony.' You will, however, be exiled among the nations, and they will speak to you in this manner [lit., according to this word]; henceforth there is none of whom one may seek or inquire"). The last clause is as obscure in the Aramaic translation as in the original.

230. Cf. Ezek. 16:6 (MT "And when I passed by you and saw you weltering in your blood, I said to you, 'By your blood live; by your blood live'" = TJ "When the memory of the covenant with your fathers came before Me, I revealed Myself to redeem you; for it was revealed before Me that you were afflicted by your enslavement. So I said to you, 'Because of the blood of circumcision I shall have consideration for you,' and I said to you, 'Because of the blood of the Paschal lambs I will redeem you'"). Cf. also T.B. Ker. 9a, where the same idea is expressed—namely that the redemption from Egyptian bondage was made possible by the observance of circumcision and the offering of the Paschal lamb. Cf. also Mekhilta on Exod. 12:23.

231. Cf. Is. 5:10a ("... ten acres of vineyard shall yield but one bath ..." = TJ "... for the sin that they did not give tithes, an area of ten wagon-loads of [the fruits of] a vineyard will yield one bath").

tion in time of trouble,[232] and the saved remnant always consists of the righteous who fulfill the Torah.[233] Indeed, when the resurrection of the dead will take place, it will be those who observed the Torah who will be revived by the miraculous "dew of light;"[234] for they who fulfill the precepts of the Torah are valued by God more highly than the purest gold.[235]

6. Prayer

The importance of prayer is frequently stressed in TJ. In line with rabbinic thinking on the subject,[236] TJ regards prayer as an indispensable substitute for the sacrifices which could no longer be offered after the destruction of the Temple.[237] Prayer, according to TJ, is the key for personal redemption.[238] Even the Aramaic term for the word praying, צלי, assumes a

---

232. Cf. *ibid.* 26:20a (MT "Come, my people, enter your chambers, and shut your doors behind you" = TJ "Come, my people, provide [lit., make] yourself good deeds which shall protect you in time of distress"). On the concept that Torah prayer, and acts of charity are more effective than sacrifices in averting evil decrees, cf. T.B.R.H. 18a; Yev. 105a; T.Y.R.H. II, 6, 58c; T.Y. Sanh. I, 2, 18c; *et passim.*

233. Cf. Is. 37:32a; II Kings 19:31a (MT "For out of Jerusalem shall go forth a remnant, and they that escape out of Mount Zion" = TJ "For out of Jerusalem shall go forth the remaining righteous ones, and the remnant of those who uphold the Torah out of Mount Zion"). On the great reward to be granted for the observance of the commandments, cf. Midr. Tanh. לך לך 1.

234. Cf. Is. 26:19 (MT "Your dead shall live . . .; for your dew is the dew of light . . ." = TJ "You are quickening the dead . . . ; for your dew is the dew of light for those who observe your Torah . . ."). Cf. T.B. Ket. 111b; "Whoever makes use of the light of the Torah, the light of the Torah will revive him." On the connection between dew and the resurrection of the dead, cf. T.Y. Ber. V, 2, 9b; T.Y. Taan. I, 1, 63d.

235. Cf. Is. 13:12 (MT "I will make . . . man more rare than the gold of Ophir" = TJ "I will love . . . those who observe the Torah more than the pure gold of Ophir").

236. Cf. Num. R. XVIII, 12; Cant. R. IV, 3; Midr. Tanh. קרח, 12; Midr. Tanh. edit. Buber, יצ, 9a, מות אחרי, 35a.

237. Cf. Hos. 14:3b, where MT ". . . we will render the fruit of our lips" (so according to LXX and Syr.; traditional Hebrew rendering: ". . . we will pay with our lips instead of bulls") is given a homiletical interpretation: ". . . let the words of our lips be accepted before you with favor like oxen upon your altar." On the concept of prayers being even superior to sacrifices, cf. T.Y. Sanh. I, 2, 18c; T.Y.R.H. II, 6, 58b; T.B. Ber. 32b.

238. Cf. Jonah 2:10b (MT "Deliverance belongs to the Lord" = TJ "The redemption of my soul is through prayer before the Lord").

special significance in TJ, where it is used only in connection with prayer directed towards God, while prayer to idols is rendered by the religiously neutral term בעי (ask, request).[239] The worst evil is one for which prayer is ineffective;[240] and failure to pray to God is liable to invoke severe punishment.[241]

In addition to regular services, there are many occasions for extraordinary prayers, first and foremost in times of trouble,[242] for example, in the face of oppression[243] or exile[244] or before an impending battle when intercession for success is vital;[245] and generally whenever perils threaten.[246] Once the danger is past, (e.g., after recovery from illness), a prayer of thanks would naturally follow.[247]

239. Cf. Jer. 11:11b (MT ". . . they will cry (יזעקו) to Me" = TJ ". . . they will pray (ויצלון) before Me"); *ibid.* 11:12a (MT ". . . they will cry (יזעקו) to the gods to whom they burn incense" = TJ ". . . they will ask (ויבעון) of the idols to whom they offer spices").

240. Cf. Is. 47:11a (MT ". . . evil shall come upon you for which you cannot atone" [or: "which you do not know how to charm away"] = TJ ". . . evil shall come upon you, against which you will not know to pray").

241. Cf. Amos 6:10b (MT "Quiet! For the name of the Lord is not to be mentioned" = TJ "Remove [viz., the dead bodies; the targumist evidently read הסר (Remove) instead of הס]; for when they were alive they did not pray in the name of the Lord").

242. Cf. Hos. 8:2, where MT "To Me they cry, My God, we Israel know You" is considerably expanded by TJ: "Whenever I bring trouble upon them, they pray before Me and say, 'Now we know that we have no God but You; deliver us, for we are Your people Israel.'"

243. Cf. Is. 38:14b (MT "O Lord, I am oppressed; be you my security" = TJ "O Lord, accept my prayer; carry out (lit., do) my request").

244. Cf. Zech. 12:10a (MT ". . . they will look on Him whom [or: to Me because] they have pierced" = TJ ". . . they will pray before Me because they were exiled"). The passage is enigmatic, and because of the Christological use made of it by the Church (cf. John 19:37), it clearly required a homiletical interpretation.

245. Cf. II Sam. 18:3b (MT ". . . therefore it is better that you send us help from the city" = TJ ". . . and now it is better that you [viz., David] should pray for us out of the city to render aid"). Thus, prior to the decisive battle against Absalom, David's projected role is to aid his army through prayer. A sermon by a "priest annointed for battle" prior to combat is prescribed in Deut. 20:1-4, and this in turn is homiletically expanded to a considerable extent in M. Soṭ. VIII, 1.

246. Cf. II Kings 3:13b (MT "The king of Israel said to him [viz., Elisha], 'No . . .'" = TJ "The king of Israel said to him, 'Please, do not mention sins at this hour [or: the sins of that wickedness]; pray for compassion for us'"). Incidentally, this passage also shows the widespread belief of the danger of mentioning sins, especially at a time of peril; cf., e.g., T.B. Ber. 19a; 60a; Ket. 8b.

247. Cf. Is. 38:9 (MT "A writing of Hezekiah king of Judah after he had been sick and had recovered from his sickness" = TJ "A writing of thanks for the miracle that was wrought for

According to the rabbis, prayer must not be regarded as a burdensome obligation fulfilled in a routine fashion without enthusiasm.[248] Since prayer is an outpouring of the soul, one should have an emotional desire and longing to pray.[249] For TJ there are no secular songs. Where singing is mentioned in the Prophetic books of the Bible, it is invariably songs of praise in honor of God.[250] In addition, prayer is also an expression of joy and exultation,[251] and worship often takes the form of joyful shouts and exclamations.[252] Yet, at the same time, TJ does not deny the value of silent prayer, and the "still small voice" heard by Elijah at Mt. Horeb is, in TJ's version, "the voice of them that praise (viz, God) in silence (or: in a whisper).[253]

Because prayer must be enthusiastic and joyful, any pessimism uttered in the course of a prayer is unacceptable to TJ.[254] Still less, are expressions of

---

Hezekiah king of the tribe of Judah after he had been sick and had recovered from his sickness"). On the importance of prayers of thanks, cf. Lev. R. IX, 7: "All prayers will be abolished, but the prayer of thanks will not be abolished."

248. Cf. M. Ber. IV, 4; T.B. Ber. 29b.

249. Cf. Is. 26:9a (MT "My soul yearns for you at night" = TJ "My soul yearns to pray before you at night"). By way of contrast, the Talmud points out that "The Holy One, Blessed be He, longs for the prayer of the righteous" (T.B. Yev. 64a). Cf. also Gen. R. XLV, 4.

250. Cf. I Kings 5:12b (MT ". . . his songs were a thousand and five" = TJ ". . . his praises [viz., of God] were a thousand and five"); Is. 26:1a (MT ". . . this song will be sung in the land of Judah" = TJ ". . . they will utter a new praise in the land of the house of Judah"); *ibid.*, 30:29a (MT "You shall have a song" = TJ "You shall have praise [viz., of God]"); Jud. 5:1a (MT "Deborah sang" = TJ "Deborah praised [viz., God]"); *ibid.*, 5:12a (MT "Awake, awake, Deborah! Awake, awake, utter a song" = TJ "Give praise, give praise, Deborah! Give praise and thanks; utter praise"). Cf. also the Targumim on Exod. 15:1, which all render Moses' song "praise;" so also Miriam's song (*ibid.*, v. 21). Similar interpretations of biblical songs are also to be found in rabbinic literature; cf., e.g., T.B. Pes. 95b; Ar. 10b; T.Y. Pes. IX, 3, 36d; Mekhilta on Exod. 15:1; Gen. R. VI, 2; Cant. R. II, 1; Midr. Tanh. בשלח 10.

251. Cf. Zech. 2:14a (MT "Sing and rejoice, O daughter of Zion" = TJ "Pray and rejoice [other versions: praise], O daughter of Zion"). The principle that one should "serve the Lord with gladness" (Ps. 100:2) is frequently reiterated in rabbinic literature; cf., e.g., T.Y. Ber. V, 1, 8d; T.B. Ber. 31a; Eruv. 65a.

252. Cf. Zeph. 3:14 (MT "Sing aloud, O daughter of Zion; shout O Israel; rejoice and exult with all your heart, O daughter of Jerusalem" = TJ "Give praise, O congregation of Zion; pray O Israel; rejoice and pray with all your heart, O congregation of Jerusalem").

253. Cf. I Kings 19:12b. On silent prayer in the Bible, cf. I Sam. 1:13. On opposition to loud prayer, cf. T.B. Ber. 24b; Sot. 32b.

254. Cf. Is. 38:10 (MT ". . . in the gates of Sheol I am deprived of the rest of my years" = TJ ". . . in the gates of Sheol, because of my memorial for good, my years have been increased"). Cf. T.B. Ber. 10a: "Even if a sharp sword lies on a man's throat, he should not abandon hope of (divine) mercy").

despair admissible.[255] Yet, optimism and joy in prayer are not enough. To be effective, prayer must be preceded by genuine repentance;[256] for persistence in sin prevents the divine acceptance of prayer.[257]

Not everyone's prayer is equally effective. TJ frequently enunciates the concept of intercession by a righteous man, with many meritorious deeds to his credit, whose prayer is more likely to be accepted than that of an ordinary person.[258] Israel, in particular, needs such intercessors badly,[259] and the prayers of prophets such as Elijah and Elisha are depicted in TJ as being "better for Israel than chariots and horsemen."[260] Even Joram king of Israel,

---

255. Cf. Ezek. 21:5a (MT "Alas [or: Ah], Lord God!" = TJ "Accept my request, O Lord God!"). See also previous note.

256. Cf. Hos. 2:4 (MT "Plead with your mother, plead; for she is not my wife, and I am not her husband; but let her put away her harlotry from between her breasts . . ." = TJ "Rebuke the congregation of Israel and say to her that she does not trouble [lit., afflict] herself in My worship, so that My *Memra* does not accept her prayer until she removes her evil deeds from her face . . ."). On the rabbinic view that prayer must be accompanied by repentence, cf., e.g., T.Y. Sanh. X, 2, 28c; T.B. Sanh. 43b.

257. Cf. Is. 1:13b, where MT "I cannot endure iniquity and solemn assembly" is paraphrased in TJ, "Your sins do not allow your prayer to be accepted at the time of your assembly." According to the Talmud (T.B. Ber. 4a), sin can cause even a divine promise to become null and void, and *a priori* prayer would be ineffective.

258. Cf. Is. 63:5a (MT "I looked, but there was no one to help; I was appalled, but there was no one to uphold" = TJ "It is revealed before Me that there is no man who has [done] good deeds, and it is known before Me that there is no man who would arise and pray for them"); Ezek. 22:30a (MT "And I sought for a man among them who should build up the wall and stand in the breach before Me for the and, so that I should not destroy it" = TJ "And I sought from among them a man before me who had [done] good deeds that he may stand up in the gates before Me and pray for mercy for the people of the land, so that I should not destroy it"); Amos 7:2a.5a (MT "How can Jacob stand?" = TJ "Who will arise and pray for [pardon for] their sins?"). The rabbinic concept of intercessory prayer both agrees and goes beyond the limits indicated in TJ. In the Talmud, it is not only the righteous man who can intercede for the nation or for individuals with the Almighty; a scholar, too, can and should be requested to pray for a sick person (T.B. B.B. 116a). Even ordinary people should be informed of a man's troubles, especially if he is sick, so that they may pray for him (T.B. Shab. 67a). By implication, such prayers, uttered by many persons, are assumed to possess heightened efficacy as compared with individual prayers. The rabbis denounced those who are able to pray for their contemporaries but fail to do so; cf. T.B. Ber. 12b; B.B. 91b. The biblical basis for this concept is to be found in I Sam. 12:23a: ". . . far be it from me that I should sin against the Lord by ceasing to pray for you."

259. See n. 258. Cf. also T.B. Sot. 49a: "Had it not been for the prayer of David, all Israel would have been sellers of rubbish" (i.e., earning a precarious livelihood).

260. Cf. II Kings 2:12a; 13:14b (MT "My father, my father the chariots of Israel and its

who was otherwise not distinguished by his piety, had to ask the prophet Elisha to pray for the three allied armies who found themselves in a waterless desert during their campaign against Mesha king of Moab.[261]

The capacity of the righteous to affect and even alter divine decrees, which is often emphasized in the Talmud,[262] is also recognized in TJ, where their spiritual, intercessory power is expanded to cover the realm of purgatory. The wicked, who are punished in hell for this misdeeds, have to endure their suffering "until the righteous say concerning them, 'We have seen enough.'"[263]

The reward of prayer is acceptance by God. Thus, the spring which revived Samson and was called En-hakkore,[264] is explained by TJ as "the well which was given through the prayer of Samson." Similarly, those who thirst for instruction and pray for it will see the fulfillment of their wish, thanks to their prayers.[265] Among the many biblical figures whose prayers were answered by God, according to TJ, are Samson's father Manoah;[266] Samuel;[267] David;[268] and Elijah.[269] King Saul's prayer, on the other hand, was not accepted.[270]

---

horsemen!'" = TJ "My master, my master, who is better for Israel through his prayer than chariots and horsemen"). This rendering is also cited in T.B. M.K. 26a, where it is attributed to Rab Joseph, the foremost Targum expert in Babylonia.

261. Cf. II Kings 3:13b, where MT "The king of Israel said to him (viz., Elisha), 'Nay . . .'" is enormously expanded in TJ: "The king of Israel said to him, 'I pray for you, do not mention the sins of that wicked woman (viz., Jezebel), (but) pray for mercy for us.'" The king's alleged request not to mention sins at a time of danger is paralleled in the Talmud, where the injunction that "a man should never provide an opening of the mouth (i.e., an opportunity for leveling accusations) for Satan," is frequently reiterated (cf., e.g., T.B. Ber. 19a; 60a; Ket. 8b).

262. Cf., e.g., M. Ber. V, 5; Taan. III, 8; T.B. Ber. 34b; Shab. 59b; Taan. 23a-25a; Ket. 103b; Sot. 12a; B.M. 106a.

263. Cf. Is. 66:24b (MT ". . . they shall be an abhorrence to all flesh" = TJ ". . . the wicked shall be judged in hell until the righteous say concerning them, 'We have seen enough'").

264. Cf. Jud. 15:19.

265. Cf. Is. 41:17. See *supra,* n. 208.

266. Cf. TJ on Jud. 13:9a.

267. Cf. TJ on I Sam. 7:9b.

268. Cf. *ibid.* 23:4a; and, especially, II Sam. 22:4 (MT "I call upon the Lord, who is worthy to be praised, and I am saved from my enemies" = TJ "David said, 'With praise I pray before the Lord, who at all times delivers me from my enemies'"); cf. *ibid.* 22:7 (MT "In my distress I called upon the Lord; to my God I called. From His Temple He heard my voice, and my cry came to His ears" = TJ "David said, 'When I am in distress, I pray before the

In assessing the positive divine response to prayer, TJ distinguishes two stages: a) acceptance in principle; b) active aid.[271] As far as Israel is concerned, there is no "favorable" time when prayer is more acceptable than at any other time. Provided the Israelites do God's will He has compassion on them; accepts their prayers; saves them whenever they are in distress; and generally helps them at all times they are in need.[272]

7. THE REWARD OF THE RIGHTEOUS AND THE PUNISHMENT OF THE WICKED

The concept of reward for the righteous (*Tsaddikim*)—as well as punishment for the wicked (*Reshaim*)—is basic to both Biblical and Rabbinic theology[273]. TJ, reflecting as it does the views of the orthodox school of R. Akiba[274], fully shares the idea that the righteous are eventually rewarded by God, while the wicked, sooner or later, get their just deserts.

What constitutes a *Tsaddik* in TJ's theology? He is first and foremost a person who not only refrains from wrongdoing[275], but actively engages in

---

Lord, and before my God I make supplication; and He accepts my prayer from His Temple, and my request is carried out before Him'").

269. Cf. TJ on I Kings 17:22a; 18:37 f.

270. Cf. TJ on I Sam. 28:6a,15b.

271. Cf. Is. 38:14b (MT "O Lord, I am oppressed, be you my security" = TJ "O Lord, accept my prayer, do my request").

272. Cf. Is. 48:8a (MT "In a time of favor I have answered you, and in a day of salvation I have helped you" = TJ "At a time when you do My will I accept your prayer, and at a time of distress I raise up for you salvation and help"). Note the contrast with Is. 55:6, where MT "Seek the Lord while He may be found; call upon Him while He is near," clearly implies a favorable time for prayer when it is more likely to be answered than at other times (cf. T.B.R.H. 18a; Yev. 49b; 105a, where the contradiction between Is. 55:6 and Deut. 4:7 [MT "... the Lord our God ... whenever we call upon Him"] is pointed out). This is significantly transformed by TJ to "Seek the fear of the Lord while you are living; ask of Him while you are in existence." Cf. also Hos. 14:9b (MT "It is I who answer and look after Him" = TJ "I, by My *Memra,* will accept the prayer of Israel and have compassion on them").

273. For a summary of the vast literature on the subject of reward and punishment in Judaism, cf. Louis Jacobs, *Principles of the Jewish Faith: An Analytical Study* (New York, 1964), pp. 350-367.

274. R. Akiba's opinions on divine reward and punishment are summed up in M. Avoth III, 15-16.

275. In the legal terminology of the Hebrew Bible, the *Tsaddik* is often the winner—or

good deeds for the benefit of his fellow man[276]. He is not merely a man of faith, but also a man of truth in all his dealings[277]. Characteristic of the *Tsaddikim* in general is their insatiable hunger and thirst for instruction in the Torah[278]. Hence they are the true aristocracy of the nation[279].

In their encounter with God, the *Tsaddikim* who carry out his wishes enjoy the privilege of divine communication in the course of which the Almighty makes his will known[280]. The relationship between God and the *Tsaddikim* is, however, by no means one-sided. In line with rabbinic thinking on the subject, TJ, too, endorses the popular concept that "the righteous decrees and the Holy One, blessed be He, fulfills.[281] God, of course, knows

---

the one who ought to win—in a lawsuit; cf. Exod. 23:7-8; Deut. 16:19; 25:1; I Kings 8:32 (=II Chron. 6:23); Is. 5:23; Prov. 17:15; 18:17.

276. Cf. Is. 32:20a, where MT "Happy are you who sow beside all waters" = TJ "Happy are you, o righteous ones, you have wrought good works for yourselves; for you are like those that sow on a well-watered field." On the twofold concept of negative restraint from evil and, conversely, the positive pursuit of good, cf. e.g., Is. 1:16-17; Pss. 34:14-15.

277. Cf. Hab. 2:4b, where MT "the righteous shall live by his faith" is significantly altered by TJ to "the righteous ones shall endure by their truthfulness".

278. Cf. Is. 32:6b (MT ". . . to leave the craving of the hungry unsatisfied, and to deprive the thirsty of drink" = TJ ". . . to make weary the souls of the righteous ones who crave instruction just like a hungry man [who] craves bread, and the words of the Torah which are like thirst for water [i.e., water for thirst; cf. Is. 55:1f.] they imagine they will nullify").

279. Cf. I Sam. 2:8a, where TJ changes MT ". . . to make them sit with princes" to "make them sit with the righteous ones, the great ones (or: the princes) of the world". This elevation of the *Tsaddikim* to the high status of princes and "the great ones of the world" is all the more remarkable in view of the fact that the virtually identical text in Pss. 113:8 is rendered literally in the Aramaic translation ". . . to make them sit with princes".

280. Cf. Is. 40:13, where the rhetorical question in MT, "Who . . . as his counsellor has instructed him?" is radically transformed in TJ to a definite assertion, "The righteous ones who do his command (lit., his *Memra*), to them he makes known the words of his good pleasure". It should be noted, though, that the literal meaning of the text, even though framed as a question, has a certain anthropomorphic connotation. In TJ, even to pose a question whether anyone could be God's counsellor and instruct him, is considered inadmissible.

281. Cf. Is. 44:26a, where MT "He confirms the word of his servants" = TJ "He establishes (or: fulfills) the words of his *righteous* servants". Cf. also a Midrashic version of TJ on Hab. 3:1, according to which the prophet Habakkuk "made a drawing (i.e., of a circle) and stood inside it, spoke up saying thus, 'As his (viz., God's) name lives and endures, I will not move from this drawing until I will be told about an extension to be given to the wicked ones (i.e., to repent) . . .'" The divine response was that if the wicked repent, they would be forgiven.

On the concept that God carries out the wishes of the *Tsaddikim*, cf. T.B. Shab. 59b; Ket. 103b; Sot. 12a; B.M. 106a; Sifre on Num. 12:13; Exod. R. XXI,2; Num. R. XVIII, 12; Deut.

who is a *Tsaddik,* and he does not need to try or test him, the trials of Abraham and Job notwithstanding[282].

The merit of the *Tsaddikim* acquired by their righteousness is enduring and cannot normally be taken away from them[283]. It is thanks to the merit of the individual righteous man as well as the *Tsaddikim* as a group that a city—and, indeed, society as a whole—can be preserved[284].

Both spiritual and material rewards are in store for the *Tsaddikim.* They are to be granted the divine light of salvation[285], and—if they labor in the

---

R.V,13; Tanh. Vaera 3; *ibid.* Naso 29; Tanh. edit. Buber I, 168; *ibid.* IV, 96; Pesik. Rabbati ch. 3, edit. Friedmann 7b. Cf. especially T.B. Taan. 23a: "You (viz. Ḥoni) have decreed (on earth) below, and the Holy One blessed be He, fulfills your word (in heaven) above"; T.Y. Taan. III,12,67a: "The Holy One, blessed be He, cancels his decree because of the decree of the righteous"; cf. Tanh. Vayera 19: "'He who obeys a command'" (Eccl. 8:5)—this refers to the righteous ones who obey the commandments of the Holy One, blessed be He; and the Holy One, blessed be He, fulfills their decree." All the passages cited are based on Job 22:28a: "You will decide on a matter, and it will be established for you.

282. Cf. Jer. 20:12a (MT "O Lord of hosts, who triest [Heb. בחן = testing] the righteous one" = TJ "The Lord of hosts chooses truth"). An omniscient God has no need to test the righteous.

283. Cf. Is. 5:23b, where MT "and the righteous they deprive of his right" = TJ "and the right (or: merit) of the righteous ones they take away from them with wickedness" (ברשע). The addition of ברשע is clearly deliberate. Only through an act of wickedness could evil people try to expunge the merit—and hence the rights—of the *Tsaddikim.* Theologically, however, righteousness is of enduring worth and cannot be expunged from the record by any arbitrary act, except by the individual concerned who may lapse into evil; cf. Ezek. 18:24ff.; 33:12ff.

284. Cf. Zech. 8:4b, where MT "each (or: every man) with his staff in his hand" = TJ "and a man whose deeds are right shall protect them". Cf. also Is. 65:8b, where MT ". . . so will I do for the sake of my servants, and not destroy everything" is expanded to ". . . so will I do for the sake of my *righteous* servants etc." It is thus only the righteous who can save society—an idea already enunciated in Gen. 18:24-32, but repudiated in Ezek. 14:12-20, where it is stated that even outstanding *Tsaddikim* can save only themselves, not their wicked countrymen. For the concept that the *Tsaddik* protects those around him, cf. Tos. A.Z.I,17 and Rashi on Num. 14:9. This idea is stated with special force in T.B. B.B. 7b, where we are told that Resh Lakish opposed the levy of an impost on rabbis for the purpose of fortifying the city wall on the grounds that "the Rabbis do not need the protection (or a wall)", adding, "If the sand which is the lesser quantity protects (the land) against the sea, how much more must the righteous men's deeds, which are numerous, protect them".

285. Cf. Is. 24:15a, where MT ". . . honor the Lord with lights (or: in the region of light, i.e., in the east)" = TJ ". . . when light comes unto the righteous ones, they shall glorify before the Lord". Cf. II Sam. 23:4a (MT "As the light of the morning when the sun rises = TJ "Happy are you, o righteous ones; you have wrought good deeds for you, so that you will shine in future like the splendor of his glory, like the light of the morning . . ."). Cf. Amos

study of Torah—wisdom[286]. They are to be privileged to dwell on God's mountains (i.e., on the mountains of Israel)[287], where they will grow and develop like tender and delicate blades of grass and like a tree planted by streams of water[288]. Because of their good deeds, the righteous shall be like those that sow on a well-watered field[289]. If they observe the Torah, they are to enjoy peace[290], long life and divine bounty in the Land of Israel[291],

---

4:13a (MT "... who makes the morning darkness" = TJ "... to prepare light for the righteous ones like the light of the morning that comes in; and he arranges to bring darkness upon the wicked ones, so as to destroy [*lit.*, break] the wicked of the earth").

The concept associating the *Tsaddikim* with light is based on Pss. 97:11a ("Light dawns on [*lit.*, is sown for] the righteous"), and is frequently reiterated in rabbinic literature. Cf., e.g., T.B. B.B. 75a: "The face of Moses is like the face of the sun". Cf. T.B. Sanh. 91b: "... 'the light of the sun shall be sevenfold, as the light of seven days (Is. 30:26a) ...'—This refers to the camp of the righteous ones". Cf. Sifre Deut. 1:10 (par. 10): "The faces of the righteous ones will in future be like the sun, the moon ..." Cf. Lev. R. XXX,2: "The righteous ones ... their faces are like the sun and the moon ..." Cf. Gen. R. III,6: "The light that was created during the six days of Creation ... was hidden away (or stored up) and it is prepared for the righteous ones in the future". Cf. Tanh. Vayakhel 10 end: "... Therefore I give you light and confer upon you the boon laid up for the righteous ones". Cf. also Komlosh, *op. cit.*, p. 367, where the Pesik. R.K., cf. XXI, edit. Buber, p. 143b, is cited for a different interpretation of Is. 24:15a.

For other passages associating the *Tsaddikim* with light, cf. Gen. R. VI,9; LXVIII,6; Lev. R. XXVIII,1; Eccl. R.I., 5.7.

286. Cf. Is. 40:29a (MT "He gives strength to the weary" = TJ "He gives wisdom to the righteous ones who weary themselves [or: faint] for the words of his Torah"). Cf. Komlosh, *op. cit.*, p. 395.

287. Cf. Is. 65:9b (MT "... My servants shall dwell thereon" [viz., "my mountains"] = TJ "... My *righteous* servants shall dwell there").

288. Cf. *ibid.* 44:4 (MT "And they shall sprout like [*lit.*, in among] grass, like willows by watercourses" = TJ "And the righteous shall grow up tender and delicate like blades [*lit.*, blossoms] of grass, like a tree that sends forth its roots by streams of water").

289. Cf. *ibid.* 32:20a (MT "Happy are you who sow by all waters" = TJ "Happy are you, o righteous ones; you have wrought good deeds for yourselves; for you are like those that sow on a well-watered field"). Cf. Komlosh, *op. cit.*, p. 386, where T.B. B.K. 17a is cited for similar concepts.

290. Cf. Is. 57:19b (MT "Peace, peace to the far ..." = TJ "Peace shall be wrought for the righteous ones who have kept my Torah from of old ...").

291. Cf. Jer. 31:6a, where MT "For there shall be a day when watchmen will call in the hill country of Ephraim" is considerably expanded in TJ to "For there is length of days and abundant goodness which he will bring upon the righteous ones who have kept my Torah from of old; their portion shall be in the Land of Israel".

including fattened herds[292] and "cream and honey"[293] (symbolizing the fat of the land) as well as the possessions of the wicked which they, the righteous, are to inherit[294].

In due course, God will "renew" the world—i.e., recreate or reform it—for the benefit of the *Tsaddikim*[295]. This idea is explained in greater detail in a Midrashic addition to TJ on Habakkuk 3:2. Accordingly, the continued provocations of the wicked before God and their failure to repent would invoke a divine promise "to renew the world from the beginning for the righteous ones".

That the *Tsaddikim* alone would be saved and escape destruction on the Day of Judgment, while the wicked would be punished is a recurrent theme in TJ's interpretation of the Prophets[296]. More concretely, the contrast

292. Cf. Is. 30:23b (MT "In that day your cattle shall graze in large [lit., wide] pastures" = TJ "The righteous ones shall be nourished [or: sustained] on their herds at that time, on the fat of young ones and fatlings"). Cf. Komlosh, *op. cit.*, p. 386.

293. Cf. Is. 7:22b (MT "Everyone who is left in the midst of the land shall feed on [or: eat] curds and honey" = "With cream and honey shall all the righteous ones that are left in the midst of the land be nourished").

294. Cf. *ibid.* 5:17, where MT "Then lambs shall graze as in their pasture, and strangers shall feed on the ruins of the stout" is allegorically expounded in TJ: "And the righteous ones shall be nourished (or: sustained) as was promised (lit., said) concerning them, and the estates (or: possessions) of the wicked ones shall the righteous ones inherit". This homiletic rendering is cited in T.B. Pes. 68a, where MT כדברם ("as in their pasture") is interpreted to mean כדברם ("as was spoken about them"). Cf. also Komlosh, *op. cit.*, p. 385.

295. Cf. Jer. 23:23 (MT "Am I ... not a God afar off?" = TJ "I, God, ... will in future renew the world for the righteous ones").

296. Cf. Is. 7:22b, where MT "everyone who is left in the midst of the land" becomes in TJ "all the *righteous* ones who are left in the midst of the land" (thus implying that only the righteous ones would be left). Similarly, *ibid.* 51:14 (MT "He who is bowed down ... shall not die [to go down] to the pit" = TJ "The righteous ones shall not die and perish [*lit.*, to destruction]"). Cf. *ibid.* 17:6, where the "gleanings" that "shall be left" (according to MT) are interpreted in TJ's expanded homiletical version as "the righteous ones" ("... so shall the righteous ones be left solitary among the kingdoms"). Similarly, *ibid.* 24:13a (MT "For thus shall it be in the midst of the earth among nations" = TJ "For thus shall the righteous ones be left solitary in the midst of the world among the kingdoms"). Cf. *ibid.* 30:18b, where MT "Happy are all who wait for him" is significantly changed in TJ to "Happy are the righteous ones who wait for his salvation"—thus clearly implying that only the righteous legitimately wait for redemption, while others are presumably not entitled to hope for salvation. The same conclusion must be drawn from Is. 37:32a (=II Kings 19:31a), where MT "... out of Jerusalem shall come forth a remnant and survivors from Mount Zion" is limited in TJ to "... out of

between the righteous and the wicked is vividly depicted in TJ on Isaiah 65:13, where the prophet, speaking in the name of God, addresses those who are addicted to heathen practices. While MT reads: "Behold, my servants shall eat, and you shall be hungry; behold, my servants shall drink, and you shall be thirsty; behold my servants shall rejoice, and you shall be put to shame", TJ identifies God's servants with the righteous[297], and the condemned sinners with the wicked: "Behold, my servants, the righteous ones, shall eat, but you, the wicked ones, shall be hungry; behold, my servants, the righteous ones, shall drink, but you, the wicked ones, shall be thirsty;

Jerusalem shall come the remnant of the righteous ones and they that have escaped of them that fulfill the Torah out of Mount Zion". What all these passages have in common is the sharp contrast between the wider application, often indeed the universality of the divine promises in MT, and their restricted application to the righteous in TJ.

The basic principle of reward and punishment is enunciated in TJ on Is. 21:12a, where MT "Morning comes (or: came), and also the night" is homiletically expounded in TJ to "The prophet said, 'There is reward for the righteous ones, and there is punishment for the wicked ones'". A similar interpretation is also offered in T.Y. Taan. I, 1, 64a: "Morning for the righteous ones, and night for the wicked ones". Cf. Is. 24:16a (MT ". . . we have heard songs of praise, Glory to the righteous one. And I said: 'I waste away! I waste away!'" = TJ ". . . we have heard praise for the righteous ones. The prophet said, 'The secret of the reward for the righteous ones has been shown to me. The secret of the punishment for the wicked ones has been revealed to me'"). Komlosh, *op. cit.,* p. 369, attributes TJ's rendering of Is. 24:16 to the influence of R. Akiba's exegetical method. Cf. Is. 31:9b (MT ". . . the Lord who has a fire in Zion, and [who has] an oven in Jerusalem" = TJ ". . . the Lord who has splendor in Zion for those who observe his Law, and he has a burning furnace of fire for those who have transgressed his *Memra*"). This is a good example of TJ's exegetical method—which agrees with that of R. Akiba—of interpreting biblical parallelisms not as expressions of the same idea in different words, but as two different statements of contrasting ideas, as in this case, reward for the righteous and punishment for transgressors.

Komlosh, *op. cit.,* observes that TJ's translation differs not only from the plain meaning of the text, but also from the rabbinic interpretation in Eruv. 19a, where the "fire in Zion" is interpreted as a reference to Gehenna. Cf. Is. 5:30b (MT ". . . darkness and distress, and the light is darkened by its clouds" = TJ ". . . if the wicked ones seek help . . ., he will bring [*lit.* he brought] distress and calamity upon them; but the righteous ones who shall be in that hour shall be hidden [*lit.,* covered] from before the evil"). Komlosh *op. cit.,* p. 380, suggests plausibly that the addition of the clause concerning the preservation of the righteous was designed to avoid concluding the chapter on a somber note. Cf. also Am. 4:13, cited *supra,* note 285.

297. So also in Is. 65:14-15, where MT "Behold, my servants shall shout for gladness of heart . . .; his servants he will call by a different name" becomes in TJ, "Behold, my servants, the righteous ones, shall utter praises for gladness of heart . . .; his servants, the righteous ones, he will call by a different (or: another) name". It is noteworthy that the role assigned by TJ to the righteous is not merely to rejoice and exult, but to praise God.

behold, my servants, the righteous ones, shall rejoice, but you, the wicked ones, shall be ashamed"[298].

The *Tsaddikim* are to be gratified with peace of mind at the discomfiture of the wicked[299], and they shall have the satisfaction of seeing the wicked go down to Gehenna[300]. There the wicked are to suffer until the righteous say, "We have seen enough"[301]. Thus, by implication, the ultimate redemption of the wicked from Purgatory will depend on the compassion of the righteous.

It also depends on the intercession of the righteous man who has good deeds to his credit whether the living but sinful people of the land are to be saved[302]. Good deeds are indeed the best protection on the day of wrath[303], since they are, as it were, constantly drawn to God's attention[304], and hence, by implication, swiftly rewarded.

Great rewards are promised or implied not only for the *Tsaddikim*, but also for ordinary people who fear God, serve Him, and generally do His will. The treasury of divine goodness—"might and salvation, wisdom and knowl-

298. Cf. *ibid.* 51:14b (MT "... he shall not want for food" = TJ "the righteous ones ... shall not lack their food").

299. Cf. *ibid.* 25:5b (MT "As heat by the shade of a cloud, so the song of the tyrants is stilled" = TJ "As the shadow of a cool rock in an exhausted land, so is the gratification [or: ease] of spirit for the righteous ones, when the wicked are humbled [or: brought low]").

300. Cf. *ibid.* 33:17 ("... your eyes shall behold the land that stretches afar" = TJ "... you shall observe and see [or: look on] them that go down to the land of Gehenna"). The person addressed in TJ is each one of the "righteous ones" in TJ's version of Is. 33:15ff.

301. Cf. *ibid.* 66:24b (MT "... they [*viz.*, the wicked ones who rebelled against God] shall be a horror to all flesh" = TJ "... the wicked ones shall be judged in Gehenna until the righteous ones say concerning them, we have seen enough").

302. Cf. Ezek. 22:30a (MT "I sought for a man among them who should build up the wall and stand in the breach before me for the land that I should not destroy it" = TJ "There was sought from them before me a man who has good deeds [i.e., to his credit], that he should stand in the gate before me and pray for the people of the land, that I should not destroy it"). Cf. also TJ on Is. 65:8, where MT "my servants" become "my righteous servants" in TJ, and they are instrumental in preventing total destruction.

303. Cf. *ibid.* 22:24 (MT "... You are a land that is not cleansed, or rained upon on the day of indignation" = TJ "... You Land of Israel are a land that is not cleansed; good deeds have not been done in it to protect it on the day of execration"). For a similar concept, cf. also T.B. Sanh. 98b: "What should a man do to be saved from the sufferings of the Messianic era (*lit.*, Messiah). He should occupy himself with the study of the Torah and the practice of kind deeds".

304. Cf. Is. Is. 62:6b-7a (MT "You who put the Lord in remembrance, take rest; and give him no rest ..." = TJ "The remembrance of your good deeds is declared [*lit.*, said] before the Lord unceasingly; and their remembrance shall not cease from before him ...").

edge"—is prepared for them[305]; their glory is like a spring whose water never fails[306]; and God accepts their prayer and saves them in time of trouble[307].

Sometimes the reward of those who do God's will and carry out His commandments is not specified[308] or else it is restricted to "those who minister before the Lord"—presumably the priests performing the Temple service[309]. However, even persons who have no positive achievements to their credit but have merely refrained from sin are to be rewarded by mighty acts on the part of the Almighty[310]. Lastly, those who have suffered humiliation and poverty shall be compensated by abundance of joy[311].

The greatest reward of all is reserved for those who "seek"—i.e., study and observe—the precepts of the Torah; for it is there that the will of God is truly manifest. They are to be granted wisdom and knowledge of the Law, and even their children and children's children will have the gifts of Torah

---

305. Cf. *ibid.* 33:6 (MT "And he [*viz.*, God] shall be the stability of your times, abundance of salvation, wisdom, and knowledge; fear of the Lord in his treasure" = TJ "And the good which you promised to do unto them that fear you shall come [*lit.*, be]; you have brought it and established it in its time, [namely] might and salvation, wisdom and knowledge; for those who fear the Lord the treasure of his goodness is prepared").

306. Cf. Jer. 17:13 (MT "... they have forsaken the Lord, the fountain of living water" = TJ "... [*viz.*, the wicked ones] have forsaken your service, o Lord, [the service] on account of which you are bringing upon them glory like a spring whose water never fails").

307. Cf. Is. 49:8a (MT "In a time of favor I have answered you, and on a day of salvation I have helped you" = TJ "At the time when you do my will I will accept your prayer, and in the day of distress I will raise up salvation and help for you").

308. Cf. *ibid.* 40:10b; 62:11b (MT "Behold, his reward is with him" = TJ "Behold, the reward of those who perform his *Memra* [word] is with him").

309. Cf. *ibid.* 23:18b (MT "Her [*viz.*, Tyre's] merchandise shall be for those who dwell before the Lord" = TJ "Her reward [or: wages] shall be for those who minister before the Lord"). The change in TJ, though apparently slight, is significant. "Dwelling" before the Lord is not necessarily confined to priests (cf., eg., Pss. 23:6b: "I shall dwell in the house of the Lord forever [or: as long as I live]"). "Ministering" before the Lord is confined to priests.

310. Cf. Is. 10:21a-22a (MT "A remnant shall return; ... a remnant of it [*viz.*, Israel] shall return" = TJ "The remnant that have not sinned ... shall return; ... the remnant that have not sinned ... for them mighty acts shall be wrought").

311. Cf. *ibid.* 29:19a (MT "The meek [or: humble] shall have increasing joy through [or: in] the Lord" = TJ "Those who have suffered [or: submitted to; *lit.*, received] humiliation shall increase their joy in the *Memra* of the Lord"). Cf. *ibid.* 14:32b (MT "In her [*viz.*, Zion] the afflicted of his people will find refuge" = TJ "In her the poor of his people shall trust and rejoice").

and intelligence[312]. No weariness shall obstruct the course of those who seek knowledge of the Law[313].

Likewise, those who observe the Torah shall be rewarded with "much peace"[314]; they shall prosper[315]; and they shall be made great and strong[316], so that they will have nothing to fear[317]. They are to enjoy superior dignity[318]. Finally, there is divine splendor in Zion for those who fulfill the commandments of the Torah[319].

The rules of conduct and reward relating to individuals also apply to Israel as a whole. It is through the worship of God that Israel gains unfailing benefits and divine glory[320]. To the extent that fear of God will be valued by

312. Cf. *ibid.* 40:14 (MT "Whom did he consult, and who instructed him, and who taught him the path of justice, and taught him knowledge, and let him know the way of discernment?" = TJ "Those who sought [or: asked] from before him he was made to understand [or: he explained] wisdom, and he taught them the way of justice, and he gave the Torah to their sons, and he has made known the way of understanding [or: intelligence] to their sons' sons"). It should be noted that in Talmudic and Midrashic literature "wisdom" is identified with Torah; cf. Tanh. Vayelekh 2; Midrash Prov. 6:32, edit. Buber, p. 57; Mishnah B.M. II, 11; T.B. Sot. 21b.

313. Cf. Jer. 2:24b (MT "All they that seek her shall not be weary ..." = TJ "All they that seek my Torah shall not be weary").

314. Cf. Is. 38:17a, where TJ "Behold, it was for my welfare (*lit.*, for my peace) that I had great bitterness" is radically transformed in TJ to "Behold, for those who observe the Torah there is much peace before you; but you bring bitterness upon the wicked". TJ's theology could not reconcile the concept of "bitterness", i.e., presumably, undeserved punishment, being for one's own good. If one does not deserve punishment, one should not be exposed to it.

315. Cf. *ibid.* 53:10b (MT "... the will of the Lord shall prosper in his hand" = TJ "... they who observe [*lit.*, do] the Torah of the Lord shall prosper when he wills it").

316. Cf. *ibid.* 42:21b (MT "... he magnifies the Torah and makes it glorious" = TJ "... he will make great those who observe [*lit.*, do] his Torah and he will make them strong").

317. Cf. *ibid.* 35:4a (MT "Say to those who are anxious of heart, 'Be strong, fear not'" = "Say to those who are eager [*lit.*, who hurry] in their hearts to observe [*lit.*, do] the Torah, 'Be strong, fear not'").

318. Cf. *ibid.* 9:6a (MT "Great [shall be] the authority" = TJ "Great shall be the dignity of those who observe [*lit.*, do] the Torah").

319. Cf. *ibid.* 31:9b (MT "... the Lord, who has a fire in Zion ..." = TJ "... the Lord who has splendor in Zion for those who observe [*lit.*, do] his Torah ...").

320. Cf. Jer. 2:13b (MT "... they have forsaken me" = TJ "They have forsaken my service [or: worship] on account of which I am bestowing [*lit.*, bringing] upon them goodness [according to another version: glory] like a spring whose water never fails"). Cf. *ibid.* 2:11b (MT "... my people have changed their glory for that which does not profit" = TJ "... my

the people of Israel will they be precious in the sight of God[321]. In practical terms, fear of God means meticulous observance of the laws of the Torah. Whenever Israel fulfills the precepts of the Torah, they are rewarded in a variety of ways. They are fruitful like a vine planted by a spring[322], and they enjoy prosperity and ease like Tyre in her heyday[323]. They prevail against their enemies and drive them out from the Land of Israel[324]. Their good deeds will protect them in time of trouble[325] and sorrow, and lamentation will depart from them[326]. Finally, the divine promises to Israel are trustworthy; for they are invariably fulfilled[327].

---

people have forsaken my service [or: worship] on account of which I bring glory upon them, but they have walked after those that do not profit them"). See also Komlosh, *op. cit.*, p. 400.

321. Cf. Zech. 8:6 (MT "If it is marvelous in the sight of the remnant of this people in these days, should it also be marvelous in my sight?" = TJ "When the fear of me will be precious in the sight of the remnant of this people in these days, they will also be precious before me"). The question in the second clause of the verse seems to be required by the context, but, in the absence of the Hé interrogative, is linguistically doubtful—hence the different interpretation, offered by the medieval commentators; cf. Rabbinic Bible. If the second clause is not a question, but a statement of fact, it would be grossly anthropomorphic. TJ's interpretation is designed to remove this difficulty without introducing a question, which is, linguistically, not apparent.

322. Cf. Ezek. 19:10a (MT "Your mother was like a vine in your blood [or: in your likeness; emendation yields: in a vineyard], planted by water . . ." = TJ "When the congregation of Israel fulfilled the Torah, it was like a vine planted by a spring of water"). Cf. Hos. 10:1a (MT "Israel is a luxuriant [or: empty] vine" = TJ "A despoiled vine is Israel, but it was a choice vine when it fulfilled the Torah"). Cf. also Jer. 17:13, see *supra*, n. 306. The comparison of Israel to a vine is based on Isaiah's parable of the vine (Is. 5:1-7) and on Pss. 80:9. Cf. also Jer. 2:21; Gen. R. XCIX, 8; Tanh. Vayehi 10.

323. Cf. Hos. 9:13a (MT "Ephraim, as I saw Tyre, is planted in a pleasant place" = TJ "When the congregation of Israel fulfills the Torah, it is like Tyre in her prosperity and happiness [or: ease]."

324. Cf. Jud. 5:2a (MT ". . . when the people offered themselves willingly" = TJ ". . . when they [*viz.*, the Israelites] returned [or: repented] to fulfill the Torah, they prevailed against their enemies and expelled them from the territory of the Land of Israel"). Cf. also *ibid.* v.4, where TJ's introductory Midrash reads in part as follows: ". . . When they (*viz.*, the Israelites) returned to it (i.e., the Torah), they prevailed against their enemies". Cf. also *ibid.* v.8a, where TJ adds a homiletical exposition not even remotely alluded to in the text: ". . . and when they (i.e., the Israelites) returned (or: repented) to fulfill the Torah, they (*viz.*, the hostile nations) could not prevail against them . . ." Cf. Komlosh, *op. cit.*, pp. 284ff.

325. Cf. Is. 26:20a (MT "Come, my people, enter your chambers, and shut your doors behind you" = TJ "Come, my people, do good deeds for yourself which will protect you in time of trouble"). Cf. Komlosh *op. cit.*, p. 396.

326. Cf. Ezek. 2:10b, where MT ". . . there were written on it (*viz.*, a scroll from heaven) lamentations and mourning and woe" is homiletically expanded in TJ to ". . . and there was

In line with rabbinic thinking that "the reward granted to the righteous ones is for the time to come",[328] TJ, too, places considerable emphasis on the life of the world-to-come, where the ultimate recompense of the righteous is to be consummated.

Just as the Rabbis frequently sought to find Biblical evidence of—or at least allusions to—the world-to-come and the resurrection of the dead[329], so also in TJ there is a marked tendency to interpret suitable verses and associate them with orthodox rabbinic concepts on the life of the world-to-come. Thus, in II Sam. 7:9a, MT "You have spoken also of your servant's house for a great while to come (i.e., for the distand future)" is rendered by TJ, "You have spoken also of your servant's house for the future world"[330]. It is impossible for any man, however powerful, to destroy souls[331]; for even the souls of the wicked do not die[332], but are subjected to punishment in Gehenna[333], so that they should on no account escape judgment for their misdeeds[334].

---

written in it that if the house of Israel would transgress the Torah, the nations would rule over them; but if they fulfill the Torah, lamentation, sorrow and groaning would cease from them".

327. Cf. Mic. 6:3a (MT "O, my people, what have I done to you?" = TJ "O, my people, what good have I promised to do for you, without having done so?").

328. Avoth II,16. Cf. T.B. Kid. 39b: "There is no reward in this world for (performing) a precept".

329. Cf. e.g., Sifre Deut. 32:2; M. Sot. IX,15 end; M. Sanh. X, 1ff.; Tos. Sanh. XIII, 1 ff.; T.B. Sanh. 90b-92a; Ber. 15b; Pes. 68a; Ket. 111a-b; Kid. 39b. Cf. also Acts 24:15.

330. So also Targum Rav Joseph's rendering of the parallel passage in I Chron. 17:17a.

331. Cf. Ezek. 17:17b (MT "... to cut off many lives" (Heb. נפשות, *lit.*, souls) = TJ "... to destroy many lands [or: cities]"). TJ, evidently assuming that נפשות has the literal meaning of "souls"—which renders it theologically unacceptable (since Nebuchadnezzar, who is the subject of the verse obviously has no power to destroy "souls")—, is forced to change the translation to something more in line with Nebuchadnezzar's real achievements. TJ's failure to render נפשות by "lives" or "people" may be due to the inner logic of the clause which describes Nebuchadnezzar's initial siege works—which in itself did not involve fighting and killing.

332. Cf. Is. 66:24b (MT "... their worms shall not die" = TJ "... their souls shall not die"). TJ's refusal to translate literally may also have been influenced by the difficulty of the concept that worms do not die. Although the general meaning of the verse is the permanent punishment of those who rebel against God, TJ, designed as it was for use in the synagogues for mass audiences, could not provide a translation which was liable to be misleading.

333. Cf. *ibid.* (MT "... their fire shall not be quenched" = TJ "... and the wicked shall be judged in Gehenna"). On the punishment of the wicked after death, see *infra*, pp.

334. Cf. Mal. 3:6b (MT "... you, O sons of Jacob, are not consumed" = TJ "... you, O

Eternal life in the world-to-come is granted to those who observe the statutes and ordinances given by God[335]. But, above all, it is the *Tsaddikim* who are rewarded with life in the world-to-come[336], since it is they who walk in the ways of God[337].

In view of the fact that even the rabbis were unable to speculate beyond generalities on the nature of life in the Great Beyond[338], it is not surprising that TJ does not add substantially to the solution of this ultimate riddle of existence. The only assumptions made by TJ are that in the world-to-come there will be eternal rejoicing[339] and the souls of those who inherit that world will be filled with delights.[340]

---

children [or: sons] of Israel, you imagine that he who dies in this world, his verdict [i.e., the verdict against him] ceases"). The purpose of this rendering is to stress the fact that death is no escape from divine judgment; cf. M. Avoth IV,22.

335. Cf. Ezek. 20:11b. 13a. 21a (MT ". . . [statutes and ordinances] by whose observance man shall live" = TJ ". . . if a man observes them he shall live an everlasting life through them"). Cf. also Targum Onkelos on Lev. 18:5a, where the Hebrew is identical with the Ezekiel text, while the Aramaic translation is likewise almost identical with that of TJ, which is likely to have been influenced by Targum Onkelos. The purpose of both Targum Onkelos and TJ may well have been to avoid the dangerous idea that long life promised in the Torah for the performance of certain commandments is meant for this world. For the dire consequences of taking such promises literally (i.e., as referring to life in this world), cf. T.Y. Hag. II,1,77b.

336. Cf. II Sam. 22:29b, where MT ". . . the Lord will lighten my darkness" is homiletically expanded in TJ to ". . . the Lord will bring me out of darkness to light, and he will let me see the world which he will in future bring about for the righteous ones". Cf. Komlosh, *op. cit.*, p. 313.

337. Cf. Hos. 14:10b (MT ". . . the righteous ones walk in them" [*viz.*, in "the ways of the Lord" mentioned immediately before] = TJ ". . . the righteous ones who walk in them shall live through them the everlasting life").

338. The primary rabbinic assumption regarding the future life is that "the world-to-come is altogether good" (T.Y. Hag. II,1,77b; cf. T.B. Kid. 39b; Hul. 142a). In other words, it is the acme of perfection, and not subject to any of the woes, sorrows and evils of this world. The real nature of world-to-come was, however, considered to be beyond human comprehension (cf. T.B. Ber. 34b), though there were certain exceptions, especially among the Midrashists who liked to delight their unsophisticated audiences with tales of future delights (cf., e.g., T.B. Taan. 31a; B.B. 75a; Lev. R. XIII,3). The classical spiritual description of the future life is to be found in T.B. Ber. 17a: "In the world-to-come there is neither eating nor drinking nor procreation nor business nor jealousy nor hatred nor competition, but the righteous sit with their (spiritual) crowns on their heads enjoying the splendor of the divine presence."

339. Cf. Is. 65:18a (MT ". . . be glad and rejoice for ever in that I am creating" = TJ ". . .

The concept of the resurrection of the dead was basic to rabbinic think-ing,[341] so much so that it was included as the second of the 18 benedictions recited three times every day. Naturally, TJ reflects rabbinic theology in this as in so many other respects. Some verses lend themselves ideally for discov-ering the idea of resurrection in the Bible. Thus, I Samuel 2:6—"The Lord puts to death and brings to life; he brings down to Sheol and raises up"—alludes unmistakably to physical resurrection. TJ interprets accordingly: "All these things are the might of the Lord who rules in the world. He puts to death, but He promised to bring back to life; and He brings down to Sheol, but He will also bring up in the eternal life."[342] Similarly, Isaiah 26:19a—"The dead shall live, their bodies shall rise"—is rendered more explicitly by TJ, and credit for the resurrection is given exclusively to the Almighty: "You (viz., God) are reviving the dead; the bones of their bodies You are raising"[343].

As in rabbinic thought,[344] so also in TJ there is some speculation on the exact nature of the resurrection. According to one Midrashic addition to TJ

---

they shall rejoice and be glad in the world of worlds [i.e., the highest of all worlds—the 'Olam Habba'] which I am creating").

340. Cf. *ibid.* 58:11 (MT "And the Lord will . . . make your bones strong, and you shall be like a watered garden" = TJ "And the Lord . . . will revive your body [or: ". . . your body shall live] in everlasting life, and your soul shall be filled with delights like an irrigated garden that is well-watered . . ."). This is one of many examples where TJ introduces the concept of the physical resurrection of the dead. See next section.

341. See *supra*, n. 329.

342. The future tense in TJ as compared to the present participle in MT is noteworthy. By limiting the resurrection of the dead to the (Messianic) future, TJ indirectly denies the resur-rection of Jesus. The Biblical resurrection cases (cf. I Kings 17:21-22; II Kings 6:36-37; Ezek. 37:1-10) are either capable of a natural explanation (cf. especially II Kings 4:34, where the prophet Elisha applies mouth-to-mouth resuscitation) or else may be taken symbolically, as was indeed done by R. Judah in the case of the dry bones revived in Ezekiel's prophecy (cf. T.B. Sanh. 92b). TJ is however, not quite consistent; cf. *infra* TJ's rendering of Is. 26:19a, where TJ renders the imperfect of MT by the present participle. This may have been due to the second half of the verse, where TJ clearly places the physical resurrection of the dead in the future.

343. On the use made of Isaiah 26:19 in rabbinic speculation on the resurrection of the dead, cf., e.g., T.B. Ket. 111a. Cf. also Is. 57:16b (MT ". . . from me proceeds the spirit" = TJ ". . . the spirits of the dead I will in future bring back"). Although here, too, it is God who revives the dead, it is not clear whether a physical or spiritual ("the spirits of the dead") resurrection is meant.

344. Cf., e.g., T.B. Ket. 111a-b; Sanh. 90b.

on Zech. 14:4, ". . . the Lord will take a large horn (Shofar) in His hand, and He will blow with it ten alarm sounds to quicken the dead." The time for the resurrection was generally believed to be the Messianic era,[345] though there was a rabbinic opinion that "there is no difference between this world and the days of the Messiah except for (Israel's) subjection to (foreign) king-doms."[346] TJ, however, designed as it was for unsophisticated synagogue audiences, tended to emphasize the miraculous aspects of the eschatological future. Thus, the resurrection was imagined not only as a supernatural event (which, of course, it must be), but as one of purely physical dimensions, with the earth opening, as it were, innumerable mouths to enable the revived dead to ascend from their graves.[347] Once resurrected, the former "dwellers in the dust" would praise God for his crowning mercy.[348]

Just as in rabbinic eschatology there are different views on the extent of the resurrection[349] and the exclusion or otherwise of individuals or types from this renewed grant of life,[350] so in TJ there are different trends regard-ing the problem whether the resurrection is to be universal or limited to the *Tsaddikim*. Thus, there are two passages where the universal quickening of the dead is emphasized;[351] while two other passages speak only of the righ-teous being raised from the dead.[352]

345. Cf. Hos. 6:2 (MT "After two days he will revive us; on the third day he will raise us up, that we may live before him" = TJ "He will revive us for the days of comfort that will come in future; on the day of the resurrection of the dead he will raise us; and we shall live before him"). The "days of comfort" undoubtedly allude to the Messianic age.

346. T.B. Ber. 34b and parallels.

347. Cf. Is. 45:8b (MT "Let the earth open, that salvation may sprout" = TJ Let the earth open, and let the dead live").

348. Cf. *ibid.* 26:19b ("Awake and sing [or: shout] for joy, o dwellers in the dust" = TJ "Let all those who were lying in the dust live and utter praise before you"). Cf. *ibid.* 42:11b (MT "Let the inhabitants of Sela sing [or: shout] for joy" = TJ "Let the dead utter praise when they come forth from their burial grounds"). TJ's rendering of Sela (lit., rock) by "the dead" was presumably influenced by the fact that tombs were hewn out of rocks; cf. espe-cially Is. 22:16.

349. It is noteworthy that in the only O.T. prose passage where the resurrection of the dead is explicitly stated, it is to all appearances limited to the truly righteous and truly wicked for their respective reward and punishment, while the average types are excluded from the resurrection; cf. Dan. 12:2: "And many of those who sleep in the dust of the earth shall awake, some to everlasting life, and some to shame and everlasting contempt".

350. Cf. M. Sanh. X, 1-3; Tos. Sanh. XIII, 1-12; T.Y. Sanh. X,1,27c-d; T.B. Sanh. 108a; 110b-111a.

351. Cf. Is. 38:16a (MT "O Lord, by these things men live = TJ "O Lord, concerning all

However, even the trend which provided for universal resurrection did not regard the wicked as deserving of everlasting life in any shape or form. Accordingly, a number of passages speak of a second death to be endured by the wicked,[353] presumably after being duly punished for their wrongdoing. In other words, their resurrection will only be temporary; they will have to submit to divine scrutiny of their deeds on the day of judgment when the power of the once mighty will be of no avail;[354] and even after their well-deserved punishment the wicked (or at least some of them) will be deprived of a share in the life of the world-to-come.[355]

While TJ generally does not refer to the resurrection or the share in the future life of specific individuals, there is one notable exception, namely the case of the High Priest Joshua son of Jehozadak who is promised personal

dead you have declared that you would bring them back to life"). Cf. *ibid.* 26:19b, see *supra;* n. 348.

352. Cf. *ibid.* 49:8b (MT "... to establish [or: restore] the land" = TJ "... to raise the righteous ones who lie in the dust"). Cf. Hos. 14:10b (MT "... and the righteous ones [shall] walk in them" [*viz.,* "the ways of the Lord"] = TJ "... and the righteous ones who walk therein shall live through them in everlasting life").

353. Cf. Is. 22:14b (MT "Surely this iniquity will not be forgiven you until you die" = TJ "Surely this iniquity will not be forgiven you until you die a second death"). Cf. *ibid.* 65:6b (MT "I will repay, yea, I will repay into their bosom" = TJ "I will not give them respite during their lifetime, but I will pay them [other version: there will be] the punishment for their sins, and I will deliver their bodies to a second death"). Here the repetition of שלמתי ("I will repay") in MT may have suggested TJ's version. Cf. also *ibid.* 65:15a (MT "... and the Lord God will put you to death" = TJ "... and the Lord God will put you to death a second time"). Cf. especially Jer. 51:39a.57a, where the "second death" is more clearly defined (MT "... and they shall sleep an everlasting sleep, and they shall not awake" = TJ "... and they shall die a second death, and they shall not awake in the world-to-come"). The concept of a second death is also to be found in the New Testament (Revelation 21:8), where it is equated with "the lake that burns with fire and brimstone" into which "the cowardly, the faithless, the polluted, the murderers, fornicators, sorcerers, idolators, and all liars" are to be cast. In the Talmud (T.B. Sanh. 92a-b) the righteous are exempted from a second death after resurrection, but others—such as the dead resurrected by Ezekiel (cf. Ezek. 37:1-10)—are assumed to have died after the manifestation of the miracle. Maimonides, on the other hand, regarded also the future physical resurrection as a temporary phenomenon. Hence even the righteous would, after a long life-span, die once again; cf. Iggerot Ha-Rambam, edit. by M.D. Rabinowitz (Jerusalem 1944), p. 364.

354. Cf. I Sam. 2:9b (MT "not by power man prevails" = TJ "... not he that has power is acquitted on the day of judgment").

355. Cf. Jer. 51:39a. 57a; see previous note. See also Rashi and Kimhi on Is. 22:14b, where the "second death" is also defined as deprivation of a share in the world-to-come.

resurrection and the company of *Seraphim*—on condition that his conduct in this world turns out to be satisfactory.[356]

Ever since the late Second Commonwealth period, the belief in hellfire punishment for the wicked was firmly held by Pharisaic and rabbinic Judaism,[357] and it also became an essential ingredient of sectarian and Christian theology.[358] Based on several Old Testament passages,[359] the idea of fiery punishment for the wicked emerges clearly in the later Apocryphal literature.[360]

It is, however, only in rabbinic literature that we meet with attempts to define more clearly the sins for which punishment in Gehenna is exacted; the duration of the ordeal; and ways of escaping this punishment by timely repentance, charity, etc.[361]

TJ generally reflects rabbinic speculation on this subject. In several passages, TJ states unequivocally that the wicked are to be punished in Gehenna.[362] The righteous—as already mentioned—are to have the satis-

---

356. Cf. Zech. 3:7 (MT "Thus says the Lord of hosts: If you will walk in my ways, and if you will keep my charge, then you shall rule my house, and you shall also have charge of my courts, and I will give you [the right of] access among those who are standing here" = TJ "Thus says the Lord of hosts: If you (*viz.*, the High Priest Joshua) will walk in ways that are right before me, and if you will keep the charge of my *Memra*, and you will also judge those who minister in my sanctuary, and you will also guard my courts; then I will revive you in the resurrection of the dead, and give you feet that will walk among these Seraphim").

357. On the concept of Gehenna in rabbinic literature, see L. Jacobs, *Principles of the Jewish Faith*, pp. 422-435; c.g. Montefiore and H. Loewe, *A Rabbinic Anthology*, pp. 581ff. Passages of special significance are to be found in Josephus, Ant. XVIII, 1,3, par. 14; Bell. 11, 8, 14, par. 163; T.B. Eruv. 19a; R.H. 16b-17a; Hag. 15a; Ned. 8b; B.M. 58b; Sanh. 108a.

358. Cf. The interpreter's Dictionary of the Bible, E-J (Nashville-New York, 1962), pp. 361ff., s.v. Gehenna.

359. Cf., e.g., Deut. 32:22; Is. 33:14; 66:24.

360. For a list of passages, cf. IDB *ibid*.

361. See *supra*, n. 357.

362. Cf. Is. 57:20a, "where a Midrashic version of TJ on MT "But the wicked are like the tossing sea" reads: "But the wicked ones shall be banished in Gehenna." Cf. *ibid*. 66:24b (MT "... their fire shall not be quenched" = TJ "... and the wicked ones shall be judged in Gehenna"). Cf. Hos. 14:10b (MT "... but transgressors stumble in them [*viz.*, in the ways of the Lord"] = TJ "... but the wicked ones shall be delivered to Gehenna because they did not walk in them" [*viz.*, in the ways of the Lord]). In the last example, TJ's rendering was designed to remove possible misconceptions, since the literal meaning of the text seems to suggest that the transgressors would "stumble" while walking in "the ways of the Lord." TJ's rendering makes it clear that the wicked are punished because they do *not* walk in the ways of the Lord.

faction of seeing the wicked posthumously burnt in hellfire[363], and they will also have the power to terminate the punishment once the wicked have received their due.[364]

It is, nevertheless, God alone who in primordial times created Gehenna as a place of punishment for sins,[365] and it is He who brings down individual sinners to *Sheol* (lit., Hades, nether world),[366] which was identified with Gehenna.[367]

The basic reason for punishment in Gehenna was transgression of God's word[368] i.e., acting contrary to His will. It goes without saying that the

363. See *supra*, n. 300.

364. See *supra*, no. 301.

365. Cf. Is. 30:33 (MT "For a burning place [or: Topheth] has long been prepared; yea, for the king it is made ready [or: he, too, is destined for Melech (= Molech)]; its pyre [or: fire-pit] made deep and wide ... the breath of the Lord, like a stream [Heb. נחל] of brimstone [or: sulfur], kindles it" = TJ "For Gehenna is prepared from of old (as punishment) for their sins; it, too—the king of the worlds prepared it by making it deep and broad. ... The *Memra* of the Lord, like an overpowering stream, brimstone kindles it"). Since an ordinary נחל is no more than a wadi which dries up in summer, it is in TJ's view inadequate to compare with the *Memra* of the Lord, hence the addition of מגבר (made mighty, reinforced, overpowering) to render the simile more appropriate. Cf. also n. 368.

366. Cf. Ezek. 31:15a (MT "On the day when he [or: it] goes down to Sheol = TJ "On the day when I brought him down to Sheol"]; *ibid.* 31:17a (MT "They went down to Sheol" = TJ "They were brought down to Sheol"); *ibid.* 32:24b (MT "... who went down uncircumcised into the nether world = TJ "... the sinners [or: the guilty ones] who were brought down to the nether world"); *ibid.* 32:27b (MT "... who went down to Sheol" = TJ "... who were brought down to Sheol"); *ibid.* 32:30b (MT "... who have gone down with the slain" = TJ "... who have been brought down with the slain"). TJ's rendering of these passages in Ezekiel may have been influenced by Ezekiel 31:16a, where God himself is the one who brings down the cedar (i.e., Assyria) to Sheol: "... when I cast it down to Sheol."

367. Cf. T.B. Eruv. 19a: "Gehenna has seven names, ... Sheol (or: nether world)..." Cf. *IDB*, E-J (New York—Nashville 1962), pp. 361ff., s.v. Gehenna.

368. Cf. Is. 12:19b (MT ... on the land of the shades you will let it [viz., the divine dew] fall" = TJ "... the wicked to whom you have given might—yet they transgressed your *Memra*—you will deliver to Gehenna"). Cf. also Jer. 17:13a (MT "Those who turn away from you [*lit.*, me] shall be written in the earth [i.e., for death]" = TJ "The wicked who transgress your *Memra* will in future fall into Gehenna"). Cf. Komlosh, *op. cit.*, p. 411. A similar homiletical expansion in TJ is to be found in I Sam. 2:8b, where MT "For the pillars of the earth are the Lord's, and he has set the world on them" is homiletically expanded in TJ to "... before the Lord are the deeds of the sons of men below revealed. He has prepared Gehenna for the wicked ones who transgress his *Memra*; but the righteous ones who do his will—for them he has completed [or: perfected] the world." Cf. Komlosh, *op. cit.*, p. 309, who suggests that TJ may have been influenced by the following verse (9), where the contrast between the

enemies of Israel, who are equated with the enemies of God, are to be delivered to Gehenna.[369]

While rabbinic views on the duration of punishment in Gehenna for different types of transgressors vary a good deal,[370] TJ tends to favor harsh retribution for the wicked in general, without explicitly discriminating between major and lesser sinners.

For example, in one passage it is stated, somewhat vaguely, that the wicked will be delivered to Gehenna because they did not walk in the ways of God.[371] In another passage, it is those indulging in heathen practices who are to be punished in Gehenna where the fire burns all day long.[372] Elsewhere we are told that the wicked are to be burned in Gehenna forever after being judged in Jerusalem.[373] It goes without saying that, in TJ, the enemies of God—in practice, the enemies of Israel—are destined for Gehenna.[374]

Hasidim rendered צדיקיא in TJ) and the wicked is vividly drawn. Cf. also T.B. Eruv. 19a: ". . . men who transgress the will of the Holy One, blessed be He . . . for whom Gehenna is made deep . . . You have provided Gehenna for the wicked ones, and the Garden of Eden for the righteous ones."

369. Cf. Nah. 1:8b (MT ". . . he will pursue his enemies into darkness = TJ ". . . he will hand over his enemies to Gehenna"). TJ's rendering of the first part of the verse (which is not very clear in Hebrew)—"And with strong anger and mighty wrath he will make an end of the nations that have arisen and destroyed the Temple of the Lord"—leaves no doubt about the identity of the enemies of the Lord with the enemies of Israel. This conclusion is further confirmed byy TJ's translation of verses 9 and 10, where TJ refers twice to "the nations that have spoiled Israel," although the Hebrew text does not remotely allude to this.

370. Cf., e.g., T.B. R.H. 16b—17a; B.M. 58b; Sanh. 108a.

371. Cf. Hos. 14:10b (MT ". . . transgressors stumble in them [*viz.*, in the ways of the Lord, mentioned earlier in the same verse]" — TJ ". . . the wicked shall be delivered to Gehenna because they did not walk in them"). TJ's interpretation was theologically essential, since the literal meaning of the text would seem to imply that the wicked, though trying to walk in the ways of the Lord, would "stumble", i.e., fail in their effort. This would mean that the repentance of the wicked is unacceptable—a concept totally at variance with Jewish theology on the subject of repentance; cf., e.g., Ezek. 18:21-23. 27-28. 32;33: 11-19; M. Yoma VIII, 8; T.B. Yoma 85b-86b.

372. Cf. Is. 65:5b (MT ". . . a fire that burns all the day" = TJ ". . . their punishment [shall be] in Gehenna where the fire burns all the day").

373. Cf. *ibid.* 33:14b (MT "Who among us can dwell with everlasting burnings?" = TJ "Who among us can dwell in Jerusalem where the wicked will in future be judged to be delivered to Gehenna for everlasting burning?").

374. Cf. Nah. 1:8b (MT ". . . darkness shall pursue his enemies" TJ ". . . his adversaries he will deliver into Gehenna").

However, as already mentioned,[375] the idea of intercession by the *Tsaddi-kim,* which seems to be alluded to in TJ on Isaiah 66:24b, somewhat lessens the harshness of TJ's concept of eternal hellfire.

8. SIN AND THE JUSTICE OF PUNISHMENT

One of the basic principles of rabbinic theology, which is unreservedly followed by TJ, is that divine justice is flawless; and that punishment both of individuals and of peoples is well-deserved, never excessive, and always fitting the offense or crime committed. God can, therefore, never be capricious or unreasonable. Like Job's friends, TJ cannot conceive of an unjust God afflicting the righteous or innocent with undeserved punishment.[376] It is thus not surprising that the Rabbis had little sympathy for Job[377] who had questioned divine justice and complained about the suffering of the righteous and the prosperity of the wicked.[378]

In line with rabbinic theology, TJ invariably interprets Biblical passages, in which the absolute righteousness of God is not sufficiently apparent, in a manner which leaves no shadow of doubt that God and His judgment are always perfect.

In accordance with rabbinic thought, TJ denies that God "brought evil" except "upon him that does it".[379] In other words, only he that commits evil

---

375. See *supra,* n. 301.

376. For a characteristic example of the rabbinic view on the workings of divine justice, cf. Tanḥuma מצורע, 4: "Why does suffering come upon the world? Because of the people, so that they should see and reflect and say, 'He that has sinned is smitten, and he that has not sinned is not smitten.'"

377. Cf. T.B. B.B. 15b—16a. Some Rabbis did, however, sympathize with Job (cf. *ibid.* 15b—16b, M. Sot. V,5), though the concensus was on the whole against him. The reason may have been partly because Job denied the doctrine of the resurrection (cf. Job 7:9; B.B. 16a) and partly because of an opinion (which was, however, disputed) that Job was a Gentile (B.B. 15b). But the main cause of the rabbinic criticism of Job was that he had dared to impute injustice to God. The Rabbis for the most part held this to be unforgivable insolence; though, in mitigation, it was pointed out that "a man is not held responsible for what he says when in distress" (*ibid.* 16b).

378. Cf., e.g., Job 9:17ff., 16:16ff.; 19:16ff.; 21:ff.; 272:ff.

379. Cf. Is. 31:2a (MT: "Yet he, too, is wise, and he brought evil" = TJ "Yet he also in his wisdom has brought evil upon him that does it").

will be subject to divine punishment. Indiscriminate evil could not conceivably be introduced by the Almighty whose anger is aroused only against the guilty, never against the innocent.[380]

Even where God is not mentioned in MT, no misfortune can befall an individual unless he has sinned and thus deserved his fate.[381] Death even at the age of 100 will ultimately be due not to old age, but to the sins of one's youth.[382]

Since, moreover, punishment must fit the crime, a mere curse would not be adequate to chastise a sinner in his old age. Instead, he is to "be driven out", presumably from this world through death.[383]

When God in his fury punishes and destroys, it is invariably the wicked and the guilty ones who are the targets of divine wrath, not the people in general.[384] TJ, moreover, cannot conceive of a God who will deliberately "lay a stumbling block" before a righteous man who has committed iniquity, so that "he shall die". Instead, it is the righteous man's sins which form the fatal stumbling block.[385]

---

380. Cf. *ibid.* 12:1a, where MT "You (*viz.*, God) were wroth with me" is significantly changed by the addition, "because I had sinned before you." The implication is that God is not angry and does not punish without cause. Cf. also Jer. 10:24a, where the prophet's willingness to accept chastisement "in just measure"—a seemingly undeserved infliction—is changed in TJ to "Bring chastisements upon them" (*viz.*, the wicked who dislike to be chastised). Cf. Komlosh, *op. cit.*, p. 410.

381. Cf. Zech. 13:6 (MT "And if one asks [*lit.*, says to] him, 'What are these wounds on your back [*lit.*, between your hands]?' he will answer [*lit.*, say], 'The wounds I received in the house of my friends'" = TJ "And if one asks him, 'Why have these blows come upon us? Is it not because of the deeds of our hands?' he will answer, 'We have rightly been smitten because of the sins of our friends [or: which I loved]'"). The Aramaic דרחימנא is ambiguous, and if the meaning is "of our friend [s]" (which would correspond closely to MT מאהבי), it would imply joint communal responsibility for individual wrongdoing—a familiar rabbinic concept, though limited to cases where one had the power to prevent one's fellow from committing a sin, but failed to do so; cf. T.B. Sanh. 27b; Sheb. 39b.

382. Cf. Is. 65:20b MT ["...the youth [or: the youngest] shall die a hundred years old"—TJ "...he that sins as a youth shall die a hundred years old").

383. Cf. *ibid.* (TJ "...he that sins at the age of hundred [or: the sinner a hundred years old] shall be accursed" = TJ "...he that sins at the age of hundred shall be driven out").

384. Cf. *ibid.* 30:27b (MT "His [*viz.*, God's] lips are full of fury" = TJ "From before him a curse upon the wicked goes forth"); Jer. 5:3a (MT "You have smitten them" = TJ "You have smitten the wicked ones"); Is. 13:5b (MT "...to destroy the whole earth = TJ "to destroy all the wicked ones of the earth").

385. Cf. Ezek. 3:20a (MT "I will lay a stumbling block before him" [*viz.*, the "righteous man" who "turns from his righteousness and commits iniquity"] = TJ "I will lay [or: put] the stumbling block of [his] sins before him").

Unlike the prophet who proclaims that "All flesh is grass, and all its goodness like flowers of the field",[386] the Targumist confines this deprecation of mankind to the wicked: "All the wicked ones are as grass, and all their power as the chaff of the field". Likewise, MT: "Grass withers, flowers fade"[387] is transformed in TJ to: "The wicked dies, his plans perish".[388]

The ultimate ruin of the wicked is indeed a recurrent theme in TJ. While those who observe the Torah are to enjoy the blessings of peace, the Almighty has a bitter fate in store for the wicked,[389] who will be worn out and stumble in their way[390] and find no rest[391] or means of escape.[392] A stumbling block on Israel's way, the wicked are to be removed;[393] their might will be like tow caught by a spark, so that the wicked and their evil deeds will perish from the earth and none shall spare them.[394]

The power ruthlessly exercised by the wicked will be weakened and dis-

386. Is. 40:6b.

387. *Ibid.* 40:7a. 8a. Cf. also *ibid.* v. 7b (MT "Indeed, the people are grass" = TJ "Therefore the wicked among the people are counted as grass"). Cf. Komlosh, *op. cit.*, p. 385, where a similar interpretation in Midr. Pss. 1:4 (edit. Buber, pp. 21–22) is cited.

388. Cf. Pss. 146:4b ("... on that day his plans perish").

389. Cf. Is. 38:17a (MT "Behold, it was for my welfare that I had great bitterness" = TJ "Behold for those who observe [or: perform] the Torah there is much peace before you; but you bring bitterness upon the wicked ones....."). See *supra*, n. 314.

390. Cf. *ibid.* 40:30 (MT: "Youths shall grow faint and weary, and young men shall surely stumble" = TJ "Sinful [or: guilty] youths shall be faint and weary, and wicked young men shall utterly stumble." Thus, it is only the sinful and wicked elements that are to suffer punishment.

391. Cf. Mic. 2:10a (MT "This is not your resting-place" = TJ "This is not a resting-place for the wicked").

392. Cf. Joel 2:3b (MT "Yeah, nothing escapes them" = TJ "Yeah, there is no escape in it for the wicked").

393. Cf. Is. 57:14b (MT "Remove the stumbling block [or: obstacle] from my people's way" = TJ "Remove the stumbling block of the wicked ones from the way of the congregation of my people").

394. Cf. *ibid.* 1:31 (MT "And the strong shall become tow, and his work a spark, and both of them shall burn together, with none to quench" = TJ "And the power of the wicked ones shall be as tow of flax, and the work of their hands as a spark of fire, as when one is placed beside the other and both burn together so shall the wicked ones perish, they and their evil deeds, and there shall be no mercy upon them"). Cf. also Zeph. 1:7a and Zech. 2:17a, where MT "Be silent (Zeph.: all flesh) before the Lord..." is transformed in TJ to "Let all the wicked ones perish from before the Lord." Cf. also the Midrashic addition in TJ on Ezek. 1:8a, where we are told that the heavenly *Hayoth* ("living creatures") would cast glowing coals of fire "on the place of the wicked ones, so as to destroy the sinners (or: guilty ones) who transgress his *Memra.*"

appear, and those that wield it will be punished and swallowed up by
Sheol.[395]

By way of contrast, the *Tsaddikim* who have faith and are sin-fearing in
their conduct will be preserved from destruction, and will not be dismayed
in times of trouble.[396]

TJ is also concerned with the extent and fairness of punishment, both for
individuals and for Israel as a whole. Where minor offenses do not appear to
merit the severity of punishment indicated in the Prophetic texts, TJ makes
appropriate changes to render the divine retribution more reasonable. Thus,
the scoffers of Jerusalem whom Isaiah denounces and threatens with
tightened bonds and a decree of destruction[397] are converted into "wicked"
men in TJ[398]—do doubt because mere mockery, however reprehensible, is
not a legally punishable act, and does not morally deserve destruction "upon
the whole land".[399]

Similarly, the divine threat to punish "all who are clothed in foreign
attire"[400] is out of all proportion to the offense and is, therefore, radically
transformed in TJ into retribution "upon all who excite themselves to worship idols".

---

395. Cf. Is. 14:5 (MT "The Lord has broken the staff of the wicked, the scepter of rulers"
= TJ "The Lord has broken the power of the wicked ones, the dominion of the sinners [or:
guilty ones]"). Cf. als Hab. 1:12b (MT ". . . and you, O Rock, have established them for chastisement" = TJ ". . . and the powerful one you have established [or: prepared] to be
punished"). Similarly, too, Is. 5:14b, where the prophet predicts that, among others, "he who
exults (or: rejoices) in her" (*viz.*, Jerusalem) will go down to Sheol. TJ, evidently aware that
joyfulness as such is not deserving of punishment, changes it to "he that is powerful among
them"—the implication here as well as elsewhere being that those who wield power are corrupted by it and are, therefore, identical with the wicked. Cf. also *ibid.* 5:15a (MT ". . . men
are brought low" = TJ ". . . the *power* of men shall be weakened [or: become feeble]").

396. Cf. *ibid.* 55:13a (MT "instead of the thorn [or: brier] a cypress shall rise; and instead
of the brier [or: nettle] a myrtle shall rise" = TJ "Instead of the wicked ones the righteous
ones shall be preserved, and instead of the sinners [or: guilty ones] those that are sin-fearing
shall be preserved"). Cf. Komlosh, *op. cit.*, p. 387, where similar interpretations in T.B. Meg.
10b are cited. Cf. *Isaiah* 28:16b (MT "He who believes will not be in haste [or: need not fear]"
= TJ ". . . but the righteous ones who believe in these things shall not be dismayed when distress [or: trouble] comes"). Cf. also *ibid.* 51:14b, see *supra*, n. 296.

397. Cf. *ibid.* 28:14a.22

398. Cf. *ibid.* 28:14a (MT "Therefore hear the word of the Lord, you scoffers . . ." = TJ
"Therefore accept the word of the Lord, you wicked men . . ." Cf.*ibid.* 28:22a (MT "Now
therefore do not scoff" = TJ "And now do not act wickedly").

399. *Ibid.*, v. 22b.

400. Zeph. 1:8.

Another example of this genre is Ezekiel's dogmatic statement that "the punishment (lit., iniquity) of the (false) prophet and the punishment of the inquirer shall be alike".[401] Since it is manifestly unfair that an ignorant, duped inquirer should be held responsible no less than a deceiving false prophet, TJ assumes that the inquirer—imagined in the role of a would-be student at a school—is guilty of a different sin, namely of refusing to study. Such an offense is considered equivalent to the iniquity incurred by a false prophet.[402]

The moral difficulty of visiting the sins of the fathers upon the children is dealt with in strict accordance with rabbinic theology, limiting such retribution to cases where children continue on the path of sinfulness trodden by their fathers.[403]

If punishment was to fit the crime, Jerusalem's and Israel's twofold punishment for their sins[404] required drastic modification by the Targumist. Jerusalem, accordingly, so far from receiving "double for all her sins",[405] is given, in TJ, "a cup of consolation from before the Lord, as if she had been smitten double (or: twice) for all her sins". A significant, though less radical, change is introduced by TJ on Jer. 16:18a, where punishment is indeed not eliminated, but altered sufficiently to exclude the concept of a double penalty.[406]

401. Ezek. 14:10b.

402. Cf. TJ on Ezek. 14:10b: "The sin (or: guilt) of him who comes to study but does not study, shall be like the sin (or: guilt) of the false prophets."

403. Cf. Jer. 2:9 (MT "Therefore I will yet contend with you, says the Lord, and with your children's children I will contend" = TJ "Therefore I will in future punish you, says the Lord, and (with) your children's children—whom I will in future punish if they will do like your deeds"). Even more explicitly is this doctrine enunciated in Jer. 32:18a, where MT "... and you requite the guilt (or: iniquity) of the fathers into the bosom of their children after them" is carefully qualified in TJ: "... and you requite (or: recompense) the sins of the fathers to their children if they continue to sin after them." This rendering agrees word for word with that of Targum Onkelos on Exod. 20:5 and Deut. 5:9. Cf. also Exod. 34:7 and Num. 14:18, where Targum Onkelos depicts the children who are to be punished for the sins of their fathers as "rebellious." Cf. also T.B. Ber. 7a, and Sanh. 27b, where the punishment of the children is limited to those who continue the sinful course of their fathers. In T.B. Mak. 24a, on the other hand, Ezekiel's insistence on personal responsibility (cf. Ezek. 18:3–4) is regarded as a flat contradiction of the Pentateuchal third and fourth generation punishment concept.

404. Cf. Is. 40:2b; Jer. 16:18a.

405. Is. *ibid.*

406. Cf. Jer. 16:18a (MT "And first I will requite [or: recompense] their iniquity and their sin double" = TJ "And I will recompense their iniquities and their sins to the second ones as

While Israel and Jerusalem are exempted by TJ from excessive punishment, such patriotic considerations (which undoubtedly influenced TJ quite apart from theological ones) do not apply to the prophet Ezekiel who is symbolically made to suffer for Israel's sins.[407] His vicarious punishment is expanded by TJ to "double for their sins".[408]

One of the most important principles of rabbinic theology is that of "measure for measure", i.e., that a person is punished or rewarded in a manner resembling his evil or good deeds.[409]

TJ adopts this principle in the interpretation of several passages.[410]

Another cardinal rabbinic principle is that neither nations nor individuals are severely punished until the measure of their guilt is complete.[411] TJ likewise introduces the concept that there is a time for final retribution

---

to the first ones"). The principle enunciated by TJ is that all sinners are equally punished irrespective of the time their wrongdoing was committed.

407. Cf. Ezek. 4:4ff.

408. Cf. *ibid.* 4:5a (MT "For I have appointed the years of their iniquity ..." = TJ "And I have given you double for their sins"). TJ's rendering is not necessarily homiletical. Apparently, TJ understood MT שְׁנֵי ("years of") as "two"—hence "double" punishment.

409. Cf. M. Sot. I, 7–9; Tos. Sot., chs. III-IV; M. Avot II, 6; T.Y. Sot. I, 7–9, 17a-b; T.B. Shab. 105b; Pes. 69a; R.H. 12a; Meg. 12b; Yev. 107b; Ned. 32a; Sot. 8b–11a; Sanh. 90a; 100a; 108a; Ḥul. 127a; Arak. 16b. Cf. also Targum Onkelos on Exod. 18:11b.

410. Cf. Is. 27:8a (MT "Measure by measure" = TJ "With the very measure with which you were measuring it shall be measured to you [or: they shall measure you]"); cf. Komlosh, *op. cit.,* p. 368; cf. Is. 21:2b, where the plain meaning of MT—"The betrayer is betraying (or: the plunderer is plundering), and the ravager is ravaging"—is completely transformed (possibly on the basis of a slightly different reading) into "The oppressors are oppressed, and the spoilers are spoiled." Similarly, *ibid.* 24:16 (MT "The betrayers are betraying; yea, they have committed the betrayal of traitors" [or: "the treacherous deal treacherously, they have dealt very treacherously"]) = TJ "Woe to the oppressors, for they shall be oppressed, and to the [spoiling of] the spoilers, for, behold, they shall be spoiled"). Cf. Komlosh, *op. cit.,* p. 366. The concept of punishment fitting the crime is also prominent in TJ's rendering of Ezek. 21:32b (MT "A ruin, ruin, ruin I will make it = TJ "Their sins which they committed— according to their sins I will punish them"). Cf. also Hos. 4:9a (MT "And it shall be like people, like priest" = TJ "And it shall be that just as they made the layman like the priest to desecrate (לְאַפָּסָא) my [other versions: their] holy sacrifices, so will I destroy (אַפֵּיס—lit., break) your honour, and I will make him that is honourable contemptible").

411. Cf. T.B. Sot. 9a: "The Holy One, blessed be He, does not exact punishment of a man until his measure (*viz.,* of guilt) is complete." Cf. *ibid.*: "The Holy One, blessed be He, does not exact punishment of a nation until the time of its punishment into exile ... The Holy One, blessed be He, does not exact punishment of a king until the time of his banishment into exile." The same principle is already implied in Gen. 15:16: "And they shall return here in the fourth generation, for the iniquity of the Amorites is not yet complete."

when the measure of sinfulness has reached its limits.[412] In fairness to the wicked, they are granted an extension to enable them to repent before the full measure of punishment is extracted.[413] Once the time comes, divine justice is inevitable and inescapable.[414]

Occasionally, TJ enumerates specific sins and crimes, and indicates the type of punishment inflicted in each individual case. Significantly, TJ makes no distinction between ritual and moral offenses, between sins committed against God and ethical misdeeds against one's fellow man. They are all equally punishable, and there is no discernible difference in the severity of retribution. Thus, failure to pay one's tithes is followed by crop failure[415]— incidentally, another example of the measure-for-measure principle of retribution. False oaths are the cause of the devastation of the land and the wasting away of its inhabitants.[416] TJ also implies that death may be the consequence of not praying to God.[417]

---

412. Cf. Ezek. 7:12a (MT "The time has come, the day draws near" = TJ "The time of retribution for transgressions has come. The day of punishment for sins is approaching." Cf. *ibid.* 35:5b (MT ". . . at the time of their calamity, at the time of their final punishment" = TJ ". . . at the time of their calamity, at the time of the retribution for their transgressions").

413. On the "respite" granted by God to the wicked to give them a chance to repent, cf. TJ on Is. 26:10a; 42:14a; 57:11b; 64:11b; Hab. 1:13b; 3:1a—2a. Cf. also Is. 21:12b, where TJ interprets the engmatic MT ("If you will inquire, inquire; come back again") as a call to those who would repent to do so while there is yet time ("If you repent, repent while you are still able to repent").

414. Cf. Is. 33:1 (MT "Woe to you, destroyer, who yourself have not been destroyed; you betrayer who have not been betrayed" = TJ "Woe to you who comes to spoil, and shall they not spoil you? and who comes to oppress, and shall they not oppress you?"). The transformation of the factual statement in MT into a question where the answer is meant to be self-evident implies the inevitability of retribution for those who engage in robbery and oppression. Cf. also *ibid.* 42:19b (MT "Who is blind as the wholehearted [or: dedicated] one? = TJ "The wicked ones will in future receive the punishment for their sins"). On the etymological connection between MT מְשֻׁלָּם ("wholehearted" or "dedicated") and TJ לאשתלמא (*lit.*, "to be paid," *viz.* retribution for sinfulness), cf. Komlosh, *op. cit.,* p. 361. Finally, the concept of the inescapability of divine justice is implicit in TJ's rendering of Hos. 6:4a, where MT "What shall I do with you, O Ephraim?" becomes in TJ "In the face of (*lit.*, From before) a true judgment, what can I do for you, of the house of Ephraim?"

415. Cf. Is. 5:10 ("For ten acres of vineyard shall yield but one bath, and a homer of seed shall yield but an ephah" = TJ "For on account of (their) sin in not giving tithes, ten acres of vineyard shall yield but one bath, and an area requiring a cor of seed shall yield but three seahs").

416. Cf. *ibid.* 24:6 (MT "Therefore a curse devours the earth; . . . . therefore the inhabitants of the earth are scorched, but few men are left" = TJ "Therefore because of false oaths

Wrongdoing towards one's fellow man is punished along similar, though not necessarily identical, lines. God's anger was likely to be aroused not so much by covetousness as such (which did not necessarily involve acts of violence or deceit), but only by acts of robbery[418] and unlawful enrichment.[419] Such acts would invariably be visited with divine punishment. Wealth obtained by violence would vanish like dust.[421] Those who had robbed houses would lose their best land;[422] while a curse would fall upon those who deceived their fellow men by using false weights and measures.[423] Even the killing of idolators may be punishable if the perpetrators of such acts become themselves addicted to idolatry.[424]

Severe punishment will also be imposed upon holier-than-thou hypocrites who pretend to be purer than everybody else. They are to be consigned to Gehenna where "the fire burns all day long".[425]

---

the earth is desolate; . . . . therefore the inhabitants of the earth perish, but few men are left").

417. Cf. Amos 6:10b ("Hush! For we must not mention the name of the Lord" = TJ "Remove [*viz.*, the corpses of the dead], for when they were alive, they did not pray in the name of the Lord"). TJ(reading הסר ["Remove"] instead of הס ["Hush," "Be silent"]) clearly implies that the death of the people was due to failure to pray.

418. Cf. Is. 57:17a (MT "Because of the iniquity of his greed [or: covetousnesss] I was angry]" = TJ "Because of the sins of their wealth which they acquired by violence was my anger upon them").

419. Cf. Jer. 17:11a–12a, where "he who gets riches but not by right (or: justice)" is doomed, according to TJ on MT *ibid.*, v. 12a ("A glorious throne"), that "punishment shall be wrought upon him from before His divine presence upon the glorious throne."

420. Cf. note 419.

421. Cf. Is. 5:24a (MT ". . . and their blossoms shall blow away [*lit.*, go up] like dust" = TJ "and the wealth which they have acquired by violence shall be as dust that flies away"). Cf. Komlosh, *op. cit.*, p. 375.

422. Cf. Mic. 1:11b (MT ". . . shall take away from you its standing place" = TJ "Your desirable houses which you acquired by violence, joining one to the side of the other [cf. Is. 5:8a]—therefore, the best of your land shall be taken away from you").

423. Cf. Mic. 6:10b (MT ". . . and the scant measure that is accursed" = TJ ". . . and false measures bring about a curse").

424. Cf. Hos. 1:4b (MT "I shall visit the blood of Jezreel upon the house of Jehu" = TJ "I shall visit the blood of the idolators which Jehu shed in Jezreel whom he slew because they had worshipped Baal [cf. II Kings 10:11]. [Now] they have turned back to go astray after the calves in Bethel. Therefore, I will account it as innocent blood upon the house of Jehu").

425. Cf. Is. 65:5 (MT"Who say, 'Keep your distance [*lit.*, to yourself], do not come near me, for I am holier than you' [or: I am set apart from you]. These things make my anger rage [*lit.*, These are a smoke in my nostrils], a fire that burns all the day" = TJ "Who say, 'Keep away, do not come near me, for I am purer than you are.' As for these, their anger is like smoke before me. Their punishment shall be in Gehenna where the fire burns all day long").

As usual, historical examples are adduced to emphasize specific punishments for certain offenses committed by Biblical personalities—in this case, by kings of Judah. Thus, the reference in Isaiah 6:1a to "the year of the death of King Uzziah" is interpreted in TJ (following II Chron. 26:19ff.) as "the year in which King Uzziah was smitten with leprosy"—no doubt as a reminder that even a successful king who generally "did what was right in the eyes of the Lord"[426] was liable to a penalty equivalent to death,[427] if he attempted to usurp priestly functions.[428]

The severity of this punishment for an outstanding king of "good" character required a significant change in Isaiah's description of his meeting with King Ahaz of Judah who was, according to II Kings 16:2 ff. and II Chron. 28:1 ff., a very bad king who not only imitated Assyrian-Aramean cults,[429] but "dealt wantonly in Judah and was faithless to the Lord",[430] even going so far as to sacrifice his son.[431] It is all the more surprising, therefore, to read in Isaiah 7:10 that "the Lord spoke further to Ahaz." Since even a prophet found it distasteful to address a wicked king,[432] it would hardly be credible that the Almighty would deign to communicate directly with such a sinful ruler, especially since the context clearly indicates that it was the prophet Isaiah who was speaking to the King. TJ accordingly alters the verse to read: "And the *prophet* of the Lord spoke further to Ahaz". While this explanation fits the context, its deliberate nature is clearly designed to avoid the impression that God ever communicated with Ahaz.

Finally, the last King of Judah, Zedekiah, whose refusal to heed Jeremiah's warning caused the destruction of the first Temple and the Babylonian exile, is taken to task in TJ on Ezekiel 12:12b. While MT reads, ". . . he (*viz.*, the prince Zedekiah) shall cover his face, that he may not see the land with his eyes", TJ significantly alters the translation to emphasize Zede-

---

426. II Kings 15:3; II Chron. 26:4.

427. Cf. T.B. Ned. 64b: "Four are accounted as dead: . . . a leper." Cf. also Exod. R. I,34 (". . . a leper is accounted as dead"), where, in addition to Num. 12:12, Is. 6:1 is also cited as an example of the affliction of leprosy being depicted as death.

428. Cf. Num. 1:51; 3:10; 18:7: "Any outsider who encroaches (*lit.*, comes near [*viz.*, to the altar to perform sacerdotal duties]) shall be put to death." Since Uzziah had attempted to offer incense in the Temple (cf. II Chron. 26:16ff.), his punishment had to be either death or an affliction like leprosy which was held to be as severe as death.

429. Cf. II Kings 16:10ff.; II Chron. 28:22ff.

430. II Chron. 28:19b.

431. Cf. II Kings 16:3. According to II Chron. 28:3, Ahaz "burned his *sons* (plural) as an offering." This may, however, be an exaggeration.

432. Cf. II Kings 3:14.

kiah's guilt, for which he was punished: ". . . he shall cover his face because
he is sinful (or: guilty), and he shall not see the land". Thus, the King has to
cover his face in shame or fear not because of some arbitrary fate, but on
account of his own misdeeds.

Not only individuals but the nations of the world are treated with justice
by the Almighty. Hence, whenever the biblical text refers to divine punishment of the earth (or the world), TJ is careful to qualify such statements by
adding the "wicked" ones who alone are the objects of divine retribution.[433]

Specifically, the nations of the world are punished by divine vengeance
for their refusal to accept the teachings of the Torah;[434] for transgressing
the divine *Memra*—a sin for which the extreme penalty of the flood was
exacted—;[435] for worshipping the sun and the moon;[436] for attempting to
do evil to David,[437] and, in particular, for refusing to admit David to Jerusalem.[438]

433. Cf. Zeph. 1:18a (MT "In the fire of his [*viz.*, God's] jealousy [or: zeal] all the earth
shall be consumed = TJ "In the fire of his retribution [or: punishment] all the wicked ones of
the earth shall perish); *ibid.* 1:18b (MT ". . . for a full, yea, sudden end he will make of all the
inhabitants of the earth" = TJ [Codex Reuchlinianus] ". . . for an end, yea, a destruction he
will make of all the wicked ones of the earth); *ibid.* 3:8b (MT ". . . for in the fire of my jealousy
[or: zeal] all the earth shall be consumed" = TJ ". . . for in the fire of my retribution [or:
punishment] all the wicked of the earth shall perish"); cf. Jer. 14:4a (MT "Because of the
earth [or: soil] which is dismayed [or: cracked]. . ." = TJ "Because of the sins of the inhabitants of the earth they are broken . . ."); Mal. 3:24b (MT ". . . and I smite the land [or: earth]
with utter destruction" = TJ ". . . and I find the whole land [or: earth] in its sin, and I smite
it utterly"). Cf. also Zeph. 1:3a, where the destruction of man and beast is threatened, but
without any motive. In TJ, on the other hand, this is explained as being due to the fact that
"the stumbling block of the wicked ones has become great" (MT "the stumbling blocks with
the wicked").

434. Cf. Mic. 5:14 (MT "And in anger and in wrath I will execute vengeance upon the
nations that did not obey" = TJ "And in anger and in wrath I will execute punishment of law
upon the nations that did not accept the teaching of the Torah"). For similar criticism of the
nations of the world for failing to obey the seven Noahide laws, cf. Mekilta on Exod. 20:2;
T.B. B.K. 38a; A.Z. 2b.

435. Cf. Hab. 3:6a (MT ". . . he looked and shook the nations" = TJ ". . . and he brought
the flood upon the people, the generation that transgressed his *Memra*").

436. Cf. Is. 24:23a (MT "Then the moon shall be ashamed, and the sun shall be abashed"
= TJ "Then those who worship the moon shall be ashamed, and those who bow down to the
sun shall be humbled").

437. Cf. II Sam. 22:48b (MT ". . . and he [*viz.*, God] brought down peoples under me" =
TJ ". . . and he crushes under me the nations that arise to do evil unto me"). Cf. Komlosh, *op.
cit.*, p. 312.

438. Cf. *ibid.*, 5:6b (MT ". . . and they [*viz.*, the Jebusites] spoke to David, saying, 'You

There are many references in TJ to Israel's sins—both general and specific—and to the various forms of divine retribution exacted for Israel's delinquencies. These misdeeds include failure to obey God[439] and study and observe the Torah;[440] wilful stubbornness;[441] failure to pray in general[442];

---

shall not come here, unless you remove the blind and the lame', [thus] saying, 'David cannot come in here'" = TJ "... and they spoke to David, saying, 'You shall not come here, unless you remove the sinners and the guilty ones who say, 'David cannot [or: shall not] come here'"). Cf. also *ibid.* v.8 (MT "... the lame and the blind who are hated by David's soul. Therefore it is said, 'The blind and the lame shall not come into the house'" = TJ "... the sinners and the guilty who are hated by David's soul. Therefore it is said, 'The sinners and the guilty ones shall not come into the house'"). Komlosh (*op. cit.*, p. 304) plausibly suggests that TJ's rendering may have been an attempt to explain why "the lame and the blind" were hated by David. This becomes more comprehensible if "the lame and the blind" are turned into "the sinners and the guilty ones." In any case, it is clear that, indirectly at least, the defeat of the Jebusites is attributed to their sinners. On the connection between sin and demoralization—and hence defeat—in battle, cf. M. Sot. VIII, 5; Tos. Sot. VII, 22.

439. Cf. Is. 28:13a (MT "The word of the Lord is to them precept upon precept, precept upon precept, line upon line, line upon line" = TJ "And this shall be the cup of their punishment: because they have transgressed the word of the Lord, and because they were commanded to observe the Torah but would not do that which they were commanded, therefore they shall be delivered up to the nations that do now know the Torah. And because they went after the desire of their soul, and did not desire to do my will, therefore they shall hope for aid at the time when I bring distress upon them, but shall have no aid or support"). It is noteworthy that TJ's homiletical expansion is not a mere deviation from MT, but represents a virtually independent theological Midrash. Cf. also *ibid.* 28:10a (MT "For it is precept upon precept, precept upon precept, line upon line, line upon line" = TJ "They were commanded to observe the Torah, but would not do that which they were commanded ... They did not hearken to the words of the prophets; they went after the desire of their soul, and did not desire to do my will"). Cf. also *ibid.* 8:14a; Hos. 6:5a (see *infra*, notes 449, 451).

440. Cf. Jud. 5:2a (MT "When men let grow their hair in Israel" = TJ "When the house of Israel rebelled against the Torah, the gentiles [or: nations] came upon them and drove them out from their cities"); cf. *ibid.* 5:4a (MT "O Lord, when you came forth from Seir" = TJ "Your Torah which you gave to Israel—when they transgressed it, the Gentiles [or: nations] ruled over them"); cf. Is. 28:13a (see n. 439); cf. *ibid.* 5:3a (MT "Now, then, O inhabitants of Jerusalem. . ." = TJ "... Behold, the house of Israel have rebelled against the Torah, and are unwilling to repent"); cf. Ez. 2:10b (MT "... and there were written upon it lamentations and mourning and woe" = TJ "... and it was written upon it that, if the house of Israel would transgress the Torah, the gentiles would rule over them"). Cf. *ibid.* 16:28a (MT "And you played the harlot with the Assyrians, because you were insatiable" = TJ "And you went astray after the Assyrians because you did not know the Torah; cf. *ibid.* 16:29b (MT "... and even with this you were not satisfied" = TJ "... and even with this you did not know the Torah"); cf. Hos. 2:5b (MT "... and I will make her like a wilderness" = TJ "... and my anger will fall [*lit.*, rest] upon her as it did upon the people of the generation that transgressed

and, in particular, refusal to worship in the Temple of Jerusalem;[443] desecration of its holy ground;[444] alliances with—and assimilation to—other nations;[445] idolatry caused in part by malicious joy and inter-tribal hostility;[446] killing of children in the service of idolatrous cults;[447] the act of estab-

---

my Torah in the wilderness"); cf. *ibid.* 4:14b (MT ". . . and a people without understanding shall come to ruin" = TJ ". . . a generation that does not reflect upon the Torah will surely be abandoned"); cf. *ibid.* 13:14b (MT "Compassion [or: repentance] is hid from my eyes" = TJ ". . . and because they transgressed my Torah, I shall remove my *Shekhinah* from them").

441. Cf. Is. 28:10a, 13a (see n. 439); cf. Hos. 8:9a (MT "For they have gone up to Assyria, a wild ass wandering alone." = TJ "For they were exiled to Assyria because they went after the desire of their soul like a rebellious wild ass.")

442. Cf. Hos. 7:10b (MT ". . . and they do [or: did] not seek him [*viz.*, the Lord], for all this" = TJ ". . . and they did not pray before me, for all this").

443. Cf. Is. 28:10 (MT "line upon line, line upon line, here a little, there a little" = TJ "They hoped that the worship of idols would be established for them, and they did not hope for the service of my sanctuary; as a small thing was my sanctuary in their eyes that they should worship there; as a small thing in their eyes was my *Shekhinah* there"); cf. *ibid.* 28:13a (MT ". . . here a little, there a little" = TJ ". . . and because my sanctuary was a small thing in their eyes that they should worship there, therefore they shall be left few in number among the nations whither they shall go into exile"); cf. Hos. 5:8b (MT ". . . after you, O Benjamin" = TJ "because . . . they did not worship before me in the Temple which is in the land of the tribe of Benjamin").

444. Cf. Ezek. 7:22a (MT "I will turn my face from them, that they may profane my hidden [or: precious] place" = TJ "I will remove my *Shekhinah* from them because they have desecrated the land of the place of my *Shekhinah*").

445. Cf. Jer. 2:25 (MT "Keep your feet from going unshod . . . But you said, '. . . I have loved strangers, and after them I will go'" = TJ "Keep your foot from attaching yourself to the gentiles [or: nations] . . . But you said, '. . . I have loved to attach myself to the gentiles [or: nations], and after the worship of their idols I will go'"); cf. *ibid.* 2:33a (MT ". . . to see lovers [*lit.*, love] = TJ ". . . to attach yourself to the gentiles [or: nations]"); cf. Mic. 4:9a (MT "Now why do you cry aloud?" = TJ "Now why are you attaching yourself to the gentiles [or: nations]?"). (While there is no connection between MT and TJ in the meaning of the verse, it is evident that TJ interprets MT עֵר [crying aloud] to be a noun [companion, fellow] rather than a verb). Cf. Ezek. 16:29a (MT "You multiplied your harlotry with the trading land of Chaldea" = TJ "You multiplied your going astray so as to attach yourself to the people of the land of Canaan, to go after the laws of the Chaldeans"); cf. Hos. 8:9b (MT "Ephraim has hired lovers" = TJ "The house of Israel has been delivered into the hands of the gentiles [or: nations] whom they have loved").

446. Cf. Jer. 2:25b (see n. 445); cf. Ezek. 21:15b (MT "Or shall we make mirth? You have despised the rod, my son, with everything of wood" = TJ "Because the tribes of the house of Judah and Benjamin rejoiced about the tribes of Israel when they were exiled on account of their having worshipped idols, therefore they [*viz.*, the tribes of Judah and Benjamin] turned back to go astray after images of wood"); cf. Mic. 1:14b (MT ". . . the houses of Achzib shall be a deceitful thing to the kings of Israel" = TJ ". . . the houses of Achzib shall be delivered to

lishing the Israelite monarchy in defiance of Samuel's warning;[448] scorning the prophets and refusing to heed their messages;[449] and failure to repent—a special topic to be discussed later.[450]

In line with both biblical and rabbinic theology, TJ postulates a day of judgment when divine wrath would explode and punishment for Israel's sins would be exacted,[451] with the result that Israel would be made to drink the cup of bitterness.[452] More specifically, Israel would be abandoned by God[453]

---

the gentiles [or: nations] because of the sins that the kings of Israel committed by worshipping in them [*viz.*, the houses] to idols"); cf. Hab. 3:7a (MT "I saw the tents of Cushan in affliction" = TJ "When the house of Israel worshipped idols, I delivered them into the hand of Cushan the sinner" [a reference to Jud. 3:8]); cf. also Is. 28:10a (see n. 443).

447. Cf. Hos. 9:13b (MT "Ephraim shall lead forth his sons to slaughter" = TJ "Those of the house of Ephraim have sinned by killing their sons for the worship [or: cult] of idols").

448. Cf. Hos. 5:8a (MT "Blow the horn in Gibeah, the trumpet in Ramah" = TJ "O prophets, raise your voices like a horn; prophesy that murderous nations will come upon them because they appointed Saul of Gibeah king over them. Cry aloud as though [you were sounding] the trumpet. Tell [them] that kings and their armies will come upon them because they did not accept the words of Samuel, the prophet from Ramah").

449. Cf. Jer. 8:18a (MT "I would take comfort against sorrow [or: grief]" = TJ "Because they used to mock at the prophets who prophesied for them, sorrow and groaning are coming upon them because of their sins"); cf. Ezek. 21:18a (MT "For there is a testing" = TJ "For the prophets have prophesied concerning them, but they did not repent"); cf. Hos. 6:5a (MT "Therefore I have hewn them by the prophets, I have slain them by the words of my mouth" = TJ "Because I warned them through the mission of my prophets, but they did not repent, I brought killers upon them, for they transgressed the word of my will"); cf. Is. 65:12a (MT "Because, when I called, you did not answer, when I spoke you would not listen. . ." = TJ "Because I sent my prophets, but you did not repent; they prophesied, but you would not hearken. . ."); cf. *ibid.* 66:4a (MT "Because, when I called, no one answered, when I spoke, they would not listen. . ." = TJ "Because I sent my prophets, but they did not repent; they prophesied, but they would not hearken . . ."); cf. also *ibid.* 28:10a (see n. 439).

450. See *infra*, p.

451. Cf. Is. 8:14a (MT "And he shall be for a sanctuary" = TJ "And if you will not hearken, his *Memra* shall be amongst you for a punishment"); cf. Hos. 5:9a (MT "Ephraim shall become a desolation in the day of punishment" = TJ "Those of the house of Ephraim shall be for a desolation on the day of retribution for sins"); cf. *ibid.* 12:9 (MT "Ephraim has said, 'Ah, but I have become rich, I have gained wealth for myself; in all my labours they shall find in me no iniquity that is sin'" = TJ "And the house of Ephraim said, 'But we have become rich, we have found power for us.' O prophet, tell them, 'Behold, all your wealth shall not be preserved for you [i.e., shall not avail you] on the day of retribution for sins'"). Cf. also *ibid.* 2:5b (see n. 440).

452. Cf. Is. 27:3a (MT ". . . I water it every moment" = TJ ". . . When they provoke me to anger (*lit.*, cause anger to be aroused before me), I make them drink the cup of their punishment").

453. Cf. Hos. 4:14b (see n. 440).

who would remove His divine presence from their midst.[454] Hence there would be no help in time of trouble,[455] and Israel would be delivered into the hands of the gentiles.[456] Because of their sins, the Israelites had been unable to drive out all the inhabitants of Canaan, but were themselves expelled from their cities.[457] Worse still, they had had to endure raids by murderous invaders[458] as well as regular invasions by kings and their armies.[459] They were—or would be—dominated by the gentile nations and their kings,[460] and they would be spoiled of their wealth.[461] Finally, their sinfulness would cause Zion to fall[462] and be consigned to the flames;[463] the Temple would be destroyed;[464] and the Land of Israel would be desolate;[465] and only few Israelites would survive among the nations.[466]

454. Cf. *ibid.* 2:5a (MT "Lest I strip her naked" = TJ "Lest I remove my divine presence from her"); cf. *ibid.* 13:14b (see n. 440).

455. Cf. Is. 28:13a (see n. 439).

456. Cf. *ibid.* (see n. 439); cf. Hos. 8:9b (see n. 445); Mic. 1:14b (see n. 446); cf. Hab. 3:7a (see n. 446); cf. Ezek. 7:22a (see n. 444).

457. Cf. Jud. 1:19 (MT "And the Lord was with Judah, and he took possession of the hill country, but he could not drive out the inhabitants of the plain. . . " = TJ "And the *Memra* of the Lord was in support of the house of Judah, and they drove out the inhabitants of the hill country [lit., mountain]; afterwards when they sinned they were unable to drive out the inhabitants of the plain. . . ."); cf. *ibid.* 5:2a (see n. 440).

458. Cf. Hos. 5:8a (see n. 448).

459. Cf. *ibid.* (see n. 448); cf. *ibid.* 5:13a (MT ". . . and he sent to King Contentious [or: to the great King]" = TJ ". . . and he sent to the King who will come to punish them").

460. Cf. Jud. 5:4a (see n. 440); cf. Is. 28:13a (see n. 443).

461. Cf. Hos. 12:9 (see n. 451); cf. Mic. 1:14b (see n. 446).

462. Cf. Mic. 4:11 (MT "Now many nations are assembled against you, saying, 'Let her be defiled, and let our eyes gaze upon Zion'" = TJ "And now many [or: great] nations shall be assembled against you, saying, 'When will she sin [or: be guilty], so that our eyes may look upon the downfall of Zion'"); cf. Jer. 4:18 (MT "Your way and your doings have brought these things upon you; this is your doom [or: evil], yea, it is bitter, for it has reached your very heart" = TJ "Your evil way and your corrupt deeds have caused these things unto you. This evil and bitterness has come upon you, O Jerusalem, until the wickedness of your heart was broken"). Cf. Komlosh, *op. cit.*, p. 414.

463. Cf. Ezek. 24:12 (MT "It [*viz.*, Jerusalem] has wearied itself with toil; yet its great filth does not go out of it, by fire [or: into the fire its rotting filth] = TJ "It is filled with misdeeds, and evildoers will not go out of it; it shall be burned by fire because of the multitude of its sins").

464. Cf. Is. 53:5a (MT "But he was wounded because of our rebellious acts" = TJ "And he will build the Temple which was desecrated because of our sins"). Cf. Komlosh, *op. cit.*, p. 392.

465. Cf. Zech. 7:14 (MT ". . . and the land was desolate after them, so that no one went to and fro; and the pleasant was made desolate" = TJ ". . . and the land shall be desolate after

Perhaps the most frequently mentioned punishment of Israel is that of exile from the Land of Israel. This was no doubt due to the fact that it was the most severe, the most lasting in its effect, and the most disastrous in its ultimate consequences. It was in line with Biblical and rabbinic theology[467]—expressed most poignantly in the opening of the *Musaph* service for the festivals[468]—that TJ attributed the exile to sin rather than to any other factor.[469] More specifically, the exile, according to TJ, was due to the fact that Israel had blindly followed the evil impulse of their heart,[470] and forgotten their divinely ordained destiny, their history studded with miracles performed by God for their deliverance.[471] Other reasons for the exile were

---

them, so that no one will go to and fro *because* they made the pleasant land desolate"). Note that TJ blames the people for the desolation of the Land of Israel.

466. Cf. Is. 28:13a (see n. 443).

467. Cf., e.g., Lev. 26:33ff.; Deut. 28:63ff.; 29:23ff.; I Kings 8:46f.; 9:5f.; II Kings 17:7–23; 21:8–15; Jer. 7:13ff.; 16:10ff.; 29:16ff.; Ezek. 6:3–10; 12:8–16; 17:11–20; 19:3–9; 22:1–15; 36:16ff.; Hos. 9:15ff.; Amos 5:21–27; 7:11–17; Zech. 7:11–14; Pss. 106:35–47; Lam. 1:3–9.18; Dan. 9:5ff.; Ezra 9:6f.; II Chron. 6:36; 33:9f.; M. Avoth V,9; T.B. Ber. 3a; 56a; Shab. 33a; Pes. 49a; Taan. 16a; Sot. 49a; Sanh. 37b; 39a; 104a; Men. 53b; Gen. R. XXXVI, 4; Num. R. VII, 10; XXIII, 14; Deut. R. II, 22; Lam. R.I, 1. Occasional views that the exile was a desirable development—even a blessing in disguise (T.B. Pes. 87b; cf. Philo, *De Legatione ad Gaium*, 281; Josephus, *Ant.* IV, 6,4, pars. 115–116)—were exceptional and by no means characteristic of rabbinic Judaism. On the general Jewish reaction to the problem of exile, cf. Haim Hillel Ben-Sasson, *Encyclopedia Judaica*, Vol. 7, art. Galut, cols. 275ff.

468. Cf. S. Singer, *The Authorised Daily Prayer Book*, 2nd Revised Edition (London, 1962), p. 319: "But on account of our sins we were exiled from our land."

469. Cf. Is. 28:2b; cf. Ezek. 39:28a = TJ "Then they shall know that I am the Lord their God; because they sinned before me, I exiled them among the nations"; cf. Hos. 10:1 = TJ "Israel is a despoiled vine, which was a choice [lit., uplifted] vine when it [viz., Israel] carried out the Torah; the fruits of their deeds caused them to be exiled"); cf. *ibid.* 10:8a = TJ "The high place of Bethel shall be desolate; the sins of Israel caused them to be exiled"); cf. also Jer. 50:7b = TJ ". . . because they had sinned before the Lord, they were removed far from his true habitation . . .").

470. Cf. Is. 57:17b (MT ". . . but he went on backsliding in the way of his heart" = TJ "I scattered their exiles because they went astray after the imagination of their heart").

471. Cf. *ibid.* 8:23 (MT ". . . but the latter has made glorious [or: has dealt a more grievous blow by] the way of the sea, the other side of the Jordan, [and] Galilee of the nations" = TJ ". . . and their remnant shall a mighty king carry into exile because they did not remember the mighty act [viz., wrought by God] by the sea, the miracles [viz., performed by God] by the Jordan, the battle of the cities of the nations"). The last clause refers to Jud. 4:13ff., where MT—מחרשת הגוים is rendered by TJ מתקוף כרכי עממיא (from the stronghold [lit., power] of the cities of the nations"). The expression כרכי עממיא is identical with the one used in our verse.

transgression of the Torah by their leaders[472] and by the people in general;[473] going astray after sorcerers[474] and false prophets,[475] while refusing to heed the true prophets;[476] despising the Temple and refusing to worship there;[477] and breaking the covenant with God and worshipping idols.[478] Other wrongs which had caused the exile were cheating in trading and especially the use of false weights and measures.[479]

472. Cf. Is. 24:1b (MT "... and he [*viz.*, God] will twist its [i.e., the land's or the earth's] surface and scatter its inhabitants" = TJ "... and shame shall cover the face of its princes [or: great men] because they transgressed the Torah, and he will scatter those that dwell therein"). "Scatter" in this context undoubtedly alludes to exile.

473. Cf. Hos. 2:1b (MT "... instead of that which was said unto them, 'You are not my people'..." = TJ "... in the place where they were exiled among the nations when they transgressed the Torah, and it was said to them, 'You are not my people'...").

474. Cf. Zech. 10:2b (MT "Therefore [i.e., because of lying "diviners" (TJ קסמא֬ = sorcerers) and dreamers (TJ נבייֵ שקרא = false prophets) mentioned in the first part of the verse] they go their way [or: wander] like sheep, they are afflicted..." = TJ "Therefore they are scattered like the scattering of sheep, they are exiled...").

475. Cf. Mic. 2:11b (MT "... and he would be the preacher for this people" = TJ "... and it shall be, as they are accustomed to go astray after false prophets, so they shall be exiled to a land of falsehood with this generation"). See also n. 474.

476. Cf. Ezek. 21:18 (MT "For there will not be a testing—what could it do if you despise the rod [or: and what if it despises even the rod]?" = TJ "For the prophets have prophesied concerning them, but they did not repent. So what will happen to them in the end? Say [that] also the tribe of the house of Judah will surely be exiled, and because of their evil deeds they will not be preserved"); cf. *ibid.* 24:6b (MT "... bring it out piece by piece; no lot is fallen upon it" = TJ "Her people has been led out into exile after [*lit.*, upon] exile because no repentance was done therein").

477. Cf. Is. 28:13a (see *supra*, n. 443).

478. Cf. Zech. 11:10 (MT "And I took my staff Grace and I broke it [or: cut it asunder], in order to annul my covenant which I had made with all the peoples" = TJ "And I brought the king of Assyria [other vss.: Sennacherib] against the king of Israel, and I exiled him, because they [*viz.*, the people of Israel] had changed the covenant that was made with them not to worship idols; therefore they went into exile among the nations"); cf. *ibid.* v. 11 (MT "So it [*viz.*, the covenant] was annulled on that day..." = TJ "And because they had changed the covenant they went into exile at that time"); cf. Hos. 10:5a (MT "The inhabitants of Samaria shall be in dread because of [or: for] the calves of Beth-aven" = TJ "Because they worshipped the calves in Bethel, a king shall come up against them with his army, and exile them. They shall take the calf of Samaria from them"). Cf. also Jud. 5:8a, where MT "They chose new gods, then war was in the gates" is homiletically expanded to "When the house of Israel desired to worship new idols that had been made recently, with which their fathers had not occupied themselves [an allusion to Deut. 32:17], nations came upom them and drove them out of their cities." This would seem to be an indirect reference to the exile.

479. Cf. Zech. 5:7 (MT "And behold, a round piece of lead was lifted up, and there [*lit.*,

Specific exiles are attributed by TJ to specific offenses of a more or less serious nature. Thus, by a novel interpretation of Hosea 7:11b, the Assyian exile of the northern tribes of Israel is attributed to Israel's Egyptian alliance which the prophets invariably opposed.[480] By way of contrast, TJ explains Jeremiah 2:18b as an indication that the exile to Mesopotamia—which could equally allude to Israel's Assyrian captivity in 721 B.C.E. or to Judah's Babylonian captivity in 587 B.C.E.—was due to Judah's erstwhile alliance with Assyria.[481] Above all, it was the breaking of the divine covenant by Judah which caused the Babylonian exile of the Judaeans and of their last King Zedekiah.[482] TJ, following the theology of the prophet Jeremiah,[483] regards Nebuchadnezzar as an agent of the Almighty who sent him to destroy the Temple and exile the people from the city of Jerusalem because they had provoked God to anger by breaking his covenant.[484] In a sense, TJ

---

this] was a woman sitting in the ephah" = TJ "And behold, despised nations exile them swiftly [or: easily] and other nations will come and dwell in their land because they were dealing [or: conducting their business] with a false measure"; cf. *ibid.* 5:8 (MT "And he said, 'This is wickedness'; and he cast her into the ephah, and he cast the weight of lead upon its mouth" = TJ "And he said, 'Because of this they became guilty and went into exile, because they were dealing [or: conducting their business] with a false measure; therefore other nations came and have settled in their place'"). With slight variations the same idea is also expressed in TJ on Zech. 5:9—10.

480. Cf. Hos. 7:11b (MT "They [*viz.*, the people of Ephraim] call unto Egypt, they go to Assyria" = TJ "They approached Egypt; they went into exile to Assyria"). The implication of this interpretation is that Israel's Assyrian exile was a punishment for Israel's Egyptian alliance—a concept based, in all probability, on Ezek. 23:8—9. On prophetic opposition to any alliance with Egypt, cf. Is. 31:1ff.; Jer. 2:18, 36f., 37:5ff.; Ezek. 16:26; 17:11ff., 23:19ff.; Hos. 7:11ff., 8:13; 9:3ff., 11:5; 12:2. Prophetic objection to reliance on—or association with—Egypt is also implied in Is. 36:6 (=II Kings 18:21) (notwithstanding the fact that scorn at reliance on Egypt is put into the mouth of the Assyrian Rabshakeh) as well as in Jer. 42:15—22; 43:8-13; 44:26—30; Ezek. chs. 30—32; and Hos. 14:4 (where the word סוס is no doubt an allusion to Egypt; cf. Deut. 17:16; I Kings 10:28f.).

481. Cf. Jer. 2:18b (MT "... Or what have you to do in the way of Assyria to drink the waters of the River?" = TJ "What do you gain by making a covenant with Assyria so as to drive you into exile beyond the other side of the Euphrates?") Cf. Komlosh, *op. cit.*, p. 401.

482. Cf. Zech. 11:14 (MT "Then I broke my second staff Union [or: Binders], annulling the brotherhood between Judah and Israel" = TJ "Then I brought Nebuchadnezzar King of Babylon against Zedekiah King of the tribe of the house of Judah, and I exiled him because they, too, of the house of Judah had changed the covenant like their brethren of the house of Israel").

483. Cf. Jer. 21:1—10; 25:9ff.; 27:2—13; 28:13f.; 32:3ff.; 34:2f. 38:2f., 17—23.

484. Cf. Midrashic addition to TJ on Is. 66:1: "Now I (*viz.*, God) do not desire it (i.e., the

regards the exile as the inevitable consequence of the absence of a king of Israel (or Judah)—presumably after the capture and abduction of Zedekiah by the Babylonians.[485]

An unusual explanation why the righteous were made to suffer the penalty of exile along with the wicked is offered in TJ's rendering of Ezekiel 21:8b-21:9a. Accordingly, the *Tsaddikim* were exiled for their own good, namely to separate them from the wicked who were doomed to perdition.[486] Sensing perhaps the injustice of such protection through exile, TJ predicts that captivity would inspire prayer and repentance, leading to the ingathering of the exiles and the restoration of Israel.[487]

It has already been shown that TJ frequently emphasizes the justice of

---

Temple) because you caused wrath before me, and therefore this decree has come forth from before me to bring Nebuchadnezzar that he may destroy it and exile you from the city of Jerusalem." Cf. also Zech. 5:11 (MT "To build a house for it [*viz.*, the ephah mentioned in v. 10] in the land of Shinar, and when it is prepared, it will be set down there in its place" = TJ "To prepare a place for them in the land of Babylon, and they shall tarry and be confined there until their time will come").

485. Cf. *ibid.* 10:2b (MT ". . . they go their way like sheep; they are afflicted, because there is no shepherd" = TJ ". . . they are scattered as sheep are scattered; they have gone into exile because there is no king").

486. Cf. Ezek. 21:8b (MT ". . . and I will cut off from you both the righteous and the wicked" = TJ ". . . and I will exile from you your innocent in order to destroy your wicked"); cf. *ibid.* 21:9a (MT "Because I will cut off both the righteous and the wicked" = TJ "Because I will exile from you your innocent in order to destroy your wicked . . ."). TJ's rendering may have been designed to avoid the theological problem raised by the spectre of divine punishment for the innocent—a problem raised already in Gen. 18:25, and presented in a particularly acute manner in Job, especially in Job 9:22ff. The problem, with special reference to Ezek. 21:8, is also discussed in the Talmud (B.K. 60a; A.Z. 4a) and the Mekilta on Exod. 12:22. Despite rabbinic attempts to find a logical solution, the rabbis conceded that "together with the thorn the cabbage is smitten" (B.K. 92a), in other words, the innocent suffer with the guilty.

487. Cf. Zech. 12:10a (MT ". . . and they shall look on him [*lit.*, me] whom they have pierced [or: because they have thrust him through]" = TJ ". . . and they shall pray before me because they were exiled"); cf. Hos. 2:1b (MT ". . . instead of that which was said unto them, 'You are not my people,' it shall be said unto them, '[You are] the children of the living God'" = TJ ". . . in the place where they were exiled among the nations when they transgressed the Torah, and it was said to them, 'You are not my people,' they shall return [or: repent] and multiply, and it shall be said to them, '[You are] the people of the living God'"); cf. Ez. 39:28a (MT ". . . because I sent them into exile among the nations, and then gathered them into their own land" = TJ ". . . because they sinned before me, I exiled them among the nations, and now that they have repented, I gathered them into their own land").

divine punishment in the case of individual sinners. The same apologetic tendency is characteristic of TJ's justification of the suffering of Israel. Whenever the Biblical text speaks of unspecified or unexplained anger against Israel or the Land of Israel, TJ usually adds an explanatory phrase to justify the harsh treatment meted out by God to his chosen people.

That there is no such thing as arbitrary punishment of Israel, but only well-deserved retribution for sins knowingly committed by the people is implicit in TJ's rendering of Isaiah 1:5;[488] but in many other passages this concept is more or less explicitly stated. While the plain meaning of numerous texts may seem to indicate excessive divine fury against Israel, TJ firmly repudiates any suggestion that the Almighty may have displayed unreasonable harshness in his dealings with Israel.

We have already seen that TJ often enumerates Israel's crimes and punishments in homiletical passages where MT does not even remotely allude to the theological concepts put forward in TJ's free rendering.[489] To that must now be added passages in which the Hebrew Bible implies unacceptable ideas of divine blows directed indiscriminately against Israel, without either explaining the sins committed by the people which would justify such harsh retribution or pointing at specific groups which alone deserve punishment and get it, while the innocent are spared. With remarkable consistency, TJ's renderings attempt to meet the inevitable questions and objections that might be raised, especially by unsophisticated synagogue audiences, against what may well seem a primitive mode of wholesale retribution, often without any evident reason.

Thus the threat of total annihilation in Jeremiah 8:13 is qualified in TJ's homiletical note explaining the divine wrath by the fact that "I gave them my Torah from Sinai, but they transgressed it".[490] The drought afflicting the land—as well as the failures of their military operations—are

---

488. MT "Why will you still be smitten, that you continue to stray away? Every head is ailing, and every heart sick" = TJ "They do not reflect (or: consider) to say, 'Why are we smitten (or: stricken)?' They continue to sin yet more; they do not say, 'Why is every head ailing, and every heart sick?'" The implicit message of TJ's rendering of Isaiah 15 is that the disasters that have befallen the nation would, on reflection, be traced back to the sinfulness of the people.

489. See *supra*, pp.

490. Jer. 8:13b: MT "... and what I gave them has passed away from them." The Hebrew text is uncertain and, by all indications, corrupt.

attributed to Israel's obstinacy in following an evil course—hence "evil will come upon them".[491]

In several passages God's anger against Israel is explained by TJ as being due to Israel's sins.[492] Where the entire country is threatened with destruction— as, for example, in Isaiah 10:23—TJ carefully qualifies the indiscriminate punishment by adding that it is the wicked ones who are to be extirpated, not the people as a whole.[493]

Those who provoke God with their sins only harm themselves,[494] and they inexorably cause calamities of every kind, including natural disasters[495] and delivery into the hands of powerful enemies[496] such as Nebuchadnezzar

---

491. Cf. Jer. 23:10 (MT ". . . the pastures of the wilderness are dried up; their course is evil, and their might is not right" = TJ ". . . the folds of the pasture are dried up; and because they went after the desire of their souls, evil shall come upon them, and their mighty men [or: warriors] shall not prosper").

492. Cf. Is. 64:4b (MT "Behold, you were angry, and we sinned" = TJ "Behold, whenever there was anger from before you against us because we had sinned . . ."). Note that MT implies that Israel's sinfulness was itself a result of the despair caused by God's anger. This unmistakable criticism of the Almighty is reversed in TJ to a defense of God whose anger against Israel was justified. Cf. Zech. 1:2 (MT "The Lord was very angry with your fathers" = TJ "There was anger from before the Lord against your fathers because they provoked anger before him"). Cf. also Mic. 4:6b (MT ". . . and those whom I have wronged [or: afflicted]" = TJ ". . . and those to whom evil was done because of the sins of my people"). Significantly, the rabbis, unlike TJ, interpreted this verse as a divine admission that, by creating the evil impulse, God had indeed wronged Israel and mankind; cf. T.Y. Taan. III, 4,66c; T.B. Ber. 31b—32a; Suk. 52b.

493. Cf. Is. 10:23 (MT "For the Lord God of hosts is wreaking a decree of destruction in the midst of all the land [or: earth]" = TJ "For the Lord God of hosts is wreaking complete destruction upon all the wicked ones of the land [or: earth]").

494. Cf. Jer. 7:19 (MT "Is it I whom they provoke? says the Lord. Is it not themselves, to their own confusion [*lit.*, to the disgrace of their own faces]?" = TJ "Do they imagine that they are provoking anger before me? says the Lord. Is it not to do evil to themselves, so that they be ashamed of their deeds?").

495. Cf. Hos. 4:3b (MT ". . . and even the fish of the sea are taken away" = TJ ". . . and even the fish of the sea shall be diminished on account of their sins"). Note that TJ also reduces the catastrophe to natural proportions. Obviously the fish of the sea would not simply vanish altogether as the literal meaning of the Hebrew יאספו would imply. To TJ, therefore, a considerably diminished quantity of sea-fishes is disaster enough.

496. Cf. Ezek. 19:14a (MT "And fire has gone out from its stem [*lit.*, out of the rod of her branches], it has consumed its [branches and] fruit, so that there is in it no strong stem [or: rod], no sceptre for a ruler" = TJ "And there came peoples that were as strong as fire because of its [lit., her] arrogant sins; they slew its people; and there were no powerful rulers within it [*lit.*, her], kings who were strong enough to subdue the kingdom"); cf. Hos. 13:9 (MT "It is

King of Babylon, who destroyed the Temple and exiled the people of Jerusalem—all because they had provoked the divine anger by their misdeeds. Likewise, the desolation of the land described in Isaiah 1:7 was not an accidental misfortune, but caused by Israel's sins[497] and their wilful refusal to repent.[498]

The same principle of unfailing divine justice which applies to Israel as a whole is also appropriate in the case of Jerusalem. Her punishment was due to the sins of her inhabitants,[499] and the diseases and plagues which had afflicted the city were attributed by TJ to acts of violence and robbery in her midst.[500] The bitter evils which had befallen Jerusalem were designed, according to TJ, to break the wickedness of the hearts of her citizens.[501]

TJ also cites more ancient historic examples of divine retribution for sins committed by Israel rather than unexplained—and possibly undeserved—misfortunes endured by the people. Thus, "In the days of Shamgar son of Anath, In the days of Jael caravans ceased",[502] not simply because Israel's

---

your destruction, O Israel, for you are against me, your help" = TJ "When you corrupt your deeds, you of the house of Israel, the nations rule over you, but when you return to my Torah [other vss.: to the Torah], my *Memra*, is in support of you"); cf. Mic. 2:8a (MT "But of late [*lit.*, yesterday or: against] my people is risen up as an enemy" = TJ "On account of the sins of my people, they are delivered to an enemy").

497. Cf. Is. 1:7b (MT "... and it is desolate [or: a desolation], as overthrown by strangers" = TJ "... and because of your sins it is desolate; it is taken away from you and given to strangers"). Cf. Komlosh, *op. cit.*, p. 358. It is likely that TJ reflects conditions after 70 C.E. when much of Judaea was in fact given by the Romans to non-Jewish settlers.

498. See *supra,* notes 476, 496.

499. Cf. Jer. 6:6b (MT "This is the city which must be punished; everywhere there is oppression within it" = TJ "This is the city whose sins are visited upon it; they are all violent men within it"). Note that TJ prefers the concrete "violent men" (or: "robbers") to the abstract "oppression." Cf. also Midrashic addition to TJ's translation of Is. 66:1; see *supra,* n. 484.

500. Cf. Jer. 6:7 (MT "As a cistern [or: well] keeps its water fresh [or: wells with its water], so she [*viz.,* Jerusalem] keeps fresh [or: wells with] her wickedness; violence and destruction [or: robbery] are heard within her; sickness and wounds are before me continually" = TJ "Like a cistern that preserves its water, so evildoers are long preserved within her; the voice of robbers and spoilers is continually heard within her before me; therefore I brought upon her sickness and wounds").

501. Cf. *ibid.* 4:18b (MT "This is your evil, yea, it is bitter; for it has reached your very heart" = TJ "This bitter evil [*lit.*, this evil and bitterness] I will bring upon you, O Jerusalem, until the wickedness of your heart will be broken").

502. Jud. 5:6a.

enemies were strong enough to make travelling unsafe (as the text implies), but because, in TJ's words, ". . . they had sinned in the days of Shamgar son of Anath". Similarly, the terrible plague inflicted by God upon the people of Beth-shemesh was not merely "because they had looked upon the ark of the Lord"[503]—an incredibly severe punishment for what would seem at worst to have been a technical misdemeanor—,but because, as TJ puts it, "they had rejoiced that they had gazed upon the ark of the Lord *when it was uncovered*".[504]

By deliberately gazing at the most sacred cult object of the nation while it was uncovered, and enjoying the sight of the "naked" ark, they had been guilty of an act of wilful desecration, for which even death was not an unfitting judgment.[505]

Perhaps the most remarkable instance of TJ's apologetic tendency regarding divine justice in relation to Israel is the interpretation of Isaiah 64:11b.[506] While the prophet bitterly complains about the apparently groundless infliction by God of terrible suffering upon Israel,[507] TJ softens the implied criticism of the Almighty by claiming that God was merely

503. I Sam. 6:19a.

504. TJ's explanation is unique, and has no parallel elsewhere. A different cause of the plague which befell the people of Beth-shemesh is offered in a marginal reading of TJ— "because they rejoiced at Israel's misfortunes and despised the ark of the Lord when it was uncovered." Conceivably, this is an allusion to the religious persecution of the Jews under Antiochus IV (during 168 to 165 B.C.E.) when the apostate Jewish Hellenists did indeed "rejoice at Israel's misfortunes," and treated the Temple—here equivalent to the ark of the Covenant—with contempt (cf. I Mac. 1:33ff., 4:41; II Mac. 3:4ff.; 4:14,32). It could, however, also refer to the Judaeo-Christian and other dissident sectarians who refused to submit to Bar Kochba, thus in effect siding with the Romans. The problem of the disproportionate punishment of the people of Beth-shemesh is also raised in the Talmud (T.B. Sot. 35a-b). The answers offered there are altogether different from TJ.

505. Since the ark was the center of the divine presence (cf., e.g., Num. 7:89; 10:35f.; I Sam. 4:5ff.; I Kings 8:6ff.), looking at the uncovered ark was almost like beholding God—and that act, in turn, constituted an offense for which a divinely ordained and miraculously executed death was exacted; cf. Exod. 33:20; Jud. 13:19–22.

506. Cf. Is. 64:11b (MT "Will you [*viz.*, God] keep silent, and afflict us sorely?" = TJ "But you are giving a respite to the wicked ones, and to those that oppress us sorely"). Cf. Komlosh, *op. cit.*, pp. 370f.

507. Cf. Is. 5:25b (MT "For all that his anger is not turned back, and his hand is still stretched out" = TJ "For all that they did not repent for their sins, so that his anger might turn back from them; and they still persist [*lit.* keep strong] in their rebellion; and yet again his blow is about to exact punishment on them").

granting a respite to the oppressors of Israel—presumably to give them an opportunity to repent.

Most of prophetic literature contains dire predictions concerning the ultimate fate of the gentiles in general, and of the nations with whom Israel came into contact in particular. As far as TJ was concerned, in addition to patriotic motives (with which we are not concerned in this context), the main theological problem was to justify sweeping prophetic denunciations of the gentiles. The divine punishment visited on them was, like that endured by Israel, neither arbitrary nor unfair, but justified by persistent and unrepentant wrongdoing.

Thus, when Jeremiah speaks about "the cities which the Lord overthrew without regret"[508]—undoubtedly a reference to the destruction of Sodom and Gomorrah[509]—, TJ adds "in his anger",[510] thus implying that the overthrow of Sodom and Gomorrah was not an act of arbitrary divine destructiveness, but one motivated by acts of provocation causing God to be "angry".

Likewise, Jeremiah's references to Moab's and Esau's (i.e., Edom's) "visitation"[511] is amended in TJ by additional words referring to their "sins". The "visitation" of Moab and Edom thus becomes not a case of blind misfortune, but a well-deserved retribution for their wrongdoing.

Finally, the sins of the Chaldees, who are denounced in the first chapter of Habakkuk in general terms for their ruthless aggression and conquests, are more precisely specified in TJ. Accordingly, their guilt was established and their eventual downfall assured because of their hubris—a boundless arrogance characteristic of conquerers throughout history—as well as for paying excessive honor to their idol.[512] Evidently, aggressive conquest as

---

508. Jer. 20:16a.

509. Cf. Gen. 19:25,29; Deut. 29:22; Am. 4:11. In all these passages, the same expression, "overthrow" (Heb. הפך), is used in reference to the destruction of Sodom and Gomorrah.

510. The same expression is used in Deut. 29:22b (MT באפו = TJ ברגזיה), and it may have influenced TJ's identical addition in Jer. 20:16a.

511. Cf. Jer. 48:44b (MT ". . . in the year of their [*viz.*, the Moabites'] punishment" = TJ ". . . in the year of their visitation for their sins"); cf. *ibid.* 49:8b (MT ". . . the time when I punish him" [*viz.*, Esau = Edom] = TJ "the time of the visitation for his sins").

512. Cf. Hab. 1:11 (MT "Then they sweep by like the wind and go on [or: Then their spirit passes over and transgresses], and they become guilty, whose own might is like their god [or: they who impute their might unto their god]" = TJ "Therefore, because his [*viz.*, the nation of the Chaldees'] spirit was haughty [*lit.*, high] upon him, he was removed from

such was not considered sinful in ancient times, unless it involved a breach of solemn covenant. The conquerer was, however, expected to maintain a due sense of humility, and to attribute his power and victories to God. If in his sinful pride he failed in this duty, retribution was sure to follow.[513]

Both the Hebrew Bible and the Talmud provide numerous examples testifying to the concept of repentance as a cardinal principle of Judaism.[514] Since "there is not a righteous man on earth who does (only) good and never sins,"[515] the gates of repentance must be open for those who genuinely regret their transgression. For, clearly, only through repentance could the sinner hope to gain salvation.

With rare exceptions, repentant sinners are welcomed back to the fold[516]. Unlike prayer, which sometimes does not pass through to the Almighty[517], "the gates of repentance are always open"[518]. Indeed, according to one opinion, "In the place where penitents stand even the wholly righteous cannot stand"[519]. In other words, the repentant sinner who has over-

---

his kingdom, and he became guilty because he paid much honor to his idol"). Cf. Dan. 4:27f. and 5:20f., which clearly influenced TJ's rendering—all the more so since Nebuchadnezzar was the King of the Chaldees (= Babylonians).

513. Cf. Dan. 5:22ff.; Is. 14:12ff.; Ezek. 28:1ff.—Israel, too, was warned against the arrogance of success and prosperity; cf. Deut. 8:11—18. Cf. also TJ on Jud. 5:13 (MT "Then he made a remnant to have dominion over the nobles and the people; the Lord made me have dominion over the nobles and the mighty" = TJ "Then one of the armies of Israel came down and broke the power of the warriors of the nations; but lo, this was not because of [Israel's] might, but the Lord broke before his people the power of the warriors of their enemies").

514. Cf. Deut. 30:8—10; I Kings 8:33—40 (= II Chron. 6:24—31); *ibid.* 8:46—50 (= II Chron. 6:36—39); II Kings 17:13; Is. 19:22; 44:22; 59:20; Jer. 3:12,14 22; 4:1; 18:11; 25:5; 35:15; Ezek. 14:6; 18:21—23,27—32; 33:9—19; Hos. 5:4; 6:1; 14:2ff.; Joel 2:12—14; Jon. 3:8—10; Zech. 1:3ff.; Mal. 3:7; Pss. 51:15; Lam. 3:40; 5:21. For the most important rabbinic teachings on the subject of repentance, cf. T.B. Ber. 10a; 34b; Shab. 32a; 153a; Pes. 54a M. Yoma VIII, 8—9; Tos. Yoma V (IV), 5—11; T.B. Yoma 85b; 86a—87a; T.Y. Yoma VIII, 6—8, 45b-c; T.B. R.H. 17b; T.Y.R.H. I, 3,57a; T.B. Taan. 16a; Sot. 47a; Kid. 40b; B.K. 94b; B.M. 58b; Sanh. 37a; 97b; 102b—103a; 105a; A.Z. 7a—b; M. Avot IV, 11; Gen. R. XXII, 13; LXXXIV, 19; Exod. R. XI, 1; XII, 1; XIII, 3; XXI, 5; XXXI, 1; Lev. R. X, 5; Num. R. VII, 10; X, 1(3); Deut. R. II, 12; Cant. R.V, 2; Lam. R. III, 43; Tanḥ. מצורע 4; Mekilta on Exod. 15:3; Pesik. R. ch. 44, edit. M. Friedmann, pp. 182b—185b.

515. Eccl. 7:20.

516. Cf., e.g., Ezek. 18:21—32; 33:11—19; T.B. Ber. 10a; Sanh. 37a.

517. Cf. Lam. 3:44: "Thou hast wrapped thyself with a cloud so that no prayer can pass through." Cf. also Lam. R. III, 44, par. 9.

518. Lam. R., *ibid.*

519. T.B. Ber. 34b.

come his moral weakness is on a higher level than "the wholly righteous" who never experienced—or never succumbed to—temptation.

In TJ, repentance—literally, return (viz., to God)—is equated to a return to God's service[520] (for a literal return to God would have anthropomorphic connotations[521]) as well as to the Torah[522]. It involves an undertaking not to sin in future[523]. Prayer without repentance is unacceptable[524]. Likewise, punishment of the wicked is no substitute for repentance—a frequent prophetic theme[525] repeated in TJ, which represents the prophet Jeremiah as complaining about the refusal of the wicked to repent despite the divine blows of punishment suffered by them[526].

The purpose of repentance is not merely to effect a change of heart in the wicked, but to transform their character radically, so that new men may emerge who are no longer recognizable in their former role. The evil men are

---

520. Cf. Jer. 3:1b (MT "... and would you return to me?" = TJ "... and return henceforth to my service"); *ibid.* 3:10a (MT "... Judah did not return to me" = TJ "... of the house of Judah they did not return to my service"; *ibid.* 4:1a (MT "If you return, O Israel" = TJ "If you return, O Israel, to my service"); *ibid.* 24:7b (MT "... for they shall return to my service"); *ibid.* 31:17b (MT "... bring me back" = TJ "... bring us back to your service"); Ezek. 14:6a (MT "... Repent ye" = TJ "... Return ye to my service"); Zech. 1:3a (MT "Return to me" = TJ "Return to my service.").

521. Cf. Komlosh, *op. cit.*, p. 397, n. 3.

522. Cf. Is. 26:10a (MT "... he does not learn righteousness" = TJ "... if they [viz., the wicked] return to your Torah ..."); *ibid.* 31:6a (MT "Turn [or: Return] ye ..." = TJ "Return ye to the Torah"); *ibid.* 58:12b (MT "... you shall be called the repairer of the breach, the restorer of streets [or: paths] to dwell in" = TJ "... you shall be called restorer[or: preserver] of the right way, one who brings back the wicked ones to the Torah"); Hos. 13:9 (MT "... in me is your help" = TJ "... when you return to the Torah, my *Memra* assists you"). Return to the Torah is also included in a homiletical expansion of TJ on Is. 1:18a, 33:13b, 42:14a, 57:19b; Jer. 31:18a, 20b; and Hab. 3:1b.

523. Cf. Hos. 2:9b (MT "... it was better for me then than now" = TJ "... it was better [or: good] for me when I was worshipping before him; from now on I will not worship idols"). It is noteworthy that a similar requirement that one must undertake not to repeat the offense is found in Maimonides' *Yad*, Hilkhot Teshuvah II,2; but not explicitly in Talmudic literature.

524. Cf. Hos. 2:4 (MT "... I am not her husband; let her therefore put away her harlotry from her face ..." = TJ "my *Memra* does not accept her prayer until she removes her evil deeds from before her face ...").

525. Cf. e.g., Is. 1:5ff.; 5:13ff.; 9:8ff.; Jer. 2:35ff.; Ezek. 16:49ff.; Hos. 13:1 1ff.

526. Cf. Jer. 5:3a (MT "Thou hast smitten them, but they felt no anguish" = TJ "As for the wicked, you have smitten them, but they have not repented").

to become righteous[527], and are to be considered as servants of God[528] equal in every respect to those who have never sinned[529]. Moreover, repentance with a perfect heart has the effect that the ex-sinner's deliberate offenses are counted as inadvertent errors to be wholly forgiven[530].

According to a Midrashic addition to Ezek. 1:8a, "the (divine) right hand is stretched out to receive sinners who return in repentance, so as to acquit them on the day of judgment, and make them inherit everlasting life". Furthermore, the wicked who fail to grasp the opportunity to turn a new leaf are not immediately condemned to suffer punishment. They are granted a respite to enable them to return to the ways of the Torah[531]. Israel, too, is granted a respite to return to the Torah[532], and the gate of repentance will

527. Cf. Jer. 15:19a (MT "If you utter what is precious, and not what is worthless ..." [or: "If you take out the precious from the vile ..."] = TJ "If you will bring back the wicked to become righteous ..."). Cf. Komlosh, *op. cit.*, p. 399.

528. Cf. Is. 42:19 (MT "Who is blind but my servant .... or blind as the servant of the Lord?" = TJ "Surely if the wicked ones repent, they shall be called my servants .... If they repent, they shall be called servants of the Lord"). Cf. Komlosh, *op. cit.*, p. 389.

529. Cf. Is. 7:3a (MT "... you and Shear-jashub ..." = TJ "... you and the rest who did not sin, and those who repented from sin ..."); *ibid.* 33:13 (MT "Hear, you who are far off, what I have done; and you who are near, acknowledge my might" = TJ "Hear, you righteous ones who have observed [or: kept] my Torah from the beginning, what I have done; and know my might, you repentant ones who have returned to the Torah recently"); *ibid.* 57:19b (MT "Peace, peace, to the far and to the near" = TJ "Peace shall be wrought for the righteous ones who have observed [or: kept] my Torah from the beginning, and peace shall be wrought for the repentant ones who have recently returned to my Torah"). The juxtaposition of the wholly righteous and the penitent sinners in all these Targumic interpretations of Scriptural verses implies equality before God.

530. Cf. Hab. 3:1b (MT "... according to Shigionoth" = TJ " ... if they [*viz.* the wicked] return to the Torah with a perfect heart, they will be forgiven, and all their sins which they committed before me shall be like inadvertent errors"). TJ connects שגינות with the root שגה— to make an error, i.e., an unintentional mistake. Cf. also T.B. Yoma 86b: "Great is repentance, for deliberate sins are accounted to him (*viz.*, the repentant sinner) as errors."

531. Cf. Is. 42:14a (MT "For a long time I have held my peace, I have kept still and restrained myself" = TJ "I have given them a respite from of old if they return to the Torah, but they have not returned"); cf. Komlosh, *op. cit.*, p. 370, n. 78; cf. Hab. 1:13b (MT "Why dost thou look on faithless men and art silent when the wicked swallows up the man more righteous than he?" = TJ "Surely it is revealed before you; why then do you look on violent men and give a respite to the wicked ones, and they swallow up those who are better than they are); *ibid.* 3:1a (MT "A prayer of Habakkuk the prophet" = TJ "A prayer which Habbakuk the prophet uttered when it was revealed to him concerning the respite granted to the wicked ones").

532. Cf. Is. 57:11b (MT "Have I not held my peace, even for a long time?" = TJ "Have I not given you a respite from of old, so that perchance you may return to the Torah?").

be revealed to Jerusalem, so that the people of the city may be shown the way of peace and truth[533].

Although God—and hence his prophets—are well aware that Israel may fail to heed the divine exhortations to repent [534], the prophets, nevertheless, continue their anguished appeals and warnings to repent while there is yet time[535] and before the divine decree is sealed[536]. Israel is also called upon to reflect upon the words of the prophets before the curses predicted by them come to pass[537]. The national strength of Israel depends on repentance; for as long as Israel fails to repent, she will continue to be in a state of weakness[538].

Israel's unwillingness to repent is deplored by the prophets[539], and

533. Cf. Jer. 33:6b (MT ". . . and I will reveal to them abundance of peace and truth" = TJ ". . . and I will reveal to them the gate of repentance, and show them so that they may walk in the way of peace and truth"). Cf. Komlosh, *op. cit.*, p. 409, on the etymological association between MT and TJ.

534. Cf. Is. 57:11b (MT ". . . but you do not fear me" = TJ ". . . but you have not returned [or: repented] before me"); Jer. 8:4b (MT "If one turns away, does he not return?" = TJ "As for returning [or: repenting], it is revealed before me that they will not return [or: repent]"). Cf. also Is. 42:14a, see *supra*, n. 531.

535. Cf. Is. 21:12b (MT "If you will inquire, inquire; come back again" = TJ "If you repent [*lit.*, return], do so [*lit.*, return] while you are still able to repent"). Cf. Jer. 3:22a (MT "Return, ye backsliding sons" = TJ "Repent [or: return], O sons who harden themselves (not) to repent [or: return]").

536. Cf. Jer. 4:1a (MT "If you return, O Israel, says the Lord, to me you should return" = TJ "If you return, O Israel, to my service, your return [or: repentance] will be accepted before the decree against you is sealed"). Cf. also Is. 55:6 (MT "Seek the Lord while he may be found, call upon him while he is near" = TJ "Seek the fear of the Lord while you are still alive; entreat [or: make supplication] before him while you still exist"). Cf. Komlosh, *op. cit.*, pp. 371–372.

537. Cf. Is. 28:19b (MT ". . . and it will be sheer terror to understand the message" = TJ ". . . before the time of the curse comes, reflect ye upon the words of the prophets"). A similar appeal to Israel for reflection and self-examination to be followed by repentance is to be found in TJ on Jer. 31:20 (MT ". . . consider well the highway, the road by which you went. Return, O virgin Israel" = TJ "Set your heart, reflect upon your deeds which you have done whether they are right; for you have gone into exile to a distant way. Now, return, O congregation of Israel").

538. Cf. Ezek. 7:13b, where the difficult MT וְאִישׁ בַּעֲוֹנוֹ חַיָּתוֹ לֹא יִתְחַזָּקוּ (*lit.*, "and no man can, because of his iniquity, strengthen his life") is rendered in TJ, "and each man takes delight in his own sins (or: in the sins of his soul), and until they will be in (a state of) repentance, they will not be strengthened."

539. Cf. Is. 5:3a; see *supra*, note 440. Cf. Jer. 8:5a (MT "Why has this people turned away in perpetual backsliding?" = TJ "Why is it that this people, the inhabitants of Jerusalem, are restraining [or hardening] themselves [מתחסנין—on the meaning, cf. Komlosh, *op. cit.*, p. 406,

attributed to the corruption of the people by prosperity and riches[540]. Nevertheless, except for the ultimate, unforgivable crime of bloodshed[541], repentance is always possible and is accepted by God[542]. He takes compassion on individuals—Jews and non-Jews alike—who repent and obey the teaching of the Torah[543]. Likewise, God is merciful to repentant Israel who returns to the Torah[544].

---

n. 5] (not) to return to my worship [or: service]; they have turned back to rebel against [*lit.*, from] my Torah, and they do not wish to return [or: repent]"); cf. Ezek. 16:23 (MT "And after all your wickedness—woe, woe to you! . . ." = TJ "What will be at the end of you for all your evil? The prophet says to her, 'Woe unto you because you have sinned, woe unto you because you have not repented'"); *ibid.* 16:28 (MT "You have played the harlot with the Assyrians, because you were insatiable; yea, you played the harlot with them, and still you were not satisfied" = TJ "You went astray after the Assyrians because you did not know the Torah; yea, you went astray after them, and did not even know repentance").

540. Cf. Is. 57:10 (MT ". . . you did not say, 'It is hopeless' [or: 'There is no hope']; you found new life for [renewal of] your strength; therefore you were not grieved [or: faint]" = TJ ". . . and you did not think of repenting [*lit.*, returning]; you multiplied great riches, therefore you did not think of repenting [*lit.*, returning]"); cf. Mic. 1:12a (MT "For the inhabitants of Maroth wait anxiously for good" = TJ "Because you were dwelling on the best of the land and hoping for [or: anticipating] good, you refuse to return to the Torah"). In this instance, TJ connects Heb. מרה with the root מרד—to rebel, hence "refuse."

541. Cf. Ezek. 24:7b—8 (MT ". . . she [*viz.*, "the blood city" of Jerusalem which has shed innocent blood] put it [i.e., the blood shed in the city] on the bare rock, she did not pour it upon the ground to cover it with dust . . . . I have set on the bare rock the blood she has shed, that it may not be covered" = TJ ". . . with premeditation and outstretched [or: raised] arm she shed it [*viz.*, the blood]; she did not shed it inadvertently so as to [be able to] do repentance for it . . . I have revealed their sins because they shed innocent blood, so that they may not be forgiven"). Cf. also Hos. 14:3, where MT "Take away (or: forgive) all iniquity" is rendered by TJ, "It is near (or: close) before you to forgive iniquity." The omission of "all" is no doubt designed to support the view that there are sins and iniquities that cannot be forgiven.

542. Cf. Jer. 4:1a (MT "If you return, O Israel, says the Lord, to me you should return" = TJ "If you return, O Israel, to my service, says the Lord, your repentance will be accepted").

543. Cf. Jonah 3:9a (cf. Joel 2:14a) (MT "Who knows, God may yet repent" = TJ "Who knows that he has sins on his conscience [*lit.*, on his hands], let him repent, so that there may be compassion [or: mercy] upon us from before the Lord"); Ezek. 34:9 (MT "Therefore, you shepherds, hear the word of the Lord" = TJ "Therefore, you wicked leaders, return to the Torah, and I will, in the future have compassion on you; obey the teaching of the Torah, and accept the word of the Lord").

544. Cf. Is. 57:18 (MT "I have seen his [*viz.*, Israel's] ways , but I will heal him; I will lead him. . ." = TJ "The way of their repentance is revealed before me, and I will forgive them and have compassion upon them"); Jer. 31:18a (MT "For after I have turned away I repented" = TJ "For when we return to the Torah, there will be compassion upon us"); Hos. 2:3 (MT "Say to your brothers, 'My people, and to your sisters, 'She has

God will forgive the transgressions of the repentant sinners of Israel and confer blessings and consolations upon them[545]; do good to Israel[546]; assist them[547]; carry out their wishes[548]; and redeem them[549].

He will perform mighty acts and miracles for them[550], thus enabling them to prevail against their enemies[551]. God will then confer on Israel the

---

obtained pity'" = TJ "O prophets, say to your brothers, O my people, return to my Torah, and I will have pity on your congregation'"); *ibid* 14:5a (MT "I will heal their backsliding; I will love them freely" = TJ "I will accept them in their [state of] of repentance; I will forgive their sins; I will have compassion on them when they freely return [or: repent]"). On the etymological connection between Heb. משובה and Aram, תיובתא cf. Komlosh, *op. cit.*, p. 406, n. 5. It is noteworthy that in all these instances unconditional divine compassion on Israel *is* changed in TJ to a conditional promise contingent on repentance and return to the Torah.

545. Cf. Joel 2:14 (MT "Who knows whether he will not turn and repent, and leave a blessing behind him" = TJ "Who knows that he has sins on his conscience [*lit.*, on his hands], let him repent from them, so that there may be compassion on him; and whoever will repent, his sins will be forgiven, and he will receive blessings and consolations . . ."). Cf. also Is. 57:18a and Hos. 14:5a (see *supra*, n. 544). On king Manasseh of Judah as a shining example of a repentant sinner (see II Chron. 33:12–13), cf. Jer. 15:4, where MT "I will make them a horror to all kingdoms of the earth because of what Manasseh . . . did in Jerusalem," is radically transformed in TJ to "I will make them a horror to all the kingdoms of the earth because they did not repent [*lit.*, return] like Manasseh . . . because he had done great things in Jerusalem").

546. Cf. Zech. 1:3 (= Mal. 3:7a) (MT "Return to me, . . . and I will return to you" = TJ "Return to my service . . . and I will make myself turn by my *Memra* to do good to you").

547. Cf. Hos. 13:9 (MT ". . . for you are against me, your help" [or: "in me is your help"] = TJ ". . . and when you return to my Torah, my *Memra* is in support of you"). See *supra*, n. 496.

548. Cf. Is. 1:18a (MT "Come now, let us reason together" = TJ "Therefore, when you will return to the Torah, you shall request from before me, and I will carry out [*lit.*, do] your request").

549. Cf. *ibid.* 30:15a (MT "By returning and rest you shall be saved" = TJ "I have said that you shall return to my Torah, have rest (*viz.*, from your enemies), and be redeemed" [or: delivered]; Jer. 3:22 (MT "Return, ye backsliding sons, I will heal your backslidings. Behold, we come to thee . . ." = TJ "Return, [or: Repent], O sons, who harden themselves (not) to return [or: repent]. I will forgive you when you repent. Behold, whenever you say, "We have returned to your service, redeem us . . .").

550. Cf. Is. 10:22 (MT ". . . a remnant of them will return. Destruction is decreed, overflowing with righteousness" = TJ ". . . a remnant that did not sin, and those who repented of sin—for them mighty acts shall be wrought that shall be mightily displayed and carried out with righteousness [or: merit]").

551. Cf. homiletical expansion of TJ on Jud. 5:4a: ". . . when they [*viz.*, the Israelites] returned to it [i.e., the Torah], they prevailed against their enemies." The same idea is conveyed by TJ in a Midrashic introduction to Jud. 5:6b: ". . . when they returned to the Torah,

blessings of peace[552] and numerical growth[553], and restore the exiles of Israel to their land[554], where they will worship before God.

On the other hand, wilful refusal to repent will have dire consequences. "Evil", i.e., calamity, would enter the gates of Jerusalem[556], and the unrepentant sinners would be severely punished.[557] For Israel, failure to

---

they (*viz.*, the foreign nations) could not prevail against them." Similarly, Hab. 3:7b, where MT "... the curtains of the land of Midian trembled" is expanded by TJ to "... when they (*viz.*, the Israelites) returned to observe [or: carry out; *lit.*, do] the Torah, you wrought miracles and mighty acts for them, and you delivered them from the hands of the Midianites through Gideon the son of Joash."

552. Cf. Is. 57:19b (MT "Peace, peace, to the far and to the near" = TJ "The prophet says, 'Peace shall be wrought for the righteous ones who have observed [or: kept] my Torah from of old; and peace shall be wrought for the repentant ones who have returned to the Torah...'").

553. Cf. Hos. 2:1b (MT "... it shall be said to them, 'Sons [or: Children] of the living God'" = TJ "... they shall return [or: repent] and multiply, and it shall be said to them, 'People of the enduring God'").

554. Cf. Ezek. 39:28a (MT "... and I gathered them into their own land" = TJ "... and now that they have repented [*lit.*, returned], I gathered them into their own land").

555. Cf. Is. 10:21 (MT "A remnant shall return, the remnant of Jacob, to mighty God" = TJ "The remnant that have not sinned, and they that have repented of [*lit.*, returned from] sin, the remnant of the house of Jacob shall return to worship [*lit.*, serve] before the mighty God").

556. Cf. Mic. 1:12 (MT "For the inhabitants of Maroth wait anxiously for good, because evil has come down from the Lord to the gate of Jerusalem" = TJ "She that was dwelling on the best [or: most beautiful] of the land, and hoping for good, refuses to return to the Torah. What will you do, seeing that [*lit.*, for] evil has come down from before the Lord to enter the gates of Jerusalem"); cf. also Jer. 15:6b (MT "I have stretched out my hand against you [*viz.*, Jerusalem] and destroyed you; I am tired of relenting" = TJ "I have raised my mighty plague [or: blow] upon you, and I destroyed, because you were able to repent [*lit.*, return] but did not"). Cf. also *ibid.* 2:19a, see *infra*, note 558.

557. Cf. Is. 5:25b (MT "For all this his anger has not turned back, and his hand is still stretched out" = TJ "for all this they did not turn back from their sins, so that his anger might be turned back from them; and they still persist in their rebelliousness; and his stroke [or: blow] will yet in future take vengeance upon them"); Hos. 1:3a (MT "So he went and took Gomer the daughter of Diblaim" = TJ "So he went and prophesied concerning them, that if they would repent (*lit.*, return), they would be forgiven, but if not—as the leaves drop from the fig-trees, so they shall drop"). This fanciful homiletical interpretation connects MT דבלים with דבילה—a dried (or: pressed) fig-cake. See Komlosh, *op. cit.*, p. 173, n. א 16. Cf. also Nahum 1:3a (MT "... and the Lord will by no means clear the guilty" = TJ "... and the Lord forgives those who return to his Torah, but those who do not return [or: repent] when he does not acquit [or: leave unpunished]").

obey the prophets and repent would bring about national calamities[558] and humiliation[559]; exposure to foreign "killers" would cause much loss of life[560], including the death of the king and, ultimately, the destruction of the Temple and the capture of its precious vessels[561] as well as deportation into exile[562].

We have already mentioned in passing that in TJ (as indeed throughout the Hebrew Bible) repentant sinners are forgiven. Divine pardon for those who abandon their evil ways is indeed a cardinal principle in TJ's theology.

558. Cf. Is. 42:14 (MT ". . . I have kept still and restrained myself; now I will cry out like a woman in labor, I will pant and I will gasp" = TJ ". . . but they did not return [or: repent]; as pangs to a woman in labor shall my judgment be revealed to them; they shall be made desolate and perish together"). See also *supra,* n. 531. Cf. Is. 65:12a (MT "I will destine you for the sword, and you will all bow [or: kneel] down to be slaughtered; because, when I called, you did not answer, when I spoke, you would not listen . . ." = TJ "And I will deliver you to the slaughter; because I sent my prophets, but you did not repent; they prophesied, but you would not hearken"); Jer. 2:19a (MT ". . . your backsliding shall reprove you. Know therefore and see that it is an evil and bitter thing that you have forsaken the Lord your God . . ." = TJ ". . . because you did not return to the Torah, punishment [or: calamity] shall be wrought upon you. Know therefore and see that I have brought evil and bitterness upon you, Jerusalem, because you forsook the service of the Lord your God . . .").

559. Cf. Hos. 7:10 (MT "The pride of Israel witnesses against him; yet they have not returned to the Lord their God, nor have they sought him, for all this" = TJ "The honor of Israel shall be humbled in their sight [*lit.,* while they are seeing it], because they did not return to the service of the Lord their God, and did not ask from before him, for all this"); Is. 66:4 (MT "I also will choose to mock them; and bring upon them that which they dread; because I called and there was none to answer, I spoke and they would not listen, but they did that which was evil in my sight [*lit.,* in my eyes] . . ." = TJ "I also will take pleasure in their destruction and they shall not be delivered from that which they dread, because I sent my prophets, and they did not repent; they [*viz.,* the prophets] prophesied, but they [*i.e.,* the people] would not hearken, but they did that which was evil before me . . .").

560. Cf. Hos. 5:6a, see *supra,* n. 448.

561. Cf. Amos 9:1a, where MT ". . . Smite the capitals so that the thresholds shake, and shatter them on the heads of all of them," is in TJ homiletically expanded to ". . . if my people Israel will not return to the Torah, extinguish (or, according to another reading, overturn) the lamp, (and) King Josiah will be slain, and the Temple (*lit.,* House) will be ruined, and the Temple courts will be destroyed, and the vessels of the Temple will go into captivity."

562. Cf. Jer. 3:8a (MT ". . . for all the adulteries of backsliding Israel I had sent her away" = TJ ". . . for all the matter that they went astray (or: erred), inasmuch as they of the house of Israel are restraining themselves from returning [or: hardening themselves not to return) to my service, I exiled them"]; cf. also Ezek. 21:18 and 24:6b, see *supra,* n. 476.

Even where, as in Isaiah 1:14b, MT "I am weary of enduring (or: bearing) them" is clear enough, leaving no doubt that the prophet sees God as unwilling to put up any longer with Israel's offenses and forgive them their misdeeds—TJ deliberately reverses the meaning of the text to "I have increased (or: multiplied) forgiveness".

Elsewhere, too, TJ emphasizes that divine wrath does not last long[563], and that God does not punish in his anger truly repentant sinners[564] Indeed, at all times God shows forbearance[565], and—with the exception of some exceptionally wicked men who are beyond redemption[566]—divine pardon is granted to those who repent and "return to the Torah"[567] or, in other words, undertake to obey and fulfill the laws of the Torah.

563. Cf. II Sam. 24:15a (MT "So the Lord sent a pestilence upon Israel from the morning until the appointed time" = TJ "So the Lord set death upon Israel from the time when the continual offering is slaughtered until it is offered up" [viz., upon the altar]). The implication of this interpretation, which is based on a disputed view in T.B. Ber. 62b, is that God's anger does not last very long; cf. Pss. 30:6 ("For his anger is but for a moment") and Komlosh, op. cit., p. 319.

564. Cf. Jer. 3:12a (MT "I will not look on you in anger" = TJ "When you repent [lit., return], I will not send my anger [or: wrath] upon you"). Cf. also Is. 9:11b, 16b, 20b, 10:4b (MT "Yet [or: For all this] his anger has not turned back" = TJ "For all this they did not repent [or: have not repented] from their sins, so that his anger should turn back [or: away] from them").

565. Cf. Is. 26:12b (MT "You have also requited all our misdeeds [lit., you have wrought for us all our works] = TJ "At all times has forbearance for our sins been shown [lit., wrought] to us").

566. Cf. II Sam. 23:6 (MT "But the ungodly, they are all like thorns that are thrown away; for they cannot be taken with the hand" = TJ "But the wicked sinful men are like thorns, which are easy [lit., soft] to pluck out when they sprout [lit., come forth]; but when a man spares them and leaves them, they become so strong that it is impossible to touch them by hand"). Although divine forgiveness is not excluded, it is clearly implied that some evil men are too dangerous to be left unpunished and do not deserve to be pardoned.

567. Cf. Is. 28:10a (MT "For it is precept upon precept, precept upon precept, line upon line, line upon line" = TJ "... the prophets prophesied unto them that, if they would repent [lit., return], they would be forgiven ..."); ibid. 57:18 (see supra, n. 544); Jer. 3:22a (see supra, n. 549; ibid. 31:18a (see supra, n. 544); Hos. 1:3a (see supra, n. 557); ibid. 2:3 (see supra, n. 544); ibid. 3:1b (MT "... though they turn to other gods and love cakes of raisins" = TJ "... though they turn after the idols of the nations, yet, if they repent [lit., return], they shall be forgiven, and they will be like a man who mistakenly said a [viz., wrong] word while [intoxicated] with wine"); ibid. 14:5a (see supra, n. 544); ibid. 14:9b (MT "... from me comes your fruit" = TJ "... from before me is forgiveness for [i.e., following] their repentance to be found"); Joel 2:14a (MT "Who knows whether he will not turn and repent" = TJ "Whoever knows that he has sins on his conscience [lit., in his hand], let him turn back from them, and

The concept of ancestral merit aiding and preserving their offspring—
even when the children do not measure up to the standards of their forefathers—is well established in both Biblical and rabbinic theology[568]. In
particular, it is the Patriarchs, Abraham, Isaac and Jacob, whose treasure-
house of merit is an unfailing source of grace for their descendants, the
children of Israel.[569]

Even when the latter are unworthy and sinful, they are saved from the
full force of divine punishment and total destruction by the inexhaustible
residue of ancestral merit.[570] This concept is fully accepted by TJ. Thus,
Abraham's willingness to obey God even to the poing of sacrificing his son
Isaac—an event perpetually invoked in the Jewish liturgy as a primary
motive for remembering Israel for good and for granting Abraham's children
forgiveness and salvation[571]—is seen in a Midrashic addition to TJ on II
Kings 3:27a as having influenced Mesha's sacrifice of his first-born son:
"He (i.e., Mesha) said thus: Surely they (viz., the Israelites) are remembered
because of the merits of Abraham who offered up his son Isaac as a burnt

---

there shall be compassion on him; and whoever will repent [*lit.*, return], his sins shall be
forgiven"); Nahum 1:3a (see *supra*, n. 557); Hab. 3:1b (see *supra*, n. 530). See also notes 544
and 545.

568. Cf. *Encyclopaedia Judaica*, Vol. 16 (Jerusalem 1971), cols. 976–978, s.v. *Zekhut
Avot*, where the important source references are cited. For additional references, cf. M.D.
Gross, אוצר האגדה Vol. I (Jerusalem 5734 (1974). pp. 333–339, s.v. זכות וחובה and C.J.
Kasowski, אוצר לשון התלמוד Vol. 12 = (Jerusalem 1963), p. 238, s.v. זכות אבות.

569. Cf., e.g., Gen. 22:16ff., 26:3ff., Exod. 6:8; 32:11ff., Lev. 33:14; 26:42, Deut. 1:8;
4:31; 7:7f.; 9:26f.; II Kings 13:23; Is. 41:8; Jer. 11:5; 33:26; Mic. 7:18ff.;
Pss. 105:41ff.; II Chron. 20:6f.; T.Y. Ta'an I, 1, 63d–64a; Exod. R. II, 5; XLIV, 1–10; Lev.
R. XXXVI, 5; Deut. R. II, 23; III, 11, 5; VI, 5; Eccl. R. IV, 3; Tanḥ וירא 23; cf. *EJ*, 13, 184,
s.v. Patriarchs and Matriarchs in the Aggadah; also n. 571.

570. Cf., e.g. Exod. 32:11ff.; Lev. 26:42; Mic. 7:18ff.; Exod. R. XLIV, 1–10; Deut. III,
11:15; Ecc. R. IV, 3; Tan.וירא 23.

571. Cf. e.g. *The Authorized Daily Prayer Book*, Eng. translation by Simeon Singer, 2nd
revised edition (London 1962), pp. 9, 62, 342f.; *Service of the Synagogue, New Year*, translated and edited by H.M. Adler and Arthur Davis, 16th edition (London, George Routledge &
Sons Lts., 1946), pp. 96f., 101, 138, 149, 159, 192; *Service of the Synagogue, Day of Atonement*, Part II, translated and edited by H.M. Adler and Arthur Davis, 13th edition, (London,
George Routledge & Sons Ltd. 1946), pp. 88, 135f., 159, 176f.,215f., 262; *Service of the Synagogue, Tabernacles*, translated and edited by H.M. Adler and Arthur Davis, 13th edition
(London, George Routledge & Sons Ltd., 1946), p. 138; A. Rosenfeld, *The Authorized Seli-
chot for the Whole Year* (London 1956), pp. 166, 168, 176, 183, 204, 232, 261, 290, 320, 390f.,
402.

offering.[572] Behold, I am offering up my first-born son as a burnt offering before you".[573]

Because of the good deeds of Israel's righteous and God-fearing ancestors, Israel's transgressions are forgiven, and they are delivered from divine wrath[574].

Even when they are punished because of their sins, God's covenant with the Patriarchs protects them from annihilation[575] and ensures their ultimate redemption and restoration—a reward for the righteous acts of Israel's forefathers,[576] who are called by God's name, and whom the Almighty created for his glory.[577]

The loving relationship between God and Israel's ancestors helps to sustain divine compassion for their descendants.[578] For Jerusalem, in particular, the good works of Israel's forefathers constitute a permanent shield both

572. On the Midrashic conncept that Isaac was indeed slaughtered by Abraham and offered up as a burnt-offering, but subsequently resurrected by a divine miracle, cf. S. Spiegel, *The Last Trial*, Eng. translation (Philadelphia, 1967), pp. 25—44.

573. The connection between Mesha's sacrifice of his son and the *Akedah* of Isaac is also noted in T.B. Taan. 4a and Gen. R. LV, 5.

574. Cf. Is. 64:4 (MT "You have struck [or: met] him who joyfully works righteousness [or: does justice], those that remember you in your ways. Behold, you were angry, and we sinned; in them [*viz.*, our sins] we have been [steeped] from of old, and shall be saved" = TJ "Established before you are the deeds of our righteous forefathers who rejoiced to do your will in truth and righteousness, in the way of your goodness and love [or: mercy] they were ever mindful of the fear of you. Behold, at all times when there was anger from before you against us because we had sinned, we were delivered by the very deeds of our righteous ancestors who are from of old).

575. Cf. *ibid.* 27:3 (MT "I, the Lord, watch over it, every moment I water it; lest any one harm it, I watch it night and day" = TJ "I the Lord keep for them the covenant of their forefathers, and I will not destroy them; but when they provoke me to anger [*lit.*, cause anger to be aroused before me], I make them drink the cup of their punishment. Yet, though their sins caused them to be punished in time past, night and day my *Memra* protects them").

576. Cf. Ezek. 16:6a (MT "And I passed by you" = TJ "And the remembrance of the covenant of your forefathers came before me, and I revealed myself to deliver you"); Jer. 31:15b (MT "And your work shall be rewarded" = TJ "And there is reward for the deeds of your righteous ancestors").

577. Cf. Is. 43:7a (MT "Every one who is called by my name, and whom I created for my glory" = TJ "All this [will be] on account of your ancestors over whom my name was called, and whom I created for my glory").

578. Cf. Hos. 11:8b (MT "My heart recoils [or: is turned] within me, my feelings of compassion are aroused together" = TJ "The word of my covenant is set from over against me; the love [or: compassion] of your ancestors is aroused [*lit.*, turned] altogether").

day and night;[579] and it is because of Israel's ancestral merit that God had caused his divine presence to rest in the Temple of Jerusalem[580].

Lastly, ancestral merit also has the added advantage that it helps to remind Israel of the good deeds of their forefathers, thereby causing them to reflect on their own deeds[581]—a necessary first step on the road to repentance.

11. Mysticism and Eschatology in Targum Jonathan

Rabbinic literature in general, and the Targumim in particular, employ the term Shekhinah (lit. Divine Presence) either as an alternative to God (especially where anthropomorphic expressions have to be avoided) or to describe the numinous immanence of God in the created universe.[582]

In TJ, the Shekhinah is both hidden and revealed,[583] both high above in heaven[584] and dwelling among men[585] and, in particular, in Zion[586] and the

---

579. Cf. Is. 62:6a (MT "Upon your walls, O Jerusalem, I have set watchmen; all day and all night they shall never be silent;" = TJ "Behold, the deeds of your righteous ancestors, O city of Jerusalem, are set in order and preserved before me, day and night, continually).

580. Cf. Midrashic addition to TJ on Is. 66:1a "Through the merits of your righteous forefathers has the Holy One, blessed be he, caused his divine presence to rest therein (*viz.*, in the Temple)".

581. Cf. Jer. 31:20 (21)a (MT "Set up waymarks for yourself ... consider well (*lit.*, set your heart on the highway, the road [or: way] by which you went" = TJ "O congregation of Israel, Be mindful of the good deeds of your ancestors [or: of the deeds of your good ancestors] ... reflect upon the deeds you have wrought whether they are right ...").

582. There is an extensive literature on the Shekhinah in all its aspects; cf. especially E. E. Urbach, חז"ל—פרקי אמונות ודעות (Jerusalem, 1969), pp. 29-52; (English translation by Israel Abrahams, *The Sages—Their Concepts and Beliefs* [Jerusalem, 1975], pp. 37-65); J. Abelson, *Immanence of God in Rabbinic Literature* (London, 1912; reprinted New York, 1969), pp. 77-149; see also A. Marmorstein, *The Old Rabbinic Doctrines of God* (London, 1927; reprinted New York, 1968), pp. 103 f.; Solomon Schechter, *Aspects of Rabbinic Theology* (New York, 1909; Schocken edition, 1961), pp. 40 ff.

583. Cf. Hab. 3:4b (MT "... there he veiled [or: hid] his power = TJ "There he revealed his Shekhinah, which had been hidden from men on his mighty height."

584. Cf. Is. 33:5a (MT "The Lord dwells on high" = TJ "The Lord ... who caused his Shekhinah to dwell in his high heaven"); *ibid.* 40:22a (MT "It is he who sits [or: dwells] above the circle of the earth" = TJ "It is he who caused the Shekhinah of his glory to dwell on his mighty height"); *ibid.* 57:15a (MT "I dwell in the high and holy place" = TJ "He dwells in the height and his Shekhinah is holy"). Cf. also Ezek 1:14a, where TJ adds a lengthy Midrashic

Temple of Jerusalem.[587] Above all, the Shekhinah dwells among Israel[586] and "summons" her when required.[587]

It would appear that the Targumists were not too sure whether the Shekhinah should dwell among men or even among Israel in the holy city of Jerusalem. Thus, the rhetorical question in I Kings 8:27a, "For will God indeed dwell on the earth?" is significantly paraphrased in TJ to "For who would think and who would imagine that the Lord would in truth choose to cause His Shekhinah to dwell among men who reside on the earth?" Even more explicit doubt on the subject is implied in Zephaniah 3:15b, where MT "The Lord is in your midst" becomes in TJ "The Lord intended (or: promised; lit., said) to cause his Shekhinah to dwell in your midst"[590]—rather

---

commentary on the *Ḥayyot* (the "living creatures" of the heavenly chariot) who "are despatched to do the will of their Master who has caused his Shekhinah to dwell on the height above them."

585. Cf. I Kings 8:27a and Zephaniah 3:15b; see main text below.

586. Cf. Ezek. 48:35b (MT "And the name of the city hencefo⸱ h shall be, The Lord is there" = TJ "And the name of the city shall be proclaimed [*lit.*, declared] from the day when the Lord shall cause his Shekinah to dwell there"); Joel 4:17a (MT "And you shall know that I am the Lord your God who dwell in Zion" = TJ "And you shall know that I, the Lord your God, caused my Shekhinah to dwell in Zion"); *ibid.* 4:21b (MT ". . . The Lord dwells in Zion" = TJ ". . . the Lord who caused his *Shekhinah* to dwell in Zion"); Zech. 2:14b and 15b (MT "I will dwell in the midst of you [*viz.*, of Zion)" = TJ "I will cause my *Shekhinah* to dwell in your midst"); *ibid.* 8:3a (MT "I will dwell in the midst of Jerusalem" = TJ "I will cause my Shekhinah to dwell in the midst of Jerusalem").

587. Cf. Hab. 2:20a (MT "But the Lord is in his holy temple" = TJ "But the Lord chose his holy Shekhinah to dwell in his holy temple").

588. Cf. Jos. 3:10a (MT ". . . the living God is among you" = TJ ". . . the living God has chosen to cause his Shekhinah to dwell among you"). See on this verse Komlosh, המקרא באור התרגום (Tel Aviv 1973), p. 275; cf. I Kings 18:36a (MT ". . . you are God in Israel" = TJ ". . . you are the Lord whose Shekhinah dwells in Israel"); Ezek. 43:9b (MT "I will dwell in their midst" = TJ "I will cause my Shekhinah to dwell among them"); Joel 2:27a (MT "I am in the midst of Israel" = TJ "I have caused my Shekhinah to dwell in the midst of the house of Israel"). Cf. also Exod. 25:8, where MT "And let them make me a sanctuary, that I may dwell in their midst" is rendered by TO: "And they shall make a sanctuary before me, so that I may cause my Shekhinah to dwell among them." Similarly also, Exod. 29:54a (= I Kings 6:13a), where MT "And I shall dwell in the midst of the children of Israel" is rendered by TO (and TJ on I Kings 6:13a), "And I will cause my Shekhinah to dwell in the midst of the children of Israel."

589. Cf. Is. 54:6a (MT "For the Lord has called you like a wife forsaken and grieved in spirit" = TJ "For the Shekhinah of the Lord has summoned you like a wife forsaken and grieved in spirit."

590. Similarly also in Zeph. 3:17a, where MT "The Lord, your God is in your midst" is rendered by TJ, "The Lord, your God, intended [or: promised; lit., said] to cause his Shekhinah to dwell in your midst."

than "The Lord caused his Shekhinah to dwell in your midst", as one would expect. Clearly some of the Targumists hesitated to permit even the Shekhinah, never mind God himself, to descend from the heavenly heights to dwell among men.[591] True, a divine intention or promise would ultimately be realized. Yet, that would still be in some mystical future. One could always leave the future to take care of itself. For the past and the present, there would be a question-mark on the Shekhinah's presence among mortal men.

Sometimes TJ substitutes the "glory" (יקרא or יקר) of God for the Shekhinah. The divine *Yekara* was imagined as radiating brightness like that of the six days of Creation.[592] Heaven itself could not contain God's *Yekara*,[593] neither was it visible to the eye of man.[594] The only possible exception would be a prophet who, while indeed unable to behold God himself,[595] may be privileged to see the divine *Yekara* resting on his throne[596] or removing itself on a cherub (conceived as a heavenly chariot) and coming to rest on the Temple altar.[597] The heavenly chariot which carries the divine

591. Note that this is explicitly stated by R. Jose, a second century Tanna, who maintained that "the Shekhinah never descended to earth" (T.B. Suk. 5a). See *ibid.* for the controversy on this and related topics. It is highly probably that this "anti-mystical" attitude was due to orthodox opposition to sectarian mystical and messianic speculations; cf., e.g., T. Hag. II, 507; T.Y. Hag. II, 1, 77 a-b; T.B. Hag. 15a; T.B. Sanh. 97b.

592.Cf. Hab. 3:4a (MT "His brightness was like the light" =TJ "The brightness of his *Yekara* was revealed like the brightness of the [days of] creation"). On the magnificent light of the six days of creation, which was removed and reserved for the righteous in the world to come; cf. T.B. Hag. 12a and Gen. R. III, 6.

593. Cf. I Kings 8:27b (MT. "Behold, heaven and the highest heaven cannot contain you (*viz.*, God)" =TJ "Behold, heaven and the highest heaven cannot contain your glory (יקרא)." Cf. Komlosh, *op. cit.*, p. 340.

594. Cf. Ezek. 1:27a-b (MT "And upward from what had the appearance of [or: what appeared to be] his loins" =TJ "The appearance of glory (יקר) upward which the eye cannot behold nor is it possible to look at it, and the appearance of glory (יקר) downward which the eye cannot behold nor is it possible to look at it"); *ibid.* 8:2a-b (MT "Below what appeared to be his loins..., and above his loins upward [or: and from his loins upward]" = TJ "the appearance of glory (יקר) downward which the eye cannot behold nor is it possible to look at it ... and the appearance of glory (יקר) upward which the eye cannot behold nor is it possible to look at it"). The gross anthropomophisms in MT required radical changes in TJ.

595. Cf. Exod. 33:20b "...no man shall see Me and live."

596. Cf. Is. 6:1a (MT "...I saw the Lord sitting upon a throne" = TJ "...The prophet said, I saw the glory (יקרא) of the Lord resting upon a (or: his) throne").

597. Cf. Amos 9:1a (MT "I saw the Lord standing beside [or: upon] the altar" = TJ "The prophet said, I saw the glory [יקרא] of the Lord removing itself on a cherub and resting upon the altar").

Yekara may, however, be revealed on special occasions to ordinary mortals.[598] Incidentally, the "chariot" vision of Ezekiel (chapter 1), the basis of Jewish mysticism and esoteric speculation, figures prominently in Targumic deviations from MT—the fundamental purpose being to avoid anthromorphic expressions and to weaken the mystical elements.[599]

Belief in the existence of angels whose function was to carry out specific missions or tasks set for them by God was almost universal among Jews during the Talmudic age.[600] Only the Sadducees denied the existence of angels.[601] TJ, in line with rabbinic theology, accepts the concept of angels, but, perhaps in reaction to the angelological speculations by various sects, tends to restrict the significance and activity of the angels. Their main role in heaven is to praise God;[602] but on earth they are somewhat less in evidence. On a number of occasions angels of God are replaced in TJ by

---

598. Cf. Hab. 3:15a (MT "You did trample [or: You have trodden] the sea with your horses" =TJ "You revealed yourself by the sea in the chariot of your glory [יקרך]"). The reference is presumably to the parting of the Red Sea at the time of the Exodus. Cf. also Hab. 3:4a (MT "...rays flashed from his hand" = TJ "...sparks came forth from the chariot of his glory [יקריה]").

599. Cf., e.g., Ezekiel 1:25a-b (MT "And there was a voice above the firmament...; they let down their wings" = TJ "And at the time when it was his [*viz.*, God's] will to cause his word to be heard by his servants, the prophets of Israel, there was a voice and it was heard above the firmament from among the cherubim beneath the firmament...; their wings were silent because of the [divine] word"). It is noteworthy that in TJ the mystical "voice" of MT is clearly identified as that of God, which, naturally, can be heard only by the prophets of God, not by ordinary people. Cf. also *ibid.* 1:20b (=1:21b)(MT "...the spirit of the living creature was in the wheels" = TJ "...like the spirit of the living creature was in the wheels"). Similarly, *ibid.* 10:17b (MT "the spirit of the living creature was in them [*viz.*, the wheels]" = TJ "like the spirit of the living creature was in them"). The deviation in TJ is significant. It is evidently designed to avoid any impression that the wheels of the divine chariot were independently endowed with the divine spirit. See also Ezek 1:14a, *supra*, note 3. Only occasionally is there an expansion on the Hebrew text; cf. *ibid.* 1:6.

600. There is a vast literature on Jewish angelology; cf. *The Jewish Encyclopedia*, Vol. 1, pp. 583-597; *Encyclopaedia Judaica*, Vol. 2, cols. 956-977 and the bibliography cited *ibid.*, col. 977.

601. Cf. Acts 8:23.

602. Cf. Ezek 1:24a (MT "...a sound of tumult like the sound of a host" =TJ "...the sound of their speech when they were thanking and blessing their everlasting master, the king of the universe [*lit.*, worlds], was like the sound of an army of angels on high"). On the function of the angels as a host praising God eternally there was virtual unanimity; cf. I Enoch, ch. 40; Tanh. Exod. 120 (Vayakhel 2); Sifre Deut. 306; T.B. Meg. 10b; Exod. R. XXIII, 7.

prophets;[603] and where a prophet or a priest is depicted as a מלאך ה' (actually, in this context "a messenger of the Lord", but translatable, "an angel of the Lord"), TJ makes sure that the angelological association be removed without trace.[604]

By way of contrast, an angel may sometimes be introduced by TJ, with a view to avoiding an anthropomorphic expression. Thus, Deborah's assurance to Barak, "Does not the Lord go out before you?!"[605] is deliberately changed in TJ to "Does not the angel of the Lord go forth to make it prosper (or: successful) before you?!" Even an angel is preferable to making God act like a human being.[606]

Satan, the angel of evil, man's heavenly "adversary" or antagonist is translated by TJ on Zech. 3:1b—2a as חטא or חטאה, i.e., "searcher of sin", "accuser".[607] This description of Satan—which contrasts with that in Job 1:6ff.; 2:1ff. (where the Aramaic translation renders סטנא[608])—agrees with that given in T.B. Baba Bathra 16a, according to which Satan "comes down and seduces (or: leads astray); then goes up (viz., to heaven) and arouses anger (viz., through his accusations); gets permission (i.e., to inflict punishment), and takes away the soul". It is the function of seducer and accuser which is emphasized in TJ rather than Satan's supernatural demonic power current in contemporary angelology.[609]

---

603. Cf. Jud. 2:1a (MT "an angel of the Lord" =TJ "... a prophet on a mission of [or: for] the Lord"); *ibid.* 2:4a (MT "... the angel of the Lord" = TJ "... the prophet of the Lord"). In Seder Olam R., ch. 20, edit. D.B. Ratner, p. 83—as well as Lev. R. I, 1 and Num. R. XVI, 20—the "angel of the Lord" is identified with Phinehas. Cf. Komlosh, *op. cit.,* p. 292. Cf. also Jud. 5:23a (MT "... the angel of the Lord" = TJ "... the prophet of the Lord").

604. Cf. Hag. 1:13a (MT "Haggai, the messenger [מלאך] of the Lord" = TJ "Haggai, the prophet of the Lord"); Mal. 2:7b (MT "...for he [*viz.,* the priest] is the messenger of the Lord of hosts" = TJ "...for he ministers before the Lord of hosts").

605. Jud. 4:14a.

606. For other examples of God "going out" in MT, which are attenuated in TJ, cf. Jud. 5:4a; Is. 26:21a; 42:13a; Mic. 1:3a.

607. So according to Jastrow, s.v. חטאה. Another plausible rendering would be, "the one who causes to sin"; cf. T.B. Baba Bathra 16a.

608. So also in Pss. 109:6b and I Chron. 21:1a. Cf. also TO on Num. 22:22a and 32b, where MT שטן (adversary) is rendered literally סטן. Similarly, also TJ on I Sam 29:4a; II Sam. 19:23a; I Kings 5:18b; 11:14a,23a,25a (where MT שטן, in the sense of a human adversary, is rendered virtually unchanged סטן).

609. Cf. *The Jewish Encyclopedia,* Vol. XI, pp. 68ff., s.v. Satan; *Encyclopaedia Judaica,* Vol. 14, cols. 902ff., s.v. Satan.

Because in rabbinic theology Satan is also the angel of death, TJ, always loath to use abstract expressions, renders Habakkuk 3:5a—"Before him (viz., God) went pestilence"—by "From before him the angel of death is sent." Thus, where there is a choice between abstract expressions—which could easily be misunderstood by unsophicticated audiences—and the employment of an angel who in the last resort is merely an instrument to carry out the will of his divine master, TJ opts to introduce an angel.

The Targumic diminution of the role of angels is particularly evident in TJ's rendering of "Seraphim", those fiery angelic beings seen by Isaiah in his first vision. In TJ, they are reduced to mere "servants" (or "ministers"— שמשיא) —albeit "holy" ones—who perform certain services in the divine court.[610] Such a mundane act as "flying" is unbecoming for a heavenly seraph who, instead, "ministers" in TJ. The grossly human act of taking a burning coal with tongs from the altar[611] is duly changed in TJ to "in his (viz., the divine servant's) mouth there was a word which he had received from before Him whose Shekhinah is on the throne of glory in the high heaven above the altar." TJ thus elevates the role of angelic beings, who are after all part of the divine host, while striving to remove the crude forms of popular imagination regarding the nature and activities of angels.

In the Hebrew Bible, the Day of the Lord is a poetic expression describing both past and future apocalyptic events.[612] Thus, in Ezekiel 13:5b, MT "the day of the Lord" becomes "the day of the anger of the Lord"[613]—the reference being to a disastrous event in the recent past. In most passages, however, "the day of the Lord" signifies a future apocalyptic event, a divine judgment upon the nations of the world, including—according to Amos 5:18 ff.—even Israel. In all these cases, TJ renders: "The day that will in future come from before the Lord".[614] This day is also identified as an eschatologi

---

610. Cf. Is. 6:2a. 6a. Elsewhere, the seraphim are semi-mythical serpent-like beings, and Targumic renderings vary accordingly; cf. Num. 20:8a, Deut. 8:15a; Is. 14:29b; 30:6b.

611. Cf. Is. 6:2b.

612. Cf. A. J. Everson, "The Day of the Lord," in *The Interpreter's Dictionary of the Bible,* Supplementary Volume (Abingdon, Nashville, 1976), pp. 209 f., and bibliography cited on p. 210.

613. Possibly, an allusion to Lam. 1:12b.

614. Cf. Is. 2:12a, 13:9a; Ezek. 30:3a; Joel 1:15b, 2:11a; Amos 5:18a, 20a; Ob. 15a; Zeph. 1:14a; Zech. 14:1a.

cal day of judgment,[615] when the might and kingdom of God would be revealed.[616]

Closely associated with the future day of judgment was also the notion of the miraculous resurrection of the dead. Indeed, ever since the Hasmonean age the physical resurrection of the dead at some undetermined future date was an integral part of Pharisaic and rabbinic Judaism.[617] TJ fully endorses the belief in the resurrection,[618] which, according to TJ, would be heralded by the sounding of the great trumpet (Shofar) by the Almighty himself.[619]

615. Cf. Is. 30:8b (MT ". . . that it may be for a future day" = TJ ". . . that it may be for the day of judgment").

616. Cf. Is. 31:5a (MT ". . . the Lord of hosts will protect Jerusalem" = TJ ". . . the might of the Lord of hosts shall be revealed over Jerusalem"); *ibid.* 31:4b (MT ". . . the Lord of hosts will come down to fight upon Mount Zion" = TJ ". . . the kingdom of the Lord shall be revealed to rest upon Mount Zion"). While MT undoubtedly refers to the divine assistance against the Assyrians, probably during Sennacherib's campaign in 701 B.C.E., TJ, unwilling to reproduce the anthropomorphic expressions of the Hebrew text, employs a terminology clearly suggesting the future divine kingdom predicted in Daniel 2:44. Cf. also Zech. 14:4a (MT "On that day his feet shall stand on the Mount of Olives" = TJ "And he shall be revealed in his might at that time upon the Mount of Olives".)

617. On the concept of resurrection in Judaism, cf. *The Jewish Encyclopedia*, Vol. X, s.v. Resurrection, pp. 382-385; *Encyclopaedia Judaica*, Vol. 14, s.v. Resurrection, cols. 96-103 and bibliography *ad loc.*

618. Cf. Is. 42:12b (MT "Let the inhabitants of Sela (סלע) sing for joy" = TJ "Let the dead give praise when they shall come forth [or: "The dead shall give praise when they come forth from their graves"]). This rendering was probably influenced by the fact that the dead were often buried in tombs cut out of the rock (Heb. סלע).

619. Cf. Zech. 14:4a, where a Midrashic version in TJ adds, "At that time the Lord shall take a (or: the) large trumpet (or: Shofar) in his hand and he shall blow ten sounds of alarm with it, in order to revive the dead."

YALE ORIENTAL SERIES

RESEARCHES

VOLUME XIV

TARGUM JONATHAN
TO THE PROPHETS

BY
PINKHOS CHURGIN

TO MY HONORED TEACHER
PROFESSOR CHARLES CUTLER TORREY
AS A TOKEN OF DEVOTION AND RESPECT
THIS BOOK IS CONSECRATED

CONTENTS

7

THE HISTORICAL BACKGROUND OF
TARGUM JONATHAN

The Aramaic rendering of the Prophets belongs to the earliest translations of the Bible which have come down to us. Its importance for the textual investigation and early Biblical interpretation cannot be overestimated. While the targumist makes little display of critical study in rendering intricate passages, and while he does not pretend to present a minutely literal translation of the Hebrew text, his reverence for the letter and transmitted reading of the text must be far have exceeded that of the Greek and Syriac translators. At the same time his translation is doubtlessly based on a sounder and exacter understanding of both the etymology and usages of the Hebrew language. Again, its value may be said to rest in the fact that, forming a distinct and independent rendering of the text, it presents a helpful source in establishing the principles pursued in the early translations. A good many emendations and assumed violations of the Hebrew text on the sole basis of the translations, so eagerly sought by the modern Biblical scholar, would thus be completely done away with. It is also a mine of Agadic exegesis, to which, in most instances, parallels are preserved in the extant sources. It cannot fail to be of considerable importance for the history of that vast literature, giving in this connection new and vivid emphasis to the religious, national and political state of mind of that age in Palestine.

The authorship of the Targum to the Prophets has been the object of protracted and diverse discussion. Tradition ascribes it to Jonathan b. Uziel, the most prominent disciple of Hillel, of the first century. This single mention in the Talmud of the authorship of Jonathan and the mystic manner in which it is related, can hardly help solve the problem. There is, furthermore, the astounding fact that in the parallel passage in the

9

Yerushalmi [1] there is complete silence of this tradition of the Babli.[2] Had this tradition been common, there could have been no possible reason for the Yerushalmi to ignore the work of the distinguished and holy Jonathan, who "when he discussed the law, a bird flying near him would be burned".[3]

The Talmudic tradition mentions Aquila's translation. Both Talmudim have set monuments to the Seventy. Is it because the Targum was originated on Palestinian soil, extensively used and known in Palestine, forming even a necessary part in the worship, that they failed to be impressed by it?

So the inference was drawn that the Aramaic version of the Bible fell in disfavor with the authorities in Palestine who, however, were distinctly pleased with the Greek translation, particularly the Greek version of Aquila.[4] The alleged reasons for

1)   Y. Megilla 1, 9.

2)   Babli Meg. 3b. Blau's contention (J. Q. R., v. 9, p. 738) has no foundation. Cases of disagreement in assigning the author of a saying are numerous. It needs no explanation and consequently cannot be made a basis for a new theory.

3)   Suk. 28a; Baba Bathra 134a; Y. Nedarim 5, 6.

4)   Berliner (Onkelos 108-110) has even the idea of a complete suppression of the official Targumim in Palestine. Weiss (Dor Dor etc., v. 1, 200) even knows exactly the time when this suppression took place and its author. It was Rabban Gamliel, of whom it is said (Shab. 115a; Tosef. 13 (14) and with some changes in Sof. 5, 15; Y. Shab. 16, 1) that he hid the Targum to Job. So then it was he who put the ban also on the official Targumim. And it was not until the time of R. Akiba that the ban was lifted. This conjecture is read by Weiss into the phrase מי גלה סתרי רבני אדם. It is evident that the whole supposition hinges on the mere finding that Rabban Gamliel forbade the use of a certain particular Targum. That the express mention of the Targum should be taken to indicate that the other Targumim were spared this interdiction seems to have escaped their observation. Furthermore, their theory is exposed to a dangerous contradiction. If the Targum was restored in the time of R. Akiba, what sense could there have been to the contention of R. Chalafta with Gamliel the younger, a contemporary of R. Akiba, with regard to his license with the Targum, and his reminder of R. Gamliel the Elder? They should not have overlooked the remarkable coincidence presented in the story of Gamliel the Elder and his grandchild. In both instances it was the Targum to Job that evoked disfavor.

such a departure will hardly stand their ground. But aside from other considerations, this assertion is flatly contradicted by the very fact that the Aramaic version was not ignored by the Palestinian authorities. Both Onkelos and Jonathan are quoted in the Yerushalmi and Midrashim,[5] while, on the contrary, the genuineness of the quotations from Aquila is doubtful.[6]

It was, then, clearly this Targum which was hit by Rabban Gamliel the Elder, and which was still regarded as forbidden.

There is little to be said of Finn's conjecture (v. 1, 56, דברי הימים) that the suppression of the Targum to the Pent. was due to the intro'duction of the Samaritan Targum with its dangerous divergencies from the Hebrew text. This he attempts to discover in the obscure saying of Mar Zutra (San. 21b).

It needs only to be mentioned that there is not the faintest hint in the Talmud of a suspension of the Targum-reading in the worship, as he would have us believe. Rosenthal (Beth Ha-Midrash 2, 276) takes the view that the reverence in which Aquila's translation was held in Pales' tine was due to the fact that Greek was spoken more than Aramaic in Palestine. It is pure imagination.

5) The reader is referred to Zunz G. V., p. 67, Notes b, c. It should be remarked that the list of citations given by Zunz represents by no means an exhaustive research. It is not my present task to cite the numerous cases which, for some reason or other, he does not cite. Suffice it to state that citations from Onkelos alone in Genesis r. exceed considerably the number of citations from Aquila taken together. Com. Lerner, An. u. Quellen d. Breishit Raba 63-65. His view that the respective citations may not represent actual quotations from the Targum, is open to question. One would be at a loss to explain the identity of these citations with the rendering in the Targum. For one of the mind of Geiger, who makes the general assertion that citations from the Targumim are not to be found except in the latter Midrashim, it will be of interest the following remark in נבחר מפנינים to Gen. r. 45,7: ודרך המדרש להביא בכמה מקומות את התרגום בפרט בשם מקום מטעם ששם התרגום ההוא היה מפורסם ונודע בעולם יותר. This is just as true of other cases.

6) Com. Field Hex. XVII. Of all the 12 respective citations, one,, on Is. 5, 6 (Eccl. r. 11, 7) belongs to Jonathan, and yet carries the name of Aquila. Luria l. c. would emend Jonathan but admits Jonathan is never mentioned in the Midrash. Einhorn (ad loc.) would have here Aquila agree with Jonathan, so Herzfeld (Geschichte II, 63). Equally, Weiss' assertion (Dor, v. 2, 123) that this implies Aquila must have made use of Jonathan needs no refutation. Another Aramaic quotation referring to Prov. 25, 11 (Gen. r. 93, 3) is partly taken from the Targum to Prov.

Yet they are not traced to their respective translators. Such is also the case in Babli, where this tradition of Jonathan's authorship is told. In all the many quotations from Targum Jonathan there is no single reference to Jonathan. These facts combine to show that both in Babylonia and Palestine this tradition was otherwise understood, and not until a comparatively late period did it succeed in gaining currency.

Aquila's authority, then, in these cases is a mistake. One other case, namely that referring to Lev. 19, 20 (Y. Kid. 1, 1 end) deals with a Halakic exposition. In the first place, it implies in no way a translatory interpretation. Further, the authority of Aquila given in the name of Jochanan is contested by Chiya who refers it to R. Laser, changing only the reference for evidence. On the other hand, in the Babli (Krithoth 11b) no authority is cited for the same interpretation. If the authority of Aquila was correctly quoted, then תרגם should be interpreted in its general sense as תרגמא is used in the Babli. His translation was not meant, and all assumptions by De Rossi (Meor Einaim, Ch. 45) and Krauss (Steinschneider Fest. 153) in this case deserve little consideration. The case of Dan. 8, 13, where Aquila is cited (Gen. r. 21, 1: Jalqut Dan. l. c.) in Hebrew, is instructive. There can be no question that the words תרגום אנקלס are an interpolation. It is Rab Huna's interpretation played on a particular form of the word and the contracted פלוני ; it should read: רב הונא פנייה, לפנימי זה, אדה"ר . It admits of no other explanation.

It is not necessary to enlarge upon these four non-Greek citations. It is scarcely necessary to state that none of these citations is to be found in the Hexapla. But of no more valid authenticity are the remaining eight Greek citations. The citation of Lev. 23, 40 (Y. Sukka 3, 5 Gem.) is a misquotation. As Field and others remarked, such a rendering is fundamentally foreign to Aquila. Besides, in Babli (Sukka 35a) this is recorded as said by Ben Azai, and deducted by the אל תקרי method. In Yerushalmi, again, R. Tanchuma is citing Aquila אמר ר' תנחומא תרג' אנקלום תרגם אקן הדר הידיר . This is striking. Aquila is always cited plainly. In the Midrash, however (Lev. r. 30, 8: Jalqut l. c.), the name of R. Tanchuma is omitted. At the same time Ben Azai is cited in the Midrash as the authority of the saying הדר זה הדר באילנו משנה לשנה while in Babli l. c. R. Abbahu is mentioned as the author, and in Yerushalmi (l. c.) R. Levi is the one who said it. It appears that Ben Azai's authority was particularly intended for the last part of the saying, namely the citation from Aquila, as if Ben Azai were citing Aquila. A reconciliation of the Babli and Yerushalmi on this point would appear to have been in the view of the compiler. That might have been the case in the Yerushalmi. According to one report, R. Tanchuma was the author of this exegetic note, just as Ben Azai is

Furthermore, Targum Jonathan is quoted in Babli, in many instances, in the name of Rab Joseph, the president of the Pumbeditha Academy, who flourished in the fourth century. Even as late as the author of a commentary on Taharoth, for a long time ascribed to Hai Gaon (flourished in the 11th Century), quotations from Targum Jonathan are given in the name of Rab Joseph, which led Zekaria Frankel, Schürer, Buhl, Winter u. Wünsche, Graetz and many others to take Rab Joseph as the

---

named as its author in the Babli; according to the other, it was Aquila's (interpretation, not translation). And both reports were united in the form it reads in the Yerushalmi. Either B. A. or R. T. made use of the semblance of the respective Hebrew word to the Greek word, a method pursued extensively by the Agadists (Com. Shab. 63b; Gen. r. 99, 7; com. Shorr החלוץ 12, 6.). It is not Aquila's translation which is quoted. Zipper's Theory (Krauss l. c.) as well as Rappaport's fine sug-gestion (ערך מלין, אתרג) employed by Krauss (l. c. 153) in this case, are superfluous. Of a similar nature is the interpretation attributed to Aquila in Lev. r. 33, 6 on Ez. 23:43. This curious explanation could hardly have found a place in the literal translation of Aquila. It does not belong to Aquila.

With reference to the allegorical interpretation of Prov. 18:21, attributed in Lev. r. 33, 1 to Aquila, it was justly characterized by Field (l. c.) along with Lev. 23:40 as "Omnino absurdae et ridiculae sunt". Com. Tanchuma Lev. מצורע 4, where practically the same idea is expressed without resorting to this Greek expression.

Questionable is the quotation from Aquila on Ps. 48, 21, cited in Y. Meg. 2, 4; Y. M. K. 3, 7. In the first place, Aquila renders על עלמות Ps. 46, 1 by ἐπίνεανιοτήτων . So a l s o i n 9:1 νεϊότητος . It stands to reason that 48, 21 was similarly rendered by him and not by the alleged ἀθανασία . This would agree with the T. rendering ביומי מליוותנא which is also indicated in the Y. (l. c.), namely בעלימות . It should also be noticed in passing that one other interpretation given there הוא ינהגנו בעולם הזה agrees with the Lxx, which renders it εἰς τοὺς εἰῶνας , which is also i m p l i e d in Cant. r. 1, 22. The Syriac Hex., as well as Jerome (Field XXVI), would lend support to such a rendering by Aquila. The rendering ἀθανασία cited in Field (l. c.) under column Ed. Prima, ought not to be take in serious consideration for obvious reasons. To all intents, this rendering of עלמות is so Midrashic that it would not find its way even into a less rigorous translation than Aq.

The quotation in Y. Shab. 6, 4 from Aq. on Is. 3:20 is not found in the Hex. The case of Ez. 16, 10 (Lam. r. 1, 1), containing a double rendering, may even be a quotation from Jon. The Lxx might as well

real author of the T. Jonathan.[7] But Rashi and Tosaphoth are
unqualifiedly right in their common explanation of this curious
occurrence.[8] It should be borne in mind that Rab Joseph himself often cites the Targum Jonathan with the introductory phrase
אלמלא תרגומא דהאי קרא, which clearly signifies he had the Targum before him.[9] Furthermore, Rab Joseph also cites Onkelos.[10] On the other hand, we have a citation from the Targum
to Esth. 3, 1, ascribed to Rab Joseph, where it is clear from the
Greek names it contains that we have a Palestinian Targum
before us.[11] Again, some of Rab Joseph's interpretations fail to
coincide with those in the Targum Jonathan.[12] In addition,

---

be meant, which here, as also in Ex. 27:16, agrees with Aq. as recorded
in the Hex., and also disagrees, just as Aq., with its version in the
Midrash. Similarly, the citation from Aq. on Gen. 17:1 in Gen. r. 46, 2;
in this case also there is no telling which Greek translation was meant,
for the Lxx contains also such a rendering (com. Field Hex., l. c.). The
ascription, again, to Aq. of citations from other sources was demonstrated
above. This might have been the case with the quotations from Aq. on
Dan. 5, 5 (Y. Joma 3, 8 Gem.) and Esth. r. 6. In the former, Aq.
is preserved in the Lxx only.

7) Keilim 29, 30 on Judges 3:16; IS. 3:23, 13:21; Ez. 17:7;
Oholoth 18 on Is. 49:22. It is interesting that the Aruch (גלד 2, גמד 2)
cites the Targum from Hai, refraining from mentioning the source, by
the same direct reference to R. Joseph ומתרגם רב יוסף.

Com. Schürer, Geschichte, VI, 149 (4th German ed); Z.
Frankel, Zu d. T., 10-12; Buhl, Kanon, 173; Winter u. Wünsche, Jüd.
Lit. 1, 65.

Winter u. Wünsche, ib., would interpret the tradition as pointing
to the authorship of Jonathan of the fragmentary Targum to the
Prophets in Codex Reuch. Com. also Weiss, Dor, 1, 200; 2, 123.

8) Rashi, Kidushin 13a; Tos. Baba Kama 3a כדמתרגם.

9) San. 94b; Moed Katan 28b; Meg. 3a.

10) Shab. 28a; Exod. 25:5, 64; Num. 31, 50; Nazir 39a; Num.
6:9; Sota 48b: Deut. 1:49, the latter ascribed to Rab Shesheth in
another recension.

11) As to the existence of a Targum to Esther at a comparatively early date, com. Megilla 17a, Mishna and Gemara 18a; Y. Meg.
2, 1. As to the assumption of Rab Joseph being the author of the
Targum to Hagiog., com. Tosafoth Shab. 115a ובידו and Megilla 21b
ובמגילה pointing out that the Targum to Hag. dates back to the
Tanaitic age, while Rashi Megilla (l. c.) asserts עשרה שאין תרגום
בכתובים.

12) Here are some illustrations: Aboda Zara 4a, R. Joseph's in-

in the instance of the Targumic citation on Is. 33:21 put in the mouth of R. Joseph in Jomma 77b, it is given in the name of Rab in Rosh Hashana 23a, and on no authority in Shek. 6, 2, Gem. It may be further stated that in some instances the authority of R. Joseph is omitted; these are introduced by the impersonal דמתרגמינן Again, it should be noticed that Onkelos to Genesis 49:27 and Gen. 30:14 is said in the name of Rab and Levi (Zebachim 54a) רב מתרגם, לוי מתרגם and San. 99b on Gen. 30:14 without מתרג׳ , and still this would not constitute sufficient evidence to place the name of Rab on Targum Onkelos. The evidence in question presses in the direction of an entirely different conclusion, and that is, that so general was the ignorance of the authorship of the official Targumim that quotations from them were permitted or had to be recalled on the authority of the one citing them.

There is no need to dwell at length on the fanciful hypothesis first formulated by Drusius and later set forth in his peculiar way by Geiger and supported by Karpeles, connecting Jonathan with Theodotion.[13] According to this theory, the Targum Jonathan is founded on the Greek translation of Theodotion, while Targum Onkelos is based on Aquila.[14] But the Theodotion version, which is rather a revised version of the Lxx than an independent rendering, and whose Pharasaic origin is open to question, and whose author shows a scant knowledge of Hebrew, could hardly become the groundwork for the Rabbinic Targum Jonathan. There is not the remotest agreement between them, either as to the principles employed or as to the rendering, except in the names of the translators, and only a

---

terpretation of Ez. 9:6; Shab. 26a on Jerem. 52:16; Shab. 54b; Kethuboth 6b on IS. 17:8, which involves an Halakic exposition cited also in Shab. 56a. This is contained in the Toseftoic addition on the margin of Codex Reuch. That Rab Joseph, however, was also an independent interpreter appears from his interpretation of Gen. 10, 2 (Joma 10a), in which he disagrees with the extant Targumim, while Ps. Jonathan agrees with R. Simoi (R. Simon in Gen. r. 37, 1).

13) Geiger, Ursch. 163; Carpeles, History (Heb.) 159.

14) Com. Rapaport זכרון לאחרונים 3; Luzzatto אגרות 214; Adler נתינה לגו׳ Introduction.

highly powerful imagination would be taken by its suggestiveness.

With the collapse of these theories; with the tradition in
complete silence over the name of the author of the official Targum to the Prophets, and in utter lack of other evidence leading
to the establishment of a tenable hypothesis, there is no use in
further attempts to solve the riddle. There was no single author
to impress tradition, and in so far as the name of the author is
concerned, the discussion should be considered as concluded.
But there is another question closely allied with this problem,
which calls for consideration. Many writers on this subject
speak of a revised redaction of the official Targumim. Some
assert that the revision was stimulated by a missionary desire
to supply the Gentile world, speaking an Aramaic dialect, with
a correct rendering of the Torah, as Luzzato, supported by Rappaport, would put it.[15] Others would look for its cause in the
careless handling by the early Aramaic translators of the Hebrew
text.[16] Berliner and Geiger adhere to the theory that the
revision was brought about by the necessity of furnishing the
congregations in the Diaspora, particularly in Babylonia, with a
unified and carefully redacted Aramaic version of the Bible.[17]

It should be first borne in mind that these theories
start from the viewpoint that these Targumim were, so
to speak, rejected in Palestine and consequently found elevation to general reverence in Bablyonia. This theory of Palestinian
disregard for the Targum is already shown to be erroneous.
On the whole, however, this theory will, on full examination,
prove to be perplexing. The question arises, how is it, that the
redactors permitted renderings to remain in the Targum which
unmistakably signify a different reading from the Masoretic
text? [18]

---

15) Luzzatto, Oheb, VIII; Rapaport l. c.

16) Meor Enaim, Ch. 45.

17) Ur. 164, Nach. Schriften 4, 103; Berliner, On. 108-110.
Com. Rapoport אגרות שד"ל p. 214. Weiss, Dor 11, 123; Deutsch in
Smith's Dictionary of the Bible 3411. Com. also Jost, Geschichte d.
Jud., v. 2, 54, Note 1.

18) Com. chapter on textual variations, group A. As to Onk.,

It is further assumed that the revision was made necessary in order to make the Targumic interpretations conform to current Halakic exposition. If this were the case, we should expect to find the Targum in complete harmony with current Halaka. But this is far from being the case. Onkelos presents a long list of cases where it differs from the formally accepted Halakic interpretations and decisions. So are the renderings of Exod. 21, 24 and Lev. 24, 19, 20 against the accepted Halaka, "transmitted from Moses and so seen at the court of every genera- tion from Joshua and on" (Maimonides 1, 6 הלכות חובל ומזיק) that a monetary and not a corporal retaliation is meant (Baba Kama 83b, 84a); Lev. 19:32 disregarding Baraitha Kidushin 32; Deut. 23:18 against Halaka. Sifri 1. c.; San. 54b; Abodah Zara 36b. (com. Maimonides יד החזקה איסורי ביאה ב, הל"א, and Magid Mishna 1. c.). In all of which the Targum undoubtedly has preserved an afterwards superseded Halaka.[19]

The same may be said, in a certain measure, of the Agada. Many are the cases both in Jonathan and Onkelos where the popular interpretations are ignored but which could hardly be ignored by a later redaction.[20] Pseudo-Jonathan and the Frag-

com. Rosenthal in Weiss' Beth Talmud, 2, 284. The adduced evidence, however, tends rather to contradict his hypothesis of a late single com- position of T. Jonathan. Com. also כרם חמד 1, 220.

19) It is instructive to notice the rendering of the respective cases in Ps. Jonathan, which conform with the Halaka. This betrays the hand of a later day editor. The Ps. Jonathan, as is generally known, con- tains some Halakic interpretations conflicting with the current Halaka, which led some writers, among them Geiger, to regard it as a mine of early, Sadducean Halaka. Com. Revel, Karaite Halaka, p. 18.

20) Some examples: Is. 17:8; Kethuboth 9b; Ezek. 1:14; Hagiga 13b; com. also the singular rendering of vv. 5, 6. Com. Hag. 1. c.; Kid 72a, referring to 2K 18:11. Both official Targumim abound with such cases.

Yawetz (תולדות ישראל v. 9, 254-264) is the author of a novel theory, namely, that Rab Joseph was the redactor of both Onkelos and Jonathan, as it is evident from the Targumic citations in the Talmud which are quoted in his name. These Targumim have originated from the Greek translation of Aquila, which was translated into Aramaic.

mentary Targum may serve as instructive illustrations. Finally, there are many inconsistencies in reference to certain prin- ciples followed in the Targum (com. groups B and C in the chap- ter on textual deviations), which would not have occurred had it proceeded from the hand of a single redactor. Nothing, again, can account for the silence in the Talmudic sources over an act of such magnitude and importance. The tradition of the Babli of the official Targumim can hardly be taken in any degree to contain the historical kernel of a single authorship. It might be assumed, on the other hand, that it does not, in sub- stance, imply that Jonathan was the author of the extant Targum or of one lost, but points to the fact that this great Rabbi was preeminently skillful in the interpretation of the Prophets. Tar- gum would then be used in this case in its acquired and more general sense. Targum as a quality is counted among the merits of the fellow student of Jonathan, Rabban Jochanan b. Zakkai.[21]

What has been said of Jonathan is true of Onkelos. There could not have been a revised redaction of the magnitude the sponsors of this theory maintained. The corruptionist hypothesis rests on the doubtful foundation that the unofficial Targumim, as Pseudo-Jonathan, to which unfavorable references are sup- posedly made in the Talmud, preceded the official Targum. But just the reverse may be true, namely, that these extra-Targumim were built upon the official Targum. Suffice it to say that the existence of "Our" Targum, stated by Tanaitic authorities, im- plies the fact that the other Targumim existed along with the official Targum.

Rab Joseph edited and put them in final shape. Hence the name of Aquila (Onk.) on the Targum of the Pentateuch and also of the Prophets (namely, the citation in Eccl. r. 11, 3 from Jonathan Is. 5:6, which was considered above) and of Rab Joseph on the Targum of the Prophets and also of the Pent. (the citation in Sota 48b). It is the queerest of theories propounded on the question of the author- ship of the Targumim. Ingenuity must fail when one identifies the literal Aquila with the interpretative Jonathan.

21)   Soferim 16, 8: אמרו עליו על רבן יוחנן בן זכאי שלא הניח פרשה ואגדות הלכות מדרש ותרגום במקרא למדו שלא מהתורה אחת , which is omit- ted in the modified version of this saying in Sukka 28a and Baba Bathra 134a; so also in אגרת דרב שרירא . Com. also Sifri Deut. 179: למען ילמד ליראה, מלמד שהמורא מביא לידי מקרא, מקרא מביא לידי תרגום תרגום מביא לידי משנה.

But this does not imply that no change was introduced in the existing official Targumim. Certain traces in the Targum carry unmistakable evidence of a Babylonian recast, which was, however, of a very limited scope.

This will be discussed later. The substance was left untouched. Consequently, we may rest assured there was no unified authorship even to the extent of a thoroughgoing redaction. But before advancing other views with regard to the authorship, we might well direct our attention to evidence preserved in the Targum.

It should be noticed at the outset that tradition assigns an early origin to the official Targumim. The same tradition which vaguely ascribed the Targum to late authorities is sponsor of the statement that they originated far back of the age of these authorities. Of Jonathan the tradition makes clear that he "said" the Targum from the mouths of the Prophets Haggai, Zachariah and Malachi. With regard to Onkelos the tradition explains that Onkelos only restored the Targum, which originated with Ezra. The latter was inferred, in the name of Rab, from the interpretation of Nehemiah 8:8, according to which מפורש carries the meaning of תרגום (R. Judan, Nedarim 37a; Gen. r. 36, end). Making all allowance, the Targum Jonathan contains evidence pointing to a comparatively early date. Evidence of a general character consists, first, of the textual deviations which abound in Jonathan as well as in Onkelos. [22] The same may be said with reference to the unacceptable Halaka, found in Onkelos. This fact points to a date when these matters were still in the balance. Why, however, they were permitted at a later age to remain in the Targum can easily be explained. There was first of all the tradition referring the Targumim to the last Prophets and Ezra, which cast a halo over them, and none would venture either to question the propriety of the ren-

---

22) Rosenfeld's long list of supposed deviations from the M. T. in Talmud (Mishpachoth Soferim, Vilna, 1883) will be found on closer examination to present no contradiction to this statement. With minor exceptions, nearly all the adduced cases are of a Midrashic nature and should be regarded as such.

dering or attempt to emend them, just because they appeared amazingly striking.

There was no cause for general alarm. The Targum was read verse for verse with the Hebrew Text, which would bring home to the reflection of the hearer the established reading.[23] Still, precaution was sought to exclude a possible impression that the Targum represents the right reading. I am persuaded to interpret the causes for the limitations placed upon the reading of the Targum in the light of this supposition.[24]

The elimination of anthropomorphisms, so persistently carried through in the official Targumim, goes back to an early period. It is a tendency which has its roots in the movement that gave rise to the 18 Tikune Soferim (Mek. Ex. 15, 7) and to the substitution of descriptive appelations (Adonai, Heaven, etc.) for the name of God.[25] In the later part of the Amoraic age a reaction set in against this tendency, which did not reappear until the Arabic Era. This principle would not have been so singularly stressed in the 4th century in Babylonia, not to speak of the 7th century. Numerous anthropomorphic substitutes were eliminated in the official Targumim by the latter redactors, to whom, it would seem, the anthropomorphic expression was no longer terrifying and repugnant.

It will be of some interest in this connection to note the relaxing of this principle in the Targum to Hagiog., which is certainly later than the Targumim to the Pent. and Prophets. This targumist does not hesitate to render literally such expressions as God laughs (Ps. 2:4; 37:13), God sees (Ps. 33:13; 35:17, 22 etc), God's eyes and eyelids (Ps. 11:4; 33:18), God's hands

---

23)   Com. Meg. 23b; Tos. Meg. 3; Rosh Hashana 27a.

24)   Com. Sota 39b and Y. Meg. 4, 1 Gem. The alleged reason שלא יאמרו תרגום כתוב בתורה becomes more sensible if interpreted to mean that the public should not suppose the Targum version to correspond to the established reading.

25)   It was this tendency which influenced both the Aramaic and the Lxx versions. Com. Z. Frankel, Vorstudien, p. 175; Einfluss, pp. 30, 82, 130; Palaest u. Alex. Shrift., 21 et seq.; Zeller, Philosophie d. Griechen, v. 3, 11; 3, 253.

(Ps. 119:73).²⁶⁾ This reavels the notions of a later generation, which would undoubtedly have come to the surface in the official Targumim, had they been its production.

The term מימרא , employed in the Targumim to cover anthropomorphic expressions, strikes me also as of early origin. It should be noticed at the outset, what a good many have missed to observe, that there is nothing in it to imply Greek influence. It represents no identity. It disavows the slightest implication of an agency. It is merely a term of speech adopted to disguise anthropomorphic presentations, for the awe-inspiring exaltation of God, hiding the face, like Moses, for fear "to look up to God". It was intended not so much to interpret or explain as to remind and evoke a higher reaction. It is fully employed in the same sense as דבר or מאמר is used in the Bible, in which image מימרא was certainly cast.²⁷⁾ In a later age, under the influence, it would seem, of the Greek Logos, this term acquired the meaning of a definite essence, an embodied heavenly power approaching an intermediary agency.²⁸⁾ The דבור calls to Moses;²⁹⁾ it visits, surrounds and kisses.³⁰⁾ In the Book of Wisdom, probably of Palestinian origin, the all-powerful word of God leaps down from heaven, "a stern warrior into the midst

---

26) L. Ginsburg in the Jewish En. Anthropo. seemingly failed to take notice of this distinction when he made the unqualified statement that the earlier Targumim retained in translation such expressions as the hand, finger, eye etc. of God. This is true of the Targum to the Hagiog. only. In Jonathan an evasive substitute is always employed in such cases. As to the hand of God, com. Joshua 22:31; 1S 5:7; 1K 18:46; Is. 5:25, 9:11, 11:11, 19:31; 3; Jer. 1:9 etc. As to finger, com. Exod. 8:15 with the exceptions of Exod. 31:18 and its parallel in Deut. 9:10, in which case, it seems, the substitute was eliminated, as in the creation story, in order to avoid an explanation that the tablets were given by some inferior power, or to escape the danger of allegorizing the fact of the tablets. Com. further Exod. 33:12, 13; 1 Kings 8:29; Is. 1:15; 43:4; Jer. 7:30.

27) In Ps. 33:6, 9; 107:20; 147:15, 18; 148:8 דבר is a descriptive term for the action of God, while in 119:89 it is descriptive of the Torah.

28) Com. Gen. r. 4, 2.

29) Lev. r. 1, 4.

30) Cant. r. 1:13.

of a doomed land".[31]   The term מימרא , then, could not have
originated in a period when it might be taken to signify a distinct
God-like power. In its use in translation it would have the effect
of investing the מימרא with all activity, God being inactive—
and nothing could be more horrible to the non-Hellenistic Jew
than a transcendentalism of the Alexandrian mould. As was
noticed before, the later Bablyonian redactors have limited in
the Targum the use of the מימרא . It is remarkable that in the
creation story all anthropomorphic expressions are, contrary to
principle, literally rendered. In most of the parallel cases in
Ps. Jonathan מימרא is inserted. The reason for that might be
found in the new significance which this term had assumed, so
that the application of this term in the creation story would
carry the implication that some other power, separate from
God, was the author of the act of the creation.[32]

The Targum to the Prophets is not wanting in more specific
evidence, although this sort of evidence is admittedly scant. This
T. is far from being Midrashic. It is primarily a translation,
and the chief concern of the translator is to find the right meaning and the interpretation of the word and phrase; it is not
seeking to explain the exigencies of the age, or to propound
the mysteries of the generations. It does, however, in a few
cases make use of allegory. In the allegorical interpretation unmistakable allusions were preserved to events which can be
placed. The events extend over many periods, which furnish
us the clue to the historical origination of the Targum.

Direct historical reference is made in the Targum to
Hab. 3:17:   ...כי תאנה לא תפרח ואין יבול בגפנים, כחש מעשה זית
The Targum interprets this to refer to the four Kingdoms ארבע
מלכיות [33] But referring to Rome, the version reads ישתיצון רומאי

_____

31) Wisdom 18:15. Com. also 16:12; 4 Esd. 6:38.

32) Com. On. Gen. 3:9, 22; 5:2; 6:3. In all these cases Ps.
Jonathan has מימרא inserted. In Gen. 8:1 there is a complete agreement
in the translation between On. and Ps. Jonathan, except that the latter has
מימרא . No explanation can plausibly account for that, except the
supposition that a later redactor, out of fear for a possible misleading inference, and who would not feel irritated over an anthropomorphic
expression, eliminated מימרא in the respective cases.

33) The reading of the extant editions וגברי עובדי כוכבים ומזלות

ולא יגבון קיסומא מירושלם. This emphasis on the tribute by the targumist is remarkable. None of the barbarities committed by the Romans inflamed his rage as did the tribute. This reference then, must have been coined at a time when the chief agitation of the people gathered around the problem of the tribute. The targumist meant the census instituted by the second Procurator Quirinius (6-7 C. E.), which aroused rebellion, being regarded by the people as bondage. Had the destruction of the Temple taken place at the time of this reference to Rome, this act would have certainly been recorded instead of the census.[34]

IS. 28:1: הוי עטרת גאות שכורי אפרים... translating allegorically: וי די יהיב כתרא לגיותנא טפשא רבה דישראל ויהיב מצנפתא לרשיעיא דבית מקדש תושבחתיה. In the same way also vv. 3, 4. Allusions are here made to the deplorable state of the High Priesthood. The reference may go to the Sadducean Hasmonean rulers, particularly to Alexander Jannaeus, who incurred the deadliest hatred of the people. This hatred of the "sinners who rose against us"; who "laid waste the throne of David in tumultous arrogance" (Ps. of Sol. 17, 4-8); who "utterly polluted the holy things of the Lord (1, 8) and had profaned with iniquities the offerings of God" (2, 3).[35] Reference to John Hyrcanus is made in Ps. Jonathan to Deut. 33:11, according to Geiger (Ur. 479), which, however, may also be equally applicable to the father of Mattathias, John, whom later authorities, mistakenly, took for a High Priest. The failure, however, of the targumist to allude to the Kingship of the sinful High Priest, speaks against this supposition. It is a safer supposition that the Herodian High Priests or the state of the High Priesthood under the Roman Procurators, when this most sacred dignity became a salable article, is here

is a later emendation, probably to escape the rigors of the censor. It should read with Lagarde, גברי יון.

34) Com. Ant. XVII, 21. As to the date of the Census, com. Schürer, Geschichte, 4th German ed. VI, erste Anhang. Com. also Hausrath N. T. Times (Eng. ed.) v. 2, pp. 74-83. It was this state of mind from which emanated the curious rendering of והמכשלה (Is. 3:6) ומגביתא, taxation, against the Agadic interpretation to mean the Law (Chag. 14b; Gittin 43b). Com also Is. 55:5.

35) Com. also 8:10, 13, 26. Com. Buchanan, Charles, Apocrypha, II, 628.

meant.[36] I am persuaded to believe that the targumist had in mind particularly the appointment by Herod of Annanel to the High Priesthood, which by right and general expectation was to belong to Aristobul III.[37]

IS. 64:11: העל אלה תתאפק is so rendered as to give vent to the general excitement of the time. It runs: העל אלין תתחסן ואת יהיב ארכא לרשיעיא דמשעבדין בנא עד עלמא ; likewise Hab. 3:1. The wicked are the rulers over the people. They are not the Gentiles, Romans, whom the T. would call either by name or by the general appelation עממיא, גוים ; רשיעיא is applied to the wicked of Israel only. I am inclined to think the allusion is made to the Herodian rulers rather than to the later Hasmonean rulers. The expression ואת יהיב ארכא could hardly have been intended for Alexander Jannaeus, whose rule was not too long, being then followed by the just rule of Alexandra. The targumist would, at the same time, place the beginning of the Herodian rule in the early days of the Antipater's political ascendency. There are other references to the Herodian rulers.

Hos. 4:13 על כן תזנינה בנותיכם is rendered על כן מזנין בנתכון דהואה לכון מבנת עממיא וכלתכון דנסבתון לבניכון מן עממיא גיפן .

---

36) Com. Ant. XX, 8, 8; Pesachim 57a; Tos. Menachoth end. אוי לי מבית ביתוס, אוי לי מאלתם. אוי לי מבית חנין, אוי לי מלחישתם, אוי לי מבית פתרוס. אוי לי מקולמוסם ; אוי לי מבית ישמעאל בן פאדי. אוי לי מאגרופם שהם כהנים גדולים ובניהם אמרכלים ועבדיהם חובטים את העם במקלות. Also Lev. r. 21, 5; Y Yoma 1, 1: ... אלא מקדש ראשון שעל ידי ששמשו באמונה שמשו בו י"ח כהנים, מקדש שני על שהיו נוטלין אותה בממון וי"א שהיו הורגין זה את זה בכשפים שמשו פ' כהנים. ומהן שמעון הצדיק מ' שנה. כיון שחזרו להיות משכירין אותו בדמים היו שנותיהן מתקצרות. מעשה באחד ששלח ביד בנו שתי מדות של כסף... ועמד אחד ושלח ביד בנו שתי מדות של זהב... אמרו כפה סיח את המנורה. Com. Yoma 9a.

37) Ant. XV, 2, 4. This reference might also be applicable to the High Priest Simon the son of Boethus, whose daughter Herod loved and married, and, in order to augment the dignity of the family, conferred upon him this high honor (Ant. XV, 9, 3). Although a priest of note, his elevation to office in this manner and the overthrow of Jesus the son of Phabet, his predecessor, brought upon him the indignation of the people and the hatred they entertained for the Herodian dynasty.

This is certainly an early T.; v. 14 is interpreted literally. Had it been the intention of the T. to soften some harsh expression flung against the morality of the Jewish daughters, it would have been followed in the other v. But the former deals a rebuke to the Herodians, who have intermarried with Gentile rulers. Herod married a Samaritan woman (Ant. 12, 2, 19); his son Alexander—Glaphira, daughter of Archelaus, King of Cappadocia (Ant. 16, 1, 2); Drusilla, the sister of Agrippa II, was prevailed upon to transgress the laws of her forebears and to marry Felix, the procurator (Ant. 20, 7, 2), while her former husband, the heathen King of Emesa and the second husband of her sister Berenice, the King of Cilicia, though circumcised, would hardly be regarded as a proselyte. The latter renounced his conversion as soon as Berenice left him (Ant. ib.). The cohabitation of Berenice with Titus (Dio Cassius 66, 15) is a further instance. It was the general reaction towards this open violation of the Law which the Rabbi would express in the only safe way through the exposition of some Prophetic utterance.

Of a more pronounced nature is the reference contained in the T. to Is. 65:4 היושבים בקברים ובנצורים ילינו — דיתבן בבתיא דבנן מעפר קבריא ועם פגרי בני אנשא דירין דירין. It is a valuable historical statement of the erection of Tiberias. Herod Antipas built it on a site strewn with sepulchres. This was resented by the orthodox Jews, who would not, on account of uncleanliness, settle there, even after the sepulchres had been removed. Herod was on that account impelled to bring pressure to bear on the first settlers, a great many of whom were strangers, poor people and slaves. (Com. Ant. 18, 2, 3; Gen. r. 23, 1). The whole incident was soon to be forgotten, as the city came to assume great eminence in the Great Rebellion, although the more scrupulous would still hesitate, until the time of R. Simon Ben Jochai (com. Shab. 34a) to settle in certain parts of it. So that this indignation of the targumist must emanate from the very time of the act of Herod. This T. belongs to 28 C. E.

I am inclined to think that the T. to Am. 6:1 נקבי ראשית מקימין שום בניהון כשום בני עממי — הגוים refers to the Herodians and their followers, who would give themselves foreign names, and were not known, like the Hasmoneans, by the Hebrew double. As it is well known, Jews during the Hasmonean rule

would unhesitatingly give themselves Greek names. But this
practice grew abominable in the sentiment of the people in the
days of the Herodian rulers. There are many references to
this effect in the Agada (Exod. r. 1, 30; Lev. r. 32, 3; Tan.
Balak 25, etc.), all of which, I suppose, emanated from that
period. Com. also Hos. 8:12.

The reference in T. to Ez. 39:16 to the destruction of Rome
is interesting. It suggests that the T. took Rome as נוג. As Gog
is the Messianic foe of Israel, one feels that in the time of
either the Great or the Bar-Kochba Rebellion, the revolutionaries, in their pious and Messianic mood, would take Rome as
the prophetic נוג, so that its overthrow is sure to come. Hence
the source of the targumic interpretation. I am also led to believe that this was the reason why the T. turns the gloomy and
miserable description of the "Servant" (Is. ch. 53) into a most
glorious presentation. The targumist, living in a time when the
Messiah stood at the head of warring armies, could hardly have
conceived those objectionable features in a literal sense. V. 5
points clearly to Bar Kochba.

Mi. 5:9, 10, 12 ...והכרתי סוסיך מקרבך והאבדתי מרכבתיך
והכרתי ערי ארצך והרסתי כל מבצריך... והכרתי פסיליך ומצבותיך מקרבך.
The T. changes the simple meaning of the words and renders
them this way:

ואשיצי סוסות עממיא מבינך ואוביד רתיכיהון (9). ואשיצי קרוי עממיא
מארעך ואפגיר כל כרכיהון תקיפיא (10). ואשיצי צלמי עממיא וקמתהון
מבינך (12).

This is a curious rendering. The second half of v. 12 is rendered literally. All other references in the Prophets to the
idolatry of Israel are rendered literally by the T. But the T. in
these verses is construed to give expression to the popular resentment of the act of Herod to construct heathen cities in
Palestine, and the erection in them of temples and statues.

Another allusion to a contemporary situation is found in
the Targum to Judges 5:11. The interpretation reads: מאתר דהון
אנסין להון ונסבין דבידיהון בית מכונת לסטין ומתובת מוכסין. There
is here the twofold reference to the robber and to the publican.
In both aspects the hint is to the last days of Jerusalem. The ab-

horrence for the publican, who was considered an outlaw,[38] was general among the people in those troublesome days. Regarding the former, the implication seems to be of the activities of the Sicarii under the Procuratorship of Felix or Festus, particularly the latter, of whom Josephus says that upon his coming Judea was afflicted by robbers while all the villas were set on fire and plundered by them.[39] The targumist is setting the mark on the facts against which his generation most vehemently reacted.

The interpretation of the T. of ויפקדם בטלאים (Is. 15:4) ומנינין באמרי פסחא is also suggestive of an event preceding the destruction of the Temple which is told in the Talmud of Agrippa I, that wishing to know the number of the people while avoiding its prohibition, he asked the High Priest to count the Paschal sacrifices.[40] I would not, however, stress this evidence. A later targumist might as well have used for exegetical purpose a current Agada.

Of more historical suggestiveness is the Targum to Ze. 11, 1 פתח לבנון דלתיך interpreted to refer to the heathen peoples and the destruction of their cities. This verse was interpreted by Rabban Jochanan b. Zakkai to imply the pending destruction of the Temple, which was generally accepted.[41] Why a targumist living in a generation impressed by the destruction of the Temple should select so strange an allegorical interpretation is hardly conceivable. It would seem that he did not know of the destruction of the Temple and was imbued with the political Messianism, which was an important factor in the Rebellions.

The Targum, however, also contains evidence pointing to a period subsequent to the destruction of Jerusalem. Is. 54:1

---

38) Com. B. Kama 113a, Mish.; Shab. 39a; San. 25b.

39) Ant. XX, 9, 10. The distinction should be drawn between the patriots and the sicarii who, to all intents, were robbers of the vilest sort and employed by Felix for the purpose of inflaming unrest to screen his outrages.

40) Pesachim 64b; Tosefta 4. Com. Wars 6, 9, 3. There are strong reasons for assuming that it was a historical reality.

41) עד שגער בו, רבן יוחנן בן זכאי אמר לו : היכל היכל מפנימה אתה מבעית עצמך, יודע. אני שסופך עתיד ליחרב וכבר נתנבא עליך זכריה בן עדוא פתח לבנון וכ"ו. Yoma 39b, and in Yerushalmi in a somewhat modified version, 6, 3 end.

the Targum interprets אֲרֵי סַגִּי יְהוֹן כִּי רבים בני שוממה מבני בעולה
בני ירושלים צדיתא מבני רומה יתבתא.

In the same sense Is. 2:5 עד עקרה ילדה שבעה ורבת בנים אמללה
is rendered in the Targum כן ירושלים דהות כאתתא עקרא עתידה
יסופון עממיא סגי דמליא ורומי גלותהא מעם דתתמליא . Jerusalem is
here seen to be desolate. Rome is in its bloom. There is still
the thirst for revenge from Rome, which also found expression
in the Targum to Is. 25:12 meaning by כרך Rome, and Ez.
39:16. Com. also Targum Is. 32:14. The targumist lived in
a period following the destruction but not too far away. Mi. 7:11
is interpreted in the T. to refer to the cessation of the persecutions of the nations: בעדנא ההיא יתבטלן גזירת עממיא . The reference is to the situation which arose in Palestine after the rebellion
of Bar Kochba. The targumist had in mind the persecutions of
Hadrian. It is hardly appropriate to the political repressions of
the Roman Procurators. It might be well applied to the persecutions of the Byzantine rulers which, however, could hardly
have found room in the Palestinian Targum, known and used
in Babylonia in the third century.

A less pronounced indication of a post-Destruction age is
suggested in the T· to Malachi 1:11 ובכל מקום מקטר מגש לשמי
rendering: ובכל עידן דאתון עבדין רעיתי אנא אקבל צלותכון... וצלותכון
כקורבן דכי קדמי.

The conception implied here that the prayer replaced the
sacrifice is an outgrowth of the age following the destruction
of the Temple, after the cessation of sacrifice. The sacrifice was
regarded with so much holy reverence by the Rabbis, that such
a conception would be considered an attempt at the divinity of
the sacrifice.[42]

Finally, the Targum to Is. 21:9 may also be of historical
contents. Here the Targum reads נפלת אף עתידא למפל בבל . The
wish is here expressed for the downfall of Babylonia. This suggests an age of persecution in Babylonia against the Jews.

---

42)   This conception has its origin in the saying of R. Jochanan
B. Zakkai: יש לנו כפרה אחת שהיא כמותה (Aboth of R. N. 4, 5). Com.
saying of R. Shmuel b. Nachmani on this verse זוהי תפלת המנחה (Jalqut l. c.). So saying of R. Eliezer גדולה תפלה יותר מהקרבנות (Berak.
32b). Com. Jalqut Eliezer קרב : מק אדם אמרו ישראל רבש"ע בזמן שבה"מ
מביא קרבן ומתכפר עכשיו אין בידינו אלא תפלה.

Babylonia in an earlier period was looked upon with admiration
by the Jews. It was only after the fanatical Sassanides had established themselves on the throne of Persia that the large Jewish
population of Babylonia began to experience the same tribulation
which their brethren in Palestine were undergoing under the
Roman rule.[43] After the new departure in the ruling dynasty,
Babylonia, like Rome, incurred the bitter resentment of the
Jews. Before the Chebarin (Magii) came to Babylonia, we
are told in Gittin 17a, the saying of R. Chiya: "God knew that
Israel could not bear the persecution of the Edomites,
so he led them to Babylonia" was true, but after their
arrival Rabbi Bar Bar Chana was right in his utterance: רחמנא או
בטולא דידך און בטולא דבר עשו. This period is implied in the
Targum to Is. 28:20 והמסכה צרה כהתכנס — ושלטון בבלאי מעיק
יסגי מרוא.

On the other hand, the fall of Babylonia is with the author
still a desire, a fervent expectation. The overthrow of Babylonia
by the Arabians is not yet in sight. There is no other allusion
in the Targum to the Arabs. So that this allusion to Babylonia
affords us a terminus ad quem.

To check up the findings, the scant evidence preserved in
the Targum to the Prophets falls apart in different groups. Some

43) Com. Saying of Rab. עתידה פרם שתפל ביד רומי Yoma 17a;
also Pesachim 54a: ומלכות פרם תנו רבנן שבעה דברים מכוסים מבני אדם...
מתי תפול. There is a striking parallel interpretation in Ps. Jonathan
Gen. 15:12 referring נפלת to Persia: דעתידא למיפל ולית לה זקיפא ומתמן...
or in the version of the Frag. דהא היא מלכותא דפרסיא דעתידא למפל ולא
תהווי לה תקומה לעלמי עלמין. It should be remarked that Ps. Jonathan
introduces here the Messianic conception of the Four Kingdoms of the
Exile, the Fourth being Edom or Rome. The targumist in this instance
dismisses Rome, placing in its stead Persia-Babylonia. In the Midrash
(Gen. r. 44, 2), on which this interpretation is based, נפלת is referred
to Edom with the parenthetic note: ויש שמחלפין נופלת עליו זו זו בבל
דכתיבה בה נפלה נפלה בבל. It is clear that both in the Midrash and
the Ps. Jon. Babylonia (or Persia) had come to be regarded as worse
than Rome, as fully expressed in the saying of Rab. At the same time,
it is made clear in the Midrash that the interpretation of נפלת as referring to Bablyonia is based upon Is. 21:9, consequently the Targum
to Is. 21:9 was either known to them and used by the Ps. targumist
or that the interpretation in the respective cases was simultanously originated. The former assumption, however, is the more plausible one.

are pointing to a pre-Destruction date, some to a period immediately following the Destruction, some, again, to a still later
period. But they do not lead to contradicting results. The evidence demonstrates in a most excellent manner the progressive
composition of the Targum until it assumed its present form.
During this long time, the Targum was submitted to changes
of different natures, when finally, before the Arabic invasion
of Babylonia, it was indorsed in the shape in which it has come
down to us.

We shall now devote our attention to a study of
the relation between the official Targumim. There is a conspicuous affinity between Onkelos and Jonathan. Most of the
early writers on this subject were struck by it but failed to
realize its extent, which consequently lead them to different conclusions. So, while De Rossi and Herzfeld were certain that
Onkelos knew the Targum to the Prophets, Zunz took the view
that Jonathan had Onkelos before him, whom he quoted in
Judges 5:26; 2 Kings 14:6; Jerem. 48:46.[44] Herzfeld would
consider all these citations as later interpolations.[45] But on
closer study of the official Targumim the cases of agreements
between them will be found to be so numerous and of such a
nature that they can be explained neither on the hypothesis of interpolation nor on the assumption of one having made use of
the other. The reader will first be referred to the chapter on general peculiarities of Jonathan. The peculiar treatment by this T.
of certain expressions, to distinguish between the holy and profane; Israel and other peoples; the belief in a second death for the
wicked, all are found in Onk. Besides, there are numerous other
cases in which both Targumim agree. I will cite here the Ps.
Jonathan only to show that there could be a different rendering in the respective cases.

Josh. 1:6 חזק ואמץ Targum תקף ואלים. So Onkelos Deut.
31:7. Ps. Jon. איתוקף ואתחייל.

ib. 1:9 אל תחת Targum תתבר   So Onk. Deut. 31:8.
Ps. Jon. תתירע.

---

44)   De Rossi Meor Enaim l. c.; Herzfeld, Geschichte l. c.; Zunz,
G. V. l. c.

45)   L. c.

ib. 3:13 ‏...וד ועמדו‎ Targum ‏רוקבא‎ . So Onk. of ‏חמת מים‎ (Gen. 21:14, 15, 19). Ps. Jon ‏זיקין דמיא‎ . In Exod. 15:8 ‏נצבו כמו נד‎ Onk. ‏קמו כשיר‎ . Ps. Jon. ‏זיקא‎ . The Targum to Psalms 33:7; 78:13 is ‏זיקא‎

ib. 7:21 ‏אדרת שנער‎ Targum ‏אצטלי דבבלי‎ . So Onk. Gen. 14:1. Ps. Jon. ‏פונטום‎ .

ib. 10:26 ‏ויתלם על חמשה עצים‎ Targum ‏צליבתא‎. So Onk. Lev. 40:19; Deut. 21:22, 23. Ps. Jon. ‏קיסא‎ .

ib. 12:5; 13:13 ‏והמעכתי‎ Targum ‏ואפיקורום‎. So Onk. Deut. 3:14. Ps. Jon. ‏אנטיקירום‎ [46].

ib. 13:3 ‏ולשבט לוי לא נתן משה נחלה, יהוה אלהי ישראל הוא‎ . Also ‏מתנן די יהב להון יי אלהי ישראל אחסנתהון‎ Targum ‏נחלתם‎ Ezek. 44:28 ‏ואחזה לא תתנו להם בישראל אני אחזתם‎ Targum ‏מתנן דיהבית להון אינון אחסנתהון‎ . This is the rendering by Onk. of Deut. 18:2 ‏עשרים וארבע מוהבותא‎ . But Ps. Jon. ‏ה׳ הוא נחלתו‎ ‏דכהונתא.‎

ib. 14:4 ‏ומגרשיהם‎ Targum ‏ורוחיהון‎. Also Ezek. 45:2; 48:17. So Onk. Lev. 25:34; Num. 35:2, 3, 4. Ps. Jon. ‏פרולין‎ .

ib. 20:1 ‏ערי מקלט‎ Targum ‏קרוי שיזבותא‎ . So Onk. Num. 35:6, 11, 13. Ps. Jon. ‏קרוי דקטלן‎.

ib. 20:5, 9 ‏גאל הדם‎ Targum ‏גאל דמא‎ . So Onk. Num. 35:19, 21, 24, 25; Deut. 19:6. But Ps. Jon. ‏תבע דמא‎ .

ib. 20:5 ‏כי בבלי דעת‎ Targum ‏ארי בלא מדעיה‎ . So Onk. Deut. 19:4. Ps. Jon. ‏בלא מתכוין‎.

ib. 23:16 ‏...ואבדתם מהרה‎ Targum ‏ותובדון בפריע מעל ארעא‎ ‏טבתא‎. So Onk. Deut. 11:17. Ps. Jon. ‏ותבדון בסרהוביא מעילוי‎ ‏ארעא משבחא.‎

Judges 5:8 ‏יבחר לו אלהים חדשים‎ Targum ‏כד אתריעו בני‎ ‏ישראל למפלח לטעותא חדתן דמקרב עבידא דלא איתעסקו בהון אבהתהון‎ Onk. to Deut. 32:17 ‏...אלהים לא ידעום חדשים מקרוב באו‎ Rendering: ‏דחלן חדתן דמקריב אתעבידו לא איתעסקו בהון אבהתכון חדתנין‎ Fragmentary Com. ‏מן כדון אתברון ולא אידכרו בהון אבהתכון‎ . Sifri l. c. and Friedmann On. and Ak., p. 65.

1S. 13:12 ‏ואתאפק‎ Targum ‏ואתחסנית‎. So Onk. Gen. 45,1. Ps. Jon. ‏למסוברא‎ .

---

46) Kohut's suggestion on these renderings (Aruch ‏אפקירום‎) will only serve the point in question.

ib. 15:7 שור Targum חגרא. So Onk. Gen. 25:18. Ps. Jon. חלוצה. [47)

ib. 23:22 והכינו Targum ואתקינו. So Onk. Exod. 16:4. Ps. Jon. ואתברדו—ל"א. ויזמנון. [47)

1K. 18:28; 5:16 ויתגדדו Targum ואתחממו. Also Jerem. 47:15. So Onk. Deut. 14:1. Ps. Jon. לא תגודון בשריכין.

2K. 5:16 ויפצר בו Targum ואתקיף ביה. So Onk. Gen. 19:3. Ps. Jon. פייס.

ib. 5:19 כברת ארץ Targum כרוב ארעאי. So Onk. Gen. 35:16; 48:7. Ps. Jon in former: סיגעי אשוון עללתא בארבע in latter: סיגעי ארעא.

ib. 6:18 ויכם בסנורים Targum בשברירא. So Onk. Gen. 19:11. Ps. Jon. בחוודרוריא. Frag. בהדבריה.

ib. 16:6 וינשל Targum ותריך. So Onk. Deut. 7:22. Ps. Jon. וינלי.

ib. 18:32 ארץ זית ודבש Targum ארעא דזיתהא עבדין משחא ומן תומריתא עבדין דבש. So Onk. Deut. 8:8. Ps. Jon והיא עבדא דבש דבש.

ib. 21:6 וענן ונחש ועשה אוב וידענים Targum ועניו ונחיש ועבד. So Onk. Lev. 19:26; 20:6; Deut. 18:10, 14. בידין וזכירן. Ps. Jon. אחידי עינין.

ib. 23:25 ובכל מאדו Targum ובכל נכסוהי. So Onk. Deut. 6:5. Ps. Jon. בכל ממונכון.

IS. 3:20 הצעדות Targum ושירי רגליא. So Onk. Num. 31:50 שירין. Ps. Jon. קדישיא מן אודניהון.

Jerem. 7:24 etc. בשררות לבם Targum בחרהור לבהון. So Onk. Deut. 29:18. Ps. Jon. בתהות יצרא ביש.

Ezek. 12:7, 8, 12 עלטה Targum קבלא. So Onk. Gen. 15:17. Ps. Jon. חומטא. Gen. r. 45, 9 אמיתתא.

---

47) Ps. Jon. agrees with On. and Jon. in Gen. 16:7; 20:1. Onkelos renders בין רקם ובין חגרא (ibid 16:14) בין קדש ובין ברד presumably influenced by 20:1 בין קדש ובין שור. Cases of this sort are numerous in Onkelos. Similar cases in Jonathan are cited in the chapter on textual deviations. But as to Ps. Jon., the rendering also of שור in 16:7; 20:1 was חלוצה as in 28:18, in which the Fragmentary concurs. Evidence for this is presented in Gen. r. 45, 9: על עין המים, באורה דחלוצה. Also Ps. Jon. to Exod. 15:22. Gronemann's (Pent. Über., p. 20) argument on this is thus a miscalculation.

‎לֹא תחלון‎. Targum ‎ואת שם קדשי לא תחללו עוד‎ ib. 20:39
So Onk. Exod. 20:22; Lev. 21:6, 12, 15; 22:32. Ps. Jon. ‎תפסון‎
But ‎ואחילו וחללו‎ (Jer. 31:4) ‎נטעו כרמים‎. So Onk. Deut. 20:6.
Ps. Jon. ‎פרקיה‎.

ib. 28:13 Targum ‎אדם פטדה ויהלם תרשיש שהם וישפה‎
So Onk. ‎סמקן ירקן וסבהלם כרום ימא וכורלא ופנתירון שבזיז אזמרגדין‎.
Exod. 28:17, 18, 19, 20. But not so Ps. Jon. and F.

‎מרחיק רגז ומסגי למעבד‎ Targum ‎ארך אפים ורב חסד‎ Joel 2:13
‎טבון‎. So Onk. Exod. 34:6. Ps. Jon. ‎חסד ...ארך רוח‎.

These cases are of special interest also for determining the
nature of the relation between Onkelos and the non-official Targumim. But of equal importance are the cases of agreement
between the official Targumim in which the non-official Targumim
concur. They also belong to Onkelos. I do not intend to raise
the question of the origin and history of the non-official Targumim to the Pentateuch. I have my own view of them, differing appreciably from those offered. But whether we assume
with Bacher that in the Fragmentary is preserved a relic of the
ancient and original Palestinian Targum on which were based
both Onkelos and Ps. Jonathan which form stages of the same
Targum,[49] or whether we choose the simpler view enunciated
by Traub u. Seligson, that Ps. Jon. and the Fragmentary are
to some extent a critical revision of Onkelos,[50] there is the
general recognition of the common ground of these Targumim
and Onkelos. The fact, therefore, that they agree with Onkelos
cannot be construed to impart to the cases in question a different
character.

Josh. 10:11; 14:6, 7 ‎מקדש ברנע‎ Targum ‎רקם גיאה‎ So Onk.
and Ps. Jon. Num. 32:8 etc.

ib. 12:2 ‎ועד היבק‎ Targum ‎יובקא‎. So Onk. and Ps. Jon. Gen.
32:23; Num. 21:24 etc.

48) This is true only when it is spoken of profanation of God
(Is. 48:11: Ez. 20:9, 14; 22:36; 27:33); profanation of the Sabbath
(Is. 56:2, 6: Ez. 20:16, 21, 24, 38). But when it is spoken of pro-
fanation of the land and temple ‎אפסא‎ is employed.

49) Z. D. M. G., v. 28, 60-63.

50) Frankel's Monatschrift, 1857, 101 et seq. Gronemann (Pent.
Übersetz., p. 8, note) also thinks that the Fragmentary and Ps. Jon.,
especially the latter, have expanded Onkelos.

ib. 11:2; 12:3 כנרות Targum גינוסר . So Onk. and Ps. Jon. Num. 34:11 etc.

ib. 12:8; 10:13, 20 אשדות Targum משפך מרמתא . So Onk. and Ps. Jon. Deut. 4:49.

Judges 1:6 ובני קיני Targum ובני שלמאה . So Onk. and Ps. Jon. Gen. 15:19 and Frag. Num. 24:21, 22.

ib. 3:8 ארם נהרים Targum ארם די על פרת . So Onk. and Ps. Jon. Gen. 24:10.

ib 17:5, 12 וימלא את יד Targum וקריב ית קרבן . So Onk. and Ps. Jon. Exod. 28:41.

1S 19:13, 16 תרפים Targum צלמניא So Onk. and Ps Jon. Gen. 31: 19, 34, 35.

2S 1:19 הצבי ישראל Targum אתעתדון . So On. Exod. 33:21 ותהי מעתד . Ps. Jon. ותתעתד — ונצבת . Also Deut. 29:9.

1K 11:36; 15:4 למען היות ניר Targum מלכו . So Onk. and Ps. Jon. Num. 21:30 ונירם .

2K 3:13 ...אל ישראל למלך ויאמר Targum בבעו . So Onk. and Ps. Jon. Gen. 19:7, 18.

ib. 5:21 ויפל מעל המרכבה Targum ואתרכין So Onk. and Ps. Jon. Gen. 24:64.

ib. 19:37 ארץ אררט Targum לארעא קרדו . So Onk. and Ps. Jon. Gen. 8:4. (Ps. Jon. דקדרון) [51] .

There is also agreement between them with regard to the belief in a second death for the wicked in the Messianic Age. So Jon. Is. 65:6; Jerem. 51:39. Both Onk. and Frag. render יחי ראובן בחיי עלמא ומותא תנינא — יחי ראובן ואל ימת Deut. 33:6 יחי ראובן בעלמא ולא ימות במותנא תנינא דבה ; Frag.: לא ימות מיתי רשיעיא . ימין ושמאל indicating direction (Is. 9:19; Ezek. 21:21; Zech. 12:6) are rendered by דרומא צפונא . So Onk. and Ps. Jon. Gen. 13:9. Is. 14:9 רפאים Targum גברין . So Onk. and Ps. Jon. Gen. 15:20. Chayjoth in אגרת בקרת [52] has brought to notice the remarkable change in the rendering of עברים by Onk. Everywhere in Gen. it is rendered עבראי but beginning with Exod. יהודאי is the rendering. The motive for that might be the exegetical saying of R. Simeon b. Jochai on Gen. 49:8:

---

51) Cited also in Gen. r. 33, 2.

52) Page 8.

אמר ר׳ שמעון בן יוחאי יהיו כל אחיך נקראין על שמך, אין אדם אומר
ראובני אנא, שמעוני אנא אלא אלא יהודי אנא.

In that Ps. Jon., with a single exception, agrees. (Gen.
43:32). But Exod. 21:2 כי תקנה עבד עברי and Deut. 15:20; 13:12
כי ימכר לך אחיך העברי או העבריה both Onk. and Ps. Jon. have
בר ישראל in order, it would appear, to avoid the misinterpretation: the slave of an Israelite (com. Mechilta l. c.). Jonathan as
a rule renders עברים — יהודאי 1S 13:3, 17; 14:11, 21; Jonah
1, 9. But Jerem. 34:9 (also 14) לשלח איש את עבדו ואיש את שפחתו
העברי והעבריה . The T. follows Onk. and Ps. Jon. rendering
לשלחא בר ישראל ובת ישראל .

Zech. 12:8 כרברבין Targum ובית דויד כאלהים . So Onk. and
Ps. Jon. Gen. 6:4 בני האלהים — רברביא .

This comparative list could be extended appreciably. But
the number of cases presented are sufficient to show the real
nature of the problem. There could be found sound explanation for the similarity between Onk. and the Frag. and
Ps. Jon. even were we not to proceed along the lines of the
theories offered, for they are exploiting the same field, the Pentateuch. Why, however, should an author of a Targum to the
Prophets seek harmony with Onkelos in many comparatively un-
important details of rendering, will hardly be possible to explain.
Could not the Targum to the Prophets have its own way of
rendering in the respective cases? Neither could it be the way of
a redactor. But this Targum, like the Mishna, Tosefta, Talmudim
and Midrashim, had no single author: there was no single revision. The inference will yield the only possible conclusion
that **there was a common source for the official Targumim. They
were originated in one and the same time; in one and the same
way, under one and the same circumstances and share a com
mon history.**
They were the product of the Aramaic rendering of the
portion from the Law and the Prophets read in public worship.
The Lxx had a similar origination, although later generations, actuated by propaganda motives, formed a different notion
of the act.[53] The official Targumim are the work of genera-

53) This view is held by most scholars. "Sie verdanken nicht
der Wissenschaft sondern dem Relig. Bedürfnisse" (Frankel, Vorstudien,

tions. They were formed and reformed through many centuries, gradually, invisibly. They were not a new attempt, supplanted none, but are the continuation of the Targumim used in the service.

Hence also the remarkable balance between the paraphrastic and literal so skillfully maintained in the official Targumim. That formed a necessary condition with the regulations of the reading in early as in later ages.

The Lxx assumed the same course. There was sought an exact rendering, a simple and ground understanding, as close to the original as possible. Literalness was insisted upon and expository rendering would only be tolerated in difficult or poetical passages, or where the danger of a misinterpretation had to be averted. I completely disagree with Zunz, Geiger, Bacher [54] and others, who insist on the priority of the Mid-rashic Targum to the literal. Their theory is wrong. It is built upon, it would seem, the doubtful foundation that the poetical and difficult passages were first to be rendered.[56] But as they can furnish no evidence it is just as safe to assert that the simpler passages involving a literal rendering were rendered either first or at one time with the poetical ones. Invoking again the Lxx, the literalness is the conspicuous feature in them and not the paraphrastic. The exposition of the Law and the Prophets held on the Sabbaths in the synagogue in Alexandria left little trace in the Lxx. Nothing approaching the Philonian exposition has

---

20). Com. Tischendorf, V. T. G. XIII; Geiger, Urschrift, 160; König, Einleitung, 103.

54) Zunz, G. V., 344; Geiger, Ur., 425. Com. Frankel, Über d. Zeit etc., Ver. Deut. Orient, 1845, 13. Bacher ib. 64, after assert-ing that the literalness of Onkelos was a later and Babylonian tendency, is not in the least disturbed when, following this assertion, he draws a list of cases in which Onkelos is expository while the Frag., the original and oldest, according to his view, is literal. Com. also Ps. Jon. Deut. 33:26 rendering the v. literally, while Onk. and Frag. are exegetical.

55) Com. Steinschneider, Jewish Lit. (Heb.) 20. He also takes the view that the Targum in essence was not different from the Midrash, assuming that the Targum originated from single translation of difficult words. Like Geiger and Bacher, he asserts (ib. 190) that from these (Midrashic) Targumim resulted the simpler and exacter understanding of the Bible. It is certainly a curious and queer process.

found room in the translation. It was the knowledge and not the
exposition of the Bible which formed the prime necessity for
instituting the reading of the translation. These writers have
exaggerated innocent sayings in the Mishna reproaching renderings of certain targumists, which are found in Ps. Jonathan.
Because they are cited in the Mishna and because they were rejected, they came at once to be regarded not only as belonging
to an early Targum but to the earliest. Consequently, the exposition preceded in point of time the literal which marked a
new departure and had been accomplished in Babylonia. But
these citations could as well belong to a later Targum. On the
contrary, the way they are quoted ‏ואלין דמתרגמין‎ [56]) clearly
signifies the existence of another Targum upon which these new
Targumim had attempted to encroach. [57])

Again, it should be borne in mind that the Agada had been
the product of a generation subsequent to the simple exposition
of the Soferim and the Zugoth. The exegetical element in the
Targumim was influenced, and on occasion determined, by the
Halaka, which also had a progressive history. But the Targum
existed before the new tendencies made their appearance.

The official Targumim thus represent the early as well
as the later recognized Targumim used in public worship.
Through common use there had been a continuous interchange
of influence between them. It is customary to consider the T.
to the Pentateuch as older than the T. to the Prophets.[58]) This
opinion rests on a questionable argument. There can be no
doubt that the introduction of the Targum in public service
dates back to a comparatively early period. But in my judgment
it had not originated before the Maccabean age.[59]) There is sufficient evidence in support of the view that Hebrew had not

---

56)   Y. Berakoth 5, 3: ‏ואילין דמתרגמין עמא דבני ישראל כמה דאנן‎
‏רחמן בשמיא‎ . The other citation in Megilla 25a reads: ‏האומר ומזרעך לא תתן‎
‏למלך‎ which carries the same implication.

57)   Com. Z. Chajoth on Megilla 25a.

58)   It is interesting to note that later tradition also assigns to the
Targum to Pent. an earlier date. Com. Sifri beginning ‏וזאת הברכה‎ .
Com. Maimonidas ‏הל׳ תפלה, יב‎ : ‏מימות עזרה תקנו שיהא שם תורגמן לעם‎
‏מה שהקורא קורא בתורה‎ ; of the T. to the Prophets he proceeds only to
repeat the regulations appearing in the Mishna.

59)   Com. Kautzsch Gram. d. Biblisch-Aram., p. 4.

only been well understood in Palestine in the time of Ezra and Nehemaia, but that it had been the vernacular tongue.[60] There is, on the contrary, no positive evidence either that Aramaic had been in those early days the vernacular among the Jews in Palestine or even that the general ignorance of the Jews of the Aramaic tongue of the period of the Kings had entirely passed. What use would that generation have for an Aramaic version of the Law ?

But whether it had been introduced in the period immediately preceding the Maccabean uprising or in the early days of Maccabean rule, it is certain that when the need of the Targum arose there had already been established the custom of reading in public service from the Prophets as a supplement to the reading from the Law. As the reading from the Law goes back to Ezra,[61] and because of the greater interest in the knowledge

---

60) Frankel, Paläst. Ex., 208, 280, consistent with his literal interpretation of the tradition that the Targum originated with Ezra, accepts the genial but useless theory put forward by De Rossi (l. c.) that Onkelos was consulted by the Greek translators. But unlike De Rossi, Frankel would not consider the Aramaic version—a corrupted rendering of the original. Rapaport, זכרון לאחרונים Let. 3, takes the same view, and it should be followed by all others of the same mind as regards the date of the origin of the Targum. To overlook the difficulty arising from an assumption that either the Targum had not been carried to Egypt, or, being in use, that it exercised no influence on the Lxx, would certainly be unforgiveable.

61) The Karaites ascribe the reading of the Haftora to Ezra (com. Neubauer, Aus Petersburger Bibliothek, p. 14); Abudraham placed its origin in the persecutions of Antiochus. But whatever cause one may unearth (com. Büchler J. Q. R. v., p. 6 et seq.), one outstanding cause was the institution of the reading of the Law in public service. The reading from the Prophets served the purpose of administering an admonition as to the holiness and observance of the Law. I completely agree with Büchler that the introduction of the reading of the Pentateuch had its origin in the festivals (J. Q. R., v. 5, p. 442). Thus the Sifra to Lev. 23:43; Sifri to Deut. 16:1; Meg. 4a, 32a. The Law was read by Ezra on the festivals of the New Year and Tabernacles (Neh. 8:2, 8, 18; 9:3). The reading on Saturday appears to have arisen later, when synagogues arose outside Jerusalem. Hence the supposition that the selection of definite portions for each festival preceded the definite apportioning of the Sabbatical reading. I disagree, however, with the motive to which Büchler attributes the origin of both the Pentateuchal

of the Law, the necessity of an Aramaic translation of the Law
might have been earlier appreciated than that of the Prophets.
But no sooner was the reading from the Prophets instituted than
the necessity of an Aramaic rendering became apparent. Although
the Greek translation of the Pentateuch leads all other books
of the Bible in point of time, not even a century passed before
the Prophets "and the other writings" were to be found in the
Greek tongue.

As far as the general ordinance is concerned, no distinction
is made between the Targum to the Law and the Targum to
the Prophets. Accordingly, it is said in Soferim 18:4 ומן הדין
לתרגם לעם ולנשים ותינוקות כל סדר ונביא של שבת לאחר קריאת התורה.
In the Mishna Meg. 21a, 23b; Yerushalmi 4, 1, 5, the Targum to the Prophets is discussed alongside with the Targum
to the Law, the limitations on the reading of the former being
less rigid than the latter for other reasons דלא נפקא מיניה הוראה .
Again in Mishna 25a; Tosefta 4 (3); Y. Meg. 4, 11 a list of
passages both from the Law and the Prophets is given which
were not to be translated. Both were not considered obligatory, so
that their omission in the service would not call for repetition,
as it is made clear in Y. Meg. 4, 6 והתרגום מעכב? אומר רב

---

and Prophetical readings, which would place their institution at nearly
the same date. One should not resort to the magical Samaritan influence
in order to find the cause for such an ordinance when it is readily
presented in Nehemia: "And on the second day there gathered themselves
together unto Ezra, the expounder, to obtain again intelligence of the
words of the Law. And they found written in the Law that the children
of Israel should dwell in booths during the feast in the seventh month.
And (they ordered) that they should publish... throughout all their cities
and through Jerusalem saying, go forth unto the mountain and fetch
leaves to make booths, as it is written (13-15)." It was the ignorance
of the people of the ordinances of the festivals which formed the cause
of the reading from the book of the Law. These passages present sufficient ground for ascribing the ordinance of the reading from the Law to
Ezra. This might also be implied in the tradition ascribing it to Moses.
Com. B. Kama 82a. The Haftora is much later, and dates to the
end of the third century or the beginning of the second century B. C.
Direct and positive evidence cannot be furnished. Early tradition is
silent over it. But what has been said above and the fact that a Greek
translation of the Prophets had already been made at that time, and also
the mention of the Prophets in Ben Sira in a manner suggesting general
acquaintance with them by the people, lend support to this view.

יובה מן מה דאנן חמיין רבנן נפקין לתעניתא וקראין ולא מתרגמין הדה.
אמרה שאין התרגום מעכב . This is in substance implied in the
saying of R. Chalafta b. Saul, Meg. 24a, as interpreted in Tosafoth l. c.

But the reading from the Law and from the Prophets in
the Sabbath service had not been definitely set as late as in the
time of the composition of the Mishna. The selection was left
to the discretion of the individual community. Any portion
from the Prophets, as from the Law, would be read.[62] The
readings were translated. Hence the rise of a Targum to all the
Prophetical books. The author of the official Targumim was
the congregation. The Targum in its first stages had no definite
shape. The reader framed the translation at the reading of the
original. Every reader had his own choice of words and his
own way of rendering. He was only conditioned to present a
close and exact rendering.

But with the persistence of the Targum and its growing
significance the free translation progressed by various degrees
to a definite and unchangeable form. Anything which endures

---

62) Com. Maimonides ונראה שלא היה: כסף משנה, הל' תפלה, יב, יב
להם באותו זמן הפטרות קבועות כמונו היום אלא כל אחד היה מפטיר ענין
שנראה לו שהוא מתיחס לפרשה. The same may be applied to the reading
of the Law. Only the reading on the festivals, including the New
Moon, Purim and Chanuka, the Four Shabbaths, Maamodoth and days
of fasting, are indicated (Babli, Meg. Mish. 30b; Y. Mish. 3, 4, 5, 6, 7).
There is no hint of a definite Sabbatical reading. The words חוזרין לכסדרן
(Y. Meg. 3, 5, 7; Babli 29a, 31a) should not be taken literally. The
interpretation of R. Ami and Jeremia Meg. 30b refers to a time when
there was a definite reading both from the Law and P. Had there been
definite portions for the Sabbatical readings from the Law, there would
certainly be also a definite selection of parallel Prophetical readings.
There could be no reason why there should be a discrimination against
the Prophetical reading. I am fully convinced that there existed a definite
Prophetical reading for each festival enumerated in the Mishna. It is
true, that in both Y. and B. the reading from the Law is given while no
mention is made of the Prophetical readings. But the Tosefto, while
registering for the festival only the readings from the Law, is, however,
indicating for the Four Sabbaths the Prophetical readings side by side
with the reading from the Law. If there had existed definite Prophetical
readings for the Four Sabbaths, there had certainly been definite Prophetical readings for the more important festivals, and yet no mention
of them is made in the Tosefto. The reason may be simple: it mentions

in humanity, as in the universe, tends to shape. It had become necessary to lay down certain rules to regulate the translation. How is the verb or adjective of a collective noun to be rendered: in singular, as in original, or in the plural? Is the literal sense to be considered or the implied meaning? How about the anthropo-morphic expressions, shall they be rendered literally to the an-noyance of the worshippers or explained away, and how? There are passages involving a Halakic interpretation of great import-ance, or a controversial point between the parties; shall such passages be left over to the intelligence of the reader, who might not be trained in the Halaka? A way of rendering had to be early devised, which the reader was to follow. The first attempts at uniformity were directed towards single phrases or words. Gradually they spread to include the less dangerous regions. The Rabbis, by concerted authority at each time, were responsible for the change. An excellent illustration is furnished us in Y. Meg. 4, 1 and Bik. 3, 4. In one case it is the rendering of טנא (Deut. 26:2). The targumist rendered מנא, but R. Jona, holding it to be improper to present the first fruits in any other receptacle than a basket, objected to this rendering and insisted upon the rendering of סלא, as the Targumim to the Pent. have it. Another case was מצות ומרורים (Exod. 12:8), which the targumist rendered פטירין עם ירקונן; the rendering ירקונן being

___

the more important, the Pentateuchal reading. The same may be said of the Mishna also.

But we know that there were no definite Prophetical readings for the Sabbath. The Mishna points out certain portions from the Prophets which are not to be read. Y. Meg. 4, 11 מרכבה ; דוד ואמנון Y. Meg. 4, 12; Babli 25a, while according to R. Eliezer בהודע את ירושלים (Ez. 16) should not be read.

Had the passages represented a definite Sabbatical reading, a sub-stitute reading would be indicated which should be read instead of the interdicted ones.

It should be borne in mind that all these portions from the Prophets cited in the Tosefta (ibid), with the exception of Ezek. 1, have not found a place on the calendar of the Haftora. The attempt of Büchler to discover the early divisions of the readings from the Law and the accompanied readings from the Prophets is highly hypothetical. Again, the definite mention of the Targum in the Mishna and Tosefta shows that the Targum was introduced before a definite order of the Sab-batical readings had been introduced.

misleading as to the proper kind, Jeremiah would force the targumist to retranslate it in a different way. The third case concerned the rendering of תורים ובני יונה (Lev. 5:7), and R. Pineas
would not allow to render תורים by פטימין. These cases demonstrate the peculiar manner in which the composition of the T.
was accomplished.

Although the official Targumim were in a definite shape in
the time of R. Akiba,[63] the process of transformation had been
still going on to a comparatively late date. It affected both the
literal and exegetical rendering. Some older exegetical renderings were rejected and replaced by others. Of the rejected, some
have been preserved in the Ps. Jonathan, which in itself is an
Aramaic Jalqut comprising also later Agadic material. Rejected
paraphrases of the Targum to the Prophets might be those which
appear on the margin in the Codex Reuch. and in some early
editions. Although the notes prefaced תרגום א' contain Agadic
material of a later date, they contain elements which might have
been first incorporated in the Targum but rejected later as not to
be read in the service. The same may be said of those ascribed to
ספר א' although being on the whole an attempt to simplify and
to supplement the extant T. Again, the duplicate renderings
which are found both in Jonathan and Onk. can be explained by
the fact that one formed the older explanation while the other
represents a more recent one but which for some reason had
not succeeded in dispossessing the older one. This explains also
the curious renderings of certain verses, one half retaining one
rendering while the other half contains a remnant of a different rendering. As rejected paraphrases may be considered the
Targum to Micah 7:3, quoted in Rashi, and another quoted in
the name of Jehuda of Paris on 2S 6:11.[64]

---

63) Com. R. Akiba's homily on Zek. 12:1 (Moed Katan 28a),
whcih shows that R. Akiba knew the Targum to this verse. Com. R.
Jehuda's saying referred to above; also Beraitha Baba Kama 17a
וכבוד עשו לו במותו זה חזקיה מלך יהודה שיצאו לפניו שלשים וששה אלף
חלוצי כתף, דברי ר' יהודה. א"ל נחמיה, והלא לפני אחאב עשו כן.

64) Com. Zunz, G. V. 80: מצא הרב זללה בשם יהודה מפריש מפוז
יונתן תרגם :27:17 Com. also Rashi, Ezek . ומכרכר תר' ירוש' טדויי ופייטוי
חטי מנית ופנג בחטי די חוש.. מפי ר' שמעון מצאתי שמצא במקרא תרגום
ירושלמי דחושלא וקלמא.

The same can be said of the selection of words in the rendering. It should be noticed at the outset that the remarkable
unity exhibited in the official Targumim is strongly emphasised
also in the wording of the translation. Once the Aramaic word
was set for a Hebrew word, you are certain to find it in each
case where this Hebrew word occurs. An illustration of this
amazing fact is presented in the rendering of the names of
peoples, countries and cities. Other instances can be picked up
at random. It demonstrates in a most emphatic way the scrupulous rigor with which the work of the Aramaic rendering had
been accomplished. If, therefore, a word is rendered in one place
one way and another way somewhere else, we are certain to
have two different Targumim of the word in question. But
apart from cases of this sort which are contained in the official
Targumim, variations have come down to us from different
sources. Concerning Onkelos variations are contained in Ps.
Jonathan. In some cases in which Ps. Jonathan has a different
Aramaic word for the Hebrew from that contained in Onk., the
Fragmentary will be found to correct it, replacing it by the one
used in Onkelos. There is, however, no means enabling us to discover which of the two represents the earlier form. They might
have had their origin in the same time. Two communities might
have coined them at the same time. Instructive instances are presented in the different renderings given by Rav and Levi of
Gen. 49:27 (Zebachim 54a); ib. 30:14 (San. 99a), Onkelos
agreeing with that of the former; R. Jehuda and Nehemia—of
Gen. 18:1 (Gen. r. 42, 6). Variations of this kind are not wanting
also in the Targum to the Prophets. Some have been preserved
in Jonathan. A good many others are contained in Talmud and
Midrashim and in the marginal notes in the Codex Reuch., under
the names of ת"א, ס"א, ל"א, פליג, ואית דמתרגמי. In a few cases
of the latter the variant will be seen to agree with Ps. Jonathan
and Fragmentary. This fact lends new support to the view of
the common source of all Targumim. The former cases shall
be considered first.

Joshua 19:8 בעלת באר Targum בעלת...; א"ל—מישר. So is
the T. of נד בעל (ib. 11:17; 12:7) בעל חרמ' (Jud. 3:3) בעלת תמר
(Jud. 20:33) etc.

Judges 6:38 הספל Targum לקנא λεκάνη; אדירים בספל

(ib. 5:25) Targum בפילי גבריא. The latter is the rendering of קבעת (Is. 51:17, 22). So is rendered קערת כסף (Num. 7:13) in Ps. Jon.; Onk. מגסתא.

Judges 8:21 השהרנים Targum ענקיא; in Is. 3:18 it is rendered by סבכיא. The latter is given to Judges by ל"א in Cod. Reuch.

1S. 19:13, 16; Ez. 21:26; Za. 10:2 תרפים Targum צלמניא. Judges 18:17, 18, 20 דמאין while ל"א has עביטא.

ib. 16 וכביר העזים Targum ונודא דעיזיא. But ל"א has וגונכא. This is the rendering of במכבר (2K 8:15) connected with כביר. Com. Kimchi l. c.

1K 22:49 תרשיש Targum אפריקא. So Jer. 10:9; Jonah 1:3. But Is. 2:16; 23:1, 14; Ezek. 27:12 ימא.

2K 5:23 חרטים Targum פלדסים. Is. 3:22 מחכיא.

Jerem. 31:28 כאשר שקדתי עליהם Targum כמו דחשבת; in the second half כן אשקד Targum כן יחדי מימרי. The same was certainly the rendering of כאשר שקדתי which is found in ס"א. Here is a case of a rejected Anthropomorphism of a latter time.

Ezek. 27:6 כתים Targum אפוליא or איטליא. Everywhere else it is rendered כתאי (Is. 23:1 etc.).

Ezek. 27: 21 קדר Targum נכט. Otherwise ערבאי (Is. 21:16, 17; 42:11; 60:7. So T. to Ps. 120:5.).

Ezek. 27:23 עדן Targum חדיב. This is the rendering of אשכנז (Jerem. 51:27).

Ezek. 40:19 התחתונה Targum מציעאה; איתדמי — ארעאה. So is the rendering of התחתונה in v. 18.

Ezek. 45:2; 48:17 ומגרשיהם—ורוחיהון. Ib. 27:28 T. פרויא. As Ps. Jon. and F. Lev. 25:34. On. וחקל רוח.

Am. 2:7; Is. 47:6 לחל Targum לאפסא. So Ps. Jon. Exod. 20:25. Is. 48:41; Ezek. 20:39 Targum תחלון. But אית דמתרגמי Am. l. c. לאחלא.

Com. further Kimchi Ezek. 40:16.

To these cases may be added the following cases, which Cod. Reuch. is at variance with the extant Targum, the latter being supported by ל"א.

Jerem. 17:7 מבטחו Targum בסעדיה; ל"א — רוחצניה. So in extant T.

Ez. 9:10 דרכם Targum חוביהון; ל"א — אורחיהין; in the extant T. פורענות אורחיהון.

Micah 3:11 ישענו Targum רחיצין ; ל"א — מסתמכין. So in the extant T.

Cases in which the marginal variations follow the Ps. Jon.: Jud. 8:11 פלנשו Targum ולחונתיה ; ל"א — ופילקתיה. So Ps. Jon. Gen. 22:24, Onk. agreeing with Jon.

1K 4:6 הבית Targum ביתא ; ל"א — קורטור. So Ps. Jon. Num. 22:18; 24:13. On. follows Jon.

Other cases of variants:
Joshua 9:5 נקודים Targum כיסנין ; '5"א — עיפושין .
Jud. 3:19 פסילים Targum מחצביא ; ל"א — גשריא .
1S 24:8 וישמע Targum ופיים ; ל"א — ישרל .
1S 30:16 נטשים Targum רטישין ; ל"א — פרסין.
2S 18:14 שבטים Targum גיסטין γαισουὶ ; ל"א—לונכיין .
IS. 3:23 הגליונים Targum מחזיתא ; ל"א — אספקלריא .
the Greek σπεκλάριον Lat. specularia. Here is presented a case, where seemingly a Greek word was replaced by its Aramaic equivalent. The same was the case with Onkelos. Bacher (ib.) has made this point clear by a comparison between Onk. and Ps. Jon. and the Frag. That is true to some extent also of Jon., which is demonstrated in the Greek and its Aramaic substitute of ומגרשיהם cited above. Still, Jonathan appears to have been more immune to such an attempt than even Ps. Jonathan. Here is an instructive case: שקל (Ez. 4:10) is rendered by the Greek פילס φόλλις while all—Onk., Ps. Jon. and Frag.—render it by סלע (Num. 7:13 etc.).

IS. 51:17 מצית Targum אעדית ; ס"א — מצית .
Ez. 44:20 כסום יכסמון Targum ספרא יספרון ; ס"א — כסמא . יכסמון .

Two cases, one in ס"א , the other in ל"א , vary with Jon. in anthropomorphisms: אלי (Jerem. 31:38) T. לותי ; ס"א—למימרי ; אותי (ib. 16:11) T. יתי ; ל"א — לפולחני . These cases and the case of Jerem. 31:27 cited above reinforce the view set forth above that later usage eliminated some anthropomorphic substitutes from the T.

The following are cases of variations found in the Talmud and Midrash.
Joshua 16:8 תאנת שלה Targum תאנת שלה . Y. Meg. 1, 12 איסכופיה דשילה .

Y. San. 2, 4. ואמרתם כה לחי Targum כדין לחייך . IS. 25:6
לקיימא .So Onk. and Ps. Jon. Deut. 4:4.

Y. Taanith 4, 5. מטול כם דלוט Targum מישא בערב . IS. 21:13
מטול רב בערב .

סדרו פתורין אקימו Targum ערך השלחן צפה הצפית IS. 21:5
סוכתא . Gen. r. 63, 9 סדר פתורא סדר מנרתא and in Cant. r.
סדרת פתורא, אקימת מנרתא, אדלקת בוצינא. מישחו, כמעט שעברתי
קבלו מלכותא — מגן. They agree with Jon. only in the rendering of
ערך השלחן. The citation from Cant. r. contains two recensions.
The rendering אדלקת בוצינא agrees with Cod. Reuch. and is
identical with the marginal note headed תרג' ירוש .

Psichta Lamentation r. on Is. 22:1, 2 כי עלית כלך לגנות —
ולאיגרא סלקין להון ; עיר הומיה — קרתא מערבבתא ; קריה עליזה —
קריה חדתא ; מהומה ומבוסה ומבוכה — יום מעורבב, יום דביזה,
יום דבכיא.
קרתא משבחתא, כרכא חדאה, ארי יום רגיש ואתדשא וקטול. .But T
ונלית Targum גליא דכסא — ויגל מסך יהודה ib. IS. 22:8
מטמורת .

אוי עיר הדמים סיר אישר חלאתה בה — ib. on Ez. 24:6
אוי מן קמא דקרתא דישפכו דמים בגווה, וחפשוישיתה לא נפקת מן גווה ;
דחפשישיתה בגווה — וחלאתה לא יצאת ממנה Targum וי על קרתא
דאשדי דם זכאי, דהיא כדורא דזיהומתיה ביה וזיהומתיה לא נפקת מניה.
Cant. r. 1:1 on Am. 8:3 והלילו שרות היכל — שבחות דהיכלא ;
Targum חלף זמרא .

Y. Shabbath 6, 4 on IS. 29:1 הוי אריאל אריאל—אריא אריא נברא
Targum מדבחא, מדבחא .

Cant. r. כמעט שעברתי on IS. 47:2 חשפי שובל — קלופי סובלתא
דנהרא ; Targum אתברי שלטוניך .

Koheleth r. טובה חכמה on 2K 18:16 ואת האומנות — מה היא
סקופיא. Targum האומנות ? בי לוי אמר ציפריא ורבנן אמרין שינגריא.
Jon. עבידין קטוליא — ועתה מרצחים on Is. 1:21 Lev. r. 4:1
קטולי נפשן . Shochar Tob 32, 2 (com. Y. San. 10, 1) on Mi. 7:8
על פשע — דאינשי חובין . Jon. ומעבר על חובין .

Similar cases are: Lev. r. 5, 2; Num. r. 10, 5 on Am. 6:4
and Lev. r. 6, 2 on Zech. 5:1, all of which represent, undoubtedly,
a different and rejected Targumic rendering. The following case
is to my mind an interesting relic of a rejected rendering. This

is in Frag. Deut. 32:1: דכן הוא מפרש ואמר טולו לשמיא עיניכון
ואסתכלו לארעא מלרע ארי שמיא כתננא ימסין וארעא כלבושא תבלי.
The rendering in Jon. is as follows: זקיפו לשמיא עיניכון ואסתכלו
בארעא מלרע ארי שמיא כתננא דעדי כן יעדו וארעא ככסותא דבליא
כן תבלי The rendering in the F. is literal. We cannot determine
which is the earlier rendering.

The process of alteration had been going on until a comparatively late date but not so late as the final redaction of the
Babylonian Talmud. That was made especially possible by the
fact that the T. was recited in the worship by heart. Reading
the Targum from a written copy was prohibited. This interdiction is indicated in Tanchuma Gen. 18:17:

ילמדנו רבינו מי שהוא מתרגם לקורא בתורה מה היא שיסתכל בכתב?
כך שנו רבותינו המתרגם אסור להסתכל בכתב. אמר ר' יהודה בן פזי
מקרא מלא הוא : כתב לך את הדברים האלה — הרי המקרא ; כי על
פי הדברים האלה — הרי התרגום שניתן בעל פה.

This passage is quoted in the Pesiqta (ed. Friedmann), p.
28. Does it imply an interdiction to put the Targum into writing?

This question was the cause of much contention. Rashi
inclined to an extreme interpretation of the prohibition to write
down all belonging to traditional exposition. So with regard
to the Mishna which, he insists, was not written down
by Rabi (Ketuboth 19b). Com. Rashi Erubin 62a, beginning
והכי נקט מגלת תענית שלא היתה דבר הלכה כתובה בימיהם : כגון
אפילו אות אחת חוץ ממגלת תענית; also Taanith 12a. He takes
the view that the Targum had not been allowed to be written
down. Commenting on the Mishna Shabbath 115a he says:
ורבותי פרשו דהאי בכל לשון דקאמר אכתובין קאי ולא אנביאין, דעפ"י
שכתובין בכל לשון טעונין גניזה, ומדומה אני מפני שמצעינו ביונתן בן
עוזיאל שאמרו תרגום הן מפרשין כך, ואני אומר אף בנביאים, אם אמר
יונתן לא כתבו ולא נתנו להכתב, והכי מפרש במס' מגלה דמאן דאסר
בכולהו אסר.

According to Rashi's teachers, with whom he disagrees, not
only was the T. to the Prophets written down, but also allowed
to be read in the service in written form; for, as Rashi himself remarks, one is dependent upon the other. For this reason
it was seemingly his teachers who would interpret the contention
between Rab Huna and Rab Chisda as referring only to the

Hagiographa, as according to the interpretation of the Gemarah they only differ on the view of those who prohibit the reading from a written Targum. Rashi, however, makes capital of the expression in the Babli Meg. 3a אונק׳ הגר אמרו as does Luzzatto (O. G. IX). But as the saying of R. Jeremia is also quoted in the Yerushalmi, it is just as well to take אמרו as an innocent substitute for תרגם of the Yerushalmi version, which does not carry this implication. The main source of Rashi's con-tention is the prohibition contained in the saying of Rabban Simon b. Gamliel, Y. M. 1, 9; Babli 8b אף בספרים לא התירו שיכתבו אלא יונית. But there are the חכמים (ib. and Shab. 115b) who differ with him, and as it is said in Soferim 15,2 אף על פי שאמר רבן שמעון בן גמליאל שאף בספרים לא התירו לכתב אלא יונית, לא הודו לו חכמים שיאמרו מעשה ברשב״ג (רבן גמליאל) שהיה עומד... ואף חכמים עמדו בדבריהם שאמרו כל כתבי הקודש ואף על פי שכתובין בכל לישון טעונים גניזה.

Furthermore, there is no implication in R. Simon b. Gamliel's saying of a prohibtion to write down the T. He only meant to say that the reading from a written T. in service does not fulfil the required Aramaic rendering. Consequently, as Rab Porath, quoted in Tosafoth (Shab. ib. ולא) rightly put it, be-cause it is not allowed to read it, is equivalent to reading the Torah by heart and דברים שבכתב אי אתה רשאי לאמרם בעלפה. The question raised there against it is thus well answered. Com. also Tos. Sota 33a כ. There is certainly not the slightest ground for an inference that no written T. to the Prophets existed. Witness the interpretation (in Babli ib.) of R. Jehuda ורבותינו התירו יונית אמר ר׳ יהודה אף כשהתירו אבותינו לא התירו אלא בספר תורה. But we well know that at that time all the books of the Bible existed in the Greek translation. There is the same base-lesness for the reason ascribed by Luzzatto (l. c.), Zunz (G. V. 65) and others to the prohibition, namely, that the T. contain-ing some Halaka, was regarded on one plane with תורה שבע״פ which was not to be written down (Temura 14b, Gittin 60b). Had this been the reason, how was the Lxx sanctioned by all the Rabbis, containing as it does so many Halakic interpretations? (Com. Z. Frankel דרכי המישנה 10 and Über d. Einfluss l. c.). It should also be noticed that the reason given for R. Simon b. Gamliel's interdiction of other than the Greek translation is

שאין התורה יכולה לתרגם כל צרכה and not because it belongs to the
דברים שבע"פ .

On the other hand, it is well known that in spite of the
interdiction on the written Halaka, the Rabbis did not hesitate
to write down for private use Halakic decisions and intercourses.
It will also be remembered that in the time of Rabban Gamliel
the Elder there was already in existence a Targum to Job. That
the interdiction passed by him on this Targum was not
due to the fact of its being written was shown above. Again,
Esther had also been translated, as it appears from the Mishna
Meg. 17a: הקורא את המגלה קרא תרגום בכל לשון לא יצא... לא צריכה
דכתיב תרגום וקרי תרגום . The reason is pointed out, for it
is written ככתבם וכלישונם . But there could be no more reason
for considering the T. to the Prophets דברים שבע"פ than the T.
to Esther.

It is clear then that the prohibition against the written T.
had only been instituted against the public reading in the service.
The reason for that was mainly to avert sharing by the T. the
same sanctity with the original. This is in essence the very
reason given for R. Simon b. Gamliel's view. And this prohibition, it would seem, was enforced even at a date when the
Mishna was already written down and allowances were made
for the written Agada (com. Gittin 60b). Rapoport (זכרון
letter 5) well expounded the case of the written Halaka when he
said that the prohibition was directed mainly against the public
discussion and was not intended to exclude it from private use.
Berliner (On. 89) rightly applied this view to the T. This view
might be substantiated by Tanchuma (ib.) ואסור למתרגם ברבים
להכתבה בתורה , which Friedmann (Pesiqta ib.) is inclined to emend
להכתב בכתב . The implied indication is that a written T.
may be permitted for private use.

There certainly were in existence written copies of the
Targum, which were restricted to personal use. One such copy
a targumist would employ in public worship and was hindered
by R. Samuel b. Isaac telling him דברים שנאמרו בפה — בפה,
ודברים שנאמרו בכתב — בכתב (Y. Meg. 4, 5). What he meant
amounted to saying that the T. should be read by heart, just
as the original is to be read from the written only.

Targum Jonathan was used by later targumists. It was
pointed out above that Targum Ps. 18 is a copy with minor
modifications, notice of which will be taken in the chapter on
Other Targumim, of the Targum to Samuel 22. T. Jonathan
was used by the targumist of Chronicles.

The T. to Chronicles exhibits pronounced and independent
characteristics. It pursues, on the whole, its own way of exposition and translation. It is more Midrashic than the official
Targumim. He will not, in most cases, let himself be influenced
by the official Targumim. In some instances he will neither follow Onkelos nor Ps. Jonathan. Yet, even this targumist made
definite and considerable use of the Targum Jonathan. The cases
in question are of a typical nature, which do not admit of an
incidental agreement. I will quote them in order of Chronicles.

.Jon. קריבך ובסרך Targum עצמך ובשרך 1 Chronicles 11:11
2S 5:1.

1 Ch. 13:7 וירכיבו את ארון Targum ואחיתו. Jon. 2S 6:3.

1 Ch. 13:9 גרן כידון. Targum אתר מתקן. Jon. 2S 6:6.

ib. מרגוהו Targum שמטן. Jon. ib.

. ואדריכלין דאומנין לבנין כותלא Targum וחרשי קיר 1 Ch. 14:1
Jon. 2S 5:11.

ויתרטישו במישר גיבוריא Targum ויפשטו בעמק רפאים 1 Ch. 14:9
Jon. 2S 5:18 reading וינטשו .

1 Ch. 14:11 בעל פרצים Targum מישר פרצים. Jon. 2S 5:20.

ib. 2S. כתבור מאן דפחר דמלי מיין Targum כפרץ מים. Jon. ib, 2S.

1 Ch. 14:15 כי יצא האלהים לפניך להכות Targum ארום נפק
מלאכה מן קדם יי לאצלחא קדמך למקטל. Jon.2S 5:24.

1 Ch. 16:3 אשפר Targum פלוג. Jon. 2S 6:19.

. Jon. דמטלל בכיורי ארזיא Targum בבית ארזים 1 Ch. 17:1
2S 7:2, 7.

ib. וארונא שרי במשכנא בגוי Targum וארון... תחת יריעות
יריעתא . Jon. 2S 7:2.

1 Ch. 17:7 אני לקחתיך מן אחרי הצאן להיות נגיד Targum
אנא דברתיך מן דירא מבתר ענא למהוי מלכא. Jon. 2S 7:8. The
usual rendering of נגיד in the T. to Chronicles is ארכון
(1 Ch. 11:2) סרכון (1 Ch. 13:1).

1 Ch. 17:9 אתר מתקן Targum ושמתי מקום . Jon. 2S 7:10.

1 Ch. 17:16 לית אנא כמיסת Targum מי אני יי אלהים . Jon. 2S 7:18.

1 Ch. 17:17 לעלמא דאתי Targum ותדבר למרחוק . Jon. 2S 7:19.

1 Ch. 17:20 בכל די שמענא Targum ככל אשר שמענו באזנינו . ואמרו קדמנא Jon. 2S 7:22.

1 Ch. 17:21 עמא יחידאי ובחיר בארעא Targum גוי אחד בארץ . עמא חד בחיר... Jon. 2S 7:23.

1 Ch. 17:25 מלכו אקים לך Targum לבנות לו בית . Jon. 2S 7:27.

1 Ch. 18:2 נטלי פרס Targum נשאי מנחה . Jon. 2S 8:2, 6.

1 Ch. 18:3 לאשנאה תחומיה Targum להציב ידו . Jon. 2S 8:3 להשיב ידו .

1 Ch. 20:3 ומסר יתהון Targum ויסר במגרה . Jon. 2S 12:13 וישם...

2 Ch. 1:14 ואשרינון בקרוי Targum ויניחם בערי הרכב ועם המלך . רתיכיא בר מן מה דהוו עם... So Jon. 1K 10:26.

2 Ch. 2:9 חטין פרנום Targum חטים מכות . Jon. 1K 5:25 חטים מכלת .

TEXTUAL VARIATIONS IN JONATHAN

Jonathan, like Onkelos, deviates in many cases from the Masoretic reading to which allusion was already made in the previous chapter. There is a way to differentiate the paraphrastic from the literal sense. Out of the obscurity of the exegetical ex-pansion there comes forth the simple, written phrase on which it rests. The Targum Jonathan, although, on the whole, far from literal adhesion to the text, is unmistakably careful to transmit both the sense and version of the text. The literal pre-dominates in the historical portions of the Prophets. Any render-ing ,then, not in accord with the Masoretic reading constitutes a deviation from the reading.

This fact was noticed by the rabbinical authorities. Rashi, while for the most part overlooking them and even following them in evident belief that they were merely of an exegetical nature, could not escape the impression that Jonathan had a different reading. Kimchi and Minchat Shai did not hesitate to point out in the plainest language some of these deviations. They have engaged the attention of later rabbinical writers as well as the modern biblical student.[1]

On close examination the deviations will be found to con-

---

1) However, Abrahm Ibn Ezra, critic as he was, would not ac-cept such a possibility. Thus he remarks in Safa Berura (9, 11, ed. Lippmann): ‏ודרך אחרת ליונתן בן עוזיאל, וכלנו יודעים, כי לא היה חכם‏ ‏אחר ר' יוחנן בן זכאי כמוהו, ולא הגיע מעלתו להיותו כחבירו יונתן. והוא‏ ‏היה גדול מכולם, וראינו במקומות רבים שתפש דרך דרש להוסיף טעם, כמו‏ ‏אלוה מתימן יבוא (חבקוק ג, ג), כי אין ספק שהוא כמו אלוה תימן... רק‏ ‏הוסיף טעם לפרש תימן מגזירת ימין כי התיו נוסף... וככה ביער בערב‏ ‏רק בעבור שאמר הכתוב ערב ולא קדר ומהשם דרש בו שהוא כמו הערב. ועוד‏ ‏שמצא עזר במלת תלינו. והנה טעמו בערב תלינו עם הערבים... וכמוהו‏ ‏(ישעיה כא, יג), גם הוא ידע כי הוא כמו כל מלכי הערב (מלכים א', טו),‏ ‏ונסתם גיא הרי (זכריה יד, ה) דרש בו משרש סתום את הדברים (דניאל‏ ‏יב, ד) ודרש ככה בעבור שלא אמר הנביא וברחתם‏. It is an unsuccessful attempt on his part to explain away renderings that represent a differ-ent reading.

52

sist of three distinct categories. Some of them represent an unquestionably different reading. With minor exceptions, they do
not admit of being explained away. The preponderate number
of these deviations consists of a difference in the pointing. Differences of this kind are found in great numbers in MSS. claiming the Masoretic sanction. They emanate from a period when
doubts still existed, as to the reading of certain words. Even
the scrupulously literal Aquila version contains variations from
the text. The Talmud presents abundant testimony to them.[2]
On the other hand, many of these deviations are either followed
by the Lxx and P. or they appear in them in a different form. Deviations of this description are here classed under heading "A".
There is another class of deviations of a mere grammatical character. There is a noticeable tendency on the part of the translator
to eliminate the more striking discrepancies either in the number
or in the person of the substantive in the sentence. So the tran-
lator renders them in either one or the other way. Sometimes he
subordinates all the forms of the sentences to the last in order.[4]
In some cases the reverse is true [5] and in some instances all
follow the one in the middle.[6] This principle is observed by
the Lxx and P. to some extent. But it does not appear to have
been consistently followed by the targumist. The number of exceptions by far exceeds the number of the cases where this
principle is enforced. Thus it is impossible to determine the
basic rule of this principle. It takes the appearance
of an arbitrary and haphazard device. At any rate, this group
of variations does not involve a dfferent reading. They appear
under heading "B".

There is another body of deviations which are very instructive for the biblical student. The targumist made it a rule to
render sentences which resemble one another, but differ in some

---

2) אמר לי ר' יהושע, ישמעאל אחי האיך אתה קורא כי טובים דודיך
או דודיך ? א"ל דודיך ; א"ל אין הדבר כן שהרי חברו מלמד עליו, לריח
שמניך Mish. Aboda Zara 29b. Com. also Gen. r. 94, 4: בתורתו של
ר' מאיר מצאו כתוב ובן דן חושים.

3) Com. More Nebuchim 3, 43.

4) Jerem. 9:5; 11:12.

5) Ezek. 11:19

6) Is. 26:8.

particulars occuring in different parts, in one and the same way.
A similar process had been pursued by the Rabbis.
It is the היקש and the נזירה שוה of Hillel and R. Ishmael b.Jose,[7]
which forms the seventh Mida [8] of the 32 Midoth enunciated by R. Eliezer. But while in the Halaka and Agada the con-
formation is sought mainly in the circumstances or in the legal
conditions of the cases involved, the targumist is interested in
the wording. The Samaritan text, as it is well known, will often
change a phrase to agree with a similar phrase somewhere else.[9]
The Lxx in some instances and the P. to a larger extent follow
the same rule. (Com. Frankel, Pal. Ex., p. 166.). There can
be little doubt that the author had been actuated by reflection. Rendering a phrase, the recollection of the other similar
phrase flashed through the mind of the translator to leave its
stamp upon his rendering. Mental activity of this sort accounts
for many misquotations from the Bible found in the Talmud.[10]
But this practice could not have originated from a mere un-
conscious play of recollection. The translator must have been
moved by something which he considered an imperative necessity. It will be observed that in most instances treated this
way the author was concerned in eliminating an outstanding di-
vergence in the version of the narrative of one and the same
fact.[11] Whether or not the translator pursued a definite rule
in applying this principle is difficult to determine. For the most
part the author is seen to make the passage second in order to
conform the one preceding it.

This kind of variation is placed under heading C. They
are of an interpretative nature. They do not point to a different
reading, as they were taken by many biblical students. I have

---

7)   Tos. San. 7, Pirkei Aboth of R. Nathan 35, and introduction
of Sifra.

8)   Com. Reifma i, Meshib Dabor (Wien, 1866).

9)   Com. Kircheim כרמי שמרון p. 37 et seq.

10)   Com. Aboda Zara 24b, citing IS 15:15   אשר חמל העם
על מיטב הצאן והבקר והמשגים והכרים : מיטב הצאן והבקר אשר חמל העם
ועל כל הצאן according to v. 9, and San. 49a, citing 2S 3:27   ויכהו שם
אל החמש — החמש according to 20:10.

11)   Com. Judges 7:7 and 20; 1S 4:21 and 19; 2S 12:21 and 22;
1K 13:9 and 17; 2K 9:19 and 18.

omitted all deviations of a doubtful character or consisting of an unrendered or added Waw or change of the preposition, which might be due to the distraction of a copyist or the Aramaic idiom.

GROUP A

	M. T.	Targ.	R.
Joshua 2:7	עַל הַמַּעְבְּרוֹת	עד	עַד (1
" 7:5	עַד הַשְּׁבָרִים	עד דתברונון	עד השברם (2
" 9:4	וַיַּעֲשׂוּ גַם הֵם בְּעָרְמָה וַיֵּלְכוּ וַיִּצְטַיָּרוּ	וַעֲבָדוּ אַף אִינוּן בְּחוּכְמָא וַאֲזָדוּרוּ	Vac. וילכו
" 11:17; 12:7	מִן הָהָר הֶחָלָק	מִן טוּרָא פְּלִיגָא	חלק (3
" 13:16	עַל מֵידְבָא	עד מידבא	עד (4
Judges 3:2	לֹא יְדָעוּם	לָא הֲווֹ יָדְעִין	ידעו (5
" 9:9	דְּמִנַּהּ מִיקְרִין... הֶחֳדַלְתִּי אֶת דִּשְׁנִי וּבֵיהּ מִתְפַּנְּקִין אֲשֶׁר בִּי		בן (6
" 11:34	אֵין לוֹ מִמֶּנּוּ	מינה	ממנה (7
" 14:15	הַלְמַסְכְּנוּתָא קְרִיתוּן הֲלֹא יְרֻשֵּׁנוּ קְרָאתֶם לָנוּ		

1) So in many MSS. of Kenn. and De Rossi. Com. Kimchi. But Onk. Gen. 49:13 has it literally.

2) So P. and in marg. Syro-Hex. Com. Field Hex. and also Arab. Kimchi's explanation lacks force. Dillmann's contention (Handbuch), "dass blosse Vervolgen passt zu dieser Wirkung nicht", missed the order of the narrative—as did Herrheimer's objection that "der Verlust von 36 Mann ist keine Zertrümerung". The same could be said with much greater force of Joshua's overpowering fright (vv. 6-9). But the current interpretation that the defeat at the descent is identical with the loss of the 36 in killed told in the beginning of the v., is not at all impressive. It is rather to be assumed, which the reading of the T. unquestionably implies, that the loss of the 36 gave cause to the ensuing defeat at the descent, where the loss, it would appear, was sufficient to cause anxiety. I am inclined to believe that the reading of the T. was הַשְׁבָרוֹם. Com. כְּלִי יְקָר. The form in itself wouldn't appear strange to the targumist, as cases of this nature are numerous.

3) So P. A. Com. Field Hex., l. c.

4) So Sebirin. Many MSS. of Kenn. and De Rossi and extant editions follow the reading of the T.

5) So P. Lxx read יָדְעָה.

6) Probably influenced by v. 13.

7) Felt by Kimchi. So Sebirin.

		M. T.	Targ.	R.
		הלא	יתנא הלכא	הלם (1
"	19:9	לינו נא הנה חנות היום	ביתו כען הכא לחוד יומא דין	הנה (2
"	20:34	מנגד לגבעה	מדרום לגבעתא	מנגב (3
"	21:10	נגדע היום שבט אחד	איתמנע	נגרע (4
1S	2:31	וגדעתי את זרעך	תקוף זרעך	זרעך (5
"	3:2	ויהי ביום ההיא	והוא ביומיא האינון	ויהי בימים ההם (6
"	6:3	אם משלחים את ארון	אם אתון משלחים	אם משלחים אתם (7
"	12:21	ולא תסורו כי אחרי התהו	ולא תסטון מבתר פולחניה ולא תפלחון לטעותא דאינו למא	כי Vac. (8
"	15:32	אכן סר מר המות	בבעו רבונא מריר מותא	סר (9
"	22:14	וסר אל משמעתך	ורב על משמעתך	סר (10
2S.	1:21	בלי משיח בשמן	דמשיח כדבמשיחא	בלי Vac. (1

---

1) Com. Kimchi. Lxx הלא vacant. In one of the MSS. of De Rossi the Keri is הלם and Ketib הלא and in two others הלם is the Ketib. Ginsburg: לסוראי הלם כתיב הלא קרי, לנהרדעי הלא כתיב הלם קרי.

2) So Lxx Lag., otherwise לין פה חנות היום are vacant. P. לערוב הנה חנות היום vacant. The T. does not render חנות.

3) Minchat Shai: בשתי מקראות ישנות כתוב מנגב. So in many MSS. of Kenn. and De Rossi.

4) Com. Onk. Exod. 21:10. Com. Minchat Shai. This reading is found in many MSS. of Kenn. and De Rossi.

5) The second את זרוע בית אביך is rendered תקוף דרע. If the targumist followed here the Masoretic reading there is hardly any reason why it occured to him a different reading in את זרע. Lxx read in both זרע while P. follows in both the Mesoretic reading.

6) So P. Probably influenced by v. 1.

7) So Lxx, P. and many MSS. of Kenn. and De Rossi.

8) So Lxx and P. Com. end of verse כי תהו המה Targum ארי למא אינון.

9) So P. Lxx סר vacant.

10) So Lxx. Com. P.

1) So P. and Arab. The suggestion that T. read בלי, as in Kenn. MSS. 30, is hardly tenable. It would seem that the T. considered this phrase to refer to מדם חללים. Com. Ehrlich Randglossen

	M. T.	Targ.	R.
`` 5:12	וכי נשא ממלכתו	ארי מנטלא מלכותיה	נשא-נשאה 2)
`` 14:14	אשר לא יאספון	דלא אפשר להון	
		דיתוספון	יאספון 3)
`` 15:23	על פני דרך את	על אפי אורח	
	המדבר	מדברא	את Vac. 4)
`` 22:44	תשמרני לראש גוים	תמניני	תשימני 5)
`` 23:13	שלישה מהשלשים	מגברי ריש משריתא	שלשים 6)
1K. 1:18	ועתה אדני המלך	ואת...	ואתה 7)
`` 1:20	ואתה אדני המלך	וכען	ועתה
`` 6:31	האיל מזוזות חמשית	מטקסין	חמושות 8)
1K. 7:3	וספן בארז	וחפא נכרין	וספן 9)
`` 8:26	יאמן נא דברך	יתקיימון כען פתגמיא	הדבר
`` 8:30	ואתה תשמע אל מקום	מאתר בית שכנתך	ממקום... מן
	שבתך אל השמים	מן שמיא	השמים 10)
`` 8:31	ובא אלה	וייתי ויומיניה	ובא ואלה 11)
`` 13:6	והתפלל בעדי	ובעי מן קדמוהי	אלין 12)

and Thenius Sarn., to which the expression כדבמשחא points. On the other hand, it is possible that the T. took בלי to mean annointing, from root בלל PS. 92:11. Ehrlich's assumption (ibid) that the T. read instead of תרומות שדי — לא די is founded on a misunderstanding of the T.

2) So P. Probably influenced by 1 CH. 14:2.

3) Exod. 5:7. But Com. T. to PS. 104:22.

4) So Lxx. P.
את is omitted in many MSS.

5) This is the reading in PS. 18:44. As the T. to PS. renders this word in accordance with the reading here, it is obvious that he intended to correct the rendering of Jonathan. The rendering of the T. is supported by P. and Lxx Lag.

6) Com. T. to vv. 23, 24 and Rashi and Kimchi. Onk. Exod. 14:7 felt by Kimchi. Com. Field Hex. Note 26. So Lag. Lxx.

7) So Lxx, P. and 250 MSS. Kimchi: רבים מהסופרים טעו בזאת המלה וכתבו ועתה באלף לפי שהוא קרוב לענין, אבל ברור הוא אצלנו כי הוא ועתה בעיין מפי ספרים המדוייקים ומפי המסורת זהו ואתה באלף וטועים בו בעיין לפי שהענין יותר קרוב.

8) But com. T. to v. 33; 7:5. Felt by Kimchi:
וי"ת מטקסין כמו חמושים.

9) So Lxx P.

10) So P., in accordance with 2 Chronicles 6:21.

11) So Lxx P.

12) Lxx omit the whole phrase.

	M. T.	Targ.	R.
`` 13:12	ויראו בניו את הדרך	ואחזיאו	ויראו 1)
`` 16:9	בית ארצא אשר על הבית	די בביתא	בבית 2)
`` 16:24	ויקן את ההר שומרון	וזבן ית כרכא	העיר ויחלמיה 3)
`` 20:33	ויחלטו הממנו	וחטפוהא מניה	ממנו 4)
`` 21:8	אשר בעירו	דבקרתא	בעיר 5)
`` 21:13	ויעדהו	ואסהידו	ויעדו 6)
`` 22:30	התחפש ובא	אנא אשתני ואיעול	אתחפש ואבא 7)
2K. 2:14	איה י' אלהי אליהו	קביל בעותי...	אהה 8)
`` 3:25	עד השאיר אבניה בקיר חרשת	עד דלא אשתארת אבנא בקרתא דלא פגרוה	עד השאיר בקיר הרסת 9)
`` 17:11	ויעשו דברים רעים	ועבדו קדמוהי	בעיניו 10)
`` 17:13	בידי כל נביאי כל חזה	ביד כל ספר	נביא 11)

1) So Lxx P. Kimchi: ת"י ואחזיאו כמו ויראו בפתח היוד מבנין הפעיל.

2) Com. Lxx. P.

3) So he renders ויבן את ההר (ib), but אדני ההר שמרן is rendered literally. It might, however, be interpretative suggested by the text, for the city—not the mountain—was called by this name. Why should the T. to Am. 3:9 render הרי שמרן literally while הר שומרון — כרכא (Am. 4:1; 6:1), although we find ערי שומרון (1K 13:32) as well, would admit of no such explanation. Cases, however, of this sort are found in the T. Kimchi (followed by Gersonide) infers from the T. that there really was a city there and Omri just strengthened it.

4) So P.; according to the Maarabai this reading is the Keri while the Masoretic reading is the Ketib.

5) Com. P. Lxx omit אשר בעירו .

6) So P.

7) So Lxx P. Felt by Kimchi. Probably interpretative suggested by what follows in the verse.

8) Or אנה (Com. 2K 20:3). Probably for anthropomorphic reasons.

9) So Lxx P. Having read הרסת and taking it to refer to אבניה the targumist changed the number.

10) Probably interpretative.

11) P. has both in plural, so that the T. might have been influenced by כל חזה .

286

	M. T.	Targ.	R.
" 21:8	ולא אוסיף להניד רגל ישראל	ולא אוסיף לטלטל ית ישראל	רגל Vac.
" 23:13	להר המשחית	לטור זיתיא	להר המשחה (1
IS. 3:12	ונשים משלו בו	וכמרי חובא	נשים (2
" 5:13	ויקירהון מיתו בכפנא וכבדו מתי רעב	ויקירהון מיתו בכפנא	מתי (3
" 8:14	והיה למקדש ולאבן נגף	ויהי מימריה בכון לפורען	למקדשו
" 8:21	וקלל במלכו ובאלהיו	ויבזי שום פתכריה וטעותיה	מלכו (4
" 10:15	בהניף שבט את מרימיו כהרים מטה לא עץ	כארמא חוטרא למימחי לא חוטרא מחי אלהין מן דמחי ביה	כהניף שבט את מרימיו (5 Vac.
" 10:34	ונקף סבכי היער בברזל	ויקטיל גברי משריתיה דמתגברין כברזלא	כברזל
" 11:16	והחרים ה'...	ויבש	החריב
" 17:2	עזבות ערי ערער	שביקין קרויהון חרבו	ערי ערער
" 21:13	ביער בערב תלינו	בחורשא ברמשא	בערב (6
" 23:3	ובמים רבים זרע שחר	דהות מספקא סחורא	סחר (7

---

1) Com. Rashi and Kimchi. It is so quoted by the R. Josi, Shab. 56b. This reading is found in one MS. Kenn.

2) Felt by Rashi, Kimchi. So Lxx. A. Com. Esther. r. 2, 2: ונשים משלו בו א״ר הוניא קופצין עליהן כבעל חוב.

3) So Lxx P. Rashi and Karo follow the T. without taking notice of the deviation. Kimchi noticed it in the T. Hitzig, Ehrlich and Krauss would read here מזי . (Com. Onk. Deut. 32, 34), which would, however, not agree with this rendering.

4) Kimchi seems to have noticed it. Though the absolute מלך is always rendered literally by the T. Com. Gray Is. In. Com. As to ובאלהיו see Dill P. Ehrlich IS.

5) Lxx P. omit כהרים מטה and have part of כהניף.

6) So Lxx P. In general the T. is apt to such an interchange, as will appear in the sequel.

7) So Lxx P. V. Kimchi also noticed it in the T. This reading of the T. was adopted by Hitz., Cheyne, Guthe and Kn.

	M. T.	Targ.	R.
IS. 29:13	יען כי נגש	חלף דאתורברב	נגש 1)
" 30:6	בארץ לביא וליש מהם אפעה ושרף מעופף	אתר דאריא בר אריון	מהם Vac. 2)
" 30:8	לעד עד עולם	לסהדו	לעד 3)
" 30:27	וכבד משאה	וקשי מלסוברא	וכבד משאה
" 38:13	שויתי	אנחנא נהמית	שועתי
" 40:6	וכל חסדו	וכל תוקפיהון	חסנו
" 40:17	כל הגוים כאין נגדו מאפס ותהו נחשבו לו	כל עממיא כלמא עובדיהון גמירא ושיצאה אינון חשיבין קדמוהי	אפס... נגדו Vac. 4)
" 43:4	ואתן אדם תחתיך ולאומים תחת נפשך	ומסרית עממיא תחותך ומלכותא חלף נפשך	ואתן עמים 5)
" 48:7	ולפני יום ולא שמעתם	ולא בסרתינון	שמעתים 6)
" 49:17	מהרו בניך	יוחון יבנון חרבתיך	בניך 7)
" 53:7	נגש והוא נענה	בעי	נגש 8)
" 54:9	כי מי נח זאת לי	כיומי דנח	כימי
" 56:11	והמה רעים לא ידעו הבין	אינון מבאשין	רעים 9)

---

1)   So in many MSS. Com. Kimchi and Seder Eliahu r. 2, 24

2)   Cort would have משם so Krauss, which would have the sup-port of the T.; still, it is not improbable that the rendering is ex-planatory.

3)   So P. V.

4)   Lxx also omit נגדו ; Lxx and P. read לאפס. There is no reason to suppose that נגדו was omitted for anthropomorphical reasons.

5)   This is suggester by the parallel; but it may also be ex-planatory. Graetz and Klost. amend איים which would have the sup-port of the T.

6)   Com. Lxx P. V.

7)   So Lxx. (Com. San. 64b: וכל בניך אל תקרא בניך אלא בוניך).

8)   So P. Sym. V. (See Dil. P. T. 2) and in many old Hebrew MSS. Com. Chayoth, Mebo Hatalmud, 25. Com. Berachoth 7b, 14a.

9)   So Lxx P. and S. Kimchi remarks: ומן התימא שתרג׳ יונתן
רעים מבאשין.

	M. T.	Targ.	R.
`` 58:3	וכל עצביכם תנגושו	אתון מקרבין	תנגשון [1]
`` 59:18	כעל גמלות כעל ישלם	מרי גמליא	בעל גמולות [2]
`` 61:3	מעטה תהלה תחת רוח כהה	רוח משבחא חלף	רוח תהלה [3]
`` 65:1	אל גוי לא קרא בשמי	דלא מצלי בישמי	קרא [4]
Jer. 6:14	וירפאו את שבר עמי	ואסיאו ית חבר כנשתא דעמי	את שבר בת עמי [5]
`` 10:24	יסרני אך במשפט פן תמעיטני	לא יתקף רוגזך בהון דלמא יזערון	יסרם... ימעטו [6]
`` 11:12	שמעו את דברי הברית ודברתם אל איש יהודה	קבלו ית פתגמא ותמלילינון [7]	ודברתם [8]
`` 11:14	בעת קראם אלי בעד רעתם	בעידן דאת מצלי עליהון בעידן בישתהון	קראך אלי בעת רעתם [9]
`` 15:14	והעברתי את איביך	ותשתעבדון וכו'	והעבדתי [10]
`` 23:26	עת מתי היש בלב הנביאים	עד אימתי אית בלבהון	עד מתי יש [11]
`` 27:8	עד תמי אתם בידו	עד דאמסר יתהון	עד תתי [12]

---

1) So Lxx. Kimchi: ומן התימה שתרגם אותו יונתן וכל תקלתכון מקרבין תרגם כמו בשין.

2) But Is. 63:7 כעל כל אשר literally.

3) It is possible to explain the rendering of the T. as suggested by the parallel רוח כהה, and would smoothen the difficulties felt by the commentators on this point.

4) So Lxx P.

5) They might, however, have been influenced by 8:11.

6) So Lxx. Com., however, chapter General Peculiarities.

7) So Lagarde. The same MS. was also before Kimchi, but in the copy of the Minchath Shai and many others the reading is ותמללון.

8) So Lxx. Com. P.

9) Lxx P. A. and many Hebrew MSS. Otherwise the T. might have been influenced by v. 12: והושע לא יושיעו להם בעת רעתם.

10) So Lxx P. Kimchi noticed it in the T. and remarks that he found this reading in many MSS. See also Kittel: Guesebrecht. Still, it is not impossible that the T. was influenced here by 17:4 והעבדתיך את איביך and hence the reading of the Lxx P.

11) So Lxx P.

12) So P.; also noticed by Giesbrecht and Cor., but it may also be interpretative.

	M. T.	Targ.	R.
" 29:12	וקראתם אתי והלכתם והתפללתם אלי ושמעתי אליכם	ותצלון קדמי ואקבל צלותכון ותבעון מן קדמי ואקבל בעותכון	וקראתם אתי ושמעתי אליכם [1]
" 31:39	וכל השדמות	וכל אדייתא	וכל הזרמות [2]
" 49:3	והתשוטטנה בגדרות	ואתחמא בסיען	בגדרות [3]
" 51:3	אל ידרך... ואל יתעל	לא ימתח... ולא	אל ידרך [4]
Ez. 1:7	וכף רגליהם ככף רגל עגל	כפרסת רגלין סגלגלן	עגל [5]
" 5:11	וגם אני אגרע	ואף אנא אקטף תקף וכו'	אגדע [6]
" 7:5	רעה אחת רעה	בישתא בתר בישתא	אחר [7]
" 10:6	אשר תרתי לכם	דיהבית לכון	נתתי לכם [8]
" 10:29	אשר אתם הבאים שם	דאתון אתן	אשר אתם באים [9]
" 12:12	פניו יכסה יען אשר לא יראה לעין היא את הארץ	חלף דחב הוא ולא יחזי ית ארעא	יען אשר לא יראה לעון את הארין [10]

1) Probably הלכתם was omitted in the text of the T. P. also omits it. Lxx omits the entire portion and begins with והתהלכתם Giesb. conjecture ונעתרתי by the T. is not justified.

2) Lxx has here the Ketib. P. omits it entirely. The reading זרמות by the T. is the only plausible explanation of the peculiar rendering of this word. שדמות is usually rendered by the T. by מישרא נחלא (1K 23:4; IS. 16:1). Com. Aruch אדייתא and אורתא.

3) Felt by Kimchi. Com. P.

4) So Lxx codd. 88, 106, P. In some MSS. לא is the Keri. Felt by Minchat Shai and Kimchi.

5) So A. Rashi follows it.

6) So P. Sym. Vulg. This is the Ketib to Madnechai, but this reading is to be found in many MSS. So in M'turgom of Eliahu Halevy under root קטף. He cites this verse reading אגדע.

7) Noticed by Kimchi.

8) So P., so Toy. was probably influenced by V. 15.

9) So Lxx P.

10) So P. Probably both of them read לעין (Com. Is. 18:9 etc.). On the other hand, we find this case עין Ketib and עון Keri (Com. 2S 16:12).

	M. T.	Targ.	R.
" 13:11	ואתנה אבני אלגביש	וית אבני אלגביש	ואת אבני אגלביש (1
" 13:21	את נפשים	ית נפשיהון	נפשם
" 14:8	ונחמתם על הרעה	על כל בישתא	על כל (2
" 14:22	מברחיו	גבורוהי	מבחריו (3
" 16:15	והשמותיהו	ואשויניה	והשימותיהו (4
	ולא כשר לך למעבד ותשפכי את זנותיך		
" 16:36	על כל עובר לו יהי	כך	לא יהי (5
" 17:21	וכדמי בניך אשר נתתי להם	ובחובת דם בנך	ובדמי בניך (6
" 18:17	מעני השיב ידו	ממסבוא לא אתיב ידיה	מעני לא השיב (7
" 19:7	וידע אלמנותיו	ואצרי בירניתיה	וירע ארמנותיו (8
" 21:19	חרב החדרת להם	דמזיעא להון	החרדת (9
" 21:21	התאחדי הימיני	אשתליפי וכו'	התחדי (10
" 21:21	השימי	ושיצי	בשין

---

1) Minchat Shai: ויונתן... נראה שהיה קורא ואת אבני אלגביש ;
Kimchi remarks that he found this reading in a MS.

2) So in some MSS. Caro l. c.

3) So Lxx, Syro Hex. and in five MSS. of Kenn. and De Rossi.

4) Noticed by Rashi and Kimchi; so also in Ald. Codd. 42, 68.

5) So P. and in some De Rossi MSS.

6) So P. and Vulg. and a great number of MSS.; the Afudi,
ch. 14, remarks: באה הכף תמורת הבית כארבע רוחות השמים (זכריה ב')
כרוח קדים (ירמיה י"ח, י"ז) כאשר ילכו (הושע ז', י"ב) כדמי בניך.

7) Probably interpretative, making the following לא referring to
מעני; also Lxx; so 28th middah of R. Eliezer. See Eliezer of Beaugency, who puts מעני עזל as an explanation of עזל. Com. Heller
על התר' הירוש.

8) So A. aliter et dimit palatium eorum. So EW. Toy וירע
Com. Kimchi. His point, however, is not clear. The T. rendering of
Jud. 8:16 ויודע is ותבב or וגבר as Kimchi had it or גרר as in Lag. or
ואלקי as cited in אבן בחן by Menachem b. Solomon.

9) So Lxx P. A. Vulg. was noticed also by Kimchi.

10) So is rendered הוחדה (v. 15). John d. Buch Ez. assumes it
represents a Syr. Ith. form.

	M. T.	Targ.	R.
" 24:26	בא הפליט אליך להשמעות אזנים	לאשמעותיך בסורא	להשמעותך 1)
" 26:2	אמלאה החרבה	דהות מליא חרובה	המלאה אמלאה 2)
" 26:20	כחרבות	בחרבתא	בחרבות 3)
" 27:6	בת אשרים	דפין דאשכרעין	בתאשר 4)
" 27:23	ונתתי יארים חרבה	ואתן נהריהון	יאריהם
" 30:12	אשור כלמד	אתור ומדי	כל מדי
" 34:26	ונתתי אתם וסביבות גבעתי	ואשרי יתהון סחור סחור	סביבות
" 39:16	וגם שם עיר המונה	ואף לתמן	שם
Hos. 4:18	סר סבאם	שלטוניהון אסגיאו	שר 5)
" 6:5	ומשפטיך אור יצא	ודיני כנהור נפיק	ומשפטי כאור יצא 6)
" 7:12	כשמע לעדתם	על דשמעו לעצתהון	עדותם 7)
" 8:5	זנח עגלך שמרון	טעו בתר עגלא	זנחו 8)
" 9:1	אל תשמח ישראל אל גיל בעמים	לא תחדון ולא תביעון	ואל גיל 9)
" 11:7	ואל על יקראהו	תערערון	יקראו 10)
" 12:1	ויהודה עוד רד עם אל ועם קדושים	עד דגלא עמא דאלהא, ואינון דהוו פלחין קדמי	עם אל... ועם קדושים 11)
	נאמן	מתקרן עמא קדישא	
" 13:10	אהי מלכך	או...	איה 12)

1) So Lxx P.

2) So Lxx; accepted by Co. Seeg. Gratz.

3) So Lxx P.

4) Com. Is. 41:19. Felt by Kimchi.

5) Felt by Kimchi.

6) So Lxx P. (Com. Nowack Die Kl. P.).

7) So Lxx P. רעתם (See Vollers Z. A. T. W., 1883, 250).

8) So P.

9) So Lxx P.

10) So P.

11) So Lxx P. Kimchi: ימי הגבעה שׁח"י עם אל כמי עם אל בפתח.

12) So Lxx P.

292

	M. T.	Targ.	R.
Am. 5:10	ושד על מבצר יבוא	ובזוזין... משליט	יביא (1
" 6:10	ומסרפו	מיקידא	מסרפו
Mi. 4:9	עתה למה תריעי רע	וכען למה את מתחברא	תרע רע (2
" 6:11	האזכה במאזני רשע	היזכון	היזבח (3
Nahum 2:3	כגאון ישראל	רבותיה לישראל	גאון
" 3:6	כראי	לעיני כל חזך	לראי (4
Zef. 3:18	אספתי ממך היו	... וי עליהון	הוי
Ze. 9:13	ועוררתי בניך ציון על בניך יון	ואגבר בנך ציון	ועודדתי (5
" 12:5	אמצה לי ישב ירושלם	אשתכח פרקן ליתבי ירושלם	אָמצא ליושבי ירושלם (6
" 14:5	ונסתם גיא הרי	ויסתתים	ונסתם (7
" 14:6	לא יהיה אור יקרות וקפאין	לא יהי נהורא אלהין עדי וגליד	וקרות (8
Mal. 2:5	ואתנם לו מורא	ויהבית	ואתן (9

---

1) So in some MSS. and Lxx P.

2) So Lxx, though in a different sense.

3) So Lxx P.

4) So Lxx P.

5) עורר לך רפאים (Is. 10:26) וייתי עלוהי ; ועורר עליו (Is. 14:9) אעירת.

6) The reading of the T. was probably אמצא found in many MSS. See Min. Shai.

7) So Sym. Ald. Codd. III, XII, 22, 23, 26. De Rossi found this reading in the Lxx. Kimchi וכן נמצא במקצת ספרים . So Kimchi ספר השרשים; also R. Eliah Halevy הגהת השרשים and Ibn Ezra pointing out this being the reading of אנשי המזרח . Com. Eich. Ein. V. 1, p. 419 (German Ed. 1787).

8) But com. Gen. 42:9 etc. See Rikmah on the change of Waw to Jod. Com. Sup. Am. 5:10.

9) So Lxx P.

GROUP B

	M. T.	Targ.	Following
Joshua 7:8	הפך ישראל ערף	קדלהון	אויבין 1)
" 8:14	והוא לא ידע כי אורב לו	ואינון לא ידעון ארי כמנא להון	וימהרו וישכימו וירוצו 2)
" 9:20	והחיה אותם	ונקים	זאת נעשה 3)
" 20:5	כי בבלי דעת	בלא מדעיה	הכה את רעהו
Judges 2:14	ביד שסים	בוזזיהון	ביד אויביהם לפני אויביהם
" 2:22	את דרך	אורחן דתקנן	ללכת בם 4)
" 20:37	והאורב החישו ויפשטו	אוחי ואתנגד	וימשך האורב ויך 5)
1S. 2:29	להבריאכם	לאוכלותהון	Implied 6)
" 6:4	כי מגפה אחת לכלם	לכולכון	ולסרניכם 7)
" 17:40	בכלי הרעים	ובתרמיליה	אשר לו וקלעו 8)
2S. 3:15	מעם איש	מלות בעלה	ויקחה 9)
" 23:5	וכל חפץ	וכל בעותי	כי כל ישעי 10)
1K. 8:46	לפני אויב	בעלי דבביהון	ונתתם
" 18:18	ותלך	ואזלתון	בעזבכם
" 21:11	כאשר כתוב	כמא דכתבת	אשר שלחה
2K. 19:4	ויפרשהו	ופרסינון	את הספרים
" 23:5	ויקטר	ואסיקו	אשר נתנו
IS 10:8	מנפש ועד בשר	נפשיהון עם פגריהון	יערו וכרמלו 11)
" 13:2	ויבא פתחי נדיבים	ויעלון בתרעהא	implied by context 12)
" 19:20	מפני לחצים	דחקיהון	וישלח להם... והצילם 13)

1) Also v. 12; so P.
2) Lxx put the whole in singular. So P.
3) So P.
4) Sbirin, followed by Lxx Lag. So P.
5) So Lxx P.
6) So P.
7) So P.
8) So P.
9) So Lxx P.
10) So P.
11) P. has it in the 2nd person. Com. Lxx.
12) P. in 2 p. f. 13) So Lxx.

	M. T.	Targ.	Following
" 21:14	בלחמו	לחמא דאתון אכלין	התיו
" 23:13	בחניו	חזותהא	ארמנתיה
" 26:8	אף ארח משפטיך קוינוך לשמך ולזכרך תאות נפש	לארח דינך סברנא לשמך ולדוכרנך תאות נפשנא	קוינוך [1]
" 26:9	נפשי אויתך... אף רוחי בקרבי אשחרך	נפשי מחמדא אף רוחי... מברכא לך	נפשי... רוחי [2]
" 26:19	יחיו מתיך נבלתי יקומון	גרמי נבלתהון	הקיצו ורננו [3]
" 30:11	סורו מני דרך הטו מני אורח	אסטיונא... אבטלונא	השביתו מפנינו [4]
" 30:13	בחומה נשגבה	כשור מתקף	כפרץ נפל
" 33:2	היה זרעם לבקרים אף ישועתנו בעת צרה	הוי תוקפנא... אף פורקננא	חננו... קוינו... ישועתנו [5]
" 33:3	מרוממתך נפצו גוים ורותה ארצם מדם	מסגי גבורן איתבדרו מלכותא	מקול המון [6]
" 34:7	ועפרם מחלב ידשן	ותרוי ארעהון מדמהון ועפרהון מתרבהון ידהן	ורותה ארצם ועפרם [7]
" 40:26	לכלם בשם יקרא	בשמהן	צבאם [8]
" 44:7	הבאתיו והצליח דרכו	ואצליחת	הבאתיו [9]
" 46:1	נשאתיכם	מטולי טעותהון	היו עצביהם

---

1) So P. Lxx. Rashi, Kimchi, Karo fellow this explanation.

2) So P.

3) So P.

4) So Lxx (see the difficult explanations of Kimchi).

5) So P.

6) P. puts for the same purpose המון in the 2nd p.

7) So Lxx. P. in מחלב only.

8) Lxx P. render in pl., influenced by Ps. 147:5.

9) So Lxx P.

	M. T.	Targ.	Following
`` 42:6	ולא יכלו מלט משא	נטליהון	ונפשם
`` 48:15	ומי כמוני יקרא	ומן כותי דין ערעינה	ויגדה ויערכה[1]
`` 51:8	כי בבגד יאכלם עש	ארי כלבושא דאכיל	כבגד...
	וכצמר יאכלם סם	ליה עשא וכעמרא	כצמר[2]
		דאחיד ביה רוקבא	
`` 57:15	מרום וקדוש אשכן	ברומא שרי וקדישא	וקדוש שמו[3]
		שכינתה	
`` 58:14	והרכבתיך... והאכלתיך	וישרינך... ויוכלינך	implied by context
Jer. 2:27	אומרים לעץ אבי אתה	אבונא את	ילדתנו
`` 7:24	במעצות	בעצתיהון	בשרירות לבם
`` 9:6	שבתך בתוך מרמה	יתבין בבית כנשתהון	במרמה מאנו
`` 10:4	במסמרות ובמקבות יחזקום	מתקיף ליה	ייפהו
`` 11:14	בעת קראם	בעידן דאת מצלי	אל תתפלל
`` 11:22	הבחורים ימותו בחרב בניהם ובנותיהם ימתו ברעב	עולמיהון יתקטלון	בניהם ובנותיהם[4]
Ez. 11:19	ונתתי להם לב אחד		
`` 11:22	ורוח חדשה... בקרבכם	ורוח דחילא אתן במעיהון	ונתתי להם[5]
`` 22:10	ערות אב גלה	גליאו	ענו בך[6]
`` 22:30	ועשתה גלולים עליה	בגוה	שפכת דם בתוכה

---

1) Lxx P. render them all in absolute.

2) So P.

3) So P. Lxx seem to have had an entirely different reading.

4) So Lxx.

5) So Lxx P. Sym. Vul.

6) So Lxx Sym.

		M. T.	Targ·	
"	23:40	ואף כי תשלחנה	ארי שלחת ועדית	רחצת כחלת...
"	26:11	לארץ תרד	ימגר	ירמס... יהרג
"	35:8	גבעותיך וגיאותיך וכל אפיקיך	ית רמתוהי וחילוהי וכל פצידוהי	הריו
"	35:10	שתי הארצות לי תהיינה וירשנוה	וארתינון	שתי הארצות[1]
"	36:20	ויבוא אל הגוים אשר באו שם	ועלו לביני עממיא	אשר באו[2]
		כאשר שממו עליך	ותארו כמה דסברו ליה	מראהו...
Hos.	10:1	כרב לפריו הרבה למזבחותיו כטוב לארצו הטיבו מצבות	אסגיאו פולחן לאגוריהון... קמתהון	לפריו... לארצו[3]
"	14:9	פריך	לתיובתהון	ואשורנו
Am.	2:3	והכרתי שופט	דינהא	וכל שריה
Mi.	5:4	עליו	עלנא	בארצנו... בארמנותינו... והקמנו
"	7:15	כימי צאתך	מפקהון	אראנו
Na.	2:14	רכבה	רתיכך	וכפיריך
"	3:7	מי ינוד לה	מן ידוי עלך	מנחמים לך[4]
Za.	14:5	ובא יהוה אלהי כל קדושים עמך	עמיה	ובא[5]

1) It is not necessary with Cor. (D. B. Ez.) to suppose a different reading by the T. Suggested by the text, the T. would not hesitate to render it as if it were in Hiph.

2) So P.; so also in Ez. 20:38; 23:44; Jerem. 51:36; Mi. 7:12, noticed by Min. Shai. In Masoreth Seder Sh'lach this is considered among those that are written in sing. and the Sebirin in pl. That the T. follows in a good many cases the Sebirin as well as the Madnechai was noticed by the Min Shai. (Com. Ez. 5:11; 13:17; 14:19; Min. Shai Jerem. 49:36; Mi. 7:12). In P'sichta Lam r. לא היה צריך קרא למימר אלא ויבואו אלא כביכול... So in many Kenn. MSS.

3) Lxx make למזבחות conform to מצבות. P. follows it closely.

4) So P. Lxx put all in the 3rd person. The reading of לך is found in many MSS.

5) So Lxx P. noticed also by Kimchi.

	M. T.	Targ.	Following
Mal. 2:15	ובאשת נעוריך אל יבגד	לא תשקד ...	ונשמרתם (1
" 2:16	כי שנא שלח... וכסה חמס על לבושו	ולא תכסי חטאה בלבושך	ברוחכם... תבגדו (2

GROUP C

. לא תדחל ולא תתבר אל תערץ ואל תחת Targum Joshua 1:9
. לא תדחל ולא תתבר On. לא תירא ולא תחת According to Deut. 31:8

. ואטמרתנון (3 Targum ותצפנו Joshua 2:4 . According to v. 6
. ותטמנם

. ית ארון קימא דיי (4 Targum שאו את ארון הברית Joshua 6:6
. וארון ברית יהוה According to v. 8

. קדם ארונא דיי (5 Targum לפני יהוה Joshua 6:8 . According
. לפני ארון יהוה to v. 7

. ואזדודו (6 Targum ויצטירו Joshua 9:4 . According to v. 12
. הצטידנו

. ובמשפך מרמתא Targum ובאשדות Joshua 12:8 . According
. אשדות הפסגה to 12:13

מתנן די יהב להון אינון Targum כהנת יהוה נחלתו Joshua 18:7
— יהוה אלהי ישראל הוא נחלתם According to 13:33 אחסנתהון
...מתנן די יהב להון .

לית לכון חולק Targum מה לכם ולי/ אלהי ישראל Joshua 22:24
במימרא . According to vv. 25, 27 ...אין לכם חלק .

כד אתרעיאו בני ישראל Targum יבחר אלהים חדשים Judges 5:8
למפלח לטעותא חדתין דמקרב אתעבידא דלא איתעסקו בהון אבהתכון.
אלהים חדשים מקרוב באו ולא שערום According to Deut. 32:17
אבתיכם .

1) So Lxx.

2) So Lxx.

3) Lxx in both places have ἔκρυψεν . Com. Jalqut l. c.

4) So P.

5) So P. V. and 4 MSS. and in 3 Kenn.

6) Many Kenn. and De Rossi MSS. read ויצטידו . So Lxx P.
Felt by Kimchi

דשרן בידיהון Targum (1 בשלשת מאות האיש המלקקים Judges 7:7
לפומהון . According to v. 6 ויהי מספר המלקקים אל פיהם .

חרבא דמקטלא Targum (2 ואמרתם ליהוה ולגדעון Judges 7:18
מן קדם . According to v. 20 ויקראו חרב לי' ולגדעון .

יטור דתנן Targum (3 משאת העשן Judges 20:38 According
to v. 40 יטור — עמוד העשן... .

והא סליק Targum והנה עלה כליל העיר השמימה Judges 20:40
שמיא לצית דקרתא תננא . According to Joshua 8:20 והנה עלה עשן
והא סליק תננא — העיר השמימה .

על... Targum והנה עלי ישב על הכסא יד דרך מצפה 1S 4:13
תרעא (4 כבש אורח . According to v. 18 על כבש אורח — בעד השער
תרעא .

ודמית חמוהא ודאתקטל Targum (5 ואל חמיה ואישה 1S 4:21
בעלה . According to v. 19 ודמית חמוהא — ומת חמיה ואישה
ודאתקטל בעלה .

ועד אבנא רבתא Targum (6 ועד אבל הגדולה 1S 6:18 . According to vv. 14, 15 האבן הגדולה .

המון משרית פלשתאי Targum (7 והנה ההמון נמוג 1S 14:16 .
According to v. 19 וההמון אשר במחנה פלשתים .

לשבחא בחנגיא Targum לשיר והמחלות 1S 18:6 . According to
21:12 (8 . משבחין בחנגיא — יענו במחולות

האית עוד גברא Targum (9 האפס עוד איש לבית שאול 2S 9:3 .
According to v. 1 האית — הכי יש עוד .

לקי בתרתין רגלוהי Targum נכה רגלים 2S 9:3 . According to
v. 13 לקי בתרתין רגלוהי — והוא פסח שתי רגליו .

---

1) So P. In some MSS. of the T. the words בידיהון לפומהון
are omitted

2) So P. In Lag. דמקטלא is omitted.

3) P. omits משאת .

4) So Lxx. Kimchi: ויונתן הוסיף בו שער שתרגם על כבש אורח
תרעא מסכי כמו שאמר בפסוק האחר בעד יד השער .

5) Com. Lxx.

6) So Lxx and many MSS.

7) So Lxx P.

8) In Lag. משמעין .

9) So Lxx P. Kimchi: ותמהתי למה תרגמו יונתן האית .

Targum (1 וישלח יואב את אוריה אל דוד 2S 11:6 ית אוריה חתאה.
According to the preceding את אוריה החתי .

Targum (2 בעבור הילד חי 2S 12:21 עד דרביא קים . According
בעוד הילד חי . to v. 22

Targum (3 עיר המים 2S 12:27 קרית מלכותא . According to
עיר המלוכה . v. 26

Targum ויצא המלך וכל העם 2S 15:17 ונפק מלכא וכל אנשי
ביתיה 4). Accordnig to v. 16 וכל ביתו וכל אנש ביתיה—ויצא המלך .

Targum שמרו מי בנער 2S 18:12 אסתמרו לי בעולימא .
According to v. 5 לאט לי לנער — אסתמרו לי בעולימא .

Targum מננה נגדו בערו נחלי אש 2S 22:13 כנומרין דנור
דלקא מימריה According to v. 9 (5 נחלים בערו ממנו—כנומרין דנור .
דלקא מימריה .

Targum (6 אשר נתן היום ישב על כסאי 1K 1:48 דיהב יומא דין
בר יתיב על כורסי . According to 3:6... ותתן לי בן ישב .

Targum (7 לא יפל משערתו 1K 1:52 משער רישיה . According
אם יפול משערת ראשו . to 1S 14:45

Targum (8 והבית הזה יהיה עליון 1K 9:8 וביתא הדין דהוה עילאי
עובר עליו ישם... According to 2 Ch. 7:21 יהי חרוב . והבית הזה אשר היה עליון לכל

Targum לית לנא (9 מה לנו חלק בדוד 1K 12:16 . According to
אין לנו חלק בדוד 2S 20:1 .

Targum (10 ולא תשתה מים 1K 13:9 ולא תשתי תמן מיא .Accord-
ולא תשתה שם מים . ing to v. 17

Targum ויהי בדבר הזה לחטאת 1K 13:34 והוה פתגמא הדין
ויהי הדבר הזה לחטאת . According to 12:13

Targum ומלך ארם צוה את שרי הרכב שלשים ושנים 1K 22:31
תלתין ותרין מלכון 11). According to 20:16 שלשים ושנים מלך .

---

1) So P. and in 2 MSS. Kenn.

2) So Lxx P. Com. Ehrlich, Randglossen.

3) So P. and in 2 MSS. Kenn.

4) In Lag. וכל עמא .

5) So Lxx P.

6) So P. Lag. ἔδωκε σήμερον ἐκ τοῦ σπερυματος μοῦ

7) So is the T. to 2S 14:11 משערת בנך . So P. here and in
2S 14:11. Lxx here only.

8) Com. P.

9) In Lag. מאלנא .

10) In Lag. תמן is omitted.

11) Literally in Lag.

According . סבהי אוביליה (1 Targum שאהו אל אמו 2K 4:19
. וישאהו ויבאהו v. 20 to

According to . מארע דרומא Targum מבעל שלשה 2K 4:42
. בארע דרומא — בארץ שלשה 1S 9:4

According . השלם (2 Targum כה אמר המלך שלום 2K 9:19
. כה אמר המלך השלום to v. 18

. אתו לותי (3 Targum מארץ רחוקה באו מבבל 2K 20:14
. ומאין יבואו אליך According to

. ואתקבר בגן עזא (4 Targum ויקבר בגן ביתו בגן עזא 2K 21:18
. בגן עזא According to v. 26

וכל אנש Targum וכל איש יהודה וכל ישבי ירושלם 2K 23:2
ירושלם . According to 2 Ch. 34:3 וכל איש יהודה ויתבי ירושלם
. ירושלם

. ברם על דארגזי קדם י׳ (5 Targum אך על פי י׳ 2K 24:3
. כי על אף According to v. 20

לא בחים . According IS. 10:7 ולהכרית גוים לא מעט Targum לא בחים
. לאספא עממין לא בחים — להרג גוים לא יחמול to Hab. 1:17

וישתארון ביה Targum ונשאר בו עללות כנקף זית IS. 17:6
. עוללין כביעור זיתא... כן ישתארו יחידאין צדיקיא בגו עלמא בין מלכותא
According to 24:13 כי כה יהיה בקרב הארץ בתוך העמים כנקף זית
. ארי כדין ישתארון יחידאין צדיקיא... —

. כל דאשתכח ביך יתקטל (6 Targum כל נמצאיך אסרו יחדו IS. 22:3
. כל די ישתכח בה יתקטל — כל הנמצא ידקר According to 13:15

בעדנא ההיא ישבחון Targum ביום ההוא יושר השיר הזה IS. 26:1
. שירו לי׳ שיר חדש (7 . According to 42:10 תושבחתא חדתא

האפשר דיימר טינא Targum כי יאמר מעשה לעשהו IS. 29:16
. היאמר חמר ליצרו According to 45:9 לעבדיה

---

1) So P. Com Lxx.

2) Com. P. Lxx εἰ εἰρηνη

3) So Lxx P. לותי is omitted in Lag.

4) Com. Lxx. Both are rendered in Lag.

5) So Lxx. Com. P.

6) The whole phrase is omitted in Lxx and P.

7) In Lag. הדא .

בדיל עובדיכון בישיא Targum רוחכם אש תאכלכם IS. 33:11
— וסערה כקש תשאם According to 40:24   מימרי כעלעולא לקשא
ומימריה כעלעולא לקשא[1] .

מי פעל ועשה קרא הדרות מראש אני יהוה ראשון ואת IS. 41:4
מן אמר אילין קים אמר ועביד... אנא ברית[2] Targum אחרונים אני הוא
עלמא מבראשית ואף עלמי עלמיא דילי אינון בר מני לית אלהא .
אני ראשון ואני אחרון ומבלעדי אין אלהים   According to 44:6 —
אנא הוא דמלקדמון אף עלמי עלמיא...[3] .

רשיעיא דאינון כחרשין הלא Targum החרשים שמעו IS. 42:18
וחרשים ואזנים למו According to 43:8 . אודנין לכון שמעו .

ובמקובין מתקיף ליה Targum ובמקבות יצרהו IS. 44:12
ובמקבין מתקיף ליה — ובמקבות יחזקום[4] According to Jer. 10:4 .

לא עבדתני Targum היאמר חמר ליצרו מה תעשה IS. 45:9
כי יאמר מעשה לעשהו לא עשני According to 29:16 .

לעלם אהי תקיפת מלכן Targum לעולם אהיה גברת IS. 47:7
תקיפת מלכון — לא תוסיפי יקראו לך גברת ממלכות According to v. 5 .

קריבא זכותי Targum קרוב מצדיקי IS. 50:8 . According to
קריבא זכותי — קרוב צדקי 51:5 .

ואביט ואין עזר ואשתומם ואין סומך ותושע לי זרעי IS. 63:5
וידיע קדמי ולית איש דיקום ויבעי עליהון Targum וחמתי היא סמכתני
According to . ופרקתינון בדרע תוקפי ובמימר רעותי סעדתינון
וידיע קדמוהי ולית אנש דיקום — וישתומם כי אין מפגיע   59:16
ויבעי עליהון ופרקינון בדרע תוקפיה ובמימר רעותיה סעדינון .

לאיתי לסוברא Targum ואת חמת יהוה נלאיתי הכיל Jer. 6:11
— ונלאיתי כלכל לא אוכל According to 20:9 . ולא יכילית למשפך
ולאיתי לסוברא ולא יכילית .

סברנא לשלם Targum קוה לשלום Jer. 8:15 . According to
סברנא לשלם — מדוע הכיתנו... 14:19 .

---

1)   It renders this way Is. 41:16:   וסערה תפיץ אותם
בעלעולא לקשא . In Lag. לקשא is omitted.

2)   So the T. renders Is. 40:12, seemingly for their similar beginning and contents.

3)   So, for the same reason, it renders 43:10: כי אני הוא לפני
אנא הוא דמלקדמין... — לא נוצר אל .

4)   See Jerem. 10:4. The rendering there was influenced by the
sequel, but the influence in this case might have been reciprocal, so
that the v. was put in the same p. in accordance with the verse here.

בכספא ובדהבא חפי ליה Targum בכסף ובזהב ייפהו . Jer. 10:4
According to Is. 40:19 ([1] . מחפי ליה — וצרף בזהב ירקענו .

Jer. 10:4 ולא יפיק Targum דלא יצטלי . According to Is.
40:20, 41:7 ([2] . דלא יצטלי — לא ימט .

Jer. 30:15 אנוש מכאבך Targum ממרעא מחתיך . According
to v. 12 . ממרעא מחתיך — נחלה מכתך .

Jer. 31:9 בבכי יבאו ובתחנונים אובילם Targum ברחמין סגיאין
אקרבינון . According to Is. 54:7 וברחמים גדולים אקבצך . וברחמין —
סגיאין אקרב .

Jer. 32:35 אשר לא צויתים ולא עלתה על לבי Targum דלא פקדית
באוריתי . According to 7:31 ([3] . אשר לא צויתי ולא עלתה על לבי —
דלא פקדית באוריתי .

Jer. 33:3 ואגידה לך גדולות ובצרות Targum רברבן ונטירן .
According to Is. 48:6 ([4] . ונטירן — ונצרות ולא ידעתם .

Jer. 41:15 וילך אל בני עמון Targum ואזל למיעבר לוה .
בני עמון . According to v. 10 . וילך לעבר אל בני עמון —

Jer. 46:8 יעלה אכסה ארץ Targum אחפי ארעא ומלאה .
According to 47:2 . ויבזון ארעא ומלאה — וישטפו ארץ ומלואה .

Jer. 48:4 נשברה מואב Targum איתברת מלכות מואב . According to 48:25 . מלכות מואב — נגדעה קרן מואב .

Ez. 11:19 ונתתי להם לב אחד ורוח חדשה אתן בקרבם Targum
ואתן לכון — לב חדש . According to 36:26 ([5] . ואתן להון לב דחיל .
לב דחיל .

---

1) So P. Rashi; Kimchi etc. curiously combine both readings.
F. Perles in J. Q. R., v. 18, p. 388, would read here יצפהו and refers
to Is. 30:22; so Kittel, both of whom refer to the T. not appreciating
the principle followed in this case. So also in Jerem. 10:19, and
curiously enough, P. there renders ירקענו in the same way as וייפהו .

2) So Lxx, except in Is. 40:20.

3) Lxx read there צויתים as here.

4) Minchat Shai sees another reading by the T. and goes so far
as to think that Rashi, who follows the T., has also had the same
reading. But Rashi does it in numerous instances where such an assumption is out of question. Kimchi remarks: וי"ת רברבן ונטירן, היה
קורא ונצורות בנו"ן .

5) Also 18:31. So P., felt by Minchat Shai. Curiously, this reading appears also in the com. of Eliezer of Beaugency (published by
Posnansky, 213). So is the reading in 3 Kenn. MSS. and 1 De Rossi.

Ez. 17:5 ויהביה בחקל טוב Targum ויתנהו בשדה זרע. According
ing to v. 8 [1] בחקל טוב — אל שדה טוב.

Ez. 29:3 דילי מלכותא ואנא Targum לי יארי ואני עשיתני כבשית. According to v. 9 [2] מלכותא — יאר לי ואני עשיתי.
דילי ואנא כבשית.

Ez. 29:6 סמך קניא רעיעא Targum יען היותם משענת קנה. According to Is. 36:6 סמך קניא רעיעא — הקנה הרצוץ.

Ez. 30:18 כעננא דסליק וחפי ית Targum היא ענן יכסנה ארעא. According to 38:16 [3] כעננא — כענן לכסות הארץ.
דסליק וחפי ית ארעא.

Ez. 31:14 עם נחתי גוב בית אבדנא Targum אל יורדי בור. According to 32:18, 24 את יורדי בור.

Ez. 31:15 ביום אחתותי Targum ביום רדתו שאולה. According
ing to v. 16 באחתותי יתיה — בהורידי אתו שאלה.

Ez. 32:5 ויתמלון חיליא Targum ומלאתי הגיאיות. According
to v. 6 [4] יתמלון — ואפקים ימלאון.

Ez. 32:18 לארעא ארעיתא Targum אל ארץ תחתיות. According
ing to 31:14 [5] לארעא ארעיתא — אל ארץ תחתית.

Ez. 32:24 דאיתמסירו לתבר Targum אשר נתנו חתיתם. According
ing to v. 23 אשר נתנו חתית.

Ez. 34:24 ועבדי דוד מלכא [6] Targum ועבדי דוד נשיא בתוכם. According to 37:24 ועבדי דוד מלך עליהם.

Ez. 36:12 ואסגי עליכון [7] Targum והולכתי עליכם אדם. According to vv. 10, 11 ואסגי עליכון — והרביתי עליכם אדם.

Ez. 41:17 על מעל הפתח Targum עד לעילא. According
to v. 20 מהארץ עד מעל הפתח.

---

1) As to the change in person, com. De Rossi V. L. V. T., l. c.

2) P. reads יאר: Lxx have v. 9 as in v. 3.

3) It also influenced Jer. 46:8.

4) Lxx have in v. 6 as in v. 5. Kittel wonders if the reading
was not ונמלאו.

5) So 26:20 בארץ תחתית.

6) Lxx have in 37:24 as in 34:24. Lag has here רבא.
However, in 37:25 the T. stands alone.

7) Ehrlich Ez. finds support in this rendering of the T. that it
is used here in the sense of increase, as in Jerem. 12:2. Equally wrong
is Jahn, ascribing a different reading to the T.

. וימשחון ית טפוסיה Targum ומדדו את תכנית   Ez. 43:10
According to v. 11   (1   . צורת הבית ותכונתו

ממון יקרהון מנהון Targum ממול שלמה אדר תפשיטון   Mi. 2:8
ממון יקרהון — ועורם מעליהם הפשיטו   According to 3:3   . נסבין
. מנהון נסבין (2

לתחות פרי Targum אל תחת גפן ואל תחת תאנה   Ze. 3:10
איש תחת גפנו   According to 1K 5:5   . גופנוהי ולתחות פרי תינוהי
. ותחת תאנתו

ואשרי בבית מקדשי... Targum וחניתי לבית מצבה   Ze. 9:8
ואני אהיה   According to 2:9   . כשור דאשא מוקף לה סחור סחור
. כשור דאשא מקף לה סחור סחור — לה חומת אש

. וי על פרנסא טפשא Targum הוי רעי האליל   Ze. 11:17
According to v. 15   רעה אוילי — פרנסא טפשא .

---

1) So P.

2) Lxx read in 2:8 עור as in 33. So P.

THE EXEGESIS IN JONATHAN

The exegetical nature of T. Jonathan is in a conspicuous manner emphasized in the report of the Talmud: 'Said R. Jeremia, others say R. Hiyya b. Abba, Targum to the Prophets Jonathan b. Uziel said it. And Eretz Israel trembled 400 para-sangs. A Bath Kol said: Who is the one who revealeth my mysteries to the children of men? Rose Jonathan b. Uziel and said: I am the one who revealeth Thy mysteries to the children of men. It is reavealed and known unto you that . . . I did it for Thy sake in order that strife may not abound in Israel." To the question why no such occurrence accompanied the act of the Targum to the Pentateuch, the ans-wer is given: "The Pentateuch is clear while the Prophets con-tain things some of which are clear, while others are ob-scure." [1]

Framed as this report is in the characteristic phraseology of the Agada it serves not only to demonstrate the prevalent view of the age as to the principal characteristic of the T. to the Prophets, its main value resting in the exegesis, but is instructive also in that it manifests the worshipful rever-ence in which the exegesis was held. It was regarded as mysteries which should not, except for a weighty reason as alleged by Jonathan, he disclosed to the uninitiated in holi-ness. It does, however, in no way indicate the nature of the exegesis. There is nothing of the mystical in it. It is governed by rules and based on principles of a kind placing it in the domain of logical hermeneutics.

The general underlying principle in the exegesis of T. Jonathan consists in an attempt to render intelligible to the fullest possible degree that which is obscure. To accomplish this the targumist does not resort to the undersense. It is the sense, the explicit and simple, which is fundamental in the exege-

---

1) Meg. 3a; Yerushalmi 1, 10.

78

sis. The object of the targumist was to translate the poetical mind of the Prophet into the lay-mind behind it. In other words, to the targumist the implication rather than the surface literalness of the passage or word involved is of chief consideration. It is, on the one hand, a desire to correctly understand the prophet,[2] and on the other hand, to make the author intelligible to others.[3] Passages which are untouched by the exegesis of the targumist, the reason is to be sought in the assumption that the passage in question was not obscure to the generation of the targumist. In determining the general nature of the exegesis of this Targum a few salient points call for recording at the outset. In the first place, the targumist in no way dismisses any passage or word unrendered due to its embarrassing nature as is frequently the case in the Lxx and P. Whether or not the targumist is assured of having found a plausible. escape or is resorting to some hopelessly obscure paraphrase, he is not evading it. On the other hand, it should be noticed that the T. appears entirely unaffected in his translation. He is not preoccupied with any particular thought, or hypothetical idea, "which assumes a connection in the train of thought which does not appear on the surface", as was the case with the Agada, Philo and the Church Fathers.[4] The aim he set for himself was translation; nothing beyond it. The targumist is inclined, however, in certain cases to parallelism of circumstances, as is the case with the Agada.

One thing, however, stands forth as peculiarly remarkable. It would appear the targumist had little regard for the historical reality of the prediction. With few exceptions he manifests no interest in the particular historical period or event of the prophecy. There is a strong inclination on the part of the targumist to shift the predicted reality to the Messianic age whenever the contents admit of such a presentation. He is this way interpreting the prophecies of "consola-

---

2) Com. Scheleiermacher, Hermenutik, etc. (ed. 1838), p. 3.
3) Immer, Hermenentik (ed. 1877), p. 10.
4) The case with the Agada needs no illustration. It constitutes one of its fundamental bases (com. particularly Maimonides preface to Seder Zerai'm end 2nd part). As to the Apostles, com. Epistle of James 2:21; Rom. 10:17.

tion" which his age of national depression and political de-
jection would hardly regard as already accomplished.[5]
In addition, there is the poetical side of the prophecy, its
overflowing richness of expression and exuberance of color in
portrayal which are not susceptible of realization, but which
were, in the belief of the people, unaware of this fact, to be
inevitably translated into reality.   Hence the tendency to
interpret the glowing description of the "consolation" in
Messianic terms. [6]   The Messianic tone is made audible
also in the prominence given in his exegesis to the
"righteous ones". In a good many instances no other reason
except to give Messianic sense to a phrase, is evident.[7] But
of significance is also the introduction of the wicked side by
side with the righteous.   In this way the M e s s i a n i c
description is complete. The Messianic epoch, as is generally
known, is in its final form rather religious and individual than
political, national. The righteous and the wicked, not the nation and nations, are the object of its justice. Finally, the
Messianic tendency has found its expression in the targumist
references to Gehenna. In the chapter on "General Peculiarities"
it will be pointed out that the Gehenna referred to by this Targum is the Messianic doom.

The major principles of the exegesis of the Targum can
be placed under four headings; namely, the allegorical, the
metaphorical, the complement and the lexical. The allegorical
shall be considered first.

The allegorical method was employed in the Agada and
by Philo, and to a larger extent by the Apostles and latter
Church Fathers.[8] But it is to be noticed that the targumist

---

5) Com. Am. 9:1; Ze. 11:7-11, particularly v. 10. On the other
hand, com. Ze. 6:5—the "four kingdoms" are not called by name.

6) Com. Is. Ch. 9, 11, 12, 6-5; Jer. 23:3-9; Hos. 6:1-4; 14:15,
etc.

7) Com. Is. 24:19-18; 25:4-5 ; Ch. 32; 33:13; Jer. 23:28; Hab.
2:4; 3:2, etc.

8) The two former need no illustration. With regard to the N. T.,
Jesus himself was addicted to it (Com. Mat. 21:42, Luk. 4:16-22). With
regard to Heb. Ch. 8, Riehm (Lehrb. p. 204, ed 1867) remarks: "The
author leaves out of consideration the historical meaning of Old Testament passages."

confines the application of this method to passages which garb
an implication. Whether or not he strikes the right point
he is distinctly approaching it. He is making no strange and
artificial combinations. In most cases his exposition falls in
line with the Agadic interpretation.

The larger portions treated allegorically by the T. are
Ez. 16, Hos. 1:2, 5, 6, 8; 3, 1-4. Ch. 16 in Ez. is turned by
the T. into a reahearsal of the History of Israel: ". . . your
habitation and your birth was in the land of the Canaanites,
there I was revealed to your father Abraham between the
pieces (Gen. 15:9-18) and I announced to him that you shall
descend into Egypt, (and that) I (shall) deliver you with an
uplifted arm, and on account of your ansectors I (will) expell
from before you the Amorites and destroy the Hitites. And
then your ancestors descended into Egypt, inhabitants in a
land which is not theirs, enslaved and oppressed. . . . The eye
of Pharaoh did not pity you, to render unto you one generous
act, to give you respite from your bondage, to have mercy on
you, and he decreed concerning you ruinous decrees to throw
your male children in the river to destroy you, while you were
in Egypt. And the rememberance of the covenant of your
ancestors came before me and I was revealed to deliver you,
for it was divulged before me that you were oppressed in your
bondage, and I said unto you by the blood of circumcision I
will pity you, and I said unto you on account of the blood of
the Passover (sacrifice) I will redeem you. And I was revealed unto Moses in the bush, for you, and I put off your
sins and swore to deliver you as I swore to your ancestors,
in order that you shall be a people serving before me. And
I delivered you from the bondage of the Egyptians. And I
lead you (forth) in freedom. And I clothed you with painted
garments from the riches of your enemies (Exod. 14:21)
and I sanctified priests from your midst to serve before me. . .
And I reformed you in the reform of the words of the Law
written on two tablets of stone and (which) I gave them
through Moses. And I gave in your midst the Ark of My
covenant and the cloud of My Glory on you and an Angel
sent from before Me leads at your head. And I gave My
Tabernacle in your midst fitted out with gold . . . and you be-

came very rich and very powerful and you prospered and ruled over all kingdoms."

Whether this exposition is right is open to question. The portion beginning with v. 7 may refer to the Kingdom of Solomon as well. But that it was allegorically framed is evident, and the T. only follows the current interpretation traceable in the Agada.[9] On the other hand, it should be noticed, the targumist asserts the dependence of his exposition on the text. On the whole, however, it runs like a Midrashic treatise. The phraseology is free in the use of parenthetical phrases and synonyms.[10] The textual form is paid little heed.[11]

Hosea, 1:2-5, 8; 3:1-4, comprising the command of God and the action on the part of Hosea to take to himself "a wife of whoredom", are interpreted in the T. allegorically. Accordingly, the rendering is put in this way: "Go and prophesy on the inhabitants of the city of the idols who increase in sin (v. 2). And he went and prophesied to them that if they repent they will be pardoned, and if not they will fall like the falling of the leaves of a fig tree (גמר בת דבלים) and they increased and committed evil deeds (vv. 3, 6, 8) and their generation, exiled among the peoples, were not acceptable (רחימין) in their deeds. And God spoke to me again: Go and prophesy on Israel who resemble a woman who is beloved of her husband and betrays him (3:1). And I redeemed them on the fifteenth of Nisan, and I put the Shekel as atonement

---

9) The interpretation of the T. as a whole is in full agreement with the Agada. It is generally accepted that this passage refers to the deliverance from Egypt (com. Sota 11b). V. 6, which the targumist refers the repeated בדמיך חיי to the blood of circumcision and Passover, is so interpreted in Seder Eliahu r. 25 (p. 138 F.); Mechilta 21,5; Pesiqta r, 15 F. (Com. Note 46). On the other hand, the interpretation of v. 10 as referring to the booty of the drowned Pharaoh is applied by the Agada to v. 7 (Mechilta), while v. 10 is interpreted as referring to the priestly garments and to the Mishkan (com. Jalqut l. c.). To the latter the T. refers v. 13, while it agrees with the former. In the interpretation of v. 11 the T. is in accord with the Agadaist (ibid).

10) Com. particularly vv. 4, 7.

11) Com. vv. 4, 5, 6, 10.

for themselves and I said that they shall bring before Me the Omer of the offering from the produce of barley." (v. 3).[12]

The allegorization in this case is somewhat peculiar. The text requires the literal conception of the act which, in its fulfilment, carries both the situation and reality of the prediction. It was taken in the literal sense by the Agada.[13] That some agadist, however, would have it allegorically interpreted and that the T. is following his interpretation is fairly certain.[14] The reason, however, for the exposition can only be the horror the targumist must have felt at the supposition that the prophet would be told by God to take a harlot to wife. The absence of such a cause is probably the reason why Zech. 6:1-9 is rendered literally.

The Servant of God is by the T. identified with the Messiah, whose approaching appearance has been expected by his contemporaries. That being the case, the allegorization on the same lines of Is. 53 must follow as a self evident result. This had been the case with all those adhering to the allegorization of the Servant of God. But the targumist is strikingly

---

12) Com. Chull 92b: "And I bought her for me for fifteen pieces of silver", R. Jonathan said: .. . for fifteen (means) this is the fifteen Nissan, when Israel was redeemed from Egypt." So Pesiqta 15. On the other hand, the latter part of the verse is interpreted differently (ibid).

13) Com. note 18. Com. Pesiqta on 3:3: תניא ר' חייא אומר : לא תזני לא תעשה פסל : ולא תהיי לאיש לא יהיו לך אלהים אחרים. Com. P'sachim 87a end. "The Holy One Blessed Be He said to Hosea: 'Thy children sinned', and he should have said: 'They are Thy chiuldren, the children of Thy favored ones, Abraham, Isaac, and Jacob, show Thy mercy to them'. Not only did he not say so, but said, 'exchange them for another people'. Said the Holy One, Blessed Be He: 'What shall I do to this aged one? I'll say to him: Go and take for yourself a harlot and have for you harlot children, and then I'll say to him, send her away from your presence; if he can send (her away), I also will send away Israel. For it is said: and the Lord said to Hosea, etc." The Agada goes on to tell that after two sons were born to him God intimated to him that it would be proper for him to divorce her. Upon which Hosea refused to comply and God then said to him: "If this be the case with your wife, being a harlot, and thy children being children of whoredom, and you know not whether they are yours or belong to others, how should it be with Israel," etc.

14) Com. Jalqut l. c.

singular. Assured that this prediction is about the Messiah, the targumist reverses the simple meaning of the words, transforming the gloomy portraiture of the Messiah into an image of magnificence and splendor, unlike the Agadist contemporaries, who would rather play thoughtfully on the humbleness and sufferings of the Messiah.[15] He was influenced by the great national movements of his time, which assumed a Messianic character. So, while he would, seemingly with this end in view, change in 52:14 the p. only as if Israel and not the Messiah is the object, he actually rewrites ch. 53, replacing it by one bearing no resemblance to the original.

Instead of the Messiah being regarded as of no form, no comeliness, of no beauty (v. 2), he becomes one of extraordinary appearance, differing from the appearance of the former Davidic Kings, his terror unlike that of the profane king; for his countenance will be a holy countenance. Whoever will see him will gaze at him (v. 3). Describing how he was despised, rejected and a man of sorrow, he makes it refer to the kingdoms whose glories will be destroyed by the Messiah. So, the rendering of the T. runs: "For our sins he will supplicate and our transgressions will be pardoned on account of him. We are considered stricken and oppressed from before the Lord." Note the rendering of v. 5: "And he will build the Temple, which was desecrated through our sins, delivered to the enemies for our transgressions, and through his teaching peace will abound for us, and by our gathering of his words our sins will be forgiven to us." In this spirit the rendering is carried on to the end of the chapter.

THE METAPHOR

Prophecy is clothed in the magnificent form of poetry. It directs its thoughts in a superfluity of imagery. The overcoming force with which the prophet perceived his vision and the vehemence with which, "like a fire," it is impelled to come forth, make the metaphor the instrumentality of prophetical

---

15) Com. San. 98a, Pesiqta Rabati 36.

speech. It is addressed in terms of nature and natural phenomena, leaving the emphatic to the layman to unveil and distinguish. The targumist made it a principle to render not the metaphor but what it represents, the event described and not the descrip- tion. It is the purpose which is of chief import to him. In a way this is with him rather a principle of translation, as in most cases there can be no claim to exegetical examination.

The parabolic metaphor is the prophetic parable which resolves itself less in event than in metaphorical presentation. The T. instead of giving the literal rendering of such a parable renders its underpoetical parallel, thus stripping it of its para- bolic nature.

Except for the substitution of the simple for the meta- phorical, the T., as a rule, in these cases keeps closely to the text stylistically as well as grammatically and synthetically. Exceptions to this rule are Is. 5:1-3; 5-7. The substitute is the one made obvious by the text, with the exception, again, of the parable in Is. 5, where somewhat far-fetched substitutes are used. Otherwise the T. will introduce its equivalent by the short phrase דהוה דמא "which is equal", and insert, where such is required for better understanding, a complementary word or phrase.

A few verses of each case of the parabolic metaphor will sufficiently illustrate the application of this principle. This will best be accomplished by placing the rendering of the T. side by side with the original.

Ez. 19:3, 6

V. 3

T.	H.
And she brought up one of her children, he became a king, and he learned to kill, killing, men he killed.	And she brought up one of her whelps, he became a young lion, and he learned to catch the prey, he de- voured men.

V. 6

T.	H.
And he went up and down among the kings, he became a king and he learned to kill, killing, men he killed.	And he went up and down among the lions, he became a young lion; and he learned to catch the prey; he devoured men.

Ez. 23:2, 5

V. 2

Son of man prophesy on two cities which are like two w o m e n who were the daughers of one mother.	Son of man, there were two women, the daughters of one mother.

V. 5

And Ohlah erred from my worship and she was wilful to err after her lovers, the Assyrians, her near ones.	And Ohlah played the harlot when she was mine, and she doted on her lovers, on the Assyrian warriors.

Ez. 31:3-15, however, is rendered by the T. in a more detached manner. This is due to the fact that while it constitutes a similitude it is framed as a comparative metaphor. Assyria is here likened to a cedar in Lebanon, around which turns the entire description. The T., translating it as a description of the greatness and strength of Assyria according to the implication, had to change the p. as well as the number. Otherwise it keeps the rendering in line with the original.

The poetical metaphor, forms of expression given in objects of nature, is treated in the same manner by the T., namely, the object represented by the description is rendered. In this case also closeness to the original is observed, while a circumscription of phraseology is predominantly maintained. But, as if it were a concession on the targumist's part to the poetical element in prophecy, the insertion, "it is equal", "like", is, with few exceptions, not employed in such cases. Examples of this sort are: Is. 2:13: "And upon all the cedars of Lebanon that are high and lifted up, and upon all the oaks of Bashan." The T. renders it: "And upon all the princes (רברביא) of the strong and powerful and upon all the tyrants (טורני) of the lands (מדינתא); or Is. 9:9: "The bricks are fallen, but we will build with hewn stones; the sycamores are cut down, but cedars will be put in their place." T.: "The chiefs were exiled but better ones we will appoint, property (נכסיא) was spoiled, and more excellent we will buy." Other examples of this sort are: Is. 10:18, 19; Ez. 9:4, 5; Hos. 7:9; Joel 2:25 etc. Finally, the targumist is not consistent in the selection of the substitute figures. (Com. רעים Jer. 2:8; Ze. 11:3 rendered by מלכיא , while in Ez. 34:2, 5, 7 etc., it is rendered by פרנסיא (עצים Ez. 24:5 and 24:10). The rendering of the T of the comparative metaphor, i. e., the metaphor employed expressly for comparison, rests on the same basis, but it is effected in a different way, namely, both the literal and the implied rendering of the metaphor in question is given. An illustration of this sort of rendering is Is. 28:2: "Behold, the Lord hath a mighty and strong one. As a storm of hail, a tempest of destruction. As a storm of mighty waters overflowing, that casteth down to the earth with violence," which the T. renders: "There is a mighty and powerful stroke coming from the Lord as a storm of hail, as a tempest, as a storm of mighty waters overflowing so will peoples come upon them and will exile them in another land for their sins." Other examples are Is. 8:6, 7; 17:6; Jer. 2:24. In this particular instance the T. introduces the necessary complement which the poetical language implies.

In other cases the T. assumes a comparative metaphor and renders it accordingly, the literal is then put after the implied one and the comparative דכן or כ is inserted. Instances of this sort are numerous. Com. Ez. 2:6; Hos. 8:7; 10:71, 16; 12:2 etc.[16]

---

16) As to the scope of the application of the metaphorical princile it should be noticed that although applied in full measure of persistency, it still has a multitude of exceptions. These excetions occur particularly in those parts of the Prophets where the T. is predominantly

The symbolic expression is rendered in the T. in its simple sense, as the text would indicate. No comparative is employed. Instances of this sort are Is. 6:6; Ez. 2:8; 3:1, 2, 3. Some meta-phorical expressions are rendered allegorically by the T., in which the T. is following a Midrashic course. The rendering is free in every respect. An instructive example of this sort is Am. 4:14: "That maketh the morning darkness and treadeth upon the high places of the earth." Targum: "To set light to the pious like the light of the morning, which is setting, to bring darkness to the wicked, to break the wicked of the land." Other examples are Is. 42:11, 57:16; Am. 8:13.

A principle extensively applied in the T. is one that may be described as the exegetical complement. This, in the first place, was intended to fill the gaps created by the poetical contraction of the prophetical style. In some cases a complement is dictated by the sense of the passage. This will be fairly well demon-strated by the following passages:

Mal. 1:4: "Whereas Edom saith we are impoverished but we will return and build." The sense of this passage requires some linking word between "impoverished" and the rest, as being impoverished, it is impossible to build. In order to fill this gap, the T. renders it this way: "We are impoverished **now we are enriched** we will return," etc.

Jer. 17:4 ‏ושמטתה ובך מנחלתך‎ the shortcomings of this pas-sage need not be pointed out. (Com. Lxx and particularly P. on this v.). The T. supplies both ‏ובך‎ and ‏מנחלתך‎ with com-plements to fill the gap, rendering: "And to you I shall render a **punishment of judgment** until I **shall exile you from your in-heritance**." Com. also Is. 10:15; Hos. 2:15; Ez. 7:13; 16:29; 38:14 etc. In other cases the passage is supplemented by the T. with a view to simplify it where such a step is considered necessary. Here are some examples: Ez. 20:29: "What is the high place whereunto ye go," which is supplemented in the T.: "whereunto ye go **to make yourself foolish**" (worshipping the idol). Hos. 2:1: "The number of the children of Israel

---

literal. Com. Jer. 51:13; Ez. 34:4; Joel 2:2, 3; 3-6; Am. 3:12, 15; 5:19; Mi. 4:7, and a few others.

shall be as the sand of the sea." The T. inserting a complement renders it: "Shall be **numerous** as the sand," etc. Other cases of this category are: Ez. 20:9; 33:24; 44:19; Hos. 2:11, 16; 8:1 etc. The T. again is inclined to provide the substantive for the pronoun in cases where it is not sufficiently obvious. Three passages from Ez. will serve the purpose of illustration. Ez. 1:4: "And out of the midst thereof." This pronoun the T. substitutes by the noun rendering: "And out of the midst **of the cloud and out of the midst of the whirlwind"** (both of which are mentioned in the v.). Ibid v. 13: "It went up and down" etc. The T. replaces the "it" by the fire. Ibid. 29:5: "Upon the field shall **it** (taking the 3rd p.) fall." Targum: "Thy corpse shall be thrown." (Com. also Ez. 45:8; Jer. 6:1.)[17]

Repetition of the same word or of identical words, considered as one of the principles governing the exegesis of Philo,[18] affords the targumist a cause for introducing an exegetical complement, thus transforming the single word into a clause. The obvious reason for this, it would appear, is the disregard of the targumist of the poetical chord of prophecy so persistently insisted upon by the T. in each exegetical turn. He was unable to resist the conviction, so effective with the Halaka and Agada, that each of the repeated words must possess independent significance and carry independent implication. However, he is not explaining it but complementing the repeated word, heading, as a rule, the clause. Here are a few illustrations: Is. 6:3: "Holy, holy, holy is the Lord of Hosts." Targum: "Holy (is He) in the high lofty heavens, the house of His Shekina; holy on the earth the work of His strength; holy in the world of worlds." Jer. 7:4: "The temple of the Lord, the temple of the Lord, the temple of the Lord are these." Targum: "Before the temple

---

17) An interesting case presents Is. 28:10. The complement is supplied in an ingenious way to obviate the difficulty in this verse. The rendering runs: "For they were commanded to observe the Law and they were commanded (to do) they wanted not to do, and prophets prophesied to them . . . and the words of the prophets they did not accept." Observe: לצו is treated thus לא צו and so with לקו.

18) Com. Siegfried, Philo, etc., p. 168, put by Briggs (Biblical Study, p. 306) in group II.

of the Lord ye worship, before the temple of the Lord ye sacrifice, before the temple of the Lord you bow three times through
the year." Com. Is. 2:19; Jer. 22:29; Ez. 16:23; 21:14;
36:3. As to identical words, com. Is. 1:2; 33:22; 43:12.

Finally it should be noticed, that though the principle pointed
out in the foregoing instances is Midrashic in nature, the complement is simple, concise, and in considerable measure keeping
within the boundaries of the text.

On one plane with the metaphorical principle rests the
lexical. This principle affects singular words or expressions
which, though not metaphorical, bear a poetical stamp, and in
reality convey more or less the idea of the meaning than the
meaning itself. Such words or expressions, instead of rendering
them according to their surface meaning, the targumist takes
them by their underlying value as suggested by the text. Instances of single verbal words: Ez. 12:13: "And I shall bring
him in Babel." Targum: "I shall exile him" etc. So also v. 16;
36:20 etc. ibid. 23:10: "they took", Targum: "they captured";
Hos. 4:3: "Therefore doth the land mourn." Targum: "Therefore shall the land be laid waste". Ibid. 13:5: "I did know thee
in the wilderness" — "I supplied your needs in the wilderness."
Instances of nouns: "And I will appoint over them four families"
— "four calamitious afflictions." In Mi. 2:3: "On this family"
— "generation; Ez. 24:8: "I gave her blood" — "I revealeth
their transgressions"; ibid. 21:37: "they blood" etc. — "the
sin of your murder." Ez. 34:2: "Prophesy on the shepherds of
Israel" — "on the leaders (פרנסיא) of Israel." Instances of expressions: "And they shall do with thee in hatred" — "and
shall revenge from thee" etc. Ez. 16:16: "not coming and not
being (so)" — "not as required nor proper; Ez. 13:17 etc.:
"put thy face" — "accept prophecy". Examples of all categories
are numerous.

In drawing a comparison between this Targum and
Onk., as well as other translations with respect to the exegetical principles, it will appear that Onk. pursues the same principles. This point was well elucidated by Luzzato in Oheb.
Ger. 31. As regards the other translations, some exceptions must
be made. The allegorical principle as well as the metaphirocal,

as applied by the Targum, are to be found neither in the Lxx nor in P. On the other hand, the principle of the exegetical complement is followed by the Lxx in Pentateuch [19] and in a lesser degree also by the P. Illustrations are: Gen. 25:22: "And she said: 'If it be so, wherefore am I'," which the Lxx render: εἰ οὕτως μοι μέλλει γίνεσθαι etc. Gen. 40:16: "in my dream" κἀγὼ ὕδεν ἐνύπνιον

In the Prophets this is evident to a lesser degree. It found, however, application in this part also. Com. Zech. 14:7: "And there shall be one day which shall be known" etc. Lxx ἔσθαι μίαν ἡ ἡμέραν καὶ ἡμέρα ἐκείνη γενεστὴ etc. So. P. Com. also P. Hos. 2:11 (8).

The lexical principle also was pursued to some extent by the Lxx, and in a lesser degree by P. Com. Gen. 13:2: "And Abram was very heavy." Ἀβρὰμ σὲ ἐν πλούσιος   So P. 15:2 עָרִירִי ἄτεκνος   . So. P. (Onk. agreenig in both instances). But com. Lxx T. Jer. 22:30, 49:3: ראשית אני — ἀρχὴ τέκνων (P. lit. Onk. Alleg.) v. 10: שבט —   ἄρχων   (P. lit. Onk. Alleg.) etc. Is. 8:4 במכני Lxx   ἐν τῃ ἐμῆ πόλει

Apart from these major principles there is an element of commentary in the exegesis of Jonathan. At the first glance it be-comes clear, that the tendency of this commentary is merely to explain away the harassing difficulty. No heed is exhibited to the text, no effort to fit it into the phraseology of the respective passages. So Mi. 2:8: ואתמול עמי לאויב... — "My people is delivered because of their sins; because of them existing peoples will inherit them." Compare also Is. 10:32, 32:19, 33:6; Jer. 4:9; Hos. 10:11; Mi. 2:11; Hab. 3:2; Mal. 1:11. But while this sort of commentary is somewhat of the nature of a homily, there is another phase of the exegesis resting on definite principles. The T. usually changes the interrogative into the categorical. This happens particularly with such interrogative phrases which, in the first place, imply a definite answer, and, in the second place, the implied answer is not given in any form. It should be observed that the Lxx in Pentateuch also employs such a

---

19) A most elucidative treatment on these points in the Lxx is found in Z. Frankel's "Über den Einfluss" etc. See particularly pp. 4, 9, 73.

device.[20]   The following are examples: Is. 66:9: "Shall I
bring to birth and cause to bring forth? Shall I that cause to
bring shut the whomb?" Targum: "I (am) the God who created
the world from the beginning. I created all men and I spread
among the people. I shall gather thy exile." Jer. 18:14: "Doth
the snow of the Lebanon fail from the rock of the field? Or
are the strange cold flowing waters plucked up?" Targum: "Behold, as it is impossible that the water snow running down
the fields of Lebanon shall cease, so will not cease rain coming
down and welling water from the source." Compare also Ob.
1:12, 15. Another interesting characteristic device of the commentary is the turning of one part of the verse into a complement of the other part. Some examples will well illustrate this
point. Is. 5:20: "Woe unto them that call evil good and good
evil, that change darkness into light and light into darkness,
that change bitter into sweet and sweet into bitter." Targum:
"Woe who say to the wicked ye are good, and unto the humble
be said you are wicked, behold when light will come to the
just will be dark for the wicked, and sweet will be the words
of my Torah to those observing them, and bitterness will come
to the wicked." Am. 5:12: "Ye that afflict the just, that take
a ransom." Targum: "Ye that afflict that just in order to take
mamon of falsehood." Compare also Ze. 11:8.[21]

---

20)   Com. Gen. 18:7; 27:36. Com. Z. Frankel, Vorstudien, p. 171.
Über den Einfluss, 76.

21)   The T. turns a comparative phrase into a resultant, treating
אם as כן . So Jerem. 22:28. Here the T. follows another principle,
namely, turning one phrase of the v. into a comparative to the preceding one. Com. Is. 8:2, in which case an Agadic interpretation is involved (Mak. 24a); 42:2.

II.

The interpretative rendering of single words or phrases is of a positive value. The interpretation is characteristic of the early Palestinian exegesis. With little exception, they are found in the Agada.

ושקרו בני ישראל Targum וימעלו בני ישראל מעל Joshua 7:1 ומעלה בו מעל (במדבר ה, יב) אין מעילה So Sifri Num. 7: שקר. בכל מקום אלא שיקור... ואומר וימעלו בני ישראל מעל בחרם. Onkelos l. c. and v. 6 has a similar rendering.

ספרא Targum ספר הישר Joshua 10:13 (also 2S 1:18) דאורייתא. Com. Aboda Zara 25b. Also Y. Sota 1, 18.

מאי ספר הישר א"ר חייא בר אבא זה ספר אברהם יצחק ויעקב. ר" אמר זה ספר משנה תורה דכתיב ביה (דברים ו) ועשית הישר והטוב.

דהוו מבטלין עסקיהון Targum רכבי אתנות צחרות Judges 5:10 רכיבין על אתנא... ומהלכין בכל תחום ארעא דישראל ומתחברין למתב על דינא...
So Erubin 54b רוכבי אתנות אלו תלמידי חכמים שמהלכין מעיר לעיר וממדינה למדינה ללמד תורה.

ורחמוהי יהון Targum ואהביו כצאת השמש בגבורתו ib. 5:31 כימי השמים. Com. Sifri Deut. 145 עתידין לאזהרא בזיהור יקריה על הארץ שיהיו פניהם של צדיקים כיום, וכן הוא אומר ואוהביו כצאת השמש.

מתלמידי נבאיא Targum מן הרמתים צופים 1 Sam. 1:1 So. מן הרמתים צופים אחד ממאתים צופים שנתנבאו להם לישראל. Meg. 14a. The Targum assumed הרמתים to be in const. state while צופים as a descriptive noun as did P. Com. Lxx.
So is the Targum to 1S 9:15 בארץ צוף — בארעא דבה נביא דיי.

ib. אפרתי Targum חולק בקודשיא בטורא דבית אפרים. siders Eli to have belonged to the Levites (1 Chronicles 6:18). (So R. Jochanan Jalqut l. c.). The בני קהת were given a portion on the Mountain of Ephraim (Josh. 21:21). The Targum in other cases (Judg. 12:5, 1K 11:26) merely transcribes it. Com., however, Berachoth 31b.

וקטיל Targum ויך בעם שבעים איש חמשים אלף איש IS 6:19 בסבי עמא שבעין גברא ובקהלא חמשין אלפין גברא. Thus the discrepancy in the number is eliminated. This interpretation agrees with Y. San. 2, 4 ר' חנינה ור' מנא, וחד אמר ויך בעם שבעים איש

(pp. 58, 59, סדר אליהו ר. and ‎ר. זו סנהדרין, וחמשים אלף מעם הארץ
‎לפיכך נפל מישראל חמשים אלף וסנהדרי גדולה עמהם), Friedmann.

‎וית שמשון Targum וישלח ה׳ את ירובעל ואת כדן ib. 12:11.
So Y. Rosh Hashana 2, 8; Babli 25a. Com. P.

‎כבר שנה דלית ביה חובין Targum בן שנה שאול במלכו ib. 13:1
‎אמר רב הונא כבן שנה שלא Y. Bikkurim 3, 3. ‎כן שאול כד מלך
‎אלא שנמחלו כל עוונותיו כתינוק בן שנה Joma 22b. ‎טעם טעם חטא.

‎ברם זכות שבטא Targum ראש שבטי ישראל אתה ib. 15:17
Com. Sota 36b on. ‎דבנימין אבוך גרמא לך די בעו למעבר בימא
Ps. 68:28 ‎היה ר׳ מאיר אומר בשעה שעמדו ישראל על הים היו השבטים
‎נוצחין זה את זה זה אומר אני ארד תחלה וזה אומר אני ארד תחלה
‎קפץ שבטו של בנימין וירד לים.
Also Tanchuma ‎ויגש 8 on the same verse.

Com. ‎וית נודא. Targum. ‎ואת כפיר העזים ib 19:13, 16
Schochar Tob as cited in the Jalqut l. c. ‎והוא מוצא את התרפים
‎בתוכה ואת העביט של עזים. Com. Kimchi l. c.

So Ze-‎בבית אולפנא Targum וישבו בניות ib 19:18, 19
bachim 54b ‎אמר רבה וכי מה ענין אצל רמה ? אלא שהיו יושבין
‎ברמה עוסקין בנויו של עולם.

ib. 23:18   ‎וימת ביום ההוא שמנים וחמשה איש נשא אפוד בד
Targum ‎וקטל ביומא ההוא תמן וחמשא גברין דכשרין למלבש אפוד
‎דבוץ. This interpretation of the expression implying that all
of them were high priests is followed in Y. San. 10, 2, Gem.
‎ויסב דואג האדומי... לא כן תני ר׳ חייה אין ממנין שני כהנים גדולים
‎כאחת אלא מלמד שחיו כולם ראויים להיות כהנים גדולים.

The T. ‎אתעתדתון ישראל Targum הצבי ישראל 2S 1:19
identified it with the root, ‎יצב. Com. Is. 21:5 Ps. Jon. Deut.
29:9. Com. Schochar Tob 22, 19:
‎אלהים נצב בעדת אל (תהלים פ״ב, א) ר׳ חני בשם ר׳ יצחק אלהים
‎עומד אין כתיב כאן אלא אלהים נצב איטימוס כמו דאת אמר (שמות
‎ה״ג, כ״א) ונצבת על הצור.
Both Onkelos and Ps. Jonathan render ‎ונצבת by ‎עתד

Com. ‎חטאיא וחיביא Targum העורים והפסחים ib. 5:6
‎שנואי נפש דוד שהיה דוד שונא עובדי ע״ז : פרקי דר׳ אלעזר 36

ib. 5:24 ‎Targum ויהי בשמעך את קול צעדה בראשי הבכאים
Com. Schochar tob 27, 2 ‎ויהי במישמעך ית קל צוחתא בריישי אילניא.

אין לך רשות לפשוט יד בהן אפילו אם היו קרבין אצלך עד שתראה
ראשי האילנות מנענעין שנאמר ויהי בשמעך את קול צעדה בראשי
הבכאים and with minor alterations in Pesiqta Rabati 8.

דחליץ ומתגלי Targum כהגלות נגלות אחד הרקים ib. 6:20
The Targum interprets רקים empty, naked. Com. Jalqut l. c.
אמרה לו משפחת של בית אבא היתה נאה ממך, חלילה להם שנראה
מימיהן פסת יד ופסת רגל ועקב מגולה.
Com. Y. Sukka 5, 14; San. 2, 4 מהו אחד הרוקים, אמרו עליו
על בית שאול שלא נראה מהם לא עקב ולא אגודל מימיהם.

Targum ויך אלחנן בן יערי את גלית הגתי ib. 21:19
ויך אלחנן בן יערי אורגים זה דוד So Jalqut l. c. וקטל דוד בן ישי
בן ישי שחננו אל; בן יערי שהיה גדול כיער.

דאתנבי לסוף Targum ואלה דברי דוד האחרונים ib. 23:1
כך ישראל כשיבא עלמא לימי דנחמתא. Com. Shochar Tob 18, 5
משיח במהרה בימינו אומרים שירה.

וכשמשא דעתיד Targum וכאור בוקר יזרח שמש ib. 23:4
לאנהרא כזהיר יקריה על חד תלת מאה וארבעין ותלתא כניהור שבעת
כוכביא שבעתא ימיא. The T. was apparently influenced in
that by Is. 30:26 with minor changes. The Midrash also interprets it in a Messianic sense. Com. Midrash Shmuel 29, end:
אין אנו יודעים מהו וכאור בקר אלא כשיאיר הקב"ה בקר של משיח
וכאור בקר בעולם הזה כעין; and in Pesachim 2a: תזריח השמש
זריחת שמש לצדיקים לעולם הבא. Com. R. Channel l. c.

ואיש יגע בהם ימלא ברזל ועץ חנית ובאש שרף ישרפו ib. 23:7
ואף על אנש דמשרי למיקרב בחובין אזלין ותקפין Targum בשבת
עלוהי עד דחפין ליה בלבוש פרזלא דלא יכלין במעי טורנין ורומחין
בכן לית פורענותיהון ביד אנש אלהין באשתא עתידין לאתוקדא יתוקדון
באתגלאה בית דינא רבא למתב על כורסיא דין למרן ית עלמא.
In a like manner runs the interpretation in סדר אליהו רבה, 3:
אבל פושעים של ישראל אינם כן אלא בקטנותם רכים ובזקנותם קשים
ומה שכרן? שמעלין ושורפין אותם בבית המקדש הגדול שלו שנאמר
ובליעל כקץ ואומר באש ישרפון בשבת.

אלין שמהת גבריא דהוי Targum אלה שמות הגבורים ib. 23:8
עם דוד גברא ריש משריתא על כורסי דינא. The interpretation of
גבורים as representing rather the learned who pronounce judgment, and not the warriors, is the favorite one in the Agada.
Com. Moed Katan 16b, Y. Mak. 6, 7 and Pesiqta r. 11.

ib. 24:15 מעידן דמתנכים Targum מהבקר ועד עת מועד
מאי עת מועד אמר שמואל משעת שחיטת So Berakoth 62b תמידא.
and in the name of R. Chiyya in התמיד עד שעת זריקתו.
Pesiqta r. 11.

IK 7:26 תרין אלפים ביתין ברטיבא. Targum אלפים בת יכיל
So Erubin 14b, Sifri Num. 42.
כתוב אחד אומר מחזיק בתים שלשת אלפים יכיל (דהי"ב ד, ה) וכתוב
אחד אומר אלפים בת יכיל כיצד יתקיימו שני כתובים הללו — אלפים
בלח שהם שלשת אלפים ביבש.

ib. 37 בירח זיו Targum זיו נצניא Com. Rosh Hashana
11a, Y. Rosh Hashana 2, 8 ההוא משום ? הכתיב נמי בחדש זיו
דאית ביה זיוא ואילניא .

ib. 8:2 בירחא דעתיקיא דקרן ליה Targum בירח האיתנים
ירחא קדמאה ובען הוא ירחא שביעאה. In the Talmud (Rosh
Hashana 11a) R. Eliezer would interpret it to refer to the
"Aboth". The T. is based on this interpretation. At the
same time it intends to account for the change of the order
of the months following Josephus (Ant. 1, 3, 3) that it was
Moses who appointed that Nisan should be the first month
for their festivals. Com. PS Jonathan Exod. 12:2.

ib. 16:34 בית מימי Targum בית האלי So P. Com. San.
113a.

2K 2:3 ויצאו בני הנבאים Targum תלמידי נבייא . (So ib.
5, 7, 15; 4:1, 38; 6:1). Com. Sifri Deut. 131: ואמר ויצאו בני
הנביאים וכי בני הנביאים היו והלא תלמידיהם היו אלא מיכן לתלמידים
שהם קרוים בנים .

ib. 12 אבי אבי Targum רבי רבי . Com. Sifri I. c. וכשם
שהתתלמידים קרוים בנים כך הרב קרוי אב, שנאמר ואלישע ראה והוא
מצעק אבי אבי ; Moed Katan 26a, where this Targum is quoted.

IS 1:23 רדף שלמונים Targum עביד לי לחבריה גבר אומרין
ורודף שלמונים : איכה Com. Pesiqta טבא בדיני ואשלם לך בדינך.
שלם ואשלם לך.

ib. 3:4 ותעלולים Targum וחלשתא. Probably according
to Chaggiga 14a אמר רב אחא בר יעקב אלו תעלי בני תעלי .

IS 4:3 כל דכתיב לחיי Targum כל הכתוב לחיים בירושלם
עלמא יחזי בנחמת ירושלים. This interpretation in a Messianic
sense agrees with San. 92b.

ib. 5:1 אשירה נא לידידי שירת דודי לכרמו כרם היה לידידי

אמר נביא אשכחיה כען לישראל דמתיל לכרמא Targum בקרן בן שמן

עשר קרנות Com. Lamentation r. 2, 3 זרעיה דאברהם רחמי.

and Menachoth 53a הן קרנו של אברהם שנאמר כרם היה לידידי.

ib. 2 ואף מדבחי Targum וגם יקב חצב בו . So Y. Sukka 4, 16

Com. מגדל זה ההיכל יקב זה המזבח וגם יקב חצב בו אלו שיתין.

שורק זה המקדש ויבן מגדל בתוכו זה מזבח וגם יקב חצב Sukka 49a

בו אלו שיתין.

ib. 10 ארי בחובא דלא יהבו Targum כי עשרת צמדי כרם

מעשריא. Com. Pesiqta D'rav Kahana, — בעון שאין מוציאין

מעשרותיהן בת עשר מידות של כרם עשר.

ib. 17 כמא דאמיר עליהון Targum ורעו כבשים כדברם

(from root דבר). Com. Pesachim 68a ר"א, כבשים כדברם ורעו

מנשיא בר ירמיה אמר רב כמדובר בם.

ib. 18 וי דמשכן למחטי צבחר נגדין Targum הוי מושכי העון

Com. Suk. 52b, San. 99a חובין בחבלי למא אזלן וסגן עד דתקיפין.

א' רבי אסי יצר הרע בתחלה דומה לחוט של בוכיא ולבסוף דומה

כעבות העגלה שנא' הוי.

Also R. Akiba, Gen· r. 22, 2; Sifri Num. 112.

ib. 6:1 בשתא דאתנגע Targum בשנת מות (2 Chronicles

26:20). So Exod. r. 1, end. Jalqut l. c. אלא שנצטרע ? וכי מת היה

ומצורע חשוב כמת. Com. Ps. Jonathan, Exod. 2:23.

ib. 2 בתרין Targum בשתים יכסה פניו ובשתים יכסה רגליו

מכסין אפוהי דלא חזי ובתרין מכסי גויתיה דלא מתחזי.

Com. Pirke d. Eliezer, 4:

ובשתים יכסה רגליו — שלט יביטו פני השכינה, ובשתים יכסה פניו —

שלא יביט בפני השכינה.

ib. 8:2 Targum ואעידה עדים נאמנים את אוריה הכהן

ואסהיד קדמי סהידין מהימנין ית לוטיא דאמרית לאיתאה בנבואת אוריה

כהנא והא אתו אף כן כל נחמתא דאמרית לאיתאה בנבואת זכריה בן

יברכיהו אנא עתיד לאיתאה.

This is exactly the interpretation of R. Akiba Makkoth 24b:

שוב פעם אחת היו עולין לירושלים כיון שהגיעו להר הבית ראו שועל

שיצא מבית קדשי הקדשים התחילו הן בוכין ור"ע מצחק אמר להן לכך

אני מצחק דכתיב ואעידה לי וכי מה ענין אוריה אצל זכריה אלא תלה

הכתוב נבואתו של זכריה בנבואתו של אוריה, באוריה כתוב לכן בגללכם

ציון תחרש, בזכריה כתוב עוד ישבו זקנים וזקנות ברחובות ירושלים.

עכשו שנתקימה נבואתו של אוריה כידוע שנבואתו של זכריה מתקיימת.

ib. 9:4 ‏ארי כל מסבהון ברשע.‏ Targum. ‏כי כל סאון סאן ברעש‏
The interpretation is based on the transposition of the two
last letters of ‏ברעש‏ . On the reading of the T. rests also the say_
ing of R. Meir, Tos. Sota 3: ‏היה רבי איר אומר מנין שבמדה שאדם‏
‏מודד מודדין לו תלמוד לומר כי כל סאון סואן ברעש.‏ Otherwise
the inference is hardly explicable. Apparently, the T. identified
‏סאון‏ with ‏שאון‏ formed from the root ‏נשא.‏ This was apparently
the underlying reading of the rendering of the Lxx, while P. and
I presume, also, Sym. read the same way and rendered it
accordingly.

ib. 10:16 ‏ותחת כבדו יקד יקד כיקוד אש‏ Targum ‏ותחות מני‏
‏יקרהון מיקד ייקדון.‏ The Targum interprets the phrase in the
terms of the current Agada that, for the purpose of rendering
the mircale of the destruction of the army of Senacherib more
pronounced, God caused the bodies of his host to be burned
within the raiments which were left intact. Com. the Syriac
Apocalypse of Baruch 63, 8: "And at that time I burned their
bodies within but their raiment and arms I preserved outwardly,
in order that still more wonderful deeds of the Mighty one
might appear, and thereby His name might be spoken of throughout the whole earth." It was, it would seem, a current Agada.
Com. Tanchuma, ‏נח,‏ 21: ‏ומנין ברשעים בשעה שעלה סנחריב לירושלים‏
‏וכל חיילותיו עמו נשרפו גופיהם ולא נשרפו בגדיהם.‏ Also Lekach
Tob, Noach 9, 23. Com. Shab. 113b (and Rashi l. c.), San. 94a
‏א"ר יוחנן תחת כבודו ולא כבודו ממש כי הא דר' יוחנן קרי ליה למאניה‏
‏מכבדותי.‏ Com. Tos. San. 52a. ‏אותם‏

ib. 13:12 ‏אוקיר אנוש מפז ואדם מכתם אופיר‏ Targum ‏אחבב‏
‏דחלי מדהבא ועבדי אוריתא.‏ Com. also 32:2. In all other cases
the rendering of these two words is literal. Here the translation
was influenced by the Messianic nature which the targumist
assumes for this prophecy. The T. takes ‏אדם‏ to imply the
observer of the law following R. Jeremiah (Sifra Lev. 18, 5):
‏היה ר' ירמיה אומר מנין אתה אומר אפילו נכרי ועושה את התורה‏
‏הרי הוא ככהן גדול תלמוד לומר אשר יעשה אותם האדם וחי בהם.‏

ib. 13:21 ‏ושעירים ירקדו שם‏ Targum ‏ושידין‏ . Com. Sifri,
Deut. 218: ‏ואין שעיר אלא שד שנאמר ושעירים ירקדו שם‏; Lev. r. 5, 1
‏וילדים ירקדון כאילין שדיא כמה דתימא ושעירים ירקדו שם.‏

ib. 17:11 ‏ביום נטעך תשגשגי‏ Targum ‏באתר דאתקדשתון‏

למהוי עם תמן קלקלתון עובדיכון. The targumist evidently took
תישגשני as based on the noun סיג, dross (Isaiah 1:25). Com.
Lev. r. 18, 3. ביום שנטעתי אתכם לי לעם עשיתם פסולת כמד"א
סיגים כסף היו.

ib. 19:25 ברוך עמי מצרים ומעשה ידי אשור ונחלתי ישראל
Targum ברוך עמי דאפקית ממצרים דעל דחבו קדמי אנליתי יתהון
לאתור וכדו דתבו מתקרן עמי ואחסנתי ישראל. The targumist
would not accept the literal and obvious meaning of this
verse placing the Egyptians and Assyrians on one footing with
Israel. In his view, therefore, the whole verse refers to Israel.
So was the view, apparently for the same rason, of the Greek
and the Syriac rendering of the verse.

Eliminating the insertions, this interpretation is found
in Hebrew ברוך עמי מצרים סדר אליהו זוטא (p. 194 Friedmann)
— עם שיצאו ממצרים, ומעשה ידי אשור — אלו שגלו לאשור והם
נחלת ישראל.

ib. 21:1 מטל משרין דאתין ממדברא Targum משא מדבר ים
Similarly Cant. r. משא מדבר ים אם ים למה מדבר אלא — כמעט
אלו ארבע מלכיות...

ib. 21:11, 12 שמר מה מליה שמר מה מליל אמר שמר אתא
נביא פריש להון ית נביאתא אמר נביא אית Targum בקר וגם לילח
אמרו Com. Y. Taanith 1, 1. אנר לצדיקיא ואית פורענות לרשיעיא.
לישעיה רבינו ישעיה וכי מה יוצא לנו מתוך הלילה הזה, אמר להם לא
כשאתם סבירין אלא בקר לצדיקים ולילה לרשעים. Com. also Pesachim
2a on 2S 23:4.

ib. 22:1 מטל נבואתא על קרתא דיתבא Targum משא גיא חזיון
בחילתא דאתנביאו עלה נבייא. This agrees with R. Jochanan (Pesichta Lam. r. 24) ר' יוחנן פתח משא גיא חזון גיא שכל החוזים מתנבאים
עליה. While Beraitha Taanith 28b would interpret it to refer
to the Tepmle. Rashi, however, would place the Beraitha in harmony with the interpretation of R. Jochanan.

ib. 8 על זין בית גנזי מקדשא Targum. על נשק בית היער
The T. was evidently prompted to this interpretation by IK
10:17, where it is called בית יער הלבנון interpreting לבנון to mean
the Temple, as he rendered 37:24 (2K 19:23), which coincides
with the explanation in Joma 39b.

א"ר זוטרא בר טוביה למה נקרא שמו יער דכתיב בית יער הלבנון לומר
Similarly Num. r. 11, 5. לך מה יער מלבלב אף בית המקדש מלבלב..

b. 17 טלטלה גבר Targum טלטלא דגברא Com. San. 25b
טלטלה גבר אמר רב טלטולא דגברא קשה...

ib. 18 Targum קלון בית אדוניך ולתמן יתובון בקלן על דלא
תנא הוא בקש קלון לבית Com. San. l. c. נטרתא יקר בית רבוניך.
אדוניו ולפיכך נהפך כבודו לקלון.

ib. 23 Targum ותקעתיו יתד. אמניה אמרכל מהימן. The targumist is of the opinion that שבנא was only אמרכל which dignity was to be transferred to Eliakim. Accordingly, he renders
סוכן (v. 15) פרנסא די ממנא על ביתא. This is the view of R.
Jehuda (Lev. r. 5, 3) לך בא אל הסוכן א"ר אלעזר כהן גדול היה,
צנף יצנפך ר' יהודה ב"ר אומר אמרכל היה. The T., however, to
(v. 18) יעדי מנך ית מצנפתא would point to the opposite view,
that Shebna was a High Priest. (Com. T. 28:1). The T.
to v. 18 has all the appearance of a Midrashic T., a portion of
which was incorporated here.

ib. 27:5 Targum או יחזק במעוזי אם יתקפון בפתגמי אוריתי
Com. San. 99b א"ר אלכסנדרי כל העוסק בתורה לשמה משים שלום
בפמליה של מעלה ובפמליה של מטה שנאמר או יחזק במעוזי.

ib. 27:8 Targum בסאסאה בשלחה תריבנה בסאתה דהויתא
תניא היה רבי מאיר אומר So Sota 8b, San. 100a. כאיל בה יכילון לך
מנין שבמדה שאדם מודד בה מודדין לו שנאמר בסאסאה.

ib. 28:7 Targum פקו פלילה טעו דינהא. So Meg. 15b,
San. 111b ואין פלילה אלא דיינים שנאמר ונתן בפלילים.

ib. 10 Targum כי צו לצו קו לקו ארי אתפקדו למעבד אוריתא
ומה דאתפקדו לא צביאו למעבד סברו דיתקיים להון פולחן טעותא ולא
(p. 19, סדר אליהו רבה Com. סברו לפולחן בית מקדשי (קו לקו)
Friedman) אתם, אי אתם כן אלא ששמין אתם טחי תפל מליעובין אתם
על דברי כאילו אין בהם ממש ועושים אתם אותן צואה שאינה צואה קואה
שאינה קואה צויתי אתכם בצאתכם ממצרים, צויתי אתכם בספר תוכחות
קויתי אתכם ארבע מאות ושמונים עד שלא נבנה הבית, חזרתי וקויתי
אתכם ארבע מאות ועשר שנים משנבנה הבית שנאמר כי צו לצו קו לקו.

ib. 29:1 Targum מדבחא מדבחא הוי אריאל אריאל According
to Midoth 4, 7 it is the היכל Pesichta Lam. r. 26. But com.
Sebachim 53a, 59b, according to Rab.

ib. 17; 32:15 Targum והכרמל ליער יחשב קרוין סגיאין יתיב
Com. Gen. r. 24, 1 והכרמל ליער יחשב לחורשי דבי אינש Com. Caro
l. c. and Rashi.

די תתובון לאוריתא Targum בשובה ונחת תושעון 30:15 .ib
תנוחון ותתפרקון. The Targum interprets בשובה to mean repentance and rendering the following as a resultant phrase. It agrees
with R. Eliezer, Y. Taanith 2, 8; San. 37b.
תניא אידך רבי אליעזר אומר אם ישראל עושין תשובה נגאלין. א"ל
רבי אליעזר כבר נאמר בשובה ונחת.

Targum ולא יכנף עוד מוריך והיו עיניך רואות את מוריך 20 .ib
ולא יסלק עוד שכינתיה מבית מקדשא ויהוון עיניך חזין ית שכינתיה
בבית מקדשא. Com. Sota 49a רב אחא בר חנינא אומר אף אין הפרגוד
ננעל לפניו שנאמר ולא יכנף עוד מוריך ר' אבהו אומר משביעין אותו
Both, it would מזיו השכינה שנאמר והיו עיניך רואות את מוריך.
appear, depend upon the interpretation of the Targum which
interprets מוריך to mean the Shekina, introducing the Temple
as a necessary complement.

ib. 31:9 תפתה Targum גהינם So Erubin 19a; Pesachim
54a; Seder Eliahu r. 29 (p. 150 Friedman).

ותנור בעיר ליה דאשא Targum ותנור לו בירושלים ib.
ר' ינאי ור"ש Com. Erubin l. c.; Gen. r. 6, 4 לרעברו על מימריה.
תרויהו אמרין אין גיהנם אלא יום שמהלט את הרשעים מה טעם הנה
והנה תנור זה : 9 ,יתרו Mek. יום בא בוער כתנור (מלאכי ג', ט')
גיהנם, שנאמר ותנור לו בירושלם.

כל דהוו מתאנחין מן קדם Targum כל אנחתה השבעתי 2 .ib
כל אנחתה השבתי כל אנחתה של בבל. So Cant. r. l. c. מלכא דבבל.

כמשכנא דלא מתפרק Targum אהל בל יצען 33:20 .ib
So Cant. r.
תני ר' אליעזר בן יעקב אהל בל יצען בל יצא ובל ינוע — כאהלי.

לא יתאמר עוד Targum לא יקראו עוד לנבל נדיב 32:5 .ib
דרש רבי יהודה בר מערבא ואיתימא Com. Sota 41b לרשיעיא צדיקיא.
רבי שמעון בן פזי מותר להחניף לרשעים בעולם הזה שנאמר לא יאמר
עוד לנבל נדיב.

Targum כי ארמן נטש משש פראים מרעה עדרים 14 .ib
Com. Lam. r. ארי בית מקדשא חרוב דהוא אתר דהוא בית חידו הוה מבו
2, 5.

טוביכן צדיקא עבדתון Targum אשריכם זרעי על כל מים 20 .ib
Com. Baba Kama לכון עובדין טבן דאתון דמן לדזרעין על שקיא.
אמר ר' יוחנן משום רשב"י מאי דכתיב אשריכם, Aboda Zara 5b, 17b
Seder Eliahu Zuta 15 (ed. F.) כל העוסק בתורה וגמילות חסדים·

אשרי מי ששם את עצמו כשור לעול וכחמור למשוא וכפרה חורשת בשדה
שנאמר אשריכם זרעי על כל מים...

ib. 33:17 יָת יָקָר שְׁכִינַת Targum מֶלֶךְ בְּיָפְיוֹ תַּחְזֶינָה עֵינֶיךָ
עָתִיד הקב"ה Com. Seder Eliahu r. 14 (p. 168 F.) מֶלֶךְ עָלְמַיָּא.
לֵישֵׁב בְּבֵית הַמִּדְרָשׁ הַגָּדוֹל שֶׁלּוֹ וְצַדִּיקֵי עוֹלָם יוֹשְׁבִים לְפָנָיו שֶׁנֶּאֱמַר מֶלֶךְ
בְּיָפְיוֹ (Eliahu Zuta 1 (p. 171 F. וּמִנַּיִן שֶׁהִיא מַעֲלֶה וּמוֹשִׁיבָהּ אֶת
נְתוּנָה נֶגֶד כִּסֵּא הַכָּבוֹד וְאוֹמֵר מֶלֶךְ . . .

ib. 40:8 מִית רְשִׁיעַיָּא. Targum יָבֵשׁ חָצִיר Com. Schochar
Tob 1, 20 (ed. Buber) and citation in Jalqut: אַבָּא תַנְחוּם
אוֹמֵר לָמָּה הַצַּדִּיקִים דּוֹמִים בָּעוֹלָם הַזֶּה לְטַבְלָא הַמְּקוּבַּעַת בְּאַבְנֵי טוֹבוֹת
וּמַרְגָּלִיּוֹת וּקְעָרַת יָרָק בְּתוֹכָהּ נָטְלָה הַטַּבְלָא וְנִשְׁפַּךְ מַה שֶּׁבְּתוֹכָהּ נִרְאָה מַה
שֶּׁבַּטַּבְלָא כָּךְ נִבְלְעוּ הָרְשָׁעִים מִן הָעוֹלָם נִרְאוּ הַצַּדִּיקִים שֶׁנֶּאֱמַר יָבֵשׁ חָצִיר.

ib. 40:10 הָא אֲגַר עוֹבְדֵי Targum הִנֵּה שְׂכָרוֹ אִתּוֹ וּפְעֻלָּתוֹ לְפָנָיו
Com. Tanchuma Gen. מֵימְרֵיהּ עִמֵּיהּ דְּכָל עוֹבָדֵיהוֹן גְּלַן קֳדָמוֹהִי.
וְכָךְ אָמַר יְשַׁעְיָה אֲבָל לַצַּדִּיקִים הִנֵּה שְׂכָרוֹ אִתּוֹ. (Noach) 12

ib. 29 דִּיהַב לְצַדִּיקַיָּא דִּמְשַׁלְּהֵן לְפִתְגָּמֵי Targum נֹתֵן לַיָּעֵף כֹּחַ
אוֹרַיְתָא חוּכְמָא. The T. was influenced by 50:4, of which this
is the rendering. So Seder Eliahu r. 17 (p. 84 F.) אֲבָל מֶלֶךְ
מַלְכֵי הַמְּלָכִים אֵינוֹ כֵן אֶלָּא יוֹשֵׁב בְּכִסֵּא שֶׁלּוֹ וּמְפַרְנֵס אֶת הַצַּדִּיקִים בְּחָכְמָה
בְּדֵעָה שֶׁנֶּאֱמַר נֹתֵן לַיָּעֵף. . . .

ib. 40:31 וְדִסְבָּרוּ Targum וְקוֹיֵ ה' יַחֲלִיפוּ כֹחַ יַעֲלוּ אֵבֶר כַּנְּשָׁרִים
לְפוּרְקָנָא דַיְיָ יִתְכַּנְּשׁוּן מִבֵּינֵי גָלוּתְהוֹן וִיתַחַדְתוּן לְעוֹלֵימְתְהוֹן. The reference here is to the Messianic era. Sifri (Num. 40) explains
it to refer to the future world which, however, might be taken
in an identical sense. Com. San. 92b, Jalqut Machiri l. c.

ib. 41:2 אֵיתֵי Targum מִי הֵעִיר מִמִּזְרָח צֶדֶק יִקְרָאֵהוּ לְרַגְלוֹ
בְּגַלֵּי מְדִינְחָא אַבְרָהָם בְּחִיר צַדְקִיָּא. This and the following verses
appear to have been generally explained to refer to the story
of Abraham's struggle with the four Kings (Gen. 14). So
Shabath 15a, San. 108b, Tanchuma l. c. 19:
מִי הֵעִיר . . . אָמַר הקב"ה אַבְרָהָם הֵעִיר אֶת עוֹלָמִי בְּצִדְקוֹ.
Com. Gen. r. 42, 1; Exod. r. 15, 50; Seder Eliahu r. 6 (p. 28
Friedman).

ib. 42:11 יִשְׁבְּחוּן מִיתַיָּא כַּד נָפְקִין Targum יָרֹנּוּ יֹשְׁבֵי סֶלַע
אַף אָבוֹת וְאִמָּהוֹת. Com. Gen. r. 13, 2, Jalqut l. c. מֵבַתָּא עֲלֵיהוֹן
בִּתְחִיַּת הַמֵּתִים כְּתִיב יָרֹנּוּ. Deut. r. 7, 3. שֶׁנֶּאֱמַר יָרֹנּוּ יֹשְׁבֵי סֶלַע
יֹשְׁבֵי סֶלַע.

ib. 21 למען צדקו Targum ישראל לזכאותה בדיל .

The T is followed by the Pesiqta 40: ואימתי ,השביעי בחדש
הקב"ה דן את העולם ומזכה אותם ? בר"ה, שהוא חפץ לזכות בריותיו.
וכן הוא אומר י' חפץ למען צדקו, שהוא חפץ להצדיק בריותיו.
Mak. 23b, Mish.: ר' חנניא בן עקשיא אומר רצה הקב"ה לזכות את
ישראל לפיכך הרבה להם תורה ומצות שנאמר י' חפץ למען צדקו.

ib. 43:4 ואתן אדם תחתיך Targum עממיא ומסרית So Mechilta 10 דנזקין מסכתא and Exod. r. 15, 3: לכך קבע להם שמחה
שהוא נפרע מאויביהם שנאמר ואתן אדם . . .

ib. 12 והשמעתי והושעתי הגדתי אנכי Targum חויתי אנא
לאברהם אביכון דעתיד למיתא אנא פרקית יתכון ממצרים כמא דקיימית
ליה. בין בתריא ואנא אשמעית יתכון אולפן אוריתי מסיני. Similarly
Jalqut l. c. והשמעתי בסיני . . . אנכי הגדתי במצרים.

ib. 44:5 זה יאמר לי' אני וזה יקרא בשם יעקב וזה יכתב ידו
Targum דין יימר מדחליא די' אנא ודין יצלי בשום יעקב ודין יקריב
קורבניה. The interpretation approaches the Midrashic explanation of the verse to refer to four estates of the righteous ones.
Aboth of R. Nathan 36 זה יאמר לי אני אלו צדיקים גמורים וזה
יקרא בשם יעקב אלו קטנים בני רשע, וזה יכתב ידו לד' אלו רשעים
שפירשו מדרכיהם וחזרו בהם ועשו תשובה, ובשם ישראל יכנה אלו גרי
אומות העולם. And in a different way in Mechilta דנזקין מסכתא)
(28 : וכך אתה מוצא בארבע כתות שהן עונות ואומרות זה יאמר לי'
אני ואל יתערב בי חטא מסגרים — זה שכולו למקום ולא נתערב בו
חטא, וזה יקרא בשם יעקב — אלו גרי צדק, וזה יכתב . . . — אלו בעלי
תשובה, ובשם ישראל יכנה — אלו יראי שמים.
Seder Eliahu r. 18 (p. 105 F.) is following Aboth of R. Nathan
מיכן אמרו לארבע כתים נחלקו ישראל באותה שעה, זה יאמר — אלו
צדיקים גמורים, וזה יקרא — אלו קטנים בני הרשעים, וזה יכתב —
אלו רשעים. The T. seems to follow this interpretation, although
it is less outspoken with regard to the last three which, however, allow themselves to be implied. Com. Sifri Deut., 119.

ib. 27 לצולה האמר Targum על בבל דאמר. Com. Y. Berakoth
4, 1; Zebachim 113a; Shab. 113a; Lam. r. Pesichta 23 (Buber)
אמר ר' יוחנן האומר לצולה חרבי זו בבל.

ib. 45:18 יצרה לשבת Targum אנשא בני עלה לאסנאה It is
so interpreted in the Talmud as implying the obligation of
human reproduction. Com. Jebamoth 62a; Gittin 41a, etc.

ib. 46:11 עצתי איש מרחק מארץ Targum רחוקא מארעא

ד"א ברצות י' דרכי איש, זה אברהם. So Gen. r. 54, 1 בני אברהם
שנקרא איש, דכתיב ביה מארץ מרחק איש עצתי.

אלהים שלחני להתנבאה ואנא Targum פתח לי אזן ib. 50:5
מהו אומר בסוף ? ה' אלהים פתח לי אוזן, 33 Pesiqta So לא סריבת.
הוא פתח לי אוזן לשמע קולו כשאמר את מי אשלח.

ארי מן קדם בישתא Targum כי מפני הרעה נאסף הצדק ib.57:1
דעתידא למיתי. The belief is here expressed that the death of
the righteous one is a signal of an approaching calamity to
escape which he is taken away from life. This was a prevalent
belief derived from the interpretation of this verse. Com.
כיון שניתן רשות למשחית . . . ולא עוד אלא שמתחיל :Baba Kama 60a
מן הצדיקים תחלה. א"ל אביי טיבותא הי לגבייהו שנאמר כי מפני הרעה...
צדיק נפטר מהעולם רעה באה לעולם שנאמר הצדיק... San. 113a
But com. Enoch 81, 9.

שלמא יתעבד לצדיקיא Targum שלום שלום לרחוק ולקרוב ib. 19
Com. דנטרו אוריתי מלקדמין ושלמא יתעבד לתביא דתבו לאוריתא.
גדול השלום שנתן לעושי תשובה שנאמר שלום שלום... :Sifri Num. 42

וגלי קדמוהי דלית גבר Targum וירא כי אין איש ib. 59:16
וא"ר יוחנן אין בן דוד בא אלא Com. San. 98b דליה עובדין טבין.
בדור שכולו זכאי או בדור שכולו חייב, בדור שכולו חייב דכתיב וירא
כי אין איש . . .

ארי לית בר מינך Targum ומעולם לא שמעו ולא האזינו ib. 64:3
משלויהם של רשעים 20 Com. Eliahu r. דאת עתיד למעבד לעבדך צדיקיא
בעולם הזה אתה למד מתן שכרן של צדיקים לעולם הבא, ואומר ומעולם
לא שמעו ולא האזינו... Com. also Shab. 63a; Exod. r. 45 end;
Esther r. 1.

כמא דאשתכח Targum כאשר ימצא התירוש באשכול 65:8
נח זכאי בדרא דטופנא. So R. Simon, Gen. r. 29, 1.

ארי דחייב עולים Targum כי הנער בן מאה שנה ימות ib. 20
בר מאה שנין יהי מאית. Com. San. 91a and Pesachim 68a. The
interpretation of the T., however, agrees with Gen. r. 26, 3.

ארי כיומי אלן חייא Targum כי כימי העץ ימי עמי ib. 22
וחייו מנין שנאמר כימי העץ. (18) Com. Tan. Gen. 2 יומי עמי.
Similarly Gen. r. 12, 5; Num. r. 13, 4. Lxx has a similar interpretation. Com. T. PS. 1:3 כעץ שתול — כאילן חיי.

Targum זכרתי לך חסד נעוריך אהבת כלולתיך Jerem. 2:2
דכירנא לכון טבות יומי קדם, רחמת אהבתכון דהימני במימרי ואזלי

בתר תרין שליחי בתר משה ואהרן במדברא ארבעין שנין בלא זודין.
אחרים אומרין... כדאי היא האמנה 3 : בשלח Com. Mechilta
שהאמינו בי שאקרע להם את הים, שלא אמרו למשה היאך אנו יוצאים
למדבר ואין בידינו מחיה לדרך אלא האמינו והלכו אחרי משה, עליהם
וקראת הלוך בקבלה מפורש And in a modified form in Seder
Eliahu r. 17 (p. 85).

מדוע אמרו עמי רדנו לוא נבוא עוד אליך Targum Jerem. 2:31
ד"א מדוע Com. Tanchuma Num. 2 אטלטילנא לא נתוב עוד לפולחנך.
אמרו, אמרו לו נתת לנו בית מקדש וסלקת שכינתך ממנו עוד לא נבוא
עוד אליך.

אילו את חביב Targum גלעד אתה לי ראש הלבנון ib. 22:6
עמלק, 2 : Com. Mechilta . קדמי מבית מקדשא דרם בריש טוריא
בקש לראות את בית המקדש והראו, שנאמר את הגלעד ואין גלעד אלא
בית המקדש שנאמר גלעד אתה לי.

וימת חנניה הנביא בשנה ההיא בחדש השביעי Targum ib. 28:17
ומית חנניה נביא בשתא ההיא שקרא ואתקבר בירחא שביעא. Com. Y.
וימת חנניה הנביא... שנה אחרת היתה, ואת אמרת כן San. 11, 5
אלא מלמד שמת בערב ראש השנה וצוה את בניו ואת בני ביתו
להסתיר את הדבר, שיוציאוהו אחר ר"ה בשביל לעשות נבואתו
של ירמיה שקר. Com. also v. 16.

ומשלם חובי Targum ומשלם עון אבות אל חיק בניהם ib. 32:18
אבהתא לבניא כד משלמין למחטי בתריהון. Likewise all Targumim
to Exod. 34:7 making it clear that the suffering sons are subject
to punishment also on their own account. This explanation is
that assumed in Berakoth 7a איני והכתיב פוקד עון אבות על בנים
וכתיב ובנים לא ימותו על אבות ורמינן קראי אהדדי ומשנינן לא קשיא,
הא כשאוחזין מעשה אבותיהם בידיהם, הא כשאין אוחזין. The reference is to San. 27b.

וישמע עבדא דמלכא Targum וישמע עבד מלך הכושי ib. 38:7
כיוצא בדבר אתה אומר וישמע עבד Com. Moed Katan 16b צדקיה.
מלך הכושי וכי כושי שמו והלא צדקיה שמו. But Sifri Num. 99
(mentioned anonymously by Rashi) would interpret it to refer
to Baruch b. Neriah.

והיה בתלתין שנין לזמן Targum ויהי בשלשים שנה Ez. 1:1
דאשכח חלקיה כהנא רבא ספרא דאוריתא. This numerical interpretation is given in Seder Olam. Com. Jalqut l. c.

מהוי הוה פתגם נבואה מן קדם Targum ... היה היה ib. 3 . . .
בארעא דישראל תב חנינות ואתמלל עמיה במדינת ארע כסדאי. So Mech.

וי"א נדבר עמו בארץ ונדבר עמו בחוצה לארץ : (פסחא בא פתיחתא)
שנאמר היה היה, היה שנדבר עמו בארץ, היה שנדבר עמו בחוצה לארץ.
Also Rab Chisda Moed Katan 25a.

ib. 24 קול המולה כקול מחנה בעמדם Targum קול מלוליהן
It seems to follow. כד מודין ומברכין ית רבונהון קימא מלך עלמיא
the homily in Gen. r. 65, 5: ומה הוא בעמדם בא עם דם, בשעה
שישראל אומרין שמע ישראל המלאכים שותקין ואח"כ תרפנה כנפיהם.
Its repetition in the v. 25 is interpreted by the T. in the same
way, the silence preceding the word of prophecy descending
upon the prophet.

ib. 2:10 וכתוב אליה קינים והגה והי Targum וכתיב ביה
דאם יעברון בית ישראל על אוריתא ישלטון בהון עממיא ואם יעברון
ית אוריתא יסוף מנהון אליא ודונא. Com. chapter General Peculiarities. However a similar evasive interpretation is found in
Sifri Num. 103, וכתוב עליה קינים קינים של רשעים, והגה של צדיקים,
והי של רשעים.

ib. 7:11 ולא מהמהם ולא נה Targum ולא מבניהון ולא מבני
Com. Gen. r. 31, 1, as interpreted rightly in נבחר מפנינים בניהון

ib. 13:5 לא עליתם Targum ולא עבדתון לכון עובדין טבין
למבעי על בית ישראל. Com. Jalqut l. c.; Esther r. 6.

ib. 16:10 ואהבשך בשש Targum וקדשית מנכון כהניא.
Com. ואהבשך בשש אילו שמונה בגדי כהונה של כהן גדול
שהיה בהם שש. The targumist, however, would interpret
ואכסך מישי as referring to the High Priest.

ib. 11 צמידים Targum אבנים לוחי תרי על כתיבין.
So Pesiqta 33 ואתנה צמידים אילו שני לוחות הברית.

ib. 12 ועטרת תפארת בראשך Targum ומלאך שליח מן קדמי
ועטרת תפארת בראשך זו : גן נעול Com. Cant. r. מדבר ברישיכון.
השכינה; Pesigta 33.

ib. 26:21 בלהות אתנך Targum כדלא הוית בלהות Kimchi וי"ת בלהות
It is, it would seem, an old Midrashic in- שתי מלים — בל הות.
terpretation. So Tanchuma Gen. 19 (Buber) מהו בלהות אתנך
ואינך, אומות העולם לא היו ולא עתידין להיות שנאמר בלהות . . .
בלהות בל היות.

ib. 28:13 מלאכת תפיך ונקביך בך Targum ברם לא אסתכלת
מלאכת תפיך... בפגרך דאיתעביד חללין ונקבין So Baba Bathra 77a.
אמר רב יהודה אמר רב אמר לו הקב"ה לחרם מלך צוו בך נסתכלתי
ובראתי נקבים נקבים באדם.

Com. Ps. Jon. and Frag. Deut. 32:18, which is the interpretation of R. Meir, Sifri Deut. 227.

ib. 45:11 Targum לשאת מעשר החמר הבת מאין תלת סבום
מנא הני Com. Menachoth 77a למסב כורא במכלתא רטיבא ביתא.
מילי אמר רב חסדא קרא האופה והבת תוכן אחד היה, מה הבת שלש
סאין, ובת גופא מנלן, אלא מהכא וחק השמן הבת The T. to v. 14 is
literal. The specification here of the number of kors is because
it forms the source for the inference of the measure of the epha.

Hos. 2:1 ...והיה במקום אשר יאמר להם לא עמי אתם יאמר להם
ויהי באתרא דאתגליאו ביני עממיא כד עברו על אורייתא Targum
ואתאמר להון לא עמי אתון יתובון ויתרבון ויתאמר להון עמיה דאלהא
קימא בזה כיוצא This interpretation agrees with Sifri Num. 131
אתה אומר לא עמי ואומר מספר בני ישראל וכי מה ענין זה לזה משל
למלך שכעס על אשתו שלח אחר סופר לבוא ולכתוב לה גט עד שלא בא
הסופר נתרצה לאשתו אמר המלך אפשר שיצא סופר זה מכאן חלוק אלא
אומר לו בוא כתוב שאני כופל לה כתובתה, לכך נאמר כי אתם לא עמי
ואומר מספר בני ישראל כחול הים. And Pesiqta 11. R. Meir,
however (Kidushin 36a), would not draw such a distinction.

ib. 2 Targum כנישתהון יום רב ארי כי גדול יום יזרעאל
So Pesachim 88a אמר ר' יוחנן גדול יום קבוץ גליות כיום שנבראו בו
שמים וארץ שנאמר כי גדול יום יזרעאל.

ib. 7 Targum מלפיהון בהיתו הובישה הורתם The T. explains
הורתם as of the root ירה to teach. It was so taken by others.
Com. Deut. r. 2, 2: א"ר שמלאי כתיב כי זנתה אמם הובישה הורתם,
שהם (הדיינים) מביישים דבריהם בפני עם הארץ. And the version
in Jalqut l. c. אמר ר' שמלאי אמר הקב"ה הדיינים מביישים דברי
...בפני עם הארץ לכך נאמר כי זנתה אמם

ib. וישקוויי Targum פרנוסי. Com. Ketuboth 65a ושקווי
דברים שהאשה משתוקקת עליהן ומאי נינהו תכשיטין.

ib. 4:7 Targum עללא להון דאסניתי כמא כרבם כן חטאו לי.
Deut. r. 2, 2 ד"א כל שהרביתי להן עושר כן חטאו לי. In a similar
way Lxx.

ib. 6:2 Targum דעתידין נחמתא ליומי יחיינו מיומים
למתי ביום אחיות מיתיא. The Messianic interpretation of this
v. was a current one. Com. San. 97a; Rosh Hashana 31a. Com
also Seder Eliahu r. 6: יחיינו מיומים זה העולם הזה וימות המשיח
ובים השלישי יקימנו זה העולם הבא.

ib. 6:7 ‏והמה כאדם עברו ברית‏ Targum. ‏ואינון כדריא קדמאי.‏
‏והמה כאדם... זה אדם הראשון,‏ 4 .,Com. R. Abahu, Psichta Lam. r
‏הכנסתיו לגן עדן וצויתיו ועבר על צווי, אף בניו הכנסתי אותם לא"י‏
‏וצויתים ועברו.‏Com. also Gen. r. 19, 7.

ib. 7:4 ‏מלוש בצק עד חומצתו‏ Targum ‏ועל דלא אדכרו נסין‏
‏(פסחא, Com. Mechilta ‏וגבורן דאיתעבידו להן ביום מסקהון ממצרים.‏
‏בא, 13 : מגיד שלשו את העיסה ולא הספיקו לחמצה עד שנגאלו,‏
‏וכן אתה מוצא לע"ל דכתיב כולם מנאפים מלוש.‏

ib. 8:4 ‏כספם וזהבם‏ Targum ‏כספהון ודהבהון דאסיקו להון‏
‏א"ר עקיבה הכל קראו תגר על הכסף‏ Com. Gen. r. 28, 7 ‏ממצרים‏
‏והזהב שיצא עמהם ממצרים שנאמר כספם וזהבם עשו להם עצבים.‏
Com. also Lam. r., Pesichta 23 (Buber), interpreting in the
same way Ez. 7:19.

ib. 11:9 ‏לא אעשה חרון אפי בקרבך קדושי לא אבוא בעיר‏
Targum. ‏לא אעביד תקוף רוגזי ולא אחליף בקרוא אוחרי עוד ירושלם.‏
Com. Eliahu Zuta 10 ‏מאותה שעה נשבע הקב"ה לעמו שלא ישנם‏
‏בעם אחר ולא ישכינם בעיר אחרת שנאמר לא אעשה חרון אפי...‏
So Eliahu r. 22.

Am. 4:12 ‏הכון לקראת אלהיך‏ Targum. ‏אתקשיט.‏ So Shab.
10a (Com. Rashi). Also Berakoth 23a.

ib. 7:7 ‏אנך‏ Targum. ‏דין.‏ Com. Lev. r. 33, 2 ‏ובידי אנך‏
‏כבעל חוב ושטרו בידו... ואומר אנך זה סנהדרי גדולה של ישראל.‏

ib. 9:1 ‏הך הכפתר‏ Targum. ‏טפי מנרתא אתקטיל מלכא יאשיהו.‏
Com. Lev. r. 33, 2 ‏הך הכפתר זה יאשיהו.‏

ib. 7 ‏הלא כבני רחימין‏ Targum ‏הלא כבני כשיים‏ . Com. On.
Num. 12:1, Sifri 99, Moed Katan 16b ‏וכי כושית היתה והלא מדיינית‏
‏היתה, אלא מה מה כושי משונה בעורו כך צפורה משונה בנויה... כיוצא בו‏
‏אתה אומר הלוא כבני כשיים, וכי כושים היו? אלא מה כושי משונה‏
‏בעורו אף ישראל משונים במצוות יותר מכל אומות העולם‏ . So Shochar
Tob 7, 18. But ib. 14: ‏כישראל חוטאים להקב"ה הוא קורא אותם‏
‏כושיים‏ .

Jona 1:3 ‏ויקם יונה לברח תרשישה מלפני י'‏ Targum ‏וקם יונה‏
‏למערק לימא מן קדם דאיתנבי בשמא דיי'‏. The targumist desired to
thus eliminate the difficulty to explain the flight of the Prophet.
Com. Mechilta ‏פסחא, פתיחתא‏ ‏וכי מלפני ה' הוא בורח והלא כבר :‏
‏נאמר אנא אלך מרוחך... אלא אמר יונה אלך לחו"ל שאין השכינה‏
‏נגלית שם.‏ The targumist, however, has struck a plain and genial
interpretation by putting a complement to ‏מלפני.‏

יסגון משיזבין כד Targum עלה הפורץ לפניהם Mi. 2:13
בקדמיתא ויסק מלך מדבר. This interpretation seems to have been
held by r. Simon b. Aba (Gen. r. 73, 3) ויפרץ האיש ר' שמעון
בר אבא אמר מלמד שנפרצה לו פרצה מעין דוגמא של עולם הבא היך
מד"א עלה הפורץ.

ארי כל Targum כי כל העמים ילכו איש בשם אלהיו Mica 4:5
Com. Shochar Tob 1, 20 עממיא יהכון לאבדון על די פלחו לטעותא.
ר' אלעזר המודעי, לעתיד לבא באין כל שרי אומות העולם ומקטרגין
על בני ישראל לפני הקב"ה ואומרים לפניו רבש"ע אלו עובדי ע"ז... הללו
יורדי לגיהנם והללו אין יורדין ? אמר להם אם כן תרד כל אומה ואומה
ואלהיה עמה לגיהנם... שנאמר כי כל העמים ילכו איש בשם אלהיו.
Cod. Reuch has יהכון לאבדון instead of יחובון.

לית גבר דביה עובדין טבין. Targum אין אשכול לאכל ib. 7:1
This interpretation is implied in Mishna Sota 47a (Y. 9,10).

בדיל קימא דעם שבטיא. Targum שבעות מטות Hab. 3:9
Com. Gen. r. 47, 7 א"ר יצחק כתיב כל אלה שבטי ישראל י"ב אלו
בני גבורה וישמעאל אינו מעמיד י"ב אלא אותן נשיאין אבל אלו מטות
ומניין שהקב"ה נשבע כמד"א שבעות מטות Also Exod. r. 44 end.
Com. also Sifri Deut. 117. : לשבטים שנאמר שבעות מטות...

בזעת ימא בחוטוריה דמשה. Targum נקבת במטיו14 ib. Com.
עשרה נסים נעשו לישראל על הים, נבקע' הים : 2, בשלח Mechilta
ונעשה כמין כיפה שנאמר נקבת במטיו...

עמא דחיבין לאשתיצאה Targum גוי כרתים Zef. 2:5
Com. Cant. r. גוי שחייב כרת, משכוני.

ליום אתגליותי למידן. Targum ליום קומי לעד Zef. 3:8 So in
שבועה היא לפני, שכל שחיכה למלכותי אני בעצמי מעיד Pesiqta r. 34
בו לטובה שנאמר ליום קומי לעד. The Agadist also took לעד to mean
to witness, from the root עוד . Com. also Exod. r. 17 end
אבל לעתיד לבא הוא עומד ודן את עולמו בעמידה... וכתיב לכן חכו לי
ביום קומי לעד

ויהושע הוו Targum ויהושע היה לבש בגדים צואים Zech. 3:3
אמר רב So San. 93a ליה בנין דנסבין להון נשין דלא כשרן לכהנותא.
פפא שהיו בניו נושאין נשים שאינן הגונות לכהונא ולא מיחה בהן שנא'
ויהושע היה לבוש בגדים צואים וכי דרכו של יהושע ללבוש בגדים צואים
אלא מלמד שהיו בניו נושאין נשים שאינן הגונות לכהונא ולא מיחה בהן.

ארי גברין כשרין למעבד Targum כי אנשי מופת המה ib. 8
כי אנשי מופת המה, איזו הם אנשים שנעשה Exod. r. 9, 1 להון נסין.

להם מופת הוי אומר זה חנניה מישאל ועזריה א"ל ידענא דצדיקא את
אלא מ"ט אהניא בך פורתא נורא וחנניה מישאל ועזריה לא אהניא בהו
כלל...

ib. 9:1 ודמשק מנחתו Targum מארע בית למהוי תתוב ודמשק
ומה אני מקיים ודמשק מנחתו עתידה : צוארך.r Com. Cant. שכנתיה.
...דמשק עד מגעת להיות ירושלים; Sifri Deut. 116.

ib. 11:12 כסף שלשים שכרי את וישקלו Targum ית ועבדו
ואיני יודע אם ל' כאן Saying of R. Jochanan רעותו גברין מקצת.
וט"ו בא"י ... כשהוא אומר ואקחה שלשים כסף הוי אומר ל"ו צדיקים.
This rendering is at the foundation of this Agada as well as
that of R. Jehuda, who finds in it the implication of the thirty
righteous ones among the Gentiles who exist by their virtue.

ib. 12:12 לבד ונשיהם לבד נתן בית משפחת Targum זרעית
והלא דברים Com. Suk. 22a . בית נתן גבריהון לחוד ונשיהון לחוד
ק"ו לע"ל שעוסקין בהספד ואין יצר הרע שולט בם אמרה תורה נשים
לבד ואנשים לבד עכשיו . . .

Malachi 1:1 מלאכי ביד Targum שמיה דיתקרי מלאכי ביד
תניא ר"י בן So R. Jehoshua b. Korcha, Meg. 15a: עזרא ספרא.
קרחא אומר מלאכי זה עזרא.

ib. 11 טהורה ומנחה לשמי מגש מקטר מקום ובכל Targum
וכי בכל מקום Com. Num. r. 13, 2 . . . וצלותכון כקורבן דכי קדמי.
מקריב קטורת ומנחה לשם הקב"ה אלא בכל מקום שישראל עומדים
ומתפללים תפלת מנחה עליה נאמר מנחה... מגש זו תפלת שחרית... מקטר
זו תפלת ערבית.

ib. 2:12 מנחה ומגיש יעקב מאהלי וענה עד יעשנה אשר Targum
ואם כהן הוא לא יהי ליה קריב קורבנא. Com. San. 82a; Shab. 55b
יכרת י'... אם ת"ח הוא לא יהיה לו עד בחכמים ועונה בתלמידים, אם
כהן הוא לא יהיה לו בן מגיש מנחה.

GENERAL PECULIARITIES

The Targum Jonathan reflects many interesting peculiarities which arose primarily from the state of mind of the age which produced the Agada and the Apocryphal literature. The Targum was read in public worship, and the translator would have to take full account of the susceptibilities of the worshipper. On the other hand, in the homilytic portions ample expression is to be found of the believes, expectations and views of that generation.

The targumist made it a principle to d i f f e r e n t i a t e between the holy and the profane. Words which are equally applied to the holy and unholy are rendered by the targumist by distinct words to maintain the difference. The Masorites follow a similar way. So that when חי is followed by the name of God it is vocalized with a patach (1S 20:3, 2S 12:15 etc.). While followed by a profane it is vocalized with a zeire. Genesis 42:15. (Com. 1S 28:26 חי יי וחי נפשך). The same tendency was made evident in the vocalization of אדני and in such forms as in the compound אדני צדק (Joshua 10:13) and אדני בזק (Judges 1:5, 6, 7). The targumist carried the principle to an extreme application.[1]

אלהים is applied both to God and the idol; the T. draws the distinction between them rendering the profane אלהם —

---

[1] Com. Geiger אוצר נחמד p. 3. Such a distinction has its parallel in the Talmud. So it is said (Shabbath 32a): "For three transgressions are women dying. Others say because they call the ארנא—ארון הקודש (box); R. Ishmael b. Elozor says: 'For the transgression of two things are the amei ha'arazoth dying: for calling the ארון הקודש Arna and because the Beth Ha-K'neseth is called Beth Am.'" No doubt, despite the unanimity of the commentaries that Arna and Beth Am are derisive, and for this reason their application to holy subjects was condemned, they desired to separate the holy from the profane. It would appear that this was urged only as a sort of mannerism. For the Talmud does not follow this distinction; in many passages Arna is employed in the sense of ארון הקודש . (Com. Berakoth 47b).

111

339

טעון . טעון — והסירו את האלהים Joshua 24:14 טעון
Judges 5:8 אלהים חדשים — טעון . 2K 19:18; Is. 33:37, 37:19
טעותהון — ונתן את אלהיהם באש . So also Jer. 2:10, 11; 11:12;
Hab. 1:11 etc. In order to avoid any semblance of imputation
of divinity to idols, the T. treats the adjective אחרים following
the profane אלהים as a noun, and אלהים as a noun in const.
state, thus rendering טעות עממיא — אלהים אחרים . So Josh.
20:16, 24; Judg. 2:12, 17, 19; Is. 26:19; Jer. 13:10,
16:11; 19:4, 13; 22:9 etc. In the same way is rendered
אלהי הנכר Josh. 20:23, 24; Jer. 5:19 etc. Probably this expression
has influenced the rendering by the T. of אלהים אחרים. Compare
ומה תלמוד לומר אל הים אחרים, אלא שאחרים : 5, יתרו Mech.
קוראים אותם אלוהות . Equally is בעלים rendered. So Jer. 2:23
טעות עממיא — אחרי הבעלים . In some cases it is rendered like
the detached profane אלהים. So Jer. 2:8 והנביאים נבאו בבעל —
לטעותא — לבעלים יזבחו Hos. 11:2 ; 13:1 לטעותא ; בשום טעותא .
לטעותא — ויאשם בבעל . Otherwise בעל is rendered by בעלא
(Jer. 7:9; 9:13 etc.).

This scrupulosity of the T. is strikingly illustrated by his
treatment of this term applied to idolatrous divinity, which is
made by the context to inevitably express godly divinity. So
אם צרך אית ביה יתפרע ליה בעלא — אם אלהים הוא Judges 6:31
This rendering which, it would appear, was suggested by such
passages as Is. 44:10; Jer. 2:8 etc., he applies also to 2K 19:18;
Is. 37:19 והמה לא אלהים as well as to the passage in Hos. 8:10
דלית ביה צרך — ולא אלהים הוא , "the unuseful one"; also Ez.
28:2, 9, in all of which the divine sense of אלהים is obvious.
But the targumist is anxious to avoid even an innocent profanation of this sort. On the other hand, when this profane
אלהים is not employed in the sense of incrimination but as a
fact the rendering is דחלתא "fear" [2]. So for instance 2K 18:33;
34:35; Is. 36:18; 37:12 : ההצילו אלהי הגוים.. איה אלהי חמת
כמספר עריך היו אלהיך 11:13 דחלתא or Jerem. 2:28; וארפד

---

[2] The Talmud also employs its Hebrew equivalent יראה
So San. 64a, 106a. Also Y. Kidushin 1; P'siqta of Rab Kohna p. 65.
On the other hand, דחלא is employed in the divine sense also. See
Proverbs 1, 7: וכפרו בדחלא תקיפא ; ריש חוכמתא דחלתא . F. Deut. 32:13
ארי שבקתון דחלא תקיפא — כי נטשתה עמך and Is. 2:6 די פרק יתהון

So also Jona 1:5 ויזעקו איש אל אלהיו — דחלתיה . Here it was only meant to state the plain reality. Com. also Ez. 28:2, 9.

In the case of the first two instances the targumist has merely identified the profane אלהים with the special name given to idols in the Bible, namely אלילים and גלולים, both of which he renders by טעון with the exception of the latter, which פולחן is in the most cases added to טעון . Com. Is. 8:8, 18, 20; 19:1, 3; Ez. 14:3; 18:6 etc. In this tendency the T. Jonathan is followed by Onkelos and the other Targumim only. With one exception, namely אלהים אחרים in the Ten Commandments (Exod. 20:3; Deut. 5:7), in which case Onkelos would not side-track the meaning, rendering them by אלהן אחרן (Ps. Jon. following On.). In all other cases On. also renders the profane אלהים — טעון (Exod. 23:24; 34:15; Deut. 12:2) and goes even with Jon. to render אל אחר — טעות עממיא . Of the other early translations no such distinction is noticeable, neither in the Pentateuch nor in any other part of the Bible, except in two cases in Lxx. These are: Num. 25:2. Com. Frankel, Über d. Ein., 175.

Usually מזבח is rendered by the targumist by the Aramic parallel מדבחא . But this rendering is applied only to the holy, to God's altar. Whenever it refers to the profane, referring to the idol either in stative or implied sense, it is rendered by אגורא, the pile. Ez. 6:4 ונשמו מזבחותיהם — אגוריכון . Hos. 8:9 מזבחות לחטא — אגורין; Is. 17:8; 27:9; Jer. 11:13; 17:12; Ez. 6:4, 6 etc. Accordingly ויאמר לפני המזבח הזה ואת מזבחותיו... (Is. 36:7) the former is rendered by אגורא the latter by מדבחא

In this case also, the Lxx and P. are making no such distinction. The only exception is the Targum Onk. and the other Targumim. They draw the same distinction and employ the same terms. Com. T. Exod. 34:13; Deut. 12:3; 7:5 etc.[3]

---

3) So the rendering by Onkelos יאכלו על הגל (Genesis 31:46) אגורא . A striking analogy to this is found in Mandaic, where עבורא is usually used to denote the worship of a false cult (Noeldke, Zeit. für Assuriologie, v. 20, p. 131). This distinction, it would appear, was not known to the Jews in Egypt in the fifth century B. C. The temple or shrine or altar of the Jews in Yeb is called אגורא (Sayce Aram. Pap. E. 14 אלה זי יהוה; J. 6 יהו אלהא ; אגורא זי יהו זי אגורא:Sachau (Aram. Pap. 1, 2). However, in Pap. 3 instead of אגורא the term em-

A distinction of this kind is traceable also in the Talmud. There is no particular name in the Talmud for the profane altar. But it has, however, special appelations for objects connected with the altar, one of which has a derisive air. So a sacrifice to an idol is called תקרובת a present.[4] Com. Aboda Zara 32b, 48b; Chullin 13b, 24a. But while the Targum to the Pentateuch reserves תקרובתא for the profane offering, the holy offering being rendered by קרבנא, תקרבתא is the judicial term, applied to idolatrous sacrifice in the Talmud using however קורבן to denote present. Com. Nedarim 20a כקרבנות מלכים; Ab. Zara 64b. So does also T. Jonathan.[5] Com. Hos. 12:2 ושמן למצרים T a r g u m וקרבנא, although Korban is joined by the Tetra-gramm (Menachoth 110a, Sifra Lev. 2). Sometimes the idolat-rous sacrifice is called זבחי מתים (according to PS 106:28) Aboth 3, 3; Aboda Zara 29b; 32b.

Instead of זבח the usual verb for sacrificing, the Talmud in several places uses the verb זבל to manure.[6] Aboda Zara 18b; Y. Berakoth 9, 1; Pesiqta r. 6.

---

ployed is בית מדבחא. I am tempted to assume that this was prompted by this very desire of differentiating the holy from the profane temple. Here, the writer is a Jew and the writing was intended for Jews, and therefore he would not use the profane name אגורא for the holy temple. The others are documents of an official nature intended for the con-sideration of a Persian official or court. The current name of a temple would be used in such a case. Sachau's assumption (ib. p. 29) that אגורא was somewhat the intimate appelation among the Jews of the synagogue (p. 12) is not impressive. On the other hand, it is interest-ing to note that the priest of the temple is called Kohan כהניא יהו אלהא (Pap. 11), while the idolatrous priest is called Komer כמריא זי חנוב (Pap. 1 and Sayce E. 15 מרדוך בר פלטו כמר לחנוב). However, there is not sufficient ground in this to justify the assumption that even then the Jews would observe a distinction to which later generations adhered. The writer might simply have used the appelation by which the Jewish priest was commonly known.

4)   תקרבת is the abbreviated form of תקרובתא. The Targum renders by it מנחה (Genesis 32:13; 20:21; Is. 18:7; Jer. 51:59 etc.).

5)   It would seem that T. Jonathan did not follow at all such a distinction. So כעם קרבנם (Ez. 20:28) is rendered by T. Jon. קורבניהן unless the translator understood it in a holy sense.

6)   In Tosefta Ab. Zara 2 there is מזבחין instead of מזבלין though in Pesiqta r. 6 רי"א יום זבול נילום. The version in Sota 36b is

Moved with this spirit, the Targum is also differently rendering Kohan according as the reference is to an Aaronite or a priest of an idol. The latter is rendered by פלחא. (So Jer. 48:7; 49:3) or, which is the usual rendering, by כומרא (2K 10:19; 17:32 etc.) which is considered by some scholars to be a trans-lation of the Persian Atharnan, the priest of the fire-worshippers. (See Aruch, Kohut כמר) . Both of them are found in the Talmud and the Agada. The priest of the idol is called משרת (San. 63b, 64a). In one passage both of them are used side by side, namely Erub. 79b. כומרא however is the usual connotation for the Kohan of the idol. But 2S 8:18 ובני דוד כהנים the rendering is רברבין (Com. Mech. יתרו, 2 : ...כל כהנים מבטלים בענין, שנאמר ובני דוד) Com. Mek. l. c. כהן מדין, ר' יהושע אומר כומר היה, : וישמע יתרו בענין שנאמר ויהונתן בן גרשם בן מנשה ובניו היו כהנים לשבט הדני

יום חגם היה. Com. also Cant. r. beginning and Gen. r. 87,3. The T. Jon. in general does not favor any distinction in this case. Thus 1K 11:8· ומזבחות לאלהיהן Targum ומדבחות . So also in 12:32; Am. 4:4 and in some other places. So Onk. Num. 24:2 לזבחי אלהיהן — לדבחי ; Deut. 32:17 יזבחו לשדים — דבחי . This principle found application in the Bible. בשת is placed for בעל ; בית און for בית אל . This might have been the reason for the peculiar vocalization of מקדשיהם (Ezek. 7:24), which is otherwise hardly explicable. (Com. Kimchi l. c.; Ew. Gramm. 215 Jahn, Das Buch Ez. l. c.). The reference here is to the idolatrous shrines (so Rashi, Kratezschmar and many others) and was so understood by the Masorites. They therefore changed the pointing as a mark of distinction. Similarly השיבו (Ezra 10:2; Nehemia 13:23) instead of נשאו . As in the judgment of the writer intermarriage is an enormous violation of the Law, he would hesitate to use the word commonly used for the act of taking to a wife.

The names of Gods should be changed into derogatory names (R. Akiba in Sifri Deut. 61). Mockery of the idol was the rule with the Hellenistic Jews also. It was for this reason that they applied the εἰδωλόθυτος to what the G e n t i l e s called ἱεϱόθυτος (Diessman, Die Hellen., p. 5). Likewise the idolatrous festival is called איד (Abod. Zara 2a), and Maimonides (in his com-mentary on Mishnayoth) says: "and it is not allowed to call them (the festivals of the idolators) מועדים because they are הבל ". Com. Rab, Aboda Zara 20a. A temple of an idol is called תרפות (Mishna Ab. Zara 29b, 32b). Its underlying meaning is not from תורפה (Aruch תרף) , but synonymous with תרפות as Tos. (Ibid 32b beginning ההולך) .

343

עד יום גלות הארץ; ר' אלעזר המודעי אומר שר היה, כענין שנאמר ובני דוד כהנים היו.

Also 2S 20:26 וגם עירא היה כהן לדוד—רב לדוד · The targumist does not consider them priests of any kind, although with regard to עירא the T. is in opposition to the view expressed in the Talmud (Erubin 63b) that he was a rightful priest. On the other hand, 1S 1:3 חפני ופנחס כהנים Targum משמשין obviously because they were sinful priests, as against Samuel b. Nachmani, who would clear them of crime (Shab. 55b). Impelled by the same consideration, the T. renders הבמה (1S 9, 12, 13, 14, 25) by אסחרותא by which he renders מושבך (1S 20:18) and לשכתה (1S 9:22) to distinguish it from the bama denoting high places of idolatrous worship which he renders by במותא (1K 13:32; 14:23 etc.), having also the meaning of heaps of ruins. (Ez. 36:2). The targumist appears to decline the talmudic view (Zebachim 112b, 118a) that the ban of bama had been lifted at that time. In order to exonerate Samuel of the sin of bama-worship, the T. rendered הבמה as denoting the place where gatherings were held with the Prophet. Hence the rendering for יברך הזבח (1S 9:13) in the essenic sense [7] ארי הוא פרים מזונא (Ant. 1, 18, 5; Berakoth 55a), while 1S 16:3, 5 is equally rendered by בשירותא . For the same reason the T. renders תרפים (Jud. 17:5) by דמאין instead of צלמניא which is otherwise the rendering of תרפים (So On. Ps. Jon. Gen. 31:19). As well said Levy (Chal. Woer.): "Um nicht einem Jüdischen Priest die Anbetung eines hömlichen götzen Bildes zuzuschreiben." So he differentiates in the rendering of אפוד . When it is used in a holy sense (1S 2:28) it is rendered אפוד but in a profane sense (1S 2:18; 2S 5:14) it is translated כדרוט דבוץ. This is the rendering of מעילים (2S 13:18). As regards other translations, the כומרא connotation for the priest of the idol is adopted by Onk. and P., while the Lxx makes no dinstinction.

Of the same character is the separation drawn by the targumist between משפט referring to that of God or Israel and that of the Gentiles. In the former case it is rendered by דינא.

7) Abudraham (שחרית ישתבח) cites a Targum Yerushalmi which would seem to be a later recenssion, this principle being disregarded. The rendering there is: ארי הוא יפרס על נכסא.

Referred to the מֹשׁפט of the Gentiles or denoting custom it is rendered by the Greek νόμος נימום . So Ez. 5:7 וכמשפטי הגוים — ואת משפטיהם אל תשמרו Ez. 20:18 ; וכנמוסי עממיא Targum ית נימוסיהן. Also Ez. 7:27; 21:25 and in one verse Ez. 11:12 וידעתם כי אני ד' אשר בחוקי לא הלכתם ומשפטי לא עשיתם וכמשפטי הגוים Targum וכנמוסי עבדתון ודיני לא הלכתון לא בקימי די עממיא. When מֹשׁפט denotes custom: 1S 2:13 משפט הכהנים מה משפט האיש (2K 1:7) ; נימום Targum משפט המלך וכו' (1S 8:9) נימום Targum וחי דרך באר-שבע Am. 8:14 Also .נמוסא Targum Applying to the holy laws, commandments or judgment it is rendered דינא . Of this sort are Is. 1:27; 3:14; 5:7; Jer. 2:12; 22:3; Ez. 20:16; 12:21, 24. Sometimes suggested by Instances of both cases are numerous. On the other hand, מֹשׁפט the contents דקשט truthful, is added. Instances of this kind are Jer. 5:1 אם איש עבוד דין דקשט Targum אם יש עשה משפט So vv. 4, 5 ; 7:5 אם עשה תעשו משפט Targum אם מעבד תעבדון Targum והבן משפט וצדקה עשה Ez. 18:19 . דין דקשוט דין דקשוט Targum והבן משפט וצדקה עשו Ez. 18:19 .דין דקשט עבד and v. 21 ויעביד דין דקשט Targum ועשה משפט . It appears from the citations that the targumist adds דקשט when מֹשׁפט is the object of עשה, did, or when this is understood by the targumist to be implied. (Jerem. 5:45). It might have appeared to him that to render מֹשׁפט in these cases by דינא alone would be obscure, as it might be taken in a profane sense. In this con‑ nection it will be notcied that ın a single case is מֹשׁפט rendered by קימא, otherwise the rendering of חק as it will appear presently. This is Jer. 8:7. However, מֹשׁפט there is also the object of עשה . The Lxx and P. in the Prophets are not fol‑ lowing such a distinction. Onk. renders חק by נימום if it refers to Gentiles. So Lev. 20:23 etc., while otherwise חק, as is the case with Jonathan, is rendered by קימא . So Lev. 20:22; 26:3 etc.; the Lxx have for חק in holy sense προςτάγματος So ibid: 20:22; 26:3 etc.

While the profane חק ibid 2:23 is rendered by Lxx νομίμος In the Talmud this term is applied to custom, manner, judicial formatlity. (Com. Gittin 43b; 65b).

The same principle the targumist applies to חק . It is ren‑ dered by נזירא when it refers either to Gentiles or idolatrous law or order. When, however, it refers to the holy laws, it is rendered by קימא covenant (the usual rendering of ברית). Instances of the latter are: Jer. 31:35; Ez. 5:6; 18:9, 10, 19, 21; Am. 2:4; Ze. 1:6; Mal. 3:22 etc. Instances of the former are: Jer. 10:3 חקות העמים Targum גזירת ; 33:25 (חקות ירח וכוכבים Targum גזירת (the same 33:34 חקות שמים וארץ; Ez. 20:18 בחקי אבותיכם אל תלכו Targum בגזירת ; 43:18 גזירת — לכל חקות So 44:5. גזירת Targumאלה חקות . In Ez. 33:9 בגזירת חייא — בחקות . In this way the T. renders Ez. 20:25 וגם אני נתתי להם חוקים לא טובים — גזירן , thus eliminating the disturbing nature of this passage. According to this rendering of the T., the assumption is that also their customs (laws) were decreed by God. Concerning the use of גזירא it will be noticed that in the Talmud it has the effect of arbitrariness. So there are hard גזירות (Makkoth 24a; Ketuboth 3b; Shab. 145b). A גזירא can be recalled, Gittin 55b; Taanith 2 גזירא עבידא דבטלא ; to the targumist it appeared to express profanity. Apart from Jonathan, no other translation adhers in this case to such a distinction.[8]

The same principle is applied by Jonathan to the rendering of נביא . In the case of the true prophet, the one sent by God, it is rendered by נביא , its Aramic equivalent. On the other hand, whenever it carries the implication of either false prophetism or, so to say, professional prophetism, נביא is rendered by ספר scribe, a term of general currency in the age of the Targum. So it renders Is. 9:14 ונביא מורה שקר — ספר . Jer. 6:13 ומנביא ועד ; Other examples of this sort are: Jer. 14:18; ומספר — כהן 18:18. In plural: Ez. 32:25 קשר נביאיה — סיעת ספראה . Ze. 7:3 ולספריא — ואל הנביאים . Note 1S 10:5 בספריא—האף שאול בנביאים.

When reference is made to a prophet of another deity, the targumer renders it literally, adding שקרא false. So Jer. 2:8 — והנביאים נבאו שקר ; 5:31 והנביאים נבאו בבעל — נביי שקרא ; וכל נביי שקרא — הנביאים. 1K 22:10 נביי שקרא; . To this cate- gory belongs also Mi. 2:5. There is annother case which is intimately connected with these cases. In the first place the T.

---

8) Kohut's identifying גזירא with חק as suggested by the render- ing of the T. (see Aruch גזר) is based on his overlooking the principle of distinction of the T.

applies the same distinction to the verb as well as to the noun. מתנבא referring to the true prophet is rendered by the T. איתנבי, referring to the false prophet it has a substitute ex-pressing ridicule. So Jer. 29:26 לכל איש ומתנבא — ומטפש (but v. 27 למה גערת בירמיה הענתותי המתנבא (מתנבא --). 1K 18:29 ויתנבאו עד לעלות המחנה — ואשטתיאו

In all these cases the Targum stands alone among other translations in observing such a differentiation.

Special regard has been paid in rendering by the targumist to Israel.[9] In the first place some harsh expressions flung towards Israel is rendered in such a way as to evaporate their sharpness. It should be remarked that in this the Targum is to some extent followed by all the Greek translations as well as the Peshitta. A few cases will be sufficient to illustrate the point.

The Piel from שוב in the sense of transgression is given a favorable turn when applied to Israel.[10] So משבה ישראל (Jer. 3:6) is rendered by the T. דמתחמנין למיתב לפולחני Lxx: κατοικία. So also P. In the same way T. Lxx P. in v. 8 A. Sym. ἡ ἀποςτροφὴ ἰσραήλ. In v. 11 the T. and P. are fol-lowing the same rendering while Lxx omit משבה. Again שובבים (v. 14) T. and P. render as in former cases, Lxx

---

9) It is generally known that Jewish-Hellenistic writers, led, it would appear, by this principle, applied ἔθνος to the Gentiles, while retaining λαός for the Jewish people. (So Wisd. 15:14. Com. Cheyne, Encyc. Biblica, Hellen.). The Lxx followed the same division in an opposite way, applying the latter to the Gentiles. Com. Gen. 23:12, 13; 42:10 etc עם הארץ — λαὸς τῆς γῆς. But Lev. 20, 2, 4 the rendering is τὸν ἔθνος, the reference being to Israel. Com. also 2 Mak. 6:3. In this connection it is of interest to note that Rashi somehow felt this peculiarity in the Targum. However, he is wrong in the illustration. Thus he remarks in Ze. 13:7: "the Targum never renders מלך ושרים when they are those of Israel except by רברב and not by שלטונין. It is first of all to be remarked that the ren-dering of שרים by רברבין is not peculiar to those of Israel. The same is applied to those of other nations also. Com. Is. 16:6; 34:6 (having both renderings used synonymously); Jer. 25:19; 39:3; 46:21, 23, and in many other instances. On the other hand we find שלטונין applied to those of Israel. So Is. 37:24 etc.

10) This is also the case in Onk. (Com. Deut. 32:6 the ren-dering of עם נבל ולא חכם. See A. Berliner, Onk. p. 120.)

347

having ἀφεστηκότες ; Sym. ῥεμβόμενοι . V. 22 שובו בנים שובבים ארפה משובתכם is rendered by T. תובו בניא דמתחמנין למיתב אישבק לכון כד תתובון .

משבותיכם, however, is rendered by the Lxx affliction (so that there is no reason to ascribe to the Lxx a different read-ing; com. Schlesner Lexicon σύντριμμα). Also ib. 5:6, 31:32. Exceptions are: Jer. 2:19; 14:17, where Lxx render in the unfavorable sense. T a r g u m and P. hold to the above rendering.

The same word is rendered in its intended sense when it refers to other nations than Israel. Note Jer. 49:4 הבת השובבה (referring to Amon) T. מלכותא טפשתא, Lxx θυγατερ ίταμίας audacious. Also Is. 47:10 קלקלתך — חכמתך ודעתך היא שובבתך Is. 57:17 forms an exception, although the reference is made to refer to Israel, the rendering by the T. and Lxx is plain. So strong, it appears, was the force of suggestion of the contents of this particular case that it was felt impossible to make other account of it. 11)

In the following case the T. is followed by Aquila in some measure. Ez. 2:10 ויפרוש אותה לפני וכתוב אליה קינים והגה והי the T., apparently disturbed by the vehemency of the prophecy, renders : וכתיב בה דאם יעברון בית ישראל על אוריתא יישלטון בהון עממיא וכד יעבדון ית אוריתא יסוף מנהון אליא ודינא ותינחתא. In this way the gloomy predcition is turned into one of con-solation. A., it seems, was also actuated by the same motive, rendering קינים — c r e a t i o n (probably from the root קנא) ; com. also Is. 28:9; 56:3; Hos. 13:14.

In his regard for Israel the T. goes farther to differentiate them from other peoples. Here are some interesting examples: Jer. 1:10 ראה הפקדתיך היום הזה על הגוים ועל הממלכות לנתש ולנתץ ולהאביד ולהרם — the T. divides the phrase, assigning its favorble part to Israel. חזי דמניתיך יומא הדין על עממיא ועל מלכותא לתרעא.

_____

11) Kimchi's Sefer Ha-Sharashim, after enumerating all the cases which the targumist as well as the Greek translations and the P. render them by its favorable meaning, remarks: "all these mean rebellion." In this point he follows Menachem Ibn Saruck. (Com. Machbereth שוב). In Machbereth Rabeinu Tam (Ed. Pilpowsky) p. 36, it is said: Hos. 8:6 כי שובבים יהיה the sinful man is called שוב , being removed from the good direction.

ועל בני ישראל למבני ולקימא ולאבדא ולפגרא. Nothing but a passionate regard for Israel could have produced such a rendering.
Com. Is. 10:25; Jer. 18:7.[12]) This scrupulous passion for Israel
is accompanied by a kind of active disregard for the gentiles.
It was the product of the catastrophies of the age. Thus the
targumist is aghast at the idea that the prophet should be overcome by the c a l a m i t i e s of other peoples. For
this reason he changes the person, and instead of the prophet
agonizing for sympathy, as the text requires, the peoples involved
are describing their sufferings. So, for instance, Is. 15:5 :
לבי למואב יזעק Targum בלבהון יימרון; Is. 16:11; Jer. 48:36
; על כן מעיהון דמואבי ולבהון... Targum על כן מעי למואב ככנור יהמו
Is. 21:3 : על כן מלאו מתני חלחלה צירים אחזוני כצירי יולדה נעויתי
על כן איתמליאו חרציהון זיעיא דחלא Targum משמע נבהלתי מראות
תעה לבבי פלצות : 4 .and v אחדתינון אטפשו מלשמע טעו מלמיחזי
טעא לבהון עקא וביעותין Targum בעתתני את נפש חשקי שם לי לחרדה
אחדונון אתר רוחצניהון היה להון לתבר. In some instances he retains the p. but alters the sense. Examples of this sort are :
Is. 16:9; Jer. 48:32 על כן אבכה בבכי יעזר גפן שבמה אריוך דמעתי
על כן כמא דאיתיתי משרין על יעזר כן איתי קטולין על שבמה Targum
אריוינך דמעתא. But otherwise is such a case treated by the
targumist when Israel is meant. The prophet's description of
his feelings towards the affliction of Israel is rendered literally.
So Is. 22:4 על כן אמרתי שעו מני אמרר בבכי אל תאיצו לנחמני על
על כן אמרית שבוקו מני אבכי במרר לא תתבעיתו Targum שוד בת עמי
לנוחמותי על תבר כנשתא דעמי.
        The Lxx are in agreement with the Targum in the rendering of Is. 15:5 and Jer. 48:31 and v. 36. The Syriac in all
these cases follows the literal meaning. The fact that Aq. and
Sym. have instead of the rendering of the Lxx of vv. 31, 36
one which is literal strengthens the supposition that the renderings of the Lxx in these cases were caused by the same motives
as lead the targumist to his. However, there is less consistence
in the Lxx with regard to this point. Com. Lxx Is. 16:9, 11.

    12)   Kimchi remarks: "And Jonathan divided this verse—the unfavorable for the Gentiles and the favorable for Israel." In the present
Rabbinic text the לבני ישראל is omitted, evidently by the censor. Com.
Exod. r. 45, 1 ...רגע אדבר על גוי אלו ישראל... ועל ממלכה אלו ישראל
לנתש... לפי שעשו אותו מעשה ובקש להשמידם.

On the other hand, this peculiar agreement between the Lxx and the Targum is another case of weight for an hypothesis of a common background of these translations.

However, Geiger (Ur. 245 et seq.), who carried this principle too far, failed to notice these renderings. He was most unfortunate in the choice of examples. Thus his assertion (p. 93) that Jer. 48:47 ; 49:6, where the restoration of Moab and Ammon is foretold, are not rendered in the Lxx, is errone- ous, for the lost renderings are found in Gmg.

Other examples are: Jer. 8:23; 13:17; 14:17; Mi. 4:5 etc. Com. particularly Ze. 8:2. Other agadists would not follow this interpretation. Com. Num. r. 20, 1. The targumist would not have been actuated by a hatred towards the respective peoples; Edom and Moab have ceased to exist at his time. It is more correct to take it as the reaction of the age against the Roman world. It is the deep-seated hatred of the time immediately preceding and following the destruction of the second Temple. It was the Prophetical writings where that generation looked for the signs of the times. The prophecies were interpreted in the terms of that period. The old oppressors of Israel, long dead, were revived in the new oppressors. Edom and Aram be- come Rome or Persia. Compassion by the prophet towards the biblical enemies would strike them as if their present oppressors were meant. Such would be horrible to them.

The targumist shares in full measure the worshipful venera- tion of the Torah manifested in the Talmud and Agada. The Torah is given by him prominence in the Prophetical books. The Torah is identified with words descriptive, in the sense they are employed, of qualities representing the will of God. The targumist is again reflecting current views which are to be found in the Agada. דעת is identified by the T. with the Torah. Is. 40:14 ילמדהו דעת Targum אוריתא [13) ; ib. 28:9 את מי יורה דעת Targum אוריתא עבדי (Hos. 6:6). Connected with it is Am. 3:10 לא ידעו עשות נכוחה ; Is. 30:10 לא תחזו לנו

---

13) Com. Alef Beitha of R. Akiba A'in: "and she ,the Torah, is called דעת , as it is written" etc.

נכחות Targum אורייתא אולפן . So also אורח IS. 2:3; Mi. 4:2 נלכה באורחותיו Targum באולפן אורייתהן מורא[14]; Mal. 2:5 Targum באור יי ואתנם לי מורא Targum אולפן אורייתי; Is. 2:5 ובאורייתא Targum ואת פעל יי לא יביטו[15]; ib. 5:12 באולפו אורייתי אורייתא[16] Targum ותהי המשרה על שכמו; ib. 9:5 לא אסתכלו Jerem. 4:5 ; אולפן אורייתא Targum נירו לכם ניר Hos. 10:12 אורייתא Targum שמר אמונים 26:2 Is. ; אורייתא Targum שברו עול (So נאמנה Hos. 5:9); ib. 27:5 יחזיק במעוזי Targum[17] אורייתי; Jer. 32:6 ומשקה צמא יחסור Targum[18] אורייתי (Com. Is. 55:1); Ze. 13:1 מקור נפתח Targum אורייתא יהי אולפן. In their related positions, whether those cases occur in metaphor or are simply conceived, they carry the significance of the all-conceived good which Israel is urged by the Prophet to follow. It was natural for the T., as it was the case with his contemporary agadists, to identify them with the Torah.

The Torah thus gains centrifugal force in the prophecy. On the observances or disregard of its precepts hinges the fate of the nation; they are punished because they transgressed the Torah (Am. 9:1; Jer. 11:16; 5:22 etc.). Other peoples suffer for their failure to accept the Torah (Mi. 5:14). On the other hand, Israel forsaking the Torah ceases to be God's people (Hos. 1:9; 2:1; Zef. 2:1). Repentance forstalls calamity, but this repentance is the return to the Torah (Is. 12:1; 31:7; Jer. 31:18; Ez. 34:1).

In this connection it is worth while noticing the Halakic element in the T. Jonathan. Of course, compared with the Pent., there is not much of Halaka in the Prophetical writings. But in a few cases, which are especially accessible to Halakic interpretation, the targumist follows the interpretation of the Halaka. All these cases occur in Ez.; the first is Ez. 24:17 פארך חבוש לראשך

14) Com. Jalqut 1. c.: "Who accepted the words of the Torah with fear."

15) Com. Midrash Shochar Tob (49): "R. Aba says, sweet are the words of the Torah likened to אור etc."

16) Com. Jalqut (prov. 8): "By me princes will ישרו (prov. 8:16), both the crown of priesthod an kingship come from the power of the Torah."

17) Com. Zeb. 116a.

18) Com. B. Kama 17a; Canticles r. 1.

The Targum renders טוטפות—פאר (Tephilin). This is in accordance with Sukka 25b: "Said R. Aba b. Zabada : A mourner
has to observe all the commands of the Torah except Tephilin; for (this is to be inferred) because God said to Ez.
פארך חבוש עליך , you are obliged to observe it while a mourner,
but no other mourner is to observe it."
Ez. 44:17 לא יחגרו ביזע Targum על חרציהון אלהין ולא יזרזון על
לבבהון ייסרון. This agrees with the Beraith Zebachim 18b (end):
"They (the priests) do not girt below their loins but against
the knuckles."
    Finally there is Ez. 44:22 והאלמנה אשר תהיה אלמנה מכהן יקחו
Targum וארמלתא די תהי ארמלתא שאר כהניא יסבון. This interpretation removes the flagrant contradiction which this interdiction presents to Lev. 3:17. It is so interpreted in Kid. 78b
משאר כהניא יקחו — מכהן יקחו.
    The Messianic hope occupies a prominent place in the
exegesis of this Targum. In addition to the Messianic sense
which the targumist is giving to passages admittedly accessible
to such a conception, he introduces the Messianic note in many
a passage that is scarcely allowing itself of such an impliation.
The targumist is following the current interpretation of that age
of intense expectation.
    In his Messianic interpretation the targumist had pre-
served many of the current ideas about the last days. On the
whole, they are identical with the Messianic description contained in the Apocryphal books, Enoch and 4 Ezra
and the Agada. The rectification of the evils of the world will
be completed on the Day of Judgment. The evil doers are given
respite in this world so that they may repent and turn to the
Torah (Hab.3:1, 2; Zef. 2:1, 2). But on the Day of Judgment
stern judgment will be meted out to the evil doers. There will be
no intercession and no escape (Is. 5:30. Com. 4 Ezra 7, 105; On.
Deut. 32:12). After the closing of the decree (the Day of Judgment) there will be no acceptance of repentance (Is. 8:22). The
world will be renewed (Jer. 23:23; Hab. 3:2. Com. Ps. Jon.
Deut. 32:1). Great wonders and miracles will appear, as in the
time of the Exodus from Egypt (Hos. 21:66; Ze. 10:11). The
Messiah, who was created from the beginning of the world and
who was hidden from the world on account of the sins of the

poeple (Mi. 4:8; 5:1; Zech. 4:7; 6:12. Com. Enoch 48, 3, 6; 62, 7)
will appear. There will be a resurrection of the death. It seems
the targumist expects both the righteous and the wicked to re-
surrect, the former to receive final judgment. (Com. Is. 38:16;
42:11; 45:8, and particularly 57:16. Com. Enoch 51, 2, 3). The
Great Court will sit to judgement (2S 23:7), the wicked will die a
second death (IS. 22:14; 65:6; Jer. 51:39, 57; com. Enoch 22, 6-
12; the Syr. Baruch 76, 4), they will be thrown in Gehenna (Is.
33:17; 53:9; Jer. 17:13; Hos. 14:10), whose fire is burning always
(Is. 65:5). In Jerusalem will the wicked be condemned to
Gehenna (Is. 33:14; com. Enoch 90:20). The righteous ones will
live the life of eternity חיי עלמא (Is. 58:11; Hos. 14:10); they will
shine 343 times (7x7x7), as the light of the seven stars in the
seven days of creation (Judges 5:31; 2S 23:4; Is. 30:26; the
extant edition of the Tanchuma Gen. 6 cites the Targum to
Judges 5:31). Com. Tanchuma ed. Buber, Gen. note 143.

INTERPOLATED TARGUM

The composite nature of T. Jonathan has been definitely demonstrated above. The T. did not escape the peculiar fate of the Greek and Syriac versions, which were preyed upon by later editors, forcing into them other material. It was all the more so an inevitable procedure with the T. Its original purpose to be merely an instrument for the instruction of the ignorant; its place in the public worship; its varied history of wandering were strong factors in rendering it susceptible to changes. It was exposed to the irresistible influences of the Midrash, which thrived in the immediate centuries following the destruction of the Second Temple. Later Midrashim crowded into the original, simple exegesis of Jonathan. The new material caused in many cases a mutilation of the original rendering, thus becoming either obscure or an overflowing rhetoric. Such portions contrast sharp-ly with the close, smooth, natural rendering of Jon. The Mid-rashic incursion is especially remarkable in the first 35 chapters of Isaiah. One need only read the T. to Jerem. or Ezekiel to be impressed by the curious difference. But in most all these cases it is impossible to release the original from the new form. In some instances the translation may represent a completely new rendering which replaced the older one. Few additions can be safely pointed out. Some of them will be found to be two different renderings put side by side. As it is generally known, duplicates of this kind are found in the ancient versions, On-kelos included. We will begin with the major portions, present-ing Midrashic portions which have made inroads into the T. Jonathan.

כד מרדו בית — בפרע פרעות בישראל בהתנדב עם Judges 5:2
ישראל באוריתא אתו עליהון עממיא וטרדונון — וכד תבו למעבד
אוריתא אתגברון אינון על בעלי דבביהון ותרכינון מכל (מעל) תחום ארעא
דיישראל — בכן על פורענות תבר סיסרא וכל מישריתיה ועל נסא ופורקנא

126

דאתעביד להון לישראל, — בכן תבו חכימיא למתב בבתי כנשתא בריש
גלי ולאלפא ית עמא פתגמי אוריתא ; בכן ברוכו ואודו.

The T. to this verse contains three different renderings
to the second half of the v. One interpreting it as implying that
when the people return to the Torah they overcome their enemies
and expel them from the land of Israel; the other taking it to
refer to the overthrow of Sisra; the third to the deliverance
from the prohibition on the study of the Law, the targumist
having in mind the Hadrian persecutions. It is hardly possible
to determine which is the older one. But the latter persisted
in v. 9 המתנדבים בעם.

Com. Seder Eliahu r. 11 (p. 52): וכדו יאי להון דיתבין בבתי
כנשתא ומאלפין ית עמא פתגמי אוריתא. במי הקב"ה נפרע מאומות
העולם ? בבני אדם שהן משכימין ומערבין לבית הכנסת שנאמר . . .
המתנדבים בעם ומברכים את הקב"ה.

ib. 3 שמעו מלכים—;שמעו מלכיא—דאתו עם סיסרא לקרבא
אציתא שלטיניא — דהוו עם יבין מלכא דכנען — לא בחלתיכון ולא
בגבורתכון אתגברתון וסלקתון על בית ישראל.
The two portions following the horizontal line are missing in
Cod. Reuch. and in Ant. Polyg. and preceded by תוס׳ in ed.
Leira, and appear in brackets in the London Polyg. and in the
Basel ed.

ib. 4 ... יי בצאתך משעיר — עלה אוריתא דיהבתא לישראל —
הוה שלטין בהון עממיא וכד תיבין לה מתגברין אינון על בעלי דבביהון,
ביום אתגליותך למתנה להון . . .
The intrusive character of the portion is obvious. It belongs
to v. 2 and is a recenssion of the first rendering. It is missing
in the Ant. Polyg.

ib. 5 הרים נזלו מפניו — טורא דתבור,—טורא יי מן קדם יי—טוריא זעו
טורא דחרמון וטורא דכרמלא ואמרין דין לדין, דין אמר עלי תשרי
שכינתיה ולי חזיא ודין לדין אמר עלי תשרי שכינתיה ולי חזיא —
(מקראות גדולות, אמשטרדם, תפ"ו), אשרי שכנתיה על טוריא דסיני
דהוא חליש וזעיר מכל טוריא — דין סיני מתרגיש . . .
It is a shortened form of the Targum on the margin of Cod.
Reuch containing a current Agada (Com. Gen. r. 99, 1) cited
in Jalqut from Jelamdenu. Refrence to this Agada is made in
T. to PS 68:16, 17. That it is an interpolation is shown in the

London Polyg., where the whole portion is placed in brackets, while in Cod. Reuch the addition is found והוה רעווא מן קדם יי ואשרי שכינתיה. It is completely omitted in Ed. Leira and in the Ant. Polyg.

ib. 8 יבחר אלהים — למפלח לטעותא כד איתרעו בני ישראל חדתין — וכד תבו למעבד אוריתא לא יכילו להון עד דאיתגברין וסליק עליהון סיסרא סנאה ומעיקא. בארבעין אלפין רישי משירין בחמשין אלפין אחדי סיפא בשתין אלפין אחדי תריסין בתמנן אלפין מחצצי גירא בר מתשע מאה רתכין דברזלא דהוו עמיה כל אלין אלפיא וכל אלין משריתא לא יכלון למקם קדם ברק וקדם עשרה אלפין גברא דעימיה...

There cannot be the slightest doubt that this Agada was on the margin to v. 2, the end of which formed על פורענות סיסרא וכל משריתיה of v. 2, which is strikingly out of all connection. Witness the beginning וכד תבו of v. 2. It was by a marginal mistake that it was introduced here, where it has no room. As to its source, com. Jalqut l. c. It appears in a shortened form in Cod. Reuch., where the version is as follows:

וכד תבו לאוריתא לא יכילו להון דכד אתא עליהון שטאה ועימיה אחדי תריסין ורומחין בארבעין אלפין רישי משיריין לא יכילו לאגתא קרבא בישראל.

In Ed. Leira it is headed by: תוספתא

ib. 11 מקול מחצצים בית משאבים — מאתר דהיי אנסין להון ונסבין מה בידיהון בית מכונת (כמנת) לסטין ומתובת מוכסין על גובין בית שקיא דמיא — לאתר דהוון נפקין בנת־ישראל לממלי מיא דלא הואה יכלין (דחלין) לאשמעא קל (טרפת) פרסת רגלאי מן קדם (כמנת) סנאה

Is is a second rendering. It is omitted in Cod. Reuch. In Leira ed. it is preceded by the following addition:

אתרא דאיתעבידא להון נסין וגבורן לדבית ישראל מלקדמין אתר . . .

ib. 16 למה ישבת בין המשפתים — למה תבתון ממשרית קרבא למתב בין תחומין — בפרשת אורחא למשמע בשורתא דא מן דא לברק אתון אמרין דילך אנחנא לסיסרא אתון אמרין דילך אנחנא כי למשמע בשורא.

This interpretation might have been intended to deal a rebuke to the half-hearted revolutionists of the Saducean party in the Great Rebellion. It is omitted in Cod. Reuch. and in ed. Leira it is headed תוספ׳; the rendering בין המשפתים — בין תחומין agrees with Onk. and Ps. Jon., Gen. 49:14.

טבתא יעל אשת חבר שלמאה דקימת—ידה ליתד תשלחנה 26 .ib
מה דכתיב בספר אוריתא דמשה לא יהוי תיקון דגבר על אתתא ולא יתקן
גבר בתיקוני אתתא אלהין ידא לסכתא . . .

It is a current interpretation in a shortened form. Com. Jalqut
l. c. (cited from Midrash Achbar):

ידיה שלחה בכישור זו יעל שלא הרגתו בכלי זיין אלא ביתד דכתיב ידה
ליתד . . . ומפני מה לא הרגתו בכלי זיין ? לקיים מה שנאמר לא יהיה
כלי גבר על אשה.

This addition is missing in Cod. Reuch., and in the Ant. Polyg.;
in ed. Leira it is headed by תום' .

דא היא נימוסא הות בישראל מלקדמין דלא מסתחרא 11:1 .ib
אחסנתא משבטא לשבטא ובכן לא היה יכול גבר למיסב
אתתא דלא הות משבטיה וכדהות אתתא דרחימת גברא הות נפקא מבי נשא
בלא אחסנתא והון אנשין קרין לה פונדקיתא דרחמית גברא דלא משבטא
וכן הות לה לאימיה דיפתח.

This Targum is cited by Kimchi l. c. and is found in ed. Leira
under heading "Tosefta". No other edition has it.

והואה לגזירה בישראל — בדיל דלא — ותהי לחק בישראל 39 .ib
לאסקה גבר ית בריה וית ברתיה לעלתא כמה דעבד יפתח גלעדאה דלא
שאיל לפנחס כהנא, ואילו שאיל לפנחס כהנא הוה פריק יתה בדמין.

It appears in a different version on the margin of Cod. Reuch.
to 12:7. The essence of this Agada is found in Gen. r. 60, 1,
holding to the view of R. Jochanan that a vow of this sort
should be redeemed by money. This author also condemns Jef-
tah for not going to Pinehas to ask the disavowal. Others think
the reverse is true. Com. Seder Eliahu r. 12 (p. 55). This portion
beginning בדיל is found in the Leira ed. headed by "Tosefta"
and is missing in the Ant. Polyg.

וצלאית חנה ברוח — ותתפלל חנה ותאמר עלץ לבי ביי 2:1 IS
נביאה ואמרית רמי קרני בי' — כבר שמואל ברי עתיד למהוי נביא על
ישראל ביומוהי יתפרקון מידא דפלשתאי ועל ידוהי יתעבדון להון נסין
וגבורן בכן ; תקיף לבי בחולקא דיהב לי ; ואף הימן בר ברי שמואל
(דהי"א ו : ח) עתיד דיקום הוא וארבע עשר בנוהי למהוי אמרין בשירה
על ידי נבלין וכינורין עם אחיהון לויאי לשבחא בבית מקדשא בכן ;
רמה קרני במתנתא דמני לי יי — ואף על פורענות ניסא דעתיד להוי
בפלישתאי דעתידון דייתון ית ארונא דיי' בעגלתא חדתא ועמיה קורבן
אשמא בכן תימר כנשתא דישראל : אפתח פומי . . .

The whole portion is missing in the Ant. Polyg.

357

The additions appear with minor modifications in all editions.
In the Basel ed. and the London Polyg., however, they are
placed in brackets. As to the interpretation that Hanna was
prophesying, com. Meg. 14a.

ib. 2   אין קדוש — ואמרת איתנביאת דאתור מלכא סנחירב על
עתיד דיקום הוא וכל חילותיה על ירושלם ונם סני יתעביד ביה תמן יפלון
פגרי משריתיה בכן יודון כל עממיא אומיא ולישניא ויימרון לית קדוש...
The whole addition is missing in the Ant. Polyg. and appears
in the Basel ed. and the London Polyg. in brackets.

ib. 3   ואל תרבו — ואמרת איתנביאת דבבל מלכא נבוכדנצר על
אתון כסדאי וכל עממיא דעתידין למשלט בישראל ; לא תסגון . . .
It is missing in the Ant. Polyg. and appears in brackets in the
Basel ed. and the London Polyg.

ib. 4   קשת גברים—יתברון — ואמרת איתנביאת יון מלכות על
קשתת דגברי יונאי ; ודבית חשמונאי : דהוו חלשין . . .
In the Basel ed. and in the London Polyg. these portions are
in brackets, and are omitted in the Ant. Polyg.

ib. 5   שבעים בלחם — דהוו : ואמרת איתנבאית דהמן בנוהי על
שבעין בלחמא — מרדכי ואסתר : כן ירושלים דהות כאתתא עקרא . . .
ורומי . . . יסופון משריה — תצדי ותחרבי.
In the Basel ed. and in the London Polyg. these portions are
ın brackets. Instead of רומי it has ארם, an intentional change,
for obvious reasons, and are missing in the Ant. Polyg.

2S 22:2 — אלהי צורי אחסה בו מגני וקרן ישעי משגבי ומנוסי
אלהי דאתרעי בי קרבני לדחלתיה תוקפי דמן קדמוהי מתיהבית לי תקוף
ופורקן לאתגברא על בעלי דבבי רוחצני — דעל מימריה אנא רחיץ ואמר
לארמא קרני בפורקניה סומכני דהוה מימרי סמוך לי — כדהויתי עריק...
This portion is missing in the Targum to Ps. That the
portion is a second and different rendering to the second half
of the verse, is evident. Its other part to the first half seems to
have been included in the first rendering. In the Ant. Polyg.
the portion דאתרעי בי קרבני לדחלתיה is omitted.
As to the rendering of צורי Com. IS 2:2; 2S 22:47, On. Deut.
32:4. And וקרן Com. IS 2:1. All of which would lend strength
to this supposition.

ib. 23:4   וכאור בקר — לכון עובדין עבדתון צדיקיא טוביכון
טבין... — על חד תלת מאה ארבעין ותלתא כניהור שבעת יומיא יתיר
מכדין תתרבון ויטב לכון דהויתון מחמדין לישני נחמתא דאתיין — הא...

This part is missing in the Ant. Polyg. This is another indication that the Targum to this verse belongs to a Midrashic T.
which was by a later editor incorporated in the T. and which
displaced the original T. In the text used by Montanus it appeared in a shortened form. Com. Cod. Reuch., Judges 5:8.

בכן על ניסא ופורקנא דיתעביד למשיחך — כי מי אל 32 .ib
ולשארא דעמך דאשתארון יודון כל עממיא וישניא וייטרון : לית אלהא...
It is an addition. The same appears in a shortened form in the
T. to 1S 2:2, which in the London Polyg. is found in brackets.
It is missing in the Ant. Polyg.

בכן על ניסא ופורקנא דעבדתא לעמך בית ישראל — חי יי 47 .ib
אודיאו ואמרו קים . . .
It is another form of v. 32. Is is missing in the Ant. Polyg.
and in the T. to Ps.

— וידבר על העצים מן הארז אשר בלבנון ועד האזוב 4:33 1K
ואיתנבי על מלכי בית דוד דעתידין למשלט בעלמא דין ובעלמא דאתי
דמשיחא.
It is a Midrashic interpretation which can in no way be read
into the verse. Had it represented the original of the T., the
same interpretation would have been applied to the second part
of the v. But the latter is rendered literally. However, the original
was displaced by the toseftoic rendering. The displaced original
is found in the Ant. Polyg.; the rendering there is as follows:
ומליל על אעיא מארזא די בלבנן ועד אזובא דנפק בכותלא ומלל על
בעירא ועל עופא ועל רחשא ועל נוניא.

ואתתא חדא מנשי — ואשה אחת מנשי בני הנביאים 4:1 2K
תלמידי נביאייה מצוחא קדם אלישע למימר עבדך עובדיה בעלי מית
ואת ידעת ארי עבדך הוה דחיל מן קדם יי' דכד קטלת איזבל ית נביא
דיי' דבר מנהון מאה גוברין ואטמרינון חמשין חמשין גברא במערתא
והוה יזיף ומוכיל להון בדיל דלא לאכלותהון מנכסיה דאחאב מן קדם
דאינון אונסא וכען נשיא אתא למסב ית תרין בני ליה לעבדין מתן ושתין
וחמשא זמנין צוווחת את עובדיה בהאי גוונא ולא הוה משגח ולא ידעה
מה למעבד לה עד דאזלא לבי קברי וצוחא דחלא דיי' ואשתמע לה קלא
מביני מיתיא מאן הדין דחלא ד' דקא בעית ארבעה איקרו דחלא ד'
אברהם יוסף ואיוב ועובדיה מתיבא ואמרה לא בעינא אלא היך דכתיב
ביה דחלא דיי לחדא וכד אודיעיה קבריה הוה קא מתפלשא בעפריה
וקא צווחא ואמרה מרי מרי היכא רוח צריך לי בשעתא דמותא כי אמרית

לך למאן את שביק לי אתיבתני ריבון עלמא רחיץ לי ואמר לי שבוק יתמך
ואנא איקיימינון וארמלתך עלי תתרחץ וכדו לא נהשכחת משיזיב ויתמי
נמי צוחי ואמרי קבלת אבא קבלן אבא, אתיב עובדיה ואמר לה זילי ליך
לגבי אלישע בפורתא דמשחא דאישתאר נביך ולברכוך ביה דאנא כד
אטמרתינהו למאה נביא וזנתיה במערתא בלחמא ובמיא לא איטפיין בו
ציני דמשחר מיניהו לא ביממא ולא בליליא לי דכר ליה נביא מילי בידי
לקודשא בריך הוא וישלים לכון מה דאוזפיתיה דהכי אמר קרא מוזיף
למרי עלמא כל מן דרחים על מסכינא ובכן אזלת ואודעתיד לאלישע
כולי האי.

This Tosefta is found in the edition Leira, which is also cited
by Kimchi (l. c.). All editions contain only the beginning of
this Tosefta without any indication of any sort to show its
toseftoic character. Here again an instructive example is presented to show how the toseftoic material was handled by later
editors. Such can be surmised was the case with other material
incorporated in the Targum but whose source we are unable
to trace. Com. Otzar Tov, v. 1, p. 10, Berlin, 1878.

Is. 10:32   עד כאן יומא רב וסגי עדן — עוד היום בנב לעמד
ליה למיעל הא סנחרב מלכא דאתור נטל ועבר תלת אונים ודבר עמיה
ארבעין אלפין גוספנין דדהב דבני מלכין קטירי תגא יתבין בהון ודבר
עמיה מאתן אלפין אחדי סיפין ורומחין דבר עמיה מאתן ושיתין אלפין
מחצצי גירין גוברין דרהטין קדמוהי מאה אלפין אורכא דמשריתיה ארבע
מאה פרסין, צואר סוסותיה ארבעין פרסין, מנין משריתיה מאתן ושתין
אלפין ריבוא חסר חד וכן אתו על אברהם כד רמו יתיה לגו נורא יקדתא
וכן עתידין למיתי עם גוג ומגוג כד ישלה עלמא קצי למתפסקרא משריתא
קדמיתא כד עברו בירדנא שתו מיא דהוו בירדנא משריתא תנינתא כד
עברו בירדנא חפרו בירין ושתו מיא אתא וקם בנוב קרית כהנא לקביל
שור דירושלם ועני ואמר לחילותיה הלא דא קרתא ירושלם דעלה ארגישית
כל משריתי ועלה כבישית כל מדינתי הא היא זעירא וחלשא מכל
כרכי עממיא דכבישית בתקוף ידי עלה קם מניד ברישיה מוביל ומיתי
בידיה על טור בית מקדשא...

All older Rabbinic editions contain this Midrashic Targum.
In the recent editions the part beginning מלכא and ending with
מיא is placed in brackets. It is omitted in Cod. Reuch. and
in the Ant. Polyg. It appears on the margin of Cod. Reuch.
in an enlarged form.

In a somewhat modified form it is told in San. 95b :
אמר רב יהודה אמר רב בא עליהם סנחריב בארבעים וחמשה אלף איש

בני מלים ויושבים בקרנות של זהב ועמהם שגלונות וזונות ובשמונים
אלף גבורים לבושי שריון קליפה ובששים אלף אחוזי חרב רצים לפניו
והשאר פרשים וכן באו על אברהם וכן עתידין לבא עם גוג ומגוג.
בתניתא תנא אורך מחנהו ת' פרסא רוחב צואר סוסיו ארבעים פרסה
סך מחנהו מאתים וששים רבוא אלפין חסר חד . . . תנא ראשונה
עברו בשתי . . . אמצעים עברו בקומה . . . אחרונים העלו עפר על רגליהם
ולא מצאו מים בנהר לשתות עד שהביאו מים ממקום אחר.
Com. also Seder Eliahu r. 8 (p. 45). They represent two versions
of a current Agada. But the following portion containing Senacherib's address is also toseftoic. It is cited in the Aramaic in
San. 95a. Furthermore, it even has the complementary portion
which was dropped at its introduction in the T.

      ib. 49:15 התשכח אשה עולה מרחם בן בטנה, גם אלה תשכחנה
— האפשר דתתנשי אתתא ברה מלרחמא על בר מעהא — מתיבא כנשתא
דישראל ואמרת אם לית קדמוהי אתנשאה דלמא לא מתנשי לי ית דעבדית
עגל דדהב. אמר לה נביא אף אלין אתנשיא : מתיבא ואמרא (ואמרת)
ליה אם אית קדמוהי אתנשאה דלמא מתנשי לי ית דאמרית בסיני נעביד
ונקבל ואמר לה מימרי לא ירחקינך.
      So in Berakoth 34b :
אמר הקב"ה כלום אשכח עולות אילים ופטרי רחמים, שהקרבת לפני
במדבר ? אמרה לפניו רבש"ע הואיל ואין שכחה לפני כסא כבודך שמא
לא תשכח לי מעשה עגל ? אמר לה גם אלה תשכחנה. אמרה לפניו
רבש"ע הואיל ויש שכחה לפני כסא כבודך שמא תשכח לי מעשה סיני ?
אמר לה ואנכי לא אשכחך.
It appears from this that a part of this Midrash was dropped
by the interpolator. The first and last are remnants of the original
Targum. It is omitted in Cod. Reuch. and First Bomberger
ed. (Com. Bacher Z. D. M. G., p. 48.)

      ib. 24, 25 אמרת ירושלים האפשר דיתנסיב מעשו רשיעא
דאמיר עליה על חרבך תחי עראה דעדי מני ואם שביא דשבא ישמעאל
דאמיר עליה דצדיקא היא ישתיזיב ? ארי כדנן אמר יי' אף עדאה דעדא
מניך עשו גברא יתנסב מניה ושביא דשבא מניך ישמעאל גיותנא דאמיר
עליה ערוד באנשא ישתיזיב — וית פורענתיך...
The latter presents an excellent example of how a combination
of this sort was accomplished. The last portion is the original
Targum, upon which was built the Midrashic interpolation.
Both portions, which unquestionably belong somewhere in the
Geonic age, appear in the current editions after the orginal and

literal rendering under the heading תא . They appear on the margin of the Cod. Reuch. under the same name, being omitted in the text; while in the first Bom. ed. they appear in a shortened form in the T. to Is. 66:5 (Bacher, p. 20).

ib. 50:10, 11 . . . מי בכם ירא — אמר נביא עתיד קודשא בריך

הוא למהוי אמר לעממיא, מן בכון . . . מתיבין עממיא ואמרין קדמוהי רבוננא לא אפשר לנא למעסק באוריתא ארי כל יומא אתגרינא דין עם דין בקרבא וכד נצחנא דין לדין אוקידנא בתיהון ושבינא (נשיהון) (על) טפלהון ונכסיהון ובחדא גונא שלימו יומנא ולא אפשר לנא למעסק באוריתא, מתיב קודשא בריך הוא ואמר להון כ' הא כולכון . . .

It is a satire particularly on Rome and Persia. Com. Aboda Zara 2b. In most all editions these portions are placed in brackets. They are missing in Cod. Reuch. and First Bom. ed.

Jer. 8:18 מבליגיתי עלי יגון — על דהוא מלעיגין לקבל נבייא דמתנבן להון דינא ותינחתא איתי עליהון מן קדם חוביהון עליהון אמר נביא לבי דוי.

It is a toseftoic addition which was probably intended for explanation. It can by itself in no way be read into the verse. It had replaced the original rendering, from which the last words remained. Com. T. to Am. 5:9

ib. 9:22 אל יתהלל חכם בחכמתו — שלמה בר דוד — לא ישתבח חכימא בחוכמתיה ולא ישתבח — שמשון בר מנוח גברא בגבורתיה, ולא ישתבח אחאב בר עמרי עתירה בעותריה.

As regards the reference to Samson, the T. seemingly was in-flluenced by Eccl. r. on 9:11. It appears on the margin of Cod. Reuch. under heading תא סא and is missing in the text.

ib. 10:11 כדנה תאמרון להום — דנא פשתגן אגרתא דשלח ירמיה נביא לות שאר סבי גלותא די בבבל ואם יימרון לכון כסדאי (עממיא) דאתון ביניהון פלחו לטעותא בית ישראל כדון תתיבו וכדון תאמרון להון טעון דאתון פלחין להון טעות דלית בהון צרוך אינון מן שמיא לא יכלין לאחתא מטרא מן ארעא לא יכלין לצמחא פרין אינון ופלחיהון ייבדון מארעא וישתיצון מן תחות שמיא אלין.

This rhetorical exposition appears in all editions. In the Cod. Reuch. it appears after the literal Aramaic of the verse. In all other editions the Aramaic is omitted. Its position in the former testifies to its being an incursion, while is position in the latter

demonstrates, as another instance, how the original was forced
out by the interpolation.

ואם על טבון דאנא מוטב — כי את רגלים רצתה . . .   ib. 12:5
לנבוכדנצר מלכא דבבל רגלאה נביא, את חזי ומתמיה ומן פון דאחזינך
מה דאנא עתיד למעבד לאהבתך צדיקיא דמן עלמא דרהטו כסוסותא
למעבד עובדין טבין קדמי ואף אמרית להון דאיתי על בניהון ברכן נחמן
הא כמיא דנחתין שטוף לירדנא.

This part appears in all editions after the complete rendering
of the v. Hence it is toseftoic. It is found fully in San. 96a:

כי את רגלים רצתה . . . אף אתה ומה בשכר ארבע פסיעות ששלמתי
לאותו רשע שרץ אחרי כבודי אתה תמיה, כשאני משלם שכר לאברהם
יצחק ויעקב שרצו לפני כסוסים על אחת כמה וכמה.

Com. also San. 26a, Cant. r. כמעט שעברתי with minor changes.

כדנן אמר יי' קול ברום עלמא — קול ברמה נשמע   ib. 31:14
אשתמע בית ישראל דבכן ומתאנחן בתר ירמיה כד שלח יתיה נבוזראדן
רב קטוליא מרמתא.

It contains a shortened Agada found in Lam. r. Pesichta, end.
That it does not belong here is evident from the two render‑
ings of רמה one being literal, the other expository. Which of
them belongs to the original is difficult to determine; probably
the former.

והוה בתלתין שנין לזמן דאישכח חלקיה כהנא — ויהי...   Ezek. 1:1
רבא ספרא דאוריתא בבית מקדשא בעזרתא תחות עולמא — בפלגות
ביומי... — לילא בתר מעלני סיהרא   The portion after the horizontal
line is missing in the Targum of the Haftora of the first day
of the Feast of Weeks in the Machzor Witri. As the Targum
to this verse beginning לזמן and ending סיהרא is Midrashic in
construction and matter, its partial omission in Machzor Witri
lends support to the hypothesis that the whole portion is an
interpolation.

וארבעא — וארבעה פנים לאחת וארבע כנפים לאחת להם   ib. 6
אפין לחדא וארבעא אפין לכל חד וחד שתת עסר אפין לבריתא חדא מנין
אפיא דארבע ברין שתין וארבעא אפין — וארבעא אפין לחדא וארבעא
גפין לכל חד וחד שתת עסר גפין לכל אפא ואפא שתין וארבעא גפין
לבריתא חדא והוו מנין גפיא דארבע ברין מאתן וחמשין ושתא גפין.
The whole portion preceded by the horizontal line is missing
in the Ant. Polyg. having instead of the second וארבעא אפין —
וארבעא גפין. It also is a case of shortened toseftoic Targum.

...לְמזרק על אתר רשיעיא לאבד חיביא — וידי אדם... ib. 8
עברי מימריה — ולקבלא בהון תיובתא דכל בעלי תיובתא . This addition is found in the Ant. Polyg. only. Com. Pesachim 119a:
אמר ר"ש בן לקיש משום ר' יהודא נשיא מאי דכתיב וידי אדם...
ידו כתיב זה ידו של הקב"ה שפרוסה תחת כנפי החיות כדי לקבל
בעלי תשובה. In Machzor Witri (ib.) there is the following
addition prefacing the literal rendering of the Targum to v. 12:
וכד חזא יחזקאל נבייא ית חזוונא דאחזי ליה שכינתא הי כמא דאחוי
לישעיה בר אמוץ נבייא בהיכלא דחזא ארבע בריין דכוונין חד לקביל
חבריה לאחזאה עינוותנותיה וכן הוה תיקוניהון אפא בקשוט —
ובריא... It is found nowhere else.

כל עתרא גיותא ויקרא — כל אבן יקרה מסכתך 28:13 ib.
מתיהיב לך . The literal translation was preserved in the toseftoic
version of this verse found on the margin of Cod. Reuch.,
entitled סם' אח, namely,כל אבנן טבן .

בכן פרנסיא רשיעיא — תובו לאוריתא — לכן רעים 34:9 ib.
ואנא עתיד לרחמא עליכון אציתון לאולפין — בכן פרנסיא קבלו פתגמא.
It is missing in Cod. Reuch.

A Midrashic Targum to 37:1 is found in Machzor Witri
in the Targum to the Haftora of the Sabbath of Passover:
והא דין גרמייא דנפקו ממצרי' בכוהון דלא איעכבו עד זמן קיצו דיי'
והוה גברא במצרי' ליומא ההוא ושמיה יאיר והוא הוה רב שיבטא
דבית אפרים אמר להון בעידנא ההוא כולהון בית ישר' הוו קיימין
בעינווא ובפוליחנא קשיא ואנן הכי הוינא עבדין יתהון מאתן ואלפין
גברין בני חילא ונפקו ממצרים ואתגאו בלא פורקנא דיי' ובכן מסרינון
יי' ביד מלכא רגת וקטל יתהון גנן ועבדוהי ואשרייני בגוי ההיא בקעתא
ובזמן פורקנא לא דבר יי' ית ישר' בההיא בקעתא דלמא יזעזעון.
This is told in San. 92a; Pirke d. E. 58. It is so interpreted
in Ps. Jon., Exod. 13:17.

ושלמתי לכם את השנים אשר אכל הארבה הילק 2:25 Joel
ואשלם לכון שניא טבתא חלף שניא דבזו יתכון פלחי — והחסיל והגזם
כוכביא אומיא ולישניא ושלטוניא פורענות חילי רבא.
It is a latter Midrash. Com. Seder Eliahu r. 20 (p. 113) :
כל גוים הנשארים בארץ לימות המשיח הולכין לארץ-ישראל ומביאים
בר לחם ומזון לתוך בתיהם של ישראל . . . ואומר אשר אכל הארבה...
אילו ארבע מלכיות שנשתעבדו בהן ישראל.
But 1:4 is rendered literally, and such was the case here, which

was displaced by the interpolation from which was left only the last part פורענות חילי רבא דשלחית בכון. This part has scarcely any connection with the interpolated exposition.

מטל כס דלוט לאשקאה ית נינוה — משא נינוה — Nahum 1:1 מלקדמין אתנבי עלה יונה בר אמתי נביא דמגת חפר ותבת מחובהא וכדי דאוסיפת למחטי תב ואיתנבי עלה נחום מבית קושי כמה דכתיב בספרא הדין.

This is toseftoic. It has displaced the original Targum to the second half of the v. It is a late one. Witness the rendering מבית קושי by האלקשי being evidently influenced by the Arabic, the vernacular of the age. In the edition used by Rashi the reading was דמבית אלקוש. Com. the rendering of המרשתי Mi. 1:1.

צלותא דצלי חבקוק נביא כד איתגלי ליה על ארכא Hab. 3:1 דיהב לרשיע הוא חבקוק נביא דצר צורתא וקם בגוה עני כן אמר חי וקיים שמיה לית אנא עדי מן צורתא הדא עד דחוין לי על ארכא דיהבת לרשיעיא מתיבא רוחא דקודשא וכן אמר ליה לחבקוק נביא על עיסק ארכא דיהבית לרשיעיא דאם יתובון לאוריתא בלבב שלם ישתביק להון ויהון כל חוביהון דחבו קדמוהי בית ישראל הא כשלותא.

Com. Shochar Tob 7, 17, ed. Buber.

וכשבא חבקוק אמר על משמרתי אעמודה ואתיצבה על מצור מהו מצור מלמד שצר צורה ועמד בתוכה ואמר איני זז מכאן עד שתודיעני דבר זה...

This Agadic interpolation is found in the Cod. Reuch., of which Buber had no knowledge. It is missing in all other edi-tions. Rashi (Taanith 23a), refers to it: כדמפרש בתרגום של תפלת חבקוק. The manner in which this reference is expressed would suggest that Rashi refers to the Targum of the Haftora of the second day of the Feast of Weeks, which was customary to read in the communities of Northern France. It is found in the Machzor Witri. On the other hand, it appears that Kimchi had no knowledge of this Targum. Probably the portion beginning על ארכא to the end, which is found in all editions, is a part of this T. J., the original being replaced by it.

י' שמעית שמע גבורתך — י' שמעתי שמעך יראתי ib. 2 מה דעבדתא בטופנא מן בראשית — ודחלתי ; — ואף על מחת פורענותא דאייתיתא על אינשי סדום כד ארגיזו קדמך שמעית וזעית י' — כמה רברבין... — בגו רוגזך דארגיזתא על רשיעיא וצדיקיא... — בגו רוגזך... ותרחם עליהון.

These exegetical interpolations are found in the Targum of the
Haftora of the second day of the Feast of Weeks in the Machzor Witri. They are not found in any other accessible edition
of the Targum. In verse 8 the words על מלכיא הוה רוגזך which
is evidently the rendering of אם בנהרים אפך, and which are
found in all editions, are missing there.

ib. 3:11 אף במעבדך נסין ליהושע — שמש ירח עמד זבלה
במישר גבעון — כד איתגברו וסליקו עלוהי חמשה מלכין מלכא דירושלם
מלכא דחברון מלכא דירמות מלכא דלכיש מלכא דעגלון ; שמשא וסיהרא
קמו במדוריהון — תלתין ושית שען.

The portions following the horizonal lines are found in Cod.
Reuch. and in Machzor Witri only. The same Targum was
used, it would appear, by the editor of the text of the other
editions, who shortened it. That the original rendering was
a literal one is evident from the comparison of these two texts.

Zech. 12:10 ואשפך על בית דוד ועל יתבי ירושלים רוח נביאה
וצלותא דקשוט ומן בתר כדן יפוק משיח בר אפרים לאנחא קרבא עם
גוג ויקטול יתיה גוג קדם תרעא דירושלם ויסתכלון לותיה ויבעון מניה
מטול מא דקרו עממיא למשיח בר אפרים ויספדון עלוהי כמא דספדין
אבא ואמא על בר יחידאי ויתמררו עלוהי כמה דמתמררן על בוכרא.

This Midrashic Targum is found in Kenn., Cod. 154, and on
the margin of Cod. Reuch., giving the source as תרג' ירוש
and in Machzor Witri. It is omitted in all other editions. It
will be seen that the Midrashic interpretation is based mainly
on the portion וספדו עליו כמספד על היחיד which, according to
this interpretation, refers to the violent death of the first
Messiah, namely the son of Ephraim or Joseph. On the other
hand, the rendering preceding and following it is close to the
text but differs slightly from the rendering of the Targum. As
to the Midrashic interpretation in general, com. Suk. 52a,
Yer. 5, 8.

Two more cases of later interpolation may be added. The
first is in Judges 10:16 ותקצר נפשו בעמל ישראל . It is rendered
literally. In the Ant. Polyg. the Targum here has the Hebrew
text. Maimonidas (Moreh Nebuchim 2, 29) makes it plain
that this portion was not rendered by Jonathan for anthropomorphic considerations. The other case is Ezek. 1:26, which
Kimchi (l. c.) says that it is not rendered by the T., but all

accessible editions do have a literal rendering. It was inserted by a later hand. The same may have also been the case
with Ezek. 1:27; 2:8, containing a peculiarly cirmumscribed
rendering.

II.

There is a considerable number of other interpolations
which are of an exegetical character. Some are recensions of the
rendering of the T. Others aim at a clarification not so much
of the text as of the rendering. They have a disturbing effect
upon the rendering. Evident interpolations of this category are
numerous. I have selected some of the most characteristic instances for the purpose of illustration. Finally I wish to call
attention that some of these duplicates were brought to notice
by Frankel (Zu Dem Targum d. Propheten, pp. 39, 40).

Duplications

אניח לעמי ישראל (ואשקיט להון) — אשקוטה   IS. 18:4

קרתא דבית שמש דעתידה למחרב — עיר החרס   ib. 19:18
One takes הרס, הרסה while the other would have it as it stands.
This passage of the T. is cited in Menahoth 110a; this duplicate
then is of a comparatively early date. It was noticed by Frankel
Zu Dem T., 40).

מריקו (וצחצחו) זינא — משחו מגן   ib. 21:5

אתיב לשכנתא מלותכון — ובל יאמר שכן חליתי   ib. 33:24
אתת עלנא מחת מרע.
According to one the refernce is to the absence of the Shekina;
the other is a simpler rendering.

הא לעבדי אוריתא סגי ישׁלמד קדמך ואת—הנה לשלום   ib. 38:17
מייתי מרירא לרשיעיא בכן כד ידעית יום מותי שפיכת דמעתי בצלו
קדמך מר לי סגי.
The latter is an interpolation. It disagrees with the interpretation of the T. of הנה לשלום referring to the pious ones. That
the entire phrase: מר לי מר is rendered by the latter is evident
from the rendering — מר לי סגי.

ib. 66:20 ובכרכרות — ובתושבחן — ובכרכרן

However ובכרכרן is missing in Cod. Reuch.

Jerem. 2:3 וכשירו חציר—עללא ארמות כדמעה—ארמותא עומר

In the former Israel is likened to the priestly tithe, in the latter to the first ripened of the produce before the offering of the Omer (Com. Rashi and Kimchi l. c.).

ib. ·2:16 קדקד ירעוך — נכסך ויבזון — גבורך יקטלון.

ib. 13:19 שלומים הגלת — עובדיכון תושלמת אתקבלא — גלו שלמא.

In the former שלומים is taken in the sense of שלם ; in the latter שלם — pay.

ib. 20:8 אזעק אדבר מדי כי — ומצוח בכי — דאנא בזמן ארי מתנבי אנא מרים קלא.

Ezek. 16:6 ואראך עליך ואעבר — קדמי אבהתכון קים דכרן ועל אתגליתי למפרקכון, ארי גלי קדמי ארי אתון . . .

ib. 34:9 הרעים לכם — רשיעיא — פרנסיא ובכן.

The former read רעים ; the latter רעים . This was noticed by Kimchi. The T. renders רעים throughout this chapter by פרנסיא In Lag. רשיעיא is omitted.

Am. 6:8 יעקב גאון — דיעקב רבותא — מקדשא בית.

The last is the rendering in 8:7; the former is a duplicate.

Mica 1:10 התפלשתי עפר — רישיהון חפו — בקטמא יתפלשון

In Cod. Reuch. יתפלשון is omitted.

ib. 11 בשת עריה — בהתין ערטילאין — עריא גלן.

The latter is more literal.

ibid. האצל בית מספד — צולאי בית מספד לכון עבידו — בכין, דין לסטר דין ומקרבין אנסין דהוויתון חמדתכון בתי —

The former renders האצל as a p. n., while the latter as אצל, near. Com. Rashi and Karo l. c.

ib. 12 לטוב חלה כי — לאוריתא למיתב ומסברא — ומסברא לטב.

ib. 2:13 לפניהם הפרץ עלה — בקדמיתא כד משיזבין יסקון — ברישיהון מדבר מלך ויסק.

The former renders פרץ—משיזבין deliverers and לפניהם—בראשונה,

the former, as in the former days, while the latter understood
פרץ as king and לפניהם, in their front.

אתגלי ואזיע ארעא בחוביהון כן בלבלינון — עמדי... ib. 3:6

לעממיא — ואיתי מכולא על עם דרא ואף בתניתא כד חבו קדמוהי.
The recenssion, it is obvious, would render this v. in a symbolic
sense. The T. would render it literally. This is evident from
the literal rendering of what follows. On the other hand, the
inserted recenssion may constitute only a portion of a Toseftoic
rendering.

באתגליותך — באתיותך לוט על סנאי עמך — בזעם... 12 .ib
למתבר רשעי ארעא.
Com. Rashi and Karo; as to the rendering of בזעם Com. Ze.
1:12; Mal. 1:4.

— ואתן לך רגליך מהלכין — ונתתי לך מהלכים 3:7 .Zech
ובאחיות מתיא אחיינך.
The inserted recenssion would render it symbolically.

הא אנא מיתי — ויתגלי — הנני מביא את עבדי צמח 3:8 .ib

Insertions

(ברם וי לרשיעיא כד אתגלי) — הוי אנחם מצרי IS. 1:24

אתמנעו לכון — חדלו מן האדם אשר נשמה באפו ib. 2:22
מלאשתעבדא לאנשא למעבדה דהלא דנשמת רוח חיין באפוהי (ארי יומא
דין הוא קים ומחר ליתוהי) וכלמא חשיב הוא.

ואפי חשיכיא מבלון אתון (ומיתן — ופני עניים טחנו ib. 3:15
בדיניהון).

ועתה יושב ירושלים ואיש יהודה שפטו נא ביני ובין ib. 5:3
כרמי — (נביא אמר להון הא בית ישראל מרדו מן אוריתא ולא צבן
למיתב) כען יתבי . . .
The preceding passages of the T. make this rhetoric portion
entirely excessive.

ותחפי בהתא (על דעברו על אוריתא) — ועוה פניה ib. 24:1
There is no more necessity for a reason here than there is for
the preceding בוקק את הארץ and the following והפיץ ישביה

(תקלא למלכין — ביום קטול רב — פלגים יבלי מים ib. 30:25
ולמשריתיהון) פצידין נגדין מיין.

(הלא יבהתון בעובדיהון) דמתקיף — ויחזק הרש ib. 41:7
There is only one other such case, also evidently an interpolation,
this is Ez. 16:20. The T. as a rule knows of no such rhetorical
prefacing.

(יטרדו בגיהנם) — והרשעים כים נגרש ib. 57:20
It is found in Cod. Reuch. only.

(ובשירותי עקא — ארי רבא אנא — כי נער אנכי Jerem. 1:6
וגלו אנא מתנבי על עמא הדין).

. . . והסתכלו לחדא וחזו — כי עברו איי כתיים וראו ib. 2:10
(עממיא דגלן מכרך לכרך וממדינה למדינה נטלין ית טעותהון ומובלין
להון עמהון ובאתר דאינון שרן פרסין ית משכניהון ומקימין ית טעותהון
וסגדין להון) אידא היא אומא . . .

(כפרין — ובעידן דבשתא אתיא עליהון — ובעת רעתם ib. 2:27
בטעותיהון ו) מודן קדמי אמרין רחים עלנו.

תתקבל תיובתך (עד לא תתחתם גזירתך) — אלי תשוב ib. 4:1
Com. 31; 17, 20.

ib. 51:1 לב קמי — (היא נא מיתי על בבל ועל יתבי ארע כסדאי

. . . עממין קטולין) דרם לבהון ושפירין בקומא, רוחהון

The insertion is in fact a duplicate interpretation of the former,
interpreting לב קמי to refer to the Chaldeans by the method of
אתבש   Com. Karo, the latter takes it in a more literal sense.

Ezek. 13:19 ...ולהמית נפשות — לאמתא דלא חזי להון דימותון

(לא אתון ממיתן) ולקימא נפשן דלא חזי להון לקימא.

Two different interpretations are here obviously incorporated.
In the London Polyg. the reading is: דימותון אתון ממיתן, דתתקומן
אתון מקומן.

Whether this was a correction by the editor due to misunderstanding or it represents a different reading, it adds emphasis
to the fact that the passages in question are insertions.

ib. 16:5 לרחמא — (למעבד לכון טבא חדא) לאנהא לכון

מישעבודכון לרחמא דילהון.

ib. 16:20 ותקחי — (איכא איסגית לארגזא קדמי כנשת ישראל)

...דדברית ית בנך.

ib. 17:4 ואיבליה לארעא דבטלא מפולחנא — בעיר כנענים שמו

בארעא דכנען (ועד לא עלון בה בית ישראל) בקרית תגרין שויה.

Hos. 10:11 ואנא פרקית יתהון — ואני עברתי על טוב צוארה

מישעבוד מצרים — אעדיתי ניר תקיף מצוריהון.

Hos. 3:3 נביא אמר (לה כנשתא דישראל — כי ימים רבים

חוביכון גרמו לכון דתגלון) יומין סגיאין תתנהון לפולחני.

ib. 7:4 (בכן יגלון בפריע מקרוויהון כמא דמוחן לקימא — כלם...

מחשבת רשע) ועל דלא אדכרו נסין וגבורן דאתעבידו להון ביום מסקהון
ממצרים מעדן מיליש לישא עד לא חמא.

The inserted passage has no connection with the rest and renders
irritating the whole passage. Com. Rashi on this v.

ib. 12:1 ויהודה עד רד עם אל — ורבית יהודה הוו מתקפין

בפולחנא (עד דגלא עמא דאלהא מארעהון).

Joel 2:3 וגם פליטה לא היתה לו — ואף שיזבא לית ביה

(לרשיעיא).

ib. 4:2   דבדרי ביני פלחי מזריא... (סחור — אשר פזרו בגוים
סחור דארעא ישראל).

The inserted portion is found in extant editions, but is omitted
in all other editions, including the princeps edition of Mikraoth
Gedoloth.

Am. 7:14   מרי גיתי אנא ושקמין אית לי — כי בוקר אנכי
בשפלתא (מן קדם חובי דעמא ישראל אנא מסגיף נפשי).

ib. 9:11   בעדנא ההיא אקום את מלכותא דבית דוד — ובניתיה...
דנפלת... וכנישתהון אתקין (ותשלט בכל מלכותא ותגמר ותשיצי סגי
משריתא) והיא תתבני ותשכלל...

This portion, intended for the last three words of the verse, is
to all intent a different version of a sort of a homily, examples of
which are readily presented in the portions of the interpolated
Targumim cited above. The original version seems to have been
replaced by the interpolation.

Mica 7:1   ארי הויתי כמיסף טביא — כי הייתי כאספי קיץ
(בעדן דאבדו חסידיא מן ארעא).

The inserted passage is merely putting כמוסף טביא of the T.
in other words.

ib. 12   יום הוא ועדיך יבוא למני אשור ועדי מצור ולמני
מצור ועד — בעדנא ההיא יתכנשון גלותא דמן אתור קרוי תיקפא —
ודמן הורמני רבתא וקרוי צירא.

The latter part seems to me to belong to the first half of the v.
forming a different rendering, which was incorporated in the
T. to the second part of the v. and displaced the original. The
former renders מני as מן and אשור — אתור while the latter, impressed by the sound of the word, would render הורמני—למני,
Armenia. It was the same case with מצור. Aq. and Theod.
follow the first rendering of the T. The Lxx and P. are somewhat following the interpolated rendering.

ib. 7:14   בעלמא דהוא עתיד) — עמא דאחסנתך — צאן נחלתך
לאיתחדתא) ישרון בלחודהון.

The inserted portion is entirely disconnected with the rest, has
no reference to any part of the v. It is explaining or com-

plementing the T. It was inserted with the intention of import-
ing into this v. a Messianic air, while the T. might not have
taken the v. in this sense.

(תדכר לנו עקידת — תתן אמת ליעקב חסד אברהם 7:20 ib.
יצחק דאתעקד על דבי מדבחא קדמך).

No reference is made in this v. to יצחק The interpolator, it
would appear, was anxious to supply this mission.

(כד איתגלי ברחמתא למתן אוריתא — לפני זעמו Nahum 1:6
לעמיה כן זע עלמא מן קדמוהי) בכן...

It has no connection and makes no sense with what follows.
It can be, however, connected with the preceding v. הרים רעשו
It is probably a recenssion of the rendering of the T. of that
v. and inserted at its end and then misplaced at the beginning
of this v.

ADDITIONS

Quotations from Targum Jonathan in Talmud and Midrash, like those from Onkelos, do not carry the name of the author to whom tradition ascribes the composition of the Targum. In most of the instances in Talmud Babli Targum Jonathan is quoted in the name of Rab Joseph. In two cases Rab Joseph himself quotes it, while in other cases the quotations are introduced by מתרגמינן. In one case in the Midrash the quotation from Jonathan carries the name of Aquila. In the rest of the cases there is no indication of the source. They are just the same quotations from Jonathan. Incidental similarity cannot serve as a basis for a contrary view, particularly when some of the quotations are of an exegetical nature.

Several quotations in Yerushalmi and Midrash, which I assumed to be a different version of the targumic rendering in the respective cases, were cited above. However, there are at least two cases in which the rendering of the Targum is clearly implied. One is Y. Shekalim 2, 6, with reference to Is. 33:21:

מכאן ואילך וימד אלף נחל אישר לא אוכל לעבור אפילו לבורנין גדולה. אינה יכולה לעבור בו כ"ט וצי אדיר לא יעברנו.

This implies the rendering of the Targum of וצי. In Joma 77b the same exposition is accompanied by a quotation from the Targum.

The other case is Mech. יתרו, 9 with reference to Is. 21:9, which was quoted above (p. 29, note 43) from Gen. r., namely,

ויש מחליפים בדבר נופלת זו מלכות בבל דכתיב בה נפלה בבל.

It is based on the rendering of the Targum נפלת אף עתידא למיפל בבל. Had it not been based on the rendering of the Targum (which was well known to the scholar), there would certainly have followed a note giving the interpretation of the quotation from Is.

As regards the quotations from the Targum in Babli, it is well to notice that most of them represent interpretations of an expository nature. At least in two cases the quotations represent a different version of the targumic rendering.

146

374

Most of the quotations were referred to by De Rossi, Zunz and Frankel.

Quotations given in the name of Rab Joseph:

Moed Katan 26a on 2K 2:12 :

אביו ואמו זרבו שלמדו תורה מנלן דכתיב ואלישע ראה והוא מצעק
אבי אבי רכב ישראל ופרשיו, אבי אבי זה אביו ואמו, רכב ישראל
ופרשיו זה רבו שלימדו תורה מאי משמע כדמתרגם רב יוסף דטב להון
לישראל בצלותיה מרתיכין ופרשין.

Pesachim 68a on Is. 5:17 :

וחרבות מחים גרים יאכלו, מאי משמע, כדמתרגם רב יוסף ונכסיהון
דרשיעיא צדיקיא יחסנון.

Menachoth 110a on Is. 19:18 :

מאי עיר ההרס יאמר לאחת, כדמתרגם רב יוסף קרתא דבית שמש
דעתיד למחרב אתאמר דהיא חדא מנהון.

Joma 77b on Is. 33:21 :

יכול יעברנו בבורני גדולה ת"ל וצי אדיר לא יעברנו, מאי משמע,
כמדתרגם רב יוסף לא תזל ביה בספינת צינדין ובורני רבתא לא תגוזינה.

Aboda Zara 44a on Is. 41:16 :

ומאי משמע דהאי וישאם דוד, לישנא דזרויי הוא, כדמתרגם יוסף
תזרם וזרוח תישאם ומתרגמינן תזרינון זרוח תטלטלינון.

The interpretation of 2S 5:21 is against the rendering there of the Targum. It seems that the Agadist would render וישאם דוד in the same sense as וזרה תישאם is rendered in the Targum, namely, and David scattered them. Other Agadists would adhere to the extant rendering of the Targum. Hence the quotation in Rosh Hashana 22b. In the instance here, however, the quotation is introduced by כדמתרגם רב יוסף and also by כדמתרגמינן, one of them is seemingly an interpolation.

Joma 32b on Jer. 46:20 :

מאי קרצו אמר עולא לישנא דקטלא הוא, אמר רב נחמן בר יצחק מאי
קרא עגלה יפה פיה מצרים קרן מצפון בא בא, מאי משמע, כדמתרגם
רב יוסף מלכותא יאי הוה מצרים עמין קטולין מצפונא ייתון עלה
למבזה.

Kiddushin 13a on Hos. 4:2 :

אלה וכחש ורצח וגנב ונאף פרצו ברמים נגעו, מאי משמע, כדמתרגם
רב יוסף מולידין בנין מנשי חבריהון חובין על חובין מוסיפין

Nedarim 38a on Am. 7:14 :

עמוס דכתיב ויען עמוס ויאמר אל אמציה לא נביא אנכי ולא בן נביא
אנכי כי בוקר אנכי ובולס שקמים, כדמתרגם רב יוסף ארי מרי גיתי
אנא ושקמין לי בשפלתא.

Baba Kama 3b on Ob. 1:6 :

איך נחפשו עשו נבעו מצפוניו, מאי משמע, כדמתרגם רב יוסף איכדין
איתבליש עשו אתגליין מטמרוהי.

Berakoth 28a on Zef. 3:18 :

אמר ריב"ל כל המתפלל תפלה של מוספין לאחר ארבע שעות לר׳ יהודה
עליו הכתוב אומר נוגי ממועד אספתי ממך היו, מאי משמע דהאי נוגי
לישנא דתברא הוא, כדמתרגם רב יוסף תברא אתי על סנאיהון דבית
ישראל על דאחרו זמני מועדי דבירושלם.

The saying of R. Jehoshua b. Levi is based on the rendering of the Targum of this verse, which is: דהוו מעכבין בך
זמני מועדך. The quotation here in the name of Rab Joseph
agrees in sense with the Targum but not in the wording. This
might be explained as being a misquotation. However, the
rhetorical prefacing phrase תברא אתי..., which is missing in
our text, seems to have been in the text of the Agadist. It
was this beginning of the rendering which, it would appear,
caused the complication with regard to the reference. For what
was wanted here was to show that נוגי means delay, and the
reference here is to the rendering of this particular word in
the Targum, namely, דהוו מעכבין. But because the Targum
of this verse had as the beginning the words תברא אתי the reference was made to תברא although it was dropped from the
Targum.

Kiddushin 72b on Zech. 9:6 :

אלא לר׳ יוסי מאי וישב ממזר באשדוד, כדמתרגם רב יוסף יתבון בית
ישראל לרוהצן בארעהון דהוו דמי בה לנוכראין.

This is also a different version of the Targum to this verse.
Our Targum renders it: וייתבון בית ישראל באשדוד דהוו בה
כנוכראין.

Two quotations are said by Rab Joseph:

Sanhedrin 94b on Is. 8:6 :

א"ר יוסף אלמלי תרגומא דהאי קרא לא הוה ידענא מאי קאמר חלף
דקין עמא הדין במלכות דבית דוד דמדבר להון בניח כמי שילוחא דנגדין
בנייח ואיתרעיאו ברצין ובן רמליהו.

Moed Katan 28b on Zech. 12:11 :

נענה ר' עקיבא ואמר, ביום ההוא יגדל המספד בירושלם כמספד הדרימון,
וא"ר יוסף אלמלא תרגומיה דהאי קרא לא הוה ידענא מאי קאמר בעדנא
ההיא יסגי מספדא בירושלם כמספדא דאחאב בר עמרי דקטל יתיה
הדרימון בר טברימון וכמספד דיאשיה בר אמון דקטל יתיה פרעה חגירא
בבקעת מגידון.

Quotations preceded by ומתרגימן :

Nazir, last Mishna, according to the version in Ein-Jakob,
on 1S 1:11 :

ומורה אל יעלה על ראשו, ומתרגמינן ומרות אנוש לא תהא עלוהי.

Rosh Hashana 22b on 2S 5:21 :

מאי משמע דמשיאין ליישנא דיקוד הוא דכתיב וישאם דוד ואנשיו,
ומתרגמינן ואוקדינון דוד.

Moed Katan 2a on Is. 62:5 :

ומאי משמע דהאי בית הבעל ליישנא דמייתבותא הוא דכתיב כי יבעל
בחור בתולה, ומתרגמינן ארי כמא דמיתותב עולם עם בתולתא יתיותבון
בגויך בנייך.

Quotations without reference to the Targum:

Sanhedrin 95a on Is. 10:32 :

א"ר הומא אותו היום נשתייר מעונה של נוב. אמרי ליה כלדאי אי אזלת
האידנא יכלת לה ואי לא לא יכלת לה. אורחא דבעא לסגויי בעשרה
יומי סגא בחד יומא. כי מטו לירושלם שדי ליה ביסתרקי, עד דסליק
ויתיב מעלוי שורה, עד דחזיוה לכולה ירושלם. כי חזייה איזוטר בעיניה.
אמר הלא דא היא קרתא דירושלם דעלה ארגשית כל משריתי ועלה
בבישת כל מדינתא, הלא היא זעירא וחלישא מכל כרכי עממיא דכבשית
בתקוף ידי עלה. וקם ומניד ברישיה מוביל ומייתי בידיה על טור בית
מקדישא דבציון על עזרתא דבירושלם אמרי...

The portion beginning הלא דא is found in all editions of the
Targum, and has been considered above (p. 132). At any
rate, the portion beginning וקם ומניד is the targumic rendering
of the verse.

Shabbath 128a on Josh. 7:21 :

וארא בשלל אדרת שנער, ר' אסי אמר אסטלא דמילא.

The rendering of אדרת in Targum is איצטלא .

A quotation of the Targum to Nahum 3, 8, preceded by
מתרגמינן in Gen. r. 1 :

אמון רבתא במה דתימא התיטבי מנא אמון, ומתרגמינן האת טבא
מאלכסנדריא רבתא דיתבא בין נהרתא.

Ecc. r. 11, 3 quotes the Targum to Is. 5:6 in the name of Aquila:

תרגם עקילס הגר ועל העבים אצוה מהמטיר עליו מטר, ועל נביאיא
אפקד דלא יתנבאון להון נבואתא.

Y. Shabbath 6, 4 contains a translation of Is. 5:18-23. Some of the rendering coincide with those in the Targum, namely: השרות — הפארות ,כלילא; שיראין (Targum שירי ידיא). עיזקייא—הטבעות (Targum עזקתא). The rendering of הסהרונים — ענקיה follows the T. Jud. 8:21, to which reference is made (The T. here having סבכיא agrees with ל"א on the margin of Cod. Reuch. to Jud. l. c. having for עינקיא—סיבכיא). קדשיא as the rendering of והלחשים is the translation in the T. of בתי הנפש. There are good reasons for the supposition that this is a version of the Targum to these verses. Com. פני משה l. c.

Y. Taanith 2, 5: א"ר לוי מהו ארך אפים רחיק רגיז.

The renrering of ארך אפים in the Targum to Joel 2:13 is מרחיק רגז. (Also On. Exod. 34:6; Ps. Jon. having ארך רוח רגז). Psichta Lam. r. 16 on Jer. 4:18: ומי עשה לך דרכך ומעלליך אורחתיך בישאתא ועובדיך מרידאתא. This agrees with the Targum except that the latter has instead of מקלקליא — מרידאתא. It is to be noticed that both this and the preceding citation contain exegetical renderings.

Lev. r. 6, 4: המצפצפים והמהגין אלין המצייגין אלו דמנהמין Targum דמנצפין ודמנהמין.

Lev. r. 5, 2; Exod. r. 10:5 on Am. 6:4 מטות שן על ערסין דפיל Targum. דישכבן על ערסן דמכבשן בשן דפיל.

Can. r שחורה on Ez. 16:61 הוא דעתיה דר' יוחנן... מהו לבנות לכופרנין.

This is the usual rendering of לבנות in the Targum (com. vv. 46, 48, 49, 57), although in this verse the rendering is לאשתמעא. R. Jochanan would have here also the usual rendering.

Finally, there is the use of טעוותא for idols in Yerushalmi and Midrashim. Com. Y. Berakoth 9, 1 בבבל אינון הכא וטעוותהון ; Y. San 10, 2: ואינון הכא וטעוותהון ברומי ואינון הכא וטעוותהון עמהון. אוי לכם ולטעותכם. As טעוותא is the peculiar rendering in the Targumim of idols, it is reasonable to assume that this descriptive term came into use in the Yerushalmi from the Targum.

2.

The toseftoic portions which were examined in the chapter on Interpolated Targumim do not represent all the Midrashic additions to Targum Jonathan. Many more are to be found in the commentaries of Kimchi, Rashi and other Rabbinical sources. A great number of fragmentary Targumim are found on the margin of Cod. Reuch. All of which were collected and elaborated by Bacher (Z. D. M. G., v. 28, p. 1 et seq.).

On close examination it will be found that those fragments on the margin of Cod. Reuch. which are headed by תרגי אחי, תרגי ירויש and ספי אהי have many characteristic points in common. Hence there is no ground for an insistence on a line of division between them as is held by Bacher. They may have a common source. Or, certain fragments in each group may be assigned to an earlier date and a different source than the rest. It will be noticed that the additions to the Targum of Is. 49:24, 25, which in Cod. Reuch. is referred to תרגי ירייש is designated in the extant editions ת"א.

In the main, the fragments described as תרגי אחי, תרגי ירויש and ספי אחי contain current Agadic expositions. But while to the group of תרגי ירויש belong the larger portions, there is hardly any peculiar characteristic either with regard to material or language to justify its placing in a separate category. Furthermore, all of them exhibit a dependence on Targum Jonathan. So ירוש' on Judges 12:6 following Jon. ואחדון ליה ונכסין ליה במגיזת ירדנא ואיתקטלו... Com. also 5:4, 5 and on Josh. 14:15. It is quoting Jon. to 1K 8:27 and 2K 21:16 (Yerush. on Is. 66:6). As to ת"א and ס"א com. ת"א וס"א on Jerem. 9:22 ת"א, לא ישתבח שלמה בר דוד חכימא בחוכמתיה... on Zech. 11:8 וישיצית' ית תלתא פרנסיא... ירחיק מימרי יתהון על דנפשתהון קצא בפולחני. Also on Is. 45:7, which are so rendered in Targum Jonathan.

All these groups contain fragments which either explain or are complementing the rendering of Jonathan.

379

ירוש׳ on Josh. 22:20 והוא גברא חד לא מית בחוביה . Yerush.
והוא יתרגם באבניא ומן בתרכן גברא חד . Com. also on Judges 1:3.
ויריחו אחידא בדשין דפרזלא ומתקפא ת"א on Josh 6:1
כמה דמתרדיף ס"א on 1S 26:20 . בעברין דנחשא ת"א adds ומתאחדא
כמה דרדיף בר ניצוצא קוראה בטוריא complementing קוראה
Also explaining the Targum Josh 4:19 ירחא קדמאה לירחא — לירחא
דניסן.

So that there is scarcely any foundation for a supposition
that they represent three distinct sources. There is equally no
basis for a theory of an earlier Targum to the Prophets of
which the אח׳ ספ׳ or even ירוש׳ and ת"א are remnants.

Certain portions are admittedly late. Such, for instance as
Is. 49:24, 25 and its parallel on Is. 66:5 which have made their
way into the text of the Targum (the latter is found in the
first Bomberger edition). They bear the traces of the Arabic
era. The fact also that the ירוש׳ on 1S 17:8 interpreting
ואת ערבתם —— וית גט פטורי is not quoted by Rab Joseph, the
author of this interpretation in Babli (Keth. 9b) shows that
this Targum was not known yet at that time. Then, their
dependence on Jon. and also on Onkelos (com. ירוש׳
on Judges 18,3 following Onk. Exod. 3:5; 32:1; Deut. 5:28;
23:4; Also ירוש׳ on 1S 17:8 מרי דר׳ מימרא על אמרין אתון ואם
ה׳ איש מלחמה which is the rendering in Onk. of קרבא נצחן...,
Exod. 15:3) would tend to place their origination at a date
subsequent to that of the official Targumim.

However, although of a comparatively later date, they
have preserved some earlier and later displaced renderings of
the Targum. Here are the instances in the Yerushalmi:
במסאסא Jud. 3:31 טיזרין ; Jon. חריפין . ירוש׳ on Josh. 5:3
דתורי ; Jon. בפריש דתורי : 4:21 ית סיכת ; Jon. ית דשר ; 5:4
שמיא איתרכינו Jon. מכו ; 2K 11:12 יחי מלכא ; Jon. יצלח ;
13:21 חמון : Jon. חזי ; פולמסיא Jon. משרית ; וטלקון ; Jon.
ורמו ;16:3 בריחוק ; Jon. כתועבת ; 19:35 שלדין ; Jon. פנרין ;
ib. 37 אפכו : Jon. אישתיזבו ; Is. 21:5 בוצינא אדליקו ; Jon.
אקימו סכואין . As for those in תר׳ אח׳, ספ׳ אח׳ com. Bacher l. c.

INDEX
Biblical Passages

22:6	C. 105	30:12	C. 75
22:13—15	33 n. 193	30:15	C. 75
22:15	98 n. 206	30:21	140 n. 74
22:16	137 n. 53	31:3	108 n. 285
22:16—19	33 n. 193	31:3	47 n. 266
22:28	C. 92 n. 21	31:5	98 n. 211
22:29	C. 90	31:6	172 n. 291
22:30	C. 91	31:9	C. 75
23:5	98 n. 206; 207	31:12	47
23:10	206 n. 496	31:14	C. 135
23:11	136 n. 43	31:15	220 n. 576
23:23	133 n. 25; 135 n. 41; 173 n. 295; C. 124	31:17	99 n. 212; 211 n. 520
23:24	135 n. 40, 41; 140 n. 79	31:18	134 n. 37; 211 n. 522; 215 n. 544; 218 n. 567; C. 123
23:26	C. 61 n. 18	31:19	99 n. 212
23:28	C. 80 n. 7	31:20	211 n. 518, 522; 213 n. 537
23:39	194 n. 421		
24:7	211 n. 520	31:21	162 n. 221
25:5	210 n. 514	31:27	C. 45
25:6,7	145 n. 106	31:28	C. 44
25:9	203 n. 483	31:32	C. 120
25:14	148 n. 124	31:35	C. 118
25:19	C. 119 n. 9	31:37	111 n. 309
25:20	86 n. 127	31:38	C. 45
25:24	116 n. 355	31:38	123
25:31	144 n. 100	31:39	C. 62
26:3	134 n. 37	31:39—40	122 n. 469
26:7	101 n. 229	32:3	203 n. 483
26:10	104 n. 257; 105	32:6	C. 123
26:11	101 n. 229	32:17	136 n. 43
26:13	134 n. 37	32:18	191 n. 403; C. 105
26:16	101 n. 229	32:27	136 n. 43
26:19	134 n. 37	32:35	C. 75
27:2—13	203 n. 483	32:35	124 n. 419
27:8	C. 61	32:44	124 n. 425
27:12	33 n. 193	33:3	139 n. 67; C. 75
28:17	C. 105	33:6	213 n. 533
29:12	C. 62	33:8	139 n. 15
29:13,14	135 n. 41	33:13	124 n. 425
29:13	137 n. 53	33:17, 20—26	67 n. 18
29:16	201 n. 467	33:24—25	C. 118
29:25—26	104	32:35	161 n. 217
29:26—27	C. 119	33:26	219 n. 569
29:26	110 n. 298	34:2	203 n. 483
29:27	C. 119	34:5	9 n. 35

Ancient Versions

Rabbinic and Other Literature

Subject Index

lyre, 106
Maaseiah, 104
Maccabean Age, 64, 127
Machaerus, 80
Manasseh (king), 215 n. 545
Manasseh, 215 n. 545
Menoah, 108, 168
Marath, 214 n. 540, 216 n. 556
marriage, 41, 44, 45, 46, 49, 108
   intermarriage—42
martyrdom, 86 n. 125
Masada, 80
Mary (daughter of Eleazar), 79
Mathnan, 115
matriarchs, 109 n. 291, 200 n. 469
Mediterranean, 121
Megiddo, 94, 94 n. 175
R. Meir, 2, 103
Meni, 89 n. 171
Mephibosheth, 44 n. 234, 155, 126
Merab, 45
   marriage of Adriel—46 n. 261
mercenaries, 97
Meribbal, 41 n. 234, 155, 126
Merodach, 152, 152 n. 147
Mesha, 83 n. 111, 168, 219, 220 n. 573
   sacrifice of—153 n. 573
Mesopotamia, 71 n. 47, 80–81, 118, 121, 203
   deities of—90 n. 155
Micah, 36, 36 n. 215
   on idolatry—151, 154 n. 159
Michal, 45
   marriage to David—45, 45 n. 254, 56
   marriage to Paltiel—46 n. 261
Michmash, 78, 78 n. 82, 79, 125
Middle East, 80
Midian, 216 n. 551, 116
Midrash, 1, 10, 14 n. 82, 48 n. 285, 49, 50, 51, 59, 63, 64, 74, 76 n. 70, 88, 77 n. 73, 90 n. 159, 92, 94 n. 176, 98 n. 205, 109, 117, 123, 159 n. 203, 117 n. 312, 180 n. 338, 197 n. 439, 201, 212, 219, 220 n. 573, 221 n. 580, n. 584, 227 n. 619
Miletus, 111, 111 n. 304
Minni, 119
miracles, 86, 148, 216 n. 551, 218 n. 572
Miriam, Song of—72 n. 49, 166 n. 250
Mishael, 73

Mishnah, 5, 8, 27, 37, 42, 47, 104
Mizpah, 125 n. 435
Moab (ites), 56, 57, 115, 122, 209
   king of—18 n. 11, 168
   stone—83 n. 111
Molech, 42
Monarchy 108, 110, 199, 206, 208
   Israelite—199
moon, 196 n. 436
   new—29
   worship of—196, 196 n. 436
morality, 108, 109
Moreh (hill of), 127
"The Mortar", 111
Moses, 15, 54, 73, 134 n. 31, 138 n. 61
   death of—161
Mount Carmel, 140 n. 79, 151
Mt. Ararat, 118
Mt. Casius, 121
Mt. Gerizim, 90
Mt. Horeb, 166
Mt. of Olives, 124, 227 n. 616
Mt. Scopus, 77 n. 75
Mt. Zion, 164 n. 233, 227 n. 616
mourning, 197 n. 440
   biblical customs of—60
murder(er), 35
murder, of James—70
Musaph, 201
mysticism, 221, 223, 223 n. 591, 224
Naaman (General), 18, 94 n. 177
Nabal, 158 n. 191
Nabatean Arabs, 57, 116, 117
   Jewish attitude toward—57 n. 317
Naboth, 142 n. 86, n. 87
Nahal Hever, 83
Nahash, 56, 57
Naioth, Samuel and David at—30
Naphatali, 127
Nazirites, 11
Nebuchadrezzar (Nebuchadnezzar), 78, 78 n. 79, 79 n. 88, 97 n. 202, 203 n. 482, 204 n. 484, 206, 209 n. 511
   and Sennacherib—78 n. 79
Necho (Pharoah), 94, 94 n. 178
Negev, 114 n. 335, 120, 124
Nehemiah, 42, 95 n. 185, 111
Nergal, 90 n. 155

Index 433